SOVEREIGN FINANCING AND INTERNATIONAL LAW

Sovereign Financing and International Law

The UNCTAD Principles on Responsible Sovereign Lending and Borrowing

Edited by
CARLOS ESPÓSITO
YUEFEN LI
and
JUAN PABLO BOHOSLAVSKY

OXFORD
UNIVERSITY PRESS

OXFORD
UNIVERSITY PRESS

Great Clarendon Street, Oxford, OX2 6DP,
United Kingdom

Oxford University Press is a department of the University of Oxford.
It furthers the University's objective of excellence in research, scholarship,
and education by publishing worldwide. Oxford is a registered trade mark of
Oxford University Press in the UK and in certain other countries

First Edition published in 2013

Published in the United States of America by Oxford University Press
198 Madison Avenue, New York, NY 10016, United States of America

British Library Cataloguing in Publication Data
Data available

Library of Congress Control Number: 2013946099

ISBN 978–0–19–967437–4

Preface

The global financial crisis of 2007–08 and the protracted debt problems in the Eurozone have returned the issue of how to deal with sovereign debt to the centre of international economic policy discussions.

Enhanced responsibility of sovereign lenders and borrowers must be a key part of the current efforts to reinstate some trust in the international economic system and prevent a recurrence of the financial crisis. The United Nations Conference on Trade and Development (UNCTAD), as the focal point in the United Nations system for debt issues, has made a contribution to these efforts by developing a set of Principles on Promoting Sovereign Lending and Borrowing, which aims to support the adoption of policies that can minimize the occurrence of sovereign debt crises and improve their management when they do occur.

For many years, UNCTAD has insisted that both lenders and borrowers should share responsibilities for the origin of debt crises. For each agent, public or private, who overborrows, there is another agent, public or private, who overlends. This is the rationale for the formulation of a set of universally accepted principles which should result in changing the behaviour of both borrowers and lenders.

The Principles were developed through an extensive process of consultations with many national and international stakeholders involved in sovereign financing, and highlight the fact that transparency, accountability, and the rule of law are essential components of market stability.

This book presents several aspects of the UNCTAD initiative in detail. I hope that it can be a valuable tool for the academic and policy-making community in their deliberations on the Principles on Promoting Responsible Sovereign Lending and Borrowing and thus make a contribution towards their further refinement and global adoption.

UNCTAD is currently building consensus around the Principles with a view to garnering global support for this instrument and its implementation. Following the financial crisis, global support for the Principles would constitute an important step towards improving global macroeconomic coordination, and building a more secure and inclusive global economy.

Finally, I would like to express UNCTAD's gratitude to the government of Norway for its generous financial and political support to this initiative.

Supachai Panitchpakdi
Secretary-General of UNCTAD

Acknowledgements

This book is an independent project that stems from the conference on 'Responsible Sovereign Financing: The Search for Common Principles', organized by the University Autónoma of Madrid (UAM) and the United Nations Conference on Trade and Development (UNCTAD) in Madrid on 2 March 2012. We would like to express our sincere gratitude to all the institutions and persons that supported the conference and this book. The conference was possible thanks to a grant from the Spanish Ministry of Economy (DER2011-15755-E) under the Research Project on 'the Protection of Global Legal Goods' financed by the Ministry of Science and Research (DER2009-11436, <http://www.uam.es/glg>), UAM's Excellence Campus programme, and financial help from UNCTAD. Many people were involved in the organization of the conference. We would like to mention Paloma Blázquez and Myriam Azar, who collaborated with us from the beginning with the organization of the conference, and Rachel Gaughan, who helped us at the conference and also with a transcription of some notes for one of the chapters of this book.

The help of Thomas Colon, Alison Floyd, and Deborah Reynolds with the copyediting at different stages of the process has been crucial.

The OUP team, and particularly Merel Alstein and Anthony Hinton, have been a pleasure to work with, and we thank them for their wise advice and their patience.

Contents

Table of Cases xiii
List of Abbreviations xvii
List of Contributors xxi

INTRODUCTION

1. Introduction: The Search for Common Principles 3
Carlos Espósito, Yuefen Li, and Juan Pablo Bohoslavsky

PART I SETTING THE GLOBAL SCENE

2. The Economic Rationale for the Principles on Promoting Responsible Sovereign Lending and Borrowing 15
Yuefen Li and Ugo Panizza
3. Sovereign Debt Restructurings as Exercises of International Public Authority: Towards a Decentralized Sovereign Insolvency Law 39
Armin von Bogdandy and Matthias Goldmann

PART II LEGAL STATUS OF THE PRINCIPLES

4. Principles Matter: The Legal Status of the Principles on Responsible Sovereign Financing 73
Juan Pablo Bohoslavsky and Carlos Espósito
5. Out of Thin Air? Tracing the Origins of the UNCTAD Principles in Customary International Law 87
Michael Waibel
6. On the Comparative Foundations of Principles in International Law: The Move towards Rules and Transparency in Fiscal Policy as Examples 113
Matthias Goldmann
7. The Legal Contours of Sovereign Debt Restructuring under the UNCTAD Principles: Antagonism and Convergence between Standards of Domestic Insolvency Law and International Investment Protection Law 135
Antonis Bredimas, Anastasios Gourgourinis, and Georges Pavlidis

PART III DEBT MANAGEMENT

8. Improving Debt Management on the Basis of UNCTAD's Principles 163
Kunibert Raffer

9. UNCTAD's Principles on Public Debt and the United Nations Convention against Corruption: Links and Common Strategies 189
Juan Bautista Justo

10. Fiduciary Relations: Legal Framework and Implications for Responsible Sovereign Debt Management 213
José R. Oyola and Marie Sudreau

PART IV CHINA AS A CASE STUDY

11. China's Governmental Preferential Loans and the Performance of its Lending Responsibility 239
Meibo Huang and Dandan Zhu

12. Crisis Prevention for China as a Sovereign Creditor and the UNCTAD Principles 261
Xiuli Han

PART V EUROZONE: PROBLEMS AND SOLUTIONS

13. Restructuring a Sovereign Debtor's Contingent Liabilities 287
Lee C. Buchheit and Mitu Gulati

14. Current EU Mechanisms to Confront Sovereign Insolvency: A Normative Analysis against the Benchmark of the UNCTAD Principles 295
Ignacio Tirado

PART VI OUTLOOK AND IMPLEMENTATION

15. Reforming Sovereign Lending Practices: Modern Initiatives in Historical Context 323
W. Mark C. Weidemaier

16. Hard, Soft, and Embedded: Implementing Principles on Promoting Responsible Sovereign Lending and Borrowing 347
Anna Gelpern

CONCLUSIONS

17. Concluding Remarks in the Light of International Law 385
Robert Howse

Annex: Principles on Promoting Responsible Sovereign Lending and Borrowing 391

Index 401

Table of Cases

INTERNATIONAL COURTS AND TRIBUNALS

Permanent Court of International Justice

Brazilian Loans Case (France v. Brazil), Judgment, 12 July 1929, PCIJ, Ser. A (1929) 93
Serbian Loans Case (France v. Serbia), Judgment, 12 July 1929, PCIJ, Ser. A (1929) 93
Société Commerciale de Belgique (Belgium v. Greece), (1939) PCIJ, Rep. Series A/B No. 78 . . . . 56, 63, 107
Treatment of Polish Nationals and Other Persons of Polish Origin or Speech in Danzig Territory, 4 February 1932, PCIJ, (ser. A/B) 1932 No. 44 104

International Court of Justice

Case concerning Military and Paramilitary Activities in and against Nicaragua (Jurisdiction and Admissibility) (1984) ICJ Rep. 392 120
Case concerning Military and Paramilitary Activities in and against Nicaragua (1986) ICJ Rep.14 . . . . 104, 219
Gabčíkovo-Nagymaros Project (Hungary v. Slovakia) (Merits) (1997) ICJ Rep. 7 . . . . 63, 105
Rights of Nationals of the United States of America in Morocco (France v. US), Judgment of 27 August 1952, (1952) ICJ Rep. 212 104
Norwegian Loans Case (France v. Norway), Judgment of 6 July 1957, (1957) ICJ Rep. 9 93

European Court of Human Rights

Barberà, Messegué y Jabardo v. Spain, Judgment of 6 December 1988, Series A, No. 146 208
Beer v. Austria, Judgment of 6 February 2001 hudoc 208
Borgers v. Belgium, Judgment of 30 October 1991, Series A, No. 214-B 208
Brandstetter v. Austria, Judgment of 28 August 1991, Series A, No. 211 208
Bulut v. Austria, Judgment of 22 February 1996, 1996-II; 24 EHRR 84 208
Campbell and Fell v. UK, Judgment of 28 June 1984, Series A, No. 80 202
Demicoli v. Malta, Judgment of 27 August 1991, Series A, No. 210 208
Dombo Beheer B.V. v. Netherlands, Judgment of 27 October 1993, Series A, No. 274-A 208
Gorraiz Lizarraga v. Spain, Judgment of 27 April 2004 hudoc 208
Grainger v. UK, Application No. 34940/10 hudoc 61
Handyside v. UK, Judgment of 7 December 1976, Series A, No. 24 205
Kress v. France, Judgment of 7 June 2001, hudoc 208
Lanz v. Austria, Judgment of 31 January 2002, hudoc 208
Lobo Machado v. Portugal, Judgment 20 February 1996, 1996-I; 23 EHRR 79 208
McMichael v. UK, Judgment of 24 February 1995, Series A, No. 307-B 208
Nikoghosyan y Melkonyan v. Armenia, Judgment of 6 December 2007, hudoc 208
Ruiz Mateos v. Spain, Judgment of 23 June 1993, Series A, No. 262 208
Vermeulen v. Belgium, Judgment of 20 February 1996, 1996-I; 32 EHRR 313 208

European Court of Justice

Thomas Pringle v. The Government of Ireland, Ireland and the Attorney General, Case C-370/12, Judgment of 27 November 2012 301

Interamerican Court of Human Rights

19 Merchants v. Colombia, Judgment of 5 July 2004, Series C No. 109 210
Acevedo-Jaramillo et al. v. Peru, Judgment of 24 November 2006, Series C No. 157 210
Acosta-Calderón v. Ecuador, Judgment of 24 June 2005, Series C No. 129 210
Cantos v. Argentina, Judgment of 7 September 2001, Series C No. 85 210
Dismissed Congressional Employees (Aguado-Alfaro et al.) v. Peru, Judgment of 30 November 2007, Series C No. 174 210
Durand and Ugarte v. Peru, Judgment of 3 December 2001, Series C No. 89 210
García-Asto and Ramírez-Rojas v. Peru, Judgment of 25 November 2005, Series C No. 137 210
Goiburú et al. v. Paraguay, Judgment of 22 September 2006, Series C No. 153 210
Indigenous Community Yakye Axa v. Paraguay, Judgment of 6 February 2006, Series C No. 142 210
Juridical Condition and Rights of the Undocumented Migrants, Advisory Opinion OC-18, September 17, 2003, Inter-Am. Ct. H.R. (Ser. A) No. 18/03 (2003) 209
López-Álvarez v. Honduras, Judgment of 1 February 2006, Series C No. 141 210
Maritza Urrutia v. Guatemala, Judgment of 27 November 2003, Series C No. 103 210
Mayagna (Sumo) Awas Tingni Community v. Nicaragua, Judgment of 31 August 2001, Series C No. 79 210
Palamara-Iribarne v. Chile, Judgment of 22 November 2005, Series C No. 135. 210
Raxcacó-Reyes v. Guatemala, Judgment of 6 February 2006, Series C No. 143 210
Serrano-Cruz Sisters v. El Salvador, Judgment of 9 September 2005. Series C No. 131 210
The Right to Information on Consular Assistance in the Framework of the Guarantees of the Due Process of Law, Advisory Opinion OC-16/99, October 1, 1999, Inter-Am. Ct. H.R. (Ser. A) No. 16 (1999) 209
Tibi v. Ecuador, Judgment of 7 September 2004, Series C No. 114 210

International Criminal Tribunal for the Former Yugoslavia

Prosecutor v. Erdemovic, Case No. IT-96-22-A (I.C.T.Y., Appeals Chamber, Oct. 7, 1997) 355

Arbitration Awards

Chevron Corporation and Texaco Petroleum Corporation v. Ecuador, Interim Award of 1 December 2008, Ad hoc—UNCITRAL Arbitration Rules, IIC 355 (2008) 149
Dreyfus Brothers and Company v. Peru (French Claims against Peru), 11 October 1921, Arbitration under Chapter IV of the Hague Convention of 18 October 1907 for the Pacific Settlement of International Disputes, Permanent Court of Arbitration, (1922) 97, 267
Ethyl Corporation v. Canada, Decision on jurisdiction of 24 June 1998, Ad hoc—UNCITRAL Arbitration Rules; IIC 95 (1998); 38 ILM 708 146
Lauder v. Czech Republic, Final Award of 3 September 2001, Ad hoc—UNCITRAL Arbitration Rules; IIC 205 (2001) 146
Tinoco Arbitration (Great Britain v. Costa Rica), 18 October 1923 . . . . 96, 97, 165, 167, 168, 172, 266
Russian Indemnity Case (Russia v. Turkey), Award of the Arbitral Tribunal of 11 November 1912, (1913) 7 AJIL 178–201; (1912) 11 UNRIAA 431 106

ICSID

Abaclat v. Argentine Republic, ICSID Case ARB/07/5, Decision on Jurisdiction and Admissibility, 14 November 2011 . . . . 52, 63, 144–9, 154
Ambiente Ufficio S.p.A. and others v. Argentine Republic, ICSID Case No. ARB/08/9 Decision on Jurisdiction and Admissibility of 8 February 2013 (formerly Giordano Alpi and others v. Argentine Republic). 144, 147, 148

Ambiente Ufficio S.p.A. and others v. Argentine Republic, ICSID Case No. ARB/08/9, dissenting opinion of Santiago Torres Bernárdez, 2 May 2013 (formerly Giordano Alpi and others v. Argentine Republic) 83, 353
Azurix Corp v. Argentina, Decision on Jurisdiction of 8 December 2003, ICSID Case No. ARB/01/12; IIC 23 (2003) 145, 148
Bayindir Insaat Turizm Tecaret ve Sanayi A Ş v. Pakistan, Decision on Jurisdiction of 14 November 2005, ICSID Case No ARB/03/29; IIC 27 (2005) 148
Burlington Resources Inc v. Ecuador, Decision on Jurisdiction of 2 June 2010, ICSID Case No ARB/08/5; IIC 436 (2010) 146
Cementownia "Nowa Huta" SA v. Turkey, Award of 11 September 2009, ICSID Case No. ARB(AF)/06/2; IIC 390 (2009) 148
Continental Casualty Co v. Argentina, Award of 5 September 2008, ICSID Case No. ARB/03/9; IIC 336 (2008) 151
El Paso Energy International Company v. Argentina, Award of 27 October 2011, ICSID Case No. ARB/03/15; IIC 519 (2011) 152
Enron Corporation and Ponderosa Assets LP v. Argentina, Decision on Jurisdiction of 14 January 2004, ICSID Case No ARB/01/3; IIC 92 (2004) 11 ICSID Rep. 273 . . . 108, 146
Giovanna A. Beccara and others v. Argentine Republic, ICSID Case No. ARB/07/5 . . . . 144, 278
Giovanni Alemanni and others v. Argentine Republic, ICSID Case No. ARB/07/8 . . . . 144, 278
Gustav F W Hamester GmbH & Co KG v. Republic of Ghana (Case No. ARB/07/24), 2010 207
Impregilo SpA v. Argentine Republic, Final award, ICSID Case No. ARB/07/17 (2011) 152
LG&E Energy Corp and ors v. Argentina, Decision on Liability of 3 October 2006, ICSID Case No. ARB 02/1 . . . . 107, 151
Murphy Exploration and Production Company International v. Ecuador, Award on Jurisdiction of 15 December 2010, ICSID Case No ARB/08/4; IIC 468 (2010) 147
Pan American Energy LLC and BP Argentina Exploration Company v. Argentina, and joined case, Decision on Jurisdiction of 27 July 2006, ICSID Case No. ARB/03/13; ICSID Case No. ARB/04/8, IIC 183 (2006) 148
Phoenix Action Ltd v. Czech Republic, Award of 9 April 2009, ICSID Case No. ARB/06/5; IIC 367 (2009) 149
Saipem SpA v. Bangladesh, Decision on Jurisdiction and Recommendation on Provisional Measures of 21 March 2007, ICSID case No ARB/05/07, IIC 280 (2007) 148
SGS Société Générale de Surveillance SA v. Pakistan, Decision on Objections to Jurisdiction of 6 August 2003, ICSID Case No. ARB/01/13 146
Suez and ors v. Argentina, Decision on Liability of 30 July 2010, ICSID Case No. ARB/03/17.
World Duty Free v. Kenya (Case No. ARB/00/7), 2006 207

NATIONAL COURTS

Belgium

Elliott Associates, Brussels Court of Appeals, 8th Chamber, General Docket 2000/QR/92, 26 September 2000 68

France

French Constitutional Court, Decision No. 2004-511 DC, 29 November 2004 226

Germany

BVerfGE, Cases 2 BvM 1-5/03, 1, 2/06, Decision of 8 May 2007 68
BVerfGE, Case 1 BvR 987/58, Judgment of 14 November 1962 68

BVerfGE, Case 2 BvR 987/10, Judgment of 7 September 2011 123
NML Capital Ltd., EM Limited v. Bank für Internationalen Zahlungsausgleich (BIZ), Betreibungsamt Basel-Stadt, Bundesgericht, July 12, 2010 141

United States of America

Allied Bank Int. v. Banco Crédito Agrícola de Cártago, Case 83–7714, 18 March 1985, 757 F.2d 516. . . . . .66, 185
Aurelius Capital Partners et al. v. Argentina, 07-Civ-2715(TPG) 67
Capital Ventures International v. Argentina, 05-2591-cv, 23 March 2006, 443 F.3d 214. 67
Capital Ventures International v. Republic of Argentina, 10-4520-cv et al., 20 July 2011, 652 F.3d 266. 67
Crédit français S.A. v. Sociedad financiera de Comercio, 490 N.Y.S.2d 670 (1985). 66
Elliot Associates L.P. v. Banco de la Nación, 1999 U.S. App. Lexis 26370 (2d Cir October 10, 1999), rev'g. 12 F. Supp. 2d 328 (S.D.N.Y. 1998) 141
EM Ltd. v. Argentina, 865 F.Supp.2d 415 67
EM Ltd. v. Republic of Argentina, 389 Fed. Appx. 38 (2d Cir. 2010), cert. denied, 131 S. Ct. 1474 (2011) 353
EM Ltd. v. Republic of Argentina, 473 F.3d 463, 472 (2d Cir. 2007) 141
NML, Ltd. v. Republic of Argentina, Nos. 03 Civ. 2507(TPG), 03 Civ. 8845(TPG), 05 Civ. 2434(TPG), 06 Civ. 6466(TPG), 07 Civ.1910(TPG), 2009 WL 2568433 (S.D.N.Y. Aug. 18, 2009), aff'd 353
NML Capital v. Argentina, 05-1525-cv, Summary Order, 13 May 2005 66
NML Capital, Ltd. v. Banco Central de la República Argentina, 652 F.3d 172, 197 (2d Cir. 2011)
NML et al. v. Argentina, 12-105(L), 26 October 2012 67
Pravin Banker v. Banco Popular del Peru Case 96-7183, 25 March 1997, 109 F.3d 850. 68
State v. Crockett, S6 Okl. 124 213
Trust v. Love Funding, 13 N.Y.3d at 199, 890 N.Y.S.2d 377, 918 N.E.2d 889. 141

United Kingdom

Donegal Int'l Ltd. v. Republic of Zambia [2007] EWHC (Comm) 197 (Eng.). 278, 353
NML Capital, Ltd. v. Republic of Argentina [2011] UKSC 31, on appeal from: [2010] EWCA Civ 41 141

List of Abbreviations

Admin. Sci. Q.	Administrative Science Quarterly
AJIL	American Journal of International Law
Am. Bus. L.J.	American Business Law Journal
Am. Econ. Rev.	American Economic Review
Am. J. Comp. L.	American Journal of Comparative Law
Am. Rev. Int'l Arb.	American Review of International Arbitration
Am. U. Int'l L. Rev.	American University International Law Review
APSR	American Political Science Review
Austral. YBIL	Australian Yearbook of International Law
Berkeley J. Int'l L.	Berkeley Journal of International Law
BIS	Bank for International Settlements
BITs	bilateral investment treaties
Brook. J. Int'l L.	Brooklyn Journal of International Law
Brook. L. Rev.	Brooklyn Law Review
B.U.L. Rev.	Boston University Law Review
CACs	collective action clauses
Cap. Mkts L.J.	Capital Markets Law Journal
Chi. J. Int'l L.	Chicago Journal of International Law
CML Rev.	Common Market Law Review
Colum. J. Eur. L.F.	Columbia Journal of European Law Online
Colum. J. Transnat'l L.	Columbia Journal of Transnational Law
Colum. L. Rev.	Columbia Law Review
Corn. Int'l L.J.	Cornell International Law Journal
Corn. L. Rev.	Cornell Law Review
DSA	debt sustainability assessment
DSF	Debt Sustainabiltiy Framework (of the World Bank and the IMF, 2005)
Duke J. Comp. & Int'l L.	Duke Journal of Comparative and International Law
Duke L.J	Duke Law Journal
Econ. J.	Economic Journal
EEGF	European Economic Governance Framework
EITI	Extractive Industries Transparency Initiative
EMIR	European Market Infrastructure Regulation
Emory L.J.	Emory Law Journal
EPFIs	Equator Principles Financial Institutions
EPs	Equator Principles
ESM	European Stability Mechanism
Eur. J. Int'l L.	European Journal of International Law
Fla. St. U. L. Rev.	Florida State University Law Review
Fletcher F. World Aff.	The Fletcher Forum of World Affairs
Ford. Int'l L.J.	Fordham International Law Journal
Ford. L. Rev.	Fordham Law Review
FTAs	free trade agreements

Geo. J. Int'l L.	Georgetown Journal of International Law
Geo. J. on Poverty L. & Pol'y	Georgetown Journal on Poverty Law and Policy
Geo. L.J.	Georgetown Law Journal
German L.J.	German Law Journal
GYBIL	German Yearbook of International Law
Harv. J. Int'l L	Harvard Journal of International Law
Harv. L. Rev.	Harvard Law Review
HIPCs	Heavily Indebted Poor Countries
Hous. J. Int'l L.	Houston Journal of International Law
HRQ	Human Rights Quarterly
ICL Journal	The Vienna Journal on International Constitutional Law
ICLQ	International and Comparative Law Quarterly
ICMA	International Capital Market Association
ICSID	International Centre for Settlement of Investment Disputes
IFC	International Finance Corporation
IFIs	international financial institutions
IIAs	international investment agreements
IIF	Institute for International Finance
IMF	International Monetary Fund
Ind. J. Global Legal Stud.	Indiana Journal of Global Legal Studies
Int'l Community L. Rev.	International Community Law Review
Int'l Fin.	International Finance
Int'l Fin. L. Rev.	International Financial Law Review
Int'l J. Const. L.	International Journal of Constitutional Law
Int'l Org. L. Rev.	International Organizations Law Review
J. Comp. Gov. & Eur. Pol'y	Journal for Comparative Government and European Policy
J. Corp. L.	Journal of Corporation Law
J. Econ. Dyn. & Cont.	Journal of Economic Dynamics and Control
J. Econ. Lit.	Journal of Economic Literature
J. Fin. Econ	Journal of Financial Economics
JIBLR	Journal of International Banking Law and Regulation
J. Inst. Theor. Econ.	Journal of the Institute for Theoretical Economics
J. Int'l Arb.	Journal of International Arbitration
J. Int'l Econ. L.	Journal of International Economic Law
J. Legal Stud.	Journal of Legal Studies
J. Pol. Econ.	Journal of Political Economy
JEP	Journal of Economic Perspectives
JWIT	Journal of World Investment and Trade
JWT	Journal of World Trade
Law & Cont. Probs	Law and Contemporary Problems
LJIL	Leiden Journal of International Law
MDRI	Multilateral Debt Relief Initiative
Mich. J. Int'l L.	Michigan Journal of International Law
Minn. L. Rev.	Minnesota Law Review
MPEPIL	Max Planck Encyclopedia of Public International Law
MRDI	Management and Resources Development Initiative

N.C. J. Int'l L. & Com. Reg.	North Carolina Journal of International Law and Commercial Regulation
N.C. L. Rev.	North Carolina Law Review
NJIL	Nordic Journal of International Law
Nw. J. Int'l L. & Bus.	Northwestern Journal of International Law and Business
NYIL	Netherlands Yearbook of International Law
N.Y.U. J. Int'l L. & Pol.	New York University Journal of International Law & Politics
OECD	Organisation for Economic Co-operation and Development
OECD J. on Budgeting	OECD Journal on Budgeting
Open Econ. Rev.	Open Economies Review
Reg. & Gov.	Regulation and Governance Journal
Rev. Econ. Stud.	Review of Economic Studies
Rev. Fin. Stud.	Review of Financial Studies
SDRM	Sovereign Debt Restructuring Mechanism (of the IMF)
SGP	Stability and Growth Pact
SIFMA	the Securities Industry and Financial Markets Association
SJIL	Stanford Journal of International Law
SWFs	Sovereign Wealth Funds
TFEU	Treaty on the Functioning of the European Union
Temple L. Rev.	Temple Law Review
TESM	Treaty establishing the European Stability Mechanism
Tex. L. Rev.	Texas Law Review
Tul. L. Rev.	Tulane Law Review
U. Ill. L. Rev.	University of Illinois Law Review
UCLA L. Rev.	University of California Los Angeles Law Review
UNCAC	United Nations Convention against Corruption
UNCTAD	United Nations Conference on Trade and Development
Va. J. Int'l L.	Virginia Journal of International Law
Va. L. Rev.	Virginia Law Review
Vand. J. Transnat'l L.	Vanderbilt Journal of Transnational Law
Wash. U. L. Rev.	Washington University Law Review
Windsor Y.B. Access Just.	Windsor Yearbook of Access to Justice
Yale J. Int'l Aff.	Yale Journal of International Affairs
Yale J. Int'l Law	Yale International Law Journal
Yale L.J.	Yale Law Journal
YBILC	Yearbook of the International Law Commission

List of Contributors

Armin von Bodgandy is Director at the Max Planck Institute for Comparative Public Law and International Law, Heidelberg.

Juan Pablo Bohoslavsky is a Sovereign Debt Expert at UNCTAD.

Antonis Bredimas is Professor of International Law, National and Kapodistrian University of Athens.

Lee Buchheit is a partner based in the New York office of Cleary Gottlieb Steen & Hamilton LLP.

Carlos Espósito is Professor of Public International Law at Universidad Autónoma of Madrid.

Anna Gelpern is a Visiting Professor of Law at Georgetown and a Professor of Law at American University.

Matthias Goldmann is Senior Research Fellow, Max Planck Institute for Comparative Public Law and International Law, Heidelberg.

Anastasios Gourgourinis is Lecturer in International Law, at the National and Kapodistrian University of Athens.

Mitu Gulati is Professor of Law at Duke University.

Xiuli Han is an Associate Professor of the School of Law at Xiamen University and a Member of Collaborative Innovation Center for Global Governance and Rule of Law.

Robert Howse is Professor of Law at New York University Law School.

Meibo Huang is Professor of Economics and Director of the China Institute for International Development, Xiamen University.

Juan Bautista Justo is Lecturer of Administrative Law at Universidad Nacional del Comahue.

Yuefen Li is Head of Debt and Development Finance Branch at UNCTAD.

José R. Oyola is adviser to the International Organisation of Supreme Audit Institutions and the World Bank.

Ugo Panizza is Deputy-Director of the Centre on Finance and Development of the Graduate Institute of International and Development Studies, Geneva.

Georges Pavlidis is Academic Assistant, International Hellenic University, School of Economics and Business Administration.

Kunibert Raffer is Associate Professor at the Department of Economics, University of Vienna.

Marie Sudreau is Associate Sovereign Debt Expert at UNCTAD.

Ignacio Tirado is Professor of Law at Universidad Autónoma de Madrid and Counsel at the World Bank.

Michael Waibel is a University Lecturer at the University of Cambridge and Lauterpacht Centre of International Law.

Mark C. Weidemaier is Assistant Professor of Law at University of North Carolina.

Dandan Zhu is a PhD candidate in Economics at Xiamen University, China.

INTRODUCTION

1

Introduction

The Search for Common Principles

Carlos Espósito, Yuefen Li, and Juan Pablo Bohoslavsky

A. Sovereign Debt, the Principles, and this Book

In 2009, when the global financial crisis was scourging the world, the United Nations Conference on Trade and Development (UNCTAD) started the initiative to formulate a set of principles on responsible sovereign lending and borrowing with the political and financial support of the government of Norway. The crisis revealed the excesses, inadequacies, imperfections, and asymmetries of the financial market and the conducting of sovereign financing. The initiative aims to contribute to the global efforts in debt crisis prevention and resolution as well as to the preservation of financial stability at national and international levels.

The financial market landscape had gone through significant changes prior to the crisis, some of which have been further accentuated as a result of crisis management in the past few years. In many countries, the financial sector followed the business model of higher leverage and shorter-term funding.[1] There has also been an increase in government debt in many industrial countries.[2] Owing to the fact that large banks normally have huge holdings of government debt from different countries, banks and governments have become more interdependent.[3] With this large-scale cross-holding of debt, risk transfer between banks and sovereigns is simply natural. The changing debt composition from predominantly bank loans to bonds has also enabled a rapid contagion, as bonds change hands quickly and across borders.

[1] A. Blundell-Wignall and C. Roulet, 'Business Models of Banks, Leverage and the Distance-to-default' (2013) 103 OECD Journal, Financial Market Trend 1, 15.

[2] C. Checherita and P. Rother, 'The Impact of High and Growing Government Debt on Economic Growth An Empirical Investigation for the Euro Area', European Central Bank Working Paper Series, No. 1237 (2010) 7.

[3] Bank of International Settlement, 'The Impact of Sovereign Credit Risk on Bank Funding Conditions', Committee on the Global Financial System Papers No. 43 (2011) 37–9; and V. Tanzi and L. Schuknecht, 'Reconsidering the Fiscal Role of Government: The International Perspective' (1997) 87(2) Am. Econ. Rev. 164.

All of these transformations in the financial market took place at a pace and on a scale assisted by deregulation in the financial sector. Indeed, the boom years of a business cycle are very often accompanied by deregulation, and this super cycle was no exception.[4] When crisis struck in 2008, the involved governments were under great pressure to find quick fixes, in particular bailing out the important banks. This remedy exacerbated the sovereign debt problem, making restructurings more time consuming and painful in the absence of an internationally agreed debt workout mechanism. The financial sector 'has a comparable talent for privatising gains and socialising losses'.[5] Such a debt crisis containment and management policy is liable to give rise not only to negative feedback loops between the financial conditions of governments and the banking sector but also to the problem of moral hazard, which would encourage excessive risk-taking and over-borrowing and over-lending in the future, thus sowing the seeds of the next debt crisis. The global financial crisis has thus far led to a greater need for international efforts to build a more responsible culture in the financial market and to re-regulate the sector.

When we focus on the legal side of the sovereign financing problem, we see that most (with the exception of international official lending) sovereign debt is governed by domestic laws applicable to each case (American, Brazilian, Chinese, etc.).[6] This legal phenomenon is reinforced by the current trend of increasing domestic debt,[7] which usually fragments applicable domestic laws even more. However, as this debt touches upon global legal goods,[8] they have been subjected to international forces shaped, for example, by governments formally protecting their national lenders' interests through diplomatic complaints, claiming on their behalf in international courts and mixed commissions, establishing quasi-receivership administrators, and even taking military action against debtor countries,[9] establishing multilateral financial institutions that lend to states, and creating regional mechanisms to prevent or deal with debt crises.

These concrete international implications of sovereign debt have been exacerbated by the contemporary characteristics of the financial market and economic globalization, making debt crises hit stronger and deeper, and spread faster. Economic growth, financial stability, global governance, development, and human rights are intrinsically involved in sovereign financing and debt crises.

If financial actors'—sovereign debtors and their lenders alike—behaviours have direct and profound impacts upon those global legal goods and, consequently, can

[4] UNCTAD, *Trade and Development Report 2011* (United Nations, 2011).

[5] M. Wolf. 'Regulators Should Intervene in Bankers' Pay', *Financial Times*, 15 January 2008.

[6] A. Gelpern and B Setser, 'Domestic and External Debt: The Doomed Quest for Equal Treatment' (2004) 35 Geo. J. Int'l L. 795.

[7] See United Nations, General Assembly report on 'Recent developments in external debt', UN Doc. A/62/151, United Nations (2007) 1, 14–19.

[8] See the contributions on 'La protección de los bienes jurídicos globales' (The Protection of Global Legal Goods) (2012) 16 *Anuario de la Facultad de Derecho de la UAM*, C. Espósito and F. Garcimartín (eds); and the contributions to the symposium on 'Global Public Goods and the Plurality of Legal Orders' (2012) 23 Eur. J. Int'l L. 643.

[9] L.C. Buchheit, 'The Role of the Official Sector in Sovereign Debt Workouts' (2005) 6 Chi. J. Int'l L. 342.

be considered as international public authorities,[10] identifying the international standards that they have to follow is of great relevance. As the title of this book indicates, international law has a say in sovereign financing.

Yet, international law is very much underdeveloped in providing both substantive rules and mechanisms for the resolution of sovereign debt disputes. The historical and ideological explanation for this reality was that no international regulation is necessary to deal with sovereign debt problems and crises. However, financial crises in the era of globalization have substantially eroded such conviction and this helps to explain why, in 2012, the member states of the United Nations unanimously granted UNCTAD the explicit mandate to elaborate the Principles studied in this book.[11]

As several chapters in this book highlight, there is a fundamental legal void in sovereign financing.[12] Unlike international trade, there are no globally agreed norms or rules guiding sovereign financing, whether we focus on treaties, customary law, or case law.[13] This legal scenario has increased the collective action problems that arise when borrowers and lenders, and lenders among themselves, interact in the context of sovereign financing, provoking so-called 'sovereign debt dilemmas'.[14]

The consequences of poor global coordination based on scant, informal, and fragmented rules have been devastating in some instances.[15] The lack of clear boundaries in terms of behaviour, as well as inadequate expectations regarding the behaviour of lenders and borrowers, has subjected sovereign financing to the short-term conveniences of decision-makers and agents at the expense of the medium- to long-term economic and social interests of governments and citizens, up to and including default.

In this context of normative forlornness, the potential utility of the Principles on Responsible Sovereign Lending and Borrowing (the UNCTAD Principles) is clear. While the few principles and rules recognized by international legal sources were actually crystallized in the Principles, the major contribution of this set of principles is to coherently systematize general principles of law and best practice in the field of sovereign financing. The Principles also propose a holistic approach to debt regulation, as they are applicable to all sovereign borrowers and lenders regardless of whether they are private, bilateral, or multilateral. While this does not exclude the application of other relevant international norms,[16] it provides a systemic and comprehensive normative framework for sovereign financing. It is

[10] See A. von Bogdandy and M. Goldmann, Ch. 3 of this volume.

[11] UNCTAD XIII, 21–26 April 2012 (para. II.A.30).

[12] See J.P. Bohoslavsky and C. Espósito, Ch. 4 and M. Waibel, Ch. 5, both of this volume.

[13] A. Tanzi, 'Sull'insolvenza degli Stati nel diritto Internazionale' (2012) 95 Rivista di Diritto Internazionale 66, 67–70.

[14] J. Hay II, 'The Sovereign Debt Dilemma,' (2010) 75 Brook. L. Rev. 905.

[15] Y. Li, R. Olivares-Caminal, and U. Panizza, 'Avoiding Avoidable Debt Crises: Lessons from Recent Defaults' in C. Primo Braga and G. Vincelette (eds), *Sovereign Debt and the Financial Crisis* (The World Bank, 2011) 243.

[16] See the preamble to the UNCTAD Principles.

one step towards a greater integration of the broad framework of the international financial order.[17]

The UNCTAD Principles were meant to have a say not only in courtrooms but also in negotiating rooms.[18] This reflects the complex legal status of the Principles, their dynamic process of legalization and normative consolidation, which includes the interplay of fundamental principles of international public law—such as the prohibition of contribution to the violation of UN sanctions; general principles of law—such as due diligence; and suggested best practice—such as establishing an efficient debt management office.

As the preliminary section of the Principles explains, the causes and widespread negative effects of the global financial and economic crisis prompted UNCTAD to launch the initiative in 2009 under the broad heading 'Promoting Responsible Sovereign Lending and Borrowing'. This involves, *inter alia*, acting as a discussion forum with the aim of developing a set of principles and best practice to promote responsible sovereign lending and borrowing.

The UNCTAD Principles have three main goals. First, filling a normative gap, they aim to provide an additional layer of certainty in debt contracting. Secondly, they seek to contribute to changing behaviours, through which sovereign lenders and borrowers may achieve a higher degree of foresight in their debt management strategies brought about by more transparent processes, more information sharing, more accountability, and better allocation of responsibilities. Ultimately, such principles should reduce the prevalence of debt crises. And thirdly, they seek to create consensus around a set of well grounded principles applied to sovereign financing, which could lead to the establishment of criteria to assess whether the contracting of sovereign debt has been performed in accordance with internationally accepted principles.[19]

UNCTAD established an Expert Group in 2009, composed of world-renowned experts in law and economics, private investors, and NGOs. Senior representatives from the IMF, the World Bank, and Paris Club participated as observers. After several formal meetings and idea exchanges, the first draft of the Principles emerged in May 2011.[20]

During 2011 and 2012, six regional consultative meetings with governments took place in Buenos Aires, Bangkok, Luanda, Geneva, Jeddah, and Punta Cana in order to get their feedback on the contents and possible implementation. Around 75 countries provided their views. After a series of bilateral and high-level regional governmental consultations and subsequent refinements introduced by the project's Expert Group, the consolidated version of the Principles was launched on the occasion of UNCTAD XIII, inaugurating the project's phase of endorsement and

[17] C. Tietje, 'The International Financial Architecture as a Legal Order' (2011) 54 GYBIL 41.

[18] L. Buchheit and M. Gulati, 'Responsible Sovereign Lending and Borrowing' (2010) 63 Law & Cont. Prob. 63 (2010) 69, 86.

[19] See A. von Bogdandy and M. Goldmann, Ch. 3 of this volume.

[20] 4 May 2011, available at <http://www.unctad.info/en/Debt-Portal/News-Archive/Our-News/UNCTAD-Launches-Principles-on-Responsible-Sovereign-Lending-and-Borrowing-3052011>.

implementation. To date 12 countries (both developed and developing) have explicitly endorsed the Principles.

The General Assembly of the United Nations has repeatedly stressed the importance of this UNCTAD initiative on promoting responsible sovereign lending and borrowing. The IV United Nations Conference on the Least Developed Countries (2011) also noted in its resolutions the need to engage in more responsible sovereign lending and borrowing. More importantly, in April 2012, the mandate negotiated during UNCTAD XIII, which provides directions for the organization for the next four years, highlighted the importance of this initiative.

B. Objective and Contents of this Book

The objective of this book is simultaneously specific, broad, and far-reaching. The specificity of the project is determined naturally by the selection of the UNCTAD Principles as its special study of analysis. It is broad because the perspective of the research conducted is truly generalist: the study of the role of international law in sovereign financing and the observation of sovereign financing viewed through the lens of international law and its current fundamental debates, which encompass numerous important legal and economic issues concerning sovereign lending and borrowing. It is far-reaching because the study of the principles is not limited to an economic justification of the need for the Principles or the analysis of their legal character, but goes further, covering substantive issues of legality, normativity, administration, case studies, macro-economic implications, and possible implementation of the Principles.

As will be evident from the table of contents, this project purports to contribute to the ascertainment and progressive development of the scarce international law on sovereign financing through a legal approach that does not neglect interdisciplinary approaches needed to fully understand the problems and solutions discussed in the book. Indeed, setting the global scene in Part I of the book with a discussion on the economic rationale of the UNCTAD Principles, Yuefen Li and Ugo Panniza argue, in Chapter 2, that the Principles, in certain cases, can reduce the prevalence and costs of sovereign debt crises. Indeed, the analysis of sovereign debt trends and practices presented in this Chapter 2 shows that the Principles can potentially alter the incentive structure of the main players in the market for sovereign debt, leading to more prudent fiscal and debt management policies.

From a legal perspective, in Chapter 3, the task of setting the global scene is completed with a sophisticated analysis of the exercises of international public authority involved in sovereign debt restructurings as agreed between defaulting states and their multilateral, bilateral, or private creditors. The authors of this chapter, Armin von Bogdandy and Matthias Goldmann, are well-known for defending a general theory of publicness in international law as a framework for global governance activities.[21] Here, they apply their theory to sovereign debt

[21] See A. von Bogdandy, P. Dann, and M. Goldmann, 'Developing the Publicness of Public International Law: Towards a Legal Framework for Global Governance Activities' (2008) 9 Ger. Law J.

restructurings, and sustain that as exercises of international public authority, decisions taken in the context of sovereign debt restructurings need to be framed by public law in order to ensure their legitimacy. Their ideas are relevant not only for the faith that the authors place in legal scholarship as a means to promote such public law framework, but also for the way in which they propose a set of procedural and substantive principles to govern the public law framework for sovereign debt restructurings.

Part II of the book deals with the legal status of the UNCTAD Principles. The four chapters present a refined set of arguments covering different aspects of the legality and normativity of the Principles. In Chapter 4, Juan Pablo Bohoslavsky and Carlos Espósito argue that the legal character of the Principles, which is generally well-rooted and broadly tested in domestic laws, is not determined by its soft law shell but will depend mainly on variables affecting the extent to which each principle is supported by international law, and the intrinsic value of the Principles in persuading stakeholders that they are necessary in international sovereign financing to overcome global problems. Michael Waibel, in Chapter 5, considers to what extent existing state practice supports the Principles, and concludes that they were not produced out of thin air as there is some state practice supporting aspects of the Principles. As in the previous chapter, Waibel believes that the Principles could become a catalyst for the creation of a body of international rules regulating sovereign lending and borrowing. This idea is also supported by Matthias Goldmann's Chapter 6, which argues convincingly that the Principles have their basis in comparative and analogical reasoning.[22] His study offers an analysis of how the Principles might corroborate the formation of principles in international law—a corroboration that Goldmann establishes through the analysis of substantive fiscal policy rules on debt or deficit ceilings, and rules on fiscal transparency. The last chapter of Part II, written by Antonis Bredimas, Anastasios Gourgourinis, and Georges Pavlidis in a comparative spirit, presents a critical assessment of the relationship between the UNCTAD Principles and the law of sovereign debt restructuring. Through the analysis of domestic insolvency law and international investment law, the authors show antagonisms and convergences between the Principles and their legal environment. In conclusion they also insist on the value of the Principles experience, as a forum of experts, stakeholders, and policy-makers for discussion and debate of the public law framework for sovereign debt restructurings.

Part III of the book relates to debt management and the UNCTAD Principles. In Chapter 8, Kunibert Raffer elaborates on the ways the Principles would improve the regulation of sovereign debt markets, focusing on the creditors' side. Raffer argues that the Principles would enhance the rule of law in sovereign financing,

1375, reprinted in A. von Bogdandy et al., *The Exercise of Public Authority by International Institutions. Advancing International Institutional Law* (Springer, 2010) 3.

[22] See further the comparative study of M. Goldmann, 'Responsible Sovereign Lending and Borrowing: The View from Domestic Jurisdictions. A Comparative Survey', available at <http://www.unctad.info/upload/Debt%20Portal/RSLB_MGoldmann_02-2012.pdf>.

foster accountability for international financial institutions, give more effective protection to bona fide creditors, and help to solve difficult issues such as the 'vulture funds' problem. In Chapter 9, Juan Bautista Justo looks into the Principles and the problem of corruption. It is interesting to note that his exploration of the relationship between the Principles and the United Nations Convention against Corruption, adopted by the General Assembly of the United Nations on 31 October 2003,[23] reveals a great deal of synergy as both instruments are based on some basic standards, such as the fiduciary responsibility of government officials to citizens, transparency, and accountability. Moreover, for Justo, the interaction of these instruments may benefit from mutual advantages given the fact that the UNCAC is a hard law instrument and the Principles is a soft law instrument: UNCAC can provide for hard law support to the UNCTAD Principles, while the Principles can allow for the development of flexible and more sophisticated tools to fight corruption in the field of sovereign debt. The third contribution to this Part is a study of the concept of fiduciary responsibility as a core element of the Principles. In Chapter 10, José Oyola and Marie Sudreau use a comparative method of analysis to examine and identify agency patterns present in numerous countries characterizing fiduciary relations in the field of debt contracting.

Part IV of the book contains two studies of the UNCTAD Principles and China. In Chapter 11, Meibo Huang and Dandan Zhu present a careful description of China's sovereign lending and borrowing practices and its increasing influence in the world since 1995, and advance some suggestions for the improvement of China's preferential loans policies and practices based on the contents and directives of the Principles, including debt sustainability and transparency. Xiuli Han, in Chapter 12, conducts an analysis of the Principles from the Chinese perspective, and suggests that the Principles are significant for the standardization of China's lending practices both in the short and the long term.

Part V of the book, which relates to problems of the Eurozone, opens with a study by Lee Buchheit and Mitu Gulati in Chapter 13. The authors offer a novel analysis of contingent liabilities in sovereign debt restructurings. They show the need to reconsider the problem following the growth of guarantees on third party debt in many countries, which used them as a tool to control turbulence in their financial markets. Buchheit and Gulati affirm that ignoring this fact can undermine the sustainability of a debt restructuring agreement. However, they also admit that answers—some of which are discussed in their chapter—to the questions of whether and how to restructure contingent liabilities are not obvious. In Chapter 14, Ignacio Tirado completes Part V with a broad study of the European Union's current and recently established mechanisms to deal with sovereign insolvency. Tirado describes these mechanisms, taking into account the UNCTAD Principles, and argues that their adequate implementation should converge with the path of balance and contained borrowing provided for in the Principles.

[23] See UNGA Res A/58/4, of 31 October 2003. The Convention entered into force on 14 December 2005 and has 165 State Parties as of 24 December 2012, <http://www.unodc.org/unodc/en/treaties/CAC/signatories.html>.

However, Tirado also warns about the possible misconception of the mechanisms, which can affect international creditors; in any case, the author believes that the new system of mandatory collective action clauses (CACs), fully coherent with the Principles, should be welcomed.

Implementation defines the contributions of Part VI of the book. Mark Weidemaier opens with Chapter 15, in which he explores and ultimately questions whether the UNCTAD Principles are likely to have the effect of changing sovereign lending practices and sovereign loan contracts through consensus-building, promulgating model contract terms, and other soft law approaches. Weidemaier uses a dataset of sovereign bonds in order to demonstrate how contracts responded to past initiatives that attempted to change those same practices, finding that prior soft law efforts have not prompted changes in contracts, while more forceful interventions in the bond markets have sometimes had unanticipated effects. In Chapter 16, Anna Gelpern considers concrete strategies for implementing the Principles. Drawing on studies of soft law and new governance, and on the recent experience in promoting best practice in international finance, she argues that the best strategy for implementation consists of maintaining the current non-binding character of the Principles, while embedding implementation in multi-stakeholder arrangements for ongoing disclosure, assessment, interpretation, and adaptation. This strategy has the best chance of changing behaviour in sovereign lending and borrowing by creating constituencies for implementation and sustained compliance.

In Chapter 17, Robert Howse offers some concluding remarks from a legal perspective. He underscores two major contributions of the UNCTAD Principles: first, the qualification of a sovereign debtor's obligation to repay the debt in full in situations of economic necessity; and secondly, the reconsideration of the odious debt doctrine by establishing the purposes of serving the public good and transparency as criteria for valid sovereign debt obligations. More importantly, Howse also underlines the fact that there is no need for the Principles to become a formal international source of law in order to realize these contributions. On the contrary, Howse believes that, in line with the ideas offered by Anna Gelpern, Matthias Goldmann, Juan Pablo Bohoslavsky, and Carlos Espósito in their respective chapters, the Principles offer new and well-grounded 'normative tools for reshaping legal relations between sovereign debtors and both official and private creditors in the absence of a centralized international institution or tribunal'.

C. Concluding Remarks

As has been explained in detail elsewhere,[24] the UNCTAD Principles initiative is consistent with the ongoing gradual, political shift towards conceding increasing

[24] J.P. Bohoslavsky and Y. Li, 'UNCTAD Principles on Responsible Sovereign Financing: The Intersection of Finance, Law and Politics' in L. Buchheit and R. Lastra (eds), *Sovereign Debt Management* (Oxford University Press, forthcoming 2013).

competencies to the United Nations in addressing global economic problems. More specifically, the idea that the United Nations should be actively engaged in the debate and search for remedies on global financial issues is gaining political momentum. Besides the support to this initiative reflected in the wording of the last annual UN General Assembly resolutions, the new UNCTAD mandate unanimously agreed in Doha in 2012 including a reference to this specific initiative, and the states' endorsements of the Principles, the current efforts of the Second Committee of the UN General Assembly to promote global consensus on a debt workout mechanism must also be mentioned.[25] This is why it is not surprising that, in 2012, UNCTAD established a new initiative on Debt Restructuring Mechanism.[26]

With its universal and equal membership, neutrality, acknowledged technical capacity in the area of debt issues, and absence of conflict of interests (it is neither lender nor borrower), UNCTAD is well placed to coordinate the process of drafting and building consensus around global standards to govern in the sovereign debt realm.

Within (and due to) this global political and institutional dynamic, UNCTAD has proposed the Principles with the hope of contributing to the building of a more responsible culture in sovereign financing *ex ante* and *ex post* debt contracting, thus creating an important instrument for debt crisis prevention. Of course, good intentions are not enough. That is why this book was written: to critically assess the legal and economic implications of the Principles.

As Robert Howse emphasizes in his chapter, the authors of this book concur in the interpretation of the legal status of the Principles as a new normative tool incorporated in a soft law instrument, which may display many and different effects, with diverse degrees of normativity.[27] Of course, the caveat that Mark Weidemaier highlights on the limits to the production of change in sovereign lending practices and the possible unintended effects of the Principles must be taken into account when considering strategies for the implementation of the Principles.[28] The call for explicit endorsements from states and the special attention paid to the legal domestic roots of the Principles acknowledge the importance of official consent in this process. At the same time, given that fair laws (seeking to approach the optimal liability is crucial in this regard) exert a compliance pull compelling states, the Principles seem to have great potential in terms of implementation. It is worth mentioning that the International Organisation of Supreme

[25] 'UNCTAD's pioneer work on sovereign debt restructuring widely recognized by world-renowned experts and policy makers', UNCTAD press release, Geneva, 29 October 2012, available at <http://unctad.org/en/pages/newsdetails.aspx?OriginalVersionID=339&Sitemap_x0020_Taxonomy=Globalization%20and%20Development>.

[26] 'Norway Pledges Financial Support for UNCTAD's Project on Responsible Sovereign Financing', UNCTAD press release, Geneva, 25 October 2012, available at <http://www.unctad.info/en/Debt-Portal/News-Archive/Our-News/Norway-Pledges-Financial-Support-for-UNCTADs-Project-on-Responsible-Sovereign-Financing-25102012>.

[27] See the chapters in this volume by Anna Gelpern (Ch. 16), Matthias Goldmann (Ch. 6), and Juan Pablo Bohoslavsky and Carlos Espósito (Ch 4).

[28] See M.C. Weidemaier, Ch. 15 of this volume.

Audit Institutions (INTOSAI) is updating its international standards to audit public debt based on the UNCTAD Principles.

With a view to creating a standard at the international level, the UNCTAD Principles hope to encourage all UN member states to implement them in accordance with their national laws and domestic requirements. Currently, UNCTAD is preparing a set of detailed guidelines analysing the various contexts in which the Principles have been implemented successfully so as to provide guidance to member states upon request. These guidelines are drafted in collaboration with a broad range of stakeholders as well as the Expert Group.

From a more ambitious angle, considering the missing regulatory link between trade, finance, sovereign debt, and currency issues,[29] it would be interesting to assess whether general principles such as due diligence, good faith, and transparency can be considered as universal standards in international economic law and, if this is the case, what their concrete implications are. This approach would be consistent with a holistic interpretation of the problems that globalization has brought or exacerbated.

[29] Tietje (n. 17) 34.

PART I

SETTING THE GLOBAL SCENE

2

The Economic Rationale for the Principles on Promoting Responsible Sovereign Lending and Borrowing

Yuefen Li and Ugo Panizza

A. Introduction

If used well, sovereign debt can contribute to economic development and help in stabilizing economic fluctuations. Excessive debt, however, can also lead to costly crises, which are often followed by long periods of economic stagnation.[1] In a world of globalized and lightly regulated finance, debt crises can have large negative international spillovers. Therefore, they are no longer a matter that only concerns domestic actors. Given these large negative externalities arising from debt crises, it is surprising that there are no well-defined international laws, rules, and regulations aimed at limiting the prevalence and costs of such crises. If fact, such paucity of international laws and regulations not only concerns sovereign debt, but, as observed by Chris Brummer, finance in general: 'hard law institutions and instruments play a very limited role in the regulation of finance, especially at the global multilateral level. National authorities face, as a result, few limitations with regard to how they oversee their national markets'.[2]

The principles on promoting responsible sovereign lending and borrowing discussed in this book are an attempt to address this legal vacuum. Their objective is to maximize the development impact of sovereign borrowing while minimizing its risks and costs. The Principles aim at achieving these objectives by delineating the framework and boundaries of sovereign lending and borrowing; by clearly spelling out what should be considered as unacceptable behaviour; and by setting the standards to which the actors that participate in sovereign lending and borrowing should adhere in fulfilling their roles. In doing so, the UNCTAD

[1] The Latin American 'Lost Decade' in the 1980s is an example of a protracted economic slump caused by a devastating debt crisis.

[2] C. Brummer, 'Why Soft Law Dominates International Finance—and not Trade' (2010) 13 J. Int'l Econ. L. 623.

Principles lay out the required procedures and institutions for debt crisis prevention and resolution and specify what is expected and what should be prohibited.

While the Principles cannot guarantee that the world will never experience another debt crisis, they are an important step towards the promotion of more responsible behaviour in the realm of sovereign finance. The current crisis provides ample evidence of the need for such change in behaviour.

Over the last 200 years, more than 260 sovereign default episodes have been observed, with nearly 120 episodes during the last 30 years.[3] There are also many debt and financial crises which did not lead to a sovereign default but still carried a high social and economic cost. The existence of such crises, their cost, and the lack of a well-defined mechanism for restructuring sovereign debts are often considered a sufficient rationale for formulating a universally agreed set of principles for the promotion of responsible sovereign lending and borrowing.[4] However, costly debt crises are not a sufficient condition for an initiative aimed at modifying the behaviour of the actors in the sovereign debt market. Such an initiative would only be justified if crises are caused by specific actions, and if the implementation of the UNCTAD Principles can contribute to the prevention of debt crises or reduce their costs.

An example from the medical sciences can be illuminating. There are certain types of diseases, such as coronary artery disease, which are associated with behaviour. Therefore, it makes sense to issue dietary and exercise guidelines that can limit the prevalence of such a disease. There are, however, also medical conditions which are due to genetic problems or purely to bad luck. In such cases, preventative measures are not of great help.

Like diseases, debt crises have different origins and natures. As in the case of a patient with a poor diet, they may be due to irresponsible behaviour in debt contracting. Alternatively, they may be linked to a country's economic structure or stage of development, which is close to the analogy of genetic problems. Finally, crises may be due to back luck, as when a country is hit by a natural disasters or an external shock (such as sudden changes in commodity prices, a sudden stop in capital flows, or a contraction in global demand).

While adherence to the Principles can fully prevent debt crises that are due to misbehaviour, they may be less successful in addressing the last two types of crises. However, just as a good diet and exercise can beef up the immune system and thus also help in the presence of diseases or accidents which are not caused by unhealthy habits, adhering to the Principles may strengthen a country's overall economic situation and increase that country's resilience to various types of shocks and congenital problems.

Of course, the only way to eliminate debt crises completely is to prevent countries from borrowing. However, well-used sovereign financing can be a powerful tool for

[3] E. Borensztein and U. Panizza, 'The Costs of Sovereign Default,' IMF Staff Papers, Palgrave Macmillan, vol. 56(4), 683–741, November (2009).

[4] L. Buchheit and M. Gulati, 'Responsible Sovereign Lending and Borrowing', UNCTAD Discussion Papers, No.198 (2010), available at <http://papers.ssrn.com/sol3/papers.cfm?abstract_id=1584624>.

promoting economic development, and, even if feasible, imposing very low debt ceilings is likely to be suboptimal. It would be like trying to limit the prevalence of car accidents by making automobiles illegal. The objective of this chapter is to discuss what types of actions or deficiencies increase the likelihood of debt crises and how such failures can be addressed by the principles on responsible sovereign lending and borrowing described in this volume.

The chapter is organized as follows. Section B starts by describing recent trends in sovereign debt in developing and developed economies, then introduces the concept of Ricardian Equivalence, stating that public debt has no real effects, and discusses why Ricardian Equivalence does not hold in practice. The section concludes with a discussion of the differences between domestic and external public debt. Section C discusses the origin of debt crises and, while highlighting the importance of prudent fiscal policies, it points out that debt crises do not always have a fiscal nature and that good debt management is key for crisis prevention. Section D discusses the incentive structure of the main players in the market for sovereign debt and shows how the Principles have the potential to alter such incentives and lead to more prudent fiscal and debt management policies. Section E concludes.

B. The Importance and Magnitude of Sovereign Financing

In 1991, the total stock of public debt of high-income countries stood at approximately US$10 trillion, it remained stable at around $16 trillion in the second half of the 1990s and the first years of the new millennium and then started growing rapidly after 2003 and accelerated even more after 2007, surpassing $40 trillion in 2010 (see Figure 2.1). The debt to GDP ratio of this group of countries, which hovered at around 60 to 70 per cent over the period 1991–2007, also started growing rapidly in the last few years and has now surpassed 100 per cent. The total stock of public debt of developing countries went from approximately $2 trillion in 1992 to about $7 trillion in 2010 (see Figure 2.2). Developing countries as a group have lower debt ratios than the advanced economies. In fact the public debt-to-GDP ratio decreased from approximately 60 per cent in 1992, to about 37 per cent in 2010.

I. Does public debt matter?

Countries issue public debt for essentially four reasons: (1) to finance investment in physical or human capital; (2) to smooth business cycles; (3) to affect the intertemporal distribution of wealth; and (4) to respond to exceptional events such as war, natural disasters, or financial crises. These motives are similar to those that lead households to incur debt. However, there are important differences between public and private debt. While it is reasonable to assume that the decision of the head of a household to borrow aims at maximizing the household's welfare, the decision to contract public debt may be driven by short-term objectives and not by the maximization of social welfare. Furthermore, since negative bequests are normally

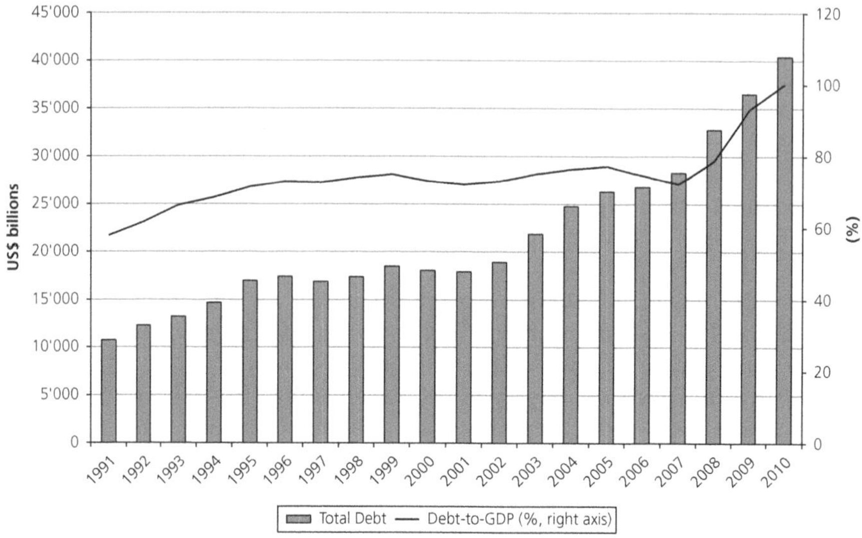

Fig. 2.1 The evolution of public debt in high income countries

Source: Authors' calculations based on an updated version of the dataset described in Panizza (2008) <http://ideas.repec.org/p/unc/dispap/188.html>.

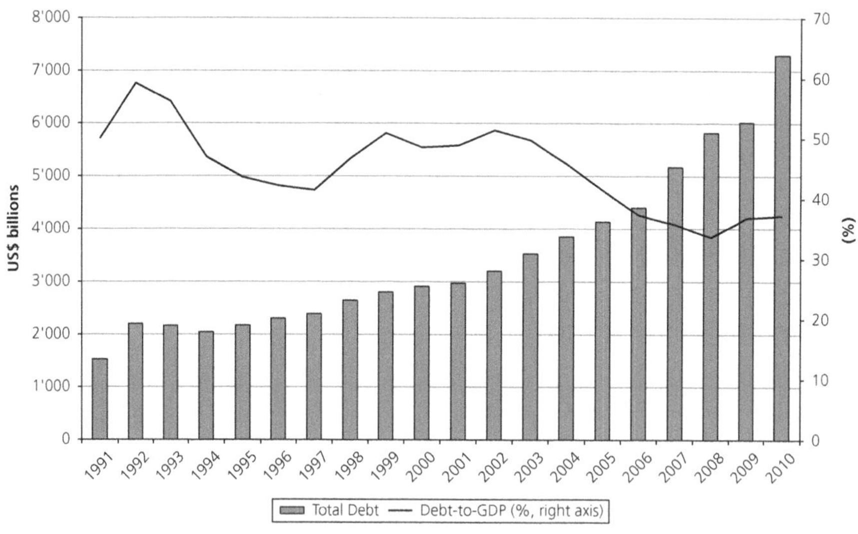

Fig. 2.2 The evolution of public debt in developing countries

Source: Authors' calculations based on an updated version of the dataset described in Panizza (2008) <http://ideas.repec.org/p/unc/dispap/188.html>.

non-enforceable, private debts cannot be forced on to future generations, but public debt can be passed on to future generations which did not have a say when the debt was contracted. Finally, the government is a large player and its borrowing decisions can have important spillovers, positive and negative, on the rest of the economy.[5]

But does public debt really matter? This seems a silly question on the basis of what we read in the newspapers every day. And yet, 'Ricardian Equivalence' states that under certain conditions public debt does not matter. While the assumptions under which Ricardian Equivalence holds are unrealistic, a discussion of this concept is helpful for a better understanding of why debt does matter. Ricardian Equivalence, which was formalized in a 1974 article by the American economist Robert Barro, is based on the intuition of the nineteenth-century British economist David Ricardo, who observed that debt needs to be financed with future taxes. Therefore, rational individuals will increase savings up to the point at which the increase in private savings fully compensates the public sector deficit that led to the issuance of new debt.[6] As a consequence, national saving, consumption, and economic growth will not be affected by the government's decision to finance a given amount of public expenditure with taxation or by issuing new debt.

The Ricardian equivalence result is based on three assumptions. First, since debt redistributes resources across generations, Ricardian equivalence can only hold if economic decisions are made by *forward-looking individuals characterized by intergenerational altruism*. Secondly, private agents can mimic the borrowing decision of the government only if they can access credit under the same conditions. As a consequence, Ricardian equivalence fails in the presence of credit constraints and it requires *perfect capital markets*. Thirdly, as distortionary taxes can have a direct effect on saving and labour supply decisions, Ricardian equivalence only holds in the presence of *non-distortionary (lump-sum) taxes*.

Since these assumptions do not generally hold, public debt tends to have real effects in the short and long run. In the presence of unutilized resources, a debt-financed tax cut or an increase in public expenditure can increase aggregate demand and speed the recovery from a recession. The long-run effect of debt is more controversial. Standard economic theory assumes that when prices and wages are allowed to adjust fully to their equilibrium level, output becomes supply determined and an increase in debt that leads to higher consumption and lower savings will also increase the interest rate, crowd out investment, and, hence, reduce output in the long run. On the empirical side, it is not clear whether debt has an effect on long-run growth.[7]

[5] For a detailed discussion, see E. Borensztein, E. Levy Yeyati, and U. Panizza, *Living with Debt* (Harvard University David Rockefeller Center for Latin American Studies, 2006).

[6] R. Barro, 'Are Government Bonds Net Wealth?' (1974) 82(6) J. Pol. Econ. 1095.

[7] Papers that find a negative relationship between public debt and economic growth include C. M. Reinhart, V.R. Reinhart, and K.S. Rogoff, 'Debt Overhangs: Past and Present', NBER Working Papers 18015 (2012). Papers that argue that public debt has no causal effect on economic growth include U. Panizza and A.F. Presbitero, 'Public Debt and Economic Growth: Is There a Causal Effect?', Money Finance Research Working Papers 65 (2012).

II. Different types of debt[8]

Problems linked to the external debt problems of advanced economies are rarely mentioned, as the discussion tend to focus on total public debt. In developing countries, however, the analysis of public debt has traditionally focused on external debt.

Past research on the debt problems of developing countries has focused on external debt for two reasons. First, while external borrowing can increase a country's access to resources, domestic borrowing only transfers resources within the country. Hence, only external debt generates a 'transfer' problem.[9] Secondly, since central banks in developing countries cannot print the hard currency necessary to repay external debt, external borrowing is usually associated with vulnerabilities that may lead to debt crises. At the same time, the external debt problems of advanced economies are often forgotten because developed economies tend to issue most of their debt in the domestic markets. To be sure, the official definition of external debt does not focus on the place of issuance but on the residence of the creditors. Therefore, countries that issue all their debt domestically but sell their bonds to non-residents do have an external debt.

However, over recent years, several developing countries have adopted aggressive policies aimed at retiring public external debt and replacing it with domestically issued debt. At the same time, some advanced economies have accumulated large external debt. For instance, 100 per cent of the debt of the United States is issued domestically. However, of the US$8.9 trillion of debt securities issued by the US Treasury and held by the public, approximately $5 trillion are held by non-residents. Therefore 56 per cent of US public debt is external.[10] Moreover, countries in the euro area no longer have complete control over the currency in which their debt is denominated and the current European crisis has many elements in common with the emerging markets crises of the second half of the 1990s. As a consequence, in the current environment of increasing financial integration, common currency areas, and open capital accounts, the traditional distinction between external and domestic debt makes less sense than in the past.

C. The Origins of Debt Crises

The current predicaments of some European countries show that debt crises can have different origins.[11] Debt crises may be due to irresponsible fiscal behaviour;

[8] This subsection draws on U. Panizza, 'Domestic And External Public Debt In Developing Countries', UNCTAD Discussion Papers 188 (2008).

[9] J.M. Keynes, 'The German Transfer Problem' (1929) 39 Econ. J. 172.

[10] These data are for December 2011. Source: US Treasury, TABLE OFS-2.—Estimated Ownership of U.S. Treasury Securities. Ownership of Federal Securities, available at <http://www.fms.treas.gov/bulletin/index.html>.

[11] For more details, see J. Bibow, 'The Euro Debt Crisis and Germany's Euro Trilemma', Levy Economics Institute, Working Paper No. 721 (2012).

they can be caused by excessive private sector debt; they may be linked to a risky debt structure; or they can be triggered by exogenous shocks.

Let us start with a comparison of the fiscal performance of the GIIPS (Greece, Ireland, Italy, Portugal, and Spain) with that of other European countries in the run-up to the crisis. Over the period 2000–07, the Greek government ran an average budget deficit close to 5.5 per cent of GDP. This was nearly three times the euro area average and twice the maximum threshold set by the Stability and Growth Pact (SGP). Portugal's average budget deficit was also much higher than the euro area average, and above the 3 per cent threshold of the SGP (see Figure 2.3). Italy and France, in contrast, had average deficits which were below the 3 per cent SGP threshold, one percentage point higher than the euro area average, and only slightly higher (half a percentage point) than Germany's average deficit. The remaining two GIIPS, Ireland and Spain, had budget surpluses over the period 2000–07.

The primary budget balance (i.e. the budget balance net of interest payment), which is the only variable under partial control of the fiscal authorities, gives an even starker picture. Over the period 2000–07, Portugal and Greece had a small primary deficit and Germany and France had a surplus which was lower than the average surplus of the euro area (see Figure 2.4). Over the same period, Ireland, Italy, and Spain had large surpluses, well above the euro area average.

Figures 2.3 and 2.4 suggest that Greece's and, to some extent, Portugal's problems are rooted in an unsustainable fiscal stance. The chronic fiscal deficits and opaque fiscal accounts that eventually led to the Greek debt crisis are a clear

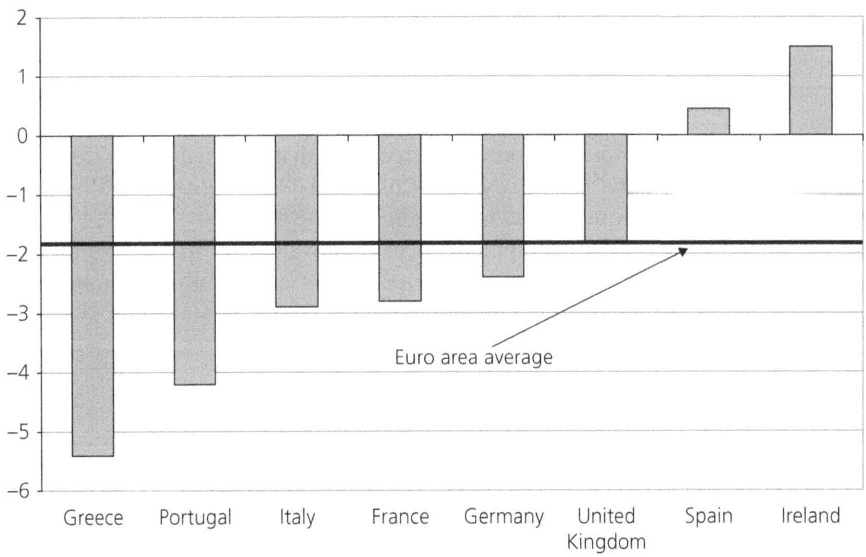

Fig. 2.3 Budget balance as a percentage of GDP (average 2000–07)

Source: Authors' elaborations based on Eurostat data.

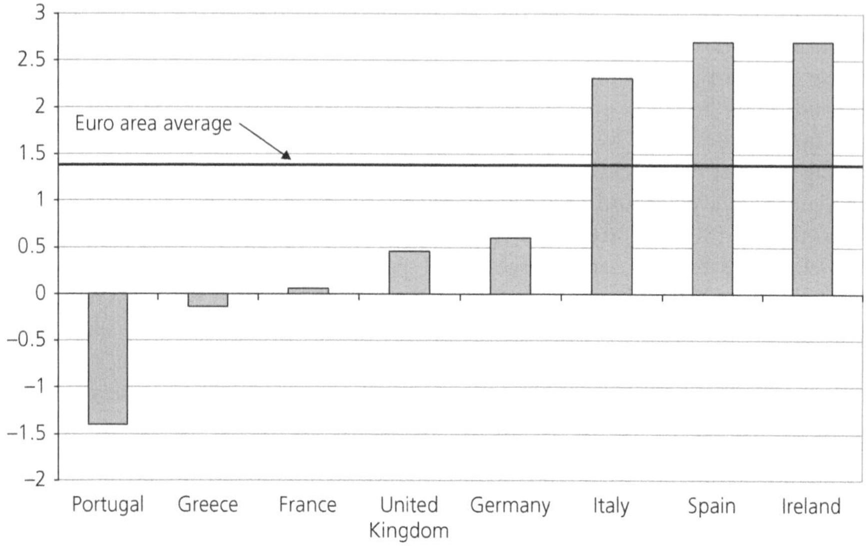

Fig. 2.4 Primary budget balance as a percentage of GDP (average 2000–07)
Source: Authors' elaborations based on Eurostat data.

violation of Principles 10, 11, and 13, which focus on avoiding over-borrowing, on providing appropriate disclosure and transparency of fiscal accounts, and require adequate debt management and monitoring.

The cases of Ireland, Italy, and Spain are, however, more complicated. Ireland's and Spain's predicaments are not of a fiscal nature, but originate in excessive domestic and external private sector debt (yet another nail in the coffin of the Lawson Doctrine). These countries are now suffering the consequences of the explosion of a housing bubble fuelled by rapid credit growth. The swing in the fiscal accounts of Ireland and Spain was brought about by the recession that followed the explosion of the real estate bubble and by the cost of rescuing their banking systems. The large fiscal deficit was a consequence and not a cause of the crisis.[12]

While the Principles do not explicitly focus on private debt, they recognize the need to pay attention to contingent liabilities.[13] This is especially important in a globalized world characterized by financial cycles and financial contagion.[14] Italy's

[12] Of course, experts in Monday morning quarterbacking now argue that the policy stance of Spain or Ireland should have been tighter during the good years. However, before 2007 there was no indication that these countries were running an expansionary fiscal policy. For instance, independent IMF estimations based on the information available in April 2007 suggested that Spain was running a large structural fiscal surplus and that the country would have kept running structural surpluses until the end of the estimation period.

[13] See Principle 4 on 'Responsible credit decisions', and see also L. Buchheit and M. Gulati, Ch. 13 of this book.

[14] A. Kose, S. Claessens, and M. Terrones, 'Financial Cycles: What? How? When?', *IMF* Working Papers 11/76 (2011).

problems did not originate in recent fiscal misbehaviour or in a housing boom. Italy was instead caught in a weak position by the global crisis due to its high debt ratio (caused by out of control fiscal accounts in the 1980s; again, a violation of the Principle that warns against over-borrowing) and lacklustre growth performance.

We thus have five euro area countries facing a debt crisis and at least three different reasons for the crisis. There is also one common factor, however. In all cases, the crisis was amplified by the fact that, by adopting the euro, these countries lost their ability to issue debt in a currency over which they have full control and to use their national central banks as lenders of last resort. Countries that join a monetary union lose an instrument of economic policy, as the debt structure of these countries becomes similar to that of emerging market countries with a large share of foreign currency debt (the original sin problem).[15] This explains why UK Gilts have now become a safe haven, with yields which are much lower than those prevailing before the crisis (see Figure 2.5), even if the debt-to-GDP ratio of the United Kingdom has grown rapidly over the past few years and remains higher than that of, say, Spain (see Figure 2.6).[16]

The Argentinian default of 2001–02 is a good example of the importance of debt composition. In the ten years preceding the default, Argentina ran a fairly moderate fiscal policy. The average deficit was 1.2 per cent of GDP and even in the deepest year of the crisis Argentina's deficit was below 3 per cent of GDP (see Figure 2.7). Debt levels were also fairly low, about 55 per cent of GDP in 2001 (see Figure 2.8). Over 2001 and 2002, Argentina ran an average budget deficit of less than 3 per cent of GDP, but the Argentinian debt to GDP ratio went from approximately 55 per cent in 2001 to 150 per cent in 2002. Argentina's sudden debt explosion was caused by the fact that about half of the country's debt was denominated in US dollars. When Argentina abandoned its dollar peg and the exchange rate went from one peso per dollar to four pesos per dollar, the local currency value of the dollar-denominated debt quadrupled. In this case, the debt crisis was not due to an irresponsible fiscal policy, but to the presence of foreign currency-denominated debt and an overvalued currency.

Debt crises can also be due to external shocks, either real or financial. Small and vulnerable economies that are hit by a large natural disaster can be pushed to the edge of insolvency and so can commodity exporters (importers) that face a sudden drop (increase) in commodity prices. External financial shocks can lead to sudden stops in capital flows which, in turn, may cause liquidity and possibly solvency crises.[17]

[15] P. De Grauwe, 'Managing a Fragile Eurozone' (2011) 12(2) CESifo Forum 40; B. Eichengreen, R. Hausmann, and U. Panizza, 'Currency Mismatches, Debt Intolerance, and the Original Sin: Why They Are Not the Same and Why It Matters' in S. Edwards (ed.), *Capital Controls and Capital Flows in Emerging Economies: Policies, Practices and Consequences* (National Bureau of Economic Research, 2007) 121.

[16] This example is originally from De Grauwe (n. 15).

[17] For a discussion of financial contagion and sudden stops, see G.A. Calvo, *Emerging Capital Markets in Turmoil: Bad Luck or Bad Policy?* (MIT Press, 2005).

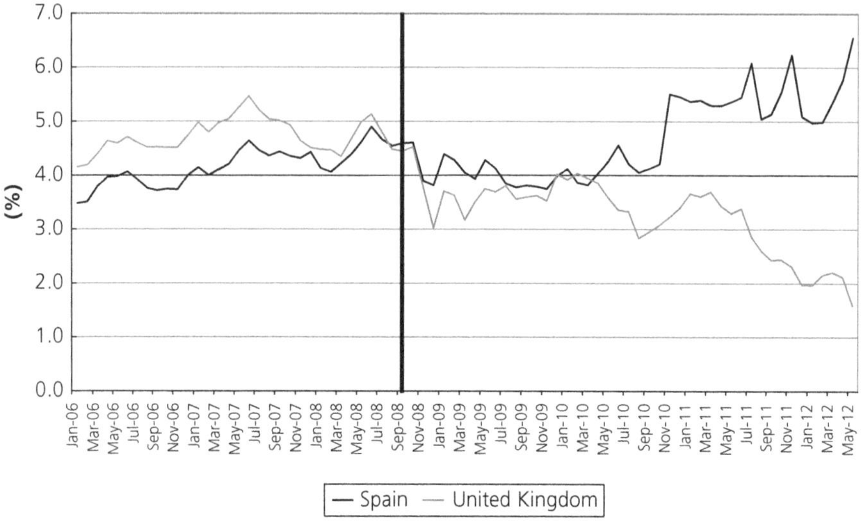

Fig. 2.5 Ten-year government bond yields (Spain versus UK)
Source: Bloomberg.

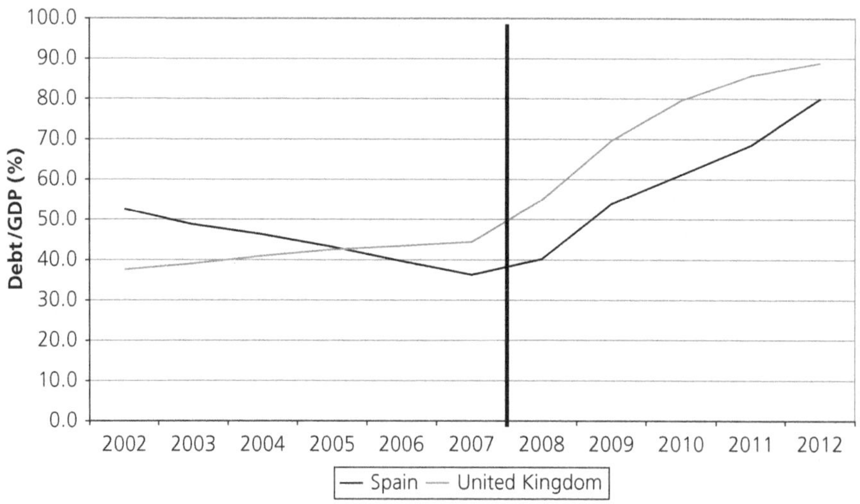

Fig. 2.6 Total gross public debt/GDP (Spain versus UK)
Source: Eurostat.

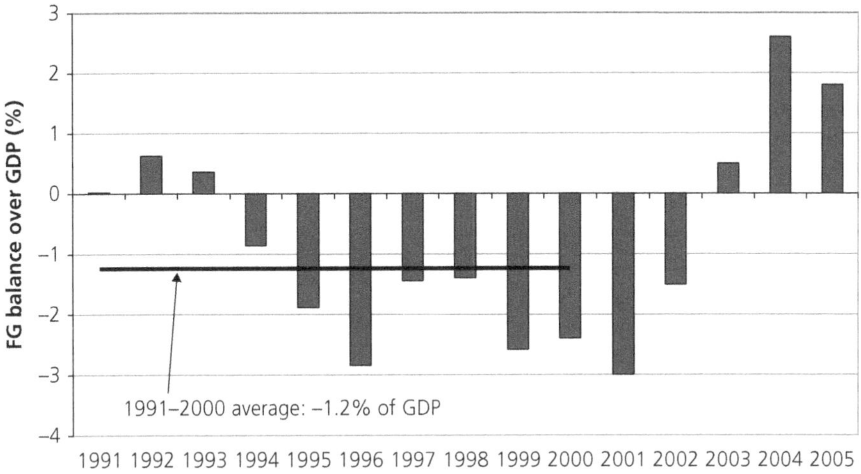

Fig. 2.7 Argentina: federal government balance over GDP

Source: JP Morgan (post-1998) and ECLAC (pre-1998) data.

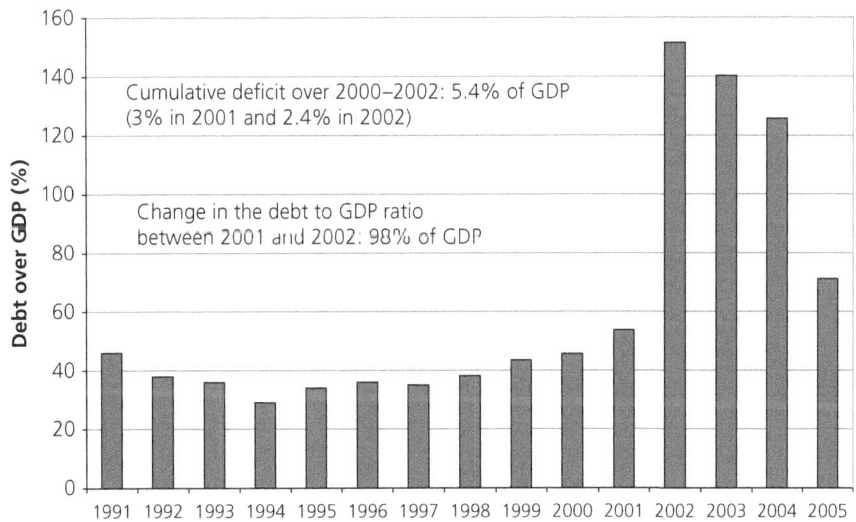

Fig. 2.8 Argentina: public debt/GDP

Source: Authors' elaborations based on JP Morgan (post-1998) and ECLAC (pre-1998) data.

Understanding the origin of crises is important both *ex ante*—in order to implement policies aimed at reducing their frequency—and *ex post*, because different types of crises require different policy responses. The previous discussion suggests that prudent fiscal policy is a necessary but not sufficient condition for the prevention of a debt crisis. Crisis prevention also requires adequate financial regulation, prudent capital account management, a wise exchange rate policy, a safe debt structure, self-insurance, and an effective international lender of last resort. Some of these crisis prevention policies are at the centre of the current version of the UNCTAD Principles and others will need further work and policy actions.

D. Why Do We Need a Set of Principles?

The previous section discussed the different natures of debt crises and highlighted a set of policy actions that can reduce the prevalence and cost of debt crises. In a perfect world, economic agents in the public and private sectors would implement these policies without the need to be guided by a set of principles. In such a perfect world, there would not be any need to create an international consensus around a set of principles for responsible behaviour. However, we have frequently been reminded, in particular by the current global financial crisis, that the world is far from perfect.

This section focuses on the incentive structure of the main players in the market for sovereign debt. We start by discussing the roots of irresponsible fiscal policies; we then discuss the roots of asset and credit booms; and conclude by analysing why agents have an incentive to under-insure. In our discussion, we will focus on both political and market failures and on how the Principles can address these failures.

I. Over-borrowing and over-lending

Over-borrowing refers to a situation in which the government borrows more than what is socially optimal.[18] For any government that over-borrows there is an actor in the private or official sector that over-lends. Why do agents over-borrow and over-lend? This is due to a mix of political and market failures.

1. Incentives to over-borrow

A benevolent social planner with full information would borrow up to the point at which the social marginal cost of an additional unit of debt (this includes principal, interest repayment, and any possible externality brought about by higher debt levels) equals the social return of an additional unit of debt-financed government expenditure. In other words, a benevolent social planner with full information would never over-borrow. Principle 14, 'Avoiding Incidences of Over-borrowing', highlights the importance of such cost-benefit analysis and is specific in establishing

[18] E. Borensztein, M. Chamon, O. Jeanne, P. Mauro, and J. Zettelmeyer, 'Sovereign Debt Structure for Crisis Prevention', IMF Occasional Papers 237, International Monetary Fund (2005).

that governments should weight the social costs and benefits of debt issuances carefully before incurring new debt obligations.

A social planner with imperfect information may not over-borrow *ex ante* but may end up doing it *ex post* if faced with an unexpected negative shock. While this observation has important practical implications, uncertainty would be irrelevant in a world with a complete insurance market. We will discuss under-insurance below, but for the moment we will maintain the assumption of perfect information and ask whether there are conditions in which policy-makers may end up over-borrowing even if they had perfect information. If the policy-maker is a benevolent social planner, the answer is no. Therefore, over-borrowing can only happen if the policy-maker's objective function is different from that of society.[19] In a nutshell, incentives to over-borrow are due to three political failures: common pool, concentrated interests, and short-termism.

The *common pool* problem has to do with the fact that public policy in general, and fiscal policy in particular, is redistributive. It is the outcome of a collective process that includes a variety of actors, each with his or her motivations and incentives, and in which the individual who enjoys the marginal benefit of an additional unit of public expenditure is different from the individual who bears the marginal cost of funding this extra unit. An example of the common pool problem is the chicken and lobster story. Assume that a restaurant offers only two dishes: chicken and lobster. Further assume that the chicken costs $10 and the lobster costs $20, and that an individual is willing to spend up to $11 for the chicken and up to $14 for the lobster. If the individual goes to the restaurant alone, she will order the chicken and obtain a consumer surplus of $1. Now assume that ten identical individuals decide to have lunch together and then split the bill. In this case, the individual marginal cost of ordering the lobster instead of the chicken is $1 ($10/10) and the individual marginal benefit of ordering the lobster is $3 ($14–$11). As consequence, each individual will order the lobster. The total bill will be $200, and each participant will need to pay $20 (the collective marginal cost of ordering the lobster is $10 per capita), resulting in a negative consumer surplus of $6.[20]

The presence of *concentrated interests* amplifies the common pool problem. When policy actions benefit a certain group and are funded with a general tax, the relatively small group of people who benefit from the policy will have strong incentives to lobby (through political donations, strikes, demonstrations, etc.) in favour of the policy. The much larger, but dispersed, group of actors that bears the cost of this action will have less incentive to act against it.

Short-termism arises from the fact that while social planners need to evaluate the cost and benefits of a policy action over an infinite horizon, policy-makers tend to

[19] There is a vast political economy literature that discusses why politicians have incentives to over-borrow and a full survey of this literature is beyond the scope of this chapter. Interested readers can find an excellent survey in B. Eichengreen, R. Feldman, J. Liebman, J. von Hagen, and C. Wyplosz, *Public Debts: Nuts, Bolts and Wories* (ICMB and CEPR, 2011).

[20] We first heard the Chicken and Lobster story from Ricardo Hausmann.

have a finite horizon which coincides with their expected term in office. Short-termism leads to a situation in which policy-makers give excessive weight to the immediate benefits of their policy actions and not enough weight to the future costs of such actions. As debt accumulation allows the postponement of the costs of public expenditure or tax cuts, self-interested and short-sighted politicians may have an incentive to over-borrow.

Summing up, even if not adhering to the best standards can have large negative effects in the long run, policy-makers are often tempted to act in their own interest because the short-run costs of violating such standards tend to be low as there is a general lack of regulations and principles that can make politicians accountable for the burden that they may leave to future generations. Unlike managers in the corporate world who are subject to the scrutiny of directors, shareholders, and regulators, policy-makers can shift liabilities to future generations without being subject to the necessary checks and balances guaranteeing that their actions are in the best interest of the citizens and state that they represent and for which they are agents.[21]

Under the title of 'Agency' for both creditors and lenders, Principles 1 and 8 tackle this issue by spelling out that actors who initiate a debt transaction '*are responsible for protecting public interest (to the State and its citizens for which they are acting as agents)*' and that '. . . any form of self-interest or speculation on the part of government officials involved in the borrowing' is wrongful. Therefore, the Principles explicitly state that policy-makers should always act in the interest of the state and its citizens and recognize that good intentions are always essential to reaching the right decision.

Lack of transparency amplifies the problems just highlighted because it allows self-interested policy-makers and other actors to hide their actions and dishonest politicians to embezzle public funds. Lack of transparency may also have negative effects in the presence of well-intentioned policy-makers. Policy analysis and decision-making require timely and accurate data. Opaque systems with poor disclosure limit the transmission of information and create serious obstacles to sound judgment for both policy-makers and market participants. Therefore, the UNCTAD Principles recommend establishing institutions and procedures (due authorization, transparency, disclosure) aimed at improving transparency and sanctioning wrongdoing and poor judgment.

2. *Over-lending*

Over-borrowing is only possible in the presence of over-lending. Why do agents in the private and public sectors over-lend? In order to provide an answer to this question we need to analyse the incentives of three types of actors: market participants, official bilateral lenders, and multilateral financial institutions. Before doing so, it is necessary to emphasize that the concept of over-lending is not as well defined as that of over-borrowing. Over-borrowing refers to a situation in which the

[21] Buchheit and Gulati (n. 4).

social cost of an additional unit of debt is higher than the social value of an additional unit of expenditure. In this case, it is clear that the decision on whether or not to incur debt should maximize the social welfare of the borrowing country. Lenders may instead have different objective functions. Presumably, private sector lenders want to maximize their own returns, and as a consequence they may find it optimal to lend more or less than what would maximize social welfare in the recipient country. As it would be absurd to require that private sector lenders should have the objective of maximizing the welfare of borrowers, the concept of private over-lending (or under-lending) needs to refer to a situation in which the lending decisions of private agents differ from what we would observe in the presence of perfect markets.

What about official sector lenders? Should official bilateral lenders maximize the social welfare of the lending country or that of the borrowing country? Should multilateral lenders maximize the social welfare of their shareholders, that of the world, or that of the borrowing country? These are difficult questions for which we do not have a clear answer. However, we will work under the assumption that official lending should maximize the social welfare of the recipient country in a way which is consistent with the budget and institutional constraints of the lending agency.

3. Procyclical private lending

The main problem with private sector lending to sovereigns has to do with procyclicality. Like Mark Twain's proverbial banker, there is evidence that the private sector is willing to lend abundant amounts when things are going well, but at times of crisis countries often face sudden stops in private financing, exactly when this financing is most needed.[22] As a consequence, the private sector tends to over-lend during good times without doing the necessary risk analysis and under-lend during bad times disregarding a country's true fundamentals. Procyclical lending has serious consequences as it leads to excessive debt accumulation during good times and liquidity (and, possibly, solvency) crises during bad times.

Procyclicality is mostly the outcome of what economic literature has called 'rational herding', a situation in which rational agents imitate each other's actions and disregard their own views and private information. Herding is partly due to asymmetric and imperfect information.[23] In good times, investors disregard the

[22] Mark Twain once said that a banker is a fellow who stands ready to lend you an umbrella when the sun is shining but wants it back as soon as it starts raining. For evidence of procyclical lending see E. Levy Yeyati, 'Optimal Debt? On the Insurance Value of International Debt Flows to Developing Countries' (2009) 20 Open Econ. Rev. 489; U. Panizza, F. Sturzenegger, and J. Zettelmeyer, 'The Economics and Law of Sovereign Debt and Default' (2009) 47 J. Econ. Lit. 651.

[23] The discussion in this paragraph and in the following four paragraphs draws from a background paper prepared by the authors for UNCTAD 'The Global Economic Crisis: Systemic Failures and Multilateral Remedies' (UNCTAD, 2009).

weakness of a given borrower and stand ready to lend at will. The same investors, however, may suddenly get scared and start a run on the assets of an otherwise safe borrower. At this point, economic theory would predict that sophisticated and better informed investors with deep liquidity step in and stabilize the market. However, if markets are perceived to be reliable, sophisticated investors will have fewer incentives to search for alternative sources of information that may put them at an advantage if a crisis were to happen. They will instead focus on the same sources of information on which everyone else is relying.[24]

Herding and excessive risk-taking during booms is also rooted in principal agent problems. Remuneration in the financial industry depends on beating some benchmark while not taking additional risk. This risk-adjusted excess return is usually referred to as Jensen's alpha (beta is the risk-adjusted return of the benchmark). While rewarding alpha may seem a correct way to assign bonuses, in practice it is very difficult to evaluate an asset manager's ability to generate alpha returns. Since alpha returns are difficult to obtain (not everybody can be above average), asset managers may try to generate fake alpha by adopting a strategy that leads to excess returns in most states of the world but hides an enormous tail risk. Financial institutions try to address this problem through their risk control departments. However, those who are in charge of risk control are often subject to the same type of incentives that dictate the behaviour of investment officers.[25] In most cases, risk officers who are too persistent in ringing bells and blowing whistles are either isolated or fired. Such distorted incentives lead to a situation in which 'bond traders are notoriously short-sighted, assuming they can get out before the storm hits: their time horizons are days or weeks, not years or decades'.[26] The change in the composition of sovereign debt in emerging market countries from predominantly syndicated bank loans to tradable instruments, together with technological innovation and globalized financial markets, contributed to the design of strategies in which, rather than following a country's fundamentals, traders follow the trend and thus amplify herding and procyclicality. The presence of long-lasting deviations from fundamental asset values is made possible by the fact that very few investors try to fight the trend.[27] Principle 4, on responsible credit decisions, cautions creditors against herding behaviour and trend-following by requiring lenders to make a realistic assessment of the sovereign borrower's capacity to service a loan and thus base their lending decisions on fundamentals rather than on current market sentiments.

[24] This is Keynes's classic beauty contest, formalized by F. Allen, S. Morris, and H.S. Shin, 'Beauty Contests and Iterated Expectations in Asset Markets' (2006) 19 Rev. Fin. Stud. 719.

[25] D. Acemoglu 'The Crisis of 2008: Structural Lessons for and from Economics', Unpublished manuscript (2008), available at <http://economics.mit.edu/files/3703>.

[26] S. Cecchetti, M. Mohanty, and F. Zampolli, 'The Future of Public Debt: Prospects and Implications', BIS Working Papers 300, Bank for International Settlements (2010).

[27] O.A. Lamont and R.H. Thaler, 'Can the Market Add and Subtract? Mispricing in Tech Stock Carve-outs' (2003) 111 J. Pol. Econ. 227.

4. Incentives to over-lend in the official sector

Unlike private lending, official sector lending tends to be acyclical.[28] There are, however, many cases in which the official sector has over-lent. Official sector over-lending is sometimes driven by excessive optimism (especially when countries adopt structural reforms that donors deem to be good for growth), but is more often driven by political considerations, commercial interests, and the incentive structure within international financial institutions.

During the Cold War, most bilateral lending (and bilateral aid) was driven by geopolitical considerations and there are plenty of examples in which brutal and kleptocratic dictators were able to accumulate large debts because they were deemed to be friendly to one of the rival blocks. Zaire (now the Democratic Republic of Congo) at the time of Joseph Mobutu is one of the most striking examples.

Worried about widespread graft, in the early 1980s, the IMF asked Erwin Blumenthal, then a senior staff member of the German Bundesbank, to monitor the activities of the central bank of Zaire. After his attempts to eliminate the siphoning of funds from the central bank accounts were stonewalled by the president and his circle, in 1982 Blumenthal issued a report stating that there was 'not any—I repeat any—chance on the horizon that the numerous creditors of Zaire will recoup their funds'.[29] And yet, the money kept flowing in, probably because in 1986 President Reagan stated that:

> President Mobutu and I have had the opportunity to review and renew one of our oldest and most solid friendships in Africa, that between the United States and the Republic of Zaire. Cooperation between the United States and Zaire under President Mobutu's leadership stretches back through 20 years and five U.S. Administrations . . . Mobutu and his people face a heavy foreign debt burden. We have encouraged Zaire to hold firm to the responsible, economic reforms it is attempting, while promising to do our best to ease the way.[30]

And so they did. Over the period 1980–90, net flows to Zaire totalled US$2.7 billion, with $1.7 billion of multilateral loans and nearly $800 million of bilateral loans (see Figure 2.9). Over the same period, Zaire's total external debt went from 33 per cent to 120 per cent of the country's GDP.

Another reason for excessive bilateral lending is export promotion or attempts to get exclusive deals with large natural resource producers. In some cases, this is just a semi-benign attempt to get access to natural resources or stimulate exports and create a level playing field with exporters in other countries that adopt the same practice. However, there are also cases, often involving military contracts, that are usually shrouded in secrecy, which entail outright corruption.

[28] For evidence, see E. Levy Yeyati, 'Optimal Debt? On the Insurance Value of International Debt Flows to Developing Countries' (2009) 20 Open Econ. Rev. 489.

[29] Blumenthal (1982) 154–5, as quoted in L. Ndikumana and J.K. Boyce, *Africa's Odious Debt: How Foreign Loans and Capital Flight Bled a Continent* (Zed Books, 2011) 2.

[30] Ronald Reagan, 'Remarks Following Discussions With President Mobutu Sese Seko of Zaire', 9 December 1986, available at <http://www.presidency.ucsb.edu/ws/?pid=36796>.

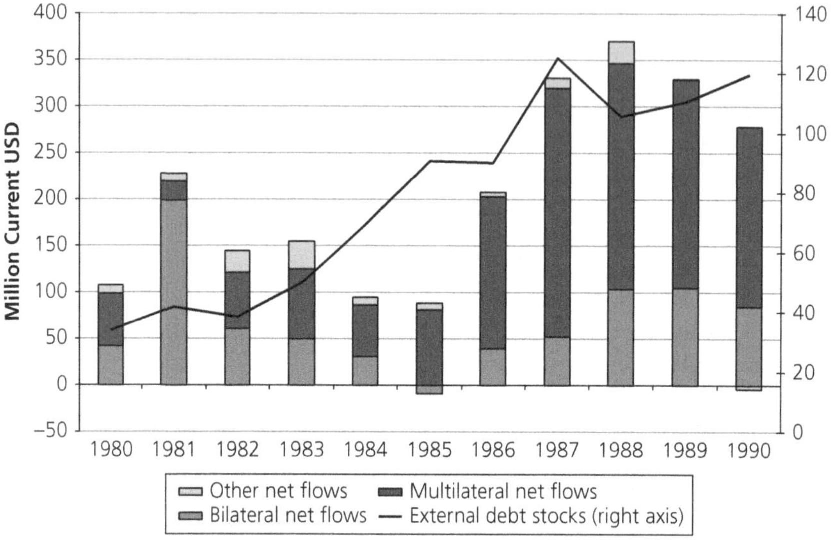

Fig. 2.9 Zaire: net financial flows and external debt to GDP ratio
Source: Authors' elaborations based on Global Development Finance data.

In response to pressure from their shareholders, multilateral financial institutions may also over-lend for geopolitical reasons. However, as in the private sector, over-lending by multilaterals is often driven by the incentive structure within these organizations. Even though they are not for profit, the multilateral and regional development banks do operate like banks. They borrow from the international capital market and make loans to countries, charging a small spread. In theory, these loans are meant to have an impact on the economic or social development of the borrowing country, but this impact is normally hard to measure. In the short run, even the success of the loan in terms of ability to repay is hard to measure because most loans have long maturities. As a consequence, careers in some international financial institutions tend to be driven by the amount of loan disbursed rather than by the developmental impact of such loans.[31]

The UNCTAD Principles have several provisions aimed at avoiding over-lending. The second and fourth Principles contain explicit safeguards against loan pushing and have important implications for making the lending process more transparent. Principle 2, on informed decisions, and Principle 4, on responsible credit decisions, emphasize that lending transactions should be grounded in responsible decisions with the best intentions for the economic development of the recipient countries,

[31] For a classic study of loan pushing in the private sector, see K. Basu, 'The International Debt Problem, Credit Rationing, and Loan Pushing: Theory and Experience', Princeton Studies in International Economics 70 (1991). For a discussion of the incentive structure within the IFIs, see A. Ebrahim and S. Herz, 'Accountability in Complex Organizations: World Bank Responses to Civil Society', Harvard Business School Working paper 08-207 (2007).

and follow pre-disbursement due diligence. The implications section of Principle 4 warns that: 'Lending beyond a borrower's reasonable capacity to repay not only risks a default on the loan in question, it adversely affects the position of all other creditors of that sovereign debt.' The principle also recognizes that, as it is reasonable to expect that private sovereign lending will be motivated by commercial considerations, lenders should have a direct economic interest in assessing the borrower's repayment capacity. Principle 3, on due authorization, also provides safeguards against irrational and self-interested lending. Principle 5 states that lenders need to take into consideration financial, operational, civil, social, cultural, and environmental implications when it comes to project financing. Transparency, which is one of the best safeguards against irresponsible practices, is the explicit objective of Principle 10. The need for transparency is further reinforced in Principle 11 which emphasizes the importance of disclosure and the publication of financing agreements.

II. Credit and asset booms

Financial crises are always based on a self-reinforcing mechanism in which high growth and low volatility lead to a decrease in risk aversion which, in turn, leads to higher liquidity and asset prices, which eventually result in higher profits and growth and even higher risk-taking.[32] The final outcome of this process is the build-up of risk and large imbalances that, at some point, will unwind. The proximate cause for the crisis may then appear to be some idiosyncratic shock, but the true cause of the crisis is the build-up of risk during good times. Therefore, rather than looking for negative shocks, the origins of the crisis are to be found in the positive shock that triggered the build-up of risk. Informational asymmetries, high leverage, and maturity mismatches make financial systems unstable and prone to boom and bust cycles. This inherent instability, together with the large negative repercussions that financial crises have on the real economy, is one of the main rationales for financial regulation.

Failures in financial regulation are partly due to an ideological bias based on the assumption that the 'market knows best' and that regulators should not try to second-guess market trends. Moreover, it is often argued that regulations cannot be successful because the regulated are better paid and have more resources and information than regulators and thus they always end up being able to circumvent regulations. However, this should be an argument for strengthening regulatory agencies and developing a regulatory structure that internalizes such asymmetries, and not an argument for abandoning regulation.

Regulators are also subject to strong, and well-financed, lobbying pressure from the financial industry. There are thus important political and economic considerations supporting the idea of a non-discretionary regulatory system. The seeds of a

[32] This subsection draws from a background paper prepared by the authors for UNCTAD (n. 23).

financial crisis are planted during boom periods,[33] but it is exactly during booms that political support for regulation reaches its lowest point (support for regulation is higher during crisis periods, when prudential regulation is not really needed because banks are not lending to start with).[34] Regulators endowed with large discretionary power may thus face pressure to adopt lax standards during periods of rapid credit expansion. A simple rule that relates capital standards to credit or asset prices growth would protect regulators from such pressure. Of course, automatic stabilizers should not exclude discretionary policies which could still play a role in periods of extreme stress.

III. Risky debt structure

Public debt management should ensure that the government's financing needs and its payment obligations are met at the lowest possible cost over the medium to long term, consistent with a prudent degree of risk.[35] Violations of this principle or the presence of market failures that limit the options of debt managers are likely to lead to debt crises originating from the presence of currency mismatches in the national balance sheet or from insufficient insurance against unexpected economic, financial, or economic shocks.

To clarify the causes and consequences of suboptimal risk mitigation let us consider a country that needs to decide on its borrowing strategy and faces an uncertain economic future. To illustrate the idea, let us assume that the country needs to borrow \$100 and that its future ability to pay will be \$120 with a 95 per cent probability and \$80 with a 5 per cent probability. Let us further assume that the country can either issue a plain vanilla bond with a 5 per cent interest rate or a contingent bond with an interest rate of 6.3 per cent if the country has high ability to pay but that requires a total payment of \$80 (i.e. the interest rate is negative 20 per cent) if the country has low ability to pay. Note that the expected interest rate on the two bonds is almost identical because $5 \approx 0.95*6.3+0.05*(-20)$.[36] Therefore, a country that wants to minimize expected borrowing costs, while also minimizing the risk of a debt crisis, will choose the contingent bond over the plain vanilla bond. In fact, a moderately risk-averse country may prefer a contingent bond even if the expected cost of this bond is slightly higher.

This example shows that, in theory, contingent debt instruments are preferable to plain vanilla bonds.[37] And yet, while contingent debt instruments (such as GDP index bonds, commodity linked bonds, and catastrophe bonds) do exist, they are rarely used. Why is that so? Again, this is a mix of political failures which reduce the demand for contingent debt instruments and market failures that reduce their

[33] C.M. Reinhart and K. Rogoff, *This Time Is Different: Eight Centuries of Financial Folly* (Princeton University Press, 2009) 8.

[34] UNCTAD, 'Trade and Development Report 2011', United Nations (2011) 93–6.

[35] A. Missale, *Public Debt Management* (Oxford University Press, 1999).

[36] We could have built a similar example by comparing the costs and benefits of local currency lending versus foreign currency lending.

[37] Note that there are also risks and limitations to the use of derivatives and contingent contracts.

supply. As a consequence, contingent sovereign debt instruments have shallow markets and command a liquidity premium.

The political failures that limit demand for contingent debt instruments are similar to those that lead to over-borrowing. Like any insurance, contingent contracts imply a premium and self-interested politicians may thus have limited incentives to enter into such contracts for which the cost needs to be paid up-front and their pay-off may come only years later and possibly benefit their successors. Moreover, contingent debt instruments tend to be relatively complex and losses associated with such instruments, even if perfectly justified, may have high political costs. Finally, countries may be reluctant to issue contingent debt instruments if they fear that their use gives negative signals on the country's willingness to service debt, on the state of its economy, or, more generally, on its commitment to good policies.[38]

The UNCTAD Principles recognize the importance of debt composition and of prudent debt management. One key implication of Principle 11 is the public disclosure of maturity, currency composition, indexation, and covenants of public debt. Moreover, key implications of Principle 13, 'Adequate Management and Monitoring', include proper debt management and a thorough knowledge of the implication of the sovereign debt portfolio through the creation of monitoring systems which account for contingent liabilities and institutions that can conduct independent, objective, professional, and timely audits of the debt portfolio. The same Principle recognizes the implication of possible negative shocks in calculating social returns and establishes that in the presence of uncertainty, governments should either set lower debt limits or engage in contingent debt contracts that can reduce the level of uncertainty.

IV. Lack of a system for the resolution of sovereign debt crises

While the principles discussed in this book can reduce the frequency and costs of debt crises, the only way to completely eliminate debt crises is to set very low debt limits. As discussed in the introduction, such a policy is likely to be suboptimal, as it would limit a country's ability to invest in high return projects and stabilize their economy.

Whereas sovereign defaults and debt crises will continue to happen, the international financial architecture is not well equipped for dealing with such events. National commercial codes contain well-defined procedures for enforcing private

[38] There are two market failures that may reduce the supply of contingent debt instruments. The first has to do with coordination problems and the need to ensure 'critical mass' for new instruments. As the appeal of a new financial instrument depends on the size and liquidity of the market, there is an externality involved in the creation and adoption of such instruments. The second market failure has to do with the creation of standards. The creation of a liquid secondary market for contingent assets requires instruments with the same features for all countries or all firms issuing them, and verifiable standards for whether the conditions that trigger payment are met. This requires coordination, standard setting, and an agency that can certify the realization of the events specified in the contingent instrument.

debt contracts and for dealing with private bankruptcies. In the case of sovereign debt, however, creditors have limited legal recourse.

Limited enforceability is partly due to the principle of sovereign immunity which protects sovereign states from lawsuits in foreign courts. However, sovereign immunity is only part of the story. Recent interpretations of US and UK law suggest that sovereign immunity may not apply to debt contracts and sovereign borrowers can waive their immunity. As a consequence, sovereign states have been successfully sued in UK and US courts. Nonetheless, the rulings of foreign courts remain difficult to enforce because creditors can only attach assets located outside a country's border and the majority of the defaulting country's assets are located within its borders.[39]

The lack of an established procedure and a clear set of rules for dealing with sovereign insolvencies often results in unfair outcomes, loss of value for both debtors and creditors, and lengthy debt renegotiations which, in some cases, do not restore debt sustainability.[40] These inefficiencies were at the root of the original proposals for the creation of a mechanism for restructuring sovereign debt.

The UNCTAD Principles recognize that there are conditions under which the sovereign will not be able to service its debts and that, at present, there is no structured system for dealing with sovereign insolvencies. As a consequence, Principles 7 and 15 aim at guiding the behaviour of lenders and borrowers in a situation in which the restructuring of sovereign debt obligations becomes unavoidable. While countries have different views on the need for creating a sovereign debt workout mechanism, the fact that a large constituency of countries supports Principles 7 and 15 is a signal of the importance of sovereign debt restructuring and the need to bring this issue to the centre of the international debate.

E. Conclusions

This chapter discusses in detail the incentives of the main actors in the sovereign debt market and shows that these incentives are not always aligned with the objective of maximizing the social welfare of the borrowing countries. In fact, there are cases in which these incentives are not even aligned with the objective of maximizing the profits of private lenders. The chapter then shows how the Principles discussed in this book can address some of the problems highlighted previously and thus reduce the costs and prevalence of debt crises.

The chapter illustrates that adhering to the UNCTAD Principles could minimize the cost and frequency of debt crises caused by irresponsible policies. However,

[39] M.C. Weidemaier, 'Sovereign Immunity and Sovereign Debt', UNC Legal Studies Research paper No. 2180228 (2012); and Panizza, Sturzenegger, and Zettelmeyer (n. 22).

[40] A study of 90 defaults and renegotiations on debt owed to private creditors by 73 countries found that debt renegotiations have an average length of over 7 years, produce average creditor losses of 40%, and lead to limited debt relief. See M. Wright, 'Restructuring Sovereign Debts with Private Sector Creditors: Theory and Practice' in C. Braga and G. Vincelette, *Sovereign Debt and the Financial Crisis: Will This Time Be Different?* (The World Bank, 2010).

debt crises do not always originate from irresponsible policies. For crises originating from negative shocks or structural situations on which policy-makers do not have any influence, the adoption of the Principles can contribute to increasing a country's resilience to crises by putting in place institutions and procedures that can reduce their economic and social costs.

The fact that the PRSLB cannot rule out the possibility of future debt crises also means that the international community should keep discussing the possibility of creating a structured mechanism for the resolution of debt crises.

3

Sovereign Debt Restructurings as Exercises of International Public Authority

Towards a Decentralized Sovereign Insolvency Law

*Armin von Bogdandy and Matthias Goldmann**

A. Introduction

The search for common principles regulating sovereign debt crises is not only of high topicality because of the pressing difficulties of several euro area Member States during the past years. Rather, excessive sovereign debt and frequent sovereign defaults have been pestering governments, citizens, and the financial sector as well as the real economy for centuries. The first traceable public-sector default in history probably occurred in the fourth century BC, when Attic city states reneged on loans from the Delian League.[1] Every step on the ladder of economic expansion bears the risk of reverberating in a sovereign debt crisis.[2] The beginning of the industrial age in the nineteenth century saw a virtual explosion in the number of sovereign defaults facilitated by increasingly developed financial markets. Carmen Reinhardt and Kenneth Rogoff have counted 83 defaults for that period on external debt alone.[3]

* This chapter was written for the Conference 'Responsible Sovereign Financing—The Search for Common Principles', convened by UNCTAD and the Universidad Autónoma de Madrid on 2 March 2012. We are grateful for the comments received from conference participants. For valuable advice we would like to thank Eyal Benvenisti, Hannah Bloch-Wehba, Juan Pablo Bohoslavsky, Thomas Earnest, Carlos Espósito, Mary Footer, Michael Ioannidis, Benedict Kingsbury, Andrea Lai, Catarina Prata, August Reinisch, Stephan Schill, Peter-Tobias Stoll, Joseph H.H. Weiler, and Chiara Zilioli; as well as participants in the Legal Theory Colloquium of the NYU Institute of International Law and Justice, in the Workshop on the Exercise of Public Authority at Tel Aviv University, and in the Max Planck Institute's Tuesday Meetings. Warm thanks to Miriam Freier and Silvia Steininger for research assistance.

[1] J. Zettelmeyer and F. Sturzenegger, *Debt Defaults and Lessons from a Decade of Crisis* (MIT Press, 2006) 3ff.

[2] Sovereign debt crises are, however, only one aspect of possible financial turmoil. On the intricate relationships between external and domestic, public and private borrowing, banking crises and debt crises, see C. Reinhart and K. Rogoff, 'From Financial Crash to Debt Crisis' (2011) 101 Am. Econ. J. 1676.

[3] C. Reinhart and K. Rogoff, *This Time is Different* (Princeton University Press, 2009) table at 91. Domestic default is more difficult to identify, see Reinhart and Rogoff 111ff.

In spite of the widespread occurrence of sovereign default, an international bankruptcy court or an international treaty stipulating rules for sovereign defaults has not yet seen the light of day.[4] Instead, sovereign borrowers and their lenders have taken recourse to unofficial, non-binding, discretionary arrangements. During the nineteenth century, the British Corporation of Foreign Bondholders facilitated negotiations about debt restructurings.[5] Broad discretion reigned at the negotiations, leading to widely differing solutions.[6] Not much has changed since then. As different as these restructurings were, one may question them in terms of effectiveness and legitimacy. As regards their effectiveness, the lack of a compulsory restructuring mechanism has caused collective action problems among creditors and allowed debtor states unwilling to undergo macroeconomic adjustments to delay restructurings.[7] In terms of legitimacy, the ad hoc solutions facilitated by the international financial institutions (IFIs), the London and Paris Clubs, and other venues might not always represent the best balance between the interests of lenders and borrowers, between private and public creditors, global north and south.[8] Since the 1970s, a considerable number of renowned authors have developed proposals for sovereign debt restructuring mechanisms,[9] geared towards addressing the collective action and legitimacy problems while avoiding moral hazard among debtor states.[10] With the rejection of Anne Krueger's proposal in 2003, these efforts experienced a painful setback.[11]

[4] There have been many proposals, though: K. Rogoff and J. Zettelmeyer, 'Bankruptcy Procedures for Sovereigns: A History of Ideas, 1976–2001', IMF Staff Papers No. 49 (2002) 470.

[5] Zettelmeyer and Sturzenegger (n. 1) 11–12.

[6] See K. Raffer, Ch. 8 and M. Waibel, Ch. 5, both in this volume.

[7] C. Trebesch, 'Delays in Sovereign Debt Restructurings. Should we really blame the creditors?', Proceedings of the German Development Economics Conference, Zurich, No. 44 (2008), available at <http://hdl.handle.net/10419/39906> (accessed 14 December 2012). Using data from 1980–2006, he reports delays caused by creditor holdouts in around 25% of the years in which a state was restructuring. Delays caused by the political opportunism of debtor governments turned out to be a significant factor for prolonged restructurings.

[8] Rogoff and Zettelmeyer (n. 4) 472, suggesting that the International Debt Commission proposed by developing states in 1979 would have provided fairer solutions for debtors than Paris Club restructurings.

[9] K. Raffer, 'Applying Chapter 9 Insolvency to International Debts: An Economically Efficient Solution with a Human Face' (1990) 18 World Development 301–11, emphasizing the difference between Chapters 9 and 11 of the US Bankruptcy Code, the latter relating to companies which may be liquidated, the former to municipalities which may not; J. Sachs, 'Do We Need an International Lender of Last Resort?', Graham Lecture at Princeton University, 20 April 1995, available at <http://www.earth.columbia.edu/sitefiles/file/about/director/pubs/intllr.pdf> (accessed 14 December 2012), advocating private lending instead of the IMF with the IMF as arbiter; L.C. Buchheit and G.M. Gulati, 'Sovereign Bonds and the Collective Will' (2003) 53 Emory L.J. 1317; A.O. Krueger, *A New Approach to Sovereign Debt Restructuring* (International Monetary Fund, 2002); C.G. Paulus, 'A Statutory Procedure for Restructuring Debts of Sovereign States' (2003) 49 Recht der Internationalen Wirtschaft 401; for a complete overview, cf. Rogoff and Zettelmeyer (n. 4) 500. Other authors have made calls for an international insolvency procedure based on philosophical, ethical, and theological reasons. See M. Dabrowski, A. Fisch, K. Gabriel, and C. Lienkamp, *Das Insolvenzrecht für Staaten* (Lit Verlag, 2003).

[10] Rogoff and Zettelmeyer (n. 3) 494–5.

[11] J.A. Kämmerer, 'Der Staatsbankrott aus völkerrechtlicher Sicht' (2005) 65 ZaöRV 651, 669.

This is an experimental paper which claims that the existing informal arrangements for the restructuring of sovereign debt can and should be considered as exercises of international public authority. The concept of international public authority has been developed as a basis for the legal conceptualization of global governance mechanisms in order to make them more legitimate and effective. Accordingly, the qualification of sovereign debt restructurings as exercises of international public authority entails important legal consequences: in the tradition of political thinking since the enlightenment, public authority is only legitimate if it is framed by public law in such a way that one may presume its acceptability for all those concerned by such exercises of authority. Our claim thus leads to a reconsideration and doctrinal reconstruction of informal sovereign debt restructurings in the light of basic principles of public law. They need to conform to a minimum of procedural and substantive standards.

This implies a major change in legal thinking about sovereign debt restructurings, which should move from a private law paradigm to one of public law:[12] it should evolve from a perception of restructurings as private law agreements or agreements governed by a horizontally structured international law as the law of coordination among sovereign states,[13] to a multidimensional approach that understands international law as the public law governing global governance and as a prerequisite of the legitimacy of restructurings.[14] As such, international law needs to take into account the rights and interests of states, citizens, and other entities affected by sovereign debt restructurings. As this chapter will show, some of the principles desirable according to this approach do already apply *de lege lata*, while others may be suggested *de lege ferenda*. The UNCTAD Principles on Promoting Responsible Sovereign Lending and Borrowing[15] provide important guidance in both respects. The public law approach set out in this chapter might add a fitting theoretical and doctrinal framework for the UNCTAD principles, linking this important instance of international norm entrepreneurship to developments in, and insights from, other fields of global governance.

This chapter will unfold in four steps. First, we will expand on our concept for the justification of international public authority and apply it to existing arrangements for sovereign debt restructurings (section B.). Secondly, the methodology used for constructing a legal framework for international public authority deserves some explanation (section C.). Thirdly, we will provide a rough sketch of the legal consequences of the authoritative character of these restructuring arrangements. In order to increase their legitimacy, they need to respect a minimum of procedural

[12] cf. in the context of investment law, S. Schill, 'International Investment Law and Comparative Public Law' in S. Schill (ed.), *International Investment Law and Comparative Public Law* (Oxford University Press, 2010) 3.

[13] On the classical sovereignist underpinnings of the law relating to sovereign debt, see O. Lienau, *Rethinking Sovereign Debt: Politics, Reputation and Legitimacy in Modern Finance* (Harvard University Press, forthcoming 2013).

[14] On the different traditions see J.H.H. Weiler, 'The Geology of International Law—Governance, Democracy and Legitimacy' (2004) 64 ZaöRV 547, 549.

[15] The text of the Principles is reproduced in the Annex to this volume.

and substantive standards (section D.I.). Also, their authoritative character should trigger a stay of proceedings against the defaulting state before domestic and international courts and tribunals (section D.II.). The concluding section reflects on the advantages and limitations of this approach (section E.).

B. Sovereign Debt Restructurings as Exercises of Public Authority

I. From global governance to international public authority

The claim that sovereign debt restructurings are exercises of international public authority is based on our previous proposals to conceptualize international institutions and their governance activities from a public law perspective.[16] This approach emerged from what we perceive as the strengths and weaknesses of the concept of global governance from the viewpoint of legal scholarship.[17] Since the mid-1990s, the concept of global governance has become a ubiquitous analytical concept in many disciplines for the description of worldwide political, economic, and social processes.[18] Four characteristic traits of this concept are of relevance for legal scholarship. First, the concept of global governance recognizes the importance of states and international institutions, but also highlights the relevance of actors and instruments with a basis in private law, or which have a hybrid nature, as well as of individuals—global governance is not just an affair of actors based on public law. Secondly, global governance marks the emergence of an increased recourse to informality: many institutions, procedures, and instruments escape the grasp of established legal concepts like binding international law. Thirdly, thinking in terms of global governance means shifting weight from actors to structures and procedures. Last but not least, as is obvious from the use of the term 'global' rather than 'international', global governance emphasizes the multi-level character of governance activities: it tends to overcome the division between international, supranational, and national phenomena.

[16] A. von Bogdandy, P. Dann, and M. Goldmann, 'Developing the Publicness of Public International Law: Towards a Legal Framework for Global Governance Activities' (2008) 9 German L.J. 1375, reprinted in A. von Bogdandy et al., *The Exercise of Public Authority by International Institutions. Advancing International Institutional Law* (Springer, 2010) 3. This section draws heavily on that text.

[17] The origins of the term 'global governance' can be traced back to J.N. Rosenau, 'Governance, Order, and Change in World Politics' in J.N. Rosenau and E.-O. Czempiel (eds), *Governance without Government* (Cambridge University Press, 1992) 1; J. Kooiman, 'Findings, Recommendations and Speculations' in J. Kooiman (ed.), *Modern Governance: New Government-Society Interactions* (SAGE Publications, 1993) 249. The concept of 'governance' was borrowed from economics. See O.E. Williamson, 'The Economics of Governance: Framework and Implications' (1984) 140 J. Inst. Theor. Econ. 195.

[18] M. Hewson and T.J. Sinclair, 'The Emergence of Global Governance Theory' in M. Hewson and T.J. Sinclair (eds), *Global Governance Theory* (State University of New York Press, 1999) 3; R. Mayntz, 'Governance Theory als fortentwickelte Steuerungstheorie?' in G.F. Schuppert (ed.), *Governance-Forschung* (Nomos Verlag, 2006) 11.

As this list of characteristic traits suggests, the concept of global governance has the merit of providing a forward-looking alternative to a so-called 'realist' (i.e. a state-centric and power-oriented) world view, and may open our eyes towards phenomena that this perspective, as well as classical accounts of international law, regularly underestimate. In this respect, sovereign debt restructuring mechanisms are a perfect example. First, they comprise a host of actors ranging from international organizations with legal capacity, such as the IMF, to 'soft' institutions like the Paris Club and private or hybrid actors like the London Club, the Institute of International Finance, or ad hoc creditors' committees.[19] Secondly, debt restructurings as well as emergency lending largely dispense with binding international legal rules.[20] Thirdly, in the absence of an international bankruptcy court, solutions are worked out in bilateral and multilateral negotiations, which sometimes span over years. Eventually, sovereign debt restructurings involve actors on all levels, ranging from international institutions and governments to individual bondholders. Although sovereign debt restructurings pre-date global governance, their current shape contains many of its typical features, such as the inclusion of private law actors and instruments, which has been on the increase over recent decades.

Thus, the concept of global governance facilitates a profound understanding of phenomena which all too easily escape the conceptual reservoir of classical international law. However, there is a price to be paid for these insights. Global governance is not a neutral, value-free terminology allowing for an impartial spectator's grasp of reality. Rather, it is by and large the offspring of so-called 'liberal' conceptualizations of international relations. As such, it stands in the tradition of institutionalist ideas such as regime theory in providing an alternative to the 'realist' world view.[21] As a consequence of its origin in this theoretical cradle, it is fraught with the normative difficulties typical of many liberal theories of international relations. Accordingly, global governance is by and large accepted and approved of as an essentially technocratic process following a little-questioned dogma of efficiency or functionality.[22]

[19] For an overview on venues and creditors involved, see U.S. Das, M.G. Papaioannou, and C. Trebesch, 'Sovereign Debt Restructurings 1950–2010: Literature Survey, Data, and Stylized Facts', IMF Working Paper WP/12/203 (2012) 14ff.

[20] While debt relief, bond exchanges, and emergency loans at some point require binding legal agreements, the direct outcomes of restructuring negotiations lack this quality. Also, the most important instruments of the HIPC Initiative, the Country Assistance Strategy, the Poverty Reduction Strategy Paper, and the Decision and Completion Point documents are neither contracts, nor binding international legal instruments. See L.F. Guder, *The Administration of Debt Relief by the International Financial Institutions* (Springer, 2009) 156–7. Further, Stand-by Arrangements and Letters of Intent, the principal instruments structuring the IMF's lending activities, are generally held to be non-binding, see A.F. Lowenfeld, *International Economic Law* (2nd edn, Cambridge University Press, 2008) 616–17.

[21] M. Barnett and R. Duvall, 'Power in Global Governance' in M. Barnett and R. Duvall (eds), *Power in Global Governance* (Cambridge University Press, 2005) 1, 7; M. Zürn, 'Institutionalisierte Ungleichheit in der Weltpolitik. Jenseits der Alternative "Global Governance" versus "American Empire"' (2007) 48 Politische Vierteljahresschrift 680.

[22] See e.g. R. Latham, 'Politics in a Floating World' in Hewson and Sinclair (eds) (n. 18) 23; M. Koskenniemi, 'Global Governance and Public International Law' (2004) 37 Kritische Justiz 241.

It did not take long for these implications to be challenged.[23] Generally speaking, critics point out that global governance involves risks to individual rights and collective self-determination, and that it may impede, rather than promote, global justice. With respect to individual rights, the striking absence of judicial review and procedural safeguards—even when international institutions have a deep impact upon individuals—meets with harsh critique. The listing of terrorist suspects by the UN Security Council without proper judicial review provides the most dramatic example of governance that would hardly be permissible in democratic states.[24] With respect to collective self-determination, international institutions are operating at a considerable distance from the communities concerned, often producing outcomes that deeply affect domestic democratic procedures, leaving domestic parliaments and other decision-makers with little influence. Recently, the legitimacy of economic and fiscal adjustment programmes negotiated as part of the Greek sovereign debt restructuring has become the subject of public contestation. Moreover, international institutions involved in sovereign debt restructurings might display features of secretive bureaucracies or might operate more in the service of the interests of particular stakeholders or states than of global justice and public interests.[25] As a result, scholars' perceptions of the concept of global governance today ranges from endorsement to rejection.[26] It facilitates the conceptualization of new phenomena, but provides no criteria for the assessment of their legitimacy problems.[27]

What should be the response to such claims of illegitimacy from a public law perspective? The starting point of a public law perspective is to ask whether the respective activities amount to an exercise of unilateral authority affecting individuals or political communities. Public law, at least in a liberal and democratic tradition, has a dual function for the rational justification of such unilateral authority: first, no public authority may be exercised that is not based on public law (constitutive

On the related liberal bias of international organizations, see M. Barnett and M. Finnemore, 'The Power of Liberal International Organizations' in Barnett and Duvall (eds) (n. 21) 161, 163–9. However, various critical perspectives on global governance have emerged. See e.g. A.D. Ba and M.J. Hoffmann (eds), *Contending Perspectives on Global Governance* (Routledge, 2005).

[23] It may suffice to cite only a few examples: A. Cohen, 'Bureaucratic Internalization: Domestic Governmental Agencies and the Legitimization of International Law' (2005) 30 Geo. J. Int'l L. 1079; R.W. Grant and R.O. Keohane, 'Accountability and Abuses of Power in World Politics' (2005) 99 APSR 29; R. Howse and K. Nicolaidis, 'Enhancing WTO Legitimacy: Constitutionalization or Global Subsidiarity?' (2003) 16 Governance 73; A.M. Slaughter, 'The Accountability of Government Networks' (2000–01) 8 Ind. J. Global Legal Stud. 347; Weiler (n. 14); M. Zürn, 'Global Governance and Legitimacy Problems' (2004) 39 Gov. Oppos. 260. For a taxonomy of different approaches, see A. von Bogdandy, 'Globalization and Europe: How to Square Democracy and Globalization' (2004) 15 Eur. J. Int'l L. 885.

[24] See, for many, C. Feinäugle, 'The UN Security Council Al-Qaida and Taliban Sanctions Committee: Emerging Principles of International Institutional Law for the Protection of Individuals?' (2008) 9 German L.J. 1513.

[25] I. Venzke, 'International Bureaucracies from a Political Science Perspective—Agency, Authority and International Institutional Law' (2008) 9 German L.J. 1401.

[26] For an overview, see Ba and Hoffmann (n. 22).

[27] For many, see M. Zürn, 'Global Governance and Legitimacy Problems' (2004) 39 Gov. Oppos. 260–87.

function); secondly, public authority is controlled and limited by the substantive and procedural standards provided by public law (limiting function).[28] Both functions imply that concerns about the legitimacy of global governance need to be translated into meaningful arguments about legality. The experience of liberal democracies teaches how important it is that legitimacy concerns can, in principle, be put forward as questions of legality. While in a pluralistic society, debates about legitimacy might potentially end up in endless contestations, public law provides standards and procedures for effective decision-making and dispute resolution without denying the contingency of the issues under consideration. This ensures the effectiveness of the ensuing decisions, while leaving those who disagree at liberty to seek their revision, or even to suggest changes to the constitutional framework in which the decisions were taken.[29]

As this section should have revealed, the main thrust of our approach is comparable to that of the Global Administrative Law project and of approaches aiming at the constitutionalization of international law.[30] We agree with these approaches to shift the attention from states to citizens as the ultimate sources of legitimacy. And like them, we are convinced that any exercise of public authority on whatever level needs to be justifiable in the light of basic principles of public law, at least for those who hold dear liberal and democratic traditions of thought. Certainly, the requirement of such a justification for authority has strong roots in the Western tradition of political theory.[31] However, Amartya Sen has recently shown in his 'Idea of Justice' that the idea of rationally justified authority has played a remarkable role in Asian and also in Islamic political thought across the centuries.[32]

[28] This idea can be found in many variations in the writings of the most eminent theorists in the enlightenment tradition. Some emphasize the limiting function of public law, e.g. J. Locke, *Two Treatises of Government* (1689) 2nd Treatise, §§ 132ff., especially at §§ 135–136; J-J. Rousseau, *Du contrat social* (1762) liv. I, chs VI and VII (especially lines 305–310; 381–386); while others emphasize its constitutive function, e.g. I. Kant, *Die Metaphysik der Sitten, Rechtslehre* (1797) §§ 43–49. For modern applications, see J. Habermas, *Faktizität und Geltung* (Suhrkamp, 1992) 167ff. (Ch. 4, sec. I); J. Rawls, *A Theory of Justice* (rev. edn, Harvard University Press, 2000) 206ff. (§ 38); J. Raz, *The Authority of Law* (Oxford University Press, 1979) 169ff.; J. Raz, *Ethics in the Public Domain* (Clarendon Press, 1994) 339ff. These ideas also pervade modern administrative law, see E. Schmidt-Aßmann, *Das Allgemeine Verwaltungsrecht als Ordnungsidee* (2nd edn, Springer, 2004) 16–18. In the context of public international law, see e.g. B. Kingsbury, 'International Law as Inter-Public Law', available at <http://www.law.nyu.edu/kingsburyb/fall06/globalization/papers/Kingsbury, NewJusGentiumandInter-PublicI1.pdf> (accessed 14 December 2012).

[29] J. Habermas (n. 28) 53ff. (Ch. 1, III.2.).

[30] B. Kingsbury, N. Krisch, and R. Stewart, 'The Emergence of Global Administrative Law' (2005) 68 Law & Cont. Probs 15; S. Cassese, 'Lo spazio giuridico globale' (2002) 52 Rivista trimestrale di diritto pubblico 323; for the constitutionalist tradition, see e.g. A. Peters, 'Compensatory Constitutionalism: The Function and Potential of Fundamental International Norms and Structures' (2006) 19 LJIL 579; S. Kadelbach and T. Kleinlein, 'International Law—a Constitution for Mankind? An Attempt at a Re-appraisal with an Analysis of Constitutional Principles' (2007) 50 GYBIL 303.

[31] cf. A. von Bogdandy and A. Dellavalle, 'Universalism and Particularism as Paradigms of International Law', International Law and Justice Working Paper No. 3 (2008).

[32] A. Sen, *The Idea of Justice* (Belknap Press of Harvard University Press, 2009) 327–35.

II. The concept and justification of the exercise of international public authority

This basic idea about the need to justify public authority raises two questions: first, what is to be understood as international public authority? Secondly, how is it possible to justify such authority on a global scale?

The public law approach to international law requires a workable concept of *international public authority*, which largely preserves the insights of the concept of global governance, while avoiding its flaws. The concept of global governance itself is insufficient for the public law approach, because it does not enable the identification of critical acts which constitute unilateral exercises of authority affecting individuals or political communities. It flattens the difference between public and private phenomena, as well as between authoritative and non-authoritative ones. The latter results from an understanding of global governance as a continuous structure or process, rather than a set of acts of specific, identifiable actors causing specific, identifiable effects. However, these distinctions are essential for the deployment of the constitutive and limiting functions of public law. Only public, authoritative acts need to be framed by public law, and the standards to be applied depend on the effects of those acts on individual rights and the self-determination of political communities. We therefore suggest the concept of the *exercise of international public authority* as a new focus, which might provide an understanding of global governance phenomena more compatible with the function of public law.

As regards the notion of the *exercise of authority*, we share the view of the proponents of Global Administrative Law that it should include, but by no means be limited to, binding international legal agreements. Rather, global governance has brought about the emergence of a multiplicity of new forms of authority on the international plane with similar effects. Soft legal instruments, but also merely factual instruments like indicators and other types of information, might affect individuals or political communities. Though unenforceable, they have the capacity to influence behaviour by setting positive or negative, material or immaterial incentives, facilitating reputational sanctions, framing issues and problems, setting agendas, instigating learning processes, using path dependencies, etc. At a certain point, this influence might grow important enough to be considered as authority requiring commensurate means of justification.[33]

The *public* character of authoritative acts thus defined depends on their legal basis. Whenever the author of an authoritative act may claim to have acted on a legal basis entitling it to enact unilateral decisions which deeply affect individuals or communities, we consider the act as one of public authority.[34] The legal basis might be part of hard or soft law, and explicit or implicit. It is an intricate

[33] The present framework could therefore be applied to the UNCTAD Principles themselves and the process of their creation, scrutinizing them for transparency, participation, and accountability.

[34] This distinguishes our approach from the ideas of Joseph Raz, for whom (legal) authority always claims to be *legitimate*, see Raz (n. 28) 28ff. We follow Habermas (n. 28) 43ff. (Ch. 1, III.(1), according to whom the legality of an authoritative act gives rise only to a refutable presumption of legitimacy.

theoretical question whether soft law should be considered part of international law proper. This depends on the particular concept of law, which is, as all basic concepts, disputed.[35] We opt for a concept of law which includes soft law, since soft law may also help to restrain authority and thereby become a constituent part of the public law framework which legitimizes the exercise of public authority by international institutions.[36] Soft law is normative because it aims at the formation and stabilization of normative expectations.[37] It can be enforced through peer pressure, reputational sanctions, deprivation of benefits, and similar incentives.[38] Still, we maintain a clear distinction between binding and non-binding international law since the breach of binding legal rules entails specific consequences, such as the possibility to impose reprisals.[39]

If the legal basis is part of *international* law, including international soft law, we consider the act to be an exercise of international public authority. Accordingly, we understand as international public authority the law-based capacity of any international institution to legally or factually limit or otherwise affect other persons' or entities' use of their liberty.[40]

One might get a better grasp of the concept of public authority and its legal framework by contrasting it with its antonym, private authority. Private authority is an exercise of liberty. It finds a basis in the consent of the parties and does not require prior legal authorization by a political community. For example, private investors are free to extend credit to states or purchase sovereign bonds at market prices and as long as such transactions are not tied to conditionalities or other political concessions. However, this does not mean that 'anything goes'. Rather,

[35] cf. only P. Weil, 'Towards Relative Normativity in International Law?' (1983) 77 AJIL 413; and U. Fastenrath, 'Relative Normativity in International Law' (1993) 4 Eur. J. Int'l L. 305; for an overview, see M. Goldmann, 'We Need to Cut Off the Head of the King: Past, Present, and Future Approaches to International Soft Law' (2012) 25 LJIL 335.

[36] M. Goldmann, 'Inside Relative Normativity: From Sources to Standard Instruments for the Exercise of International Public Authority' (2008) 9 German L.J. 1865.

[37] Despite their otherwise incompatible approaches, Habermas (n. 28) 48–9; and N. Luhmann, *Das Recht der Gesellschaft* (Suhrkamp, 1992) 134, agree on this point. However, they disagree about the meaning of 'normative expectations', see Habermas (n. 28) 70. See also F. von Hayek, *Law, Legislation and Liberty*, vol. 1: Rules and Order (University of Chicago Press, 1973) 101–2.

[38] cf. A. Guzman, *How International Law Works* (Oxford University Press, 2008) 71ff.; D. Shelton, *Commitment and Compliance. The Role of Non-binding Norms in the International Legal System* (Oxford University Press, 2000), several contributions on the issue; J. Brunnée, 'Reweaving the Fabric of International Law? Patterns of Consent in Environmental Framework Agreements' in R. Wolfrum and V. Röben (eds), *Developments of International Law in Treaty Making* (Springer, 2005) 101–26; H. Neuhold, 'The Inadequacy of Law-Making by International Treaties: "Soft Law" as an Alternative?' in Wolfrum and Röben (eds) (see previous reference) 39; R. Howse and R. Teitel, 'Beyond Compliance: Rethinking Why International Law Really Matters' (2010) 1 Global Policy 127, emphasizing the significance of international law as a benchmark providing orientation—the same should be true for soft law.

[39] This should mitigate the concerns raised against this view by J. d'Aspremont, *Formalism and the Sources of International Law* (Oxford University Press, 2011) 12; J. d'Aspremont, 'The Politics of Deformalization in International Law' (2011) 3 Goettingen Journal of International Law 503, 507–8.

[40] This definition further develops our previous position. It is identical with the definitions given to the concept of international public authority in A. von Bogdandy and I. Venzke, *In wessen Namen? Internationale Gerichte in Zeiten globalen Regierens* (Suhrkamp, forthcoming 2013); and in M. Goldmann, *Internationale öffentliche Gewalt* (Springer, forthcoming 2013).

states as well as international and regional organizations are called upon to set minimum rules for the exercise of private authority in markets in order to protect public goods and interests. Also, private actors have duties to respect human rights, although they might be based on soft law.[41]

As regards the second question about the possibility of justifying international public authority, there is no simple answer, except that any justification needs to be based on open-textured principles. In a pluralistic world fraught with different national, regional, functional, religious, and ideological actors and a corresponding multiplicity of identities and interests, the exercise of public authority is likely to be deeply contested.[42] Nothing demonstrates this better than the the adjustment measures which some members of the eurozone have implemented in the course of their restructuring. The citizens of the defaulting state and foreign bondholders might radically disagree over the necessary measures, just like economists, depending on whether they favour demand- or supply-oriented policies. The public law framework of international public authority needs to square the circle and set up legal requirements which can be expected to make international public authority acceptable to at least the most gravely affected communities and individuals to at least a satisfactory extent without taking a position on specific policy issues. These principles are therefore likely to deal with issues of competence, procedure, review, and human rights.

In this respect, we do not consider state consent as a fully sufficient legal requirement for the justification of international public authority anymore. International public authority might affect people in states other than those which have given their consent.[43] Also, global governance has broadened and increased the authority exercised by international institutions, sometimes as tools in the hands of powerful hegemons, sometimes as relatively independent agents of their member states.[44] This requires looking into new perspectives for the justification of international public authority. With a global parliamentary assembly remaining unfeasible for the foreseeable future, contemporary approaches emphasize participation, deliberation, procedural fairness, transparency, respect for fundamental human rights, and accountability as additional ways of ensuring the legitimacy of international public authority.[45] These proposals find support in modern political

[41] cf. the OECD Guidelines for Multinational Enterprises and the UN Guiding Principles on Business and Human Rights.

[42] See only N. Krisch, *Beyond Constitutionalism. The Pluralist Structure of Postnational Law* (Oxford University Press, 2011) Ch. 7.

[43] On the limits of consent, cf. Weiler (n. 14) 557–8.

[44] Venzke (n. 25).

[45] From the rich literature, see only Grant and Keohane (n. 23); R. O. Keohane and A. Buchanan, 'The Legitimacy of Global Governance Institutions' in R. Wolfrum and V. Röben (eds), *The Legitimacy of International Law* (Springer, 2008) 25–62; D. Dyzenhaus, 'Accountability and the Concept of (Global) Administrative Law', International Law and Justice Working Paper No. 7 (2008); S. Cassese, 'Administrative Law Without the State? The Challenge of Global Regulation' (2005) 37 N.Y.U. J. Int'l L.& Pol. 663. Art. 11 TEU positivizes this approach, see J. Mendes, 'Participation and the Role of Law after Lisbon: A Legal View on Article 11 TEU' (2011) 48 CML Rev. 1849.

theories such as those by Amartya Sen, John Rawls, and Jürgen Habermas.[46] Even if implemented, they might not necessarily elevate the legitimacy of international public authority to the level enjoyed by domestic public authority. But they would establish a new, additional strand of legitimacy for international public authority by giving citizens and political communities other than the states represented in the respective institution a say, whether directly, through domestic or supranational parliaments, or other institutions like NGOs.[47] This might provide at least some protection against illegitimate exercises of authority, which give sway to unfettered special interests. Alternatives to this sobering outlook seem to be scarce, especially if one considers that Habermas's plea for a refurbished General Assembly representing both states and citizens[48] probably overstretches the idea of representation and overlooks its pitfalls.[49]

III. Applying the Concept to Sovereign Debt Restructurings

The preceding theoretical considerations enable us to qualify the existing international mechanisms for the restructuring of sovereign debt as institutions exercising international public authority. We confine the following analysis to the most important venues for debt restructurings, namely the IMF, the Paris Club, and the London Club, and comparable venues of private creditors. For the purposes of this chapter, we use the term 'restructuring' as comprising not only the act by which the parties actually reschedule or reduce the debt of the troubled state, but the entire bundle of measures comprised in a sovereign debt workout, including conditionalities and adjustment measures in the context of lending into arrears. One might further subdivide such a broad concept of restructuring into more specific standard instruments of international public authority[50] at the disposal of different actors, like lending into arrears, Agreed Minutes and other instruments for rescheduling or relief, and arbitration or adjudication (if applicable). Restructurings might be triggered by a default, i.e. the failure of a state to make a due payment, or by an announcement of the troubled state that its financial situation requires a restructuring.[51]

[46] J. Rawls, *Justice as Fairness. A Restatement* (Harvard University Press, 2001); J. Habermas, 'Hat die Konstitutionalisierung des Völkerrechts noch eine Chance?' in J. Habermas, *Der gespaltene Westen* (Suhrkamp, 2004) 113; J. Habermas, 'The Constitutionalization of International Law and the Legitimation Problems of a Constitution for World Society' (2008) 15 Constellations 444–55; Sen (n. 32).

[47] This idea originates in the debate about the dual strands of legitimacy within the European Union. See J. Habermas, *Zur Verfassung Europas. Ein Essay* (Suhrkamp, 2011) 68; In the context of global governance, see Habermas (2004) (n. 46) 159; A. Peters, 'Dual Democracy' in J. Klabbers, A. Peters, and G. Ulfstein (eds), *The Constitutionalization of International Law* (Oxford University Press, 2009) 263; S. Besson, 'Institutionalising global *demoi*-cracy' in L. Meyer (ed.), *Legitimacy, Justice and Public International Law* (Cambridge University Press, 2009) 58.

[48] Habermas (2011) (n. 47) 87.

[49] cf. Sen (n. 32) 87ff.; C. Möllers, 'Expressive versus repräsentative Demokratie' in R. Kreide (ed.), *Transnationale Verrechtlichung. Festschrift Brunkhorst* (Campus Verlag, 2008) 160.

[50] On the concept of 'standard instruments', see Goldmann (n. 36).

[51] Das, Papaioannou, and Trebesch (n. 19) 12–13.

There can be little doubt about the *authoritative* character of IMF lending in case of sovereign debt crises, although the nature of the underlying arrangements is contested.[52] Procedurally, IMF lending requires a decision of the IMF Executive Board. Substantially, states need to meet the conditionalities applicable to the lending instrument in question, including an economic adjustment programme agreed in letters of intent and memoranda of understanding concluded with the IMF.[53] As soon as the borrowing state effectively receives financial support, these soft legal instruments acquire an authoritative character. The state is expected to meet the goals set out therein. If it fails to do so, it faces sanctions like the withholding of the subsequent tranche, which is not unlikely to happen since the introduction of performance targets.[54] This would seriously impede the entire restructuring process. Indirectly, conditionalities and adjustment programmes bear important consequences for the citizens of the defaulting state and affect the ability of that state to service its external and domestic debt, thereby impacting upon the interests of third party creditors. IMF lending therefore qualifies as an exercise of *international* and *public* authority because it has a legal basis in the Articles of Agreement of the IMF,[55] a binding international treaty enjoying nearly universal membership. It corresponds to the traditional way in which collective action by public actors is realized on the international plane.

The Paris Club, by contrast, lacks a basis in binding international law. Still, we contend that the Agreed Minutes, which conclude Paris Club negotiations about debt restructurings, constitute exercises of international public authority. First, they are to be considered as exercises of *authority* as they affect the financial situation of the defaulting state by stipulating the details of the deal between the borrower and its lenders, including whether there will be relief and the conditions of any debt restructuring. Backed by the economic power of its members, the Paris Club has the capacity to implement effectively the formally non-binding Agreed Minutes and frame and stabilize the normative expectations of all actors involved or affected, including the citizens of the defaulting and lending states.[56] Moreover, the comparability of treatment clause requiring the state not to grant more favourable conditions to other creditors affects these very creditors, as well as the ability of the defaulting state to further lighten its financial burden.[57] Secondly, the Agreed Minutes are exercises of *public* authority because they are based on the normative

52 On this contentious issue, see Lowenfeld (n. 20) 616f.

53 IMF Guidelines on Conditionality, 25 September 2002, para. 9ff., available at <http://www.imf.org/External/np/pdr/cond/2002/eng/guid/092302.pdf> (accessed 14 December 2012).

54 IMF Guidelines on Conditionality (n. 53) para. 11.

55 Articles of Agreement, Art. V(3)(a), (b), and (c).

56 On the effects of debt restructurings on human capabilities as understood by Amartya Sen and Martha Nussbaum, see Dabrowski et al. (n. 9) 35–48.

57 <http://www.clubdeparis.org/sections/composition/principes/comparabilite-traitement> (accessed 14 December 2012), see D. Josselin, 'Regime interplay in Public-Private Governance: Taking Stock of the Relationship Between the Paris Club and Private Creditors Between 1982 and 2005' (2009) 15 Global Governance 521, 531; see also Das, Papaioannou, and Trebesch (n. 16), emphasizing the discretion the application of the comparability principle gives to the Paris Club.

framework of the Paris Club, which enables Club members to exercise unilateral authority against debtor states. Although of non-binding character, this framework comprises a set of procedural and substantive principles as well as fairly standardized terms for restructurings.[58] It not only serves the interests of creditor states, but also those of debtor states, at least rudimentarily since the Paris Club began granting debt relief in the late 1980s. Since that time, the Paris Club has also enjoyed a near monopoly on restructurings of bilateral debt.[59] One might therefore conclude that the Paris Club and its legal framework reflect the implicit consensus of many creditor and debtor states to use the rules and procedures of this venue for restructurings of bilateral debt. Thirdly, the Agreed Minutes are exercises of *international* public authority because this normativity is generated by the common will of states, more precisely government representatives of various states. They constitute an implicit form of international soft law.[60]

Qualifying restructurings negotiated between states and representatives of commercial creditors as exercises of international public authority is a more difficult task. Such negotiations take place in the London Club, the Institute of International Finance, or other venues, which convene in creditors' committees on an ad hoc basis.[61] At close inspection, such restructurings might under certain circumstances be characterized as exercises of *authority*: for the debtor state, the effects of such restructurings are comparable to those of Paris Club Agreed Minutes. For creditors, participation might not be so voluntary after all. In fact, without such venues as the London Club, creditors would be faced with a huge collective action problem leaving everybody worse off than if they participated in a common restructuring of a debtor to which they have a significant exposure.[62] While such reschedulings might therefore be qualified as authoritative for their parties, their *international* and *public* character is less obvious. No explicit hard or soft agreement authorizes the London Club or other venues to carry out their activities. Nevertheless, we consider implicit consent on the part of states or international organizations as sufficient for the establishment of a legal basis (hard or soft) for the exercise of international public authority. In this respect, we follow the general tendency in international law of recognizing that implicit or even tacit consent may give rise to international obligations.[63] In the case of the London Club, the IMF has repeatedly shown its support for the Club's restructuring activities. One might regard it as an implicit expression of consent that the IMF has even compelled creditors and debtors to engage in London Club restructurings by its lending policies. Prior to

[58] <http://www.clubdeparis.org/sections/composition/fonctionnement-du-club/reunions>; <http://www.clubdeparis.org/sections/composition/principes/cinq-grands-principes>; <http://www.clubdeparis.org/sections/types-traitement/reechelonnement/termes-de-traitements> (accessed 14 December 2012).

[59] L. Grard, 'Le Club de Paris et les dettes publiques des Etats' in D. Carreau and M.N. Shaw (eds), *The External Debt* (1992) 197, 228.

[60] J. Bentham, *Introduction to Principles of Morals and Legislation* (1789), Ch. XVII, § 2, para. XXV.

[61] On the functioning of the London Club, see Zettelmeyer and Sturzenegger (n. 1) 12ff.

[62] See L.C. Buchheit and R. Reisner, 'The Effect of the Sovereign Debt Restructuring Process on Inter-Creditor Relationships' (1988) U. Ill. L. Rev. 493, 500, 514.

[63] See S. Szurek, 'Article 11, Convention of 1969' in O. Corten and P. Klein (eds), *The Vienna Conventions on the Law of Treaties* (Oxford University Press, 2011) 188, 197–8.

1989, debtors had to reach an agreement in principle with their creditors in order to qualify for funds under stand-by arrangements.[64] In 1989, the Fund launched its policy of lending into arrears in order to facilitate the restructurings of sovereign debt with private creditors and the corresponding adjustment programmes.[65] It now requires countries to enter into negotiations with its *private* creditors in order to receive up-front public sector support.[66] The London Club in turn endorses IMF support by requiring borrowers to seek IMF assistance.[67] In addition, not only the IMF, but also state practice implicitly approves of London Club negotiations as an indispensable mechanism for the restructuring of sovereign borrowers' commercial debt. For example, the exchange of syndicated loans for Brady Bonds was facilitated not only by the IFIs, but also by some governments of creditors which pledged collateral.[68] As a sign of such official endorsement, IMF staff have been regularly present at negotiations in the London Club.[69] Thus, it is not far-fetched to say that the London Club and similar venues for the private sector have often struck their deals at least with the implicit approval of the IFIs as well as of a considerable number of states. Therefore, such restructurings have been authorized at least on a non-binding basis, which justifies their characterization as exercises of international public authority.

In summary, all of the international instruments for restructuring considered here qualify under certain conditions as exercises of international public authority. It does not take much fantasy to extend the same reasoning to further instruments aimed at debt sustainability such as the Heavily Indebted Poor Countries Initiative (HIPC), the Multilateral Debt Relief Initiative, or the Vienna Initiative and also qualify them as exercises of international public authority. Remarkably, in *Abaclat v. Argentina* the tribunal recognized the existence of an informal restructuring mechanism consisting of the mentioned venues.[70] It is not by accident that the previous sentence uses 'mechanism' in the singular: The above considerations should not lead to the conclusion that each venue and each act has to be examined in isolation. Rather, we hope that this text has demonstrated so far that each debt crisis triggers a series of acts carried out by several actors in multiple venues.

[64] S. Hagan, 'Sovereign Debtors, Private Creditors, and the IMF' (2002) 8 Law and Business Review of the Americas 49, 51.

[65] On the effects of restrictive IMF policy on lending into arrears to private creditors, see L. Simpson, 'The Role of the IMF in Debt Restructurings: Lending Into Arrears, Moral Hazard and Sustainability Concerns', UNCTAD G-24 Discussion Paper Series No. 40 (2006) 9, claiming it had a pro-creditor basis.

[66] See 'The Chairman's Summing Up—Fund Involvement in Debt Strategy', Executive Board Meeting 89/61, 23 May 1989; 'The Acting Chairman's Summing Up on Fund Policy on Arrears to Private Creditors—Further Considerations', Executive Board Meeting 99/64, 14 June 1999; and 'The Acting Chair's Summing Up—Fund Policy on Lending into Arrears to Private Creditors—Further Consideration of the Good Faith Criterion', Executive Board Meeting 02/92, 4 September 2002; cf. Hagan (n. 64) 52–3.

[67] Josselin (n. 57) 526.

[68] Lowenfeld (n. 20) 686–7.

[69] Zettelmeyer and Sturzenegger (n. 1) 22.

[70] *Abaclat v. Argentine Republic*, ICSID Case ARB/07/5, Decision on Jurisdiction and Admissibility, 14 November 2011, § 40.

Sometimes only a holistic view of the entire process might allow the identification of those acts which need to be qualified as public authority. This is one important lesson learned from the research on global governance. For example, in the recent Greek crisis, the Institute of International Finance, which represented the private sector creditors in the talks about a restructuring of the debts owed to them by Greece early in 2012, negotiated the terms of a restructuring of Greek sovereign bonds which do not refer to adjustment measures to be implemented by Greece.[71] The restructuring might therefore appear to be entirely voluntary and free of negative effects for the population. However, this outcome coincided with the agreement between the Greek government and the Eurogroup on the terms of a second bailout package, conditional upon the fulfilment of a number of adjustment measures. The understanding on the second bailout endorses the private sector agreement, and underlines its significance for the materialization of the second bailout package.[72] One might consider this as evidence of public sector endowment for the restructuring negotiated with the private sector.

C. Method: How the Law Governing International Public Authority Emerges

Qualifying sovereign debt restructurings as exercises of public authority is not an end in itself. It makes it necessary to develop a more substantial legal regime in order to ensure the legitimacy of the authoritative acts in question in accordance with the approach discussed earlier (section B.II.). This raises difficult methodological questions. How could such a legal regime possibly come into existence in an effective and legitimate way? The following is only a brief summary of issues which have been set out elsewhere in necessary detail.[73]

For the foreseeable future, a binding treaty regulating the legitimacy of sovereign debt restructurings is unlikely to come along, in spite of the urgency of the need. But the advancement of public law does not hinge on legislation or treaty-making alone. Rather, the history of public law provides ample illustration for the incremental emergence of legal concepts and principles by way of discursive interactions between practice and scholarship. Most continental legal orders saw a turn to the so-called 'legal method' during the nineteenth century.[74] In particular

71 Ministry of Finance of the Hellenic Republic, PSI Launch Press Release, 21 February 2012, available at <http://www.minfin.gr/portal/en/resource/contentObject/id/7ad6442f-1777-4d02-80fb-91191c606664> (accessed 21 February 2013).

72 Eurogroup statement, 21 February 2012, available at <http://consilium.europa.eu/uedocs/cms_data/docs/pressdata/en/ecofin/128075.pdf> (accessed 21 February 2013).

73 A. von Bogdandy and M. Goldmann, 'The Exercise of Public Authority through National Policy Assessment: The OECD's PISA Policy as a Paradigm for a New International Standard Instrument' (2008) 5 Int'l Org. L. Rev. 241, 270ff. This section quotes from that text.

74 A. von Bogdandy, 'The Past and Promise of Doctrinal Constructivism: A Strategy for Responding to the Challenges Facing Constitutional Scholarship in Europe' (2009) 7 Int'l J. Const. L. 364–400. However, the legal method never thrived in England and France as much as elsewhere on the continent.

in Italy and Germany, the legal method saw a steep rise in popularity because it allowed a reaction to perceived deficits in the legitimacy of the governments of the day, which were characterized by constitutional arrangements that fell short of parliamentary democracy and gave a strong role to governments controlled by monarchs. At the same time, the administrative apparatus had to master an ever-increasing range of problems, which in turn caused the bourgeois elite to demand respect for its liberty and property. In this situation, practice readily adopted the legal method.[75] It allowed advancement of the legal order through the development of new concepts and principles. This is to be imagined as a dialectical process involving scholarship and practice, and including both deductive, principled reasoning guided by the idea of the *Rechtsstaat* as well as inductive analyses of existing legal rules and practice.[76] The resulting doctrinal concepts and principles had the advantage of being considered, on the one hand, as existing parts of the legal order which explain its deeper structure, and on the other as providing legitimacy because of their consistency with the overarching idea of the *Rechtsstaat*.[77] It was a win-win situation: the administration obtained effective instruments, and the citizens some basic safeguards against arbitrary state action, which are small by contemporary standards but meant some progress in those days.

This sometimes rather intuitive process might have prompted pragmatic, efficient, and somewhat legitimate solutions, but they were far from being uncontroversial. Thus, the legal method soon came to be accused of providing a mere apology for existing power structures.[78] Indeed, most of the advocates of the legal method in the nineteenth century had little interest in democratic reform.[79] However, our age is profoundly different from the nineteenth century. Scholarship is not expected to justify governmental power. There is thus no need to follow a Hegelian approach in order to disguise the contingency of doctrinal constructions. Instead, a modern version of doctrinal constructivism should face the political implications of legal concepts head-on in an open, deliberative

[75] On the parallel developments in Germany and Italy, see M. Stolleis, *Geschichte des öffentlichen Rechts in Deutschland*, vol. 2 (Beck, 1992) 318–19; and P. Schiera and R. Gherardi, 'Von der Verfassung zur Verwaltung: bürgerliche Staatswissenschaft in Deutschland und Italien nach der nationalen Einigung' in E. Volkmar Heyen (ed.), *Wissenschaft und Recht der Verwaltung seit dem Ancien Régime* (Klostermann, 1984) 129–46, 140–4.

[76] Stolleis (n. 75) 330–48; a good illustration for the 'legal method' is provided by Laband's distinction of formal and material laws, see W. Pauly, *Der Methodenwandel im deutschen Spätkonstitutionalismus* (Mohr Siebeck, 1993) 177–86.

[77] For an insightful analysis into the nature of doctrine (*Dogmatik*) in continental legal orders, see N. Luhmann, *Rechtssystem und Rechtsdogmatik* (1974) 9–23. On the impact of *Dogmatik* on courts and legislators: C. Möllers, 'Methoden' in W. Hoffmann-Riem, E. Schmidt-Aßmann, and A. Voßkuhle (eds), *Grundlagen des Verwaltungsrechts*, vol. 1 (Beck, 2006) 121–75, marginal notes 35–37; Schmidt-Aßmann (n. 28) 4–6.

[78] W. Wilhelm, *Zur juristischen Methodenlehre im 19. Jahrhundert* (Klostermann, 1958) 159; S. Mastellone, *Storia ideologica d'Europa da Stuart Mill a Lenin* (Sansoni, 1982) 158. Well-known is the turn against the legal method by Rudolf von Jhering, *Der Kampf ums Recht* (1872).

[79] S. Cassese, *Cultura e politica del diritto amministrativo* (Il Mulino, 1971) 17.

exchange of ideas, which might lead to the consolidation of legal principles applicable to exercises of international public authority guided both by current practice and the normative ideas deployed previously (section B.II.). In developing such principles, legal scholarship should be aware of the limits of doctrinal constructivism: it is unable to achieve 'justice' in the sense of objectively right, ideal solutions fostering nothing but the common good. All those notions have become essentially contested concepts. The principles will therefore relate to issues of competence, procedural fairness, review, and human rights, but less to substantive standards.

In fact, this process of doctrinal constructivism has already begun with respect to sovereign debt restructurings. We try to demonstrate in the following that important legal concepts and principles ensuring the legitimacy of sovereign debt restructurings already exist *de lege lata* in the form of general principles of law, customary international law, or the institutional soft law governing the Paris Club and other venues.[80] Other elements might be desirable *de lege ferenda* and should be proposed to practitioners, interest groups, policy-makers, judges, and academia. The UNCTAD Principles provide an important contribution to both *de lege lata* and *de lege ferenda* aspects.[81] Domestic and international courts might play a crucial role in developing and enforcing such standards. For example, they might choose to give effect to restructurings only if they meet a minimum level of legitimacy. In other fields, domestic and international courts have already started to coordinate their efforts in order to agree on common principles.[82]

D. Elements of a Legal Framework for Sovereign Debt Restructurings

This section elaborates proposals as to how the legitimacy of the exercise of international public authority relating to sovereign debt restructurings might increase by developing a legal framework comprising procedural and substantive aspects (section D.I.). Further, sovereign debt restructurings legitimized by such a legal framework might cause repercussions for cases before domestic and international courts and tribunals (section D.II.).

80 On customary international law, see M. Waibel, Ch. 5 of this volume; on general principles of law, see M. Goldmann, 'Responsible Sovereign Lending and Borrowing: The View from Domestic Jurisdictions', Survey Written for UNCTAD (2012), available at <http://www.unctad.info/upload/Debt%20Portal/RSLB_MGoldmann_02-2012.pdf> (accessed 14 December 2012); and M. Goldmann, Ch. 6 of this volume.

81 On the role of such codes of conduct, see N. Roubini and B. Setser, 'Improving the Sovereign Debt Restructuring Process: Problems in Restructuring, Proposed Solutions, and a Roadmap for Reform', conference paper (2003, on file with the authors) 14–15.

82 cf. E. Benvenisti, 'Reclaiming Democracy: The Strategic Uses of Foreign and International Law by National Courts' (2008) 102 AJIL 241–74.

I. Legal requirements for sovereign debt restructurings

1. Procedural requirements

The following is only an illustrative list of procedural rules and principles which have to be considered as necessary or desirable elements of the legal regime of sovereign debt restructurings, provided that one follows the reasoning that sovereign debt restructurings have a public and authoritative character. Some of these rules and principles are already part of the positive law. The list is by no means intended to be exhaustive.

As regards the relationships between borrowers and lenders, the public law approach requires both sides to participate in negotiations on debt restructurings at the request of a borrower who is unable or might become unable (and not unwilling) to service its debts.[83] Deductively, the public law approach militates in favour of such a duty. The community of states has over time created and supported certain informal mechanisms for the authoritative resolution of sovereign debt crises through multilateral negotiations. In a public law context, the ability to act and to make decisions (i.e. a *competence*) indicates a responsibility to act, at least in situations where issues of public concern are at stake.[84] The participants in authoritative restructurings do not resemble private citizens who may choose to contract whenever they please, but Members of Parliament, who have a responsibility towards the community, or even more administrative agencies which need to deal with matters falling within their competence.

Inductively, the duty to participate in restructuring negotiations has received at least some recognition in contemporary international law.[85] There is considerable agreement about this result, although the reasoning may differ. Some derive this duty from the *erga omnes* character of human rights obligations.[86] Others derive it from the obligation to strive for a peaceful settlement of disputes contained in the UN Charter.[87] Again other scholars argue that the practice of the Paris Club might have created customary law to that effect.[88]

[83] On the criterion of the inability to pay, cf. J.A. Kämmerer, 'State Bankruptcy' in R. Wolfrum (ed.), *Max Planck Encyclopedia of Public International Law* (Oxford University Press, 2009) marginal note 2.

[84] This thought might even become a doctrine of general international law as part of the responsibility to protect, see UN General Assembly, 2005 World Summit Outcome, UN Doc. A/RES/60/1, para. 26. It is to be stressed that this does not imply that in all cases a court may find a breach of an obligation in case of inaction. Rather, in such situations, the competent institutions enjoy discretion.

[85] The PCIJ in *Société Commerciale de Belgique (Belgium v. Greece)* (1939) PCIJ Rep Series A/B No. 78, did not find customary law to exist. See also R. Dolzer, 'Staatliche Zahlungsunfähigkeit: Zum Begriff und zu den Rechtsfolgen im Völkerrecht' in J. Jekewitz et al. (eds), *Festschrift Partsch* (1989) 531–54, 536ff.

[86] Kämmerer (n. 11) 657.

[87] M. Bothe and J. Brink, 'Public Debt Restructuring—the Case for International Economic Co-operation' (1986) 29 GYBIL 107.

[88] Grard (n. 59) 228; A. Reinisch, 'Debt Restructuring and State Responsibility' in D. Carreau and M.N. Shaw (eds) (n. 59) 537, 547ff.; C. Tietje, *Die Argentinien-Krise aus rechtlicher Sicht: Staatsanleihen und Staateninsolvenz* (Archon, 2005) 18, suggesting the existence of a customary principle of cooperative debt management.

But along these lines of argument it might be difficult to extend this duty over private creditors. Only general principles of law might do so, provided they become part of domestic law. General principles of law may be derived from deductive reasoning as well as from municipal law comparisons, abstractions, and analogies, insofar as such provisions are applicable to the international level.[89] One might argue that a duty to negotiate debt restructurings follows from the general principle to act in good faith.[90] However, such a line of argument would be fraught with uncertainty. In addition or in the alternative, one might derive a general principle of law obliging creditors to participate in debt restructurings from the compulsory character of domestic insolvency proceedings. Domestic actors do not have a choice whether to participate in insolvency proceedings or not.[91] Rather, they need to respect the applicable law as well as any decision by a bankruptcy court, i.e. exercises of public authority which may modify their claims unilaterally. This reflects the fact that insolvency proceedings raise questions of distributive justice such as the fate of employees and creditors, which in many cases defy a contractual solution. The absence of obligatory bankruptcy procedures for public entities, with the exception of municipalities in the United States and a few other countries,[92] does not militate against this analogy, as states might use their public law instruments in order to develop ad hoc solutions in case of subnational insolvencies.[93] As has been emphasized previously, on the international level, such ad hoc solutions with effects equivalent to those of domestic bankruptcy procedures already exist, even though their legitimacy might raise questions. From this consideration, a general principle of law obliging creditors to participate in international debt restructurings appears to follow by analogy: if domestic law considers the duty to participate as an essential aspect of legitimate bankruptcy proceedings and as a prerequisite to achieve the distributive purposes of insolvency proceedings, there are good reasons to recognize this idea as a general principle of law. Essential public interests should not be left to the discretion of individual creditors or creditors' committees, but to legitimate and authoritative restructuring mechanisms. It would be therefore desirable for domestic and international courts and tribunals, provided that they are called upon to apply general principles of law, to recognize this duty as having at least a *de lege ferenda* character. For this purpose, UNCTAD Principles 7, 9, and 15 provide valuable guidance by stipulating that cases of financial necessity should be resolved by negotiated restructurings.

[89] H. Lauterpacht, *Private Law Sources and Analogies of International Law* (Archon, 1970) 67ff.; R. Wolfrum, 'Sources of International Law' in R. Wolfrum (ed.), *Max Planck Encyclopedia of Public International Law* (Oxford University Press, 2011), marginal note 35; calling for a new approach which sees general principles more as an argumentative playing field: J. Ellis, 'General Principles and Comparative Law' (2011) 22 Eur. J. Int'l L. 949–71. For a taxonomy of principles, see M. Goldmann, Ch. 6 of this volume.

[90] Slightly optimistic: Dolzer (n. 85) 538–9; Tietje (n. 88) 18.

[91] cf. Goldmann, 'Responsible Sovereign Lending and Borrowing' (n. 80) 39ff.

[92] cf. 11 U.S.C., Chapter IX; see n. 140 on other jurisdictions.

[93] For examples, see G.E. Kodek, 'Nationale Regelungen der Insolvenz von Gebietskörperschaften—ein Modell für die Regelung der Staateninsolvenz?' in G.E. Kodek and A. Reinisch (eds), *Staateninsolvenz* (Bank Verlag Wien, 2011) 145–62.

Another procedural requirement which one may derive from many theories on procedural legitimacy is the idea of an inclusive decision-making process. All those affected by a restructuring should have the opportunity to influence authoritative decisions—either directly or indirectly through representatives, notice-and-comment procedures, or the like.[94] This requirement might challenge the practice of some existing restructuring mechanisms and call for improvements. First of all, the population of the debtor state is heavily affected by a restructuring, especially by the related adjustment programme, but often lacks the power to influence it effectively. In the Paris and London Clubs, the population is represented by its government. However, the default or near-default might prove how manifestly some defaulting governments might have ignored their responsibility towards their people. Also, given the gravity of the decisions taken, in particular the adjustment measures, it seems doubtful whether traditional state consent is always sufficient. One might want to think about strategies for improving the 'ownership' of the adjustment measures by those affected.[95] Of course, the ability to act quickly and efficiently is of great importance in acute crises. But this ability needs to be balanced against the need for inclusive decision-making, which might in turn generate some support for the adjustment measures among the affected citizens. One way of doing so is by setting goals and letting the state in default choose the means. This is the intent behind the abolition of structural performance criteria in IMF lending conditionalities.[96] Another solution might consist of involving domestic stakeholders, in particular domestic parliaments, at an early stage, seeking their continuous input and support. Also, one might question the wisdom of separate negotiation rooms in the Paris Club for the creditors and the defaulting state, which only meets with the Chair.[97] These considerations might to some extent be derived from the general principle of good faith,[98] but should otherwise be understood as suggestions *de lege ferenda* in order to increase the legitimacy of sovereign debt restructurings, as well as their effectiveness. By requiring prompt, efficient, and fair rearrangements, UNCTAD Principle 15 provides argumentative support for such efforts. Domestic insolvency law, by contrast, seems of little help in this respect because it applies to private individuals and entities which cannot be equated with states and their duties towards their populations. In fact, insofar as public entities may be subject to

[94] See section B.II. of this chapter. On notice-and-comment procedures, see R. Stewart, 'US Administrative Law: A Model for Global Administrative Law?' (2005) 68 Law & Cont. Probs 63–108.

[95] Since the end of the Cold War, 'ownership' has become a guiding principle for the international financial institutions. For an early manifestation, see J.H. Johnson, 'Borrower Ownership of Adjustment Programs and the Political Economy of Reform', World Bank Discussion Paper No. 199 (1992); on its meaning, see P. Dann, *Entwicklungsverwaltungsrecht* (Mohr Siebeck, 2011) 216–19. For a proposal on how to improve ownership of conditionality, see O. Eldar, 'Reform of IMF Conditionality: A Proposal for Self-Imposed Conditionality' (2005) 8 J. Int'l Econ. L. 509.

[96] IMF, GRA Lending Toolkit and Conditionality: Reform Proposals (2009), available at <http://www.imf.org/external/np/pp/eng/2009/031309a.pdf> (accessed 14 December 2012).

[97] cf. <http://www.clubdeparis.org/sections/composition/fonctionnement-du-club/deroulement-d-session> (accessed 14 December 2012).

[98] K. Raffer, 'Ein Insolvenzverfahren für Staaten—Gebot ökonomischer Ratio' in G. Kodek and A. Reinisch (eds), *Staateninsolvenz* (2011) 33.

insolvency proceedings, most domestic laws attach greater leverage to public interests than in purely private proceedings.[99]

Further, like the relationship between creditors and the debtor state, inter-creditor relationships need to be designed in a way which ensures the legitimacy of the negotiated agreement. In this respect, it needs to be ensured that all creditors of the same group have an equivalent influence on the terms of the rescheduling while the negotiations are ongoing, whether directly or through representatives. The practice of sovereign debt restructurings has not always respected this consideration.[100] In London Club creditors' committees, a small group of banks represents a much larger number of institutional creditors during negotiations.[101] Some restructurings therefore experienced holdouts by small banks that had been excluded from the negotiations.[102] Further, it might be worthwhile to rethink voting requirements. The consensus requirement for Paris Club restructurings serves to ensure that the taxpayers in creditor states that eventually need to bear the losses are not deprived of their influence.[103] But majority voting might be an option for smoothing decision-making, rendering the restructuring less costly for creditors. In return, the transparency of the negotiations might be increased in order to make sure that no essential interests of creditor states are violated. As far as only private actors are concerned, as in the London Club, we do not see any obstacle to majority voting with numbers of votes proportionate to the sums owed, as in domestic insolvency proceedings. One might, however, opt for minimum thresholds in order to safeguard the interests of small creditors. In this context, Collective Action Clauses provide a good example.

The relationship between different groups of creditors might also receive some guidance from the principle of inclusiveness. The Paris Club's comparable treatment clause, which prohibits the debtor from agreeing with other bilateral and private creditors on other than comparable terms, predetermines the negotiations with those other creditors. It seems difficult to justify this clause bearing in mind the intergovernmental nature of the Paris Club and the capacity of its members to represent their populations. First, not every private creditor might be represented by his or her government in the Paris Club. Secondly, Paris Club members negotiate not only for their citizens' financial interests, but primarily for their own interests. Therefore, some kind of coordination between the different fora, or at least a right of other creditors to be heard by the Paris Club, seems necessary in order to address tensions between private and public creditors as they have arisen in the past.[104] An interesting idea in this respect are the Principles proposed by the Council on Foreign Relations, which recommend coordination between private

[99] Goldmann, 'Responsible Sovereign Lending and Borrowing' (n. 80) 41.

[100] Buchheit and Reisner (n. 62) 500, 514.

[101] K. Hudes, 'Coordination of Paris and London Club Reschedulings' (1984–85) 17 N.Y.U. J. Int'l L. & Pol. 553, 560.

[102] Das, Papaioannou, and Trebesch (n. 19) 17.

[103] cf. the Paris Club Five Key Principles, available at <http://www.clubdeparis.org/sections/composition/principes/cinq-grands-principes> (accessed 14 December 2012).

[104] Josselin (n. 57); Raffer (n. 6).

creditors steering committees and the Paris Club.[105] UNCTAD Principle 7 points in the same direction by requiring lenders 'to behave in good faith and with cooperative spirit'.

Transparency and disclosure are important concerns for discursive approaches to the legitimacy of international public authority. Only if the parties of a restructuring know what is at stake will they be able to find an acceptable solution. Transparency and information sharing is already required by defaulting states under existing IMF and Paris Club legal frameworks.[106] UNCTAD Principles 11 and 13 corroborate these rules. Further, the second explanatory paragraph of Principle 15 states that the rescheduling itself should also be transparent. This might be necessary in order to promote its acceptance by stakeholders in the affected state. By contrast, the Best Practices for Formation and Operation of Creditor Committees elaborated by the Institute of International Finance requires a high level of confidentiality from committee members.[107] While there is indeed reason to protect the confidentiality of sensitive business information, the prohibition for bilateral and multilateral creditors to participate in the negotiations and for all parties to publicly comment on progress is hard to justify from a discursive perspective. Rather, the applicable rules should balance the diverging interests. In this respect, the Best Practices seem to be slanted towards business interests.

A final procedural issue to be discussed here is whether the legitimacy of sovereign debt restructurings would be enhanced by the availability of a court or arbitration tribunal with the jurisdiction to resolve disputes arising from negotiated restructurings (as opposed to creditor holdout litigation, cf. section D.II.). This would certainly strengthen the legitimacy of debt restructurings.[108] One might not have to design and set up new courts or tribunals for this purpose, but rather rely on existing domestic and international judicial institutions.

2. *Substantive issues: human rights*

The development of substantive legal requirements for sovereign debt reschedulings faces the problem that in a modern understanding of democracy which would be commensurate to pluralistic, post-traditional societies, there is no fixed standard of distributive justice from which one might derive such requirements.[109] Only the protection of fundamental human rights should be uncontroversial from the angle of the theoretical framework advanced here. Apart from human rights, doctrinal

[105] cf. Hagan (n. 64) 66.

[106] IMF Articles of Agreement, Art. IV; the Comparability of Treatment Clause is part of the Five Key Principles of the Paris Club (n. 103).

[107] Institute of International Finance, Principles for Stable Capital Flows and Fair Debt Restructurings, 2011 Report on Implementation by the Principles Consultative Group, 39, available at <http://www.iif.com/download.php?id=FwM6aDbqca0=> (accessed 14 December 2012).

[108] cf. C.G. Paulus, 'Ein Insolvenzrecht für Staaten' in M. Dabrowski, *Die Diskussion um ein Insolvenzrecht für Staaten* (2003) 231–59.

[109] See section C. of this chapter.

constructivism may only engage in the formation of institutional frameworks and procedural principles for the elaboration of legitimate substantive standards.

The relationship between human rights and sovereign debt restructurings has not yet been fully explored in scholarship and practice. This opens a perspective for doctrinal constructivism, but also for the future development of the UNCTAD Principles and other international instruments. Some possible contours of this development might be sketched here. The protection of fundamental human rights, especially economic, social, and cultural rights, requires a viable state with effective institutions for the maintenance of at least a minimal standard of basic public services such as education, health, and security. States owe this duty to their citizens. Even if one considers adjustment programmes as necessary in sovereign debt crises, they must avoid discriminatory or otherwise unjustified regressions of economic, social, and cultural rights. This has been confirmed by the European Committee of Social Rights, which established that certain labour market reforms adopted by Greece in the course of its debt crisis violated the European Social Charter.[110] Some scholars argue that these rights apply *de lege lata* to sovereign debt restructurings by virtue of the *erga omnes* effect of human rights obligations.[111] This view finds confirmation in the recent Maastricht Principles on Extraterritorial Obligations of States in the Area of Economic, Social and Cultural Rights.[112] Understanding sovereign debt restructurings as exercises of international public authority strongly corroborates this view. The public law approach should prevent conditionalities and adjustment programmes from becoming the twenty-first century equivalent to the granting of concessions or transfer of property from debtor to creditor states in the nineteenth and twentieth centuries.[113]

Certainly, the financial interests of creditors are not to be discarded lightly. Their claims might fall under the definition of 'property' in human rights treaties or of 'investment' under BITs or the ICSID Convention.[114] However, the European Court of Human Rights grants states a rather broad margin of appreciation in exceptional economic situations.[115] One might also consider such measures as an inherent risk of sovereign debt instruments, which is taken into account in pricing. Indeed, research has revealed that investors' long-term returns from sovereign debt have often been positive, even in cases of default and restructuring.[116]

[110] European Committee of Social Rights, Complaints No. 65/2011 and 66/2011, decisions on the merits of 23 May 2012.

[111] T. Pfeiffer, 'Zahlungskrisen ausländischer Staaten im deutschen und internationalen Rechtsverkehr' (2003) 102 Zeitschrift für vergleichende Rechtswissenschaft 141, 160–1; Dolzer (n. 85) 547; R.T. Hofmann and M. Krajewski, 'Staatsschuldenkrisen im Euro-Raum und die Austeritätsprogramme von IWF und EU' (2012) 45 Kritische Justiz 2–17.

[112] Reproduced in (2012) 34 HRQ 1084.

[113] Zettelmeyer and Sturzenegger (n. 1) 16.

[114] On possible ECtHR cases against Greece, see L. Thomas, 'Hedge Funds May Sue Greece if It Tries to Force Loss', *New York Times* (18 January 2012), B1; on the prospects of cases against Greece brought before ICSID tribunals, see O. Sandrock, 'Ersatzansprüche geschädigter deutscher Inhaber von griechischen Staatsanleihen', Recht der Internationalen Wirtschaft (2012) 429.

[115] e.g. *Grainger v. UK* App. 34940/10, para. 37 (with further references).

[116] Zettelmeyer and Sturzenegger (n. 1) 26ff.

It is clear that effective, legitimate sovereign debt reschedulings require further substantive standards. One particularly salient example is the question of preferential status for IFIs, which Anna Gelpern has termed the 'seating chart' of international debt restructurings.[117] In this respect, it is not quite settled that the IMF and other multilateral institutions should enjoy priority over other creditors, thereby depleting the value of their investment. Some argue that priority should be granted to more senior loans which involve lower funding costs for the affected state.[118] However, given that IMF lending might bridge some time until a more sustainable solution is negotiated, there are good policy reasons for granting such loans preference.[119] Some even argue that customary law already recognizes the preferential position of the IMF.[120]

Nevertheless, developing such a seating chart would exceed what modern doctrinal constructivism may achieve without betraying its own convictions about the essentially contested character of the idea of justice. Therefore, doctrinal constructivism might only call for the elaboration of substantive standards by inclusive institutions in deliberative decision-making processes. The UNCTAD Principles constitute an interesting example of an inclusive, deliberative law-making process involving many representatives and experts. This might contribute to the increasing support they receive. Unfortunately, they are unspecific about the seating chart problem. A contrasting example are the Principles for Stable Capital Flows and Fair Debt Restructurings elaborated by the Institute of International Finance, which stipulate, among others, that multilateral institutions should be responsible for providing interim financing.[121] Even though the Principles were endorsed by the Paris Club, one may wonder to what extent they are the result of a fair and inclusive standard-setting procedure lending credibility to the distributive consequences of such a statement.

Other substantive issues that the legal framework for sovereign debt restructurings should address relate to the preventive side of debt crises. The availability of legitimate and efficient mechanisms for sovereign debt restructurings might at least in theory create moral hazard. They might be abused by states that are able, but genuinely unwilling, to pay their debts in time and consider restructurings as preferable to sustainable debt practices.[122] In this respect, the preventive aspects

117 A. Gelpern, 'Building a Better Seating Chart for Sovereign Restructurings' (2004) 53 Emory L.J. 1119; see also J.P. Bohoslavsky, 'Lending and Sovereign Insolvency: A New Criterion to Distribute Losses among Creditors' (2010) 2 Goettingen Journal of International Law 387.

118 P. Bolton and D.A. Skeel, 'Inside the Black Box: How Should a Sovereign Bankruptcy Framework be Structured?' (2004) 53 Emory L.J. 763.

119 e.g. German Ministry for Economic Cooperation and Development, *Internationale Insolvenzregelungen für Entwicklungsländer*, Stellungnahme des Wissenschaftlichen Beirats beim BMZ (BMZ Spezial Nr. 014), Mai 2000, Bonn: BMZ (AG1–14/91).

120 Reinisch (n. 88) 552; C. Holmgren, *La renégociation multilatérale des dettes: le Club de Paris au regard du droit international* (Bruylant, 1998) 159.

121 Institute of International Finance, Principles for Stable Capital Flows and Fair Debt Restructurings, 2011 Report on Implementation by the Principles Consultative Group, 33, available at <http://www.iif.com/download.php?id=FwM6aDbqca0=> (accessed 14 December 2012).

122 Sovereign defaults are usually preceded by lending booms, which might lead to irresponsible behaviour. See Zettelmeyer and Sturzenegger (n. 1) 6ff.

of the UNCTAD Principles constitute an extremely important building block in the construction of a stable international restructuring mechanism and an international insolvency law. Needless to say, the public law approach requires such principles to be developed in a legitimate setting.

These few examples might illustrate that the recognition of existing mechanisms for debt restructurings as exercises of public authority entails a good deal of practical and theoretical work in order to make these exercises of public authority rationally justifiable to all those affected while preserving their effectiveness.

II. Effects for domestic and international courts and tribunals: a stay on proceedings?

Domestic litigation, and even more so, international arbitration by private creditors and the enforcement of the judgments or awards received, may restrict the ability of states to implement restructurings.[123] A recent series of cases against Argentina before domestic and international tribunals has underlined the severity of this threat.[124] Several strategies have been devised in order to curb such holdout litigation. Debevoise proposed considering sovereign debt contracts as exchange contracts according to Art. VIII(2)(b) of the IMF Articles of Agreements, which would enable the debtor state to prevent their enforcement in other jurisdictions by imposing export regulations.[125] However, courts so far have not followed this view.[126]

More successful have been attempts to invoke necessity as a defence in claims against financially distressed states. This story, which begins with the *Serbian Loans* case and presently continues with ICSID disputes, is well known among lawyers and does not need to be reiterated here in full.[127] However, necessity as a defence is unsatisfactory from the perspective of the public law approach for several reasons. First, a defaulting state may not invoke necessity if it has contributed to the situation of necessity.[128] This requirement has limited the ability of defaulting states to use this defence effectively, since a sovereign default is typically the result

[123] On ICSID, see K.P. Gallagher, 'The New Vulture Culture: Sovereign debt restructuring and trade and investment treaties', IDEA Working Paper 02/2011; M. Waibel, 'Opening Pandora's Box: Sovereign Bonds in International Arbitration' (2007) 101 AJIL 711. A positive view is taken by K. Halverson Cross, 'Arbitration as a Means of Resolving Sovereign Debt Disputes' (2006) 17 Am. Rev. Int'l Arb. 335.

[124] ICSID, *Abaclat v. Argentine Republic*, Case ARB/07/5, Decision on Jurisdiction and Admissibility, 14 November 2011; on domestic cases, see later in this section.

[125] W. Debevoise, 'Exchange Controls and External Indebtedness: A Modest Proposal for a Deferral Mechanism Employing the Bretton Woods Concept' (1984) 7 Hous. J. Int'l L. 157; see Rogoff and Zettelmeyer (n. 4) 479–80.

[126] Tietje (n 88) 10–11, with references to the opinion of the German Federal Court of Justice on the point that exchange contracts do not include sovereign debt instruments.

[127] Kämmerer (n. 11) 659; see also the PCIJ in *Société Commerciale de Belgique (Belgium v. Greece)* (n. 85).

[128] cf. Articles on State Responsibility, Art. 25(2)(b); *Gabčíkovo-Nagymaros Project (Hungary v. Slovakia)* (Merits) [1997] ICJ Rep 7, 46.

of multiple causes, including mistakes of the defaulting government.[129] Secondly, the legal consequences of invoking necessity do not correspond to the policy objectives of sovereign debt restructurings. Necessity only entitles a state to a temporary stay of proceedings, which ceases as soon as the economic or financial situation improves. This does not necessarily coincide with the successful completion of a debt restructuring. Also, a state might have to pay damages to its creditors for the delay.[130] Thirdly, the invocation of necessity is unrelated to the procedural and substantive legitimacy of debt restructurings. While it might be a strong indication for a situation of necessity if a large number of creditors enters into negotiations with the defaulting state, unilateral, non-negotiated default does not necessarily bar a state from establishing an emergency and invoking the defence of necessity.

After the failure of the IMF proposal for a Sovereign Debt Restructuring Mechanism, states massively increased the use of Collective Action Clauses (CACs) in their debt instruments, which had hitherto been a common feature only in debt instruments governed by English law.[131] So far, CACs have proved to be at least a partially effective means against holdout creditors. However, they suffer from certain practical and normative drawbacks. In practical terms, they only apply to new debt, not to old debt with long maturities. Also, large vulture funds are in a position to buy enough bonds of one issue to obstruct the restructuring. The majority required under CACs for the approval to a change in payment terms is the majority (usually 75 per cent or 85 per cent) of the holders of one particular bond, not of all outstanding government debt.[132] Normatively, CACs might raise some of the legitimacy concerns set out in the preceding sections. They make the financial survival of a state dependent on the goodwill of its creditors, irrespective of the rights and interests of the people in the defaulting state.[133]

These considerations lead us to suggest another solution. We argue that there is an emerging general principle of law backed by reasons of legitimacy according to which authoritative international sovereign debt restructurings lead to a stay of

[129] For a critique of the ICSID awards on necessity cf. S. Schill, 'International Investment Law and the Host State's Power to Handle Economic Crises' (2007) 24 J. Int'l Arb. 265–86; C. Binder, 'Changed Circumstances in Investment Law: Interfaces between the Law of Treaties and the Law of State Responsibility with a Special Focus on the Argentine Crisis' in C. Binder et al. (eds), *International Investment Law for the 21st Century* (2009) 608–30; M. Waibel, 'Two Worlds of Necessity in ICSID Arbitration: *CMS* and *LG&E*' (2007) 20 LJIL 637.

[130] Kämmerer (n. 83) marginal note 10; Waibel (n. 129). On damages, cf. Articles on State Responsibility, Art. 27(b).

[131] For data on the use of CACs, see M.C. Weidemaier, Ch. 15 of this volume. On the political process leading to the rise in CACs see R. Quarles, 'Herding Cats: Collective-Action Clauses in Sovereign Debt—The Genesis of the Project to Change Market Practice in 2001 Through 2003' (2012) 73 Law & Cont. Probs 29.

[132] Gallagher (n. 123) 12; J.E. Fisch and C.M. Gentile, 'Vultures or Vanguards?: The Role of Litigation in Sovereign Debt Restructuring' (2004) 53 Emory L.J. 1043, 1094–5; C.C. Wheeler and A. Attaran, 'Declawing the Vulture Funds: Rehabilitation of a Comity Defense in Sovereign Debt Litigation' (2003) 39 SJIL 253, 264–5.

[133] R.K. Rasmussen, 'Integrating a Theory of the State into Sovereign Debt Restructuring' (2004) 53 Emory L.J. 1159, 1163–4.

international and domestic enforcement actions against sovereign debtors. Deductively, such a principle is, first, a corollary of the idea that sovereign debt restructurings need to respect essential human rights.[134] Only one single, centralized proceeding or a number of closely coordinated proceedings may enable a state to regain the capacity necessary for safeguarding essential human rights and avoid disastrous shocks to the domestic and global economy. Secondly, only one single, or multiple coordinated proceedings may ensure that all creditors are treated equally and that any priorities are applied consistently. Thirdly, it is appropriate to apply stays by analogy to sovereign defaults, because the only fundamental normative difference between defaulting states and defaulting private entities is that the former cannot be liquidated. This militates *a fortiori* in favour of the imposition of stays of enforcement proceedings in sovereign default cases, because such a defence would facilitate the orderly resolution of a sovereign debt crisis while ensuring the maintenance of the essential functions of a state. Thus, from a teleological point of view, the transfer of this principle of private insolvency law to sovereign defaults seems adequate.

Inductively, we argue that there is growing evidence that ongoing negotiations about sovereign debt restructurings as well as their implementation might have *de lege lata* the effect of a stay on court proceedings. A general principle of law to this effect seems to be on the rise.[135] In practically all domestic jurisdictions, bankruptcy filings of private entities trigger a stay on enforcement actions.[136] Although domestic law might vary in some details from one legal order to the other, in particular as some jurisdictions require prior court approvals, on an abstract level there is a high degree of convergence: authoritative, centralized insolvency proceedings bar individual enforcement against the creditor in default.[137] This also shows that the 'sanctity of contract' invoked by the Principles prepared by the Institute of International Finance is a myth.[138]

What is the rule in private sector insolvencies is increasingly applied to defaults in the public sector. First, domestic legislation in some jurisdictions provides for some form of stay in case of defaulting public entities. Under Chapter 9 of title 11 of the US Code, automatic stay is applicable in bankruptcy procedures against municipalities.[139] Other states that have enacted bankruptcy legislation for subnational entities include Brazil, Bulgaria, Hungary, Romania, and South Africa.

[134] cf. section D.I.2. of this chapter.

[135] In this sense, see already Dolzer (n. 85) 546–7.

[136] International Law Association, 'State Insolvency: Options for the Way Forward', Report for the Hague Conference (2010) 23. Paulus (n. 9) 404; Waibel (n. 123) 750.

[137] cf. only 11 U.S.C. § 362 and German Code of Civil Procedure, § 240; German Insolvency Code, § 89. Differences are due to the fact that in Germany, stays require court approval, but the execution of judgments usually does not require adversarial enforcement proceedings before courts. The general principle has been recognized by international tribunals, cf. ICSID, *Noble Ventures Inc. v. Romania*, Case ARB/01/11, which emphasizes that restructurings under municipal law are not arbitrary measures under the fair and equitable treatment standard, cf. Waibel (n. 123) 750. However, willful breaches and abuse could lead to a violation, cf. C. Schreuer, 'Fair and Equitable Treatment in Arbitral Practice' (2005) 6 JWIT 357, 380.

[138] See IIF Report (n. 121) 33.

[139] 11 U.S.C., §§ 901(a), 362.

It routinely includes some form of stay on enforcement.[140] Even in the absence of formal bankruptcy proceedings, there is legislation in some legal orders recognizing that creditors may not obtain and enforce judgments for the full amount of their debt against insolvent sovereign debtors. After the Second World War, Germany passed legislation which annulled, with few exceptions, all domestic government debt of the Reich, thereby mooting ongoing and future enforcement action.[141] The 2010 United Kingdom Debt Relief (Developing Countries) Act reduces claims of private creditors against countries participating in the HIPC proportionate to the relief granted to them under the initiative. Although the legislation in Germany and the United Kingdom technically does not impose stays, it serves the identical purpose, namely ensuring the orderly resolution of debt crises through international negotiations while preserving the equality of creditors.

Secondly, state practice and some case law show the acknowledgement of the importance of stays of proceedings in case of international debt restructurings, thereby recognizing the latter as authoritative, which justifies applying essentially the same rules as in domestic insolvency proceedings. Since the 1930s, bilateral lenders have routinely granted financially distressed states a moratorium on their debt during international negotiations.[142] This might be a corollary of the duty to cooperate in sovereign debt restructurings.[143] The situation is less clear with respect to private creditors, which usually reserve the right to file suits and require states to waive their jurisdictional immunities. However, some precedents stir hopes that more and more courts might recognize automatic stay as a legal consequence of sovereign debt restructurings. In 1985, the Supreme Court of New York recognized this principle in a suit against Venezuela, basing it on the duty of the plaintiff to respect creditor solidarity.[144] Another line of reasoning originates in the first decision in *Allied Bank Int. v. Banco Credito Agricola de Cartago*. In 1984, the US Federal Court of Appeals for the Second Circuit ruled against a holdout creditor since Costa Rica seemed to be negotiating in good faith at the time. When the restructuring later amounted to a rather unilateral suspension of payments, the first ruling was reversed.[145] A more recent example of this line of reasoning is provided by the 2005 summary order rendered by the same court in *EM Ltd v. Argentina* and *NML Capital v. Argentina*. Although formally this order lacks precedential value, it has been widely cited for the remarkable considerations of the judge, who decided that 'the District Court acted well within its authority to vacate the remedies in order to avoid a substantial risk to the successful conclusion of the debt restructuring. That restructuring is obviously of critical importance to the economic health of a nation'.[146] At around

[140] M. Waibel and L. Liu, 'Subnational Insolvency: Cross-Country Experiences and Lessons', World Bank Policy Research Working Paper No. 4496 (2008) 26.

[141] Allgemeines Kriegsfolgengesetz, § 1(1), 5 November 1957, Bundesgesetzblatt III, No. 653–1.

[142] Zettelmeyer and Sturzenegger (n. 1) 15.

[143] cf. section D.I.1. of this chapter.

[144] Supreme Court of New York, *Crédit français S.A. v. Sociedad financiera de Comercio*, 490 N.Y. S.2d 670 (1985); Dolzer (n. 85) 539.

[145] Case 83–7714, 18 March 1985, 757 F.2d 516; cf. Rogoff and Zettelmeyer (n. 4) 475.

[146] *EM Ltd v. Argentina*; *NML Capital v. Argentina*, 05-1525-cv, Summary Order, 13 May 2005.

the same time, the Italian Corte di Cassazione recognized that the need to safeguard essential public interests and human rights justified extending immunity over Argentina's emergency laws, even though it had waived its immunity for the bonds in dispute. The underlying rationale is the same, even though the court presents it as a combination of arguments relating to necessity and immunity.[147] The 2011 judgment of the US Court of Appeals for the Second Circuit in *CVI v. Argentina* seems to endorse its earlier line of reasoning, although only indirectly.[148] In this case, the Court upheld the attachments received by CVI on Argentina's reversionary interest in collateral pledged for Brady bonds (i.e. when exchanging Brady bonds, Argentina would receive the pledged collateral, which CVI would then have 'confiscated' pursuant to the attachment orders). However, the Court based its decision primarily on the argument that the attachments concerned only a relatively small sum (US$100 million), while the volumes of the planned restructuring and thus of the expected reversionary interest were much larger. Therefore, the Court concluded that the attachment would not obstruct Argentina's finances. If one reverses this argument, attachments could principally be vacated in case they obstruct restructurings.[149] In what is at present the latest case in the Argentinian debt saga before US courts, the same court upheld the District Court's injunction obliging Argentina to make ratable payments to holdout creditors whenever it made payments to creditors which had participated in the exchange. Again, it emphasized that this did not threaten the implementation of Argentina's restructuring plan and would not trigger a new financial and economic crisis.[150]

Certainly, the mentioned cases represent only part of the entire picture. Judges at the US Federal Court for the Southern District of New York rendered dozens of judgments in favour of vulture funds attempting to reclaim the nominal amount of their debt against Argentina in which they did not recognize that Argentina had a legitimate interest in having the proceedings stayed until the conclusion of its restructuring.[151] Other particularly infamous decisions are those of a Belgian court granting Elliot Associates enforcement of a US judgment in Belgium by allowing interception of Peru's interest payments to non-holdout creditors cleared by a

[147] Corte di Cassazione, Sezione Unite Civile, n. 11225, 27 May 2005, (2005) 88 Rivista di diritto internazionale 856; see Waibel (n. 123) 757.

[148] *Capital Ventures International v. Republic of Argentina*, 10-4520-cv et al., 20 July 2011, 652 F.3d 266.

[149] See also the decision of the 2nd Circuit in *Capital Ventures International v. Argentina*, 05-2591-cv, 23 March 2006, 443 F.3d 214, 217, regarding the risk that the order of attachment might create 'confusion' among the creditors participating in the exchange offer (obiter dictum): 'we can conceive, perhaps, of a situation in which an order of attachment might be against the public interest for some reason not addressed in the CPLR (statute)'.

[150] *NML et al. v. Argentina*, 12-105(L), 26 October 2012, 26.

[151] e.g. *EM Ltd v. Argentina*, 03-Civ-2507(TPG), opinion on motions for attachment and restraints, 7 April 2010; see also the impressive list of judgments against Argentina in a restraining order of 15 January 2010 in the case *Aurelius Capital Partners et al. v. Argentina*, 07-Civ-2715(TPG), totalling more than US$500m. But see also in this as well as 11 other cases the order of the same court of 28 March 2012 lifting an earlier restraining order concerning funds of the Argentinian central bank held at the Federal Reserve Bank of New York in order to enforce judgments of a total worth of over $2.2bn (*EM Ltd v. Argentina*, 865 F.Supp.2d 415).

Belgian company,[152] and the decision of the German Federal Constitutional Court in the Argentinian Bond case, which refused to give recognition to the defence of necessity in cases confronting states and private investors.[153] However, in a 1962 judgment concerning Germany's post-war default on its domestic debt, the latter court recognized that sovereign defaults justified highly intrusive measures including the legislative cancellation of debt without compensation because of the high significance of the state for politics and the economy in general and the ensuing impossibility of liquidating all of the state's assets.[154] And it should be kept in mind that the US cases against Argentina address a massive, unilaterally imposed haircut on sovereign debt. It is not certain that the courts involved would come to the same conclusions in cases against a state extending an invitation to all creditors to participate in fair and transparent negotiations either directly or through representatives. Another way in which courts might change their views in the long run emerges from the 1997 decision in *Pravin Banker v. Banco Popular del Peru.* In that case, the defaulting state attempted to reach a negotiated exchange of defaulted debt into Brady bonds. The US Federal Court of Appeals for the Second Circuit only declined to stay proceedings as a matter of comity because the US government considered participation in a Brady plan restructuring as a strictly voluntary matter.[155] In this respect, it is interesting to note that the amicus brief submitted by the US government in the *NML v. Argentina* case decided in October 2012,[156] while formally insisting on the voluntary nature of debt restructurings, stresses that this should not allow individual creditors to thwart an entire restructuring process.[157]

For the foregoing reasons, it seems possible to identify a normatively justifiable conviction across legal orders that both private and sovereign debt restructurings must not be jeopardized by holdout litigation or arbitration. All requirements for the emergence of a general principle of law are met.[158] By requiring prompt, fair, and effective restructurings in case of financial necessity, UNCTAD Principles 7, 9, and 15 corroborate these efforts. As a general principle of law, the stay on proceedings would have to be applied by international courts and tribunals,

[152] *Elliott Associates*, Brussels Court of Appeals, 8th Chamber, General Docket 2000/QR/92, 26 September 2000; for a meticulous critique, see L.C. Buchheit and J.S. Pam, 'The *Pari Passu* Clause in Sovereign Debt Instruments' (2004) 53 Emory L.J. 869; further holdout litigation is listed in U. Panizza, F. Sturzenegger, and J. Zettelmeyer, 'The Economics and Law of Sovereign Debt and Default' (2009) 47 J. Econ. Lit. 651, 655–9.

[153] Cases 2 BvM 1–5/03, 1, 2/06, decision of 8 May 2007, BVerfGE 118, 124.

[154] Case 1 BvR 987/58, Judgment of 14 Novermber 1962, BVerfGE 15, 126, 140–4.

[155] Case 96-7183, 25 March 1997, 109 F.3d 850, 855. Cf. Panizza, Sturzenegger, and Zettelmeyer (n. 659).

[156] See n. 150.

[157] Brief for the United States of America as Amicus Curiae in Support of Reversal, Case 12-105-cv (L), 4 April 2012, <http://blogs.reuters.com/felix-salmon/files/2012/04/US-Br.pdf> (accessed on 14 December 2012).

[158] In the taxonomy used by M. Goldmann in Ch. 6 of this volume, this principle would have to be characterized either as a general principle of law, or as a guiding principle about to mature to a general principle.

including ICSID arbitral tribunals.[159] For the latter, there are also good policy reasons to grant automatic stay. A powerful argument has been made that ICSID dispute settlement is conditional upon the protection of essential public interests.[160] Sovereign debt restructurings aim at preserving the financial survival and stability of states and should therefore be respected.[161] Additionally, legitimate restructurings of this kind could hardly be said to violate fair and equitable treatment or national treatment clauses contained in bilateral investment treaties.

Domestic courts and tribunals would only be immediately bound by such a general principle of law if the legal order in which they operate gives direct effect to them.[162] Otherwise, only their state is obliged to respect this principle as a matter of international law. In order to avoid state responsibility arising from continuing holdout litigation, it would have to pass appropriate legislation. Beyond the scope of strict legal obligations, it should be borne in mind that the more legitimate and effective international debt restructurings are, the more domestic and international judges and arbitrators will have reason to defer to them and put a stay on creditor suits and enforcement action.

E. Conclusion

Conceptualizing sovereign debt restructurings as exercises of international public authority involves a daunting task for practice and legal scholarship. It requires uncovering the full extent of the implications of sovereign debt restructurings for all affected parties and underlines the need to bring these mechanisms out of the shadow of informality. Like all exercises of public authority, they must not escape the reach of public law. This insight calls for a good dose of doctrinal constructivism in order to develop rules which protect the interests of all parties involved, including states, citizens affected by adjustment measures, and commercial and other private creditors, as well as international institutions. We hope that the public law approach advocated in this chapter and its underlying principles might guide the development of such rules and principles and provide useful insights and arguments for the support of legal rules and principles that make international debt restructurings both more legitimate and more efficient.

[159] cf. ICJ Statute, Art. 38(1)(c).

[160] Schill (n. 12); B. Kingsbury and S. Schill, 'Investor-State Arbitration as Governance: Fair and Equitable Treatment, Proportionality and the Emerging Global Administrative Law', International Law and Justice Working Paper No. 6 (2009).

[161] On the connection between sovereign debt and domestic stability, see M. Goldmann, 'Sovereign Debt Crises as Threats to the Peace: Restructuring under Chapter VII of the UN Charter?' (2012) 4 Goettingen Journal of International Law 153.

[162] An example would be Art. 25 of the German Basic Law. According to Wheeler and Attaran (n. 132) 266ff., comity as a doctrine of US law might lend itself to such purposes. This is confirmed by the case referred to in n. 155.

Nevertheless, legal scholarship is unable to legitimize substantive rules with serious distributional consequences since there is no objective idea of justice on which they could be based. Instead, they require a political decision. In that respect, initiatives like the UNCTAD Principles constitute a necessary and important step on the road towards a decentralized, yet incrementally developing, international insolvency law for the regulation of sovereign debt restructurings.

PART II

LEGAL STATUS OF THE PRINCIPLES

4

Principles Matter

The Legal Status of the Principles on Responsible Sovereign Financing

*Juan Pablo Bohoslavsky and Carlos Espósito**

A. Introduction

Except for the case of international intergovernmental lending, typically ruled by public international law, sovereign lending and borrowing is an activity that usually takes place under domestic law, so it is only natural to ask why international law should have a say in this matter. First, it is obvious that preventing sovereign insolvencies, promoting global financial stability, and facilitating the attainment of the Millennium Development Goals are of genuine interest to the international community—a community ruled by international law. In fact, actors and interests of the international community are repeatedly present in debt issues. This is, most probably, because when certain sovereign borrowers' and their lenders' decisions have deep and broad consequences for markets and societies, these decisions might be considered, from the international financial law perspective, as actions of public authorities which should respect the applicable public law regime developed at the international level.[1] Secondly, if a sovereign insolvency cannot be prevented, this involves not only a single and common sovereign debtor but also a multiplicity of laws and jurisdictions, nationalities, locations, goals, and types of lenders.[2] This situation also comprises the economic basis of the sovereign debtor, its fiscal and regulatory powers. All this brings questions of state responsibility to bear, which, once discussed in international disputes, highlights the need for at least some minimum legal guidelines at the international level.[3]

* The authors wish to thank Pal Borresen, Yuefen Li, Marie Sudreau, Jean D'Aspremont, and Matthias Goldmann for their comments on early drafts of this chapter. The views and conclusions reflected in this chapter are solely those of the authors and are in no way intended to reflect the views of any of the institutions with which the authors are affiliated.

[1] See A.von Bogdandy and M. Goldmann, Ch. 3 of this book.

[2] The approach of Global Administrative Law may be helpful to understanding this multilayered structure. See B. Kingsbury, N. Krisch, and R.B. Stewart, 'The Emergence of Global Administrative Law', IILJ Working Paper 2004/1 (Global Administrative Law Series) <http://www.iilj.org>, available at <http://ssrn.com/abstract=692628>.

[3] But see E. Posner, *The Perils of Global Legalism* (Chicago University Press, 2009) 8, 'if a world government is not possible, then solving global collective action problems is also not possible'.

It is therefore not surprising that there have been several international official and private initiatives that have proposed principles or guidelines to be applied to sovereign borrowing and lending. However, none of these initiatives has resulted in the creation of effective and enforceable legal means. This chapter examines the legal status of the Principles on Responsible Sovereign Lending and Borrowing (UNCTAD Principles), elaborated by an expert group established in 2009 and coordinated by UNCTAD.[4] Are the Principles different in this regard? Will they become law, soft or hard? This chapter tries to advance some clues to answer these questions.

The latest financial crisis has not prompted effective coordination between countries in order to overcome the problems through systemic solutions and global macroeconomic policy coordination.[5] Indeed, many countries have embarked on unilateral strategies to deal with the crisis, such as protectionism and subsidies to financial and non-financial sectors.[6] Another implication of this lack of coordination is the prevailing absence of basic rules on sovereign insolvency or, in plain English, a deep uncertainty on how property rights will be affected in case of insolvency. This provokes problems in terms of both efficiency and fairness in international financial markets, and it becomes more and more pernicious as globalization advances and interconnections become more intense: crises hit harder and spread faster.

It is obvious that sovereign lending and borrowing constitutes an area in which rules are scant,[7] even when needed in a minimalist formulation. This strengthens the idea that principles matter. Disputes among creditors and between debtors and creditors need to be resolved in an efficient and fair way and, of course, legal *lacunae* cannot be a valid argument for not applying the rule of law in this area. The current case-by-case practical application of a few rudimentary principles in sovereign lending and borrowing does not really help to prevent or minimize crises.

The structure of this chapter is as follows. Section B. outlines and elaborates on the content and implications of the UNCTAD Principles from the perspective of the formal sources of international law. As will be seen, while there are only a few rules derived from international conventions and international customary law, legal provisions distilled from the constitutional, contract, and bankruptcy laws of national legal systems have been crucial in shaping the Principles. Section C. moves the discussion forward in order to consider the legality of the Principles from the viewpoint of informal international law-making.[8] This analysis of the

[4] UNCTAD, 'Draft Principles on Responsible Sovereign Lending and Borrowing', Geneva, May 2011, available at <http://www.unctad.info/upload/Debt%20Portal/Principles%20drafts/Principles%20Consolidated_jan%2010.pdf>.

[5] J.K. Sundaram (ed.), *Reforming the International Financial System for Development* (Columbia University Press, 2010).

[6] United Nations, 'Report of the Commission of Experts of the President of the United Nations General Assembly on Reforms of the International Monetary and Financial System', 21 September 2009, available at <http://www.un.org/ga/econcrisissummit/docs/FinalReport_CoE.pdf>.

[7] J. Grigienė and A. Mockienė, 'Can a Sovereign State Declare Bankruptcy?' (2010) 3 Baltic Journal of Law & Politics 125.

[8] J. Pauwelyn, R.A. Wessel, and J. Wouters (eds), *Informal International Lawmaking* (Oxford University Press, 2012).

Principles as a soft law instrument will be helpful to ascertain the legal character of the Principles and whether they have a low or high degree of bindingness. The conclusion underscores the utility of fragmenting and defragmenting the legal status of the Principles considered as a whole as a soft law instrument, while framing this specific discussion in the current general debate on the sources of international law.

B. The Principles and their Legal Formal Basis

As a result of the discussion within the Expert Group that provided technical assistance to UNCTAD, in January 2012 a set of principles on responsible sovereign lending and borrowing emerged.[9] The draft has crystallized a range of principles separately applied to lenders and sovereign borrowers.

The principles (called *responsibilities* in the draft) to be applied to lenders are: (a) lenders should acknowledge the fiduciary duty of government officials to the state (and its citizens), which has implications in terms of preventing corruption; (b) lenders should take informed decisions based on realistic assessments (due diligence), and determine whether the financing is duly authorized and valid under the law of the borrower; (c) lenders should investigate the likely effects of financing a project; (d) lenders must not participate in transactions that contribute to violation of UN sanctions; (e) in the context of restructuring, lenders should behave in good faith and with cooperative spirit to reach a consensual, speedy, and orderly rearrangement.

On the other hand, principles to be applied to sovereign borrowers consist of: (a) government officials have a fiduciary responsibility towards citizens; (b) debts must be honoured unless the economic circumstances of the borrower prevent its full/timely repayment or a judicial authority rules that a legal defence has arisen; (c) there must be due authorization and a transparent decision-making process; (d) broad disclosure of the contractual terms and the economic situation must be made; (e) borrowers should investigate the implications of projects to be financed; (f) borrowers should implement adequate management strategies and monitoring systems, including proper audits; (g) governments should weigh costs and benefits when seeking loans so as to avoid negative instances of over-borrowing; (h) if a restructuring becomes unavoidable, it should be undertaken promptly, efficiently, and fairly, seeking a consensual agreement supported by a supermajority of creditors, avoiding opportunistic and discriminatory behaviour, respecting seniority of debts, and ensuring that all stakeholders share an equitable burden of losses.

What is the legal basis of these principles? Our perspective is international, so the answer requires a proper reference to the sources of international law. A simple and generally accepted way to proceed is by reference to Article 38 of the statute of the

[9] 12 January 2012, available at <http://www.unctad.info/en/Debt-Portal/News-Archive/Our-News/UNCTAD-Releases-Consolidated-Principles-on-Responsible-Sovereign-Financing-310112>. Reproduced in the Annex to this book.

International Court of Justice, which mentions that the primary legal sources of international law are international conventions, international custom, and general principles of law, while secondary sources are judicial decisions and the teachings of the most highly qualified publicists.[10]

International conventions do not offer much in terms of rules to be applied to sovereign financing. Still, there are a few principles that are indisputably supported by conventional law. On the one hand, lenders and borrowers are not allowed to violate UN sanctions (Article 25, UN Charter);[11] on the other hand, corruption in sovereign financing is wrongful, and transparency and accountability are mandatory in state contracting (Articles 9, 15ff., and 34, UN Convention against Corruption).[12] These rules were adopted by the Principles (see Principles 1, 6, 8, 9, 10, 11, and 13).

International customary law is also rather sparing in its provision of rules on sovereign financing.[13] First, a reference to the golden rule of *pacta sunt servanda*[14] is appropriate. This generic rule may be limited by the public law defence of state of necessity, based on the economic or political circumstances that render impossible the full or timely repayment of the debts.[15] Secondly, the Paris Club supports the idea of parity among creditors, since it works on the basis of equitable burden-sharing where each sovereign creditor has to extend debt relief in proportion to its exposure to the debtor country and the debtor is expected to seek comparable relief from the private sector.[16] These rules were also adopted by UNCTAD's draft in Principles 7, 9, and 15.

One could further affirm that financial assistance violating or helping to breach norms of *jus cogens* is also wrong (Article 53, Vienna Convention on the Law of

[10] See A. Pellet, 'Article 38' in A. Zimmermann et al. (eds), *The Statute of the International Court of Justice. A Commentary* (2nd edn, Oxford University Press, 2012) 731. We are of course fully aware of the limits of Art. 38 of the ICJ Statute, but this is not the place to tackle those problems or discuss new approaches to the sources of international law. Rather, we follow the advice of Pellet that Art. 38 'deserves neither over-praise nor harsh indignity' (at 734), and use it as a reference and starting point for our discussion on the Principles. Cf. J. D'Aspremont, *Formalism and the Sources of International Law. A Theory of the Ascertainment of Legal Rules* (Oxford University Press, 2012) 150, arguing that 'law-ascertainment in international law must be conceived independently from article 38, which was not only conceived to serve another purpose, but leaves too much room for non-formal law-ascertainment'.

[11] See A. Peters, 'Article 25' in B. Simma et al. (eds), *The Charter of the United Nations. A Commentary* (3rd edn, Oxford University Press, 2012) 787.

[12] On this specific issue, see J. Justo, Ch. 9 of this book.

[13] In a way, this limited scope of customary international law in global finance makes the current debate on withdrawing from international custom an abstract issue in this particular field. On this debate, see C. Bradley and G.M. Gulati, 'Withdrawing from International Custom' (2010) 120 Yale L.J. 202.

[14] On this matter, state practice with a sense of obligation is overwhelming, as shown by M. Waibel in Ch. 5 of this book. In any case, we understand this basic rule also as a general principle of law, and not necessarily limited to interstate law as in a restrictive interpretation of the Vienna Convention on the Law of Treaties (1969), Art. 26. See the discussion by M. Waibel and R. Howse in this regard in Chs 5 and 17 of this book.

[15] International Law Commission's Articles on State Responsibility, Art. 25.

[16] G. Vitale, 'Multilateral Sovereign Debt Restructuring: The Paris Club and the London Club' in B. Einchengreen and R. Portes (eds), *Crisis? What Crisis? Orderly Workouts for Sovereign Debtors* (Center for Economic Policy Research, 1995) 123.

Treaties 1969). Whether or not a link between a loan and a *jus cogens* violation exists depends on a case-by-case assessment.[17] While the Principles are not explicit in this regard, their preamble nonetheless indicates that '*this set of principles should apply without prejudice of other international rules concerning the action of lenders or borrowers*' (emphasis added).

Case law in this area is rather limited, mixed, and sometimes contradictory.[18] Therefore this legal source does not yet offer a logical and systemic body to resolve (even less so to prevent) disputes on sovereign lending and borrowing. On the other hand, scholarly writing, even when sometimes robust and sophisticated, cannot itself be a primary legal source, but can only help to interpret primary sources.

The insufficiency of legal guidance regulating sovereign lending and borrowing forces us to turn to general principles in order to fill this gap.[19] This unavoidable need makes a theoretical discussion on whether rules or principles prevail in case of conflict futile.[20] In the absence of rules, principles are needed.

Even when general principles do not require a formal, written indicator representing the states' consent—whether through written agreement or explicit practices—implicit consensus can be derived from domestic orders.[21] Of course, we are aware that, in the beginning, general principles were introduced in order to solve problems of *non-liquet*;[22] they were not conceived as mere abstractions from domestic orders. However, we believe that today it is fairly uncontroversial to accept that comparative law is a strong legal tool that may lead to the crystallization of a general principle of international law.[23] In any case, we need to determine how to identify applicable principles. The Statute of the ICJ alludes to general principles recognized by nations,[24] not *all* nations,[25] but to be truly

[17] S. Michalowski and J.P. Bohoslavsky, 'Ius Cogens, Transitional Justice and other Trends of the Debate on Odious Debts. A Response to the World Bank Discussion Chapter on Odious Debts' (2010) 48 Colum. J. Transnat'l L. 67.

[18] See generally M. Waibel, *Sovereign Defaults before International Courts and Tribunals* (Cambridge University Press, 2011).

[19] A. Reinisch, 'The Need for an International Insolvency Procedure' (1994) 2 *Zeitschrift für das gesamte Bank- und Börsenwesen* 119.

[20] R. Alexy, *A Theory of Constitutional Rights* (Oxford University Press, 2002) 83–4. The ICJ, nevertheless, 'tends to treat [rules and principles] as synonymous'. See M. Mendelson, 'The International Court of Justice and the Sources of International Law' in V. Lowe and M. Fitzmaurice (eds), *Fifty Years of the International Court of Justice: Essays in Honour of Sir Robert Jennings* (Cambridge University Press, 1996) 63, 80, and the case of the *Gulf of Maine*, ICJ Reports 1984, 246, 288–90, para. 79, both cited by Pellet (n. 10) 834, para. 255.

[21] A. Verdross, *Die Quellen des universellen Völkerrechts* (Rombach & Co. GmbH, 1973) 128. On this function of the general principles, see M.C. Bassiouni, 'A Functional Approach to "General Principles of International Law"' (1990) 11 Mich. J. Int'l L. 776; E. Olufemi and L. Chim, 'General Principles of Law, Soft Law and the Identification of International Law' (1997) 28 NJIL 4.

[22] Pellet (n. 10) 832, para. 250.

[23] See J. Ellis, 'General Principles and Comparative Law' (2011) 22 Eur. J. Int'l L. 949.

[24] We are not going to deal with the issue of exclusion and colonialism here. That is the reason why we have not mentioned the word 'civilized' to qualify nations. The broad review by Goldmann includes all sorts of countries, representing a broad sense of the international society, beyond exclusionary and colonialist qualifications. See M. Goldmann, Ch. 6 of this book.

[25] C. Ford, 'Judicial Discretion in International Jurisprudence: Art. 38 (1) (c) and "General Principles of Law"' (1994) 5 Duke J. Comp. & Int'l L. 76.

general principles they must reflect a legal rule of broad spectrum as provided for or acknowledged by the municipal law of states. Having said this, we favour an analytical and functional approach to identify general principles transposable at the international level. This means understanding the rationale behind the way in which domestic laws solve certain problems,[26] a process that requires qualitative evaluation and abstraction. That is the reason why particularities among legal systems can exist and general principles still be recognized as having the force of law. As a general rule, in a way derived from the principle of equality among states, a general principle should be identified in the main legal systems of the world.

Domestic legal orders provide the raw material for carrying out comparative surveys in order to identify general principles of law in the field of sovereign financing. Due diligence, good faith,[27] transparency, fiduciary duty, and *pacta sunt servanda* seem to be preliminary, deeply rooted principles in European and American legal orders.[28] A wide-ranging comparative study has been conducted by Matthias Goldmann, who reaches the conclusion that 'most of the principles contained in the Principles are to be qualified as generally accepted guiding principles, or as emerging principles. Some of them might even be considered to have acquired the status of (emerging) general principles of law'. Goldmann further asserts that: 'There is no principle contained in the Draft which would not, at least on an abstract level, find some support among the domestic legal orders under examination.'[29]

For instance, there is one area in which it might already be said that domestic law strengthens the degree of normative force of the UNCTAD Principles: restructuring. When one examines the substantive principles in comparative perspective, the common denominators are evident,[30] as the 2004 United Nations Commission on International Trade Law's 'Legislative Guide on Insolvency Law' demonstrates.[31] The objectives that private insolvency law should normally attain[32] give sense to the

[26] T. Tridimas, *The General Principles of EU Law* (Oxford University Press, 1999) 38.

[27] On these two principles already applied by international tribunals, see B. Cheng, *General Principles of Law as Applied by International Courts and Tribunals* (Cambridge, Grotius Publications, 1987) 121, 218.

[28] T. Graziano, *Comparative Contract Law* (Palgrave Macmillan, 2009); T. Kilmas, *Comparative Contract Law* (Carolina Academic Press, 2006); S. Sánchez-Lorenzo (ed.), *Derecho contractual comparado. Una perspectiva europea y transnacional* (Civitas Thomson-Reuters, 2009).

[29] M. Goldmann, 'Responsible Sovereign Lending and Borrowing: The View from Domestic Jurisdictions. A Comparative Survey Written for the United Nations Conference on Trade and Development', UNCTAD Working Document, February 2012, Geneva, available at <http://www.unctad.info/upload/Debt%20Portal/RSLB_MGoldmann_02-2012.pdf>.

[30] See Goldmann (n. 29). For a comparative analysis, see generally H. Schier, *Towards a Reorganization System for Sovereign Debt* (Martinus Nijhoff, 2007).

[31] See broadly UNCITRAL, 'Legislative Guide on Insolvency Law', United Nations, New York (2005), available at <http://www.uncitral.org/pdf/english/texts/insolven/05-80722_Ebook.pdf>.

[32] Provide certainty in the market; maximize the value of assets; strike a balance between liquidation and reorganization; ensure equitable treatment of creditors; provide for timely efficient and impartial resolution of insolvency; preserve the insolvency state to allow equitable distribution to creditors; ensure a transparent and predictable insolvency law; grant recognition of creditors' rights and establish clear rules for ranking of claims; establish a framework for cross-border insolvency. See UNCITRAL, 'Legislative Guide on Insolvency Law (n. 31).

similarities that the spirit and contents of UNCTAD's and UNCITRAL's proposals present.[33] There is always one fundamental problem: a common debtor cannot repay its debts to its creditors in full and/or in a timely fashion. This comparative approach rests on the assumption that sovereign bankruptcy law is functionally comparable to insolvency principles at the domestic level.

The fact that principles coming from domestic laws offer a goldmine of sound and consolidated rules to deal with sovereign insolvency is nothing new. There is a growing and broadening tendency to systematize principles distilled from domestic legal systems in order to build a sovereign insolvency architecture—especially taking Chapters 9 and 11 of the U.S. Bankruptcy Code as models. The notable similarities in domestic bankruptcy laws facilitated the work of creating the SDRM proposed by the IMF, since, for instance, the standstill and approval of the reorganization plan are deeply-rooted principles in domestic laws. Even when departing from a very different perspective, the Fair and Transparent Arbitration Procedure proposed by Jubilee 2000 also emulates domestic bankruptcy principles, such as the procedural right to be heard that parties potentially affected by the process should enjoy.[34]

Having said that, our understanding is that general principles, as reflected in the UNCTAD Principles, cannot only be derived from domestic laws but also from principles governing international relationships,[35] including resolutions of the UN General Assembly,[36] the IMF,[37] or other international institutions representing a considerable majority of the international community.[38]

Finally, the Principles contain a few recommendations based on best practice, for example, in its suggestion to establish a debt management office (Principle 13) or to

[33] Insolvency as a legal defence, good faith on the borrowers' and lenders' sides, cooperative spirit, speedy and orderly resolution, consensual rearrangement, respect for seniority, equitable treatment of stakeholders.

[34] J. Kaiser, 'Taking Stock of Proposal for More Ordered Workouts' in B. J.A. Ocampo and S. Spiegel (eds), *Overcoming Developing Country Debt Crisis* (Oxford University Press, 2010) 441; A. Pettifor, 'The Jubilee 2000 Campaign: A Brief Overview' in C. Jochnick and F. Preston (eds), *Sovereign Debt at the Crossroads. Challenges and Proposals for Resolving the Third World Debt Crisis* (Oxford University Press, 2006) 297.

[35] See B. Simma and P. Alston, 'Sources of Human Rights Law: Custom, Jus Cogens, and General Principles' (1988–89) 12 Austral. YBIL 82, 102: 'general principles can now be accepted in an international setting. Principles brought to the fore in this "direct way", so to speak, would (and should) then percolate down into domestic fora, instead of being elevated from the domestic level to that of international law by way of analogy'. See also S. Kadelbach and T. Kleinlein, 'International Law—A Constitution for Mankind? An Attempt at a Re-appraisal with Analysis of Constitutional Principles' (2007) 50 GYBIL 340.

[36] See UN General Assembly, 65th Session, 20 December 2010, Resolution on External Debt (A/RES/65/144), stressing the importance of responsible lending and borrowing, emphasizing that creditors and debtors must share responsibility for preventing unsustainable debt situations. This idea has also been addressed during UNCTAD's 6th and 7th Debt Management Conference in November 2007 and November 2009, respectively.

[37] The IMF Agreement, Art. 5 § 3.b. elaborates on the assessment of the situation of the sovereign borrower before disbursing funds; while Art. 6 § 1.a and § 1.b.ii establish restrictions to the actual use of the borrowed funds.

[38] N. Petersen, 'Customary Law without Custom? Rules, Principles, and the Role of State Practice in International Norm Creation' (2008) 23 Am. U. Int'l L. Rev. 308.

recognize the legislative branch as having an active role in sovereign borrowing (Principle 1). Best practices do not amount to general principles, but can coexist perfectly with general principles of law.

C. The Legal Force of the Principles as a Soft Law Instrument

Section B. has already included a reference to the main formal sources of international law[39]—i.e. treaties, customary international law, and general principles of law—with regard to sovereign borrowing and lending. We arrived at some preliminary conclusions: on the one hand, there are no international treaties regulating sovereign lending and borrowing; on the other hand, the sources of law in sovereign financing issues are not found in customary international law; and therefore, one must rely on other applicable norms, rules, or principles,[40] formal or informal, if we want to minimally coordinate sovereign borrowing and lending at an international level.

The UNCTAD Principles aspire to be regarded at minimum as a relevant informal source of law, but also in certain aspects as a formal source of international law, as explained in section B. with regard to some principles which are embodied in international treaties, customary international law, or general principles of international law.

The idea of informal sources of law is meant to be broadly understood in this chapter, meaning both rules made by processes which are not formal and rules identified through criteria which are not formal, such as persuasiveness.[41] This idea has its similarities with the concept of 'informal international law-making' as it may be recognized in the way in which it deals with certain formalities concerning the output, the process, or the actors implicated in the formation of the norms.[42] In our case, the instrument, the process, and the actors involved in the making of the Principles are all informal, i.e. the instrument is not an international treaty, it did not stem from a formal process of international cooperation, and it has not been negotiated by traditional diplomatic actors.

There is no doubt that the UNCTAD Principles are embodied in a soft law[43] instrument, a sort of informal law output that is certainly neither a treaty nor

[39] See e.g. I. Brownlie, *Principles of Public International Law* (7th edn, Oxford University Press, 2003) 3–29.

[40] See (n. 20).

[41] We thank Jean D'Aspreamont for making this point more clear.

[42] See generally J. Pauwelyn, 'Informal International Lawmaking: Framing the Concept and Research Questions' in Pauwelyn, Wessel, and Wouters (eds) (n. 8) 13–34.

[43] See C. Chinkin, 'The Challenge of Soft Law: Development and Change in International Law' (1989) 38 ICLQ 850; P-M. Dupuy, 'Soft Law and the International law of the Environment' (1991) 12 Mich. J. Int'l L. 420; G. Abi-Saab, 'Eloge du "droit assourdi". Quelques réflexions sur le role de la soft law en droit international' in *Noveaux itineraries en droit: Hommage à François Rigaux* (Bruylant, 1993) 59; H. Hillgenberg, 'A Fresh look at Soft Law' (1999) 10 Eur. J. Int'l L. 499; D. Shelton (ed.), *Commitment and Compliance: The Role of Non-Binding Norms in the International Legal System* (Oxford University Press, 2000); A. Boyle, 'Soft Law in International Law Making' in M. Evans (ed.), *International Law* (3rd edn, Oxford University Press, 2010) 122. See also K.W. Abbott and D. Snidal,

'international customs as evidence of a general practice accepted as law'.[44] The Principles, however, may be considered persuasive enough to influence the interpretation, application, and development of other rules of law[45] and may become recognized as legal rules by themselves. In other words, the Principles may turn out to be relevant either as soft law or emerging hard law.

Indeed, soft law is a 'multi-faceted concept',[46] which has several meanings. Soft law is not a formal, binding source of international law in itself,[47] but a kind of intermediary international legal tool which assists in the development and application of general international law in varied ways.[48] As such, soft law should be distinguished from hard law in that only the latter has the capacity to be formally binding. From this perspective we have generally described the collective Principles as an instrument of soft law. This means that they form an instrument which contains principles, best practices, guidelines, or standards whose degree of formal bindingness depends on its specific relationship with formal sources of international law, including the general principles of law recognized as sources of international law.[49] Of course, it can be said that the Principles are not formally binding international law, however, as has been sustained, 'the concept of an instrument's binding nature, though it has an undeniable heuristic value, is theoretically elusive and is not a meaningful criterion for a theoretically sound distinction between different kinds of instruments expressing different kinds of commitments'.[50] In a word, the soft law character of the instrument does not necessarily determine *ex ante*, in absolute terms, nor forever its normative effects.

The predominance of soft law instruments in the regulation of finance at a global multilateral level is manifest, and also slightly surprising when compared with the role of treaties in other international economic areas such as trade.[51] Considering international trade law, there is also another important difference: international financial law lacks a formal institutional structure, such as the WTO; and it is

'Hard and Soft Law in International Governance' (2000) 54 International Organization 421. For critical views of the concept, see P. Weil, 'Towards Relative Normativity in International Law' (1983) 77 AJIL 413; J. Klabbers, 'The Undesirability of Soft Law' (1998) 67 NJIL 381; J. D'Aspremont, 'Softness in International Law: A Self-Serving Quest for New Legal Materials' (2008) 19 Eur. J. Int'l L. 1075.

[44] Statute of the International Court of Justice, Art. 38(1)(b).

[45] See A. Boyle and C. Chinkin, *The Making of International Law* (Oxford University Press, 2007) 223.

[46] Boyle and Chinkin (n. 45) 229.

[47] See S. Besson, 'Theorizing the Sources of International Law' in S. Besson, and J. Tasioulas (eds), *The Philosophy of International Law* (Oxford University Press, 2010) 163, 171.

[48] cf. Jean D'Aspremot's idea of the programmatic virtue of soft law in D'Aspremont, *Formalism and the Sources of International Law* (n. 10) 130–1: 'The use by international lawyers of non-formal criteria of law-identification with the hope of contributing to the subsequent emergence of new rules in the *lex lata*'.

[49] See section B. of this chapter.

[50] M. Goldmann, 'Inside Relative Normativity: From Sources to Standard Instruments for the Exercise of Public Authority' (2008) 9 GYBIL 1865, 1907.

[51] C. Brummer, 'Why Soft Law Dominates International Finance—And Not Trade' (2010) 13 J. Int'l Econ. L. 623. See also C. Brummer, *Soft Law and the Global Financial System* (Cambridge University Press, 2011). And see A. Gelpern, Ch. 16 of this book.

governed or coordinated by agencies or in fora with important participatory deficits. These differences may have consequences for matters of compliance,[52] and they directly affect the requirements of publicness[53] and the rule of law, particularly in connection with the sources[54] of international law and its procedural and substantive legitimacy. This does not diminish, however, the important role that soft law has been playing as a coordinating mechanism in the field of international financial law.[55] Indeed, there are many reasons to prefer and choose soft law instruments and regimes over hard law in the field of international finance, with a combination of general incentives[56]—including the fact that soft law mechanisms may represent cheaper, faster, more flexible, and more efficient ways of rulemaking—and specific features of the field—such as the prevailing actors, mostly financial technocrats,[57] and the rapidly and constantly changing nature of financial markets.[58]

We have already mentioned the basis of the UNCTAD Principles, which generally stem from domestic and international norms and present a full and coherent set of rules and principles which purport to influence significantly the creation of a more reasonable normative structure. In this sense, the Principles play the role of a social architect more than that of a policeman.[59] The process of attaining the status of a universal standard will be gradual;[60] unlike the Universal Declaration of Human Rights, the most influential non-binding instrument of all, the Principles must be discussed, tested, and applied in order to prove their reasonableness and to achieve the necessary consensus to be considered persuasive as a whole set of norms.[61]

[52] See the concluding remarks by R. Howse in Ch. 17 of this volume, and also R. Howse and R. Teitel, 'Beyond Compliance: Rethinking Why International Law Really Matters' (2010) 1 Global Policy 127.

[53] A. von Bogdandy, P. Dann, and M. Goldmann, 'Developing the Publicness of Public International Law: Towards a Legal Framework for Global Governance Activities' (2008) 9 German L.J. 1375.

[54] Besson (n. 47) 163–85.

[55] Brummer (2010) (n. 51).

[56] cf. Abbott and Snidal (n. 43); G. Shaffer and M.A. Pollack, 'Hard vs Soft Law: Alternatives, Complements, and Antagonists in International Governance' (2010) 94 Minn. L. Rev. 706. Also M.A. Pollack and G.C. Shaffer, 'The Interaction of Formal and Informal Lawmaking' in Pauwelyn, Wessel and Wouters (eds.) (n. 8) 241ff., arguing that informal international law-making 'has not replaced formal lawmaking, but exists alongside it, with multiple, overlapping formal and informal procedures often addressing the same substantive issues in world affairs'.

[57] Brummer (2010) (n. 51) 634.

[58] Brummer (2010) (n. 51) 637.

[59] G. Abi-Saab, 'Eloge du "droit assourdi". Quelques réflexions sur le role de la soft law en droit international' in *Noveaux itineraries en droit: Hommage à François Rigaux* (Bruylant, 1993) 68: 'non pas le droit cassant du justicieer ou du gendarme, mais celui, plus discret et malléable, de l'architecte social, auquel sied à la perfection la dénomination "droit assourdi"'. But see Gelpern (n. 51), defining broader functions of soft law in combination with new governance for sovereign debt.

[60] See G. Abi-Saab, 'Les sources du droit international: essai de deconstruction' in *Le droit international dans un monde en mutation—Liber Amicorum en homage au Professeur Eduardo Jiménez de Aréchaga* (Fundación de Cultura Universitaria, 1994) 29, who in his concluding remarks (at 47–9) puts emphasis on the idea that international law emerges not with a 'big bang' but through a progressive social process.

[61] Boyle and Chinkin (n. 45) 225: 'Use of soft law techniques does not diminish the need for consensus among states, however'.

Indeed, the UNCTAD Principles have been conceived as an instrument which aims at persuading and influencing the conduct of states and other subjects on sovereign borrowing and lending. However, can the Principles seriously affect the way courts decide sovereign debt cases? Might these Principles affect the conduct of states or the decisions of international organizations? Can the stakeholders claim that the Principles should be taken into consideration on sovereign debt decisions? We believe that these questions could be answered in the affirmative; we are convinced that the Principles have the force to become persuasive enough to influence the interpretation, application, and development of other rules of law[62] or even to become recognized as legal rules in themselves. This is what happened when the Norwegian Minister of International Development expressed the intention, in 2012, that Norway will review its loans to developing countries using the Principles as a basis for this.[63] Besides the updating and reformulation of the international standards applied to debt audits based on the UNCTAD Principles that is currently carried out by the International Organisation of Supreme Audit Institutions (INNTOSAI), it is also worth mentioning that a dissenting opinion in a recent International ICSID arbitration decision on jurisdiction and admissibility mentioned the UNCTAD Principles as relevant law when deciding a dispute on public debt.[64]

In other words, the Principles may become relevant either as soft law or (emerging) hard law.[65] These statements require some clarification, particularly in relation to the interplay of instruments of soft law and formal sources of international law, including the general principles of law.[66]

Generally speaking, as a soft law instrument, the legal implications of the UNCTAD Principles are twofold: the Principles' potential binding effect will strongly depend on the specific link between each principle and the legal sources of international law; and their persuasiveness will be associated with their intrinsic economic and political utility in overcoming global problems.

As general principles can be derived both from domestic laws and from principles governing international relationships[67]—including resolutions of the UN General Assembly or of other international institutions representing a considerable majority of the international community—[68] the existence of the Principles reinforces the idea that general principles were identified and recognized in the field of sovereign lending and borrowing. The annual UN General Assembly resolutions on external

[62] See Boyle and Chinkin (n. 45) 223.

[63] 'Norway first in the world to review loans to developing countries', press release, 17 August 2012, available at <http://www.regjeringen.no/en/dep/ud/press/news/2012/loan-review-developing-countries.html?id=697585>.

[64] *Ambiente Ufficio S.p.A. and others v. Argentine Republic*, ICSID Case No. ARB/08/9 (formerly *Giordano Alpi and others v. Argentine Republic*), dissenting opinion of Santiago Torres Bernárdez, 2 May 2013, available at <http://www.italaw.com/cases/1750>.

[65] cf. Gelpern (n. 51), defending the appropriateness of soft law and new governance for sovereign debt.

[66] On general principles of law, see e.g. the classic book by B. Cheng, *General Principles of Law as Applied by International Courts and Tribunals* (n. 27). For studies of specific courts and tribunals, see F.O. Raimondo, *General principles of law in the decisions of international criminal courts and tribunals* (Martinus Nihjoff, 2008); and A.D. Mittchell, *Legal Principles in WTO Disputes* (Cambridge University Press, 2008).

[67] See Simma and Alston (n. 35); and Kadelbach and Kleinlein (n. 35).

[68] N. Petersen, 'Customary Law without Custom? Rules, Principles, and the Role of State Practice in International Norm Creation' (2008) 23 Am. U. Int'l L. Rev 308.

debt in 2010, 2011, and 2012 stressed the importance of responsible lending and borrowing, emphasizing that creditors and debtors must share responsibility for preventing unsustainable debt.[69]

Is it likely that the UNCTAD Principles—as a unique and integral legal framework—will demand further, more effective ways to induce compliance? This will depend on the will of states to reach formal and multilateral consensus, and the persuasiveness of the Principles. As they seem to be part of most national legal cultures (with all the *domestic quality tests* that this implies, already passed), their intrinsic value can indeed presumably operate to promote consensus on the emergence of new rules.[70] Indeed, to date 12 (developed and developing) countries have explicitly endorsed the Principles.[71]

As regards the comparative law methodology explicitly or implicitly relied upon in this piece,[72] one must bear in mind that the common characteristics that a rule may have in different legal systems do not necessarily give rise to a common principle of quality at the international level or applicability to subjects of international law, such as states.[73] Apart from verifying the basis of the principle itself, one must appropriately synthesize and adapt it to the level at which one plans to explore its application, which can create the necessity to conciliate principles. This is the abstracting methodological step in searching for general principles.

It is particularly in this aspect that the systematization conducted by the Expert Group established by UNCTAD can play a critical role in the evolution of international law. The way in which principles relate to each other and the particular implications of each of them constitute a legal interpretative task where domestic principles are translated systematically into general principles applied at the international level.

For example, the voluntary basis of restructuring, as provided for in Principle 15, means that debtors or creditors cannot arbitrarily decide how to modify their rights and obligations. They must agree. But what if they do not? At the domestic level the institutional framework offers a neutral authority (a judge) who will decide to force a reorganization plan (*cramdown*) or let the debtor go bankrupt and liquidate its assets. In the global sovereign realm there is no such authority and states cannot—at least in legal books—be dissolved because of their unpaid debts. So how is this voluntary principle applied to states? At this point the fibre of the principle must be captured and adapted to public finance and theory of state.[74]

69 UN General Assembly Resolutions 65/144 of 20 December 2010, 65/144 of 4 February 2011, and 66/189 of 14 February 2012 on external debt sustainability and development.

70 On the programmatic virtue of informal sources, see d'Aspremont (n. 10) 130–1. Also, on soft law as precursor and basis of legal norms, see L. Blutman, 'In the Trap of a Legal Metaphor: International Soft Law' (2010) 59 ICLQ 605, 617–19.

71 'Principles on sovereign lending and borrowing: UNCTAD kick starts endorsement process', UNCTAD press release, 22 April 2012, available at <http://www.unctad.info/en/Debt-Portal/News-Archive/Our-News/Principles-on-sovereign-lending-and-borrowing-UNCTAD-kick-starts-endorsement-process-Doha-22-April->.

72 See Goldmann (n. 24). See also Ellis (n. 23).

73 See K. Pistor, 'The Standardization of Law and its Effect on Developing Countries' (2002) 50 Am. J. Comp. L. 97.

74 On this argument, see R. Rasmussen, 'Integrating a Theory of the State into Sovereign Debt Restructuring' (2004) 53 Emory L.J. 1159.

Both parties must negotiate under the guidelines of Principles 7 and 15, looking for an agreement which is reached when a supermajority of creditors and their sovereign debtor coincide on how to modify their original contractual terms. Requiring unanimity of creditors or allowing a debtor to unilaterally or arbitrarily punish its creditors through a haircut are not valid options.

Indeed, the only legal system that established a specific law for sovereign insolvency—Chapter 9 of the US Bankruptcy Code—has recognized most of the principles on restructuring now identified by UNCTAD.[75] Of course, the fact that within the US domestic realm the sovereign bankruptcy procedure is monitored by a court makes a notable institutional difference with regard to sovereign insolvencies where no universal debt restructuring mechanism has been established. Despite this crucial fact, one can still affirm that all of these concepts—sovereigns can go bankrupt, debtors and creditors should act in good faith, the basis of rearrangement is consensual, a supermajority of creditors is needed to modify contracts, seniority of debts should be respected, discrimination of creditors is prohibited, and all stakeholders should make equitable sacrifices in a context of insolvency—are general, substantive principles present across legal systems.

Procedural principles and institutional designs are concerned with the way in which substantive legal principles are applied. This is why procedures and institutions should be inspired by substantive principles, and develop the methods to reach their goals. Certain basic substantive principles should be followed regardless of the authority appointed to make these decisions and the mechanism established to channel the disputes.

D. Conclusion

The UNCTAD Principles have systematized a range of rules, principles, and best practices that present a variety of legal statuses. A few of them derived from international conventions and customary law, and some are typical best practices identified in certain areas of international finance. On the other hand, most of the Principles might be considered—in the terminology of international law—to be general principles derived from domestic legal orders. Those which are not fully developed in *foro domestico* may be recognized and validated on the international plane.[76]

This legal-based approach seems to be corroborated by the Preamble to the Principles:

> The normative contribution of these Principles lies not in the creation of new rights nor obligations in international law but in identifying the basic principles and best practices applied to sovereign lending and borrowing and in elaborating the implications of these standards and practices for lenders and borrowers.

[75] K. Raffer, 'Applying Chapter 9 Insolvency to International Debts: An Economically Efficient Solution with a Human Face' (1990) 18 World Development 301. See also K. Raffer, Ch. 8 of this volume.

[76] See Simma and Alston (n. 35), and accompanying text.

The Principles therefore have the capacity to express many different examples of bindingness depending on their background norms of international law. In that sense, the nuanced approach proposed in this chapter may have great benefits to better determine the nature of the law revealed by each one of the Principles and all of them taken as a whole incorporated into a soft law instrument. Moreover, the non-binding character of the instrument is not essential when considering the normativity and persuasiveness of specific principles purporting to govern certain conduct.

The contents of the UNCTAD Principles are not ambiguous but their legal status is dynamic. The current soft law status of the Principles presents an important and specific benefit even beyond the soft law's general contractarian advantages studied earlier. This expands the range of instruments available for cooperation among states, making regulation more likely (than in a situation in which only binding instruments are possible) in certain topics.[77] This presumably has some positive impacts in terms of effectiveness in the provision of public goods related to sovereign financing.

The Principles advance along a path and at a pace that do not necessarily match those of the debate on sovereign debt workouts. The Principles do not imply institutional reforms, such as an international debt restructuring procedure, a global economic coordination council, statutory reforms of the Bretton Woods institutions, or changes to the global reserve system.[78] They actually recognize that to date, no universal sovereign debt restructuring mechanism has been established. The Principles systematized in a coherent body the scant core and substantive international law principles on sovereign lending and borrowing to be applied on a global scale. Their soft law option seems to be aware of the driving forces and pulse of the current *politics of deformalization of international law* while not ignoring the relevance of the state consent materialized through both official endorsements and mirroring principles existing in most domestic legal orders.

[77] T. Meyer, 'Review Essay—Towards a Communicative Theory of International Law' (2012) 13 Mel. J. Int'l L. 921.

[78] See Y. Akyüz, 'Policy Responses to the Global Financial Crisis: Key Issues for Developing Countries' in Sundaram (ed.), *Reforming the International Financial System for Development* (Columbia University Press, 2010) 105.

5

Out of Thin Air?

Tracing the Origins of the UNCTAD Principles in Customary International Law

*Michael Waibel**

A. Introduction

UNCTAD's Principles on Responsible Sovereign Lending and Borrowing are an innovative set of informal governance standards for sovereign borrowing and lending. Independent of the desirability of the Principles, it is important to consider whether they depart in important ways from the existing practice on sovereign lending and the resolution of sovereign defaults, or whether they merely confirm some trends already under way in state practice. The chances of general acceptance of the Principles by states are greater if state practice already supports aspects of the Principles, both in a technical sense and in the informal practices of central players in sovereign debt crisis resolution, such as the Paris Club and the IMF.

As major political events, responses to sovereign debt crises are often driven by economic and political considerations, and shaped by the interests of a variety of actors. Almost invariably, important stakeholders, including states and private creditors, prefer discretion over rules. This preference has generally resulted in policy responses to sovereign debt crises that manifest a striking inconsistency across time and location, and vary considerably by political, social, or economic conditions and other specific circumstances.[1] For example, Poland's sizeable foreign debt was restructured on untypically generous terms in 1991 following the collapse of communism and the rapid transition to a market economy under the Balcerowicz Plan.[2] Similarly, Iraq, in the wake of the US invasion, received unprecedented debt relief for a country of its level of development. In both cases,

* I thank Juan Pablo Bohoslavsky, Carlos Espósito, Matthias Goldmann, Robert Howse, and Yuefen Li for discussions, an anonymous reviewer of OUP for comments, and Dan Peat for his help in preparing this chapter.

[1] L.C. Buchheit and M. Gulati, *Responsible Sovereign Lending and Borrowing*, UNCTAD Discussion Paper, 198 (2010) 5–8.

[2] J. Williamson (ed.), *The Political Economy of Policy Reform* (Institute for International Economics, 1994) 566.

substantial debt relief was a policy priority for the United States and other Western countries.[3] In other cases, such strong political backing from the major capital exporting countries for substantial debt relief was absent.

The Principles on Responsible Sovereign Lending and Borrowing project was borne of the initiative of UNCTAD in the wake of the global financial crisis of 2008, and followed by the Report of the Secretary General of the United Nations on External Debt Sustainability and Development.[4] This report expressed concern over the consequences of excessive borrowing for the developmental path of the least developed countries, and vulnerable low- and middle-income countries. Recognizing the costliness of debt crises and the desire for increased stability within the international financial system, the report called for rule-based procedures for sovereign debt, along with increased data and research to establish early warning systems, mechanisms for mitigating debt default and increased transparency in international debt dealings.[5] The United Nations, in the UN General Assembly Resolution of 4 February 2011[6] and within the framework of the fourth UN Conference for Least-Developed Countries, held in Istanbul from 9 to 13 May 2011,[7] further affirmed its commitment to the UNCTAD initiative, and reiterated the importance of durable solutions to the debt problems faced by developing countries.

Faced with the unenviable task of systematizing an international process with an 800-year history of ad hoc solutions, UNCTAD proposed the second draft of the Principles at UNCTAD's eighth Debt Management Conference in November 2011, and the consolidated version in Doha in April 2012.[8] The Principles drew upon the work of an Expert Working Group, encompassing members with legal, economic, and civil society backgrounds, and the Group of Advisory Countries (open to all countries participating in the project).[9] Now is the time to consider the importance and the implications of the Principles for future sovereign debt lending and borrowing, and the support the Principles find in state practice.

This chapter focuses on the Principles that set out standards for sovereign borrowing and lending measures that have a manifestly international character—those that would be capable of constituting state practice on the international level.

[3] M.A. Weiss, 'Iraq's Debt Relief: Procedure and Potential Implications for International Debt Relief', CRS Report for Congress, 29 March 2011; B. Momani and A. Garrib, 'Iraq's tangled web of debt restructuring' in B. Momani and M. Lamani (eds), *From desolation to reconstruction: Iraq's troubled journey* (WLU Press, 2010) 157: 'Eventually, however, the United States was able to use the United Nations Security Council to limit Iraq's reparation payments to its creditors. Then the US also managed to have the Paris Club offer its most generous of terms to any middle-income country ever received: 80 per cent debt write-off and generous repayment conditions. With pressure exerted on the IMF, the US also managed to have the Fund underestimate the Iraqi ability to repay their debt.'

[4] UN Doc. A/65/155.

[5] UN Doc. A/65/155, paras 72–73.

[6] UN GA Resolution A/RES/65/144, para. 3.

[7] UN Doc. A/CONF.219/L.1, para. 11.

[8] C.M. Reinhart and K.S. Rogoff, *This Time is Different* (Princeton University Press, 2009) ch. 6.

[9] UNCTAD, 'Responsible Lending and Borrowing—About the Project', available at <http://www.unctad.info/en/Debt-Portal/Project-Promoting-Responsible-Sovereign-Lending-and-Borrowing/About-the-Project>.

Those Principles not dealt with are predominantly concerned with information gathering and provisions related to sovereign borrowing and lending, but the execution of which takes place on the domestic level. Examples include due diligence on the borrower's capacity to pay, *ex ante* investigations, transparency of obligations, and audits. A convergence of domestic practices related to sovereign lending and borrowing is desirable, giving the benefits of increased predictability and lower transaction costs, yet could only become an international obligation via the conclusion of a treaty requiring states to act in such a way, or as a 'general principle of law recognized by civilized nations', a principle found in virtually all legal systems.[10]

If the Principles reflected widespread agreement among states on sovereign lending and borrowing, one would expect some convergence in the way states borrow and creditors lend with the substantive content of the Principles. The Principles are premised on a dearth of consistent state practice in sovereign lending and borrowing. Even when it exists, state practice is rarely accompanied by *opinio juris*. Only if a sufficient body of state practice with the requisite *opinio juris* was identifiable for a certain Principle, could one conclude that such Principle had already attained the status of custom, binding upon all states as customary international law. This chapter considers the extent to which the Principles reflect existing state practice, drawing upon the past 200 years of sovereign borrowing and default. Whilst generally finding a dearth of state practice, the chapter nevertheless locates instances of state practice that lend support to some of the Principles, notably Principles 1, 7, 8, 9, and 15. And yet even convergence of practice behind these Principles is not uniform and consistent.

The UNCTAD Principles, which aim to institute transparency, fairness, and responsibility within the realm of sovereign lending, represent a major innovation for sovereign lending practices. Whereas they do not simply codify existing international custom, and are progressive in character, they could, over time, foster consensus on harmonized standards that could be incorporated into the domestic legal infrastructures for sovereign borrowing in all jurisdictions and, in turn, give rise to more consistent state practice and jurisprudence. This demonstrates the innovative character of the Principles.

B. The Importance of State Practice in Relation to the Principles

State practice is one of the two elements constitutive of customary international law, the other being the belief that the state is required to act that way due to the existence of a legal obligation, called *opinio juris*.[11] Over the last few decades,

[10] Statute of the International Court of Justice, Art. 38(1)(c). See J.P. Bohoslavsky and C. Espósito, Ch. 4 and M. Goldmann, Ch 6, both in this volume.

[11] *North Sea Continental Shelf (Germany v. Denmark; Germany v. The Netherlands)*, 20 February 1969, ICJ Rep. 3 (1969) 44.

private lenders have accounted for the lion's share of lending to developed and middle-income countries. Their acts do not constitute state practice and can play no role in the formation of customary international law. Most of the acts underpinning lending to states are thus 'invisible' from the point of view of international law. This includes, for instance, the acts of banks as creditors in the London Club. The predominance of private lenders is a major reason for the dearth of state practice in the area.

Acts of states within international organizations may count as state conduct. The latter half of the twentieth century saw the increased prominence of various multilateral lending institutions, such as the IMF or the World Bank, in the realm of sovereign lending. This leads to the question of whether the acts of the international organizations themselves or acts of states within the framework of international organizations constitute an element in the formation of custom, given their membership and recognition as subjects under international law.[12]

Acts by international organizations in themselves are incapable of constituting state practice. Conversely, acts of states taken within the framework of international organizations are capable of constituting state practice. In this way, international organizations can play an important indirect role in the formation of customary international law. The prime example is UN General Assembly resolutions. The UN Charter provides states with the opportunity to manifest their state practice within the framework of General Assembly debates.[13] The acts of states in international organizations may evidence existing customary norms, crystallize customary norms by fortifying accumulated state practice, or act as a focal point in the process of convergence towards a new norm of general international law.[14]

In relation to the UNCTAD Principles, state practice is important in two ways. First, the existence of state practice accompanied by *opinio juris* could found the claim that one, or several, of the Principles embody a customary international legal obligation. Custom as a source of law is powerful, in that it is the only type of international law that can create universal obligations without express consent from states. If the Principles, or parts thereof, represent customary international law, the substance of the Principles would be legally binding upon all states.

Secondly, state practice could show convergence upon a particular process or method of action in international sovereign lending practice, without being supported by the requisite uniformity of state practice or the necessary *opinio juris* to amount to customary international law. Thirdly, the Principles, in whole or in part, could reflect soft law.[15] As Higgins has highlighted: 'Legal consequences can

[12] *Interpretation of the Agreement of 25 March 1951 between the WHO and Egypt*, Advisory Opinion, ICJ Rep. (1980) 89–90, para. 37, and *Legality of the Use by a State of Nuclear Weapons in Armed Conflict*, Advisory Opinion, ICJ Rep. (1996) 78, para. 25.

[13] cf., B. Cheng, 'United Nations Resolutions on Outer Space; "Instant" International Customary Law?' (1965) 5 Indian Journal of International Law 40.

[14] E. Jiménez de Aréchaga, 'International Law in the Past Third of a Century' (1978-I) 159 *Recueil des Cours* 31; and B. Sloan, 'General Assembly Resolutions Revisited' (1987) 58 BYBIL 39, 69.

[15] See J.P. Bohoslavsky and C. Espósito, Ch 4 of this book.

also flow from acts which are not, in the formal sense, "binding"'.[16] Despite their non-binding character, rules of a soft character entail legal consequences by shaping states' expectations as to what constitutes desirable behaviour.[17]

Most importantly, converging state practice could demonstrate the willingness of states to adopt non-binding rules (such as the UNCTAD Principles), that could in turn catalyse greater convergence of state practice, and increase the likelihood of states deciding to elevate the Principles to custom in due course. Even if the Principles do not reach the status of custom at present, adoption of the Principles as standard practice increases the stability of domestic legal mechanisms and processes on sovereign debt and may help to preserve international financial stability. For example, transparent *ex ante* analyses of the impact of public borrowing could help to prevent the build-up of debt sustainability problems. The Principles also enhance the legitimacy of international institutions, such as UNCTAD, that promote and spearhead the convergence of practice in this area. State practice is, therefore, an important consideration, even if such practice currently falls short of establishing the existence of customary law.

C. The General Trend—Ad Hoc Solutions for Specific Problems

As noted in the introduction to this chapter, the responses to sovereign debt crises are diverse, and often dependent on the political and economic context. There is a widespread view in the financial and policy community that in matters of sovereign financial distress, discretion is preferable to rules, allowing policy-makers to tailor the policy prescription to the specific circumstances of each case. The belief is widely held that each case is different, and that therefore, a cookie-cutter approach would lead to undesirable results.

Creditors are heterogeneous, and lending takes a variety of forms. The lender may be another country, an international or regional institution, or a private party. There is also considerable diversity among private lenders that account today for the bulk of lending to high- and middle-income countries. They range from banks, insurance companies, and asset managers to individuals who buy sovereign bonds to save for retirement.

Responses to sovereign debt crises as ad hoc solutions are driven largely by extra-legal considerations. The resolution of sovereign financial distress is frequently a highly technical matter, driven by the desire to develop pragmatic solutions for concrete problems. Often, the legal considerations that influence sovereign debt restructurings do not lend themselves to abstraction in the form of general legal principles or customary international law. Some of the boundary parameters of restructuring sovereign debt are legal in character, yet many of the primary constraints are economic and political. For the most part, this body of restructuring practice cannot claim the status of customary international law.

16 R. Higgins, *Problems and Process: International Law and How We Use It* (Clarendon Press, 1994) 25.

17 A.T. Guzman and T. Meyer, 'International Soft Law' (2011) 2 Journal of Legal Analysis 171, 175.

Creditor states have dealt with sovereign debt defaults over the course of the last 200 years in a variety of ways. States have always had much discretion when acting via diplomatic channels in protection of their nationals, a corollary of the longstanding right of the state of nationality under international law.[18] This creates a spectrum of acts on the part of the state, from refusal to act because the buying of government debt abroad is 'speculative',[19] to official intervention. Lord Palmerston, the mid-nineteenth century British Foreign Secretary, summed up this approach as follows: 'it is for the British Government entirely a question of discretion, and by no means a question of International Right, whether they should or should not make this matter a question of diplomatic negotiation.'[20]

Among the most assertive examples of diplomatic intervention were several cases of military intervention at the turn of the twentieth century, combining a desire to enforce arbitral awards,[21] and broader foreign policy motives unrelated to the repayment of debt.[22] An illustrative example is the campaign undertaken by Germany, the United Kingdom, and Italy against Venezuela in 1902, with the aim of establishing a preferential claim over Venezuelan assets for the fulfilment of the latter's sovereign debt obligations. The intervening states blockaded Venezuelan customs houses and launched a military campaign that caused, among other things, the loss of three Venezuelan warships and severe damage to Venezuelan ports.[23] The option of using force to enforce sovereign debt was prohibited only in 1945 by Article 2(4) of the UN Charter, creating a general ban on the use of force in international relations, unless either authorized by the UN Security Council or in self-defence. The Drago-Porter Convention had outlawed the use of force to recover sovereign debt without prior recourse to arbitration, though it left open an important loophole if the debtor state refused to submit to arbitration.[24]

Another option short of military intervention was the exercise of a quasi-receivership power over the debtor state,[25] directly controlling sources of revenue, such as national monopolies,[26] customs houses,[27] or train companies,[28] in order

[18] e.g. Vertrag zwischen der Republik Österreich und der Bundesrepublik Deutschland zur Regelung vermögensrechtlicher Beziehungen vom 15. Juni 1957, BGBI. Nr. 119/1958 and Arts 22 and 23 of the State Treaty, cf. I. Seidl-Hohenveldern, *The Austrian-German Arbitral Tribunal* (Syracuse University Press, 1972).

[19] e.g. Lord Palmerston's Memorandum on the British Government's position, quoted in R. Phillimore, *Commentaries upon International Law*, vol. 2 (London: Butterworth's, 1882) 9–11.

[20] Quoted from Phillimore (n. 19) 9–11.

[21] e.g. *The Cerruti Arbitrations (Italy v. Colombia)* and *Pacifico Claim (Great Britain v. Greece)*, blockade to pressure Greece to compensate a British national, Daniel Pacifico, for losses of his private property.

[22] e.g. the Franco-British intervention in Mexico in 1862, in E.W. Turlington, *Mexico and Her Foreign Creditors* (Columbia University Press, 1930) 141.

[23] e.g. *The Venezuelan Preferential Case* in M. Waibel, *Sovereign Defaults before International Courts and Tribunals* (Cambridge University Press, 2011) 30–5.

[24] Waibel (n. 23) 35–8.

[25] Waibel (n. 23) ch. 3.

[26] e.g. The Greek International Financial Commission of Control (from 1898 onwards).

[27] e.g. the Fiscal Administration of Haiti, examined in 'The Proposed Loan Conventions between the United States and Honduras and the United States and Nicaragua' (1911) 5 AJIL 1044.

[28] e.g. the Young Loan to the German government in 1930, repayable via an annual DM660m tax on the German Railway Company for a period of 37 years.

to repatriate moneys due. Such acts normally resulted from collective creditor initiative, and were formalized in international agreements between the debtor state and its creditors. A leading example is the International Financial Commission in Greece, which was established by the major official creditors of Greece in 1898, and played an important role in Greek economic life up to the outbreak of the Second World War.[29]

Negotiation has often taken centre stage in restructuring sovereign debt, especially after the Second World War.[30] The advent of the Bretton Woods institutions provided a platform for private creditors and states to negotiate such restructuring agreements, which often seemed the best outcome that creditors could hope for faced with a state whose debts were unsustainable. The negotiations helped to ensure that there would be substantial, if partial, repayment of the debt. The Paris Club became the primary forum for debtor states and their official creditors conducting negotiations, and has provided guidance to sovereign debt restructurings more generally through non-binding principles it developed, such as comparability of treatment. However, the members of the Paris Club conclude bilateral agreements with the debtor country outside a formalized legal framework. Negotiations are undertaken on a country-by-country basis.[31] As a result, the agreements reached are generally not apt to form either a sufficiently coherent body of state practice to create customary international law, nor are bilateral agreements concluded under Paris Club auspices accompanied by *opinio juris*.

A further possibility for the peaceful resolution of sovereign debt default incidents has been to bring creditor claims before international courts and tribunals, including mixed claims commissions,[32] arbitral tribunals,[33] and the Permanent Court of International Justice (PCIJ) and the International Court of Justice (ICJ).[34] In the late nineteenth century and the first half of the twentieth century, the rule of absolute sovereign immunity closed national courts to creditors seeking to force a sovereign to fulfil their debt obligations. As a result, ad hoc arbitral tribunals and mixed claims commissions frequently attempted to 'fill' the gap left by the lack of available judicial settlement on the national level.

[29] Convention between the United Kingdom, France, Greece, and Russia to facilitate the conclusion of a loan by the Greek government. Signed at Paris, 29 March 1898, 1898 (C.8856) Treaty series. No. 9, 1898.

[30] M. Waibel, 'The Diplomatic Channel' in J. Crawford, A. Pellet, and S. Olleson (eds), *The Law of International Responsibility* (Oxford University Press, 2010) 1085.

[31] A. Rieffel, *Restructuring Sovereign Debt: The Case for Ad Hoc Machinery* (Brookings Institution Press, 2003); The Paris Club, 'The Evian Approach', available at <http://www.clubdeparis.org/sections/types-traitement/reechelonnement/approche-d-evian>. Michel Camdessus, former Chairperson of the Paris Club and IMF Managing Director, famously called the Paris Club a 'non-institution', see J.C. Trichet, 'Official Debt Rescheduling' in H. Mehran (ed.), *External Debt Management* (International Monetary Fund, 1984) 126.

[32] e.g. the Mexican-US, Venezuelan-US, and Colombian-US mixed claims commissions.

[33] e.g. the Iran-US claims commission.

[34] The *Serbian Loans Case (France v. Serbia)*, Judgment, 12 July 1929, PCIJ, Ser. A (1929) A20; *Brazilian Loans Case (France v. Brazil)*, Judgment, 12 July 1929, PCIJ, Ser. A (1929) A21 before the Permanent Court of International Justice, and the *Norwegian Loans Case (France v. Norway)* before the International Court of Justice, Judgment, 6 July 1957, ICJ Rep. (1957) 9–95.

From the 1960s, the increasing recognition of restrictive of sovereign immunity, especially in the two most important financial centres (London and New York), enabled creditors to sue debtor states in national courts on their commercial transactions (*acta iure gestionis*). One result was a decline in arbitration and other ad hoc dispute resolution before international courts and tribunals arising out of sovereign debt. As testament to this change, most debt instruments of developing countries now contain jurisdictional clauses submitting to the national courts of global financial centres in case of disputes, especially the English and New York courts. The situation is different as regards developed countries, whose debt often either contains no express reference to any dispute resolution procedure or limits litigation to the courts of the debtor country itself.

Even those lending agreements that contain arbitration clauses, such as World Bank lending, are generally dormant, with creditors preferring debt-restructuring negotiations with the debtor state, as opposed to formal dispute settlement. Cases before the World Court are rare, with just two cases involving sovereign debt before the PCIJ, and one case before the ICJ.[35] In 1957, the ICJ rejected the *Norwegian Loans Case* at the jurisdictional stage.[36] The *Brazilian* and *Serbian Loans* cases illustrated that there was no bar in principle to the submission of legal disputes that concern exclusively domestic law to the Court if the state of the creditor's nationality chose to exercise diplomatic protection.

Even so, the PCIJ played no substantial role in resolving the wave of sovereign defaults in the 1920s and 1930s. The jurisdictional limitation that only disputes between states can be brought before the ICJ has greatly limited the appeal of the PCIJ and the ICJ in economic disputes generally and in sovereign debt disputes specifically. In addition, in the sovereign debt field, creditors, based on considerations such as cost, efficacy, and the need to resolve disputes quickly, often favour renegotiation over formal dispute settlement before other international courts and tribunals.

Whilst the method of enforcing sovereign debt obligations is but one facet of Principle 7 regarding debt restructurings, the examples of the diverse methods of pursuing the same aim illustrate the wider state practice of sovereign borrowing and lending. From the previous examples, one is able to see that a variety of extra-legal factors come into play when dealing with sovereign debt, which motivate diverse policy responses. The latest example is the response by Eurozone governments to the sovereign debt crisis in Greece. Nowhere else is ad hoc improvisation in crisis resolution more apparent.

The prevalence of ad hoc responses to sovereign financial distress is explained by the foreign policy aims pursued by governments, including considerations of international stability. For example, faced with the threat of a disorderly default by the Russian Federation in 1998, the world's second largest nuclear power, creditor states gave priority to stability over full repayment of debt.[37] States do

[35] *Serbian Loans Case* (n. 34) A20. [36] *Norwegian Loans Case* (n. 34) 9–95.

[37] For an insider's account of Russia's default, see M.G. Gilman, *No Precedent, No Plan: Inside Russia's 1998 Default* (MIT Press, 2010).

not behave as they do because they feel bound by any rule of customary international law, but instead act in their best interests within a complex matrix of facts and political considerations at any given time.

D. The Limited Convergence of State Practice

Notwithstanding considerable variation in policy responses, it would be mistaken to conclude that state practice on sovereign debt has shown no convergence whatsoever over the past 200 years. If one considers the history of sovereign debt, two factors are important. First, states have been subject to increasing limitations upon what measures they may take in relation to sovereign debt. This limitation reduces the options left open to states and, in that limited respect, increases convergence of practice. The leading example is the general prohibition on the use of force, contained within Article 2(4) of the UN Charter. Since 1945, states have breached this prohibition on various occasions, but no state has used military force since 1945 to enforce sovereign debt obligations.

Secondly, the advent of the IMF and the World Bank has concentrated state practice within certain international organizations' frameworks. The Paris Club, despite its informal character, is another forum. Whilst not regularizing the treatment of sovereign lending and default in a rules-based legal framework, these institutions have undoubtedly created common elements that are routinely taken into account in designing sovereign debt restructurings—such as an informal entitlement to debt relief if certain performance targets are met under the Heavily Indebted Poor Countries (HIPC) initiative or the need for roughly equal burden sharing between different types of creditors.[38] Partly due to these factors, some elements of dealing with sovereign debt crises show a degree of convergence. If we trace the history of sovereign default, we can see a limited corpus of state practice identifiable in four notable areas.

I. Principles 1 and 8—the duty of government officials to protect the public interest

Principle 1 of the UNCTAD Principles states that 'Lenders should recognise that government officials involved in sovereign lending and borrowing transactions are responsible for protecting the public interest (to the State and its citizens for which they are acting as agents)', and Principle 8 provides that 'Governments are agents of the State and, as such, when they contract debt obligations, they are responsible to protect the interests of their citizens. Where applicable, borrowers should also consider the responsibility of lenders' agents towards their organisations.' Taken

[38] See e.g. the Paris Club participation in the Heavily-Indebted Poor Countries Initiative (HIPC), The Paris Club, 'HIPC Initiative', available at <http://www.clubdeparis.org/sections/types-traitement/reechelonnement/initiative-ppte>.

together, therefore, these principles encapsulate an obligation—on the part of both the debtor and the creditor—for public officials to protect the public interest of their citizens.

Some instances of state practice furnish examples of limitations on the acts of government officials when borrowing on behalf of their state. First, there is the doctrine of odious debt.[39] Whilst the exact definition of odious debt is unclear, it is generally formulated as the possibility of raising the nature of the regime that borrowed when a creditor claims repayment.[40] The idea of odious debt is traced back to the contributions of a Russian jurist, Alexander Sack, in the early twentieth century,[41] and to the *Tinoco* arbitration in 1923.[42]

Tinoco ruled Costa Rica under a short dictatorship from 1917 to 1919, after which he was forced to flee following a popular uprising. The succeeding government promptly issued the Law of Nullities No. 41, invalidating all of Tinoco's acts when he was in office, including sovereign debt issued during that period. Whilst not recognized by the majority of the international community, the Tinoco government had managed to borrow under a debt facility with the Royal Bank of Canada, whose claim for repayment was supported by the British government. An arbitral tribunal, composed of a sole arbitrator (US Chief Justice Taft), was convened to settle the dispute. Costa Rica advanced four claims supporting invalidity of the debt, namely, first that the Tinoco government was not a *de facto* government in control of the state; secondly, that the government was not a *de jure* government in international law; thirdly, that the government assumed power in violation of the old Costa Rican constitution; and fourthly, that the British were stopped from recognizing the validity of debt signed under Tinoco by virtue of their non-recognition of the regime.

Taft rejected all of the Costa Rican contentions, relying on the *de facto* governmental power exercised by dictator Tinoco over the majority of the territory, and the rule of international law that a change of government—regardless of legitimacy—does not affect a state's obligations in international law.[43] The arbitrator continued, however, to hold that Costa Rica was not liable for debts taken on by the Tinoco government, as the debts were of an 'odious' character. The arbitrator based his holding on two grounds. First, he explained that the debt taken on by Tinoco was used solely and exclusively to the benefit of the Tinoco brothers,[44] and secondly, that the Royal Bank of Canada was aware of the illegitimate purpose of the loans.

[39] R. Howse, *The Concept of Odious Debt in Public International Law*, UNCTAD Discussion Paper, 187 (2007) 10–16; and J. King, 'The Doctrine of Odious Debt in International Law: A Restatement' (2013) 89 BYBIL (forthcoming).

[40] M. Gulati, L. Buchheit, and R.B. Thompson, 'The Dilemma of Odious Debt' (2007) 56 Duke L.J. 1201.

[41] A.N. Sack, *Les Effets des Transformations des Etats sur leurs Dettes Publiques et Autres Obligations Financières* (Recueil Sirey, 1927).

[42] *Tinoco Arbitration (Great Britain v. Costa Rica)*, 18 October 1923, (1924) 2 ILR 34–39, (1924) 18 AJIL147–74, (1922) 116 BFSP 438–43, 1 UNRIIA 369.

[43] *Tinoco Arbitration* (n. 42) 154.

[44] Bucheit, Gulati, and Thompson (n. 40).

An arbitral tribunal constituted by the Permanent Court of Arbitration (PCA), in *French Claims against Peru*, dealt with a similar subject matter.[45] In that case, the Peruvians advanced the claim that they were not obliged to repay a loan modified under the Piérola regime on the basis that the regime was not the legitimate government of the state, and hence could not borrow on behalf of the state. The tribunal held that the widespread support that the Piérola dictatorship enjoyed across large parts of Peru sufficed to rebut the contention that the dictatorship was not a *de facto* government, and confirmed that debt issued under the Piérola regime was valid. Further, recognition of the regime by many states and in some court rulings was adequate to conclude that a law of nullity did not apply to debt instruments concluded with foreigners who had acted in good faith.[46]

A more recent example of the invocation of the doctrine of odious debt was by the Commission for Auditing the Public Debt established by the Ecuadorian government, under President Correa, charged with the task of investigating the possibility that some Ecuadorian debt need not be repaid because of its 'illegitimate' or 'odious' character.[47] In 2008, the commission found significant irregularities with much of the Ecuadorian debt issued in the preceding decade. The Ecuadorian government, specifically invoking the illegality of the debt instruments, deliberately defaulted on two debt instruments in late 2008. It gave debt holders the option of a new debt instrument with a two-thirds haircut; 91 per cent of the bondholders accepted the new instruments. Odious debt was also variously mentioned in the lead-up to Iraq's debt restructuring in 2005.[48]

Existing state practice, however, does not provide strong support for a doctrine of odious debt. It runs up against the firmly entrenched rule that sovereign debt needs to be repaid. Whether this is more than a strong expectation on the part of creditors and states are obliged under international law to repay their sovereign debt governed by some domestic law is an open question. This issue will be explored further in relation to Principle 9 on the binding character of debt obligations.

Of the cases frequently cited in favour of the argument that the legitimate repudiation of odious debt is a rule of custom, all except one hold that the defence is not valid, and that the relevant sovereign debt must be repaid. The notable exception is the *Tinoco* arbitration, the holding of which is narrow (improper use of *all* the funds borrowed, to the *knowledge* of the creditor). Indeed, a similar situation would be virtually unthinkable today, when even the most ambitious 'dictator *du jour*' would steal only part of the loan, with the rest being used,

[45] *Dreyfus Brothers and Company v Peru ('French Claims against Peru')* (*France v. Peru*), 11 October 1921, Arbitration under Chapter IV of the Hague Convention of 18 October 1907 for the Pacific Settlement of International Disputes, Permanent Court of Arbitration, (1922) 16 AJIL 480–4; I UNRIAA 215–22. See Waibel (n. 23) 138–41.

[46] Award, 11 October 1921 (1922) 16 AJIL 480.

[47] Comisión de Auditoría Integral del Crédito Público, Informe de la subcomisión jurídica, 23 September 2008.

[48] P. Adams, *Iraq's Odious Debts* (Cato Institute, 2004); S. Negus and J. Reed, 'Iraq seeks further deal on debt relief', *Financial Times* (London), 2 December 2004; J. Chung and S. Fidler, 'Why Iraqi debt is no longer a write-off', *Financial Times* (London), 16 July 2006.

however ineffectively, for the benefit of the citizens of the state.[49] Such limited support for an odious debt doctrine inevitably leads one to the conclusion that it has not yet reached the status of custom, and nor will it do so in the foreseeable future.[50]

State practice suggesting a further limitation upon the conduct of public officials in international law may be deduced from the support given to UN General Assembly (GA) resolutions by states and from the conclusion of treaties proscribing certain acts of governmental officials. Both have the potential to manifest the requisite state practice and *opinio juris* to found a claim of customary law.[51] The UN Convention against Corruption, which entered into force on 14 December 2005, and its mandating GA resolutions[52] provide an illustrative example. Chapter III of the Convention, regarding Criminalization and Law Enforcement, contains 27 provisions obliging states to regulate the conduct of public officials in domestic law.[53]

For present purposes, five articles are relevant. First, Article 15 obliges parties to the Convention to criminalize the offer of a bribe to a public official, or the solicitation or acceptance of a bribe by that public official. Article 16 similarly obliges criminalization of the offer of a bribe to a foreign government official, or the solicitation or acceptance of a bribe by the same. Article 17 provides that parties shall adopt domestic legislation against 'the embezzlement, misappropriation, or other diversion by a public official for his or her benefit or for the benefit of another person or entity'. Further, Articles 19 and 20 provide that parties will consider adopting legislation criminalizing both the abuse of power of public officials (i.e. not fulfilling the duties of public office in order to gain personal enrichment), and illicit enrichment ('that is, a significant increase in the assets of a public official that he or she cannot reasonably explain in relation to his or her lawful income').

The UN Convention against Corruption currently has 159 parties, manifesting widespread support for banning certain corruptive practices of public officials.[54] Reports of the Secretariat of the Convention suggest that states are, generally, implementing the obligations contained within Chapter III.[55] The Inter-American Convention on Corruption and the 2010 amendments to the 1997 OECD Anti-Bribery Convention also address the demand side of corruption on the part of officials, in addition to the supply side from those seeking to obtain favour from

[49] Bucheit, Gulati, and Thompson (n. 40) 1219.

[50] See A. Gelpern, 'What Argentina and Iraq Might Learn From Each Other' (2005) 6 Chi. J. Int'l L. 391, 406.

[51] *North Sea Continental Shelf* (n. 11) 44. See also A. Roberts, 'Traditional and Modern Approaches to Customary International Law: A Reconciliation' (2001) 95 AJIL 757, 758–9.

[52] GA Resolutions 55/61 of 4 December 2000, 57/169 of 18 December 2002, and 58/4 of 31 October 2003.

[53] See J. Justo, Ch. 9 of this volume.

[54] UN Convention Against Corruption, 'List of Parties', available at <http://www.unodc.org/unodc/en/treaties/CAC/signatories.html>.

[55] UN Convention Against Corruption Secretariat, 'Implementation of chapter III (Criminalization and law enforcement) of the United Nations Convention against Corruption: Thematic report prepared by the Secretariat', 25 August 2011, UN Doc. CAC/COSP/2011/2.

public officials.[56] Gelpern explains how Transparency International monitoring led to the gradual strengthening of the international instruments for fighting corruption, culminating in the 1997 OECD Anti-Bribery Convention.[57]

All states reviewed in the first year of the first review cycle had implemented measures to criminalize the bribery or acceptance of bribes of public officials, and the embezzlement of funds by public officials, and most states had criminalized the abuse of functions by public officials.[58] The implementation of the Convention in domestic law is only the first step. Importantly, the enforcement of the obligations at the domestic level is critical. In addition, the majority of states have yet to put measures in place to criminalize the bribery of foreign public officials, or illicit enrichment. Nevertheless, an analysis of the state practice surrounding the UN Convention against Corruption does suggest that there may be a customary rule—either in the nascent stages of existence, or in the stage of crystallization into custom—obliging states to proscribe certain illicit acts of public officials, particularly acts which involve the public officials of that state.

The UNCTAD Principles, however, go much further than either the doctrine of odious debt, or the obligations against corruption contained within the UN Convention against Corruption. The Principles call on public officials to *protect* the public interest, as opposed to an obligation not to harm the public interest, as embodied by odious debt and the Convention against Corruption. The distinction is slight, but important. In effect, the UNCTAD Principles do not just prescribe certain behaviour of public officials. Instead, they encourage officials to act positively in protection of the public interest. One could quite easily imagine that an incompetent—but not malevolent—public official could be acting contrary to the Principles, without contravening the domestic legislation implementing the Convention against Corruption.

State practice has converged towards the regulation of the acts of public officials engaged in international relations, regardless of whether such state practice constitutes custom. This convergence has, however, been to limit the potential malicious acts of public officials (in other words, a *negative* obligation, or obligation to refrain from certain acts), and not an attempt to provide best-practice guidance of conduct for public officials. The UNCTAD Principles represent an innovation in this respect, by providing a *positive obligation* to public officials to act in order to protect the public interest.

[56] Inter-American Convention Against Corruption, 27 May 1996, 35 ILM 724, Art. 6; see further G.D. Altamirano, 'The Impact of the Inter-American Convention against Corruption' (2007) 38 University of Miami Inter-American Law Review 487–547; OECD, Annex I, Good Practice Guidance on Implementing Specific Articles on the Convention on Combating Bribery of Foreign Public Officials in International Business Transactions, Recommendation of the Council for Further Combating Bribery of Foreign Public Officials in International Business Transactions, 18 February 2010–C (2010)19.

[57] See A. Gelpern, Ch. 16 of this volume.

[58] The first year of the first cycle comprised a review of 28 states parties, UN Convention Against Corruption Secretariat, 'Country reviews: organization and schedule of reviews Background paper prepared by the Secretariat', 26 November 2010, UN Doc. CAC/COSP/IRG/2010/CRP.12.

II. Principle 7—the duty of a creditor to act in good faith towards debt re-arrangements

Principle 7 of the UNCTAD Principles institutes a duty on the creditor to enter into good faith negotiations when sovereign default is imminent, providing that: '*In circumstances where a sovereign is manifestly unable to service its debts, all lenders have a duty to behave in good faith and with cooperative spirit to reach a consensual re-arrangement of those obligations. Creditors should seek a speedy and orderly resolution to the problem.*' This principle is to be read in conjunction with Principle 15, which contains the obligations of the debtor sovereign, and will be dealt with later.

As noted in section C.I., the states of nationality of creditors have historically adopted a variety of approaches when faced with a sovereign debtor on the brink of insolvency, including military interventions and quasi-receivership of the state. Renegotiation was to be approached with a diplomatic eye, conscious of the possibility of a disorderly default on the debt, and the political benefit that renegotiation may bring to the creditors. Perhaps the most intensive periods of inter-sovereign debt renegotiation were those of the inter-allied debt arising from the First World War, and of German external debt arising after the Second World War.

At the end of the First World War, the United States held over US$4.3 billion of UK debt, lent to the British to support the war effort.[59] The British argued that this debt was taken on to support not only the British war effort, but also that of continental allies (particularly France).[60] The British contended that they therefore should not be held solely accountable for the outstanding debt. The Americans rejected that argument, and declined the British suggestion of general debt forgiveness,[61] based on popular opinion in the United States at the time and the negative light in which the Congress viewed debt cancellation as a matter of principle. As a result, the Americans and British entered renegotiation of the debt on 8 January 1923, with an agreement in principle reached on 31 January. Congress approved the renegotiation on 28 February 1923.[62]

The agreement restructured $4.6 billion of debt, including the wartime loans, with the weak state of the post-war British economy reflected in a forgiving repayment schedule in the early years. Similar renegotiations were pursued, via the World War Foreign Debt Commission, and agreements concluded with other

[59] Combined Annual Reports of the World War Foreign Debt Commission with Additional Information regarding Foreign Debts Due the United States (Government Printing Office, 1927), Report for Fiscal Year 1923, 64 (hereinafter 'FDC').

[60] FDC (n. 59) 72.

[61] FDC (n. 59) 68.

[62] Address of the President of the United States to the Congress, 7 February 1923, Submitting the Report of the World War Foreign Debt Commission on the Proposed Settlement with Great Britain; Agreement for the Funding of the Debt of Great Britain to the United States, 18 June 1912, FDC 106–13.

European debtors in the following decade.[63] Whilst reaching specific agreements with each debtor sovereign, the US Commission did approach renegotiations with a degree of structure. The two paramount concerns of the Commission were, first, to remove sovereign debt as a factor of international tension and, secondly, to uphold the sanctity of sovereign financial obligations.[64] The Commission pursued these objectives by taking into account each state's capacity to pay,[65] whilst insisting on full repayment of the principal sum of debt.[66]

What motives did the United States as a creditor have in renegotiating the post-war debt of the allies in the interwar period? The reconstruction of allied states in Europe was seen as being the key factor in the stability of international relations in the post-war period, and renegotiation reduced uncertainty for debtor states regarding the payment schedule, thereby facilitating reconstruction. Some debt relief on interest payments and stretching out the repayment obligations over a long period of time would allow the allied governments to fulfil their functions and provide the basis for economic growth to resume. Renegotiation, in this case, was entered into with good faith, and based on broader, political objectives.

France, the United Kingdom, and the United States established the Tripartite Commission on German Debt in April 1951, with the purpose of renegotiating pre-Second World War external German debt in the light of Germany's defeat in 1945. The Commission proposed haircuts of between 62 and 75 per cent on debt claims against the defunct Reich, providing Germany with a sound financial position going into the important London Debt Conference of 1953.[67] The Conference enabled a comprehensive agreement between both sovereign and private creditors and Germany, and was notable for its emphasis on the actual ability of Germany to pay, instead of an emphasis on the extent of its legal obligation to pay.[68]

Similar conclusions can be drawn from the renegotiation of post-Second World War debt compared to the renegotiation of inter-allied debt in the wake of the First World War. The willingness to renegotiate with good faith on the part of the creditors was forthcoming partly because of the desire to see the quick reconstruction of a stable Germany (of particular importance to keep Germany in the Western camp), and partly because states widely recognized that the post-war German economy could not service the German Reich's debts in full. A cooperative solution was in the interest of the defeated debtor, and more importantly, in the interest of the United States and other creditors, in particular once the scale of the challenge posed by communism became apparent.

[63] Agreements were concluded with Finland (12 March 1924), Poland (November 1924), Lithuania (December 1924), Latvia (September 1925), Belgium (June 1925), Czechoslovakia (October 1925), Romania (December 1925), and Italy (April 1926).

[64] FDC (n. 59) 37.

[65] FDC (n. 59) 59.

[66] Public No. 155, 69th Congress, H.R. 6773, 28 April 1926.

[67] D. Vagts, 'Sovereign bankruptcy: In re Germany (1953), In re Iraq (2004)' (2004) 98 AJIL 302.

[68] G.R. Delaume, *Legal Aspects of International Lending and Economic Development Financing* (Dobbs Ferry, 1967) 53.

In the latter half of the twentieth century, sovereign debt renegotiations have increasingly taken place in the framework of formal or informal international organizations, notably under the auspices of the Paris Club of sovereign creditors, the London Club of private creditors, and the IMF.

The Paris Club is an informal organization of 19 permanent member states, all of which have considerable exposure to sovereign debt. The role of the Club is to provide a forum that allows sovereign creditors to discuss and, if necessary, renegotiate the conditions of sovereign debt. Although the Paris Club is an informal organization, it follows several guiding principles, including making restructuring conditional upon manifest economic inability of the sovereign to meet its external debt obligations, meaning in practice that the debtor must have 'a current program supported by an appropriate arrangement with the IMF'.[69]

According to the relative gravity of the debtor state's economic situation, the Paris Club proposes a variety of debt concessions or restructuring measures, with the most concessional being those concluded under the HIPC initiative (which provides for coordinated action by the whole international finance community, including the international financial institutions). Agreements reached within the framework of the Paris Club have, as the agreed minutes of negotiations state,[70] no legal force, but must be implemented into a legally binding bilateral agreement signed between each creditor and the debtor state. To date, the Paris Club has reached 423 agreements, covering a total of $556 billion of debt.[71]

The IMF and World Bank mainly renegotiate, or grant concessions to, countries under the HIPC initiative or the Multilateral Debt Relief Initiative (MDRI). The 'decision point' (i.e. the qualification of a sovereign's eligibility to participate in the programme) of both programmes is composed of objective indicators to measure the gravity of the country's indebtedness. For example, whilst each international institution is separately responsible for setting conditions for debt relief, the IMF provides that a debtor will be eligible for relief under the HIPC initiative if the debtor is:

> ... eligible to borrow from the World Bank's International Development Agency ... and from the IMF's Extended Credit Facility, faces an unsustainable debt burden that cannot be addressed through traditional debt relief mechanisms, has an established track record of reform and sound policies through IMF- and World Bank-supported programs, and has developed a Poverty Reduction Strategy Paper (PRSP) through a broad-based participatory process in the country.[72]

[69] Club de Paris, 'Conditionality', available at <http://www.clubdeparis.org/sections/composition/principes/cinq-grands-principes>.

[70] Club de Paris, 'Agreed Minutes', available at <http://www.clubdeparis.org/sections/services/glossaire/definitions/proces-verbal-agree>.

[71] Club de Paris, 'Key Figures', available at <http://www.clubdeparis.org/sections/donnees-chiffrees/chiffres-cles>.

[72] IMF, 'HIPC External Factsheet', available at <http://www.imf.org/external/np/exr/facts/hipc.htm>.

In summary, creditors often realize that full repayment in cases of protracted lack of debt sustainability is unlikely and will harm the debtor country's future economic growth. Nevertheless, it is difficult to contend that state practice thus far manifests an obligation to renegotiate sovereign debt on the part of official and private creditors—whether the debtors are least-developed countries, fragile post-war economies, or advanced countries.[73] Creditors renegotiate debt for a variety of political and economic considerations (e.g. the stability of the international financial system, the desire for aid development, or the realization of the impossibility of full repayment). States exercise their discretion to renegotiate in good faith, but they do not renegotiate because they believe they are obliged to do so. As such, whilst state practice does seem to support renegotiation in good faith, the *opinio juris* necessary to create a rule of custom is absent.

III. Principle 9—the binding character of debt obligations, and the defence of necessity

Principle 9 of the UNCTAD Principles provides that:

A sovereign debt contract is a binding obligation and should be honoured. Exceptional cases nonetheless can arise. A state of economic necessity can prevent the borrower's full and/or timely repayment. Also, a competent judicial authority may rule that circumstances giving rise to legal defences have occurred. When, due to the state of economic necessity of the borrower, changes to the original contractual conditions of the loan are unavoidable, Principles 7 and 15 should be followed.

Principle 9 contains two distinct but related propositions. First, it states that sovereign debt obligations should be honoured. Secondly, it implies that legal defences, including that of necessity, should be available for those debtors that, as a last resort, need to avail themselves of them.

The first part of the Principle refers to the contractual sanctity of debt. It is crucial to distinguish the sanctity of debt as a matter of the domestic governing law from the principle of *contracta sunt servanda* internationally. In the rare cases where one government lends to another on the basis of a treaty, there is indeed an international legal obligation to abide by the terms of the treaty. The situation is less clear-cut as far as sovereign borrowing under some domestic law is concerned. Howse suggests that these cases need to be viewed as fundamentally distinct:

...the concept of pacta sunt servanda concerns treaties, that is to say, state-to-state agreements that evidence the intent of the States in question to be bound in international law. When States enter into loan contracts with other States, do they intend that the obligations in question be international law obligations, private law obligations or both?[74]

[73] M. Meetarbhan, 'Vers un droit international de la dette exterieure?' in D. Carreau and M.N. Shaw (eds.), *La dette extérieure/The external debt* (Martinus Nijhoff, 1995) 512–13.

[74] R. Howse (n. 39).

Only treaties are covered by the international principle of *pacta sunt servanda*. Official lending between two states on the basis of treaties constitutes only a small fraction of modern sovereign lending.

Pacta sunt servanda in respect of treaties has been an important principle of international law from early on, though on its own it is insufficient to ground an alleged breach of international law. It was, for example, the concept of the faithful fulfilment of obligations upon which Grotius based the very unity of the community of nations.[75] Prominent jurists throughout the decades echoed a similar sentiment, such as, among others, Pufendorf,[76] Suarez,[77] and Vattel.[78] More contemporary theorists have similarly placed great importance on the principle. Kelsen, for example, suggests that the principle is the very underpinning of a legal system (the '*Grundnorm*'),[79] the presupposition on which all legal normativity rests.

Many decisions echo this doctrinal support. The PCIJ, for example, in the *Polish Nationals in Danzig* case,[80] held that 'the assumption runs that States will in good faith observe and carry out the obligations which they have assumed'.[81] The Court's successor confirmed the sanctity of interstate obligations in, among other cases, the *Military and Paramilitary Activities in Nicaragua* case,[82] and the *Rights of US Nationals in Morocco* case.[83]

The principle of *pacta sunt servanda* is also found in Article 26 of the Vienna Convention on the Law of Treaties 1969 (VCLT). That provision reads: 'Every treaty in force is binding upon the parties to it and must be performed by them in good faith.' Note that a debt instrument concluded in writing between sovereign states constitutes a treaty under Article 2(1)(a) of the VCLT. The International Law Commission commentary on the Vienna Convention states that the sanctity of international obligations 'is the fundamental principle of the law of treaties'.[84] The Convention currently has 111 parties.[85] Both the support found in jurisprudence for the principle, and the state practice of adhering to and upholding the principle—including the support culminating in its inclusion in the VCLT—demonstrate that the principle of *pacta sunt servanda* is essential to the orderly conduct of international affairs.

Whilst there is no doubt that states are bound by the principle of *pacta sunt servanda* in relation to treaties they have voluntarily entered into, debts governed by private law and often held by private entities form a different category. Contracts

[75] H. Grotius, *De Jure Belli ac Pacis*, lib. III, ch. 25, sec. 1.

[76] S. Pufendorf, *Elementorum Jurisprudentiae Universalis*, lib. I, ch. 12.

[77] F. Suarez, *Tractatus de Legibus*, lib. II, ch. 18, sec. 9.

[78] E. Vattel, *Le Droit des Gens*, liv. II, ch. 15, secs 219–222.

[79] H. Kelsen, 'Droit Interne et Droit International' 14 (1926) *Recueil des Cours* 303.

[80] *Treatment of Polish Nationals and Other Persons of Polish Origin or Speech in Danzig Territory*, 4 February 1932, PCIJ, (ser. A/B) 1932 No. 44.

[81] *Treatment of Polish Nationals* (n. 80) 24.

[82] *Military and Paramilitary Activities in Nicaragua (Nicaragua v. US)*, Merits, 27 June 1986, ICJ Rep., 14 (1986), 135, para. 270.

[83] *Rights of Nationals of the United States of America in Morocco (France v. US)*, Judgment, 27 August 1952, ICJ Rep., (1952), 212.

[84] ILC, 'Commentary on the Vienna Convention on the Law of Treaties' (1966) II YBILC 211.

[85] As of 24 January 2012.

governed by private law do not generally fall under the protective umbrella of the international *pacta sunt servanda* rule. As a general rule, breaches of contractual obligations, without more, do not breach international law. That non-payment of debt governed by some domestic law does not generally breach international law does not, however, imply that debt obligations are not binding as a matter of the governing law.

There is unanimous support today for the proposition that debt obligations are binding as a matter of their governing law on the state. The principle of the sanctity of obligations voluntarily undertaken also resonates in domestic legal systems.[86] It is rare for states that restructure their debt obligations or default on their debt to dispute that the obligations are binding. It has long been established that they are not merely debts of honour, but binding legal obligations. One of the rare cases where a government took the view that the debt obligations were not binding was the Soviet repudiation of Czarist debt in 1917—predictably, creditor countries firmly opposed the Soviet view that because a new regime had assumed power, the debts incurred by the Tsar were no longer binding.

As a matter of domestic law under which they borrow, states are generally bound by a domestic variant of *contracta sunt servanda*. Just like its international law counterpart, however, *contracta sunt servanda* is rarely an operative principle. It establishes the general principle that contractual obligations are binding, but leaves open the question of when non-performance of the obligation is justified and what the consequences of breach are.

Notwithstanding these uncertainties, the first proposition of Principle 9 of the UNCTAD Principles reflects a well-established rule of general international law, albeit one that gives virtually no practical guidance. States are obliged to repay debt incurred under treaty by virtue of international law and debts incurred under contract as a matter of the applicable domestic law. The binding character of debt obligations, as a matter of international law in case of treaties and as a matter of domestic law in case of contractual borrowing, is beyond doubt. All the controversy centres on the circumstances when non-performance of obligation is justified and the consequences of non-performance.

The second part of Principle 9 provides that a state of necessity may cause a situation in which breach of the sovereign's debt obligations is excused.[87] The defence of necessity to a breach of obligations under international law has a long track record before international tribunals and courts. It is paradigmatically formulated in Article 25 of the ILC Articles on State Responsibility, which is recognized as being declarative of the state of customary law.[88] State practice supports the ILC article on the defence of necessity. Perhaps the most instructive examples of state practice are General Assembly Resolution 56/83 of 2001 commending the

[86] e.g. of the French Civil Code, Art. 1134: 'Duties imposed by contract are absolute, contracts entered into freely and voluntarily are held to be sacred and shall be enforced.'

[87] Waibel (n. 23) ch. 5.

[88] *Gabčíkovo-Nagymaros Project (Hungary v. Slovakia)*, Judgment, 25 September 1997, ICJ Rep. (1997) 7, paras 50–51; see also J. Crawford, *The ILC Articles on State Responsibility: Introduction, Texts and Commentaries* (Cambridge University Press, 2002) 183.

articles, and comments of state representatives in the Sixth Committee of the United Nations.[89] Whilst recognition of the existence of the defence in international law is undeniable, its use in practice in the sovereign debt context is highly limited,[90] conditional upon the breach of the obligation being the '*only* way for the State to safeguard an *essential* interest against a *grave and imminent* peril' (emphasis added).[91]

The *Russian Indemnity Case* stands as authority for the proposition that a defence of financial necessity is in principle available to states that are suffering from particularly acute economic problems.[92] The Ottoman Empire defaulted on its debt twice at the end of the nineteenth century, in 1875 and 1876, following the costly Crimean War with Russia. As a result of the first default, creditors reached an agreement with the Ottoman government, which created the Ottoman Debt Council, a body charged with supervising payments of the restructured debt and protecting the interests of bondholders.[93] When revenue accrued by the Council swelled, in 1903, due to a back payment made by Bulgaria on an outstanding annuity, the Council increased the interest rate payable to bondholders by a quarter of one per cent. After an arbitral decision affirmed the ability of the Council to alter the interest rate payable on debt, Turkey promptly defaulted upon such payments.

The *Russian Indemnity Case* resulted from a dispute over Turkey's default on interest payments to Russian holders of bonds issued as indemnity for damage caused throughout the Russo-Turkish War (1877–78), starting in 1902. Turkey contended that the breach of obligation was excused due to the failing state of the Turkish economy at the time. The tribunal responded to Turkey's claim with the following: 'l'obligation pour un Etat d'exécuter les traités peut fléchir *si l'existence même de l'Etat* vient à être en danger, si l'observation du devoir international est... *self destructive*' (emphasis added).[94] Ultimately, the tribunal did not accept

[89] UN Doc. A/55/609.

[90] See Crawford (n. 88) 183.

[91] Article 25, 1 (a), *ILC Articles on Responsibility of States for Internationally Wrongful Acts, with Commentaries* (2001) II YBILC, Part Two, 81. ILC Articles on State Responsibility, Art. 25 provides:
Article 25. Necessity

1. Necessity may not be invoked by a State as a ground for precluding the wrongfulness of an act not in conformity with an international obligation of that State unless the act:
   (a) is the only way for the State to safeguard an essential interest against a grave and imminent peril; and
   (b) does not seriously impair an essential interest of the State or States towards which the obligation exists, or of the international community as a whole.
2. In any case, necessity may not be invoked by a State as a ground for precluding wrongfulness if:
   (a) the international obligation in question excludes the possibility of invoking necessity; or
   (b) the State has contributed to the situation of necessity.

[92] *Russian Indemnity Case (Russia v. Turkey)*, Award of the Arbitral Tribunal of 11 November 1912, (1913) 7 AJIL 178–201; (1912) 11 UNRIAA 431.

[93] D.C. Blaisdell, *European Financial Control in the Ottoman Empire: A Study of the Establishment, Activities, and Significance of the Administration of the Ottoman Public Debt* (Columbia University Press, 1929).

[94] *Russian Indemnity Case* (n. 92) 180.

the defence put forward by Turkey. On this basis, states finding themselves in financial distress of the gravest character could argue that they are entitled to some flexibility in their debt service.

A similar claim was made in the *Société Commerciale de Belgique*[95] case before the PCIJ. In that case, the debtor state (Greece) argued that its economic crisis of 1932 constituted an event of *force majeure* (though Greece invoked necessity), and that full repayment of two arbitral awards to the Belgian creditor bank would place Greece's public services and security in danger.[96] Belgium also agreed in principle with the possibility of the defence, but denied its applicability to the case.[97] The court decided that it lacked jurisdiction to review the capacity of the Greek state to pay the awards, and hence that such a defence could not be substantiated in this case. It did, however, seem to imply that a defence of financial necessity was possible in theory.[98]

In the *Serbian Loans* and *Brazilian Loans* cases, before the PCIJ, both Serbia and Brazil argued that the economic distress caused by the First World War amounted to *force majeure* and should allow the states to claim debt relief.[99] The court rejected the contention that economic dislocations caused by the First World War could, in any way, alter the sovereign debt obligations of the debtor states.[100]

Modern invocations of the defence can be found in Argentina's submissions to numerous ICSID arbitral tribunals following its financial crisis at the turn of the twenty-first century. The question of how successful these attempts to rely on necessity will be is still open. In *LG&E v. Argentina*,[101] the arbitral tribunal accepted the defence of financial necessity whereas, in *CMS v. Argentina*,[102] the tribunal rejected the defence, based on the same facts. Argentina also attempted to utilize the defence in the *Enron*[103] and *Suez*[104] arbitrations. In these cases the defence was unsuccessful for two reasons. First, the tribunals held that there was always more than one option of action open to the Argentine government to tackle the crisis. In other words, it did not fulfil the criterion found in Article 25 of the ILC Articles on State Responsibility of being the *only* route of action open to

[95] *Société Commerciale de Belgique (Belgium v. Greece)*, 15 June 1939, PCIJ, Ser. A/B (1939), 160.

[96] F Paddeu, 'A Genealogy of Force Majeure in International Law' (2011) 82 BYBIL 1–114, 50–2.

[97] Paddeu (n. 96) 162–63.

[98] Paddeu (n. 96) 178.

[99] See *Serbian Loans Case* and *Brazilian Loans Case* (n. 34).

[100] *Serbian Loans Case* (n. 34) 4. *Brazilian Loans Case* (n. 34) 120.

[101] *LG&E Energy Corp., LG&E Capital Corp. and LG&E International Inc. v. Argentine Republic* (Decision on Liability, 3 October 2006), 21 ICSID Rev 203 (2007); 46 ILM 36 (2006).

[102] *CMS Gas Transmission Company v. Republic of Argentina* (Award, 12 May 2005) ICSID Case No. ARB/01/8; (2005) 44 ILM 1205, paras 214ff, 304ff.

[103] *Enron Corporation and Ponderosa Assets, LP v. Argentine Republic* (Award, 22 May 2007) ICSID Case No. ARB/01/3, paras 304–309.

[104] *Suez, Sociedad General de Aguas de Barcelona S.A. and Vivendi Universal S.A. v. Argentine Republic* (Decision on Liability, 30 July 2010) ICSID Case No. ARB/03/19, para. 258 and *AWG Group v. Republic of Argentina* (Decision on Liability, 30 July 2010) UNCITRAL arbitration, para. 258; *Suez, Sociedad General de Aguas de Barcelona S.A. and InterAgua Servicios Integrales del Agua S.A. v. Argentine Republic* (Decision on Liability, 30 July 2010) ICSID Case No. ARB/03/17, para. 236.

the state.[105] There was no discussion of whether this criterion, formulated ostensibly for the security context, was a workable one in relation to economic crises. Secondly, Argentina was deemed to have contributed to its position of financial necessity, and therefore could not avail itself of the defence of necessity, as per Article 25(2)(b).[106] These two conditions for necessity tend to render necessity inoperable as a defence in the context of financial crises.[107]

The Argentina cases highlight that a state that wishes to avail itself of the defence cannot be responsible for contribution to the problem that causes the state of necessity.[108] Indeed, these limits are difficult to attain if one talks of a state of necessity of a financial character.[109] Necessity, as currently formulated in customary international law, is ill-suited to international economic law generally and the sovereign debt context in particular. Only in the most extreme scenarios, such as duress, would a state be able to claim that it did not contribute in some way to a situation of financial necessity. Conversely, other actors—including international creditors—will invariably have contributed to a sovereign debt crisis. Even if one excluded *de minimis* contributions by the debtor state, necessity thus construed remains inoperative in the economic context because both the debtor state and creditor have contributed to the situation of necessity.

The transposition of necessity to the financial context raises other questions. A first is whether necessity extends beyond the interstate plan and could conceivably suspend repayment obligations of a state due to private creditors.[110] A second is whether a successful invocation of necessity based on a sovereign debt crisis would excuse the state indefinitely from full repayment or whether its effect is merely to suspend the repayment of the debt. Article 27 of the ILC Articles leaves this question open. The answer is critical to determining whether necessity is a useful defence for sovereign debtors. A suspension could provide breathing space for the debtor, and give it time to conclude a restructuring with its creditors. Creditors will factor the effect of necessity into the negotiations and their demands for repayment. Should necessity result in repayment, they are likely to insist on full repayment of the principal. For countries suffering from serious over-indebtedness that clouds their growth and development prospects, this would risk assuring that no debt relief on the principal obligation would be provided. The likely result is that necessity would offer little assistance to such states.

In state practice, the plea of financial necessity as a means to excuse *prima facie* breaches of international obligations is not new. The ILC Articles on State Responsibility firmly enshrined it as part of the customary law of state

[105] e.g. *Enron Corporation and Ponderosa Assets, LP v Argentine Republic* (Decision on the Application for Annulment of the Argentine Republic, 30 July 2010) ICSID Case No. ARB/01/3, para. 369, *Suez v Argentina III* (n. 103) para. 260; *Suez v Argentina I* (n. 104) para. 238.

[106] *Suez v Argentina III* (n. 103) para. 263, *Suez v Argentina I* (n. 104) para. 241.

[107] cf. A. von Bogdandy and M. Goldmann, Ch. 3 of this volume.

[108] ILC Articles on State Responsibility, Art. 25 (2)(b).

[109] M. Waibel, 'Two Worlds of Necessity' (2007) 20 LJIL 637.

[110] A. Reinisch, 'Sachverständigengutachten zur Frage des Bestehens und der Wirkung des völkerrechtlichen Rechtfertigungsgrundes "Staatsnotstand"' (2008) 68 *Zeitschrift für ausländisches öffentliches Recht und Völkerrecht* 3.

responsibility. But the defence of financial necessity appears underdeveloped and has almost no practical application under the prevailing case law. A defence of financial necessity, as understood by current international law, is unlikely to succeed in rebutting non-respect of sovereign debt obligations even if it may theoretically be available.

It is important to note that Principle 9 does not conflict with the current conception of financial necessity in international law—the principle in effect distinguishes between the recognition of a state of economic necessity (the third sentence of Principle 9) and the availability of necessity as a legal defence (the fourth sentence of Principle 9), the application of which is to be determined by a competent judicial authority in accordance with international law. As worded, the UNCTAD Principles hence do not increase the scope of the defence of necessity, but defer to the strict limits of the defence in general international law, as set out in Article 15 of the ILC Articles on State Responsibility. Soft law cannot overcome the limitations of the defence in current customary international law. An international court or tribunal could only uphold a defence based on a legal rule, though it may take soft law into account.[111]

IV. Principle 15—the debtor's obligation to undertaking restructuring in a prompt, efficient, and fair manner

Principle 15 resembles Principle 7 in that it institutes obligations of conduct during restructuring procedures. Principle 15 deals with the obligations of the debtor, as opposed to creditors. It provides that: '*If a restructuring of sovereign debt obligations becomes unavoidable, it should be undertaken promptly, efficiently and fairly.*' The commentary to the Principle expands on these provisions, explaining that extended restructuring negotiations are undesirable for all concerned, that the inclusion of collective action clauses in agreements may encourage collective behaviour, and that the debtors should not arbitrarily distinguish between creditors when concluding renegotiated agreements.

Some instances of debt restructuring have been undertaken following these principles. Three are particularly notable. A first example of is Iraq's debt restructuring following the fall of Saddam Hussein's regime in 2003. Iraq's outstanding debt totalled US$129 billion when the Hussein regime collapsed, which was restructured using commercial techniques without the benefit of collective action clauses, leaving just $39 billion of outstanding debt. The restructuring process was preceded by UN Security Council Resolution 1483 (2003), passed in the wake of the US-led intervention in Iraq. That resolution, among other issues, highlighted 'the desirability of [the] prompt completion of the restructuring of Iraq's debt'.[112]

Sovereign debt restructuring undertaken within the Paris Club framework is subject to the 'comparability of treatment' principle, which captures the idea that

[111] See A. von Bogdandy and M. Goldmann, Ch. 3 of this volume.

[112] UN Security Council Resolution 1483 (2003), UN Doc. S/RES/1483 (2003), para. 22.

debtors ought not give more favourable renegotiated terms to creditors outside the Club than they do to its members.[113] The idea underlying this principle is echoed in a large number of modern restructuring agreements, reflected by the inclusion of *pari passu* clauses,[114] burden sharing clauses,[115] mandatory prepayment clauses,[116] negative pledge clauses,[117] and cross-default clauses.[118] Its goal is clear: to establish fair burden sharing across all creditors.

In these cases we find that extra-legal considerations, such as the desire to secure further loans, dominate legal motivations for such acts, negating the *opinio juris* of such acts. State practice amassing behind the values that Principle 15 includes therefore does not support a claim of customary international law, but does suggest that, in due course, an obligation to conduct restructuring negotiations in a prompt, efficient, and fair manner foreshadowed in Principle 15 may crystallize into customary international law.

E. Conclusion

The UNCTAD Principles were not produced out of thin air. UNCTAD's Principles reflect, to a considerable degree, how states and creditors of states act, even if these acts are generally not accompanied by *opinio juris*. The Principles aim to guide sovereign lending and borrowing comprehensively, in line with modern governance standards. Their informal character follows the predominant preference in international finance for discretion rather than hard rules. Their voluntariness increases the chances of acceptance by states and creditors, while states and creditors always retain the option of not conforming their conduct to the content of the Principles.

This chapter has shown that states have traditionally not been subject to rules in this area of sovereign debt, and their acts were instead driven by a combination of foreign policy interests, domestic politics, and economic interests. These factors resulted in a wide variety of policy responses to situations of sovereign financial distress, and a lack of formation of customary law regulating sovereign borrowing and default. There is also virtually no directly relevant treaty law on the subject, with the possible, and contested exception of bilateral investment treaties.[119]

Since their formal launch in Doha in April 2012, 13 states have endorsed the Principles.[120] The UN General Assembly has referred to the Principles on three occasions. UNCTAD received a unanimous mandate in Doha to continue its work

[113] R.A. Morales 'Equality of Treatment of Creditors in the Restructuring of Foreign Debt' in Carreau and Shaw (eds.) (n. 73) 381–3.

[114] See e.g. the Philippine Public Sector Restructuring Agreements, s. 7.01(f).

[115] See e.g. the Philippine Public Sector Restructuring Agreements, s. 5.03(b), and the 1985 Mexican Restructuring Agreement, s. 5.03(b).

[116] e.g. the Philippine Public Sector Restructuring Agreements, s. 4.01(b).

[117] Philippine Public Sector Restructuring Agreements, ss 8.03–8.04.

[118] Philippine Public Sector Restructuring Agreements, s. 10.10(f) and (g).

[119] M. Waibel, 'Opening Pandora's Box: Sovereign Bonds in International Arbitration' (2007) 101 AJIL 711.

[120] In mid-November 2012. More states are expected to endorse the Principles in due course.

on implementing the Principles.[121] Furthermore, some national parliaments have also expressed their support of the Principles.[122] All of these are early and promising signs of the acceptance of the Principles by some states in different parts of the world. At the same time, the voluntary endorsements by 13 states of the non-binding Principles does not, for the time being, affect customary international law. Customary international law will only change once state practice consistently conforms to the content of the Principles, and states conform their conduct because they believe they are bound to act in such a manner.

In spite of the prevailing ad hoc approach to resolving sovereign debt crises, this chapter has noted that some state practice prior to the promulgation of the Principles supports aspects of the Principles. First, the UN Convention against Corruption, among others, evidences broader international consensus that acts of bribing public officials are illicit, including as far as sovereign debt is concerned. Whilst state practice does proscribe acts of bribery and corruption, it does not—as the UNCTAD Principles do—impose broader obligations on public officials to protect the interests of their constituents in sovereign borrowing.

Secondly, the chapter has examined the motivations of creditors in debt renegotiations to try to establish whether they are obliged to negotiate in good faith. Even though good faith is in fact often discernible in debt renegotiations and states and other creditors refer to the desirability of such negotiations with increasing frequency, this tendency towards good faith is attributable to a variety of extra-legal factors and not accompanied by *opinio juris*.

Thirdly, state practice affirms the binding character of debt obligations, typically governed by domestic law. There is consensus on the binding character of debt obligation, though generally the binding character results from the applicable domestic law rather than international law. Recall that the volume of sovereign borrowing under treaty in recent decades is tiny. Conversely, debtor states are unlikely to be able to rely successfully on necessity—a concept as it presently exists in customary international law that is ill-suited to the financial realm. Finally, debtor state conduct in debt restructurings was examined. Just like the conduct of creditors, the conduct of debtors has historically been guided by extra-legal factors, such as a desire to guarantee access to the global debt markets. Here too, the requisite *opinio juris* for a customary obligation to arise is lacking.

This chapter limited itself to those Principles supported by a body of state practice. Those that were not examined are the provisions that have less support in existing state practice. These Principles are hence much more in the nature of contributing to the progressive development of international standards on sovereign debt, and typically would take effect via the domestic legal system or changes in borrowing and lending practices. These include Principles 2, 3, 4, 5, 10,

[121] <http://www.unctad.info/en/Debt-Portal/News-Archive/Our-News/Principles-on-sovereign-lending-and-borrowing-UNCTAD-kick-starts-endorsement-process-Doha-22-April->.

[122] <http://www.unctad.info/en/Debt-Portal/News-Archive/Our-News/Parliamentary-Support-of-the-Principles-on-Responsible-Sovereign-Lending-and-Borrowing-23112011>.

11, 12, and 13, which aim at instituting notions of transparency and due diligence into sovereign debt dealings.

UNCTAD's non-binding Principles could be an important catalyst for change in sovereign borrowing and lending practices. They promise to guide conduct in an area of international relations previously left largely to the domestic sphere, but one that is increasingly of international concern. Adherence by states and creditors to these written principles could be monitored by independent third parties, such as UNCTAD or civil society. This channel of accountability could in due course create domestic constituencies that support moving away from discretion in sovereign debt restructurings. On this basis, the formulation of binding international rules regulating sovereign lending and borrowing may become feasible.

6

On the Comparative Foundations of Principles in International Law

The Move towards Rules and Transparency in Fiscal Policy as Examples

*Matthias Goldmann**

A. Introduction

The UNCTAD Principles on Promoting Responsible Sovereign Lending and Borrowing (the UNCTAD Principles) constitute a soft law instrument endorsed by an international organization and a growing number of states. This raises the question of their legal status.[1] While the legal nature of soft law has been under dispute for decades,[2] there might be more to the UNCTAD Principles, or at least to some of them, than just soft law. A few of them might reflect customary law, although state practice appears to be inconsistent in many respects.[3] Others might express general principles of law in the sense of Article 38(1)(c) of the Statute of the ICJ, or different kinds of principles which remain below this threshold. This contribution deals with such principles. It requires first some theoretical considerations about the nature of general and other principles of law, their status, and establishment. They emerge in a gradual manner from a convergence of domestic public and private law, which might be reinforced by international soft law codifications. This requires studying domestic legal systems in a comparative perspective, which is the object of a longer survey that has been prepared for UNCTAD.[4] In this chapter, I explain the taxonomy of principles and the

* This chapter draws considerably on a study I wrote for UNCTAD entitled 'Responsible Sovereign Lending and Borrowing: The View from Domestic Jurisdictions. A Comparative Survey', available at <http://www.unctad.info/upload/Debt%20Portal/RSLB_MGoldmann_02-2012.pdf> (accessed 16 January 2013). I would like to thank all colleagues mentioned in that document who helped me in its preparation. I am grateful to Silvia Steininger for editorial assistance.

[1] On this issue see also J.P. Bohoslavsky and C. Espósito, Ch. 4 of this volume.

[2] See M. Goldmann, 'We Need to Cut Off the Head of the King: Past, Present, and Future Approaches to International Soft Law' (2012) 25 LJIL 335.

[3] See M. Waibel, Ch. 5 of in this volume.

[4] See note* to this chapter.

methodology used for their establishment in the survey (section B.). Afterwards, I analyse convergence in two matters of fiscal policy, namely transparency in fiscal policy-making (section C.), and substantive restrictions to borrowing (section D.). I have selected these two fields for this contribution because the UNCTAD Principles reflect and reinforce important international trends in both of them.

B. General and Not So General Principles in International Law

This section argues that from the perspective of legal theory, legal principles are nothing but legal rules of a more abstract, general character, not a category of norms that would be logically different from rules (section B.I.). In international law, one should distinguish various types of principles besides general principles of law (section B.II.). The establishment of general principles or other forms of principles in international law is facilitated by studies in comparative law (section B.III.).

I. Legal theory: rules and principles

Although the concept of 'principles' enjoys widespread usage in domestic and international law and legal discourse, its meaning has been subject to a major dispute among legal theorists. The controversy revolves around the distinction between rules and principles. Since the norms[5] stipulated in the UNCTAD Principles are designated as 'principles', it seems worthwhile inquiring into the nature of principles from a theoretical vantage point.

The dispute over the distinction between rules and principles confronts positivist and non-positivist scholars. It originates in the claim of positivists like H.L.A. Hart that law is adequately described as a system of primary and secondary legal rules.[6] Non-positivist scholars like Ronald Dworkin have argued that judges do not apply legal rules in a mechanical, syllogistic fashion. Rather, as Kant established, rules cannot determine the conditions of their own application to facts. This requires a meta-rule.[7] Dworkin finds such meta-rules in the interpretive practice of courts, which determine the meaning of a certain legal rule in the light of 'principles' or 'policies'; the former expressing fundamental requirements of justice or fairness of the community, the latter social, economic, or other political objectives.[8]

Dworkin is of the opinion that legal rules and principles are two categorically different types of norms. In the case of two conflicting rules, one rule categorically prevails over the other, while in the case of conflicting principles, the prevalence of one or the other depends on the specific circumstances of the situation.[9] Based on Dworkin, Robert Alexy even goes as far as to consider principles as 'commands

[5] I use 'norm' as a general term comprising both rules and principles, legal and non-legal ones.

[6] HLA Hart, *The Concept of Law* (2nd edn, Oxford University Press, 1961) 79ff.

[7] I. Kant, *Kritik der reinen Vernunft* (2nd edn, Preussische Akademie der Wissenschaften, 1900) 131ff.

[8] R. Dworkin, *Taking Rights Seriously* (Duckworth, 1977) 22.

[9] Dworkin (n. 8) 24–6.

to be optimized', i.e. as values which need to be weighted and balanced against each other, whereas rules must be fully obeyed as long as they are valid.[10]

Although the distinction between rules and principles allows a good grasp of the interpretive work required by judges and other law appliers, one might have doubts about both the amalgamation of principles with values as proposed by Alexy, and the categorical distinction between rules and principles on which Dworkin insists. As regards the idea of principles as value-laden goals requiring optimization, Jürgen Habermas has pointed out that this would charge courts with the task of assigning a specific weight to each value that enters the equation in a specific case. This would be incompatible with the idea of a liberal, pluralistic society characterized by disagreement about the significance of specific values. Therefore, Habermas considers principles as abstract, general types of legal norms.[11] This, however, causes the categorical distinction between rules and principles to collapse. As H.L.A. Hart had emphasized in response to Dworkin, principles are only slightly different from rules in that they are relatively more abstract and general, not categorically different.[12] Dworkin implicitly concedes that rules and principles differ only to a small extent when he elaborates that it might often be difficult to figure out whether a certain norm is a rule or a principle.[13]

Thus, for the purposes of this contribution, I take principles to be just another form of rules, although of a rather abstract and general character. They may serve as guidelines for the interpretation of other, more specific rules, especially if they are in conflict with one another. They may further guide the application of rules by analogy. But it is also possible to base an argument about the legality of a certain act on its conformity with a specific legal principle. For example, while some acts might be more or less respectful of basic rule of law principles like due process rights, other acts might be qualified as illegal for violating that very principle.

II. Taxonomy: the legal status of principles in international law

While general principles of law in the sense of Article 38(1)(c) of the ICJ Statute are an integral part of binding international law, it does not seem that all stipulations contained in the UNCTAD Principles reach this threshold.[14] This, however, does not render them legally insignificant. There are a host of other functions and corresponding legal statuses that principles might have in a legal system. In this respect, I use the following taxonomy of legal principles, which is based on a proposal by Armin von Bogdandy.[15]

[10] R. Alexy, 'On the Structure of Legal Principles' (2000) 13 *Ratio Juris* 294; R. Alexy, Theorie der Grundrechte (2nd edn, Suhrkamp, 1994) 75–7.

[11] J. Habermas, *Faktizität und Geltung* (Suhrkamp, 1992) 255, 309–17.

[12] Hart (n. 6) 260ff. (Postscript).

[13] Dworkin (n. 8) 27.

[14] An overview of the current legal status of each UNCTAD Principle is reproduced in the Annex to this chapter.

[15] This largely follows the taxonomy proposed by A. von Bogdandy, 'General Principles of International Public Authority: Sketching a Research Field' (2008) 9 German L.J. 1909, 1910ff.

Some principles reflect existing international law, in particular *general principles of law* in the sense of Article 38(1)(c) of the Statute of the ICJ. Despite their bias in favour of a universalistic understanding of international law as a legal order,[16] general principles have been recognized as a proper source of international law—at least since the adoption of the ICJ Statute.[17] This is why Koskenniemi designates them as 'normative' general principles.[18] They are usually extrapolated from domestic legal orders by means of analogical and comparative reasoning.[19] Most legal orders should be familiar with a principle considered to be a general principle, but not necessarily all.[20] In addition, general principles of law typically appear in diverse legal orders such as international, supranational, and domestic ones. Principles which are contingent upon the existence of specific institutions which only exist on the domestic level may not be considered general principles.[21] For example, basic parliamentary practices, even though in use in all democratically elected parliaments, may hardly become general principles, because they might be inapplicable on the international level. A further indicator for the existence of a general principle of law is its applicability both in public law and private law contexts, even though this criterion should not be overstretched, since the distinction itself as well as its significance varies from one legal order to another.

From general principles of law in the previously-described sense, Koskenniemi distinguishes what he designates as *'descriptive' general principles*.[22] Such principles are considered to be implicit in other rules of international law and therefore do not constitute a source of international law of their own. Those principles represent more or less the international law equivalent of the principles Dworkin has in mind in the context of his interpretive theory of law. Of course, it would be mistaken to overlook the synthetic character of such principles. They are interpretations of existing international legal rules. Semantic pragmatism teaches that the meaning of language, and thus of legal rules, is determined by their usage in a specific context.[23] This approach finds increasing support in international legal scholarship.[24] On this basis, each interpretation of the law with respect to a specific context both confirms

[16] R. Kolb, *La bonne foi en droit international public* (Presses Universitaires de France, 2003) 24–5.

[17] Before, the legal status of general principles was heavily disputed, see A. Verdross, 'Les principes généraux de droit dans le système des sources du droit international public' in Université de Genève, Faculté de Droit, *Recueil d'etudes de droit international en hommage à Paul Guggenheim* (Imprimerie de la Tribune, 1968) 521, 521–2.

[18] M. Koskenniemi, 'General Principles: Reflexions on Constructivist Thinking in International Law' in M. Koskenniemi (ed.), *Sources of International Law* (Ashgate, 2000) 360, 364–5.

[19] H. Lauterpacht, *Private Law Sources and Analogies of International Law* (first published 1927, Archon, Hambden, 1977) 67ff. From this type of general principle of law, one needs to distinguish general principles of international law, cf. G. Gaja, 'General Principles' (2007) MPEPIL paras 17ff. They are not relevant for this study.

[20] According to Gaja (n. 19) paras 16, the ICJ is reluctant to recognize general principles when this would require controversial discussions of comparative law.

[21] V.D. Degan, *Sources of International Law* (Martinus Nijhoff, 1997) 103.

[22] M. Koskenniemi (n. 18) 365–6.

[23] L. Wittgenstein, *Tractatus logico-philosophicus. Tagebücher 1914–1916. Philosophische Untersuchungen* (16th edn, Suhrkamp, 2004) 262 (§ 43).

[24] From the recent literature, see J. d'Aspremont, *Formalism and the Sources of International Law. A Theory of the Ascertainment of Legal Rules* (Oxford University Press, 2011) 198–9; I. Venzke, *How*

and further develops the meaning of the applied norm. Since these rules should therefore better be understood as constructions on the basis of existing international legal rules, rather than as discoveries of their inherent content, it might be difficult, if not futile, to properly distinguish them from 'normative' general principles in case the latter can be derived both from international and domestic legal practice.

Apart from general principles in their normative and descriptive variant, modern legal orders are characterized by various types of non-binding principles. This would open the discussion on the legal status of soft law. Since this issue cannot be dealt with here conclusively, I confine myself to stating that I generally consider international soft law to be a form of law, though distinct from binding international law, and that one should distinguish different types of soft law by virtue of a set of formal parameters such as their source. This reveals their effective authority.[25]

The UNCTAD Principles, as a compendium of stipulated norms, represent one such type of soft law. They constitute an act of an international organization seeking 'soft' adherence by states. Such adherence should be considered 'soft', since it does not seem to be intended to trigger in case of breach the same consequences as a breach of a binding rule of international law. Despite their soft nature, the authority of the UNCTAD Principles is strengthened by the inclusive, deliberative character of the process that led to their adoption.[26]

But in addition to the soft legal character shared by all of the UNCTAD Principles, some of the provisions in this document might represent other types of soft principles. One of them might be characterized as *guiding principles*, i.e. standards enjoying broad, though not necessarily universal acceptance in domestic and/or international legal orders. In contrast to general principles of law, their application might be more controversial. In that respect, they might constitute a step in the development of new general principles of law. But apart from that, guiding principles can also relate to a particular sector or institution of domestic or international legal orders which has no equivalent on the other level, such as the previously-mentioned parliamentary practices, or specific rules addressing international relations. It would be misleading to consider such rules as general principles 'of law', implying that they exist in every (modern) legal order. Analagous to general principles of law, guiding principles might be derived from domestic law, or extrapolated from other international soft law. One might designate the former as 'normative guiding principles' and the latter as 'descriptive guiding principles'. But in accordance with what has been said about semantic pragmatism, not only would

Interpretation Makes International Law. On Semantic Change and Normative Twists (Oxford University Press, 2012) 30.

[25] M. Goldmann, 'Inside Relative Normativity: From Sources to Standard Instruments for the Exercise of International Public Authority' (2008) 9 German L.J. 1865.

[26] On the significance of inclusion and deliberation for the legitimacy of acts of international organizations, see A. von Bogdandy, 'The European Lesson for International Democracy: The Significance of Articles 9–12 EU Treaty for International Organizations' (2012) 23 Eur. J. Int'l L. 315, 325ff., 331ff.

the term 'descriptive' be misleading, it would also be very difficult to distinguish one form from the other, since indications for guiding principles will often appear in domestic as well as international legal systems. In any case, designating a provision of the UNCTAD Principles as a guiding principle would strengthen its authority.[27]

From guiding principles, I distinguish what I call *emerging principles*. In contrast to guiding principles, they express trends rather than settled convictions. They are about to gain support among domestic and/or international legal orders, but their acceptance may not yet have reached the dimensions required for guiding principles. The authoritative character of emerging principles is therefore more limited.

Finally, *structural principles* is a category used to describe an empirical regularity, without attributing a specific normative preference to it. It is therefore a category that guides the analysis and understanding of a legal order, but does not possess a legal character or represent an emerging trend. For the purposes of this contribution, for a rule to amount to a structural principle, it needs to exist in several legal orders, yet without reflecting a clear trend or normative preference. Usually, structural principles emerge when domestic legal orders feature a number of divergent solutions to a specific problem.

The comparative survey carried out on the UNCTAD Principles has revealed that the legal status of its individual provisions usually ranges between that of general principles of law and structural principles. An overview of the results is reproduced in the annex to this chapter. One should not imagine these characterizations and therefore the relationship among the various provisions of the UNCTAD Principles to be fixed. Rather, principles move up and down as a function of changes to the domestic and international legal orders, making the qualification of a certain principle at a given time a challenging task. In this respect, the implementation of the UNCTAD Principles in domestic legal orders might have an impact on the status of some of their provisions in international law.[28]

III. Methodology: comparative law and analogies

How can the legal status of the provisions of the UNCTAD Principles be established according to the taxonomy developed in the preceding section? This is a daunting task requiring comparative research and analogical reasoning.

Establishing the existence of a general principle of law requires comparative legal analysis showing its existence in a wide variety of legal orders.[29] Comparative law is about comparing functions, not terminologies. It rests on the conviction that every legal system deals with fundamentally similar economic, political, and social problems.[30] Certainly, it is not easy to identify similar economic, political, or social

[27] See also J.P. Bohoslavsky and C. Espósito, Ch. 4 of this volume.

[28] cf. A. Gelpern, Ch. 16 of this volume.

[29] L.C. Green, 'Comparative Law as a "Source" of International Law' (1967–68) 42 Tul. L. Rev. 52.

[30] See K. Zweigert and H. Kötz, *An Introduction to Comparative Law* (3rd edn, Clarendon Press, 1998) 34ff.

problems. What looks similar at first sight might have different implications in different societies. Also, different legal rules for similar problems might stem from different cultural traditions or epistemological structures, which the functional approach tends to overlook.[31] However, in the case of public debt issues, such difficulties of comparative law are mitigated by the fact that the legal framework for public debt instruments is relatively homogeneous all over the world, and that cultural differences are considerably less significant for budgeting rules than for family or criminal law. Also, sovereign debt crises are administered by a number of international institutions, some formal, like the IMF, others informal like the Paris and London Clubs. It therefore seems possible to identify similar structures and functions and to compare the laws applicable to them, even though the markets for developed and developing states' debt differ in certain respects, especially with regard to the applicable law.

This chapter, as well as the aforementioned larger comparative survey, mainly compares law as a normative phenomenon, i.e. as legislation, rule-making, and adjudication, and not as social reality. One could criticize it for this blindness towards social reality. Certainly, the actual role of law and its relationship with politics might be different from one society to another.[32] However, the purpose of this chapter and the comparative survey is predominantly normative. It asks to what extent the principles reflect existing *normative convictions*, not necessarily existing *social reality*. To that effect, the comparative survey was based on reports from 15 jurisdictions, which were chosen to compile an adequate representation of developing, emerging, and developed economies, as well as lenders and borrowers.[33]

Together with comparative legal research, one might take recourse to analogies in order to establish whether some provisions of the UNCTAD Principles constitute general principles of international law, or at least guiding principles. The contribution by von Bogdandy and Goldmann demonstrates the need for analogical reasoning.[34] In domestic contexts, with the exception of criminal law, courts usually use analogies in order to fill lacunae in the law. An analogy requires (1) a lacuna in the positive law which appears to be normatively inconsistent; (2) and a second legal rule which appears to be normatively appropriate to fill the lacuna by virtue of a general principle expressed in that second rule.[35] In international law, there is an intrinsic connection between analogies and general principles of law. Unless the latter originate genuinely on the international level, they consist of

[31] On cultural differences, see J. Bell, 'Comparative Law and Legal Theory' in W. Krawietz, N. MacCormick, and G.H. von Wright (eds), *Prescriptive Formality and Normative Rationality in Modern Legal Systems* (Duncker & Humblot, 1995) 23, 26; on structural differences, see G. Samuel, 'Comparative Law and Jurisprudence', (1998) 47 ICLQ 818, 827ff.

[32] cf. U. Mattei, 'Three Patterns of Law: Taxonomy and Change in the World's Legal System' (1997) 45 Am. J. Comp. L. 5, 12ff.

[33] Argentina, Brazil, Chile, China, Egypt, France, Germany, India, Japan, Mexico, Nigeria, Russia, Tanzania, the United Kingdom, and the United States.

[34] A. von Bogdandy and M. Goldmann, Ch. 3 of this volume.

[35] K. Larenz and C.-W. Canaris, *Methodenlehre* (3rd edn, Springer, 1995) 202ff. For a powerful defence of analogical reasoning, see L.L. Weinreb, *Legal Reason. The Use of Analogy in Legal Argument* (Cambridge University Press, 2005) 65ff.

extrapolations of widely shared concepts of domestic private or public law to the international level.[36] For example, the concept of estoppel, usually considered a general principle of law, was derived from domestic legal orders where it enjoys almost universal acceptance, albeit with varying terminology. Comparative law is thus at the basis of such general principles. It is a prerequisite for any transfer of legal principles from domestic law to the international level by way of analogy.

Some international lawyers have doubted that analogies in international law are permissible. They fear that analogies might unduly extend international obligations to which states have given their consent.[37] The International Court of Justice (ICJ), by contrast, has taken recourse to analogies in a number of cases. For example, in the *Nicaragua* case, it applied principles of treaty law to unilateral declarations pursuant to Article 36(2) of its Statute.[38] Indeed, analogies appear to be necessary elements of every legal order. They are almost inevitable since it is impossible to lay down a specific rule for every case which may ever arise.[39]

However, analogical reasoning has its limits. Explicit conventional or customary rules might render impossible the analogical application of a rule with the opposite content. Also, the specific institutional context of domestic and international levels of government need to be taken into account when considering whether an analogy might be appropriate, or whether the widespread acceptance of a rule in domestic legal orders might justify considering it as the expression of a general principle of law.

The preceding methodological remarks should reveal the contingency of analyses in comparative law and the extrapolation of their results to the international level.[40] Nevertheless, if legal scholarship engages in a transparent, rational discourse which is open to criticism, it might render its exercise in 'doctrinal constructivism' by way of comparative and analogical reasoning acceptable for a wider audience, and in particular those affected by the principles effectively created.[41]

C. Transparency in Fiscal Policy-making (Principle 10)

After the theoretical overture, the remainder of this contribution seeks to put theory into practice and demonstrate the construction of principles by way of comparative

[36] cf. Lauterpacht (n. 19) 60ff.

[37] e.g. D. Anzilotti, *Corso di diritto internazionale*, Vol 1 (4th edn, Athenaeum, 1955) 106.

[38] *Case concerning Military and Paramilitary Activities in and against Nicaragua* (Jurisdiction and Admissibility) (1984) ICJ Rep. 392, 420; for further examples, see A. Bleckmann, 'Analogie im Völkerrecht' (1977–78) 17 *Archiv des Völkerrechts* 161; S. Vöneky, 'Analogy in International Law' (2008) MPEPIL paras 7ff.

[39] Weinreb (n. 35) 13.

[40] Criticizing the prevailing practice: J. Ellis, 'General Principles and Comparative Law' (2011) 22 Eur. J. Int'l L. 949.

[41] cf. A. von Bogdandy, 'The Past and Promise of Doctrinal Constructivism: A Strategy for Responding to the Challenges Facing Constitutional Scholarship in Europe' (2009) 7 Int'l J. Const. L. 364, 371ff.

legal research. I begin with a comparative analysis of UNCTAD Principle 10, which addresses transparency requirements for borrowers in fiscal policy.

In the first place, Principle 10 identifies formal requirements for approval and oversight of borrowing. In this respect, this principle is a corollary of Principle 3 on due authorization: lenders may only be obliged to ensure proper authorization on the part of the borrower if the approval process is transparent. Principle 10 has the underlying assumption that legislative involvement may reinforce the transparency of borrowings. In addition, transparent procedures for debt approval might enhance prudential borrowing practices, since this increases the likelihood that unsustainable debt practices will be criticized and stopped. Insofar as this is the case, the idea of transparency relates closely to that of responsible borrowing (Principle 14, see later).

The transparency of borrowings touches upon the general issue of fiscal transparency. This topic has received much attention from policy-makers during the last decade. It is the IMF in particular which promotes fiscal transparency among its members.[42] Its programme for fiscal transparency relates to both the decision-making process and the transparency of fiscal data (Principle 11). Many of the countries under examination have made their fiscal process more transparent over the last few years. In particular, emerging countries have adopted fiscal responsibility laws which strengthen transparency and accountability in the decision-making process.[43] The European Union recently adopted the European semester, an *ex ante* review of domestic budget proposals at the Union level.[44] In the light of these developments, which leave almost none of the states under consideration in the aforementioned comparative survey unaffected, one might speak of a guiding principle of transparency in fiscal policy-making. Issues of particular significance for the transparency of the decision-making process include the involvement of the legislature (section C.I.), mid-term financial frameworks (section C.II.), and transparency on the level of sub-state entities (section C.III.).

I. Influence of the legislature

In all examined jurisdictions, the legislature is involved in the adoption of the budget and the approval of borrowings. Beyond that general level, however, there are significant differences. As regards the approval of the budget, the relationship between the legislative and executive powers varies from one jurisdiction to another. In most jurisdictions under examination, and in particular in the United States,[45] the legislative bodies play a central role in the adoption of the budget. France's 2001 organic law on financial bills expanded the powers of parliament. It is

[42] e.g. IMF (2007) Manual on Fiscal Transparency.

[43] cf. I. Lienert, 'Should Advanced Countries Adopt a Fiscal Responsibility Law?,' IMF Working Paper No. 254 (2010).

[44] Regulation 1466/97 as amended by Regulation 1175/2011, Art 2a [2011] OJ L306/12ff.

[45] Regarding its budgetary powers, Congress has been characterized as the most powerful parliament in the world. Cf. J.R. Blöndal, D.-J. Kraan and M. Ruffner, 'Budgeting in the United States' (2003) 3 OECD J. Budgeting 18.

now entitled to receive detailed information and performance estimates about proposed expenses from the executive in the course of the budgeting process. Except for the United States, jurisdictions with bicameral legislatures tend to concentrate budgeting powers in one chamber.[46]

By contrast, in some jurisdictions, the role of the legislature is a more reactive one. For example, in Chile, the budget proposal is considered approved unless parliament vetoes it within 60 days. In India, parliament needs to approve the annual financial statement, but may not modify certain items. In the United Kingdom, the executive could in principle accrue expenses without parliamentary approval, but the influence of parliament is guaranteed by its exclusive right to levy taxes. In this way, parliament may only decrease expenditures proposed by the government. Government presents a budget report twice a year, which includes data on spending and debt. There is no budgeting committee for *ex ante* examinations of the budget.[47] In China, the National Peoples' Congress adopts the budget, but may not amend it. While additional revenues do not require budget amendments, additional debt always needs legislative approval.[48]

Beyond these differences, in many of the jurisdictions examined, the budget is concretized in a process extending over various stages from pre-budget proposals to the final vote (if applicable). Also, the budgets of the examined jurisdictions generally included the budgets of the armed forces. One exception is Chile, whose armed forces are entitled to 10 per cent of the revenues of the state-owned copper mining company, which are kept off the budget. However, in 2011, a Bill was introduced in order to abolish this privilege. By contrast, Article 197 of the new Egyptian constitution gives the National Defense Council the right to prepare the budget of the armed forces, while the House of Representatives only approves an overall budget.

Like the annual budget, decisions about the incurrence of debt and the extension of official guarantees are subject to legislative approval in practically all jurisdictions under examination. Such approvals are sometimes made in connection with the adoption of the annual budget law. Notable exceptions to this rule are India and the United Kingdom, where public debt, strictly speaking, does not require legislative approval. However, in both jurisdictions, parliament has indirect control over public debt through its power over the budgetary process or taxation. In addition, the Indian constitution grants parliament the power to set a debt ceiling, which it has not done yet, and to limit the total amount of official guarantees, of which it has made use.

The extent to which the legislature controls the incurrence of debt also varies. In the United States, Congress has delegated the power to borrow money to the Treasury Department up to a specific debt ceiling. Beyond that, Congress has

[46] I. Lienert and M.-K. Jung, 'The Legal Framework for Budget Systems' (2004) 4 OECD J. Budgeting 70–1.

[47] On budgeting committees, see Lienert and Jung (n. 46) 71–2.

[48] Chinese Budgetary Law, Art. 53. For a detailed analysis see S. Deng and J. Peng, 'Reforming the Budgeting Process in China' (2011) 11 OECD J. Budgeting 75.

imposed a 'pay-as-you-go' rule which is meant to impose self-discipline on congressional spending. After the Gramm-Rudman-Hollings Act of 1985, which set obligatory debt ceilings, had been declared unconstitutional, Congress enacted legislation requiring every legislative project creating expenses or cuts in revenues not provided for in the budget to identify a source of funding.[49] Pay-as-you-go later became a House and Senate rule and has been reintroduced with broad exceptions into legislation in 2010.[50] So far, the rule has not prevented aggregate debt from rising, making it necessary to raise the Congressional debt ceiling repeatedly. A similar pay-as-you-go rule applies in Argentina. In Germany, the federal government may veto any legislative project which reduces revenues or causes costs not provided for in the current budget.[51] However, it should not come as a surprise that this rule remained largely without any practical impact in a parliamentary system of government.

In the United Kingdom, the Treasury enjoys considerable discretion regarding the issue of bills and loans. By contrast, in Brazil, the Chamber of Deputies has to approve each tranche specifically within an overall debt limit set by the Senate. In Germany, the Constitutional Court decided in 2011 that not only does the total amount of guarantees extended to credit operations by international institutions require parliamentary approval, but the budget committee also needs to approve of each credit facility set up by such institution with the consent of the German government, provided that it involves considerable financial risks for Germany.[52] In Chile, the legislative approval of debt with maturities exceeding the presidential term requires a higher majority.

A minority of the jurisdictions under examination allow the executive to have recourse to emergency borrowings under certain, restrictive conditions.[53] Most jurisdictions, however, require such borrowings to be subject to parliamentary approval.

In summary, since the legislature is involved in borrowings in all jurisdictions under examination, either directly or indirectly by virtue of its power over the budget or taxation, one could speak of a guiding principle. It could not be considered a general principle of law because it hinges on the political system in place in a particular state. Not all UN member states have parliamentary assemblies on the domestic level. Beyond that, there is great variance in detail. In general, it seems that in jurisdictions influenced by the common law, with the notable exception of Nigeria, the legislature plays a more reduced role. Some models, like the pay-as-you-go rule, have the status of structural principles, but are too context-sensitive to be considered as emerging principles.

[49] cf. the Budget Enforcement Act (1990) which succeeded the Gramm-Rudman-Hollings Act and expired in 2002.

[50] Statutory Pay-As-You-Go Act, 12 February 2010, 111th Congress, Public Law 139.

[51] Basic Law, art. 113(1).

[52] Bundesverfassungsgericht, judgment of 7 September 2011, Case 2 BvR 987/10 et al.

[53] Argentina, Brazil, France, and India. The issue is currently under debate in the US. In the UK, government does not require parliamentary approval for the incurrence of debt.

II. Medium-term financial frameworks

The purpose of medium-term financial frameworks is to make fiscal policy more forward-looking and to guide expectations. Not all countries develop and maintain medium-term financial frameworks as of yet. The more developed economies and some emerging ones now regularly use this planning tool.[54] Sometimes the framework expands over three years, as in the case of Germany or France, and sometimes over five years, as in Mexico, the United Kingdom, and the United States. China and India use five-year plans which contain growth targets, but do not include deficit or debt targets. EU legislation obliges Member States to set up medium-term budgetary frameworks extending over at least three years,[55] to submit stability programmes defining, *inter alia*, a medium-term budgetary objective ranging between -1 per cent of GDP and surplus, as well as adjustment paths towards that objective.[56] Considering the fact that medium-term financial frameworks have gained such popularity during recent decades, one might consider their establishment as an emerging principle.

III. Budget transparency in sub-state entities

Although greater transparency is increasingly required for the budgets of sub-state entities, there is little uniformity in the way this is supposed to be achieved.[57] Among federal states, one can distinguish two competing structural principles. The first is what I call the 'control model' and the second is the 'incentive model'. Under the control model, state debt is subject to federal approvals or debt ceilings.[58] Under the incentive model, federal states enjoy budgetary autonomy, including the right to borrow money. In the United States, instead of mechanisms of control, a strict no-bailout rule imposes budgetary discipline. Germany seems to be moving from the incentive model to the control model. It recently introduced a dynamic constitutional debt ceiling for state budgets.[59] Also, being part of the euro area and subject to its Stability and Growth Pact, there was a need to establish a committee of federal and state governments charged with the task of ensuring overall budgetary stability.[60]

In most examined jurisdictions, the budgets of local governments are subject to governmental approval or supervision.[61] This has proved to be very effective as a

[54] Reported for Germany, France, Chile, Japan, Nigeria, and the UK. In the US, the case is controversial.

[55] Directive 2011/85/EU, Arts 9–10 [2011] OJ L306/41–7.

[56] Regulation 1466/97 as amended by Regulation 1175/2011, Art. 2a [2011] OJ L306/12ff.

[57] This term is meant to comprise federal states, devolved administrations, and local governments.

[58] e.g. Argentina, Brazil, India, and Mexico. Devolved administrations in the UK may only borrow to meet short-term cash flow needs.

[59] See section D.II. of this chapter.

[60] Gesetz zur Errichtung eines Stabilitätsrates und zur Vermeidung von Haushaltsnotlagen, 10 August 2009, BGBl. I (2009) 2702.

[61] e.g. Brazil and Germany.

means for curbing structural deficits.[62] Also, local governments can increase transparency by reaching a decision in town councils or, as in China, local peoples' congresses. To this extent, one might speak of a guiding principle of budgetary supervision.[63]

D. From Discretion to Rules on Borrowing (Principle 14)

I. The debate about rules versus discretion

Principle 14 urges states to keep the total amount of their debt under control and establishes certain proposals to this effect. This recalls the old debate over whether and to what extent macroeconomic policy-making should follow certain specified rules, or should be left to the discretion of policy-makers.

The theory of optimal control argues that policy-makers should always choose the best available option. This militates against rules as guideposts for decision-making, and in favour of discretion allowing a deviation from previous policies under changed circumstances.[64] However, discretionary decision-making involves a number of problems. It is impossible to identify the best available option in a given situation with certainty. Knowledge about future developments suffers from intrinsic uncertainty, because market reactions and government action cannot be predicted.[65] This amounts to an argument in favour of rules for macroeconomic policy: it makes government action more predictable and therefore reduces uncertainty for market participants, thus in turn making their reactions more predictable. The most remarkable example for rules-guided policy-making has been monetary policy-making. Today, many jurisdictions have independent central banks that ensure price stability in accordance with transparent policy rules,[66] such as the Taylor rule.[67] The move towards rules on price stability is generally considered a success and an appropriate means for preventing excessive inflation or deflation.[68]

Some argue that fiscal policy should follow this example.[69] Enhancing the credibility of policy-making might avoid market disturbances and lower financing costs.[70] Also, rules-based fiscal policy would provide a bar to special interests of

[62] U. Wagschal, 'Allheilmittel oder Budgetmimikry: Wie wirksam sind Verschuldungsgrenzen zur Haushaltskonsolidierung?' (2011) 9 J. Comp. Gov. & Eur. Pol'y 352, 361.

[63] This principle had not been identified in the comparative survey, see note* to this chapter.

[64] Cautiously advocating such an approach: S. Fisher, 'Dynamic Inconsistency, Cooperation and the Benevolent Dissembling Government' (1980) 2 J. Comp. Gov. & Eur. Pol'y 93.

[65] F.E. Kydland and E.C. Prescott, 'Rules Rather than Discretion: The Inconsistency of Optimal Plans' (1977) 5 J. Pol. Econ. 473.

[66] The most prominent example is probably the European Central Bank, cf. Art. 127(1) TFEU.

[67] J.B. Taylor, 'Discretion versus Policy Rules in Practice', Carnegie-Rochester Conference Series on Public Policy (1993) 195–214.

[68] cf. Remarks by Governor Ben S. Bernanke before the National Economists Club, Washington, D.C., 21 November 2002, on file with the author.

[69] e.g. C. Wyplosz, 'Fiscal Policy: Institutions versus Rules' (2005) 191 National Institute Economic Review 64; J.B. Taylor, 'Reassessing Discretionary Fiscal Policy' (2000) 14 JEP 21.

[70] G. Kopits and S. Symansky, 'Fiscal Policy Rules', International Monetary Fund Occasional Papers No. 162 (1998) 6ff.

elected representatives and provide a counterweight to their short-term interests in the benefits of deficit spending.[71] Fiscal policy rules constitute a means to achieve intergenerational justice, since future generations have no voice even in the most transparent and representative decision-making processes. Also, as the European sovereign debt crisis has amply shown, increasingly global markets might allow financial turmoil to spread into other jurisdictions. On the other hand, fiscal policy rules have a price. They might weaken the decision-making power of democratically elected representative bodies and reduce the flexibility necessary for crisis management. Empirical evidence about the success of fiscal policy rules is relatively scarce and reveals a mixed pattern.[72]

II. The move towards rules on borrowing

Principle 14 picks up an important trend in practice. A growing number of states have adopted substantive rules intended to keep borrowing at a sustainable level.[73] There seems to be the conviction that procedural safeguards, such as those addressed by Principle 10, might not suffice to protect states against excessive debt. The nature and content of these substantive provisions varies greatly. In some states, debt or deficit ceilings are included in the constitution or in legislation. Other jurisdictions have introduced debt ceilings in the form of non-binding commitments. The content of these rules sometimes reflects diverging fiscal policy approaches. While some rules are relatively rigid, others allow for more flexibility in counter-cyclical spending. This section focuses on the main models in use in the jurisdictions under examination, namely the Golden Rule and numerical debt ceilings.[74]

1. The Golden Rule

Strictly speaking, the Golden Rule addresses expenditure. Usually, it states that debt may only be incurred for investments which generate revenues exceeding the cost of financing. In Nigeria, government may only borrow for capital expenditures and human development at low interest rates and with reasonably long amortization periods.[75] In the United Kingdom, an informal Golden Rule applies which

[71] W.R. Keech, 'Rules, Discretion, and Accountability in Macroeconomic Policymaking' (1992) 5 Governance 259, 268.

[72] Sceptical: U. Wagschal (n. 62); A. Schick, 'Post-Crisis Fiscal Rules: Stabilising Public Finance while Responding to Economic Aftershocks' (2010) 10(2) OECD J. Budgeting 1; more optimistic: A. Fatás and I. Mihov, 'The Case for Restricting Fiscal Policy Discretion' (2003) 118 Quarterly Journal of Economics 1419; A. Alesina and T. Bayoumi, 'The Costs and Benefits of Fiscal Rules: Evidence from U.S. States', National Bureau of Economic Research Working Paper No. 5619 (1996); identifying contextual factors as reasons for success or failure: P. Manasse, 'Deficit Limits, Budget Rules and Fiscal Policy', IMF Working Paper No. 120 (2005).

[73] Some countries include those rules in their fiscal responsibility laws. However, fiscal responsibility laws are mainly about issues of transparency and accountability, cf. Lienert (n. 43).

[74] For further approaches, cf. Wagschal (n. 62) 358ff.; Schick n. 72.

[75] Fiscal Responsibility Act (No. 31, 2007), s. 41.

requires government to borrow only for investments and not in order to fund structural deficits. The Mexican constitution allows deficit spending for projects which directly increase public revenue, but otherwise contains a zero deficit rule. An exemption applies in case of national emergencies.[76] The constitution of Brazil also contains a Golden Rule, but exempts borrowings approved by parliament for specific, defined purposes from its scope of application.[77]

The German constitution contained a Golden Rule from the late 1960s until 2009. Like many others, it did not prevent an enormous increase in public debt during that period. In the opinion of some observers, the Golden Rule suffered, first, from an overly broad definition of 'capital expenditure', which included expenditures not generating any direct revenue, if at all, and secondly, from generous exceptions for periods of general economic deterioration as well as for separate budgets.[78]

2. *Numerical debt or deficit ceilings*

Since the Golden Rule and other expenditure rules do not set an overall limit to debt or budget deficits, many jurisdictions have adopted numerical debt or deficit ceilings (the latter are sometimes called balanced budget rules). Some of them are defined in absolute terms. For example, US legislation establishes a fixed debt ceiling without reference to any economic indicators. However, as Congress may lift this limit if the need arises, the rule, just as the pay-as-you-go rule mentioned earlier in relation to Principle 10, is at the crossroads of procedural and substantive rules. It primarily serves to restrict the authority of the Treasury to issue debt without congressional approval.

Other ceilings are referenced to macroeconomic indicators. For example, the European Stability and Growth Pact and the rules on budgetary discipline stipulated in Article 126(2) of the Treaty on the Functioning of the European Union cap budgetary deficits at 3 per cent of GDP and aggregate debt at 60 per cent of GDP. Economic deteriorations might justify larger debt ratios.[79] Following the EU example, Mercosur established similar numerical targets of 3 per cent of GDP for annual deficit and 40 per cent of GDP for overall deficit in 2000;[80] and the Andean Community followed a year later with targets of 3 per cent and 50 per cent

[76] Mexican Constitution, art 73(8). Additional exceptions apply for monetary policy and conversion operations.

[77] Constitution of Brazil, art. 167(3).

[78] The concept of capital expenditure ('Investition') is defined in German Law on Budgetary Principles (Haushaltsgrundsätzegesetz), s. 10(3), No. 2. Among others, capital expenditures comprise expenditures for all construction projects and for all credits extended by the federal government, whatever public revenue or other economic benefit they may generate, if at all. The previous version of Art. 115(2) contained an exception for separate budgets.

[79] The meaning of these terms is specified in Regulation 1467/97, as amended by Regulation 1056/2005.

[80] Declaración presidencial sobre metas y mecanismos de convergencia macroeconómica, Florianópolis Summit, 15 December 2000, on file with the author.

respectively.[81] Those targets were stipulated in a presidential declaration and a report. These documents are not legally binding, although they are of the highest political significance.

Many emerging and developed economies have adopted such referenced numerical debt or deficit ceilings. The Indian Financial Responsibility and Budget Management Act obliges government to reduce the fiscal deficit to 3 per cent of GDP, and the revenue deficit to zero by 2008–09. This target has not been met. The last two Finance Commissions, a constitutional body convoked every five years, recommended non-binding aggregate debt ceilings of 75 per cent and 68 per cent of GDP respectively. Brazil, Nigeria, and the United Kingdom have committed to numerical debt ceilings in addition to their Golden Rules. In Brazil, the Senate has set the aggregate debt ceiling at 60 per cent of current net revenues. In the United Kingdom, the non-binding Sustainable Investment Rule requires government to keep debt at a level of 40 per cent of GDP.[82] The 2010 Fiscal Responsibility Act stipulates targets for the reduction of net borrowings and net debt until 2016.

Numerical debt or deficit ceilings do not need to use GDP as a point of reference. In fact, this might be a problematic indicator for developing states with a large informal sector where GDP is neither easy to measure, nor a good indicator for public revenue. Thus, the Tanzanian debt ceiling is set at a ratio of the country's foreign exchange earnings, and the aggregate service cost may not exceed 30 per cent of the average annual recurrent revenue.[83]

Since the time around the outbreak of the financial crisis, there has been a trend towards more flexible numerical debt or deficit ceilings, which include exceptions for catastrophies and times of crisis, making them increasingly complex.[84] An early example is the Nigerian Fiscal Responsibility Act. Accordingly, the aggregate fiscal deficit shall not exceed 3 per cent of the estimated GDP or any level deemed sustainable by the National Assembly. The ceiling may be exceeded if the President determines the presence of a threat to national security.[85] In the light of its mixed experience with the Golden Rule, Germany opted for a cyclically adjusted, flexible numerical deficit ceiling in 2009 modelled after a Swiss rule from 2001. Accordingly, the cyclically adjusted annual net budget deficit may not exceed 0.35 per cent of nominal GDP. The deficit may be larger during cyclical downturns, but such additional debt needs to be levelled out during times of economic prosperity. Actual deficits in excess of the limit allowed under this rule need to be tracked and consolidated once their sum exceeds 1.5 per cent of GDP.[86] An exception from

[81] Final Report of the Fifth Regular Meeting of the Andean Community Advisory Council of Treasury or Finance Ministers, Central Banks, and Economic Planning Officers, 21 June 2001, para. 4, available at <http://www.comunidadandina.org/ingles/documentos/documents/caracas21-6-01.htm> (accessed 16 January 2013).

[82] cf. HM Treasury, Code for Fiscal Stability (1998) 16.

[83] Government Loans, Guarantee and Grants Act of 1974, as amended in 2003, s. 3.

[84] A. Schaechter, T. Kinda, N. Budina, and A. Weber, 'Fiscal Rules in Response to the Crisis—Toward the "Next Generation" Rules. A New Dataset', IMF Working Paper No. 187 (2012).

[85] Fiscal Responsibility Act (No. 31, 2007), s. 12.

[86] Basic Law, arts 109(3) and 115(2).

these limits applies in case of natural disasters.[87] The proceeds arising from new debt are not subject to any restrictions. Some of the concepts of this rule are unclear. The effectiveness of the rule hinges on their interpretation.[88]

While Spain soon followed the German example, in France, a legislative project to introduce a similar debt ceiling did not materialize in 2011. However, in order to reinforce the credibility and implementation of the deficit and debt ceilings under the Stability and Growth Pact, the Member States of the European Union, with the exception of the United Kingdom and the Czech Republic, recently concluded a Treaty on Stability, Coordination and Governance in the Economic and Monetary Union.[89] Since its entry into force in 2013, the Member States have had to adopt constitutional deficit ceilings. The rule required by the Treaty closely follows the German model and obliges states to achieve a balanced budget on a cyclically adjusted basis comprising all levels of government. According to Article 3(1)(b) of the Treaty, a country will be considered to be in compliance with the balanced budget rule if it achieves the medium-term objectives as defined under the Stability and Growth Pact. The cyclically adjusted deficit may not exceed 0.5 per cent of nominal GDP. In contrast to the new German debt ceiling, the Treaty allows for temporary deviations from the balanced budget rule in 'exceptional circumstances', which are defined as an unusual event outside the control of the state. Such deviations may not, however, endanger medium-term fiscal sustainability.[90] The reference to sustainability makes this exception more restrictive than the exception contained in the old German Golden Rule for periods of general economic deterioration. Further, Article 4 of the Treaty, as well as secondary legislation, obliges states to reduce their aggregate debt at an average rate of one-twentieth per year if it exceeds the threshold of 60 per cent of nominal GDP.[91] Failure to comply with recommendations of the Council concerning the prevention or correction of an excessive deficit entails semi-automatic sanctions which can only be avoided by a negative vote of the Council.[92]

Chile has adopted a flexible numerical debt ceiling which is even more ambitious. Under its Structural Balance Policy Rule, higher revenues during periods of prosperity need to be netted out with lower revenues during economic downturns. The rule aims at a surplus of 1 per cent of GDP in order to meet future contingent liabilities, such as guaranteed minimum pensions. The rule was first introduced in 2001. After the successful completion of a trial period as a non-binding commitment, it was cast into legislation in 2006, yet without specifying a surplus target.[93]

[87] Basic Law, art. 115(6). Such debt is conditional upon the adoption of a repayment plan.

[88] For a critical analysis, cf. H. Kube, 'Article 115' in T. Maunz and G. Dürig (eds), *Grundgesetz-Kommentar*, Vol. 7 (Beck, 2009) paras 140ff.

[89] The text of the Treaty is available at <http://european-council.europa.eu/media/639235/st00tscg26_en12.pdf> (accessed 31 May 2013).

[90] Treaty on Stability, Coordination and Governance in the Economic and Monetary Union (n 89) Art. 3(3).

[91] Regulation 1467/1997 as amended by Regulation 1177/2011, Art. 2(1a) [2011] OJ L306/33–40.

[92] Regulation 1173/2011, Arts. 4, 5 and 6 [2011] OJ L306/1–7.

[93] Fiscal Responsibility Law (Law No. 20.128).

So far, the rule has stabilized financial conditions and increased the financial credibility of the Chilean government.[94]

3. Rules for federal and local entities

It is common for federal states to put in place substantive provisions limiting the debt that may be incurred by federal entities. Some of these provisions are the result of sub-national debt crises.[95] Thus, in Argentina, the debt of provinces may not exceed 15 per cent of governmental transfers to these entities. The Brazilian debt ratio applies to all levels of government. The German constitution applies the same numerical debt ceilings to states,[96] and budgetary framework legislation requires all levels of government to spend money in efficient and parsimonious ways.[97] In India, if states owe money to the Union government, they need its consent if they want to incur additional debt.[98] Mexican states are prohibited from taking on external debt and need to register their domestic debt with the federal government. In the United States, federal law does not limit borrowings by states. However, almost all states have adopted some restrictions on debt. There is a great variety of different approaches. Some states require government to propose a balanced budget. In the State of New York, for example, new debt requires a referendum.[99] Other states require supermajorities for new debt.[100] Again, procedural and material restrictions flow into one another. There is a fierce debate about the effectiveness of these rules.[101]

Local governments are often subject to Golden Rules. For example, in Germany, budgets are subject to a Golden Rule allowing only for capital expenditures.[102] China imposed a strict zero deficit rule in 1994, prohibiting local governments from incurring budget deficits or issuing bonds.[103] However, local governments set up highly leveraged investment vehicles. Now that this 'off-balance sheet' debt has reached a critical level, the central government has set up a pilot programme under an exception contained in the 1994 rule in order to facilitate debt management. Shanghai was the first city to issue bonds under this rule.[104]

[94] J. Rodríguez et al., 'Structural Balance Policy in Chile' (2007) 7(2) OECD J. Budgeting 59, 74ff.

[95] L. Liu and M. Waibel, 'Subnational Insolvency: Cross-Country Experiences and Lessons', World Bank Policy Research Working Paper No. 4496 (2008) 3ff.

[96] Basic Law, Art. 109(3).

[97] Law on Budgetary Principles (Haushaltsgrundsätzegesetz), s. 6.

[98] Constitution of India, art. 293(3).

[99] However, this requirement is not considered to apply to debt for capital expenditures by state enterprises.

[100] For an overview, see U. Wagschal (n. 62) 369ff.

[101] e.g. R.P. Inman, 'Do Balanced Budget Rules Work? U.S. Experience and Possible Lessons for the EMU', NBER Working Paper No. 5838 (1998).

[102] e.g. the Law on Local Communities of the State of Baden-Württemberg, s. 87(1).

[103] Budget Law of the People's Republic of China (1994), art. 28.

[104] cf. 'The bounty of the muni: Shanghai borrows in its own name for the first time in decades', *The Economist*, 19 November 2011.

4. *Interim conclusion*

There are strong indications for at least an emerging principle, if not a guiding one, obliging states and other public entities to raise material restrictions to sovereign debt. Not all countries have adopted such policies, but their number is steadily on the rise. Most of these models do not prohibit countercyclical deficit spending. This may be considered a guiding principle. Apart from this, the approaches pursued vary widely. At this time, the Golden Rule, the distinction between numerical ceilings referenced to economic indicators and ceilings without such reference, or the approach falling between flexible and rigid types of numerical ceilings, reflect at best structural principles. This implies that although countries usually follow one or several models, no model may be considered to fit all cases or to be normatively superior. Indeed, some of the models of recent origin still need to pass the test of practice. Rigid rules might have the propensity to cause shocks, while the more recent flexible rules are sometimes difficult to apply or more likely to be abused. This might give a role to international surveillance mechanisms.

III. International surveillance

The introduction of substantive restrictions on borrowing often goes along with the establishment of international mechanisms for surveillance. Member States of the European Union are subject to a budgetary review process under the Stability and Growth Pact.[105] Although the deficits of this process as it currently stands have become notorious, enforcement of the rules of the Pact has now become semi-automatic.[106] The Andean Community set up a surveillance mechanism in 2003 for the fiscal convergence targets of 2001. Apart from these peer review mechanisms, some international organizations provide data analysis. Periodic publications such as the 'IMF Fiscal Monitor', the 'OECD Economic Outlook', as well as 'Government at a Glance' and the 'World Bank Public Expenditure Reviews', provide extensive data and policy analysis. Thus, although the potential of peer review has not been fully explored in all regions of the world, one might speak of an emerging principle. However, any further steps in this direction might have to make precautions in order to safeguard the legitimacy of international surveillance, especially with respect to domestic legislatures. The implementation of Principle 14 should be conducted while bearing in mind other Principles which endorse the goal of legitimacy for borrowing decisions.

E. Conclusion

The comparative law perspective on some provisions of the UNCTAD Principles regulating fiscal policy reveals that the UNCTAD Principles reproduce and confirm

[105] Arts 121, 126(3)–(14) TFEU. [106] See n. 86.

existing trends in domestic and international law. Fiscal policy, which had long been one of the last resorts of unfettered state sovereignty, now appears regularly on the agendas of international summits and organizations. This constitutes a logical consequence of the globalization of financial markets and the increasing interconnectedness of macroeconomic policy. At the moment, international legal principles on fiscal policy mostly have the status of soft law. It remains to be seen whether there will be a formation of hard law.

The comparative analysis of fiscal policy rules also illustrates how the legal status of each individual provision contained in the UNCTAD Principles can be examined. A more extensive analysis is available in the previously-mentioned comparative survey compiled for UNCTAD. For the purposes of this chapter, the examples included in the preceding sections might suffice to demonstrate the potential of principles as a category for tracing and taxing developments in international law. Due to their particular nature, which transcends the dividing lines between soft and hard as well as between domestic and international law, they are especially valuable as an analytical tool in areas where treaty law has not been forthcoming and where progress in international law depends on the gradual emergence of customary rules or general principles. But even if hard international law should not emerge in this way, the examples provided here might have shown that soft international legal principles might also have repercussions for domestic law and set in motion significant trends in policy-making, especially if reinforced by the UNCTAD Principles. In this respect, the Principles exercise an important consolidative function.

Annex: Overview on the Legal Status of the UNCTAD Principles[107]

No.	Principle	Legal qualification
1.	Agency	General principle of law
2.	Informed decisions	Guiding principle (structural asymmetries between lenders and consumers require due diligence in case of consumer loans)
		Emerging principle (lender due diligence in the case of non-consumer loans)
3.	Due authorization	General principle of law (*prima facie* authorization)
		Emerging principle (invalidity of loans to public entities without proper authorization)
4.	Responsible credit decisions	Emerging principles (duty of lender to assess borrower's capacity)
		General principle of law (responsibility for abusive credits)

[107] Reproduction from the Comparative Survey, see note* to this chapter.

5.	Project financing	Guiding principle (*ex ante* environmental impact assessment by lenders) Emerging principle (duty of private lenders to conduct social and financial impact assessment)
6.	International cooperation	General principle of law (contracts violating sanctions are null and void, cf. Principle 9)
7.	Debt restructurings	General principles of law (see Principle 15)
8.	Agency	General principle of law
9.	Binding agreements	General principles of law (nullity of contracts resulting from corruption or in a violation of binding international sanctions; natural disasters give rise to a defence for reasons of economic necessity) General Principle of Law (inability to pay due debts triggers insolvency proceedings)
10.	Transparency	Guiding principles (transparent fiscal policy-making; involvement of legislature; surveillance of local governments) Emerging principle (medium-term financial Frameworks) Structural principles (pay-as-you-go; incentive model versus control model in federal states)
11.	Disclosure	Guiding/general principle of law (right of access to information) Guiding principle (public availability of budgets)
12.	Project financing	Guiding principle (*ex ante* environmental impact assessment by borrowers; post-disbursement evaluation of ODA) Emerging principle (post-disbursement project evaluation in general).
13.	Adequate management and monitoring	Guiding principles (conduct of audits; high level of education of auditors; independence of external auditors; publicity of reports) Emerging principle (external auditors)
14.	Avoiding over-borrowing	Emerging or guiding principle (material restrictions on sovereign borrowing) Structural principles (different models) Guiding principle (countercyclical deficit spending permissible) Emerging principle (international surveillance of fiscal policy)
15.	Restructuring	General principles of law (interdiction of parallel proceedings; stay on claims during restructurings; equality of creditors; right to pro rata payments; priority of secured creditors; majority decision-making)[108] Guiding principle (good faith during insolvency proceedings) Emerging principle (HIPC debt relief is an insolvency procedure which renders the previously-mentioned general principles of law applicable)

[108] The application of these principles depends on the existence of a restructuring procedure.

7

The Legal Contours of Sovereign Debt Restructuring under the UNCTAD Principles

Antagonism and Convergence between Standards of Domestic Insolvency Law and International Investment Protection Law

Antonis Bredimas, Anastasios Gourgourinis, and Georges Pavlidis

A. Introduction

The present chapter critically assesses the relationship between the UNCTAD Principles on Responsible Sovereign Lending and Borrowing (the UNCTAD Principles)[1] and their normative environment, and more specifically, the parallel universes of domestic insolvency law and international investment law. The underlying aim of the chapter is to bring to the surface both the antagonism and convergence between the Principles, and standards of domestic insolvency law and international investment law regarding the issue of sovereign debt restructuring.

Our analysis is organized in a three-fold fashion: the chapter first revisits domestic insolvency law and identifies the drawbacks of the statutory and the contractual approaches to sovereign insolvency by juxtaposing them with UNCTAD Principles 7, 'Debt Restructurings',[2] and 15, 'Restructuring',[3] combined with Principle 9, 'Binding Agreements'.[4] Then, the discussion turns to the

1 UNCTAD, Principles on Responsible Sovereign Lending and Borrowing (Amended and Restated as of 10 January 2012), the text of which is included in the Annex to this book.

2 '*In circumstances where a sovereign is manifestly unable to service its debts, all lenders have a duty to behave in good faith and with cooperative spirit to reach a consensual re-arrangement of those obligations. Creditors should seek a speedy and orderly resolution to the problem.*'

3 '*If a restructuring of sovereign debt obligations becomes unavoidable, it should be undertaken promptly, efficiently and fairly.*'

4 '*A sovereign debt contract is a binding obligation and should be honored. Exceptional cases nonetheless can arise. A state of economic necessity can prevent the borrower's full and/or timely repayment. Also, a competent judicial authority may rule that circumstances giving rise to legal defense have occurred. When,*

corpus of international investment protection law, which has dealt and continues to deal with claims from private lenders against sovereign borrowers. Finally, an attempt to put the UNCTAD Principles to the test in concrete debt-crisis work-outs, such as the 2012 Greek Debt Restructuring, is made.

B. Sovereign Debt Restructuring under the UNCTAD Principles in the Light of Domestic Insolvency Law

The menacing mutation of the recent financial crisis into a sovereign debt crisis has renewed the theoretical discussion on debt restructuring, a debate that recurs in times of major economic crises. It is generally admitted that in the era of bond finance and integrated financial markets, sovereign debt must be restructured in a timely, equitable, and orderly manner in order to mitigate problems, such as contagion, moral hazard, collective action, inter-creditor equity, and vulture litigation.

The need to establish a set of rules to deal with sovereign state insolvency was identified as early as 1776 by Adam Smith, who was also the first to draw the analogy between the bankruptcy of persons and the bankruptcy of sovereign states. The analogy was rediscovered after several major default cycles in international economic history (during the 1930s, 1980s, and 1990s).[5] In the aftermath of the crisis in Argentina, the Krueger proposal on a Sovereign Debt Restructuring Mechanism (SDRM) built on this analogy and came close to fruition.[6] The failure of this project adds to a series of proposals which attempted to transpose features of

due to the state of economic necessity of the borrower, changes to the original contractual conditions of the loan are unavoidable, Principles 7 and 15 should be followed.'

5 See K. Rogoff and J. Zettelmeyer, 'Bankruptcy Procedures for Sovereigns: A History of Ideas, 1976–2001', IMF Working Paper WP/02/133 (August 2002), available at <http://www.imf.org/external/pubs/ft/wp/2002/wp02133.pdf>, 3–7. On the so-called 'Brady Plan', see Power, 'Sovereign Debt: The Rise of the Secondary Market and its Implications for Future Restructurings' (1996) 64 Ford. L. Rev. 2701, 2719–23; P. Pazartzis, 'La renégociation des dettes: l'example allemand (1953) et indonesien (1970)' in D. Carreau, M. Shaw (eds.), *La dette extérieure* (Martinus Nijhoff, 1995) 124–36.

6 On the SDRM proposal, see IMF, 'Sovereign Debt Restructuring and Dispute Resolution', speech by Ms Anne O. Krueger, First Deputy Managing Director IMF, at Bretton Woods Committee Annual Meeting (6 June 2002), available at <http://www.imf.org/external/np/speeches/2002/060602.htm>; IMF, 'The Design of the Sovereign Debt Restructuring Mechanism—Further Considerations', Prepared by the Legal and Policy Development and Review Departments, 14 August 2002, available at <http://www.imf.org/external/np/pdr/sdrm/2002/081402.pdf>; M.C. Malaguti, 'Sovereign Insolvency and International Legal Order' (2009) 11 Int'l Community L. Rev. 307, 318–20. Cf. the criticism of the SDRM proposal advanced by K. Raffer, 'The IMF's SDRM—Simply Disastrous Rescheduling Management?' in C. Jochnick and F.A. Preston (eds), *Sovereign Debt at the Crossroads—Challenges and Proposals for Resolving the Third World Debt Crisis* (Oxford University Press, 2006) 246ff. One could also note that the proposal for the establishment of a European Crisis Resolution Mechanism (ECRM), put forward by the think-tank Bruegel, foresees debt restructuring in the Eurozone under the oversight of the Court of Justice of the European Union, and a set of rules for the provision of financial assistance. F. Gianviti et al., 'A European Mechanism for Sovereign Debt Crisis Resolution: A Proposal', Bruegel Blueprint Series (November 2010) available at <http://www.bruegel.org/download/parent/446-a-european-mechanism-for-sovereign-debt-crisis-resolution-a-proposal/file/928-a-european-mechanism-for-sovereign-debt-crisis-resolution-a-proposal-english>.

domestic bankruptcy law and firm reorganization law into the context of sovereign insolvency but were never put to the test. It would be interesting to examine how the UNCTAD Principles differ from all these proposals and to assess their added value in theoretical and in practical terms.

To begin with, debt restructuring is dealt with by UNCTAD Principles 7 and 15, which belong respectively to Part I, entitled 'Responsibilities of Lenders to Sovereign Borrowers', and Part II, entitled 'Responsibilities of Sovereign Borrowers to Lenders'. According to this structure, as well as the wording of UNCTAD Principles 7 and 15, emphasis is given to the creditors' and borrower's behaviour during the debt restructuring process. An analogy can be drawn here with domestic bankruptcy law, which imposes obligations not only on the insolvent person or organization, but also on its creditors.

While the UNCTAD Principles 7 and 15 aim to balance the conflicting interests of the sovereign borrower and its lenders, the question remains whether they can in fact deliver on the promise, by facilitating lenders' coordination and assuring the equitable treatment of all parties. To this end, the present chapter examines the UNCTAD Principles in the light of domestic insolvency law, and, more specifically, in the light of the general common features of bankruptcy law and firm reorganization law applied in most domestic jurisdictions.

I. Scope and types of domestic bankruptcy proceedings

Under domestic law, a distinction is commonly made between liquidation proceedings (such as Chapter 7 of the US Bankruptcy Code) and reorganization proceedings (such as Chapter 11 or Chapter 9 of the US Bankruptcy Code).[7] In the first case, the assets of the bankrupt person are realized as a pool in accordance with the legal order of priorities, commonly known as the ladder of priorities. In the second case, the debtor and its main creditors conclude an agreement for the reorganization of the business, with or without judicial intervention; the debtor may continue conducting business or be in possession of the property as a fiduciary. Of course, a debt workout or exchange offer can be achieved even without entering insolvency proceedings.[8] The UNCTAD Principles clearly opt for a scheme similar to reorganization.[9]

Domestic insolvency procedures have two basic purposes:[10] on the one hand, they establish *ex ante* rules for the orderly liquidation of assets or the reorganization

[7] See also the Greek Bankruptcy Code (Law 3588/2007), Arts 99–131 on the reorganization proceedings and Arts 132–161 on the liquidation proceedings.

[8] P. Bolton, 'Toward a Statutory Approach to Sovereign Debt Restructuring: Lessons from Corporate Bankruptcy Practice Around the World', IMF Working Paper WP/03/13 (January 2003), available at <http://www.imf.org/external/pubs/ft/wp/2003/wp0313.pdf> 11.

[9] See also K. Raffer, 'Applying Chapter 9 Insolvency to International Debts: An Economically Efficient Solution with a Human Face' (1990) 18 World Development 301, proposing an international insolvency procedure modelled after Chapter 9, which applies bankruptcy reorganization principles to municipalities.

[10] Group of Ten, 'The Resolution of Sovereign Liquidity Crises: A Report to the Ministers and Governors Prepared Under the Auspices of the Deputies' (May 1996), available at <http://www.bis.org/publ/gten03.pdf> 10.

of a business through a structured negotiation process between the creditors and the debtor; on the other, they may enable a viable enterprise to continue doing business, by providing the debtor with temporary protection from its creditors and access to interim finance. The UNCTAD Principles have similar, though not identical, functions: on the one hand, they establish *ex ante* rules for the orderly restructuring of sovereign debt, but not for the liquidation of assets; on the other, they provide the debtor with protection from its creditors through the use of Collective Action Clauses (CACs), which can prevent individual bondholders from commencing litigation (CACs on majority enforcement).[11]

Bankruptcy cases can be categorized into two types: voluntary and involuntary (e.g. US Bankruptcy Code § 301 and § 303). In voluntary bankruptcy cases, the debtor triggers the bankruptcy process by petitioning the bankruptcy court. In involuntary bankruptcy cases, which are rarer, the petition in bankruptcy is filed by the creditors, who have the responsibility to show that the debtor is not generally paying its debts as they become due. Domestic bankruptcy laws, which commonly make the distinction between voluntary and involuntary bankruptcy cases, differ as to the conditions they apply to each case.[12] The UNCTAD Principles adopt a voluntary approach to debt restructuring, whereby the debt restructuring process is triggered by the sovereign borrower. Of course, things could hardly be otherwise, since there is no legal basis, no legal procedure, and no international forum for lenders to file a petition in bankruptcy for sovereign borrowers. The initiative to commence restructuring negotiations belongs to the sovereign borrower; nevertheless, the borrower has the responsibility 'to move in a timely fashion' in order to 'commence the process of a consensual debt rearrangement'.[13] The voluntary approach in the UNCTAD Principles is, therefore, put into perspective by the borrower's responsibility not to procrastinate in commencing the restructuring process.

II. The institutional setting for bankruptcy proceedings

At the institutional level, the UNCTAD Principles do not provide for the establishment of an independent 'court-like entity', such as an arbitration panel with the functions and powers of a bankruptcy court.[14] Such an entity, acting as a neutral adjudicator, would considerably facilitate the restructuring process. Under domestic bankruptcy law, the bankruptcy court generally legitimizes the commencement

[11] For criticism of the efficiency of CACs in general, see A. Gelpern and G.M. Gulati, 'Public Symbol in Private Contract: a Case Study' (2006) 84 Wash. U. L. Rev. 1627.

[12] See the Greek Bankruptcy Code (Law 3588/2007), Art. 5, which allows for both possibilities.

[13] The need to restructure debt promptly was also identified in the context of the SDRM debate, see Rogoff and Zettelmeyer (n. 5) 6.

[14] Under the SDRM proposal, the powers of the dispute resolution forum would include administrative functions (notification to creditors, registration of claims, and administration of the voting process), dispute resolution and injunctive relief. Rogoff and Zettelmeyer (n. 5) 12. Cf. H.C. Lee, 'Efficient and Inefficient Debt Restructuring: A Comparative Analysis of Voting Rules in Workouts' (2007) 40 Corn. Int'l L.J. 661, regarding the US and South Korea legal framework on voting in debt restructuring.

of the bankruptcy proceedings and the imposition of a payments moratorium,[15] whilst it also decides disputes. In some jurisdictions, especially in continental European practice, the bankruptcy court tends to be much more involved in the process.[16] However, it remains possible that the restructuring may take place 'by the agreement and consensus of the parties, and not by imposition from some international institution'.[17] Thus, the approach adopted by the UNCTAD Principles, where there is no bankruptcy court,[18] remains feasible and has been put effectively to the test in the context of domestic law.

Moreover, the UNCTAD Principles do not provide for the appointment of a trustee or receiver, the official who is appointed to administer the bankruptcy estate. The powers of the trustee or receiver (preference avoidance, fraudulent transfer actions, rejection of certain executory contracts, etc.) differ from one jurisdiction to another.[19] In general, this person is empowered to liquidate assets and distribute the product of the liquidation according to a scheme of priorities. In the case of reorganization proceedings (e.g. US Bankruptcy Code § 1108), domestic law may even empower the trustee to operate the business of the debtor. Nevertheless, the trustee is not an integral part of reorganization proceedings, since the debtor can also act as trustee of the business (debtor in possession).[20] It can be argued that Principle 15 introduces a similar reorganization scheme, where the sovereign borrower remains in possession of its assets, but owes a duty of care to the creditors ('The borrower should avoid opportunistic behaviour and arbitrary discrimination among creditors'). In any case, as the G-10 Deputies Working Group stated in 1996, 'it would be neither appropriate nor possible to replace the authorities responsible for the economic policies of a sovereign state with a "new management"'.[21] For the same reason, contrary to domestic reorganization proceedings, where the creditors can be left with ownership of the reorganized company, the debt restructuring under the UNCTAD Principles cannot produce such a result in the context of sovereign insolvency. As the ILA Study Group points out, the solution in this case is IMF or other official conditionality.[22]

[15] See the Greek Bankruptcy Code (Law 3588/2007), Arts 4–11 on the powers of the competent bankruptcy court. See also ILA Sovereign Insolvency Study Group, 'State insolvency: options for the way forward', The Hague Conference (2010) 25.

[16] Bolton (n. 8) 15.

[17] C.G. Oechsli, 'Procedural Guidelines for Renegotiating LDC Debts: An Analogy to Chapter 11 of the U.S. Bankruptcy Reform Act' (1981) 21 Va. J. Int'l L. 305, 333.

[18] The adoption of the UNCTAD principles does not exclude the use of arbitration as a means of resolving disputes.

[19] See the Greek Bankruptcy Code (Law 3588/2007), Arts 7 and 67–81 on the appointment and powers of the bankruptcy receiver.

[20] On the risks associated with this situation, see L. Weiss and K.H. Wruck, 'Information Problems, Conflicts of Interest, and Asset Stripping: Chapter 11's Failure in the Case of Eastern Airlines' (1998) 48 J. Fin. Econ. 55; L.M. LoPucki, 'The Debtor in Full Control: Systems Failure under Chapter 11 of the Bankruptcy Code?' (1983) 57 American Bankruptcy Law Journal 99.

[21] Group of Ten (n. 10) 10. Cf. V. Paz, 'Restructuring of Sovereign Debt and Crisis Argentina: Payment Out of Central Bank Reserves' (2011) 26 JIBLR 40, 43–6, discussing the domestic political repercussions in Argentina of the creation of the 'Bicentennial Fund' to repay the country's sovereign debt.

[22] ILA Sovereign Insolvency Study Group (n. 15) 24.

Contrary to domestic bankruptcy law (e.g. US Bankruptcy Code § 541ff.), the UNCTAD Principles do not provide for the equivalent of the 'estate' that is created on commencement of bankruptcy cases. Under domestic bankruptcy law, the estate usually includes most assets and property interests of the debtor at the time of case commencement (several exclusions and exemptions from the estate are provided for).[23] There is no procedure for the liquidation of the estate and the distribution of the proceeds to the creditors; there is also no legal elimination (discharge), but a restructuring of debts owed by the sovereign borrower, so that one can still speak of a 'fresh start' for the borrower.

III. Paving the path to an orderly debt restructuring

The importance of protection from litigation, in other words a stay of litigation while negotiations are ongoing, is more than evident. Previous studies have identified the threat that a 'race to the courthouse' might pose to orderly negotiations.[24] A 'run' by creditors produces unfair results among similarly situated creditors and further damages the financial situation of the borrower. For this reason, domestic bankruptcy laws (e.g. US Bankruptcy Code § 362) impose an automatic stay that prohibits the commencement or continuation of actions or proceedings, including the enforcement of judgments, against a debtor or the estate, for the collection of a claim that arose before the commencement of the bankruptcy case.[25] The UNCTAD Principles do not deal with this issue explicitly. According to Principle 7, 'all lenders have a duty to behave in good faith and with cooperative spirit to reach a consensual rearrangement'. It can be argued that a 'race to the courthouse' while negotiations are ongoing is a free-riding decision that undermines cooperative solutions and violates the principle of good faith. However, there is no formal bankruptcy protection of the automatic stay and the acts of the free-rider cannot be treated as void *ab initio* or voidable.[26] The UNCTAD Principles restrict individual debt-collection actions in an indirect manner, i.e. through their support for the use of CACs. For instance, the G-10 model CACs prohibit individual legal action and allow litigation to be instituted solely by the permanent representative at its own discretion or upon instruction of at least 25 per cent of bondholders. According to the same model clauses, recovery proceeds are distributed pro rata to all holders, '*thus limiting the appetite for disruptive litigation*'.[27] In this manner, the application

[23] See the Greek Bankruptcy Code (Law 3588/2007), Art. 16 on the bankruptcy estate.

[24] R.J. Barnett et al., 'On Third World Debt' (1984) 25 Harv.Int'l L.J. 83, 85; IMF, 'Note on an International Debt Adjustment Facility for Sovereign Debtors', EBS/95/90, 26 May 1995 (unpublished; Executive Board Internal Report).

[25] cf. the Greek Bankruptcy Code (Law 3588/2007), art. 25 on the stay of litigation.

[26] Bolton (n. 8) 20, arguing that a stay on debt collection actions is less critical in the sovereign debt context.

[27] Group of Ten, 'Report of the G-10 Working Group on Contractual Clauses' (September 2002), available at <http://www.bis.org/publ/gten08.pdf> Annex 2.

of the UNCTAD Principles and the use of CACs can protect the sovereign debtor from unsettling litigation and collection actions.[28]

Domestic laws do not enunciate clear principles on the issue of vulture litigation,[29] with some notable exceptions (NY Judiciary Law § 489). For instance, the *champerty* defence, known under common law, can be applied in the restructuring context under specific conditions,[30] although 'the prohibition of champerty has always been limited in scope'.[31] The UNCTAD Principles deal with this problem explicitly. Principle 7 clarifies that a creditor is acting abusively if the creditor 'acquires a debt instrument of a sovereign in financial distress with the intent of forcing a preferential settlement of the claim outside of a consensual workout process', perhaps mindful of the *Eliot Associates v. Peru* litigation,[32] and the cases of vulture litigation that followed.[33] The problem of proving the intent of the investor remains; the acts of purchasing sovereign chapter in the secondary market at a discount and declining to participate in a sovereign debt workout are not sufficient, by themselves, to characterize a creditor as a reprehensible 'vulture'.[34]

In the case of reorganization proceedings, the debtor and the creditors conclude a plan for repayment of debts, a plan that is confirmed by the bankruptcy court and becomes binding (see e.g. US Bankruptcy Code § 941ff., § 1121ff.).[35] The same

[28] Experience does not confirm that the threat or the act of litigation, or isolated instances of 'rogue creditor' behaviour would necessarily disrupt the debt restructurings; A.C. Porzecanski, 'From Rogue Creditors to Rogue Debtors: Implications of Argentina's Default', (2005–06) 6 Chi. J. Int'l L. 311, 314.

[29] On the issue of vulture litigation in the context of sovereign debt, see: C. Wheeler and A. Attaran, 'Declawing the Vulture Funds: Rehabilitation of a Comity Defense in Sovereign Debt Litigation' (2003) 39 SJIL 253; J. Fisch and C.M. Gentile, 'Vultures or Vanguards: The Role of Litigation in Sovereign Debt Restructuring' (2004) 53 Emory L.J. 1043; L.C. Buchheit and J.S. Pam, 'The Hunt for Pari Passu', (2004) 23 Int'l Fin. L. Rev. 20; J.I. Blackman and R. Mukhi, 'The Evolution of Modern Sovereign Debt Litigation: Vultures, Alter Egos and Other Legal Fauna' (2010) 73 Law & Contemp. Probs 47.

[30] See e.g. R.L. Cohen and R.M. Schwartz, 'Champerty and Claims Trading' (2003) 11 American Bankruptcy Institute Law Review 197.

[31] *Trust v. Love Funding*, 13 N.Y.3d, 199, 890 N.Y.S.2d 377, 918 N.E.2d 889.

[32] *Elliot Associates L.P. v. Banco de la Nacion*, 1999 U.S. App. Lexis 26370 (2d Cir 10 October 1999), rev'g. 12 F. Supp. 2d 328 (S.D.N.Y. 1998). It is worth noting that Elliott Management Corp. has taken up Argentinian bonds, and pursues litigation, via its affiliates, NML Capital, Ltd and EM Ltd, before US, UK, and Swiss courts. See: *EM Ltd v. Republic of Argentina*, 473 F.3d 463, 472 (2d Cir. 2007); *NML Capital, Ltd v. Banco Central de la República Argentina*, 652 F.3d 172, 197 (2d Cir. 2011); *NML Capital, Ltd v. Republic of Argentina* [2011] UKSC 31, on appeal from: [2010] EWCA Civ 41; *NML Capital Ltd, EM Limited v. Bank für Internationalen Zahlungsausgleich (BIZ)*, Betreibungsamt Basel-Stadt, Bundesgericht, 12 July 2010. See also: 'Argentine defaulted bonds dispute reaches the US Supreme Court', *Mercopress* (18 January 2012), available at <http://en.mercopress.com/2012/01/18/argentine-defaulted-bonds-dispute-reaches-the-us-supreme-court>; 'Gauchos and gadflies Creditors' decade-long battle with Argentina shows just how tangled sovereign defaults can be', *The Economist*, 22 October 2011, available at <http://www.economist.com/node/21533453>.

[33] For a recent overview of the relevant (domestic) case law, see e.g. P. Wautelet, 'Vulture Funds, Creditors and Sovereign Debtors: How to Find a Balance?' in M. Audit (ed.), *L'insolvabilité souveraine* (LGDJ, 2011) 104–19.

[34] L.C. Buchheit and G.M. Gulati, 'Responsible Sovereign Lending and Borrowing', UNCTAD Discussion Paper No. 198 (April 2010), available at <http://www.unctad.org/en/docs/osgdp20102_en.pdf> 2.

[35] cf. the Greek Bankruptcy Code (Law 3588/2007), Arts 107–131 on the reorganization plan. Also, note that 'cramdown authority, under which creditors could be forced to accept a rescheduling'

scheme was proposed in the context of the SDRM project, under which the agreement would become binding on all registered creditors once the vote was certified by the Sovereign Debt Dispute Resolution Forum.[36] The restructuring agreement is an integral part of the UNCTAD Principles,[37] as well as the Principles for Stable Capital Flows and Fair Debt Restructuring in Emerging Markets of the Institute of International Finance (IIF Debt Restructuring Principles).[38] More specifically, the restructuring agreement can become binding for the dissenting bondholders, if the sovereign bond contract contains CACs and the clauses' requirements are satisfied. The use of CACs has the advantage of forcing dissident creditors to go along with a broadly acceptable settlement, which is a typical feature of formal bankruptcy proceedings.[39] Thus, the UNCTAD Principles adopt the supermajority rule in debt restructuring decisions[40] in order to deal with the creditor-holdout problem;[41] nevertheless, there is no confirmation of the restructuring agreement by a court or court-like entity.

Under domestic bankruptcy law (e.g. Chapters 7, 9, and 11 of the US Bankruptcy Code) the bankruptcy court appoints committees, which represent the creditors, communicate with the debtor, facilitate creditors' access to information, etc. Representative creditors' committees would be given a role under the SDRM as well, 'to address both debtor-creditor and intercreditor issues'.[42] The use of CACs is mentioned in Principle 15 and collective representation clauses are the simpler form of CACs, although there is no universal conception and application of CACs in bond contracts. Collective representation clauses 'typically provide procedures for the organization of bondholders and the designation of a representative'.[43] The

is, indeed, a common feature of domestic bankruptcy laws: D. Tarullo, 'The Role of the IMF in Sovereign Debt Restructuring' (2005–06) 6 Chi. J. Int'l L. 287, 303.

[36] Rogoff and Zettelmeyer (n. 5) 10.

[37] According to UNCTAD Principle 15, 'the debtor should seek an agreement with the supermajority of creditors to modify the original contractual terms'; its twin provision, UNCTAD Principle 7, imposes on lenders the responsibility to 'reach a consensual rearrangement'.

[38] cf. Institute of International Finance (IIF), 'Principles for Stable Capital Flows and Fair Debt Restructuring in Emerging Markets', available at <www.iif.com/download.php?id=4fyB5BGIKzU=> Principle 3 ('Good Faith Actions').

[39] Buchheit and Gulati (n. 34) 9. According to Bolton and Jeanne, 'a policy that encourages the adoption of such clauses . . . by making their use mandatory, could achieve the same effect as a restructuring under a bankruptcy regime'. P. Bolton and O. Jeanne, 'Structuring and Restructuring Sovereign Debt: The Role of a Bankruptcy Regime', IMF Working Paper WP/07/192 (August 2007), available at <http://www.imf.org/external/pubs/ft/wp/2007/wp07192.pdf> 5.

[40] As noted by J. Sgard, 'Bankruptcy Laws: Part of a Global History' in D. Ma and J.-L. van Zanden (eds) *Law and Long Term Economic Change: An Eurasian Perspective* (Stanford University Press, 2010) 200: 'Over centuries and across countries, majority rule and judicial confirmation explain why bankruptcy laws have always revolved around the core vertical axis whereby the sovereign enforces, protects, and regulates private rights—though by intervening into them.'

[41] S. Schwarcz, 'A Minimalist Approach to State Bankruptcy' (2011) 59 UCLA L. Rev. 322, 328.

[42] Rogoff and Zettelmeyer (n. 5) 10. According to IIF Debt Restructuring Principle 3: 'The appropriate format and role of negotiation vehicles such as a creditor committee or another representative creditor group . . . should be determined flexibly and on a case-by-case basis.' On the issue of creditors' representatives in the case of the syndicate loans in the 1980s, see J. Fisch and C. Gentile, 'Vultures or Vanguards?: The Role of Litigation in Sovereign Debt Restructuring' (2004) 53 Emory L. J. 1047, 1055–8.

[43] Group of Ten (n. 10) 16.

powers given to the general assembly of bondholders and to the representative, as well as the voting procedure and thresholds, may vary significantly. In any case, it is positive that the UNCTAD Principles support the use of CACs, including collective representation clauses.

The amount of disclosure that creditors are entitled to receive, via their committees, varies from country to country.[44] In the context of private sector bankruptcies, companies generally have to deliver 'a statement of affairs explaining the causes of the insolvency, elaborate financial statements, details of the plan itself... the circumstances giving rise to the filing, and risk factors'.[45] UNCTAD Principle 11 requires full disclosure and accurate representation of information at the time the debtor incurs a debt.[46] It can be argued that disclosure at the moment of restructuring is also covered by Principle 11, which requires debtors, as a general obligation, to 'make public disclosure of their financial and economic situation'.[47] Furthermore, UNCTAD Principle 10 explicitly refers the issue of transparency and the responsibility of the borrower to avoid 'transactions or accounting techniques that have the effect of misrepresenting the true nature or extent of a sovereign's debt picture'.

In the context of sovereign debt restructuring, UNCTAD Principle 15 refers to the seniority of debts, which finds its roots in domestic bankruptcy law providing that creditors who have a security interest or collateral are paid before unsecured creditors. Still, the UNCTAD Principles do not determine priority levels for the claims of unsecured creditors, contrary to domestic law (see e.g. US Bankruptcy Code § 507). Respecting the seniority of debts would not exclude giving seniority to new financing, a proposal favoured by several authors in order to provide an incentive for the assumption of additional risk.[48] It is perhaps in this respect that Schwarcz evokes the US Bankruptcy Code (US Bankruptcy Code § 364(a)–(d)) as a helpful precedent on how the trustee can attract new-money loans while protecting existing creditors.[49]

All in all, UNCTAD Principles 7 and 15 display a veritable degree of coherence with standards of domestic insolvency law. Indeed, it appears that, even as they currently stand, they have sought, to a great extent, to capitalize on domestic law insolvency conceptions. The next section of this chapter will, then, attempt to juxtapose them with the realities of modern investment protection law.

[44] See the Greek Bankruptcy Code (Law 3588/2007), Arts 109 and 131 on the disclosure of information.

[45] ILA Sovereign Insolvency Study Group (n. 15) 25.

[46] cf. IIF Debt Restructuring Principle 1 ('Transparency and Timely Flow of Information').

[47] More specifically, UNCTAD Principle 11 requires that borrowers provide, *inter alia*, the following information: '(i) accurate and timely fiscal data; (ii) level and composition of external and domestic sovereign debt including maturity, currency, and forms of indexation and covenants; (iii) external accounts; (iv) the use of derivative instruments; and, (v) details of any kind of implicit and explicit sovereign guarantees.'

[48] Rogoff and Zettelmeyer (n. 5) 28.

[49] Schwarcz (n. 41) 347.

C. Sovereign Debt Restructuring under the UNCTAD Principles in the Light of International Investment Protection Law

This section assesses the UNCTAD Principles in the light of the legal protection afforded to individuals under international investment agreements (IIAs), comprising of the 2,676 concluded bilateral investment treaties (BITs),[50] as well as free trade agreements (FTAs) equipped with provisions on investment protection.[51] This is particularly important since two arbitral tribunals, constituted under the auspices of the International Centre for Settlement of Investment Disputes (ICSID),[52] reached majority decisions accepting that they had jurisdiction to hear the *Abaclat and ors v. Argentina* and *Ambiente Ufficio S.p.A. and ors v. Argentina* claims, alleging a number of breaches of the Italy-Argentina Bilateral Investment Treaty (BIT) protective guarantees resulting from the Argentinian debt and payment default in 2001.[53] While the 2001 Argentinian crisis resulted in a saga of investment arbitrations addressing the negative effects on foreign investments of Argentina's regulatory measures taken in response, the ICSID Tribunals' decisions in *Abaclat and ors v. Argentina* and *Ambiente Ufficio S.p.A. and ors v. Argentina* are the first arbitral decisions related to the non-payment of sovereign bonds *after* a sovereign debt restructuring. Hence, it would appear that the shift of sovereign bond litigation from domestic litigation to international arbitration indicates that 'Pandora's box' is starting to open, if not already open,[54] as a 'a relatively low-cost and unbureaucratic procedure... and a superior solution to the enforcement and adjudication issue' regarding sovereign bonds,[55] especially given that sovereign

[50] As at the end of 2008. UNCTAD, 'Recent Developments in International Investment Agreements (2008–June 2009)' (2009) 3 IIA Monitor 2.

[51] As, e.g. the North American Free Trade Agreement (NAFTA) whose Chapter 11 provides for protection for investors and investments in NAFTA countries. North American Free Trade Agreement, 17 December 1992, 32 ILM 289 (Parts 1–3); 32 ILM 605 (Parts 4–8).

[52] Convention on the Settlement of Investment Disputes between States and Nationals of Other States, 17 October 1966, 575 UNTS 159.

[53] See *Abaclat and ors (Case formerly known as Giovanna A. Beccara and ors) v. Argentina*, Decision on Jurisdiction and Admissibility of 4 August 2011, ICSID Case No ARB/07/5; IIC 504 (2011), where the initial claim in 2006 numbered 180,000 Italian holders of Argentinian bonds, reduced to 60,000 after Argentina's second voluntary bond exchange offer in 2010; *Ambiente Ufficio SpA and ors (Case formerly known as Giordano Alpi and ors) v Argentina*, Decision on Jurisdiction and Admissibility of 8 February 2013, ICSID Case No ARB/08/9; IIC 576 (2013), involving initially 119 and now 90 holders of Argentinian bonds. Moreover, there is at least one (known) additional, and currently pending, investment claim against Argentina regarding the non-payment of sovereign bonds, namely *Giovanni Alemanni and ors v. Argentine Republic* (ICSID Case No. ARB/07/8). Further on the background and various aspects of the Argentinian crisis, see J.J. Falcone, 'Argentina's Plight: an Unusual Temporary Solution to a Sovereign Debt Crisis' (2004) 27 Suffolk Transnational Law Review 357, 359–70.

[54] M. Waibel, 'Opening Pandora's Box: Sovereign Bonds in International Arbitration' (2007) 101 AJIL 411, 715.

[55] S.L. Schwarcz, 'Idiot's Guide to Sovereign Debt Restructuring' (2004) 53 Emory L.J. 1189, 1210.

debt instruments fall under the scope of the intra-EU BITs of a number of EU Member States.[56]

An important advantage to opting for international investment arbitration under ICSID rules regarding the non-payment of sovereign bonds lies in the modalities regarding the recognition and enforcement of arbitral awards. Under Articles 53 and 54 of the ICSID Convention, Contracting States have an obligation to abide by and comply with arbitral awards rendered under the auspices of ICSID, recognizing them as binding and enforcing them as if they were 'final judgment[s] of a court in that State'.[57] Non-compliance with ICSID awards may also have indirect repercussions: Following the *U.S. Section 301* petitions of Azurix Corp. and Blue Ridge Investments, L.L.C., before with the Office of the US Trade Representative, Barack Obama, President of the United States of America, issued a Proclamation on 26 March 2012, suspending Argentina's designations as a Generalized System of Preferences (GSP)[58] beneficiary 'because it has not acted in good faith in enforcing arbitral awards in favor of United States citizens or a corporation, partnership, or association that is 50 per cent or more beneficially owned by United States citizens'.[59] One could even point out that the vulture funds' shift to international arbitration is to be considered as a response, first, to the limited effectiveness of sovereign bond litigation before domestic courts,[60] and, secondly, to the enactment of domestic legislation curtailing the scope of (domestic)

[56] D. Strik, 'Investment Protection of Sovereign Debt and Its Implications on the Future of Investment Law in the EU' (2012) 29 J. Int'l Arb. 183, 185–94.

[57] See H. Cross, 'Arbitration as a Means of Resolving Sovereign Debt Disputes' (2006) 17 Am. Rev. Int'l Arb. 335, 354–65; S.A. Alexandrov, 'Enforcement of ICSID Awards: Articles 53 and 54 of the ICSID Convention' in C. Binder et al. (eds.), *International Investment Law for the 21st Century: Essays in Honour of Christoph Schreuer* (Oxford University Press, 2009) 322–37; C. Schreuer et al., *The ICSID Convention: A Commentary* (Cambridge University Press, 2009) 1096–184; M. Waibel, *Sovereign Defaults before International Courts and Tribunals* (Cambridge University Press, 2011) 318–20.

[58] On the GSP in the context of the multilateral trade regime, see e.g. dos Santos et al., 'Generalized System of Preferences in General Agreement on Tariffs and Trade/World Trade Organization: History and Current Issues' (2005) 39 JWT 637; L. Bartels, 'The WTO Legality of the EU's GSP + Arrangement' (2007) 10 J. Int'l Econ. L. 869.

[59] *Presidential Proclamation—To Modify Duty-free Treatment Under the Generalized System of Preferences and for Other Purposes, by the President of the United States of America*, The White House, Office of the Press Secretary, 26 March 2012, available at <http://www.whitehouse.gov/the-press-office/2012/03/26/presidential-proclamation-modify-duty-free-treatment-under-generalized-s>. Under US law, to be eligible for GSP, beneficiary countries are required to comply with final awards rendered under ICSID rules.

[60] See e.g. H.T. Liendo III, 'Sovereign Debt Litigation Problems in the United States: A Proposed Solution' (2007) 9 Oregon Review of International Law 107, 127–40; U. Panizza et al., 'The Economics and Law of Sovereign Debt and Default' (2009) 47 J. Econ. Lit. 651, 655–9; L. Alfaro, N. Maurer, and F. Ahmed, 'Gunboats and Vultures: Market Reaction to the "Enforcement" of Sovereign Debt', available at <http://www.econ.ucla.edu/workshops/papers/History/Maurer,%20Gunboats%20and%20Vultures,%20version%205.2.pdf> 17–21; J.C. Hatchondo and L. Martinez, 'Legal Protection to Foreign Investors' (2011) 97 *Federal Reserve Bank of Richmond Economic Quarterly* 175, 183–4. *Contra*, see, *inter alios*, J. Goren, 'State-to-State Debts: Sovereign Immunity and the Vulture Hunt' (2009–10) 41 Geo. Wash. Int'l L. Rev. 681, 694–701. Cf. also the argument advanced by M. H. Miller and D. Thomas, 'Sovereign Debt Restructuring: The Judge, the Vultures and Creditor Rights' in R.W. Kolb (ed.), *Sovereign Debt: From Safety to Default* (Wiley, 2011) 217–22, according to which, holdout litigation and judge-mediation may in fact positively contribute to orderly sovereign debt restructurings.

litigation against developing countries/debtors.[61] Thus, it is apt to assess the UNCTAD Principles on debt restructuring in the light of international investment protection law.

I. UNCTAD Principle 7: Creditors' good faith conduct

UNCTAD Principle 7 ('Debt Restructurings') prescribes that: '*In circumstances where a sovereign is manifestly unable to service its debts, all lenders have a duty to behave in good faith and with cooperative spirit to reach a consensual re-arrangement of those obligations.*' The rationale behind UNCTAD Principle 7 is somehow similar to the one behind the insertion of the so-called 'waiting period' or 'cooling-off period' clauses in IIAs, i.e. provisions that require the lapse of a certain time period (usually, between six and 18 months) since the date when the dispute arose and before instituting arbitration proceedings. Such clauses in IIAs aim to provide an opportunity for entering into good-faith negotiations, or even mandatory recourse to domestic courts, *before* resorting to investor-State arbitration. While it has been argued that 'The question as to whether a mandatory waiting period is jurisdictional or procedural has limited practical significance',[62] disagreement has in fact arisen between investment tribunals regarding whether non-compliance with 'cooling-off'/'waiting' clauses under IIAs constitutes a jurisdictional bar or merely a 'procedural' requirement.[63] So, while early investment awards took the latter view,[64] more recent arbitral awards have strongly opted for the former,[65] perhaps in

[61] For instance, in the UK the Debt Relief (Developing Countries) Act 2010 (c. 22) limits the amount of money that commercial creditors can recover from certain developing countries; in Belgium, see Loi du 06/04/2008 visant à empêcher la saisie ou la cession des fonds publics destinés à la coopération internationale, notamment par la technique des fonds vautours, available at <http://reflex.raadvst-consetat.be/reflex/pdf/Mbbs/2008/05/16/109374.pdf>. For further details, see International Development Association and International Monetary Fund, 'Heavily Indebted Poor Countries (HIPC) Initiative and Multilateral Debt Relief Initiative (MDRI)—Status of Implementation', Prepared by the Staffs of IDA and the IMF, Approved by Otaviano Canuto and Reza Moghadam, 14 September 2010, available at <http://www.imf.org/external/np/pp/eng/2010/091410.pdf> 21–3.

[62] C. Schreuer, 'Of Waiting Periods, Umbrella Clauses and Forks in the Road' (2004) 5 JWIT 231, 239.

[63] R.D. Deutsch, 'An ICSID Tribunal Denies Jurisdiction for Failure to Satisfy BIT's "Cooling-Off" Period: Further Evidence of a Sea Change in Investor-State Arbitration or a Meaningless Ripple?' (2011) 33 Hous. J. Int'l L. 589, 602–3.

[64] e.g. *Ethyl Corp. v. Canada*, Decision on jurisdiction of 24 June 1998, Ad hoc—UNCITRAL Arbitration Rules; IIC 95 (1998); 38 ILM 708, paras 74–88; *Lauder v. Czech Republic*, Final Award of 3 September 2001, Ad hoc—UNCITRAL Arbitration Rules; IIC 205 (2001), para. 187, where the Tribunal did not read the six-month waiting period in the applicable BIT as 'a jurisdictional provision, i.e. a limit set to the authority of the Arbitral Tribunal to decide on the merits of the dispute, but [rather as] a procedural rule that must be satisfied by the Claimant'; *SGS Société Générale de Surveillance SA v. Pakistan*, Decision on Objections to Jurisdiction of 6 August 2003, ICSID Case No. ARB/01/13; IIC 223 (2003) 18 ICSID Rev—FILJ 301; (2003) 42 ILM 1290, para. 184, where the Tribunal similarly held that compliance with such a waiting period clause does not constitute 'a condition precedent for the vesting of jurisdiction'.

[65] See e.g. *Enron Corp. and Ponderosa Assets LP v. Argentina*, Decision on Jurisdiction of 14 January 2004, ICSID Case No. ARB/01/3; IIC 92 (2004) 11 ICSID Rep 273, para. 88, holding that a six-month negotiation period requirement is 'very much a jurisdictional one'; *Burlington Resources Inc v. Ecuador*, Decision on Jurisdiction of 2 June 2010, ICSID Case No. ARB/08/5; IIC 436 (2010), para. 312: 'The six-month waiting period requirement of Article VI is designed precisely to provide the State with an opportunity to redress the dispute before the investor decides to submit the dispute to

the context of what has been characterized as a 'half-hearted revival of the local remedies rule'.[66] Nevertheless, compliance with mandatory waiting/cooling-off periods, even if a jurisdictional requirement proper, may still not prove to be considered as an absolute prerequisite in the context of investment arbitration in relation to the non-payment of sovereign bonds, as was the exactly the case in the decisions of the *Abaclat* and *Ambiente Ufficio* Tribunals. While it was an established fact in both cases that the claimants did not abide by the 18 months' litigation requirement under Article 8(2) and (3) of the Argentina-Italy BIT,[67] the majorities of both Tribunals decided that this did not constitute a bar to their jurisdiction, albeit for different reasons.

More specifically, the *Abaclat* Tribunal approached the issue in the following terms: 'The relevant question is not "could the dispute have been efficiently settled before the Argentine courts?", but "was Argentina deprived of a fair opportunity to address the dispute within the framework of its own domestic legal system because of Claimants' disregard of the 18 months litigation requirement?".'[68] Then, the *Abaclat* Tribunal moved to find that a 'weighting of interests of the Parties', i.e. between the host State's right to have a fair opportunity to address the dispute domestically, on the one hand, and the bondholders' right to efficient dispute resolution, on the other, was in order.[69] In this fashion, the Tribunal concluded that Argentina's right was more theoretical than real, since it would not have been possible for Argentina to adequately address the dispute domestically within the 18-month period; hence, the claimants' relevant interests outweighed Argentina's.[70]

Notwithstanding the vigorous dissent of one member of the *Abaclat* Tribunal,[71] and relevant criticisms in the literature[72] and later arbitral

arbitration'; *Murphy Exploration and Production Co. International v. Ecuador*, Award on Jurisdiction of 15 December 2010, ICSID Case No. ARB/08/4; IIC 468 (2010), paras 140–157, stating that a six-month waiting period requirement 'is not about a mere formality', non-compliance with which may be excused.

[66] C. Schreuer, 'Calvo's Grandchildren: The Return of Local Remedies in Investment Arbitration' (2005) 4 The Law and Practice of International Courts and Tribunals 1, 4.

[67] Article 8 of the Argentina-Italy BIT, should a dispute between a foreign investor and the host State arise, provides for 'amicable consultations' between the parties to the dispute (para. 1), coupled with a requirement of prior recourse to the host State's courts for an 18-month period before initiating investment arbitration (paras 2 and 3).

[68] *Abaclat and ors v. Argentina* (n. 53) para. 581.

[69] *Abaclat and ors v. Argentina* (n. 53) para. 582.

[70] *Abaclat and ors v. Argentina* (n. 53) paras 583–584.

[71] Arbitrator Abi-Saab found no basis in the BIT from which the 'weighting of interests' element/test could possibly derive, the will of the Parties to the Treaty eventually being substituted by 'purely subjective judgment' by the Tribunal and coming very close to an *ex aequo et bono* ruling. Moreover, he strongly doubted whether barring the claim would indeed deprive claimants of 'an important and efficient dispute settlement means' (as the majority of the *Abaclat* Tribunal decided), since the bondholders could pursue remedies inside *and* outside Argentina (i.e. under the contractually selected foreign *fora* in the bond instruments, or even the Italian courts). *Abaclat and ors v. Argentina* (n. 53) (Dissenting Opinion of Georges Abi-Saab), paras 27–33.

[72] See e.g. S. Wordsworth, 'Case Comment: *Abaclat and ors v Argentine Republic*: Jurisdiction, Admissibility and Pre-conditions to Arbitration' (2012) 27 ICSID Review 255, 257–9, criticizing the majority's decision in *Abaclat* to treat the 18 months requirement as relating 'to the conditions for implementation of Argentina's consent to ICSID jurisdiction and arbitration', rather than jurisdiction.

practice,[73] regarding the majority's reasoning, the more recent *Ambiente Ufficio* Tribunal (again, by majority) maintained the same stance towards the consequences of the non-observance of the 18-month period by claimants and overruled Argentina's jurisdictional objection, albeit following a different route.[74] Thus, it could reasonably be argued that if arbitral practice is to follow the *Abaclat* and *Ambiente Ufficio* Tribunals, then, effectively, 'cooling-off'/'waiting' clauses in IIAs are to be rendered null in sovereign bond arbitration cases. Ergo, it is perhaps in this respect that one could perhaps wish for further elaboration on creditors' good faith obligations under UNCTAD Principle 7 when sovereigns are indeed manifestly unable to service their debt.

It is worth further pointing out that the commentary to UNCTAD Principle 7 features a concrete reference to the prohibition of *abus de droit*, i.e. in cases where a 'creditor that acquires a debt instrument of a sovereign in financial distress with the intent of forcing a preferential settlement of the claim outside of a consensual workout process is acting abusively'.[75] Investment tribunals may resort to the general principle of prohibition of abuse of rights and/or process so as to ensure proper administration of international justice.[76] Barring frivolous and *mala fides* exercises of the right to adjudicate,[77] as a defence 'to what may otherwise be a valid

[73] See *ICS Inspection and Control Services Ltd v Argentina*, Award on jurisdiction of 10 February 2012, PCA Case No. 2010–9; IIC 528 (2012), paras 263–73, where the Tribunal held that non-compliance with the 18 months requirement barred the claimant from initiating investment treaty arbitration, noting that 'judicially-crafted exceptions must find support in more than a tribunal's personal policy analysis of the provisions at issue', so that it could not trace the existence of a 'futility exception' in interpreting the BIT. Hence, the Tribunal, having previously taken note of the decision in *Abaclat*, concluded that 'futility', *in any event*, had not been demonstrated to its satisfaction.

[74] See *Ambiente Ufficio SpA and ors v Argentina* (n. 53) paras 597–607, where the Tribunal interpreted Art. 8 of the Argentina-Italy BIT using Art. 31(3)(c) of the 1969 Vienna Convention on the Law of Treaties (VCLT), to find that a ' futility exception' was applicable, as is the case with the exhaustion of local remedies rule in the field of diplomatic protection. cf. *ICS Inspection and Control Services Ltd v Argentina* (n. 73) paras 267–268, where the Tribunal undertook the same interpretative exercise and reached the opposite conclusion, noting that it could *not* 'create exceptions to treaty rules where these are merely based upon an assessment of the wisdom of the policy in question, having no basis in either the treaty text or in any supplementary interpretive source, however desirable such policy considerations might be seen to be in the abstract'. Further, on the scope and inherent limitations of interpretation under Art. 31(3)(c) VCLT, see A. Gourgourinis, 'The Distinction between Interpretation and Application of Norms in International Adjudication' (2011) 2 Journal of International Dispute Settlement 31, 49–51.

[75] UNCTAD Principles (n. 1) 7.

[76] See C. Brown, 'The Relevance of the Doctrine of Abuse of Process in International Adjudication' (2010) 7 Transnational Dispute Management, available at <http://www.transnational-dispute-management.com> especially at 7–8.

[77] *Azurix Corp. v. Argentina*, Decision on Jurisdiction of 8 December 2003, ICSID Case No ARB/01/12; IIC 23 (2003), paras 92–96; *Bayindir Insaat Turizm Tecaret ve Sanayi A Ş v. Pakistan*, Decision on Jurisdiction of 14 November 2005, ICSID Case No. ARB/03/29; IIC 27 (2005), paras 169–172; *Pan American Energy LLC and BP Argentina Exploration Co. v. Argentina, and joined case*, Decision on Jurisdiction of 27 July 2006, ICSID Case No. ARB/03/13; ICSID Case No. ARB/04/8, IIC 183 (2006), para. 52; *Saipem SpA v. Bangladesh*, Decision on Jurisdiction and Recommendation on Provisional Measures of 21 March 2007, ICSID Case No. ARB/05/07, IIC 280 (2007), paras 145–154; *Cementownia 'Nowa Huta' SA v. Turkey*, Award of 11 September 2009, ICSID Case No. ARB(AF)/06/2; IIC 390 (2009), paras 156–157.

claim',[78] is designed so as to 'to prevent an abuse of the system of international investment protection under the ICSID Convention, in ensuring that only investments that are made in compliance with the international principle of good faith and do not attempt to misuse the system are protected'.[79] Indeed, this was highlighted in *Abaclat and ors v. Argentina* when addressing the theory of abuse of rights as a more specific facet and expression of the more general principle of good faith. The Tribunal draw a distinction between 'material' and 'procedural' good faith requirements, the latter pertinent at the jurisdiction and admissibility stage, in contrast to the latter which can be examined both at the jurisdiction and the merits stages.[80]

Ergo, the potential implications and usages of the previously-mentioned dicta by investment tribunals in current and future investment arbitrations related to the non-repayment of sovereign bonds are obvious. For example, in *Abaclat and ors v. Argentina* the Tribunal has already dismissed Argentina's procedural abuse of rights objections, still leaving for the merits the tackling of the issue where material good faith requirements were met by the Claimants in view of Respondent's allegations related to Italian banks' alleged behaviour consisting in the breach of various selling restrictions and other related obligations.[81]

II. UNCTAD Principle 15: Prompt, efficient, and fair debt restructurings

According to UNCTAD Principle 15 ('Restructuring'), sovereign debt restructuring is to be undertaken 'promptly, efficiently and fairly', echoing domestic insolvency law conceptions. But, perhaps a closer look at the 'fairness' element in UNCTAD Principle 15 may warrant more analysis. To elaborate, it is exactly that principles of fairness and equity,[82] taking into account bondholder participation in the restructuring, price of bond acquisition (as often distinct from their face-value), as well as the haircut percentage, may perhaps be seen as per se equitably barring vulture-type claims before investment tribunals. In any event, it is suggested that The UNCTAD Principles could have at least attempted to provide more guidance on the scope and modalities of 'fairness' in sovereign restructuring, not only internally (i.e. with respect to the modalities of the restructuring per se), but also externally (i.e. with respect to its potential impact on holdout bond-litigation).

The 'internal' aspect is especially crucial if one turns to one of the 'implications' of UNCTAD Principle 15, which reads: 'The borrower [in the context of sovereign

[78] *Chevron Corp. and Texaco Petroleum Corp. v. Ecuador*, Interim Award of 1 December 2008, Ad hoc—UNCITRAL Arbitration Rules, IIC 355 (2008), para. 137.

[79] *Phoenix Action Ltd v. Czech Republic*, Award of 9 April 2009, ICSID Case No. ARB/06/5; IIC 367 (2009), para. 113.

[80] *Abaclat and ors v. Argentina* (n. 53) paras 646–650.

[81] *Abaclat and ors v. Argentina* (n. 53) paras 651–653.

[82] See e.g. A. Gourgourinis, 'Delineating the Normativity of Equity in International Law' (2009) 11 Int'l Community L. Rev. 327.

debt restructuring] should avoid opportunistic behaviour and arbitrary discrimination among creditors; and it should respect the voluntary basis of the process and the seniority of debts.' It is in this respect, then, that one can trace an instance of normative convergence in terms of the omnipresent in international investment arbitration, prohibition of arbitrary, unreasonable, and/or discriminatory measures, expressed via IIA clauses on national (NT) and most-favoured nation treatment (MFN),[83] clauses prohibiting arbitrary, unreasonable, or discriminatory measures,[84] or even, the fair and equitable treatment (FET) standard.[85] Still, one can also note that, as Edwin Borchard wrote in the early 1950s: 'While the private law of bankruptcy is governed by the principle of equality of claims in the distribution of the debtor's assets (*par condicio creditorum*), differential treatment of the holders of foreign government bonds in case of default is the rule.'[86]

Borchard's view appears to be applicable in the contemporary context: it is often propounded, in terms of economic analysis, that differential treatment between domestic and foreign bondholders serves the viability of debt restructuring per se.[87] In this respect, one could then argue that even the otherwise dynamic, by design, non-discrimination standards in IIAs appear too rigid to accommodate the practical economic and political realities of sovereign debt restructuring. In other words, one could posit that there is much more to be written regarding the coexistence of the elements of 'efficiency' and 'fairness' in UNCTAD Principle 15.

It is precisely due to the *sui generis* characteristics, modalities, and goals of sovereign debt restructuring that the 'arbitrary discrimination' element in the commentary of UNCTAD Principle 15 should have taken into account the need to provide sovereigns in financial distress the necessary flexibility in rescheduling their debt. It would, accordingly, have been welcome if, instead of an unavoidably vague reference to 'fairness' in the treatment of creditors, UNCTAD Principle 15

[83] For instance, see T. Waelde, 'The Serbian Loans case—a Precedent for Investment Treaty Protection for Foreign Debt?' in T. Weiler (ed.), *International Investment Law and Arbitration: Leading Cases from the ICSID, NAFTA, Bilateral Treaties and Customary International Law* (Cameron May, 2005) 411–14; A. Szodruch, 'State Insolvency—Consequences and Obligations under Investment Treaties' in R. Hofmann and C. Tams (eds.), *The International Convention for the Settlement of Investment Disputes: Taking Stock After 40 Years* (Nomos, 2007) 159–60; Waibel (n. 57) 273–6.

[84] e.g. V. Heiskanen, 'Arbitrary and Unreasonable Measures' in A. Reinisch (ed.), *Standards of Investment Protection* (Oxford University Press, 2008) 89–109.

[85] On the *problématique* regarding the potential overlaps between NT and MFN clauses with IIA provisions on arbitrary, unreasonable, or discriminatory measures or FET, see A. Newcombe and L. Paradell, *Law and Practice of Investment Treaties: Standards of Treatment* (Kluwer, 2009) 288–90 and 306–7, respectively.

[86] E. Borchard, *State Insolvency and Foreign Bondholders. Volume I. General Principles* (Yale University Press, 1951) 340.

[87] See e.g. G. Roubini, 'Why should the foreign creditors of Argentina take a greater hit/haircut than the domestic ones: On the economic logic, efficiency, fairness and legality of "discriminating" between domestic and foreign debt in sovereign debt restructurings', available at <http://cdi.mecon.gov.ar/biblio/docelec/nber/books/arg/roubini.pdf>; A. Erce and J. Díaz-Cassou, 'Creditor Discrimination During Sovereign Debt Restructurings', Banco de España Documentos de Trabajo N. 1027 (2010), available at <http://www.bde.es/webbde/SES/Secciones/Publicaciones/PublicacionesSeriadas/DocumentosTrabajo/10/Fic/dt1027e.pdf> 11–28; UNCTAD, 'Sovereign Debt Restructuring and International Investment Agreements', IIA Issues Notes No. 2 (July 2011), available at <http://ase.tufts.edu/gdae/publications/UNCTADSovereignDebt.pdf> 4.

directly and more substantially tackled the issue of their, sometimes unavoidable, differentiated treatment. For instance, UNCTAD Principle 15 could have explicitly taken into account the so-called 'funding problem' in sovereign debt restructuring (i.e. a sovereign debtor is likely to need to borrow anew to meet the exigencies of its debt restructuring),[88] and, hence, consider instances where the differentiated treatment of creditors constitutes the only means to address it.

III. UNCTAD Principle 9: Sovereigns' financial necessity defence

UNCTAD Principle 9 ('Binding Agreements') makes reference to a 'state of financial necessity' preventing 'full and/or timely repayment' of sovereign bonds capable of operating as a legal defence before a 'competent judicial authority'. As one can reasonably infer, what the drafters of Principle 9 had in mind when including the scenario of a sovereign's financial necessity resulting in an inability to service its debt, essentially corresponds to the case of successful invocation of either 'non-precluded measures' (NPM) clauses in IIAs, or the customary necessity defence enshrined in Article 25 of the ILC Articles on State Responsibility.[89] So, while it appears that UNCTAD Principle 9, *inter alia*, is expressive of the view that financial necessity indeed constitutes a legitimate ground justifying the full and/or timely repayment of sovereign debt, further elaboration and analysis is needed. For, the majority of investment arbitral awards that have so far dealt with the Argentinian crisis and have addressed respective defences, have, albeit with two notable exceptions,[90] not entertained Argentina's treaty or customary necessity arguments on various grounds,[91] pointing, *inter alia*, to the fact that

[88] S.L. Schwarcz, 'Facing the Debt Challenge of Countries That Are "Too Big To Fail"' in R.W. Kolb, (ed.) *Sovereign Debt: From Safety to Default* (Wiley, 2011) 426.

[89] ILC Draft Articles on the Responsibility of States for Internationally Wrongful Acts with Commentaries', (2001) II(2) YBILC Art. 25:

> 1. Necessity may not be invoked by a State as a ground for precluding the wrongfulness of an act not in conformity with an international obligation of that State unless the act: (a) Is the only way for the State to safeguard an essential interest against a grave and imminent peril; and (b) Does not seriously impair an essential interest of the State or States towards which the obligation exists, or of the international community as a whole. 2. In any case, necessity may not be invoked by a State as a ground for precluding wrongfulness if: (a) The international obligation in question excludes the possibility of invoking necessity; or (b) the State has contributed to the situation of necessity.

According to the ILC Commentaries: 'For a plea of necessity to be precluded under subparagraph (2) (b), the contribution to the situation of necessity must be sufficiently substantial and not merely incidental or peripheral'. For the crucial difference between NPM clauses and the customary necessity defence, see A. Gourgourinis, 'General/Particular International Law and Primary/Secondary Rules: Unitary Terminology of a Fragmented System' (2011) 22 Eur. J. Int'l L. 993, 1022–6. It is worth noting, that even the successful invocation of the customary necessity defence (a secondary rule) enshrined in ILC Art. 25 may only temporarily suspend the sovereign's obligation to service its debt, by virtue of ILC Art. 27 ('Consequences of invoking a circumstance precluding wrongfulness'). Arguably, and to the extent that they do not explicitly provide otherwise, the successful invocation of NPM clauses in IIAs (as primary rules proper) may not have such a time-limited effect.

[90] *LG&E Energy Corp. and ors v. Argentina*, Decision on Liability of 3 October 2006, ICSID Case No. ARB 02/1; IIC 152 (2006); (2007) 46 ILM 36, paras 226–261; *Continental Casualty Co. v. Argentina*, Award of 5 September 2008, ICSID Case No ARB/03/9; IIC 336 (2008), paras 234–6.

[91] See further, C. Binder, 'Non Performance of Treaty Obligations in Cases of Necessity: from "Necessity knows no Law" via the "Law(s) of Necessity" to Interfaces between different "Laws of

Argentina's macroeconomic policies in fact 'substantially' contributed to its situation of necessity,[92] as well as that there existed other means available to Argentina to address its financial distress.[93] It is in this respect that, indeed, the threshold for invoking necessity appears to be insurmountably high,[94] so that UNCTAD

Necessity"' (2008) 13 Austrian Review of International and European Law 6; J. Youngjin and D. H. Sangwook, 'What to Do With the Dilemma Facing the State of Necessity Defense Under the Investment Treaties and How to Interpret the NPM Clause?' (2011) 12 JWIT 397.

[92] See e.g. *CMS Gas Transmission Co. v. Argentina*, Award of of 12 May 2005, ICSID Case No. ARB/01/8, IIC 65 (2005), para. 329:

> The issue, however, is whether the contribution to the crisis by Argentina has or has not been sufficiently substantial. The Tribunal, when reviewing the circumstances of the present dispute, must conclude that this was the case. The crisis was not of the making of one particular administration and found its roots in the earlier crisis of the 1980s and evolving governmental policies of the 1990s that reached a zenith in 2002 and thereafter. Therefore, the Tribunal observes that government policies and their shortcomings significantly contributed to the crisis and the emergency and while exogenous factors did fuel additional difficulties they do not exempt the Respondent from its responsibility in the matter.

Suez and ors v. Argentina, Decision on Liability of 30 July 2010, ICSID Case No ARB/03/17; IIC 442 (2010), para. 264:

> The Tribunal finds that a combination of endogenous and exogenous factors contributed to the Argentinian crisis at the beginning of this century. Among Argentina's contributing factors to the crisis were excessive public spending, inefficient tax collection, delays in responding to the early signs of the crisis, insufficient efforts at developing an export market, and internal political dissension and problems inhibiting effective policy making. In listing these factors, the Tribunal does not by any means intend to minimize the substantial external forces that were buffeting the Argentinian economy. Its intent is to show that Argentina itself contributed to its situation of emergency.

Impregilo SpA v. Argentine Republic, Final award, ICSID Case No ARB/07/17; IIC 498 (2011), para. 358:

> ... the Arbitral Tribunal recognizes that international market forces and events taking place in, *inter alia*, Mexico, Southeast Asia, and Russia affected adversely the economy of Argentina, culminating in the crisis of the early 2000s. Yet, the Arbitral Tribunal has been persuaded by substantial evidence proffered by Impregilo that Argentina's own economic policies over several years prior to the crisis rendered the economy of the country vulnerable to exogenous shocks and pressures, and impacted adversely the sustainability of its economic model on the national and local levels. The Arbitral Tribunal notes, by way of example, Argentina's long-term failure to exercise fiscal discipline, including control of provincial spending and of the subsidization of the Provinces by the central Government; and its inability to adopt labor and trade policies consistent with the country's currency board. The resulting high public indebtedness and inflexibility in Argentina's markets hampered substantially the country's ability to cope with external shocks, leading to the 2001 crisis. It follows that Argentina contributed significantly to the 'situation of necessity' within the meaning of para. 2 (b) and therefore failed to meet the criterion under that paragraph. [footnote omitted].

See also the more extensive analysis in *El Paso Energy International Co. v. Argentina*, Award of 27 October 2011, ICSID Case No. ARB/03/15; IIC 519 (2011), paras 649–665.

[93] See e.g. *Suez and ors v. Argentina* (n. 91) para. 260:

> ... Argentina could have attempted to apply more flexible means to assure the continuation of the water and sewage services to the people of Buenos Aires and at the same time respected its obligations of fair and equitable treatment. The two were by no means mutually exclusive.

[94] A. Reinisch, 'Necessity in Investment Arbitration' (2010) 41 NYIL 137, 152–5.

Principle 9 could be effectively rendered devoid of legal significance if one sticks with the view of the majority of investment awards dealing with the Argentinian financial crisis.

Hence, it would seem that, mindful of the contemporary stance of the majority of investment tribunals with respect to the invocability of the financial necessity defence, the UNCTAD Principles, could have provided more detail on the interplay and individual effect (from the point of view of the law on state responsibility) of the endogenous and exogenous factors surrounding sovereign default,[95] or perhaps could have also pointed to the effect of debt restructuring as a pertinent element in the context of a necessity defence excusing the inability to service sovereign bonds.

IV. The prospective role for the UNCTAD Principles in investment treaty arbitration

A last, general, comment pertains to the potential normative effect of the UNCTAD Principles in future investment arbitration cases related to sovereign bonds: according to the UNCTAD Principles' Preamble:

> The normative contribution of these Principles *lies not in the creation of new rights nor obligations in international* law but in *identifying, harmonizing and systematizing* the basic principles and best practices applied to sovereign lending and borrowing and in elaborating the implications of these standards and practices for lenders and borrowers at the international level. This set of principles should *apply without prejudice* of other international rules concerning the action of lenders or borrowers.[96]

In other words, the UNCTAD Principles *prima facie* claim to partly represent a 'codification' exercise, to borrow the wording of the Statute of the International Law Commission (ILC),[97] with respect to the rights of sovereign borrowers and their lenders at the international level; importantly, they do not seek to eventually replace existing international standards (such as those derived from investment protection law) but rather opt for their *inter se* coexistence.

Accordingly, even if the UNCTAD Principles per se qualify as soft law,[98] this should not be understood as undermining their prospective importance in the

[95] cf. the noteworthy attempts made by, *inter alios*, A. Reinisch, 'Debt Restructuring and State Responsibility Issues' in D. Carreau and M. Shaw (eds.), *La dette extérieure* (Martinus Nijhoff, 1995) 561–3; A. Alvarez-Jiménez, 'Foreign Investment Protection and Regulatory Failures as States' Contribution to the State of Necessity under Customary International Law: a New Approach Based on the Complexity of Argentina's 2001 Crisis' (2010) 27 J. Int'l Arb. 141, 160–77.

[96] UNCTAD Principles (n. 1) 3 (Preamble) (emphasis added).

[97] Statute of the International Law Commission, Art. 15, adopted by the UN General Assembly in Resolution 174 (II) of 21 November 1947, as amended by Resolution 485 (V) of 12 December 1950, and Resolutions 984 (X) of 3 December 1955, 985 (X) of 3 December 1955, and 36/39 of 18 November 1981. On the extent to which the UNCTAD Principles reflect existing state practice, see M. Waibel, Ch. 5 of this book.

[98] See J.P. Bohoslavsky and C. Espósito, Ch. 4 of this volume. On the definition and normative qualities of soft law, see e.g. H. Neuhold, 'Variations on the Theme of "Soft International Law"' in I. Buffard et al. (eds), *International Law between Universalism and Fragmentation: Festschrift in Honour*

context of international economic adjudication.[99] It is, perhaps exactly, in this context that the *Abaclat and ors v. Argentina* investment Tribunal in its Decision on Jurisdiction and Admissibility referred to the description/definition of sovereign default as defined by a non-governmental entity, namely the credit rating agency Standard & Poor's,[100] as well as to the practices (and principles derived therefrom) of the Paris and London Clubs regarding sovereign debt workouts.[101] Hence, one should not be surprised if investment tribunals in the future make direct reference, albeit as soft law, to the UNCTAD Principles, or even incorporate them in their reasoning. This serves as another indication of the importance of the content and direction that the Principles have acquired, or may acquire in the future.

D. Synthesis: the 2012 Greek Debt Restructuring

Since UNCTAD Principles 7 and 15 seek to introduce a comprehensive and systemic approach to debt restructuring, it would be suitable to attempt to examine how these principles fit with the actual management of recent debt crises, especially in the case of the EU countries that face the spectre of insolvency, when the global financial system is threatened with a domino effect in terms of government bankruptcies.[102] This intriguing exercise would allow us to see whether Principles 7 and 15 are indeed designed to effectively deal with novel complex and extreme situations, as a means of identifying strengths, weaknesses, and problems in their wording and to make recommendations for their interpretation. While the recent Greek debt restructuring (the largest in history) is ongoing, and the analysis herein does not and cannot claim to be exhaustive, it can still serve as an illustrative example/test for *prima facie* assessing the limited effectiveness of the UNCTAD

of Gerhard Hafner (Martinus Nijhoff, 2008) 343; D. Shelton, 'Soft Law' in D. Armstrong (ed.), *Routledge Handbook of International Law* (Routledge, 2009) 69; D. Thürer, 'Soft Law' in R. Wolfrum (ed.), MPEPIL online edition (2009), <http://www.mpepil.com>.

[99] For this point, see I. Seidl-Hohenveldern, 'International Economic Law: General Course on Public International Law' (1986) 198 *Recueil des cours* 68–71; W.W. Park, 'The Procedural Soft Law of International Arbitration: Non-governmental Instruments', in L.A. Mistelis and J.D.M. Lew (eds.), *Pervasive Problems in International Arbitration* (Kluwer Law International, 2006) 143–53; G. Kaufmann-Kohler, 'Soft Law in International Arbitration: Codification and Normativity' (2010) 1 Journal of International Dispute Settlement 1, 5–13.

[100] *Abaclat and ors v. Argentina* (n. 53) para. 28.

[101] *Abaclat and ors v. Argentina* (n. 53) paras 32–37.

[102] For an apt legal analysis of the EU law framework on sovereign bailouts, see C. Stephanou, 'Building Firewalls: European Responses to the Sovereign Debt Crisis' in O. Hieronymi and C. Stephanou (eds), *International Debt: Economic, Financial, Monetary, Political and Regulatory Aspects* (Palgrave Macmillan, 2012) 127. More specifically, on the European Financial Stability Facility (EFSF) and the 'no bail-out' clause, see P. Athanassiou, 'Of Past Measures and Future Plans for Europe's Exit From the Sovereign Debt Crisis: What is Legally Possible (and What is Not)' (2011) 36 European Law Review 558, 559–65; on the possible legal basis (again, from the EU law perspective) for the decision creating the European Stability Mechanism (ESM) and providing for the mandatory insertion of CACs and extension of maturity terms in the sovereign bonds of EU Members, see J. Gott, 'Addressing the Debt Crisis in the European Union: the Validity of Mandatory Collective Action Clauses and extending Maturities' (2011) 12 Chi. J. Int'l L. 201, 219–26.

Principles in the case of *sui generis* sovereign debt workouts, such as the 2012 Greek Debt Restructuring.

I. A brief overview of the 2012 Greek debt workout

The loss of the creditworthiness of the Greek government at the beginning of 2010 was the triggering event for the creation of the mechanism to support the Greek economy in the spring of 2010.[103] The reasons that led to the creation of the '*support mechanism*' are described in Council Decision 2010/320/EU,[104] as well as in paragraphs 1 to 3 of Article 1 of Law 3845/2010.[105] Greek gross public debt at the end of 2009 stood at 115 per cent of GDP, a debt ratio among the highest in the European Union (the reference value of the Treaty is 60 per cent of GDP). The package of May 2010 was premised on the assumption that Greece would re-establish its access to the bond markets by 2012.[106] Still, and as the debt crisis unfolded, Greece could not return to capital markets for funding. Thus, the decisions of the Eurozone Summit of 26–27 October 2011 opened a new chapter in the management of the crisis in the Eurozone. The decisions involved a Private Sector Involvement (PSI) package, in essence a bond exchange, to assure the sustainability of Greek debt.[107] As far as the timing of the bond exchange is concerned, the Greek government had to roll over bonds (€14.4 billion) in March 2011.

In its fifth review of Greece (December 2011), the IMF estimated that the Greek PSI would need to involve a haircut of 50 per cent, a bondholders' participation of nearly 100 per cent, and interest rates of around 4 per cent. In the same document,

[103] cf. C.M. Reinhart and K.S. Rogoff, *This Time Is Different: Eight Centuries of Financial Folly* (Princeton University Press, 2009) 99ff. According to these authors, Greece, Ecuador, and Honduras are among the few countries that have spend more than half of their existence in a state of sovereign bankruptcy or debt restructuring. According to the same study (at 121), from 1827 to 2003, European countries in default had a ratio of public debt to public revenues of 4:1. In Latin American states the ratio was 5:1. In 2009, Greek public revenues (excluding loans) amounted to €50bn; external debt was about €300bn. Thus, the ratio of debt to revenues was at least 6:1. On the dimensions and institutional contours of the 2007–09 international financial crisis, as well the regulatory gaps in the system of international financial law, see C. Gortsos, *Fundamentals of Public International Financial Law: International Banking Law within the system of Public International Financial Law* (Nomos Verlagsgesellschaft, 2012) 127–31, 283–6.

[104] [2010] OJ L145/6ff.

[105] On Law 3845/2010, Greece's Stand-by-Agreement with the IMF and the 2010 loans to Greece from the eurozone countries, see A. Bredimas, 'Memorandum of Understanding, Stand-by-Agreement (FMI) et Accord d'emprunt de la Grèce avec les Etats membres de l' Eurozone: leurs conclusions souls l'angle du droit international et constitutionnel', in S. Perrakis (ed.), *States in the 21st Century International Community* (Ant. N. Sakkoulas Publications, forthcoming).

[106] W.R. Cline, 'Sustainability of Greek Public Debt', Peterson Institute for International Economics Policy Brief 11–15, available at <http://www.iie.com/publications/pb/pb11-15.pdf> 2.

[107] Still, one must also to consider the consequences of PSI in the long-term. 'Debt restructurings are no free lunches for sovereigns' (F. Moss, 'Debt Resolution Mechanisms: Should there be a Statutory Mechanism for Resolving Debt Crises?', paper presented at the Eighth UNCTAD Debt Management Conference, Geneva, 14–16 November 2011, available at <http://r0.unctad.org/dmfas/docs/DMconf2011/Moss_ECB.pdf>), since they implicate significant reputational costs; indeed, the more drastic the haircut, the longer is the loss of market access and the higher are borrowing costs for the sovereign in the future.

the IMF recommended the 'legislation of CACs in domestic law bonds'. This would be an effective means to coerce participation, since more than 90 per cent of the bonds to be exchanged were governed by Greek law. Developments in the first trimester of 2012 confirmed the IMF's approach. The two important developments leading to the bond exchange have been, first, the adoption of the Greek Bondholder Act (Law 4050/2012),[108] introducing CACs in the bond contracts that were governed by Greek law, and, secondly, the successful conclusion of the negotiations between the Greek government and the representatives of the bondholders over the terms of the exchange.

On 24 February 2012, the Greek Ministry of Finance launched an official public offer for the exchange of Greek government bonds.[109] The offer closed on 8 March 2012 with an overall participation of 83.7 per cent of all PSI-eligible debt (€172 billion of bonds issued or guaranteed by the Greek government).[110] Although there was an extension of the invitation period for some categories of bonds (foreign-law bonds and bonds issued by state enterprises and guaranteed by the Greek government)[111] and a deferral of the settlement date to 11 April 2012, the offer can be considered as a successful one, from a technical point of view. The quorum required by the Greek Bondholder Act was achieved, as well as the qualified majority (two-thirds of the participating principal) consenting to the bond exchange.[112]

The next step in the restructuring process was the activation of the CACs. According to the press release of the Greek Ministry of Finance on 9 March 2012:

[108] Law 4050/2012, 'Rules on the amendment of titles issued or guaranteed by the Hellenic Republic with the bondholders' agreement', *Government Gazette* A 36/23.02.2012. See also Act No. 5 of the Ministerial Council, *Government Gazette* A 37/23.02.2012.

[109] The full terms of the invitation have been made available in electronic form only through <http://www.greekbonds.gr>. To sum up, there are two types of titles to be delivered at settlement: (1) new bonds having a face value equal to 31.5% of the face value of the debt exchanged (2) notes of the EFSF maturing within 24 months and having a face value equal to 15% of the face value of the debt exchanged. Each participating holder also receives detachable GDP-linked securities of Greece with a notional amount equal to the face amount of the new bonds. See Ministry of Finance, 'PSI Launch Press Release', 21 February 2012.

[110] P. Monokroussos and P. Petropoulou, 'Greek PSI: Public offer results, debt exchange timeline and impact on sovereign liquidity & solvency', *Greece Macro-Monitor—Eurobank Research* (9 March 2012), available at <http://www.eurobank.gr/Uploads/Reports/FOCUS%20GREECEPSI%20March%209%202012.pdf>. As these authors observe:

> ...as per the EU Summit Statement of 26–27 October 2012, a temporary EFSF credit enhancement (up to €35bn) will be provided to ensure collateral eligibility of Greek sovereign bonds in ECB liquidity operations. Presumably, the EFSF credit enhancement will remain in place for as long as Greece's sovereign debt rating remains on 'selective default' as a result of the debt swap. This amount is not included in the €100bn figure (new EFSF/IMF financing).

[111] For these two categories, bondholders' participation was not so high; holders of approximately €20bn tendered their bonds (69% of such eligible instruments). For a proposal in favour of super-collective-action clauses, allowing a qualified majority of the all bondholders to decide the restructuring of all the bond issues, see K.M. Kletzer, 'Sovereign Bond Restructuring: Collective Action Clauses and Official Crisis Intervention', IMF Working Paper WP/03/134 (June 2003), available at <http://www.imf.org/external/pubs/ft/wp/2003/wp03134.pdf>.

[112] See Act of the Governor of the Bank of Greece of 9 March 2012 (unofficial translation), available at <http://www.isda.org/uploadfiles/_docs/Act_of_the_Bank_of_Greece_9_March_2012.pdf>, which certified the consent of the bondholders to the proposed amendments.

The Republic has advised its official sector creditors that upon confirmation and certification by the Bank of Greece as process manager under the Greek Bondholder Act (Law 4050/2012), it intends to accept the consents received and amend the terms of all of its Greek law government bonds, including those not tendered for exchange pursuant to the invitation, in accordance with the terms of the Greek Bondholder Act.

After the activation of the CACs, the level of participation in the bond exchange will rise to 95.7 per cent of the overall outstanding amount (€197 billion). The success of the PSI deal, which is expected to bring a significant upfront nominal reduction in privately-held Greek debt, is combined with another positive development for Greece, i.e. the approval of the new bailout package that covers government's borrowing needs in the period 2012 to 2014.

II. A first take on the features of the Greek PSI in the light of the UNCTAD Principles

In *prima facie* consistency with UNCTAD Principle 7, the majority of the lenders of the Greek government appear to have recognized that circumstances necessitate the restructuring of sovereign debt, entering into the negotiations and accepting a generous haircut, with the help of the IIF, which assumed a key role in coordinating the action of private bondholders. From the bondholders' point of view, some elements of the package are of special significance to investors:[113] the use of English law, the use of a co-financing structure with the EFSF loan to Greece, the use of GDP-linked securities in the event of higher Greek growth than anticipated in the economic programme. This brings us to a major issue of the Greek PSI programme: its voluntary character.

In practice, the outlines of the deal where decided at the Eurozone summit of 26–27 October 2011. As far as incentives are concerned, the enhancement of the quality of the exchanged debt could not guarantee a high participation rate. An imposition of CACs through domestic legislation, as the IMF has proposed, seemed a more effective approach to debt restructuring. Nevertheless, this solution was very controversial and could hardly qualify as a voluntary one, at least for the dissenting bondholders. An issuer's unilateral change of the original terms and conditions of an obligation can be considered as a *de facto* restructuring;[114] furthermore, the process leads to the issuance of new debt with less favourable terms than those of the original issue without adequate offsetting compensation.[115] Ergo, the Greek PSI's voluntary character was a key aspect of the problem of how

[113] Steering Committee of the Private Creditor-Investor Committee for Greece (PCIC), Statement by Charles Dallara and Jean Lemierre, IIF Press Release, 9 March 2012.

[114] On the changes of local law, see: L. Buchheit, 'Restructuring a Nation's Debt' (2010) 29 Int'l Fin. L. Rev. 46, 47–8.

[115] See Standard & Poor's, 'Retroactive Application of Collective Action Clauses Would Constitute a Selective Default By Greece', 10 February 2012, and 'Rating Implications of Exchange Offers and Similar Restructurings, Update', 12 May 2009.

to avoid a credit event in the market for credit-default swaps (CDS)[116] and a declaration by rating agencies that Greece is in default.

The ISDA Credit Derivatives Determinations Committee met on 9 March 2012, to examine the Greek debt restructuring and to determine if a credit event had occurred under section 4.7 of the ISDA 2003 Credit Derivatives Definitions. It resolved unanimously that a Restructuring Credit Event had indeed occurred with respect to Greece, following the exercise of CACs to amend the terms of Greek bonds, 'such that the right of all holders of the Affected Bonds to receive payments has been reduced'.[117] On their part, credit rating agencies also considered Greece to have defaulted.[118] It is in this respect that the existence of the 'consensual rearrangement' element, inherent in UNCTAD Principle 7, in the case of the Greek PSI would, at the least, appear to be in doubt.

With respect to UNCTAD Principle 15 and fairness in creditors' treatment, one could identify at least three outstanding issues: *first*, on 17 February 2012, Greece and the ECB completed a side-deal,[119] i.e. a separate debt exchange on bonds held by the ECB under the Securities Market Programme. The new bonds are identical to the old ones in all aspects, except the issue date and International Securities Identification Number (ISIN). In this manner, the new bonds held by the ECB have not been included in the PSI debt exchange in March 2012 (the exchange offer covered bonds issued on 31 December 2011, or earlier), and are to be serviced

[116] In the case of CDS transaction using the standard ISDA documentation, the parties agree to be bound by the decisions of the competent ISDA Credit Derivatives Determinations Committee. According to the Depository Trust & Clearing Corporation's data (Trade Information Warehouse), the total net exposure of market participants in Greek CDS protection was approximately $3.2 billion as of 2 March 2012.

[117] ISDA Press Release, 'ISDA EMEA Determinations Committee: Restructuring Credit Event Has Occurred with Respect to The Hellenic Republic', 9 March 2012, available at <http://www.isda.org/companies/HellenicRepublicCDS/HellenicRepublicCDS.html>. Outlining the restructuring scenarios which could trigger CDS, see M. Waibel, 'Steering Greece's Debt Restructuring Through the CDS Quicksand', 7 March 2012, available at <http://ssrn.com/abstract=2017772> 24–31. On the other hand, if such a restructuring were not declared a credit event, the sovereign CDS market would undoubtedly suffer a severe stroke: A. Sibert, 'Debt Restructuring: Ramifications for the Euro Area', Draft Briefing Note—European Parliament's Committee on Economic and Monetary Affairs (June 2011) 12.

[118] Standard & Poor's Ratings had lowered the sovereign credit ratings on Greece to 'Selective Default' following the retroactive insertion of CACs in the Greek bond contracts on 23 February 2012. Nevertheless, following the PSI deal, the rating agencies considered selective default to have been cured. For instance, Fitch withdrew the ratings on the old bonds and assigned a 'B-' rating to Greece's new government bonds issued in the context of the debt exchange. According to Moody's Investors Service, the Greek debt exchange represents a 'distressed exchange', and therefore a debt default, 'because (i) the exchange amounts to a diminished financial obligation relative to the original obligation, and (ii) the exchange has the effect of allowing Greece to avoid payment default in the future.' Moody's Investors Service, 'Moody's comments on Greek debt exchange', 9 March 2012, available at <http://www.moodys.com/research/Moodys-comments-on-Greek-debt-exchange–PR_240125>.

[119] 'ECB Concludes Greek Bond Exchange', *Wall Street Journal*, 17 February 2012, available at <http://online.wsj.com/article/SB10001424052970204059804577229341521642580.html>. The ECB had its own Greek bond holdings (approximately €50bn) acquired though the Securities Market Programme, as well as Greek bonds placed by banks as collateral for ECB liquidity: Z. Darvas, 'Debt restructuring in the euro area: a necessary but manageable evil?', Draft Briefing Note, European Parliament's Committee on Economic and Monetary Affairs (June 2011) 23.

in full, in contrast to other Greek Government bond creditors affected by the imposition of CACs under Law 4050/2012.[120] *Secondly*, holders of foreign-law Greek bonds may be found to enjoy '*de facto* seniority' over Greek-law bondholders, in the context of the Hellenic Republic's workout.[121] *Thirdly*, the impact of the Greek PSI on domestic creditors is perhaps the most serious consequence.[122] One could then reasonably speculate that these three instances of discrimination among creditors will come to the forefront of legal counsels' argumentation. In this fashion, UNCTAD Principle 15 as it currently stands, and albeit establishing an otherwise readily accepted by all affected parties generic proposition for 'fair treatment', may only to a limited extent, if at all, provide meaningful guidance to arbitrators and judges before whom sovereign bonds cases are brought; and this serves as but another indication that further in-depth analysis is merited, so that the UNCTAD Principles indeed achieve their goal.

E. Concluding Remarks

The UNCTAD Principles have indeed been put forward in a very timely fashion: in February 2012, the US District Court entered permanent injunctions restraining payments to holders of restructured Argentinian debt, until Argentina complies and services in full the bonds held by the Elliott Management Corporation vulture

[120] Given the key role of the ECB in the Eurozone rescue plan for Greece, one could draw an interesting parallel with the principle that sovereign debt owed to international organizations is never rescheduled: see e.g. P.R. Wood, 'Debt Priorities in Sovereign Insolvency', (1982) 1 Int'l Fin. L. Rev. 4, 7. In this sense, it is interesting to note, for instance, that the League of Nations loans were afforded more favourable treatment by virtue of the fact that they 'formed part of a powerful and useful reconstruction machine'. League of Nations, Second Annual Report of the Committee for the Study of International Loan Contracts (1936) 9, 16–22, as cited in Borchard (n. 85) 341, footnote 13. Accordingly, in the 1930s, Greece's League loans were granted front rank over other liabilities. On Greece's League Loans, see e.g. W.H. Wynne, *State Insolvency and Foreign Bondholders: Selected Case Histories of Governmental Foreign Bond Defaults and Debt Readjustments* (Yale University Press, 1951) 349–57.

[121] On the *de facto* and *de jure* seniority in debt restructurings, see P. Bolton and O. Jeanne, 'Structuring and Restructuring Sovereign Debt: The Role of Seniority' (2009) 76 Rev. Econ. Stud. 879. On the Greek PSI, see G.M. Gulati and J. Zettelmeyer, 'Making a voluntary Greek debt exchange work' (2012) 7 Cap. Mkts L.J. 169, especially at 182–3. For instance, the Hellenic Republic made timely payment of the principal as well as the interest due on approximately €435m of bonds maturing on 15 May 2012, not tendered for exchange, emphasizing that this decision 'does not prejudice future decisions on the treatment of the remaining bonds not tendered in the PSI exchange'. Hellenic Ministry of Finance, Press Release, 15 May 2012, available at <http://www.minfin.gr/portal/en/resource/contentObject/id/bec9c833-6dd5-46d8-8383-9ade14498e3d>.

[122] A major issue in the context of the 2012 Greek Debt Restructuring was the exposure of domestic banks to Greek sovereign bonds, hence imposing the need for their recapitalization. See, in this respect, A. Blundell-Wignall and P. Slovik, 'A Market Perspective on the European Sovereign Debt and Banking Crisis', OECD Journal: Financial Market Trends 10 (2010), available at <http://www.oecd.org/dataoecd/19/9/46970598.pdf> 16; C. Gortsos, 'The Impact of the Current Eurozone Fiscal Crisis on the Greek Banking Sector and the Measures Adopted to Preserve its Stability' in O. Hieronymi and C. Stephanou (eds), *International Debt: Economic, Financial, Monetary, Political and Regulatory Aspects* (Palgrave Macmillan, 2012) 164.

fund.[123] Argentina has appealed against the district court's orders and, in its appellant brief submitted to the US Appeals Court, emphasized the negative repercussions of the non-reversal of the permanent injunctions for the eventual success of the Greek debt restructuring;[124] at the same time, the probability of the initiation of investment arbitration and domestic litigation proceedings against Greece, by holdout bondholders, has already been highlighted,[125] and recently materialized.[126] In other words, the challenges ahead for the UNCTAD Principles are by now both visible and substantial. Ergo, the conclusion reached in this contribution is that, while a veritable degree of coherence between standards of domestic insolvency law and, to a lesser extent, international investment law regarding sovereign debt restructuring is indeed maintained in the UNCTAD Principles, international discourse on the matter will benefit from a 'monistic' furtherance of exchange of views and standard-setting coordination between an enlarged pool of experts, stakeholders, and policy-makers. The UNCTAD Principles, being 'still open for discussion and debate' according to their Background Note, constitute a remarkable initiative with potentially far-reaching effects regarding sovereign debt; still, their elaboration must continue. This chapter points precisely to specific facets of the treatment of debt restructuring therein that, perhaps, require revision and further elaboration, towards developing a set of commonly accepted and effective principles and practices relating to and aiming at the success of sovereign debt workouts.

123 *NML Capital Ltd v. Republic of Argentina*, 09-cv-01707, U.S. District Court, Southern District of New York (Manhattan).

124 US Court of Appeals for the Second Circuit, *NML Capital Ltd v. Republic of Argentina*, Brief of Defendant-Appellant (The Republic of Argentina), 21 March 2012, available at <http://newsandinsight.thomsonreuters.com/uploadedFiles/Reuters_Content/2012/04_-_April/Argentina_brief.pdf> 2, 24, and 46.

125 See e.g. K.P. Gallagher, 'The New Vulture Culture: Sovereign Debt Restructuring and Trade and Investment Treaties', IDEAs Working Paper Series, Paper No. 02/2011, available at <http://ase.tufts.edu/gdae/publications/GallagherSovereignDebt.pdf> 17–18; L. Buchheit and M. Gulati, 'How to Restructure Greek Debt', in: *Greek Debt—The Endgame Scenarios*, 18 April 2011, available at SSRN: <http://ssrn.com/abstract=1807011> 24. According to press reports, the Spanish hedge fund Vega Asset Management resigned from the private creditors' steering committee, opposing the proposed terms of the bond exchange and considering 'all available legal options'. T. Wilkes and S. Sassard, 'Hedge funds hunker down for Greek debt standoff', Reuters (13 January 2012), available at <http://www.reuters.com/article/2012/01/13/us-hedge-funds-greece-idUSTRE80C0KJ20120113>. Moreover, the Greek PSI appears to have attracted the attention of vulture funds, which are said to have long been gearing up for litigation and arbitration against the Hellenic Republic: e.g. C. Whittall et al., 'Vulture funds prepare to battle Greek default', *International Financing Review* (16 February 2012), available at < http://www.ifre.com/vulture-funds-prepare-to-battle-greek-default/20048814.article>.

126 On 20 May 2013, the Secretary-General of ICSID registered a request for the institution of arbitration proceedings against Greece regarding the claims by a Slovak financial institution and its shareholder against Greece arising under the 2012 Greek debt restructuring. *Poštová banka, a.s. and ISTROKAPITAL SE v Hellenic Republic*, ICSID Case No. ARB/13/8.

PART III

DEBT MANAGEMENT

8

Improving Debt Management on the Basis of UNCTAD's Principles

*Kunibert Raffer**

A. Introduction

Responsible sovereign borrowing and lending practices are a legal and economic necessity for the proper functioning of financial markets, as well as an ethical desideratum. As any economic textbook states, markets need reliable frameworks to operate efficiently. Thus, the WTO was propagated as a rule-based system. However the WTO might really function, and whatever the effects of its rules as practised may be, it is quite interesting that a similar need has not yet been identified in the case of sovereign debt in spite of many grave problems caused by this asymmetry, as Li and Panizza argue in more detail, in Chapter 2 of this volume. Sovereign lending still has no comparable international framework. UNCTAD's Principles are a first and important initiative to avoid repeating many problems of the past. They also protect bona fide creditors, who otherwise recoup less in the case of default with or without proper procedures. UNCTAD quite rightly observes that the 'contribution of these Principles lies not in the creation of new rights nor obligations in international law';[1] it should be recalled, however, that elements of the Principles are already the law of the land in many, and sometimes all, municipal legal systems. Bohoslavsky and Espósito and Goldmann, in Chapters 4 and 6 respectively, argue that the Principles are well-rooted and broadly tested in domestic law. Due authorization under Principle 3, or the due diligence implications of Principle 2 are the best examples. Unfortunately, such very basic legal necessities have not always been observed in sovereign lending.

To be meaningful, responsibility must be made economically relevant by re-instilling market incentives, notably risk. The economic interest of lenders must be brought to bear. Lender liabilities that exist in any municipal law must be introduced into the international arena in order to avoid a two-tier global legal system that is not only unjust and in contradiction to jurisprudence as *ars boni and*

* I am indebted to Juan Pablo Bohoslavsky for useful comments.

[1] UNCTAD, Principles on Promoting Responsible Sovereign Lending and Borrowing, reproduced in the Annex of this book.

aequi but also rigs the market. Fair play, not fair game, must be the cornerstone of international financial markets when it comes to Southern sovereigns.

This chapter elaborates the implications of some of UNCTAD's Principles, focusing in particular on creditors where the need to introduce appropriate rules is seen as more urgent. It shows that until the Second World War several principles were routinely applied, triggering economic consequences. In a way, the rule of law and a proper economic incentive system were more frequently upheld than at present. It then discusses the economic role of risk and its legal implications, the relation between prospective social returns and interest rates, and the necessary differentiation of responsibilities depending on whether lenders purely grant credits or also engage in further activities, such as designing or monitoring projects, an issue virtually only relevant for official lenders. The chapter shows that the instruments to implement Principle 5 already exist, although they seem to have fallen into oblivion. Finally it discusses the well-known fact that a debtor may become incapable of honouring all contractual obligations, a sad fact of life dealt with by Principles 7 and 15. This calls for a—preferably consensual—solution. In doing so, this chapter also puts the fervently discussed problem of holdout creditors, often called 'vultures', into proper perspective.

B. Sovereign Lending before 1945: More in Line with the Rule of Law, UNCTAD's Principles, and Economic Reason

Military interventions and threats notwithstanding, economic mechanisms mostly prevailed before 1945. Risk was allowed to play its role. Legal principles, such as debtor protection and debtor rights, were generally accepted. After some negotiation and foot-dragging, claims were in most cases reduced by agreement. The management of the Egyptian debt crisis of 1876 is an economic success story contrasting vividly with current no-state-insolvency policies. How this debt accumulated is not of interest here, nor is the background of Anglo-Egyptian relations, only the technicalities of the solution. Private creditors decided to use Egyptian insolvency law as the yardstick to solve the crisis. After a surprisingly short time this concept was economically successful for creditors and the debtor alike. The administrator, a hard-nosed nineteenth century capitalist, managed this crisis much better and more quickly than international public sector institutions nowadays. He lowered taxes and postal fees, for example, financed expenditures in public health and education, and encouraged improvements in irrigation. Wages and pensions were paid out in full. Briefly, the principle of debtor protection was *de facto* applied.[2]

After Mexico's default of 1914 the US Ambassador proposed following Egypt's example, but did not prevail against creditors. The United States invaded Mexico

[2] K. Raffer, *Debt Management and Development—Protection of the Poor and the Millennium Development Goals* (Elgar, 2010) 2.

and occupied Veracruz, although the Hague Convention of 1907 had outlawed the use of force in the case of sovereign debts. After years of debt management—the country was practically run by creditors at times—debt service was finally geared to Mexico's capacity to pay. Eventually, creditors received less than 10 per cent of face values. The Egyptian solution would most probably have delivered a better result more quickly and cheaply for everyone involved.

Generally, though, sovereign debtors, including Southern Countries (SCs), were treated much better and more correctly before the Bretton Woods Institutions (BWIs) became debt managers. Two highly illuminating issues are presented in more detail in section B.I. and II.

I. Authority to sign

Especially during the nineteenth century, international tribunals held that states were not bound by contracts made by someone without proper authority, so-called *ultra vires* contracts. When Venezuela's President Páez had his consul improperly enter into contracts that fell within the legislature's authority, claims under these contracts were rejected. In 1922, Costa Rica refused to honour a contract between the former dictator Federico Tinoco and a British oil company, a concession granted by him and approved by the Chamber of Deputies. The constitution would have required approval by both chambers. The new government repudiated the contract on the grounds that those who had entered it had acted *ultra vires*.[3]

Checking whether a person signing on behalf of a legal entity actually has the authority to sign (UNCTAD's Principle 3) is one fundamental obligation of creditors. If the official or person signing has no authority, the contract naturally does not bind the debtor. It is legally null and void, non-existent as far as this unrepresented debtor is concerned. The very law rests on the condition that one can only be bound by contracts freely entered into and signed by oneself or—especially in the case of legal entities—by someone properly authorized to do so. Otherwise the debtor might not even be aware of the loan. Checking the authority to sign is an obligation of creditors. Lenders, who do not fulfil it, do so at their own peril, unless they lend to an SC. Although this is self-evident and such checks are routine for Northern corporate or sovereign debt, this principle has *de facto* been waived in sovereign lending supported by Northern governments and International Financial Institutions (IFIs). There is no valid reason for such discrimination. By basic legal principles, substantial parts of sovereign debts are null and void.

One clear illustration of the problem may suffice. Article 75 of the Argentine constitution reserves the authority to incur sovereign debts to Congress. Article 76 prohibits Congress from delegating this prerogative to the administration. Sovereign debts multiplied under the military dictatorship from $7.8 billion in 1975 to $46 billion in 1984 without a single loan raised in the proper, constitutional way. One may argue that the existence of a dictatorship violating human rights obliged

[3] cf. Raffer (n. 2) 2–3.

creditors in particular to check whether all formal requirements had been obeyed. Relevant information was readily available, public knowledge and should have been respected by lenders unless they wanted to support the military dictators. When a citizen, Alejandro Olmos, started legal proceedings against the government 'and others', the verdict by Criminal Judge Jorge Ballesteros on 14 July 2000 ruled that a large part of Argentine debt resulted from 'measures which were intended to benefit private companies and businesses'.[4] This verdict established irregularities in no fewer than 477 credit operations, as two members of Argentina's Congress, María América González and Mario Cafiero, recalled in a letter (dated 29 July 2004) to the Securities and Exchange Commission, Washington, DC, c/o Mr Russell Clause. No debtor, except SCs deprived of self-evident rights, would be expected to 'honour' such 'contracts' in full. Not that any irregularity need necessarily void a contract totally. But these facts certainly give reason to make thorough checks, which were not conducted in the Argentine case. Argentina's unilateral debt reduction, though second best from the point of view of economics and the rule of law, has meanwhile corrected the debt burden somewhat, arguably optimizing under given restraints. Clearly, the creditors losing money were no longer those lending during the dictatorship.

This cornerstone of law, unconditional necessity in all municipal laws, must also become routine in sovereign lending. Unfortunately, it has not always been protected by those municipal courts to whose jurisdiction sovereign debtors submitted by waivers of immunity.

When I proposed verifying debts as part of my international Chapter 9 (US Chapter 9, Title 11) approach,[5] as is routine in any domestic case, the need and even the possibility of doing so were hotly denied by IFI personnel in discussions. Meanwhile, the IMF[6] also demands specific checks regarding, 'for example, the authority of an official to borrow on behalf of the debtor', echoing my demand, nearly in my own words.[7] Over decades this self-evident obligation was ignored. It still has no practical relevance. Neither IFIs nor any other creditors have encouraged debtors to consider such debts null and void and to act upon that conclusion. There has not even been any attempt to uphold the basic legal principle that those binding a legal entity must have the authority to do so, even though that is plain vanilla in any transaction with Northern governments and corporations. The comparatively civilized legal practice of the nineteenth century still remains out of reach for one group of debtors. Following UNCTAD's principles would provide

4 A. Pettifor, L. Cisneros, and A. Olmos Gaona, *It Takes Two to Tango: Creditor Co-responsibility for Argentina's Crisis—and the Need for Independent Resolution* (Jubilee Plus, NEF, 2001) 8.

5 K. Raffer, 'Applying Chapter 9 Insolvency to International Debts: An Economically Efficient Solution with a Human Face' (1990) 18(2) World Development 309.

6 IMF, 'The Design of the Sovereign Debt Restructuring Mechanism—Further Considerations' (2002), available at <http://www.imf.org/external/np/pdr/sdrm/2002/112702.pdf> 68 (accessed 2 March 2013).

7 K. Raffer, 'What's Good for the United States Must Be Good for the World: Advocating an International Chapter 9 Insolvency' in Bruno Kreisky Forum for International Dialogue (ed.), *From Cancún to Vienna, International Development in a New World* (Kreisky Forum, 1993) 68 or <http://homepage.univie.ac.at/kunibert.raffer/kreisky.pdf> (accessed 2 March 2013).

relief. Unfortunately, Argentina suffered greatly from these illegal debts. But creditors as a group suffered as well, especially bona fide creditors, because they eventually lost more money than they would have under an early solution and correct application of fundamental legal principles, as illustrated later. Ultimately, private creditors had to pick up the bill. Protecting claims without proper legal foundations, the public sector shares the responsibility for many of Argentina's troubles and for present creditor losses. While private creditors may have tried to cover up errors, the public sector has allowed and encouraged them to do so, disregarding the very foundations of the rule of law, which the public sector should preserve. The legal framework, especially in those countries whose courts were chosen under waivers of immunity, did not work properly.

Although legal norms—including the authority to sign—are public knowledge, borrowers may helpfully increase transparency. Debt management offices could disclose this information in an easily accessible way.

II. The Famous *Tinoco* Case: Odious Indeed but not Really Odious Debts

Contrasting Costa Rica in the 1920s with present practices is highly informative. Costa Rica also challenged 'odious debts' entered into between Tinoco and the Royal Bank of Canada, passing a law to renounce them. Great Britain invoked arbitration. Chief Justice Taft, of the US Supreme Court, was the sole arbitrator. While holding that Tinoco's government was a legitimate *de facto* government capable of binding the state to international obligations, he held that the Royal Bank of Canada 'knew' that the funds in question were to be used for the personal expenses of the retiring ruler and his brother. Thus, the bank could not expect repayment by Costa Rica.[8] If the Royal Bank of Canada had been able to prove that its funds had been put to legitimate government uses, its claim would have been upheld. Comparing this decision with present debt management, one cannot help noting differences.

Although customarily cited as a case of odious debts, Taft's arbitral award simply applied due diligence as demanded by UNCTAD's Principle 2, and arguably its Agency Principle. The problem boils down to equal treatment before the Law. No lender lending to a corporation's CEO, executive director, or to a cabinet minister in an OECD country, knowing that this money would be embezzled but lending nevertheless, could even dream of having this claim 'honoured'. Quite to the contrary, lawsuits for damages by the legal entity and quite possibly penal law consequences would follow.

Unfortunately, even official creditors have not always obeyed customary due diligence standards. Jeffrey Winters[9] coined the term 'criminal debts'. These are

[8] P. Adams, *Odious Debts: Loose Lending, Corruption, and the Third World's Environmental Legacy* (Earthscan, 1991) 167–9.

[9] J. Winters, 'Criminal Debt, written statement for Combating Corruption in the Multilateral Development Banks', Hearing before the Committee on Foreign Relations, US Senate, 108th

debts originating from loans IFIs disbursed to corrupt governments, such as Suharto's Indonesia, knowing that large parts of these loans would be embezzled. The parallels with the *Tinoco* case are obvious. Unlike the *Tinoco* case, Indonesia had to 'honour' these debts. Such criminal debts amounted to 25 to 33 per cent of all loans. They had routinely been embezzled with the lender, the International Bank for Reconstruction and Development (IBRD), in full knowledge. Compared with Taft's award, this is a considerable drop in legal standards.

Similarly, commercial banks were accused of facilitating capital flight in Latin America and Africa in the 1980s,[10] thus rendering the economic situation of their debtors even more untenable. If risk and normal legal responsibility had not been eliminated, banks could not have had an interest in debilitating their debtors. This problem would not have arisen to the same extent. All legal systems contain norms protecting debtors against either overly cavalier attitudes by creditors or creditors carelessly financing illegal activities, embezzlement, or fraud. Such laws may sometimes be quite strict. Unless the debtor is an SC, any creditor suspected of lending with full knowledge that employees, politicians, or functionaries would redirect these funds into their own pockets, will face trouble. In the Philippines, firms connected to the Marcos clan borrowed government-guaranteed loans to go bankrupt after disbursement, leaving the government to pick up the bill. According to the *New York Times* (30 March 1986) such loans amounted to $9.59 billion, a considerable chunk of the country's total sovereign debt at that time. It is difficult to believe that this practice had gone unnoticed by creditors and that they had followed due diligence as requested by Principle 2. In the case of any other debtor but a Southern sovereign, creditors would have had to foot the bill for their behaviour, either by losing money in an insolvency or by legal challenge to their claims with or without such insolvency.

Creditor dominated debt management after the 1970s contrasts vividly with earlier rule of law based debtor-creditor relations, as the arbitral award in the 1922 *Tinoco* case or the general application of *ultra vires* proves. Generally, domestic laws enforce much higher standards of lender accountability. In several countries professional creditors may also be held accountable for damages created by negligently granted credits.

Unfortunately, inequality before the law does not stop at embezzlement, and an extension of UNCTAD's Principles seems advisable to cover debts assumed under pressure. Principle 3 could possibly be stretched to cover it, but it does not

Congress, 2nd session, 13 May (2004), available at <http://foreign.senate.gov/imo/media/doc/WintersTestimony040513.pdf> (accessed 2 March 2013); cf. also K. Raffer, 'International Financial Institutions and Financial Accountability' (2004) 18(2) Ethics & International Affairs 61, 61–2; or <http://www.carnegiecouncil.org/publications/journal/18_2/articles/5019.html/_res/id=sa_File1/5019_EIA_18.2_Raffer_Article.pdf> (accessed 2 March 2013).

[10] On this topic, see D. Duwendag, 'Kapitalflucht aus Entwicklungsländern: Schätzprobleme und Bestimmungsfaktoren' in A. Gutowski (ed.), *Die internationale Schuldenkrise; Ursachen—Konsequenzen—Historische Erfahrungen* (Duncker & Humblot, 1986) 115–49; or M. Jr Pastor, 'Capital Flight from Latin America' (1990) 18(1) World Development 1–18; But cf. qualification of Chilean results by Raffer (n. 2) 271–2.

explicitly say so. The IBRD[11] informed early on that 'governments in many of these countries were forced to assume the losses suffered as a result of the external debts of private banks and corporations, which further worsened the burden on the budget'. Chile in the early 1980s is one prominent example of such 'socialized' debts, which had initially been incurred without any government involvement and while the government declared that it would neither intervene in private contracts nor bail out private debts.[12] Banks tried to cover themselves after the crisis broke. Without protection by official creditors or Northern governments, however, this open breach of the law would not have been possible. The BWIs did not even criticize this practice of forcing 'retroactive guarantees' of already defaulted private debt on other, totally different debtors considered less risky because they were denied insolvency protection. Over quite some time they simply ignored it. The very same practice would, in any other case but that of a Southern sovereign, have had legal consequences, including quite possibly penal law consequences. Although this *ex post* socialization made debt management more difficult, the BWIs and Northern governments insisted on punctual service of these illegal debts as well, thus anointing them with international 'respectability'. In all cases except those of Southern sovereigns such debts would be legally null and void.

Before 1945, the fact that full repayment could not be enforced despite invasions and gunships was also a restraint, not always as efficient as one would have wished, but always working and facilitating sound solutions.

C. Economic Risk and Creditors' Duties and Liabilities

It seems useful to clarify the difference between risk and the duties or liabilities of creditors. Risk and liability are necessary systemic elements of the framework markets' need to function.[13]

I. The role of risk

Risk is the hazard of losing money, even without any fault on the part of the lender. It cannot always be avoided even if creditors apply the highest standards of care and caution. It exists both with sovereigns and other debtors. External shocks, individual catastrophes, or unforeseeable events can change the debtor's circumstances drastically, resulting in losses in spite of every possible precaution and state-of-the-art analysis of creditworthiness. Even model creditors may lose money if external shocks, such as natural disasters, render debtors insolvent. Without any fault of creditors, such shocks can change the terms of the initial contract. On the other

[11] IBRD, *World Debt Tables 1988–89*, Vol.1 (1988) xx.

[12] Raffer (n. 2) 14–15.

[13] This part draws on K. Raffer, 'Risks of Lending and Liability of Lenders' (2007) 21(1) Ethics & International Affairs 85; reprinted in C. Barry, B. Herman, and L. Tomitova (eds), *Dealing Fairly with Developing Country Debt* (Blackwell, 2007) 127.

hand, unwise creditor decisions may increase risk. Economically, risk serves as an incentive to assess in a careful manner the ability of debtors to service debts. Errors and negligence in assessment bring about losses.

Risk makes creditors cautious; it is the main incentive against loose lending. This useful mechanism has been eliminated in sovereign lending, producing massive misallocations of funds. In sovereign syndicated lending it was claimed that countries would always exist and thus always repay. This idea does not, of course, stand up to scrutiny, as the history of sovereign lending shows. But it was highly influential and led to the misallocation of funds on a global scale.

After 1970, however, a fundamental change occurred in international lending practices vis-à-vis SCs. Receiving signals that their governments would protect them, commercial banks lent aggressively, disregarding the most elementary rules of prudent banking. OECD governments and multilateral institutions encouraged and applauded the 'successful recycling of Petrodollars'. Since the crisis broke, and in spite of quantitative evidence,[14] OPEC has been used as a convenient scapegoat for the debt crisis. At present the European Union is repeating this failure, guaranteeing all future lending to euro-members.

Eventually risk asserted itself, as both massive losses by the private sector and insufficient losses by multilateral institutions show. In the meantime, though, the mistaken belief in riskless loans influenced lending in a very damaging way, causing a massive misallocation of funds. Without proper checks and assessments, money was thrown at developing countries—and it is no wonder that most countries have little to show for it.

Once the IMF and the IBRD had established themselves as 'debt managers', they propagated the illusion that everything would eventually be repaid. The illiquidity theory, the Baker Plan claiming that everything must be repaid, 'forced lending' (commercial banks were encouraged to lend the same percentages of new funds necessary to keep a debtor afloat as the percentages of their existing claims vis-à-vis that debtor), or the catchphrase 'growing out of debts' (the idea that growth would soon render debts payable; that countries were illiquid, not insolvent) bear witness to this aberration.

Eliminating risk totally by political fiat is, of course, impossible. While still insisting on full repayment first (Venice Terms, 'Baker Plan'), economic facts eventually forced official creditors to accept reality. Thus, '100 per cent debt relief' is meanwhile propagated by bilateral creditors for some countries. Although IFIs are still protected politically, they too have started to reduce their claims. Finally, the G-7 decision at Gleneagles officially recognized that multilateral debts can be unpayable too.

If the debtor is insolvent rather than illiquid, debts start accumulating on paper further beyond an insolvent debtor's economic capacity to repay. Debts

[14] K. Raffer and H.W. Singer, *The Foreign Aid Business: Economic Assistance and Development Co-operation* (Elgar, 1996) 123–33; K. Raffer and H.W. Singer, *The Economic North-South Divide, Six Decades of Unequal Development* (Elgar, 2001) 133–7.

that can never be repaid because of increasing gaps between economic capacity and payments contractually due—I named them 'phantom debts'[15]—must increase eventually. As anyone familiar with basic mathematics can verify, creditors unwilling to grant sufficient relief when necessary, increase (their own) irrecuperable debts. Total debts are pushed to ever more unrealistic heights, making reductions to economically sustainable levels appear costlier and costlier on paper as the share of phantom debts increases. Phantom claims are generated. Existing only on paper they nevertheless compromise the debtor's economic future. They also allow creditors to exert pressure. 'Forgiving' them may mean losing political power but certainly not money. One cannot lose money already lost. Cancelling phantom debts simply means ceasing to play the Emperor's New Clothes, acknowledging the naked economic truth.

Until September 1995, the BWIs officially denied that multilateral debts could be a problem. If they had actually financed viable projects and programmes, these debts would have been self-liquidating, thus really no problem. Unfortunately, multilateral claims were not earning their own debt service. A pervasive preoccupation with new lending, identified for the IBRD by internal documents,[16] is certainly one reason. It is IBRD-President Wolfensohn's great merit to have acknowledged the reality that multilateral claims can become phantoms too, and to have acted appropriately.

Substantial shares of present debt were caused by creditors delaying necessary reductions over decades. As early as 1992 the IBRD declared 'early recognition' of a solvency crisis and speedy settlement '*important for minimizing the damage*', adding that 'protracted renegotiations and uncertainty damaged economic activity in debtor countries for several years.... It took too long to recognize that liquidity was the visible tip of the problem, but not its root'.[17]

A functioning credit market, as opposed to sovereign lending, limits the amount of risk creditors can shift onto debtors. If interest hikes are too large, debtors are driven to insolvency. Functioning markets make creditors lose money in spite of unduly shifting risk. This also applies to punitive interest rates: if they are too high, they push debtors into insolvency and cannot be paid.

II. Differentiating public and private lender responsibilities

All legal systems establish duties creditors must comply with in order to enjoy full legal protection of their contractual rights. Not complying with such duties may give rise to damage compensation payments. Establishing and enforcing

[15] Raffer (n. 2) 41, 191–5; K. Raffer, 'Schemes for Resolving the External Debt Problem' in OPEC Fund for International Development (ed), *Financing for Development, Proceedings of a Workshop of the G-24 held at Nigeria House, New York, September 6–7, 2001*, Pamphlet Series No. 33 (2002) 143.

[16] The so-called Wapenhans Report (IBRD, 'Effective Implementation: Key to Development Impact, Report of the World Bank's Portfolio Management Task Force' Washington, DC, 1992) is still the best known but by no means only example; for more sources see Raffer and Singer (1996) (n. 14) 173–80.

[17] IBRD, *World Debt Tables 1992/93*, vol. 1, 10–11 (emphasis in original).

these principles is the duty of governments, both with regard to domestic and international debts. While the private sector has no further duty but to abide by laws passed by others, governments also have the obligation to preserve the foundation of the rule of law, including international law, and to safeguard human rights. As legal entities on their own not passing but obeying laws, sovereign wealth funds are private creditors. In virtually all municipal laws, responsibilities differ depending on the economic participation of lenders. Lenders only granting loans have the duty to check the authority to sign, not to suborn executives, public servants, or politicians or help them to embezzle funds—as in the *Tinoco* case. Due diligence standards also require checks of the economic viability of projects and proper information of the client. If lenders are fully subject to risk, it is in their very own interest not to lend unless they have complied with the demands of UNCTAD's Second Principle. If they do not comply, they are very likely to lose money. Requesting that the usual standards should also be applicable to sovereigns, the Second Principle calls for the reintroduction of market risk and an end to the global two-tier legal system.

There is no reason why the same standards should not be applied to sovereign lending. However, responsibility as demanded by Principle 5 needs economic consequences as in the case of *Lloyds*,[18] or is likely to remain little more than an admonition more honoured in the breach than the observance. Going beyond mere lending by also giving advice, Lloyds had to pay damages when prices in the property market fell and its clients suffered losses because its manager had not pointed out the risks clearly. Without the obligation to compensate damage caused by not doing one's advising, monitoring, or project planning with proper care, there is no economic incentive to avoid such damages. If negligence or even *dolus* in inflicting damages triggers another loan to finance the repair of damage done, one has an economically perverse incentive system. Improper decisions are rewarded but good management is not. This Principle is mainly relevant for official lenders, although private creditors finance projects too. One must discuss whether and how such economic consequences can be introduced.

IFIs claim that the economic consequences of allowing Principle 5 to function cannot be applied to their own lending. Usually, they also claim to be preferred creditors and that such preference is mandatory to allow them to comply with their tasks. From this they deduce that their claims must be unconditionally preferred and that even the idea of damage compensation is against their statutes. However, without an economic incentive—the loss of money if these responsibilities are neglected—Principle 5 remains declaratory or, to put it in more legal wording, a *lex imperfecta*. The fact that the statutes of all IFIs demand the behaviour requested by Principle 5 corroborates this point quite clearly.

The mechanisms for enforcing the keynote of Principle 5 already exist, although they seem to have fallen into oblivion, or—as the *Lloyds* case shows—are not

[18] J. Gapper and R. Gourlay, 'Damages Win Leads Lloyds to Rethink Advice', *Financial Times*, 5 September 1995, 9.

applied to SCs. The most important multilateral financiers all have clauses that make it possible. It can be shown that the status of preferred creditor is alien to the statutes of all IFIs. The impression quite successfully created over decades that multilateral claims are entitled to preferential treatment is absolutely unfounded. In fact, IFIs have undone their founders' intention of subordinating IFI claims in order to foster development financing and to reassure private flows, *de facto* reversing it into the opposite. The problem is most clearly illustrated by the handling of the Euro crisis. Illegally enforced *ex post* preference for the public sector unsettles private creditors and was, quite correctly, one reason for the downgrading of several euro countries. Also, there is no hindrance for IFIs to undergo legal procedures, either in courts of law or in procedures of arbitration. Thus any disagreement regarding project implementation can be solved in a legally correct and economically advised way. Neglecting these duties can lead to economic consequences. In addition, IFIs can fully participate in any insolvency proceeding.

At Bretton Woods, normal legal redress was seen as a matter of course. The statutes of the IBRD and the International Development Association are clearest. The IBRD's founders understandably wanted lending to be subject to some market discipline—as also proved by clauses allowing the IBRD to be sued or allowing members legal redress via arbitration, designing mechanisms that would allow the Bank to shoulder its fair share of the risks involved—another clear sign that no preference in treatment was and still is wished as these clauses are part of the presently valid statutes.[19]

Article VII.3 of the IBRD's Articles of Agreement explicitly allows actions against the Bank except by members or persons acting for or deriving claims from members. Years later, International Development Association's statutes (Article VIII.3) mirrored those of the IBRD.

Members are not allowed to sue the IBRD but are referred to arbitration to avoid giving a member's court adjudication authority. The Bank's founders might well have been concerned about the sufficient neutrality of national courts, but they guaranteed full legal relief. Like the IBRD's former General Conditions (Section 10.04), its present General Conditions for Loans (of 1 July 2005, Section 8.04) stipulate that: 'Any controversy between the parties to the Loan Agreement or the parties to the Guarantee Agreement, and any claim by any such party against any other such party . . . not . . . settled by agreement . . . shall be submitted to arbitration by an arbitral tribunal.'

Bank and country (guarantor country and borrower if these are not identical) appoint one person each. Both sides agree on a third arbitrator. The President of the International Court of Justice or the UN Secretary-General appoints this 'umpire' if the parties fail to agree. Section 8.04 contains the necessary

[19] For details and quotes, see K. Raffer, 'Preferred or Not Preferred: Thoughts on Priority Structures of Creditors', Paper presented at the 2nd Meeting of the Sovereign Insolvency Study Group of the International Law Association, 16 October, Hosted by the Legal Department, International Monetary Fund (2009), available at <http://homepage.univie.ac.at/Kunibert.Raffer/ila-wash.pdf> (accessed 19 October 2012).

procedural provisions. In parentheses one may add that they are plain vanilla in international law, or equivalent to my proposal on how to establish ad hoc insolvency panels.[20]

Although borrowers other than governments can demand arbitration as well, people suffering project-inflicted damage remain excluded, a shortcoming that one could change with the stroke of a pen. And it must be changed. In most cases affected people cannot exert pressure on their own governments, let alone borrowers, to represent them appropriately against multilateral financiers. Governments and public entities may not wish to sue for several reasons.

Mirroring the IBRD, the Inter-American Development Bank is not immune either. It can be sued (Article XI.3 of its statutes). Once again 'members or persons acting for or deriving claims from members' are barred. However, and unfortunately from a legal point of view, independent arbitration is restricted to countries that are no longer members or that have already decided to leave the Bank. The spirit of Bretton Woods is no longer fully present to install the rule of law and economic sense, but at least members leaving are not denied legal relief.

The Asian Development Bank may be sued, although Article 50 already limits this possibility to 'cases arising out of or in connection with the exercise of its powers to borrow money, to guarantee obligations, or to buy and sell or underwrite the sale of securities'. However, it 'may waive any of the privileges, immunities and exemptions conferred under this Chapter in any case or instance, in such manner and upon such conditions as it may determine to be appropriate in the best interests of the Bank' (Article 50.1). This qualification has to be noted: it is not legal principles, equity considerations, fairness, or legally proper behaviour, but the Bank's best interest that determines such a decision. However, assuming that correct and sound management as well as sound economic and legal principles *are* in the very interest of the Bank, this is nevertheless equivalent to allowing a general waiver. The Asian Development Bank's property and assets are immune from all forms of seizure, attachment, or execution before the delivery of final judgment. Arbitration is restricted to former members (including members 'on the way out').

Article 52 of the statutes of the African Development Bank on judicial proceedings mirrors Article 50 of the statutes of the Asian Development Bank. The Board of Directors may waive immunity 'in cases where its action would in its opinion further the interests of the Bank' (Article 59). Arbitration is only foreseen for former members or 'a member upon the termination of the operations of the Bank'.

However, its *General Conditions Applicable to the African Development Bank Loan Agreements and Guarantee Agreements (Non Sovereign Entities)*, in Section 10.04, stipulate that 'any controversy between the parties to the Loan Agreement and the Guarantee Agreement and any claim by a party against the other party arising under the Loan Agreement and the Guarantee Agreement' not settled amicably may be

[20] cf. Raffer (n. 5) 304; K. Raffer, 'International Debts: A Crisis for Whom?' in H.W. Singer and S. Sharma (eds), *Economic Development and World Debt* (Macmillan, 1989) 61.

submitted to arbitration. Section 10.04 of the *General Conditions* for 'Sovereign Entities' repeats this verbally.

The European Bank for Reconstruction and Development writes off losses and submits to arbitration (also foreseen for the IBRD)—which proves that Multilateral Development Banks, if properly managed, can survive financial accountability and market risk. Its clientele, however, does not comprise SCs.

The IMF differs from Multilateral Development Banks. Article IX.3 of its Articles of Agreement grants it total immunity 'except to the extent that it expressly waives its immunity for the purpose of any proceedings or by the terms of any contract'. The Fund could institutionalize legal relief and the rule of law by adding one clause in any agreement with debtors that waives immunity pursuant to this Article.

Obviously, this is explained by the fact that the IMF was initially intended to help member countries overcome short-term dollar/gold-parity problems by unconditional short-term drawings (loans). It would be difficult to perceive any need for legal procedures and redress in the case of an emergency helper unconditionally giving money, except in cases such as criminal debts. Such eventuality probably made the Fund's founders insert this waiver to provide for proper legal dispute settlement. When conditionality became enshrined in the IMF's statutes in 1969, the appropriate change regarding immunity was not made for whichever reason, although its founders would doubtlessly have stipulated the possibility of legal redress as with the IBRD if they had approved conditional drawing. Arguably, this was the first step towards establishing legal double standards globally. Nevertheless, the IMF may not only submit to arbitration or courts, but contractual clauses stipulating this remain expressly allowed. Nothing in its statutes prevents the Fund from applying civilized legal standards. On the contrary, the existence of this waiver may be seen as an encouragement to do so if and when appropriate.

Preferred creditor status is alien to IFI statutes. It cannot prevent loan losses, let alone immunize against damage compensation. Over decades, IFIs have successfully nurtured the completely unfounded perception that IFI claims would be entitled to preferential treatment. Contrary to what they assert, the technical concept of preferred creditors does not apply to IFIs. The IMF knows that it enjoys no legal or contractual preferred creditor status, as one can read on its very own homepage.[21] No IFIs are preferred creditors, as their own homepages and Articles of Agreement document.[22]

All IFIs have established loan loss reserves (officially often called precautionary reserves) that allow haircuts to be absorbed. These reserves have been paid for by client countries via higher spreads. In other words, borrowers have already paid insurance fees for cases of default, but are denied the benefits already paid for by insurance

[21] J. M. Boughton, *Silent Revolution: The International Monetary Fund 1979–1989* (IMF, 2001) 820; available at the IMF homepage <http://www.imf.org/external/pubs/ft/history/2001/ch16.pdf> 820 (accessed 2 March 2013).

[22] Raffer (n. 19) 15; K. Raffer, 'Delivering Greater Information and Transparency in Debt Management' in UNCTAD (ed), *Proceedings of the Fifth Inter-regional Debt Management Conference Geneva, 20–22 June 2005* (UN, 2007) 79–88, available at <http://r0.unctad.org/dmfas/speakerspapers.htm> (accessed 19 October 2012).

premia if and when the insured event occurs. There is no reason why these reserves should not be used for their unique, official, and rightful purpose: to cover losses.

III. Abusive credits

Abusive credits are a special case of neglecting creditor duties. This is a concept familiar in particular to French, Belgian, and Italian jurisprudence. Juan Pablo Bohoslavsky[23] surveyed laws and judicial practice in eight countries, establishing creditor liabilities for loose lending in order to extract common principles from national, domestic laws to transform the theory of the responsibility for abusive granting of credit into a general principle of international law. He argues that such 'abusive credits' should also have consequences in international law, and thus be made applicable to cases of sovereign insolvency. This concept holds lenders liable for damages inflicted on other creditors by lending with disregard for the most basic principles of risk evaluation, thus hiding the debtor's real situation and postponing the insolvent borrower's crash, thereby increasing other creditors' losses. In private business such behaviour triggers an obligation to compensate for damages.

Bohoslavsky argues that such loans granted without following the most elementary prudential guidelines in the analysis of credit risk should be subordinated to those not classified as abusive and impaired by abusive lending. Subsequent creditors, in particular those harmed by having been induced to make loans because of abusive lending to a party that could not or would not repay them, could file claims against the abusive grantors generating such false appearances. However this concept is in a very early stage at present. It still needs to be made applicable to cases of sovereign insolvency. Abusive credits inflict damages on bona fide creditors and mislead them. These credits generate misallocation of capital in international capital markets. Subordinating such credits in order to enforce the due diligence standards demanded by Principle 2 is one logical conclusion. It should be noted that even the IMF could be taken to court because of such abusive conduct if it used its authority under Article IX.3, obeying the obvious intention of its founders.

Argentina illustrates the practical relevance of this demand. Well before the September 2001 augmentation, IMF staff estimates had been carried out to establish what percentage of debt would have to be cut in order to reach sustainability. As a memo to management dated 26 July 2001 noted: 'While the results are highly sensitive to the assumptions, the staff estimates that a haircut of between 15 and 40 per cent is required, depending on the policy choice.'[24] The IMF nevertheless went on lending, increasing the amount of debt unpayable by its

[23] J.P. Bohoslavsky, 'Consecuencias jurídicas y económicas del crédito abusivo (Especial referencia al endeudamiento soberano)', Tesis doctoral (Doctorado Europeo) Facultad de Derecho, Universidad de Salamanca (2006); J.P. Bohoslavsky, 'Lending and Sovereign Insolvency: A Fair and Efficient Criterion to Distribute Losses among Creditors' (2010) 2(1) Goettingen Journal of International Law 387.

[24] IMF, Independent Evaluation Office, 'Evaluation Report: The IMF and Argenina, 1991–2001' (2004) 90, footnote 95, also at <http://www.imf.org/external/np/ieo/2004/arg/eng/pdf/report.pdf> (accessed 19 October 2012).

own assessment. Requesting and enforcing preference over others, this means that the Fund knowingly increased the haircut that private creditors had to suffer later on as well as its own income from undue borrowing.

The case of Greece is even worse. At the end of 2009, her public debt had reached 115 per cent of GDP. When the first proposals to implement a haircut or some form of sovereign insolvency were published, this ratio was around 120. The so-called 'rescue mission' by the European Union and the IMF consisted of granting more credits and made Greece's debt grow to nearly 170 per cent. In March 2011, the IMF thought it possible that given a banking shock, 'debts would jump to over 200 per cent of GDP before declining'.[25] A 'voluntary' 50 per cent-haircut by the private sector alone was supposed to allow the country to reduce to 120 per cent again by 2020. Eventually, private creditors lost more. New official loans overcompensated the haircut and Greece ended up with more debt. Even if things had worked out as declared, Greece would have been back to square one in 2020, to that 120 per cent that had made 'rescue operations' necessary—a clear failure of EU-IMF policies. Public abusive lending in tandem with *de facto* preferred creditor status make larger and larger haircuts of the private sector mathematically necessary. If the proposal by Gros and Mayer[26] to halve (all of) Greece's debts in early 2010—at that time virtually all Greek sovereign debt was owed to the private sector—had been implemented, the country would have been afloat again, with a Maastricht conform debt-GDP ratio of some 60 per cent. One may even discuss whether a smaller haircut would not have sufficed. One of the authors, incidentally, was the chief economist of Deutsche Bank. By lending instead of solving the problem, official creditors made things worse, finally increasing losses and damaging Greece and private creditors in particular.

D. Prospective Social Returns and Interest Rates

In order to avoid over-borrowing, Principle 14 demands the weighing of costs and benefits and that borrowing should not take place if expected social returns are not at least equal to interest rates. This is both correct and in line with textbook cost-benefit analysis. Textbooks, though, focus on rich countries, where cost-benefit analysis was developed. Economically, it is no doubt a necessary minimum condition, but just meeting it may still create mismatching problems for a country with debt and borrowing problems. First, social returns often do not accrue as quickly as debt servicing becomes due and in line with these obligations: a liquidity mismatch.

[25] IMF, 'Greece: Third Review under the Stand-By Arrangement—Staff Report'; IMF Country Report No. 11/68, March (2011) 10, available at <http://www.imf.org/external/pubs/ft/scr/2011/cr1168.pdf> (accessed 19 October 2012).

[26] T. Gros and D. Mayer, 'How to Deal with Sovereign Default in Europe: Towards a Euro(pean) Monetary Fund' (February 2010); updated version (17 May 2010) available at <http://www.ceps.eu/book/towards-european-monetary-fund>; cf. the comment by K. Raffer, 'An EMF with a Sovereign Insolvency Mechanism' (April 2010), available at <http://homepage.univie.ac.at/kunibert.raffer/Berlin10-EMF.pdf> (accessed 19 October 2012).

Second, pecuniary returns will often accrue in domestic money: a currency mismatch unless the country borrows in its own currency or only finances export activities. Thirdly, it may be that not enough of these returns will accrue to the sovereign financing projects or they may accrue only after several debt service payments have been made. At going tax rates, recovering the state's costs from pecuniary benefits of private investors caused by the project is likely to last several years.

In the case of concessional interest rates this is less pronounced because debt service can be covered with comparably lower income streams. But even so, often useful investments cannot produce sufficient monetary returns for debt service. Institution building, the social agenda, and projects for the poor are examples. Raffer and Singer[27] therefore proposed that these projects must be financed by grants unless a country is sufficiently liquid, which is, however, extremely unlikely in the case of most poor SCs.

Cash strapped economies should equate financial return to interest. This means that laudable and necessary social expenditures, for example the Millennium Development Goals (MDGs) in poorer countries must be—largely at least—financed by grants. In the Millennium Declaration, all UN member states (including rich countries) promised: 'We will spare no effort to free our fellow men, women and children from the abject and dehumanizing conditions of extreme poverty...we are committed to making the right to development a reality for everyone and to freeing the entire human race from want.' Logically, implementing necessary anti-poverty measures requires financial efforts. Achieving the MDGs is directly connected with the idea of debtor protection, with a proper and fair solution to the debt problem. Supporting debtor countries in their efforts to achieve the MDGs without creating future debt problems has meanwhile become one of the officially declared aims of debt management. So it should be hoped that grants (or lending with a grant element of virtually 100 per cent) will be forthcoming on a sufficient scale.

E. Impossibility of Payment and a Non-Conflicting Way Out

Although *pacta sunt servanda* is a fundamental legal, economic, and ethical principle, all legal systems recognize circumstances where contractual rights can no longer be enforced, or indeed cease to exist. Whenever the right of creditors to payments collides with the economic incapability of honouring all debts, the principle recognized generally (not only in the case of debts) by all civilized legal systems that fulfilment must not be enforced at the cost of inhuman distress, of violating human rights and human dignity, means that debtor protection enjoys unconditional priority. The occasional incapability to repay fully is a fact of life. Any lending system must therefore incorporate a solution to this problem.

[27] Raffer and Singer (1996) (n. 14) 209.

Protracted restructurings are usually injurious to all concerned parties, as UNCTAD's Principles put it in a nutshell.

Naturally, a consensual agreement is always preferable and is indeed reached in many cases of non-sovereign bankruptcy. Ideally, an arbitral award or an insolvency court's verdict should just rubber-stamp the solution agreed on by the parties. However, for a range of reasons this is not always possible. Therefore all legal systems have a formal procedure with cram-down authority. Its mere existence makes solutions easier, and—as Krueger put it—often leads to agreements 'in the shadow of the law'[28] without formal procedures. If outcomes are acceptable to all, this may save everyone a lot of trouble, not least debtor countries and their inhabitants. Collective Action Clauses (CACs) are very helpful, arguably even necessary in order to achieve such agreements. But CACs are also useful in the case of formal sovereign insolvency procedures. Helping creditors to organize, to be able to act more quickly and efficiently, CACs are a useful component of any sovereign insolvency rather than a contradiction to it. The proper functioning of fair insolvency procedures depends on the full ability of parties to defend their legal and economic interests. Creditors must be able to act efficiently. Whatever helps them to do so is welcome. Options from the pre-Brady 1980s, such as debt-for-nature swaps may be used as well.

All historical cases of sovereign debt overhang prove that debts must eventually be reduced by substantial amounts. The IMF presented research results for the period 1970–2002 that 'suggest that while large debt reductions have often occurred in conjunction with debt defaults there are cases where they have been brought about by a combination of strong economic growth and fiscal consolidation'.[29] However, 19 out of 26 cases 'were associated with a debt default'. There is an evident need for a fair mechanism that avoids unnessary conflict, which in the end is better for creditors and debtors alike.

Creditors may meanwhile see a fair mechanism in a more favourable light. Richards[30] identified a clear trend towards unilateral exchange offers as a technique for restructuring sovereign debt, understandably creating great concerns with creditors. Argentina has already been mentioned. Ecuador put pressure on creditors via her debt audit commission. The point was not whether Ecuador could pay but whether Ecuador should pay. After quite an unpleasant debate she received a large reduction from creditors. Dubai made an exchange offer. Nigeria obtained a large reduction from the Paris Club after a resolution to repudiate debts had passed parliament. In 2005 Grenada restructured her sovereign debt, eliminating the unconditional enforcement right in bonds governed by New York law. Belize—presently offering offering bondholders just 20 per cent in a unilateral restructuring attempt—followed suit.

[28] A. Krueger, 'A New Approach to Sovereign Debt Restructuring', Address at the Indian Council for Research on International Economic Relations, Delhi, 20 December 2001, available at <http://www.imf.org/external/np/speeches/2001/122001.htm> (accessed 19 October 2012).

[29] IMF, *World Economic Outlook* (September 2003) 140.

[30] M.B. Richards, 'The Republic of Congo's Debt Restructuring: Are Sovereign Creditors Getting their Voice Back?' (2010) 73(4) Law & Cont. Probs 273.

When Congo (Brazzaville)—after a series of restructurings in which creditors were either completely bypassed or slighted after initial overtures for dialogue—responded favourably to promoting a negotiated solution over unilateral exchange offers, this was seen as 'a ray of sunshine cutting through the shadow cast by the cases of Ecuador and Argentina'.[31] It was 'the first negotiated debt restructuring conducted in conformity with the Principles [for Stable Capital Flows and Fair Debt Restructuring in Emerging Markets] in the wake of the reaction to the SDRM and the Argentine crisis'. These are clear signals that the time of virtually unrestricted creditor decisions is coming to an end.[32] In a way it was a return to what had been customary before the First World War.

My preferred insolvency model, the Raffer Proposal, aims at consensual outcomes as the ideal. But as ideals are not always realized, the panel of arbitrators must have the authority to decide if necessary. As all facts and arguments would have been presented by the parties and the population exercising the right to be heard (by representation), arbitral decisions are very likely to affect small sums only, overcoming deadlocks if there are any. As this model has been presented frequently, I will only refer to the literature quoted in this chapter.[33]

I. Holdouts: the 'vulture' problem and bona fide creditors

Vulture hunting has become a popular pastime but detracts from the real problem. Criticizing these holdouts, unpleasant as some may be, allows critics to feel moral outrage and the satisfaction of fighting evil. Yet they are barking up the wrong tree while totally ignoring the fact that holdouts only use the legal framework that governments provide. This fundamental difference between private creditors that are subject to laws and official creditors that are making them and are obliged to defend decent legal standards, must not be obfuscated. Northern governments carry a large part of the blame for the admittedly unsatisfactory situation by not allowing time-tested and necessary protective mechanisms routine within their own jurisdictions to work equally on the international stage.

Public sector failure is the illness, of which various forms of incorrect debts and the 'vulture problem' are but symptoms. The issue of holdout creditors, called 'vultures' by NGOs and Northern governments, is just another sad effect of the official sector neglecting its very reason for existing: to safeguard the rule of law and sound economic principles.

Putting things into a proper context—some might prefer to call this playing the role of devil's advocate—one has to recall a few matters:

(1) Buying debts at discounts is not a unique feature of SC debts, but common practice. Legally, 'vultures' exercise their rights in a way that is no different from what happens every day in practically any country. Risk-averse creditors

[31] Richards (n. 30) 298. [32] Richards (n. 30) 283.

[33] e.g. Raffer (n. 2) 78–113; Raffer (n. 5); Raffer (n. 7); further literature at <http://homepage.univie.ac.at/Kunibert.Raffer> (accessed 19 October 2012).

sell claims at a discount, hoping to cut their losses. New owners try to get full repayment to which they are legally fully entitled, with varying success. Once debtors are insolvent, however, they are protected. This makes economic sense and is also legally of advantage in order to give creditors a fair deal. Recognizing that full payment to all bona fide creditors is or may be impossible, insolvency proceedings automatically stay individual lawsuits to safeguard fairness to anyone affected. It is mainly for economic reasons that they prevailed over debt slavery and debt prisons. 'Vultures' are grounded. Unlike present clumsy attempts to force litigators not to use their right, a stay within an insolvency mechanism is correct and fair. All creditors are party and can defend their interests, thus influencing the outcome. No one is forced to accept what has been decided without their participation, for example by the Paris Club. Some official creditors have occasionally sold their claims to 'vultures', all have prevented SC debtors from buying back their own debts themselves at secondary market prices, as had been the going practice in the nineteenth century. While this practice produces its own problems (most notably moral hazard), countries openly buying their own debts on secondary markets would certainly have curbed the 'vulture business'. One wonders why official creditors suddenly show great compassion for debtors in litigation, a problem for which they are responsible.

Just exempting SC debts after and because of Paris Club decisions would violate constitutional rights in any jurisdiction. Constitutional amendments would be needed in all creditor countries; without a written constitution, the United Kingdom is a special but not an easier case. This would fundamentally change the foundation of Western legal systems—it is a non-starter. But even if all creditor governments were willing to amend their constitutions, this process would take a fairly long time. Notably, the US constitution is technically difficult to change. Citing an officially non-existent 'institution', the Paris Club, as justification, is unlikely to make things any easier.

(2) The Paris Club has violated other creditors' basic rights. These have not even been heard. There is no perceptible legal procedure at all on which duties to reduce claims could be based. Private claims remain perfectly valid and enforceable. This shows clearly when debtors are sued in a Paris Club country: they must pay. The legal problem described seems to explain why Club-members force debtors to get 'comparable treatment' from other creditors: to avoid exerting direct pressure, which would result in lawsuits. Logically, debtors are denied any legal protection against dissenting creditors as there is no basis for it.

Ten of the 44 cases of litigation[34] were filed within Heavily Indebted Poor Countries (HIPCs) themselves. Barring miscarriage of justice, creditors are bound to win, although not necessarily the whole amount. Incidentally, eight

[34] IDA & IMF, 'Heavily Indebted Poor Countries (HIPC) Initiative and Multilateral Debt Relief Initiative (MDRI)—Status of Implementation' (2007), available at <http://www.imf.org/external/pp/longres.aspx?id=4208> 32 and 105.

of these 44 cases were 'in arbitration'. Litigating creditors—the pariah group at the moment—are much more prepared to accept fair arbitration than official creditors that thus destroyed the very foundation of any legal system that one must not be judge in one's own cause. Official creditors have done everything possible to avoid giving up their present dominant role in debt management.

(3) Economically and legally, the enforcing of 'comparable treatment' by governments would in essence be a 'taking', as prohibited by the 5th Amendment of the US Constitution or equivalent constitutional guarantees elsewhere. It would be a case of private property subject to unbridled, uncompensated qualification by government, without just compensation, not to mention the denial of anyone's most basic right to defend his or her interest. While constitutions differ, this unjustified expropriation would violate any constitution of Paris Club member countries.

The UK Treasury recognizes that suing for full payment is 'the creditor's legal right'[35] and: 'Even once a country reaches Completion Point, creditors retain their legal rights to enforce claims against the country concerned.'[36] Furthermore, 'The debts concerned are property rights protected by the Human Rights Act',[37] since the Paris Club's decision 'is not legally binding'.[38] On the other hand, 'the Government has already taken vigorous action . . . within the existing legal framework' against holdouts. Unsurprisingly, 'these methods cannot prevent creditors intent on pursuing their claims through the courts from doing so'.[39] It remains to be seen whether this will change dramatically without a proper insolvency framework. Such a framework would break this deadlock.

(4) While this may be morally less gratifying, basing debt cancellations on the fact that debts are unpayable, on the rule of law, and equal rights to all debtors globally, will not only bring relief sooner but largely in an economically equivalent way. Whether x billions go because of odiousness, illegality by whichever definition, or because they cannot be paid, the result is always x billion less. The point is which way Southern debtors are likely to get meaningful relief more quickly. The arguments that there must not be two different standards between debtors depending on geographical location and that the foundations of the rule of law as well as human rights have to be respected whatever the passport of those affected, are absolutely unbeatable. There is no counter-argument, and certainly none any politician would dare voice.

Summing up, the conclusion that holdouts act 'abusively'[40] needs qualification. One has to differentiate between 'original' creditors and those buying cheaply on

[35] HM Treasury, 'Ensuring effective debt relief for poor countries: a consultation on legislation' (2009) 5.

[36] HM Treasury (n. 35) 14.

[37] HM Treasury (n. 35) 25.

[38] HM Treasury (n. 35) 25.

[39] HM Treasury (n. 35) 19.

[40] As stated by the UNCTAD Principles, Principle 7.

the secondary market. Those holding out after they actually delivered goods or services have certainly every moral right to insist on payment and to defend against the imposition of decisions by other actors which have been reached without their having even the slightest opportunity to be heard, let alone to exercise all their rights as a party, as well as with illegal preference enforced for some creditors. One should note that this differs radically from any insolvency mechanisms where all creditors have full party rights. All have full legal relief, and quite in contrast to diktats by official creditors they are supposed to obey without even being heard. In this regard creditor protection is severely lacking and urgently needed. Greece, where one additional step in the preference ladder was squeezed in *ex post* and *contra legem*, is just one outstanding example. Full repayment to those legally entitled to it is certainly not a preferential settlement.

Professional investors, who buy claims on secondary markets in order to profit from enforcing full repayment, are another creditor type. This happens every day with non-sovereign debts. Thus, 'vultures' are not an exception but the rule. In non-sovereign cases, though, debtors are protected by insolvency proceedings, or 'protection from creditors'. It must be stressed that official creditors deny this protection to sovereign debtors. Only the lack of a proper, prompt, fair, and efficient insolvency mechanism allows 'vultures' to fly, otherwise they would be grounded.

Coming back to the duties of creditor governments to guarantee and safeguard the rule of law and equality before the law without undue discrimination, one cannot avoid mentioning that the 'vulture' business only came into existence because Northern countries allowed it. Champerty laws would have prohibited 'vulture' actions but they were raised in vain because champerty was redefined by US courts in a way that fostered and encouraged holdouts. It is extremely interesting that those campaigning against 'vultures' turn a totally blind eye regarding actions of courts within creditor states. Apparently, 'vultures' seem morally more rewarding targets. In any case, the 'vulture' debate casts a convenient veil over the real problem of global inequality: the fact that SCs and their inhabitants are denied basic rights by Northern official creditors, remaining the only type of debtor still denied insolvency protection.

Elliott Associates' famous litigation with Peru, which ignited and encouraged followers, is a perfect illustration. Reuter's Salmon[41] describes the case as follows:

> A federal district court in New York initially ruled against Elliott, finding that the fund had purchased the debt 'with the intent and purpose to sue' and 'rejected each and every opportunity to participate in Peru's restructuring.' Elliott appealed and won. Then the fund began working the political system in New York. With the help of a lobbying firm in Albany, Elliott, through a subsidiary, persuaded the New York legislature to change an obscure law governing compound interest, increasing Elliott's payout by $16 million, for a total, including interest, of $58 million. It was done so quietly that Peru's lawyers didn't find out until after the fact. A few years later the New York State Assembly eliminated another

[41] F. Salmon, 'Elliott Associates goes to Albany, again', Reuters, 16 June 2010, available at <http://blogs.reuters.com/felix-salmon/2010/06/17/elliott-associates-goes-to-albany-again> (accessed 19 October 2012).

law that Peru had used to defend itself. Three months after the bill became law, Singer gave the lead sponsor, State Assembly Member Susan John, a $2,500 campaign donation.

The observation may be added that this was precisely the type of *ex post* legislation that makes creditors choose courts outside their sovereign debtor's jurisdiction.

The Brussels court that found in favour of Elliott made its debatable interpretation on the basis of an *ex parte* motion by Elliott: 'Had Peru had an opportunity to respond we think that the court would not have leapt quite so easily to its conclusion.'[42] Arguing that the court's interpretation was wrong and should be disregarded, Gulati and Klee point out that the court interpreted the *pari passu* clause in a way different from the market understanding. Only hearing one side must have been quite helpful. The authors formulate graphically: 'What the Brussels Opinion does is to put a large hammer in the hands of holdout creditors, thereby enabling them to cause even more disruption in restructurings'[43] and encouraging others to follow suit.

Reinisch[44] points out that the court of appeal in New York also stated that US interest in Peru's successful rescheduling was (in its view) less important than the interest of New York as a financial centre as one of the reasons for the verdict. This recalls the Costa Rican case *Allied Bank International v. Banco Credito Agricola de Cartago* in 1984, in which the US Court of Appeals for the Second Circuit granted US insolvency protection to Costa Rica, based in part on legal grounds and what it had called 'principles recognized by all civilized nations',[45] but also on the assumption that this was consistent with US policy. Rehearing the case, the court reversed itself when the executive branch, as *amicus curiae*, clarified that supporting Costa Rica was not US policy. It did not reverse its legal points, though. This Court, too, specifically named US 'interest in maintaining New York's status as one of the foremost commercial centres in the world' as one reason for the final judgement. Grave economic problems and legal reasoning were subordinated to what the court perceived to be New York's commercial interest, even though it seems unlikely that a different judgment would have done perceptible harm to its standing as a financial centre.

If the first court's verdict in *Elliott* and its correct reasoning had been upheld, the 'vulture business' would not have prospered as it actually did. The court of appeal's view that someone buying distressed debts and having a record of suing for full repayment had not done so in the case of a debtor already in distress for some time,

42 M. Gulati and K.N. Klee, 'Sovereign Piracy' (2001) 56 Business Lawyer 638.

43 Gulati and Klee (n. 42) 638.

44 A. Reinisch, 'Sachverständigengutachten zur Frage des Bestehens und der Wirkung des völkerrechtlichen Rechtfertigungsgrundes "Staatsnotstand"' (expert opinion for the Bundesverfassungsgericht, the German Constitutional Court) (2005) 41, available at <http://investmentarbitration.univie.ac.at/fileadmin/user_upload/int_beziehungen/Personal/Publikationen_Reinisch/staatsnotstand_bverfg_28_2_06.pdf> (accessed 19 October 2012); cf. M. Waibel, Ch. 5 of this volume.

45 UNCTAD, *Trade and Development Report 1986* (UNCTAD, 1986) 142; cf. also K. Raffer, 'Internationalizing US Municipal Insolvency: A Fair, Equitable, and Efficient Way to Overcome a Debt Overhang' (2005) 6(1) Chi. J. Int'l L. 363; *Allied Bank International v. Banco Credito Agricola*, 757 F2d 516 (2d Cir 1985).

is severely at odds with logic. Meanwhile small organizational changes largely hinder a repetition of the Peruvian case. When proposing the IMF's insolvency model, Krueger[46] also points out that it is not absolutely clear whether Elliott's strategy would 'survive legal challenge in future cases'.

The important and apparently overlooked point is that 'vultures' are only able to fly because governments and Northern courts allow them to. Rather than clarifying legal prohibitions so that problematic interpretations by courts would be precluded, New York changed the law in favour of professional holdouts. These facts were never criticized or attacked by NGOs, even though law-makers could easily solve the problem.

II. Losses by bona fide creditors and the rule of law

Losses depend substantially on whether the rule of law is obeyed or flouted, for example by granting illegal preferential treatment to some creditors. Table 8.1 illustrates the effects of unfounded claims (classified as odious, illegitimate, or in whichever way), unpayable debts, and preferred creditors. Let us assume that country A has total debts of 100, but is only able to service a debt stock of 50 (50 is unpayable), and that A actually gets insolvency protection, no doubt a heroic assumption still when it comes to SCs. To simplify, we only consider a one-off debt stock reduction.

Table 8.1 Haircuts of bona fide creditors under different assumptions

Differentiation of creditors	Haircuts of private creditors
None	
No preference, all debts fully recognized	50%
Claims amounting to 40 null and void*	16.67%
IFIs exempt	
All other debts fully recognized	83.33%
40 null and void, 40 (IFIs) exempt	50%
IFIs treated lawfully	
40 plus 10 of IFI claims null and void	0%
40 plus all IFI claims null and void**	0%

* To simplify matters, including any form of impaired claims economically resulting in recuperated claims ultimately being less than nominal claims initially demanded, thus the amount of money 'lost' for legal reasons.

** In this extreme case, the debtor country still has money left that would be needed to service 30.

[46] A. Krueger, 'International Financial Architecture for 2002: A New Approach to Sovereign Debt Restructuring', Address at the National Economists' Club Annual Members' Dinner, American Enterprise Institute, Washington, DC, 26 November 2001, available at <http://www.imf.org/external/np/speeches/2001/112601.htm> (accessed 19 October 2012).

If all debts have to be honoured and no creditor is preferred, the haircut would be 50. With 40 null and void, A's remaining debt stock is 60, of which 10 still have to go in order to align A's capacity to pay to debt service due. Economically, this would not matter for A: 50 would go one way or another, although based on very different legal titles. For A's creditors, though, the results differ strongly. In the former case every creditor would receive half of their claims. In the latter case, those whose claims are voided would receive nothing, while recognized creditors would receive 83.33 per cent. As economic facts eventually assert themselves—what cannot be paid goes unpaid—denying debtors the rule of law has considerable effects on creditors, both unduly discriminated-against bona fide creditors, and unduly protected ones.[47] Official creditors allowing or supporting violations of the rule of law cause substantial negative effects for private bona fide creditors. Treating perfectly legal and legitimate debts like debts lacking such solid foundation inflicts grave injustice. Classifying and differentiating debts may thus be seen as more in the interest of bona fide creditors, even though the application of universally recognized legal principles would have avoided substantial damage to debtor countries and their peoples. In an insolvency procedure respecting existing legal principles, private bona fide creditors would recover more than under present public creditor domination and increasing discrimination against the private sector.

Quite noteworthy distributional effects are exacerbated by IFIs securing themselves privileged treatment as *de facto* preferred creditors, in breach of their own statutes.[48] This undue privilege is especially problematic in the poorest countries, where large percentages of sovereign debts are multilateral, and IFIs have influenced economic policies substantially. But it pops up in Greece too. Official creditors have repeatedly attached conditionalities to debt relief that are not connected to economic necessities and have quite often worsened crises.

The position of bona fide private creditors has deteriorated, as was shown previously with the example of the recent Greek crisis, where a new layer of preferences has been established *ex post, contra legem*, and after the public sector had vigorously encouraged, even urged private lenders to invest in what regulators declared to be riskless instruments. This preference ladder illegally subordinates private claims not only to the IMF but also to EU claims. As investors had been enticed to invest in Greek sovereign paper marked by regulators and credit rating agencies as virtually riskless, this is doubly unfair. Regulators—ultimately our governments—encouraging the build-up of unsustainable debts are also getting preferences. In fact, with regard to Greek debts, the European central bank is the biggest holdout, or as some would say 'vulture'. True, the Statement by the euro area heads of state in December 2010 reaffirmed that the haircut in Greece is unique and exceptional. Like many other EU statements before, this bold statement is unlikely to survive even the first reality test.

The haircut necessary for discriminated creditors to align capacity to pay and debt service would be 83.33 per cent if IFIs were allowed to continue breaking the

[47] cf. Raffer (n. 22); and Raffer (n. 45) 371–7.
[48] cf. Raffer (n. 45) 45, 371–7.

law. If 40 were voided but no IFI claims, a stock of 20 of non-IFI debt would remain, but only 10 could be serviced (servicing capacity 50, IFI stock 40). Treated 'comparably', non-IFIs would lose half of their face values, unless they chose to litigate. Under fair and equal treatment, they would only lose 16.67 per cent. If they win their cases, which is likely at present, they lose nothing. Considering mathematics and IFI-statutes, even private creditors without 'vulture-intentions' may be induced to litigate. Paying insurance against loan losses also remains more costly as long as IFIs remain unduly preferred. This economically perverse incentive system, rewarding failure, has caused substantial misallocations and damages. Instead of attacking vultures one should attack illegal and illegitimate, self-serving IFI behaviour and those governments aiding and abetting it. Breaches of law by IFIs have cost the poor much more dearly than any sum recovered by 'vultures'. Inexplicably, this problem gets practically no attention.

F. Conclusion

This chapter has elaborated on the implications of UNCTAD's Principles further, focusing mainly on creditors. Comparing early sovereign lending and the present situation, it has argued that the position of debtors has worsened. Unlike nowadays, legal principles were usually also respected in the case of SCs. The argument of this chapter shows that legal redress for quite a few problems exists but continues to be denied to SCs. It has also discussed the discrimination against private creditors that meanwhile even risks destroying capital markets, at least in one major region of the globe. The bottom line is simple: abolishing the ruling legal double standard would be a great improvement and support the meaningful implementation of important UNCTAD Principles.

9

UNCTAD's Principles on Public Debt and the United Nations Convention against Corruption

Links and Common Strategies

Juan Bautista Justo

A. Introduction

This chapter explores the relationship between the Principles of UNCTAD on responsible sovereign lending and borrowing[1] (the Principles) and the United Nations Convention against Corruption[2] (UNCAC).

To that effect, it tackles the need to establish some lawfulness in the field of public indebtedness, which these principles intend to satisfy, and tries to determine the role of the UNCAC in achieving this goal. The Principles suggest applying the core standards of the rule of law in the domain of sovereign loans—in terms of the fiduciary nature of authority prerogatives,[3] publicity, and accountability—aspects that constitute the conceptual basis of the UNCAC as well.[4]

This correlation of objectives creates the need to consider the way these two initiatives complement each other, trying to identify the advantages that they can offer one another. As a first approach, I will suggest that the UNCAC can contribute to the strengthening of the Principles, since it gives them—as a means of hard law—a powerful form of regulatory support. If we bring the rules of that convention to the field of state credit transactions we offer UNCTAD's proposal the backing of a binding source of international law, which would generate a significant

[1] UNCTAD, Consolidated Principles on Promoting Responsible Sovereign Lending and Borrowing, included in the Annex of this volume.

[2] United Nations, General Assembly Resolution 58/4 of 31 October 2003 (A/58/422). Annex: UN Convention Against Corruption (entered into force 14 December 2005), available at <http://www.unodc.org/unodc/en/treaties/CAC/index.html>.

[3] Transparency International defines corruption as 'the abuse of entrusted power for private gain', available at <http://www.transparency.org/whatwedo>.

[4] K. Annan, 'Message' in UNODC, *Global Action against Corruption. The Merida Papers* (2004) 1: 'Corruption is a major obstacle to political stability, and to successful social and economic development. Our only hope of removing this obstacle is through the effective application of the rule of law.'

transformation to its juridical nature and enable many of the actions it favours to gain support within a treaty.

In turn, the Principles can play an influential role in implementing the UNCAC more effectively in the field of government credit, an area which is especially sensitive to the scourge of corruption as a result of the absence of regulations and the significance of the financial transactions involved.

Indebtedness is, in fact, one of the most challenging public factors in the struggle against corruption, since—despite the seriousness, scope, and extent of its consequences within the community[5]—it still holds some weaknesses as regards publicity, assessment, and accountability that both the Principles and the UNCAC can help to resolve. Therefore, a complementary reading of these global initiatives is of strategic value.

B. The Principles: Main Features and Soft Law Status

UNCTAD's Principles assemble a series of international standards that focus on the prevention of reckless lending and borrowing of public loans.[6]

Their Preamble makes clear that their regulatory contribution 'is not the creation of new rights or obligations on international law, but the determination, standardizing and classification of the basic principles and the best practices for the lending and borrowing of state loans and analysis of the consequences of these standards and practices for lenders and borrowers on an international scale'.[7] The Principles

[5] As a result of those implications, 'when certain sovereign borrowers' and their lenders' decisions have deep and broad consequences on markets and societies, these decisions might be considered, from the international financial law perspective, as actions of public authorities which should respect the applicable public law regime developed at the international level.' (A. von Bogdandy and M. Goldmann, Ch. 3 of this volume). UNCAC is a clear emergent of that international public law regime. See A. von Bogdandy, P. Dann, and M. Goldmann, 'Developing the Publicness of Public International Law: Towards a Legal Framework for Global Governance Activities' (2008) 9 German L.J 1375, 1381–2.

[6] The Principles join other sectoral initiatives aimed at ensuring transparency, such as the Extractive Industries Transparency Initiative (2002), the Equator Principles for Financial Institutions (2005), the Wolfsberg Anti-Money-Laundering Principles for Private Banking (2000), the FIDIC Code of Ethics and Business Integrity Management System of the International Federation of Consulting Engineers, and the Sustainable Development Charter of the International Council on Mining and Metals (2002). There are also instruments to help companies to organize themselves against corruption, e.g. the ICC Rules of Conduct to Combat Extortion and Bribery (published by the International Chamber of Commerce in 1977 and revised on various occasions, most recently in 2005), the Business Principles for Countering Bribery (Transparency International), the World Economic Forum's Partnership against Corruption Initiative (launched in January 2004), the OECD Guidelines for Multinational Enterprises (revised in 2000), the Principle 10 in Global Compact (2010). See A. Posadas, 'Combating Corruption Under International Law' (2000) 10 Duke J. Comp. & Int'l L. 2.

[7] UNCTAD, 'Draft Principles on Responsible Sovereign Lending and Borrowing', Geneva, January 2012, available at <http://www.unctad.info/upload/Debt%20Portal/Principles%20drafts/SLB_Principles_English_Doha_22-04-2012.pdf>.

are, in this sense, considered collectively as an agent of soft law that aims to promote and consolidate, in both states and the private sector, voluntary practices based on a set of rules that, despite lacking a binding force, build strong expectations as regards the behaviour of their recipients.[8]

These rules try, in this way, to take advantage of the great potential in soft law, which offers the possibility of combining strong flexibility—from the absence of a binding nature—with an increasing ability to penetrate operators' practices due to their argumentative force. Soft law's tools can result in essential legal developments, since they define the significant social expectations regarding the behaviour of both public and private individuals. In other words, they show the expected way to proceed even when they are non-mandatory, and that entails a considerable persuasive force, far superior to coercion.[9]

With this influence, the first thing that the Principles expect from lenders is respect for the role of government officials that participate in the transactions as supporters of the public interest, with the consequent avoidance of complicity with corrupted practices in the borrowing process (Principles 1 and 9).

That crime-free environment is not, however, the only goal of this initiative. Lenders are also supposed to act under standards of due diligence in order to assist their sovereign clients to make informed, authorized, and legal financial decisions (Principles 2, 3, and 6). That requirement includes a realistic evaluation of the state debtor's reimbursement capacity (Principle 4) and of the possible effects of the projects whose financing caused the loan to exist (Principle 5). Finally, in case of the sovereign's inability to pay its debts, good faith and a cooperative spirit are expected from lenders, so as to reach a consensual restructuring of such obligations and provide a speedy and orderly way out of the problem (Principle 7).

The Principles also express clear requirements for sovereign borrowers. Based on governments' responsibility to protect their citizens' best interests (Principle 8), they impose standards of transparency in the process for obtaining financing and assuming sovereign debt obligations (Principles 10 and 11) and require a strict assessment of the costs and benefits of each sovereign loan (Principles 13 and 14), including the evaluation and diffusion of the financial, operational, civil, social, cultural, and environmental consequences of the projects for which the financing was requested (Principle 12). The obligations assumed under those rules must be fulfilled, and in the case of a state of economic necessity or a change in circumstances, an immediate, efficient, and fair restructuring must be followed (Principles 9 and 15).

[8] J.P. Bohoslavsky and C. Espósito, Ch. 4 of this volume; A. Guzman and T. Meyer, 'International Soft Law' (2010) 2 Journal of Legal Analysis 171; R. Higgins, *Problems and Process: International Law and How We Use It* (Cambridge University Press, 1994) 25.

[9] K.W. Abbott and D. Snidal, 'International Regulation without International Government: Improving International Organization Performance through Orchestration' (2010) 5 Review of International Organization 315.

C. The UNCAC: Main Features and Hard Law Status

The UNCAC is the first global instrument in the field of the fight against corruption.[10] As stated in Article 1, its objective is to prevent and combat this scourge efficiently, facilitate international cooperation and technical assistance, and promote integrity, accountability, and proper management of public affairs and public property.

Implementing the UNCAC incorporates the fight against corruption with a selection of themes affected by the legalization process of international relations,[11] or the internationalization of law, depending on the focus. This phenomenon implies—especially since the middle of the twentieth century—that areas which were traditionally destined for the domestic domain, and released within the scope of sovereign relationships, are increasingly regulated at an international level, with the subsequent limitation to state action in both spheres. We can see the same tendency within the fields of human rights, commerce, or investments, among others, and its three typical characteristics are:

(1) the explicit establishment of minimum levels of action on the part of public authorities;[12]

(2) preventing states from invoking their domestic legal systems, their cultural traditions, or any other aspect of their national identity to justify their distancing from those minimum levels;[13] and

(3) the creation of international bodies—courts, groups of experts, or peers—with the ability to control the compatibility of governmental practices with those minimum levels of action, and to declare a state's international liability in case of infringement.

The presence, to varying degrees, of each and every one of these aspects identifies the legalization process of international relations and allows us to distinguish three different stages within it:[14]

[10] The UNCAC was adopted in 2003 and entered into force on 14 December 2005. To date, 160 states have become parties to the convention. The treaty was the result of two years of negotiation by 130 governments, starting with the Vienna Declaration issued at the Tenth UN Congress on the Prevention of Crime and the Treatment of Offenders in April 2000. The Vienna Declaration resulted in the UN General Assembly adoption of Resolution 55/61 in December 2000, requesting the analytic reports necessary for a convention, and Resolution 55/188 of the same year proposing the establishment of a group of experts on international illegal corruption-related cash flows. See B. Michael, 'What Does the UN Convention on Corruption Teach Us About International Regulatory Harmonisation?' (2003), available at <http://ssrn.com/abstract=512082 or http://dx.doi.org/10.2139/ssrn.512082>.

[11] K.W. Abbott and D. Snidal, 'Values and Interests: International Legalization in the Fight Against Corruption' (2002) 31 J. Legal Stud. 141.

[12] UNODC, *Legislative Guide for the Implementation of the United Nations Convention against Corruption* (2006) § 21.

[13] Vienna Convention, Art. 27 and the UNCAC, Art. 65.

[14] K.W. Abbott et al., 'The Concept of Legalization' (2000) 54 International Organization 401; B. Koremenos et al., 'The Rational Design of International Institutions' (2001) 55 International Organization 761, 761–2; A. Boyle, 'Some Reflections on the Relationship of Treaties and Soft Law' (1999) 48 ICLQ 901.

(1) *precision* of rules, when we go from the ambiguity of political commitments to the clear definition of what is demanded, permitted, or prohibited by the establishment of minimum levels;

(2) *obligation*, when it is explicitly assumed—through the rule of inadmissibility of domestic law invocation and the principle of *pacta sunt servanda* (agreements must be kept)—that the undersigned are *legally* bound to a commitment from which they cannot step aside and that their actions will be measured against that commitment; and

(3) *delegation* of decision-making powers, when a third party is given the authority to interpret and apply the rules that derive from the commitment.

The degree to which these three dimensions are present determines whether an international instrument is closer to hard or soft law. Therefore, the concept of legalization is gradable: from the ideal type—where the three dimensions are at a maximum; passing through 'hard' legislation—where the three dimensions (or at least obligation and delegation) are high; to different forms of 'soft' legalization that combine these attributes; and finally to the total absence of legalization as another ideal type.

The UNCAC clearly adopts a high degree of legalization of anti-corruption actions, with intense levels of precision and compulsoriness and increasing progress as regards delegation.[15] From this perspective, it constitutes a typical instrument of hard law whose creation is attributable to the acknowledgement that only with a coordinated, uniform legal framework at the international level it is possible to fight the scourge of corruption.[16] This reality led, despite some conflicts,[17] to the development of binding instruments to fight against corruption at a global level, and the UNCAC is the utmost expression of this tendency.[18]

[15] One of the main criticisms aimed at the UNCAC is the lack of a body with powers to sanction non-compliant states. The shortfall in supervision was partially offset by the Conference of States Parties through the issuance—in 2009—of Resolution 3/1, that sets a review mechanism. The Conference also agreed to two five-year review cycles, with the first on Chs III (Criminalisation and Law Enforcement) and IV (International Cooperation), and the second cycle on Chs II (Preventive Measures) and V (Asset Recovery). The mechanism included an Implementation Review Group, which met for the first time in June–July 2010 in Vienna and selected the order of countries to be reviewed in the first five-year cycle, including the 26 countries (originally 30) in the first year of review.

[16] UNCAC's Preamble expresses the conviction that corruption is no longer a local matter but a transnational phenomenon that affects all societies and economies, making international cooperation to prevent and control it essential.

[17] See A. Cliff, '*The Failure to Negotiate Effective International Measures Against Transnational Bribery*' (2011) 53 Harv. Int'l L.J. Online, <http://www.harvardilj.org/2011/12/online_53_cliff>; Abbott and Snidal (n. 11).

[18] At the Global and Inter-Regional Level: UNCAC; United Nations Convention against Transnational Organized Crime (UNTOC); OECD Convention on the Bribery of Foreign Public Officials in International Business Transactions (OECD Convention); Revised Recommendation of the Council of the OECD on Combating Bribery in International Business Transactions. Africa: AU Convention on Preventing and Combating Corruption (AU Convention); SADC Protocol against Corruption (SADC Protocol); ECOWAS Protocol on the Fight against Corruption (ECOWAS Protocol). Americas: The Inter-American Convention against Corruption (OAS Convention). ASIA: ADB-OECD Action Plan for Asia-Pacific. Europe: Council of Europe Criminal Law Convention; Council of Europe Civil Law Convention; Resolution (99) 5 of the Committee of Ministers of the

On this basis, the UNCAC is characterized by the treatment of a wide range of themes. Through its articles, the convention establishes that state parties shall adopt measures within four broad fields.[19]

In first place, the UNCAC bases the achievement of its goals on *prevention*, imposing upon state parties the development and implementation of coordinated and effective anti-corruption policies that promote the participation of society and reflect the principles of the rule of law, integrity, transparency, and accountability. Those policies must be supervised by an independent and specialized body.

Prevention measures also include the endorsement of efficiency, transparency, and objective criteria in decision-making in most of the crucial areas of government, such as the recruitment, promotion and retirement of public officials, funding of candidatures and political parties, procurement, public finances, and the organization of public administration. To those ends, the UNCAC calls for different means, like codes of conduct; the protection of whistle-blowers; restrictions on the professional activities of former public officials—to avoid conflicts of interest; public participation in the fight against corruption—with a strong defence of the freedom to seek, receive, publish, and disseminate information concerning corruption; and a comprehensive domestic regulatory and supervisory regime for banks and non-bank financial institutions in order to deter and detect all forms of money laundering.

The second area in which UNCAC bases the international anti-corruption strategy is *criminalization and law enforcement*, demanding the global establishment of the bribery of a public official (national or foreign, or from a public international organization),[20] the embezzlement, misappropriation, laundering of proceeds of crime, and the obstruction of justice as criminal offences,[21] accompanied by the liability (criminal, civil, or administrative) of legal persons for participation in those transgressions, without prejudice to the liability of natural persons.

In order to avoid impunity related to those crimes, the UNCAC imposes duties such as the regulation of a long statute of limitations period in which to commence proceedings, the confiscation of proceeds of crime and instrumentalities used in the offences, and the protection of witnesses, experts, victims, and people who report any corruption case. Finally, states must ensure that entities or people who have suffered damage as a result of an act of corruption have the right to initiate legal proceedings against those responsible for that damage, in order to obtain compensation.

Council of Europe: Agreement Establishing the Group of States against Corruption; Resolution (97) 24 of the Committee of Ministers of the Council of Europe: Twenty Guiding Principles for the Fight against Corruption; European Union Convention on the Protection of the Communities' Financial Interests and the Fight against Corruption and two Protocols.

[19] M. Boersma, 'Catching the "Big Fish"? A Critical Analysis of the Current International and Regional Anti-Corruption Treaties', Maastricht Faculty of Law Working Paper (2008–9).

[20] See Cliff (n. 17).

[21] Additionally, state parties are required to consider criminalize trafficking in influence, abuse of functions, illicit enrichment, bribery, and embezzlement in the private sector.

International cooperation constitutes the third mechanism by which the UNCAC proposes to achieve its objectives. To that end, it develops an exhaustive regulatory regime for the extradition of people who have committed crimes of corruption, and demands from the state parties the widest measure of mutual legal assistance in investigations, prosecutions, and judicial proceedings in relation to the offences covered by the UNCAC, as well as the implementation of joint investigations.

Finally, in order to mitigate one of the aspects of the economic damage caused by corruption and to deter illegal practices by the elimination of its benefits, the UNCAC establishes *asset recovery* as its fourth purpose, with great significance placed on reparation for victims.

In this sense, the treaty requires the widest measure of cooperation and mutual assistance in the return of assets of proceeds of crime. In order to achieve this, it demands the establishment of regulations requiring financial institutions within its jurisdiction to verify the identity of customers, to take reasonable steps to determine the identity of beneficial owners of funds deposited into high-value accounts, and to conduct enhanced scrutiny of accounts sought by or maintained by or on behalf of individuals who are, or have been, entrusted with prominent public functions, as well as their family members and close associates.

With this wide range of commitments and tangible objectives, the approval of the UNCAC enabled the anti-corruption struggle to be transferred from the regional territory in which it was held to a global space,[22] all thanks to the indisputable binding force of the treaty as a primary source of international law. These marked aspects of hard law—resulting from a strong presence of the components of precision, obligation, and delegation—constitute the chief attraction of the UNCAC for the Principles.

D. Synergy between the UNCAC and the Principles

I. The UNCAC as the trojan horse of the Principles in the area of hard law

The UNCAC's four pillars of prevention, criminalization, cooperation, and asset recovery impose a series of obligations on the state parties whose transfer to the sovereign debt arena may be decisive, offering the Principles the endorsement of a binding source of international law. Many of the suggested practices in UNCTAD's initiative are directly welcomed by this international treaty, and that sets them in a different place from that of soft law which they were initially considered to occupy.

In fact, the UNCAC is the typical example of the legalization of international relations in the anti-corruption struggle. It constitutes a highly legalized instrument,

22 P. Webb, 'The United Nations Convention Against Corruption: Global Achievement or Missed Opportunity?' (2005) 8 J. Int'l Econ. L. 191.

with precise rules that are legally binding[23] and whose fulfilment is increasingly verified by international conventional bodies: the Conference of the State Parties to the Convention and the Implementation Review Group.

And it is precisely this quality as a source of legal obligations for states that allows the UNCAC to bring significant advantages to the Principles.

1. Binding force

The possibility of assimilating certain Principles to the UNCAC—as we will see in section E—would allow them to have access to the binding legal framework that they lacked from the start.[24] The UNCAC is the Trojan horse for the Principles as a primary source of international law, since states must fulfil this treaty in their indebtedness operations and with that they should put into practice many of the liability standards proposed in UNCTAD's document. For instance, to comply with Article 9 of the UNCAC, they must establish objective and competitive processes for the selection of lenders and, by doing so, they put into practice Principles 8, 10, and 11.[25]

Naturally, the Principles' contents and purposes are not reduced to the struggle against corruption and they are far from being absorbed into the UNCAC. There is a significant range of aspects not covered by this convention that relate to matters of political appraisal and institutional responsibility typical of the sovereign credit area. However, that does not alter the synergy between both instruments: it is not about competitiveness, but shared use for those aspects on which they agree. The UNCAC sets the minimum anti-corruption guidelines for indebtedness practices and the Principles develop them in relation to their particular field.

2. A regulatory framework that penetrates the domestic system

Secondly, the UNCAC makes a strong contribution to building the system of standards and acceptable practices claimed by the Principles.

As an instrument of hard law, this convention has a direct effect on domestic jurisdictions, imposing duties for measures of execution, adjustment of internal practices, and fitting of the state actions to its dispositions. This turns it into an excellent instrument to enable the Principles to penetrate governmental practices in every country. The implementation of the UNCAC through legislative, administrative, or judicial measures creates a background of direct permeability for the Principles. It is far easier for the Principles to be accepted in each country when they

[23] It is true, however, that the binding force of the treaty's norms varies. The UNCAC's provisions can be grouped into the following three categories: a) mandatory provisions, which consist of obligations to legislate; b) measures that state parties must consider applying or endeavour to adopt; c) measures that are optional (UNODC (n. 13) §§ 11 and 12).

[24] See T. Meyer, 'Soft Law as Delegation' (2009) 32 Ford. Int'l L.J. 906.

[25] C.R. Yukins, 'Integrating Integrity and Procurement: The United Nations Convention against Corruption and the UNCITRAL Model Procurement Law' (2007) 36 Public Contract Law Journal 307.

have the institutional, regulatory, and conceptual backup of the most advanced anti-corruption instrument in the world.

These attributes not only provide a formal setting for states to promote the fulfilment of the Principles in the field of indebtedness in a more effective way but also broaden their domain. As a matter of fact, if we verify the assimilation of a Principle to an UNCAC standard, most of the states that ratified the convention could not step aside from that Principle in a consistent way without jeopardizing their reputation. To date, almost every country in the world has assumed a series of commitments whose transfer to the field of sovereign indebtedness is embodied by the Principles.

3. A universe of national bodies of enforcement

The national offices that are in charge of credit operations are internal conventional bodies of the UNCAC, and therefore must spontaneously comply and enforce the convention as a complement to the Principles.

As a matter of fact, UNCAC's implementation task depends on two subsequent levels of engagement: first, on the spontaneous work of the judges, legislators, administrators, and other national authorities of the state, who oversee its fulfilment and act as internal conventional bodies, in the sense that they operate at the time when a treaty is applied within a country; and secondly (and only in a complementary role to the initial work done by the local authorities) we find bodies created by the UNCAC, namely the Conference of the States Parties and the Implementation Review Group, in charge of overseeing its fulfilment outside the country. These are conventional supranational bodies, as they operate exclusively on that level, and their role is to enhance the national work.

This coordination between the internal and supranational levels ratifies the importance of the local authorities' work and identifies the responsibilities involved. It is not enough to establish supranational bodies that fight corruption, it is also necessary for this fight to be accompanied, or in fact preceded, by cultural and hermeneutic incorporation to ensure the spontaneous compliance of each state party. This starts to work when the local authorities assume the role they are entrusted with as the first level of the system and unofficially verify, at every step, that their actions adequately follow the regulatory plexus they must supervise. In this way, the main role in the struggle against corruption is still played by domestic law and state practices, but it is necessary to transfer the regulatory and interpretative framework imposed by the UNCAC to the national level as a whole.

When national authorities are set up as domestic conventional bodies—agents for enforcement of the treaty within a country—the UNCAC directly penetrates the local decision-making area without the need for a superstructure. This arrangement, which is the visible expression of a design guided by efficiency directives, places the local system as a necessary, rather than merely possible, subject for the implementation of the treaty. The effectiveness of the UNCAC depends on the faculty, and especially on the obligation, of the country's officials to verify that the decisions they make or apply follow the convention rules, and to refrain from moving forward if they receive a negative response as regards their compliance. Thus, the system of UNCAC aims at the effective implementation of the prevention, criminalization, cooperation, and asset recovery measures through spontaneous action by states in their daily practices. As a result of this, all domestic bodies charged with the preparation and execution of credit operations are enforcement bodies of the UNCAC, and consequently of the Principles associated with that convention. This implies that the field of application of those standards would increase significantly.

To summarize, the UNCAC offers the UNCTAD's Principles the legal framework of an instrument with binding force, and of direct application by national authorities. This allows them to gain ground in a way which is highly unusual for an instrument of soft law, at least in the short term.

II. The Principles mould the UNCAC in the field of sovereign indebtedness

The Principles were conceived as an instrument of soft law. Their lack of binding force, however, is far from being a weakness. On the contrary, that non-binding nature constitutes an essential requirement for the current state of the legalization of sovereign indebtedness as it allows a certain degree of flexibility in an area that is being developed and remains subject to debate.

From this perspective, the Principles offer the UNCAC the advantages set out under the following four headings:

1. Greater dynamism to combat corruption

Even though the use of hard law is beneficial in order to plan relationships and consolidate commitments, the same obligatory characteristics that generate these advantages imply costs, especially because of limited flexibility.[26]

From this perspective, the positive characteristics of soft law focus our attention on the benefits that the Principles can bring to the UNCAC. Their lack of binding force offers more flexibility for negotiation, which means agreements can be reached on the anti-corruption fight in the field of indebtedness in a cheaper and less severe way.[27] Moreover, this flexibility allows people to participate in a process that is being developed and learn from the subsequent experiences (for example the cases of Argentina or Greece), which enhances the ability to adapt to vertiginous changes.[28]

[26] K.W. Abbott and D. Snidal, 'Hard and Soft Law in International Governance' (2000) 54 International Organization 422.

[27] C. Brummer, 'Why Soft Law Dominates International Finance—And Not Trade' (2010) 13 J. Int'l Econ. L. 630.

[28] K.W. Abbott and D. Snidal, 'Strengthening International Regulation Through Transnational New Governance: Overcoming the Orchestration Deficit' (2009) 42 Vand. J. Transnat'l L. 501:

> Old Governance is rooted in "hard law", its regulations are legally binding and mandatory. Hard law rules are generally uniform across regions and categories of actors and are enforced

In the same vein, the absence of the binding nature of rules motivates states to be more cooperative and to make more concessions than they would otherwise. It also allows them to approach a broad diversity of regulations better, as it offers instruments that are more suitable for experimentation and revision,[29] and employed by a wider range of bodies: the private sector and NGOs rather than state parties only.

Lastly, soft law avoids the costs of various negotiations, the risks of internal ratification, and political problems, sometimes achieving a far superior level of effectiveness than that of treaties if its operators are convinced. This compelling force allows governmental and private practices to be modelled, which leads—in this case—to the development of sources like customs or treaties.

This whole range of positive attributes can be mentioned in connection with the Principles and on the role they are called to play in the struggle against corruption in public credit operations.

2. *Better capacity for a multi-sector response*

The Principles can contribute to a more effective fight against corruption in the field of external indebtedness. They furnish specific knowledge, references, and sustainable practices that provide the UNCAC with content in this field.[30] In section E, I explore how certain Principles need to have the scope of anti-corruption mandates in the field of credit operations, which illustrates how they can complement and give substance to the UNCAC's requirements.

3. *Orientation to overcome gaps or deficits in the UNCAC*

The Principles fill many gaps in the UNCAC with respect to the practice of external indebtedness, and allow this treaty to deal better with changes in the international scenario.[31] In aspects where the UNCAC does not offer guidance or discusses a case in a vague or non-mandatory way, the Principles can reaffirm the relevance of valid

> by legal procedures backed by civil, administrative, or criminal sanctions. New Governance relies on more flexible norms and procedures throughout the regulatory process. The emerging Transnational New Governance system relies heavily on voluntary principles, codes, procedures, and (to the extent states and IGOs are involved) soft law. Private schemes lack authority to promulgate hard law; they also lack the capacity for coercive enforcement, relying on economic and social pressure from consumers and other constituencies, potential commercial benefits, and the implicit threat of state regulation to induce firms to adopt and comply with their norms. Even when the state is involved, Transnational New Governance relies on New Governance techniques rather than Old Governance coercive regulation.

(at 529–30).

[29] D.M. Trubek and L.G. Trubek, 'Hard and Soft Law in the Construction of Social Europe: The Role of the Open Method of Coordination' (2005) 11 European Law Journal 343, 353.

[30] See also Trubek and Trubek (n. 29) 355–9.

[31] D. Shelton, 'Introduction: Law, Non-Law and the Problem of Soft Law' in D. Shelton (ed.), *Commitment and Compliance: The Role of Non-Binding Norms in the International Legal System* (Oxford University Press, 2000); C. Chinkin, 'The Challenge of Soft Law: Development and Change in International Law' (1989) 38 ICLQ 850, 866.

anti-corruption practice.[32] For example, Article 12 of the UNCAC introduces optional measures to combat conflicts of interests, whereas Principle 10 implies that conflict situations will not be allowed to be reached, being in this way more effective than the hard law instrument.

4. Greater emphasis on prevention

Lastly, one of the most valuable contributions of the Principles to the UNCAC is that they compensate for the excessive zeal of the treaty in penalization measures, which is combined with a tendency to neglect other issues—from administrative, regulatory, and financial law—that play a decisive role in the prevention and remediation of corrupt practices. A clear example of this deficit can be appreciated in Article 34, which turns something into a voluntary practice that should clearly be mandatory for any country that wishes to combat corruption efficiently. In other words, the Principles can replace this style, somewhat biased towards criminalization, present in the UNCAC.[33]

III. Corollary

The Principles and the UNCAC complement each other to strengthen the prevention of corrupt practices within the sovereign indebtedness' arena. The UNCAC provides the framework of a structured system of rules with the category of a treaty, and the Principles provide a specialized perspective and flexibility, i.e. the necessary guidance for the convention to be applied to that field.

If a state party to the UNCAC has not yet implemented any mechanisms to apply the convention in the field of indebtedness, the Principles will guide this process and will be useful at a global level to bring practices into line with a binding international instrument.[34] Moreover, a complementary reading of both initiatives allows us to avoid the risk of fragmentation.[35]

[32] See M. Waibel, Ch. 5 of this book.

[33] The Inter-American Convention against Corruption also focuses too heavily on criminalization.

[34] C. Chinkin, 'Normative Development in the International Legal System' in D. Shelton (ed.), *Commitment and Compliance: The Role of Non-Binding Norms in the International Legal System* (Oxford University Press, 2000).

[35] As the 2006 ILC report states:

> What once appeared to be governed by 'general international law' has become the field of operation for such specialist systems as 'trade law,' 'human rights law,' 'environmental law,' 'law of the sea,' [or] 'European law' each possessing their own principles and institutions. The problem, as lawyers have seen it, is that such specialized law-making and institution-building tends to take place with relative ignorance of legislative and institutional activities in the adjoining fields and of the general principles and practices of international law. The result is conflicts between rules or rule-systems, deviating institutional practices and, possibly, the loss of an overall perspective on the law.

International Law Commission, 'Fragmentation of International Law: Difficulties arising from the Diversification and Expansion of International Law', Report of the Study Group of the International Law Commission, finalized by Martti Koskenniemi. A/CN.4/L.682 of 13 April 2006, 11.

As a result, the UNCAC can help countries to adopt the Principles and amend their credit practices, while the Principles can help them to apply the UNCAC within that field. *Both initiatives aim, all in all, to strengthen the regulatory and institutional ability of states to bring lawfulness to the field of sovereign indebtedness.* And therein lies the synergy.

E. The Fight against Corruption in the Field of Sovereign Indebtedness

Many of the obligations imposed on state parties by the UNCAC have a direct impact on public credit operations. The ones that stand out are the following.

I. Independent control bodies to prevent corruption in debt transactions

Article 6 of the UNCAC requires states to guarantee the existence of an independent body[36] in charge of preventing corruption by means of the implementation of coordinated and effective policies that promote the participation of society and reflect the principles of the rule of law, proper management of public affairs and public property, integrity, transparency, and accountability.

In the field of sovereign indebtedness, this demand implies that:

(a) The existence of this type of body is not optional, but mandatory for states. Credit borrowing does not escape this rule, and therefore governments must guarantee the effective presence of an anti-corruption body in that area. It is not necessary for it to belong to that specific sector, but it must be able to operate in that field.[37]

(b) This anti-corruption body shall have a guaranteed independence and the necessary material resources and specialized staff to carry out its functions in an effective manner. The distinctive feature of independence lies in the absence of any unlawful influence or conditioning of a state body by another state body, or an individual.

For that directive to come to fruition we shall consider:

(1) the way its members are appointed, giving priority to coordinated mechanisms with the necessary involvement of the deliberating body, following the

[36] The body or bodies referred to in this article may be the same as those referred to in Art. 36. UNODC, *Travaux Préparatoires of the Negotiations for the Elaboration of the United Nations Convention against Corruption* (2010) 83.

[37] Governments can assign corruption prevention responsibilities to one or more state agencies. The legislative guide for the implementation of the UNCAC establishes that 'Article 6 is not intended to refer to the establishment of a specific agency at a specific level. What is needed is the capacity to perform the functions enumerated by the article', UNODC (n. 13) 16.

carrying-out of a pre-selection procedure that guarantees the principles of publicity, concurrence, equity, and citizen scrutiny;

(2) the duration of the public office—controlling officials with decision-making power shall have a permanent position and fixed salaries;

(3) the existence of barriers against external pressure through coordinated dismissal procedures, based on grounds of proven inadequate performance of their duties; and

(4) the appearance of independence, i.e. citizens' perception of such a requisite as a value worth keeping in a democratic society.[38]

These components must guide the development of the control body's establishment rules, setting any discretionary schemes of appointment, authority, and dismissal aside, or the presence of hierarchical bonds between the controlled person and the one who exerts the control.

(c) This body is given a role of a preventive nature by the UNCAC, which means that control shall be exerted prior and not subsequent to the entry into force and execution of agreements. In the field of public credit, there should be prior and integrated control on the development and implementation processes of a contract. From this point of view, control should be considered as a formal requisite of validity of the agreement with regard to the terms of Principle 3.

(d) The exclusion of credit operations from external control and the assignment of auditing to hierarchically dependent bodies are not compatible with Article 6 of the UNCAC.

All of this is consistent with Principles 1, 3, and 8, which reaffirm the fiduciary nature of the decision-making prerogatives on indebtedness,[39] in that public authority shall not be exerted for the interest of the person in charge. State bodies act, by definition, for the benefit of a third party and are responsible for the temporary administration of this third party's interests.[40] Control is a logical consequence of this representative bond, as it is part of the electors'—the citizens'—capacity to verify at all times that the elected—government officials—follow those rules. The loss of that possibility entails a definitive alienation of faculties that the democratic system does not accept.

II. Transparent, competitive, and objective credit borrowing procedures

Article 9.1 of the UNCAC legally binds states to establish systems of procurement based on transparency, competition, and objective criteria in decision-making.[41]

[38] ECHR, *Campbell and Fell v. UK* (App 7819/77) (1984).

[39] See J. Oyola and M. Sudreau, Ch. 10 of this volume.

[40] See O. Lienau, *Rethinking Sovereign Debt: Debt and Reputation in the Twentieth Century* (Harvard University Press, forthcoming 2014).

[41] Competition, integrity, and transparency are typically viewed as the core, or pre-eminent, goals in any sound procurement system. See S.L. Schooner, 'Desiderata: Objectives for a System of Government Contract Law' (2002) 11 Public Procurement Law Review 103.

Such systems shall address, *inter alia*:

(1) the public distribution of information relating to procurement procedures and contracts to promote the concurrence of tenders;

(2) the establishment, in advance, of conditions for participation, including the selection and award criteria;

(3) the use of objective and predetermined criteria in order to facilitate the subsequent verification of the correct application of the rules or procedures; and

(4) an effective system of domestic review, including an efficient system of appeal, to ensure legal recourse and remedies in the event that the rules or procedures established in the regulation are not followed.

Through these accurate directives, Article 9 of the UNCAC directly and immediately imposes an obligation on state parties to adapt their domestic law to those norms and procedures. That general obligation implies the adoption of measures in two aspects: first, the abolition of norms and practices of any nature that entail a violation of the conventional directives; and secondly, the implementation of rules and the development of practices that lead to effective compliance with those directives. The obligation derived from the first aspect is not fulfilled as long as the rule or practice that is in violation of this obligation remains a part of the legal system, and therefore can be satisfied through its modification, abolition, annulment, or amendment. In the second assumption, the conventional obligation is fulfilled by the implementation of regulations and practices that lead to compliance with rights, that is to say, by positive measures.

If we transfer those parameters to the interpretation of the obligation to amend provided for in Article 9.1 of the UNCAC, we can conclude that it entails—from the first aspect—the abolition of any state practice that implies the establishment or ratification of procurement procedures that do not apply the principles of transparency, competition, and objectivity. In this way, the exemption of credit contracts from mechanisms that abide by those principles constitutes a breach that must be remedied by their amendment or annulment, or by the establishment of a system that complies with the convention mandates.

In this case, the agreements and other resolutions adopted pursuant to rules that do not respect the principles established in Article 9.1 of the UNCAC are contrary to that convention. This implies that, leaving aside the possibility of establishing precise exceptions of legal range, a direct agreement with a bank or an agent or disrespect for the directives of Article 9.1, compromise the validity of the agreement in terms of Principle 3. This is consistent with the demands of Principles 8, 10, and 11, which ensure the fiduciary role of government officials, and their subsequent duties of publicity and accountability.

National legislators are not allowed to exempt credit contracts from the requirements of transparent, competitive, and objective procedures. The applicable international regulation determines the way to draw up state contracts, and this should be respected since it represents an essential requisite for its existence. As a consequence, all contracts that do not adjust to those rules shall be sanctioned with invalidity.

III. Accountability of government officials who participate in agreements

Article 9.2 of the UNCAC legally binds states to adopt the appropriate measures to promote transparency and accountability in the management of public finances. Such measures shall encompass, *inter alia*: '*(i)* procedures for the adoption of the national budget; *(ii)* timely reporting on revenue and expenditure; *(iii)* a system of accounting and auditing standards and related oversight; *(iv)* effective and efficient systems of risk management and internal control.'

This directive is not only consistent with Principle 11, but also implies that public officials who carry out the operation shall render accounts with respect to the financial benefits it produces, pursuant to Principle 14.

IV. Conflicts of interest

Article 12 of the UNCAC makes states responsible for adopting measures to prevent corruption and to enhance accounting and auditing standards in the private sector. To achieve this, it allows them—not obliges them—to take the initiative to prevent conflicts of interest by imposing temporal restrictions on the professional activities of former public officials or the employment of public officials by the private sector after their resignation or retirement.

The prevention of conflicts of interest is, therefore, an optional measure by the UNCAC. Nevertheless, and from the point of view of the synergy proposed here, the rules of transparency included in Principle 10 highly recommend the strict regulation of conflicts of interest. Only by doing this is it possible to achieve the aim of transparency in processes to obtain financing and ensure the adequate approval and supervision for official credit borrowing.

V. Right of access to information on corruption and to data on loans

Article 13 of the UNCAC binds states to 'promote the active participation of individuals and groups outside the public sector... in the prevention of and the fight against corruption'. To do that, states must, among other things, enhance transparency and promote the contribution of the public to decision-making processes and ensure that the public has effective access to information.

Along these lines, the UNCAC imposes an obligation on states to respect, promote, and protect the freedom to seek, receive, publish, and disseminate information concerning corruption, and it specifies that this freedom may be subject to certain restrictions that depend on specific requisites.

In this way, the UNCAC joins the global tendency anticipated in Article 10 of the European Convention for the Protection of Human Rights and Fundamental Freedoms and Article 13 of the American Convention on Human Rights.[42] These

[42] According to the Interpretative Notes for the Official Records (*Travaux Préparatoires*) of the Negotiation of the United Nations Convention Against Corruption, 'The intention behind paragraph 1

rules embrace the principle of maximum disclosure, which establishes that all information regarding a state is presumed to be accessible. This access is, therefore, an essential condition for the validity of the state authorities' performance in a democratic society. Thus, the principle of maximum disclosure imposes not only a negative obligation on states which consists in avoiding any practice that may cause a cut in public access to information, but also a positive obligation that involves adopting all the necessary measures to ensure the execution of this right, in practice, by any citizen.

Moreover, the UNCAC's provision seems to go a step further as, unlike other instruments that regulate the subject of freedom of information, it is not limited to protecting access to and dissemination of public information, but extends to *all* information related to corruption, without distinction, including, hence, *private* information. In any case, the regulation itself authorizes the possibility of imposing restrictions based on the law, paying attention to the honour and reputation of third parties, and allowing certain reservations to protect privacy.

Along the same lines, Article 13.1 establishes that the right to information on corruption is subject to a system of restrictions that shall be: (a) previously provided for by law, as a means to ensure that they are not left to the discretion of the public power in each case; and (b) necessary to guarantee respect for the rights or reputations of others or the protection of national security or public order or public health or morals.[43] Other than these, there are no restrictions to the access of information in the framework of UNCAC, and the state should prove under which assumption each limitation should be framed.

The state should be compelled to demonstrate that, with the establishment of restrictions on access to information on corruption, it has met all the prerequisites and the decision on this point should meet the requirement of due foundation. According to this requirement, the confidentiality of credit operations should be authorized by law and the circumstances should fall within any of the exceptions precisely envisaged by the UNCAC—otherwise, it would represent a restriction that is prohibited by that treaty or Principle 11.

So rules that generically authorize public officials to limit access to credit transactions or agreements in an unrestricted way are not valid. Legislation should settle the causes of secret operations, out of which public access to them fully applies, as prescribed by Principle 11.

(d) is to stress those obligations which States Parties have already undertaken in various international instruments concerning human rights to which they are parties and should not in any way be taken as modifying their obligations', A/58/422/Add.1, § 17.

[43] That restrictions imposed must be necessary means that, among several options for reaching the target, the one which restricts the right to a lesser degree must be chosen. Whilst the adjective 'necessary' is not synonymous with 'indispensable', neither does it have the flexibility of such expressions as 'admissible', 'ordinary', 'useful', 'reasonable', or 'desirable'; rather, it implies a 'pressing social need', ECHR, *Handyside v. UK* (App 5493/72), 1976.

VI. Liability of legal persons that participate in offences related to credit operations

In accordance with Article 26 of the UNCAC and Principles 4, 5, and 6, state parties shall establish a system of liability for legal persons involved in corruption crimes. This requirement is mandatory. Like other international initiatives that recognize the variety of approaches used by the different legal systems and adapt to them, the second paragraph of Article 26 indicates that, subject to the legal principles of each state, the liability of legal persons may be criminal, civil, or administrative. In consequence, the state party to the convention is not bound to establish criminal liability if that is incompatible with its constitutional principles. In those cases, a civil or administrative liability should be enough to fulfil the requisite requirements.[44] This implies that there should not be domestic regulations to exempt legal persons of their liability for the illegal performance of their bodies.

At this point, the strong development of businesses' responsibility for complicity plays a key role, and although today it mainly depends on human rights violations, it has effects on the corporate complicity framework through acts of corruption.[45] A new field of corporate liability emerges from this convention clause.

VII. International regime of invalidity for corruption in sovereign debt contracts

Article 34 of the UNCAC—in accordance with Principles 6, 8, 9, 10, and 11—requires in a general way that each state should take measures to address the consequences of corruption. However, it allows—but does not oblige—states to '*consider* corruption a relevant factor in legal proceedings to annul or rescind a contract, withdraw a concession or other similar instrument . . . '.

In this way, the first part of Article 34 includes a binding regulation that can kick-start the development of a state contract annulments system for the violation of international rules in the development and execution of those bonds. Nevertheless, when it has to move forward from that initial mandate, the provision leaves the decision on the consequences of civil or administrative law to the sole discretion of the state parties, which is debatable. The margin of appreciation as regards the possible measures does not, however, make the main rule of the regulation less strict: the consequences of a corrupt act should be eliminated, and if that entails the annulment of acts or contracts, so be it. Otherwise, the effectiveness of the conventional mandate included in Article 34 would be compromised.

There is, however, an inconsistency in a convention that seeks to prevent and eradicate corruption and includes a wide range of criminalization measures, but which also considers the annulment of the state measures deriving from those

[44] UNODC (n. 12) § 334.

[45] C. Rose, 'The Application of Human Rights Law to Private Sector Complicity in Governmental Corruption' (2011) 24 LJIL 715.

crimes as optional. It would be a contradiction to bind states to categorize crimes but to leave the decision to annul the contracts resulting from these crimes to their discretion.

Furthermore, the tendency of international law shows that the annulment of acts and contracts resulting from corruption is not optional.[46] Moreover, that measure is a fundamental precondition for any minimally effective practice in the fight against this scourge. Thus, far from being left to 'whether the State Parties wish to consider' corruption as a 'relevant' factor to annul or rescind a contract, this is a binding measure.

So, the non-optional nature of the nullity of a contract based on corruption can be considered a general principle of law accepted in international regulation.[47] As sustained in an arbitration case of ICSID, 'a contract inciting or favouring the corruption of civil servants goes against the transnational public policy and, if such proves to be the object of the consultancy contract, it has no option other than to declare its nullity'.[48] It then concludes that 'in light of domestic laws and international conventions relating to corruption, and in light of the decisions taken in this matter by courts and arbitral tribunals... bribery is contrary to the international, public policy of most, if not all, States or, to use another formula, to transnational public policy. Thus, claims based on contracts of corruption or contracts obtained by corruption cannot be upheld'.[49]

It should be emphasized that respect for the rules of the UNCAC is crucial for the borrower, and it even generates a duty of due diligence to verify the transparency of the operation, since the nullity of the contract will directly affect its chance of being enforceable, as comment on Principle 9 clearly states.[50]

All in all, there are parameters that make the validity and efficacy of sovereign contracts conditional on the fulfilment of the relevant regulations as regards the form and procedures for their making and execution, and Principle 3 requires borrowers to duly exercise reasonable diligence in verifying that validity.

[46] The Civil Law Convention on Corruption in Europe, Art. 8 states: 'Each Party shall provide in its internal law for any contract or clause of a contract providing for corruption to be null and void.'

[47] M. Goldmann, 'Responsible Sovereign Lending and Borrowing: The View from Domestic Jurisdictions. A Comparative Survey' (2012) 43, 55, available at <http://www.unctad.info/upload/Debt%20Portal/RSLB_MGoldmann_02-2012.pdf>.

[48] ICSID, *World Duty Free v. Kenya* (Case No. ARB/00/7), 2006, § 155; *Gustav F W Hamester GmbH & Co KG v. Republic of Ghana* (Case No. ARB/07/24), 2010, §§ 123 and 124.

[49] ICSID, *World Duty Free v. Kenya* (n. 48) § 157. See S. Schill, 'Illegal Investments in International Arbitration', Max Planck Institute for International Law, Working Papers Series (2012); J.N. Summerfield, 'The Corruption Defense in Investment Disputes: A Discussion of the Imbalance between International Discourse and Arbitral Decisions' (2009) 6 Transnational Dispute Management; J.W. Yackee, 'Investment Treaties and Investor Corruption: An Emerging Defense for Host States' (2012) 52 Va. J. Int'l L. 723; G. Sacerdoti, 'Corruption in Investment Transactions: Policy Initiatives, Legal Principles and Arbitral Practice', Bocconi Legal Studies Research Paper No. 1931598 (2011); H. Raeschke-Kessler, 'Corruption in Foreign Investment. Contracts and Dispute Settlement between Investors, States, and Agents' (2008) 9 JWIT 1.

[50] See UNCTAD (n. 7) 9: 'In some cases the circumstances surrounding the incurrence of a sovereign loan may give rise to a legal defense pertaining to the performance of that contract by the sovereign borrower. Creditor complicity in the corruption of government officials in the borrowing process is one.'

VIII. Compensation for individuals affected by detrimental credit operations derived from acts of corruption

Article 35 of the UNCAC demands that state adopt the necessary measures 'to ensure that the entities or persons[51] who have suffered damage as a result of an act of corruption have the right to initiate legal proceedings against those responsible for that damage in order to obtain compensation'.

The interpretation notes explain that 'the intention of this article is to establish the principle that the state parties should ensure that they have the mechanisms to allow persons or entities that have suffered damage to initiate legal proceedings, in the proper circumstances, against those who commit acts of corruption'.[52]

Article 35 does not demand compensation or restitution for the victims. However, there should be measures, legislative or of a different nature, to address procedures through which that compensation or restitution could be obtained or claimed.[53]

A decisive aspect in achieving the efficacy demanded by Article 35 of the UNCAC is equality of arms. There is usually no point of comparison between the power of victims—generally, the citizens of the debtor country affected in their rights as a result of the economic losses caused by illegal debt transactions—and that of corrupt public officials or businessmen. The purpose of Article 35 will in fact be compromised if measures are not established to compensate for this inequality.

To be precise, the equality of arms principle, as part of the notion of the fair trial established by the European Court of Human Rights and the Inter-American Court of Human Rights, requires all parties to be given a reasonable opportunity to present their cases under conditions that do not place each party at a *substantial disadvantage vis-à-vis his opponent*,[54] ordering the existence of an *adequate balance* between the parties.[55]

On that basis, it is necessary to introduce measures compensating for actual inequality that may exist between parties into various aspects of administrative and legal procedures. This concept is not limited to the obligation to avoid substantial differences between opponents, but extends to the removal of existing ones produced by economic, social, or any other factors.

[51] The expression 'entities or persons' is deemed to include states, as well as legal and natural persons (n. 42) § 37.

[52] See n. 42, § 38.

[53] UNODC (n. 13) § 460.

[54] ECHR, *Dombo Beheer B.V. v. Netherlands*, (App 14448/88) (1993); *Kress v. France*, (App 39594/98) (2001); *Beer v. Austria*, (App 30428/96) (2001); *Nikoghosyan y Melkonyan v. Armenia*, (App 11724/04) (2007); *Ruiz Mateos v. Spain*, (App 12952/87) (1993); *Lobo Machado v. Portugal*, (App. 15764/89) (1996); *Vermeulen v. Belgium*, (App 19075/91) (1996); *Barberà, Messegué y Jabardo v. Spain*, (App 10590/83) (1988).

[55] ECHR, *Gorraiz Lizarraga v. Spain*, (App 62543/00) (2004); *Borgers v. Belgium*, (App 12005/86) (1991); *Demicoli v. Malta*, (App 13057/87) (1991); *Brandstetter v. Austria*, (App 11170/84) (1991); *McMichael v. UK*, (App 16424/90) (1995); *Lanz v. Austria*, (App 24430/94) (2002); *Bulut v. Austria*, (App 17358/90) (1996).

In this sense, the function of equality of arms is to require corrective factors to be established, that favour equality for those who are unequal for other reasons, and to enable fair solutions to be found, in material relationships as well as in proceedings.[56] That purpose has been outlined in four directives:[57]

(1) In order for a due, legal process to exist, the person must have the chance to defend their rights and interests in an effective way, and under equal procedural requirements vis-à-vis their opponent and other citizens in general. Equality should be practised, under these circumstances, not only between parties, but also between them and third parties in general.

(2) To ensure their real guarantees, the person whose right is under consideration should have procedural tools available that contribute—in practice—to the protection, reinforcement, or defence of their exercise of rights.

(3) Depending on this, to reach its objectives, the state process should recognize and solve the actual inequality factors present for those persons whose rights or obligations are subject to the decision of the public authority. In this way, the principle of equality before the law is met, as is the subsequent prohibition of discrimination.

(4) A way of fulfilling the mandate of solving these inequalities and avoiding a presumed discriminatory omission is to adopt compensation measures. These contribute to the reduction or elimination of obstacles and deficiencies that stop or reduce the efficient defence of self-interest. If there are no such means of compensation, widely recognized in the various sources of the procedure, we cannot say that those who are disadvantaged benefit from due, legal processes under conditions of equality, vis-á-vis those who do not face these obstacles.

The equality of arms principle, created from the contributions of both America's and Europe's human rights courts, briefly requires the interested party to be given a reasonable opportunity to present his or her case under genuinely equal conditions. To that end, the rules or acts of procedure should anticipate compensation measures to reduce or eliminate the obstacles and deficiencies that stop or reduce the efficient defence of rights. Full respect for this rule constitutes an essential requirement for the fulfilment of the regulations of Article 35 of the UNCAC.

The 'Guiding Principles on Business and Human Rights: Implementing the United Nations "Protect, Respect and Remedy" Framework'[58] also offer useful

[56] IACHR, AO-18/03, 2003. [57] IACHR, AO-16/99, 1999.

[58] UN, Human Rights Council, A/HRC/17/31, 2011. See also, 'State obligations to provide access to remedy for human rights abuses by third parties, including business: an overview of international and regional provisions, commentary and decisions', A/HRC/11/13/Add.1, 2009; B. Mares, (ed.), *The UN Guiding Principles on Business and Human Rights* (Brill, 2012); J. Knox, 'The Ruggie Rules: Applying Human Rights Law to Corporations', Wake Forest University Legal Studies Paper No. 1916664 (2011); R.C. Blitt, 'Beyond Ruggie's Guiding Principles on Business and Human Rights: Charting an Embracive Approach to Corporate Human Rights Compliance', University of Tennessee Legal Studies Research Paper No. 158 (2011).

guidance to understanding the reparation remedies in Article 35 of the UNCAC. They emphasize the need to avoid creating barriers in compensation for damages, especially those that derive from, among others, high costs or difficulties in gaining legal representation due to lack of resources or other incentives for lawyers to advise the complaining parties within this sphere, or from the lack of adequate options to present joint claims or establish representation procedures (like civil, joint complaints and other collective action procedures). This prevents complaining parties from obtaining adequate compensation at an individual level. All of this is worsened by the initial disadvantage that the victims experience, usually belonging to the most neglected sectors of society.

So, for the adoption and entry into force of the action described in Article 35, states should apply the standards of *simplicity*, *promptness*, and *effectiveness*, developed in the framework of human rights law as regards the effectiveness of remedies in favour of victims.[59] The directive of effectiveness implies that the resource is suitable to fight the violation and that it is effectively applied by the relevant authority, which means that it can solve or give answers on how to solve the said violation.[60] Resources that turn out to be false, given the general conditions a country is in or the circumstances surrounding a given case, cannot be considered effective. This can happen, for example, when such resources prove to be useless in practice, or when the body in charge of the decision-making process is not sufficiently independent to make that ruling impartially, or additionally when there are insufficient means to execute that body's decisions, or for any other situation that represents a form of justice denial, as is the case when there is an unacceptable delay in justice.[61]

Article 35, in a way consistent with Principles 1 to 5, implies that victims—for example, the citizens of a country—should be able to rely on a regulatory instrument that allows them to claim compensation from those responsible—public officials or bankers—for damages that arise from illegal credit borrowing or lending. That legal action should respect the principle of equality of arms and satisfy the

[59] IACHR, *López-Álvarez v. Honduras*. Judgment of 1 February 2006, Series C No. 141; *García-Asto and Ramírez-Rojas v. Peru*, Judgment of 25 November 2005, Series C No. 137; *Palamara-Iribarne v. Chile*, Judgment of 22 November 2005, Series C No. 135; *Acosta-Calderón v. Ecuador*, Judgment of 24 June 2005. Series C No. 129; *Serrano-Cruz Sisters v. El Salvador*, Judgment of 9 September 2005. Series C No. 131; *Tibi v. Ecuador*, Judgment of 7 September 2004, Series C No. 114.

[60] IACHR, *Acevedo-Jaramillo et al. v. Peru*, Judgment of 24 November 2006, Series C No. 157; *Goiburú et al. v. Paraguay*, Judgment of 22 September 2006, Series C No. 153; *Raxcacó-Reyes v. Guatemala*, Judgment of 6 February 2006, Series C No. 143.

[61] IACHR, *Dismissed Congressional Employees (Aguado-Alfaro et al.) v. Peru*, Judgment of 30 November 2007, Series C No. 174; *19 Merchants v. Colombia*, Judgment of 5 July 2004, Series C No. 109; *Maritza Urrutia v. Guatemala*, Judgment of 27 November 2003, Series C No. 103; *Cantos v. Argentina*, Judgment of 7 September 2001, Series C No. 85; *Mayagna (Sumo) Awas Tingni Community v. Nicaragua*, Judgment of 31 August 2001, Series C No. 79; *Durand and Ugarte v. Peru*, Judgment of 3 December 2001, Series C No. 89; *Indigenous Community Yakye Axa v. Paraguay*, Judgment of 6 February 2006, Series C No. 142.

effectiveness and accessibility requirements.[62] Thus, Article 35 of the UNCAC creates at the international level an autonomous and independent compensatory remedy that must be enforced by states[63] and can function as a crucial instrument for the decentralized fight against corruption.

F. Conclusions

Corruption could be said to constitute the combined effect of monopoly of power plus discretion in decision-making in the absence of accountability.[64] By observing the dynamics of external indebtedness, the lack of a clear legal framework, and the increased levels of discretion for participating officials, we can acknowledge that this is a field where corruption can flourish easily.

In this scenario, the UNCAC and the Principles can join together to play a key role in the fight against corruption within a particularly complex field. Both initiatives have compatible objectives and contents and offer stimulating mutual advantages. From this perspective, the hard law of the UNCAC can play a decisive role in helping the Principles by giving them a binding character, whereas the Principles allow the development of flexible and tailored tools to fight against corruption in the arena of credit contracts. With those mutual benefits, they aim, all in all, to introduce rule of law techniques to the field of sovereign indebtedness. That is the synergy and the opportunity we must not lose.

62 The European Civil Law Convention on Corruption, Art. 4 states:

1. Each Party shall provide in its internal law for the following conditions to be fulfilled in order for the damage to be compensated:
   i) the defendant has committed or authorised the act of corruption, or failed to take reasonable steps to prevent the act of corruption;
   ii) the plaintiff has suffered damage; and
   iii) there is a causal link between the act of corruption and the damage.

63 UNCAC, Art. 65.

64 R.F. Klitgaard, R. Maclean Abaroa, and H.L. Parris, *Corrupt Cities: A Practical Guide to Cure and Prevention* (ICS Press, 2000).

10

Fiduciary Relations

Legal Framework and Implications for Responsible Sovereign Debt Management

*José R. Oyola and Marie Sudreau**

A. Introduction

The Consolidated version of the Principles, dated 10 January 2012, refers in Principles 1 and 8 to the responsibility owed by government officials to the state to protect the public interest.[1] This formulation is tantamount to establishing a fiduciary relationship in the form of agency between governments and citizens. The public interest, which is defined as '*something in which the public, the community at large, has some pecuniary interest, or some interest by which their legal rights or liabilities are affected*',[2] corresponds to the general interest or will of the nation's citizens.[3] While these interests are difficult to categorize, it can be said that their overarching aim is to promote the nation's welfare.[4]

In this chapter we look into the implications of defining governments as agents of the state in terms of the identification and allocation of responsibilities in sovereign debt contracting. The status of state as principal imposes *de facto* fiduciary

* Disclaimer: the views of the authors in this chapter are not necessarily the opinions of the institutions.

[1] Consolidated Principles on Responsible Sovereign Lending and Borrowing, UNCTAD, January 2012.

[2] *State v. Crockett*, 56 Okl. 124, 206 P. 816, 817 quoted in J. D. Montgomery, 'Public Interest in the Ideologies of National Development' in C.J. Friedrich (ed.), *The Public Interest* (Atherton, 1962) 218.

[3] S. Peter, *Public Interest and Common Good in International Law* (Helbing Lichtenhahn Verlag, 2012) 6.

[4] There are two main conceptions of the public interest: a voluntarist and a utilitarian conception. In Western philosophy, some conceptions (e.g. Rousseau's) regard the state or society as a collective entity, commanding citizen obligations that dominate individual or self-interested objectives. Other 'utilitarian' conceptions of public interest (e.g. Smith and Bentham's) focus on individual welfare or value, and invoke some assumption justifying interpersonal comparisons of value or satisfaction. See *International Encyclopedia of the Social Sciences 2008* available at <http://www.encyclopedia.com/topic/Public_interest.aspx#2>. The sovereignist public interest discussion has to be differentiated from that about 'community interest' under the international law; see I. Feichtner, 'Community Interest', *Max Planck Encyclopedia of Public International Law*, available at <http://www.mpepil.com.>.

responsibilities on governments. In the common law tradition, fiduciary responsibilities are twofold; they embody the duty of loyalty and the duty of care, a breach of which may lead to an action in equity.[5] In civil law countries, fiduciary responsibilities are equally present but they are framed by statutory contractual law and entail duties related to the ethics of contracts.[6] Whilst most governments have included fiduciary duties in the codes or statutes regulating public servants' conduct, they do not seem to have done so consistently at all government levels, especially in regard to sovereign debt contracting.

Governments' responsibilities to their citizens are shaped by the degree of integration of fiduciary duties in their legal framework. This chapter starts to disentangle the thread of governmental fiduciary responsibility embedded in professional conduct patterns in governmental agencies and lenders involved in sovereign debt contracting. With this in mind, various types of states and governments' laws are examined to see how they have integrated fiduciary responsibility in practice, and specifically with regard to sovereign debt contracting.

This chapter seeks to ground the Principles in domestic law with a view to explaining why they constitute customary law, if not general principles of law. The chapter examines fiduciary relationships in governments and states and clarifies the intricacies of this concept on theoretical and practical levels. The chapter then identifies the sources and extent of integration of fiduciary responsibilities, followed by conclusions on the status of fiduciary relationships in sovereign debt contracting practices.

The chapter analyses legal instruments from 14 different jurisdictions (Afghanistan, Algeria, Australia, Brazil, Canada, China, Ecuador, France, Greece, Japan, Kenya, Saudi Arabia, South Africa, and the United States) chosen on the basis of the following considerations: diversity of economic profile, geographical representation, legal systems, state types, governmental structures, and debt profiles.

The chapter does not dwell on enforcement mechanisms, as it does not attempt to measure the effectiveness of fiduciary duties. However, it is important to identify enforcement mechanisms, especially in the context of auditors-executive relations because these mechanisms constitute indicators of a fiduciary relation. Future research should cover this important area.[7]

[5] If a fiduciary relation is established, the appropriate remedies will be found in equity law, however, a breach of duty of care or loyalty may also be a breach of contract and can result in damages or injuries, which fall under contractual, tort or criminal law. J. Law and E. A. Martin. *A Dictionary of Law* (Oxford University Press, 2009).

[6] For instance, see the French civil code, Titre III, art. 1134—Des contrats ou des obligations conventionnelles en général (available at <http://lexinter.net/Legislation/contrat.htm>), which stipulates that contracts must be executed in 'good faith'.

[7] Due to time constraints, data collection stopped at the main pieces of legislation. Future research could examine ministerial decrees and monitoring reports, which also provide information on fiduciary duties embedded in the process of implementing policies. When needed, the chapter relies on secondary sources to fill gaps. Data collection was also limited due to unavailable sources and language barriers. Some texts could not be translated into English for lack of an official version or access to official translators. This absence of evidence does not mean that fiduciary relationships do not exist in a specific country.

The analysis carried out in this chapter is of a comparative nature.[8] Differences in legal functions are examined to establish the existence of fiduciary relations (including duties) and their variations. Although they are not central to a functional comparative analysis, political and social aspects are at times highlighted to provide perspective on certain aspects of the fiduciary relationship. These may not be explicit in the law, and yet they have a clear influence over professional conduct in sovereign debt contracting. The detailed analysis of the actual implementation and enforcement of fiduciary duties is beyond the scope of this chapter.

B. Fiduciary Relationships in Governments and States: Conceptual Considerations

I. Definition of fiduciary relationship

Black's Law Dictionary, defines fiduciary relationship as a 'relationship under which one person is under a duty to act for the benefit of the other on matters within the scope of the relationship'.[9] The process of trusting someone for the completion of a task can be called 'entrustment'. For the principal (the 'entrustor'), this process implies a loss of control, whereas for the agent (the 'fiduciary'), it leads to the acceptance of specific obligations.

Fiduciary relationships can arise when a complex task, such as sovereign debt contracting, cannot be performed well by the entrustor, who has the power to perform the task but lacks the capacity to perform it effectively and efficiently.[10] In many countries, the legislature has the constitutional power to borrow on behalf of the state but legislators lack the organizational framework and technical skills that are needed to conduct sovereign debt contracting in an efficient and effective manner. In this circumstance, the legislature may choose to assign the power to borrow to a financially competent fiduciary in the executive branch, and impose reporting and accountability requirements to monitor the executive's sovereign debt-related actions.

As shown by its legal definition and the previous example, fiduciary relationships are defined by two essential components: an agency relationship[11] and the resulting

[8] Literature on comparative law includes debates on cultural and structural differences, which have an impact on the comparative analysis of national laws. See G. Samuel, 'Comparative Law and Jurisprudence' (1998) 47 ICLQ 818, 827ff.; and J. Bell 'Comparative Law and Legal Theory' in W. Krawietz, N. MacCormick, and G. H. von Wright (eds), *Prescriptive Formality and Normative Rationality in Modern Legal Systems* (Duncker and Humblot 1995) 23, 26.

[9] *Black's Law Dictionary* (7th edn, 1999) B.A. Garner (ed.).

[10] Etymologically, the word 'fiduciary' comes from the latin 'fiduciarius', which means holding in trust. A fiduciary relation stems from a relationship of trust, emerging out of the need to rely on someone to do something. This process can be called 'entrustment' or 'delegation'.

[11] This could also be a relationship of trust, or other relation entailing a delegation of power. Agency constitutes a type of fiduciary relation, the authors chose to refer to the agency relation not only because it is a concept common to all legal systems (as opposed to trust, which is mostly found at common law) but also because it entails the delegation of powers (not only property), which makes it more encapsulating.

fiduciary duties. According to Frankel,[12] the agency relationship is heavily influenced by the complexity of the expected fiduciary services and the cost of monitoring the quality of those services. Agents are defined by the powers they receive to act solely on behalf of their principal. In the context of states and governments, the definition provided by Criddle and Fox-Decent focuses on the vulnerability of the entrustor (principal) in its relation to the fiduciary (agent) who holds '*discretionary powers of an administrative nature*' but may not be able to exercise them.[13]

In the case of sovereign debt contracting, the legislature is faced with a difficult trade-off: in order to carry out sovereign debt contracting effectively and efficiently, it must surrender or 'entrust' most of its borrowing powers to an agent or a fiduciary in the executive.[14] However, the cost of monitoring the quality of sovereign debt contracting services provided by the agent or the fiduciary will be very high because of the technical complexity of those services and the fact that it may take years to discover their underlying benefits (if any) and other associated issues. In this case, the legislature would be vulnerable to two significant issues: misappropriation and receiving low-quality services.

Fiduciary relationships may give rise to several issues among which two are worth highlighting.

First, state agents can misappropriate the powers inherent in sovereign debt contracting for personal gain. This possibility will depend on three conditions:

(1) there is an opportunity to commit fraud caused by internal control weaknesses in sovereign debt operations;
(2) there are financial or personal incentives for state agents to commit a fraud; and
(3) agents have an attitude or rationalization to justify their actions to themselves, their friends, and relatives.[15]

In general, it can be costly to discover such a misappropriation, difficult to prove in a court, and its occurrence may be discovered only after the perpetrators have left their positions. Secondly, the likelihood of poor performance that is costly to monitor, may be more prevalent in many countries than the risk of personal fraud. The recent introduction of performance benchmarks in sovereign debt management may eventually help fiduciaries to adopt best management practice. However, systematic efforts to improve debt management have not yet been adopted in a majority of countries.[16] In order to reduce these risks inherent in surrendering the sovereign power to borrow, fiduciary duties are imposed on state agents.

[12] T. Frankel, 'Fiduciary Duties' in P. Newman (ed.) *The New Palgrave Dictionary of Economics and The Law* Vol. 2 (1998) 127.

[13] E.J. Criddle and E. Fox-Decent, 'A Fiduciary Theory of Jus Cogens' 34 (2009) Yale J. Int'l L. 331, 349.

[14] For a discussion on the legislative delegation process see M. Pečarič, 'Delegated Legislation—A Mixture of General Principle of Law and Individual Mind' (2011) 5(3) ICL Journal 400.

[15] These are known as the 'fraud triangle'; see Statement on Auditing Standards No. 99, Consideration of Fraud in a Financial Statement Audit (2002).

[16] See Debt Management Performance Assessment Tool, available on the World Bank website <http://treasury.worldbank.org/bdm/pdf/DeMPA_Tool_English.pdf>.

The first issue of misappropriation is mitigated by fiduciary duties, which require state agents to be honest and loyal, i.e. to refrain from misappropriating the power to engage in sovereign debt contracting for personal gain.[17] In many countries, a code of ethics is used to define specific types of behaviour that support this duty. For example, state agents in several countries must submit personal financial statements that show their investments, and must refrain from making specific investments based on insider information.[18] A breach of these duties would occur if an agent who is in a fiduciary position with the state uses its powers for personal gain. Depending on the country's funding sources, a costly breach is more likely to occur at the senior management level, where an override of internal control is possible. The ethical dimension of this category of legal duties lies in their tendency to promote what can be considered 'good behaviour' without any underlying utilitarian consideration.[19]

The second issue of poor performance in the execution of sovereign debt contracting is mitigated by performance-related fiduciary duties, which requires state agents to perform their duties using their best skills and the tools that the experts in their profession would use. According to Frankel (at common law), the duty of care requires fiduciaries to: '(1) gather pertinent information; (2) focus—pay attention—and deliberate before making a decision; and (3) use their skills in the process'.[20] Civil law provides for a larger spectrum of performance-related obligations, which are also more specific since they are often codified.

Thus, fiduciary relations can be sustained if laws or contracts provide the necessary support to enable the monitoring of the performance of fiduciaries, who would otherwise be likely to abuse the trust given to them were it not for efficient control mechanisms.[21] In modern societies, the rule of law is the warrant of such controls thereby enabling the establishment fiduciary relations. External controls such as social values or politics are equally important in this respect.[22]

In most countries fiduciary assignments are influenced by economic, social, and political factors that create significant differences across countries. Still, despite the differences that will be evidenced in section B.II., Frankel's insight referring to the complexity of sovereign debt contracting and the high cost of monitoring its quality is valid for countries where the constitutional power to borrow belongs in the

[17] The idea that governments that contract potentially illegitimate debts are held accountable to their citizens on the basis of fiduciary relationships was first argued in L.C. Buchheit and G.M. Gulati, 'Responsible Sovereign Lending and Borrowing', Prepared for UNCTAD (2010), available at <http://ssrn.com/abstract=1584624>.

[18] See section C.I., on State-Government relation.

[19] Although discussions on ethics and law are beyond the scope of this chapter, further information can be found in C. Perelman, *Ethique et droit* (2nd edn, Alain Lempereur, 2012).

[20] Frankel (n. 12) 130.

[21] K.S. Cook, *Trust in Society*, Vol. II in the Russell Sage Foundation Series on Trust (2003) xiii, where the author argues that the reduction of vulnerability in the face of contact with strangers is best achieved through the use of contracts and insurance schemes.

[22] R. Kraiem, 'Leaving Money on the Table: Contract Practice in a Low-Trust Environment' (2004) 42 Colum. J. Transnat'l L. 25.

legislature. In most countries, a well-defined fiduciary relationship tends to arise as a 'best' solution to the challenge of conducting sovereign debt contracting efficiently and effectively, while also making it accountable.

II. Challenges to the concept of governmental fiduciary relationships

Fiduciary principles exist both at common law and civil law but through different legal means. Fiduciary law originates in a common law concept in equity linked with property law. Though civil law countries also have fiduciary principles inscribed in their legislation, they were not originally used in the same contexts. Common law fiduciary duties protect the beneficial ownership of a property or power of which the legal control or ownership has passed to a different person. Civil law fiduciary duties are meant to ensure that a contract is concluded ethically both in regard to its terms and to the conditions leading to its conclusion.[23] Given these differences, one may argue that recognizing fiduciary duties at the international level may be difficult in practice.[24] An international principle recognizing fiduciary relationships between states and governments may just be what states need to overcome the legal gaps of incomplete jurisdictional approaches.[25] In the end, the harmonization of standards depends on courts' interpretation and jurisprudence.[26] The establishment of a 'fiduciary principle', such as the one released by UNCTAD, could increase the capacity of courts to make such jurisprudence. Indeed, the source of fiduciary duties is ultimately not as important as their essence (i.e. a relationship based on trust) and their objectives (i.e. avoiding unethical and unfair situations and maintaining the quality of public service). Having said this, even from a comparative law perspective, the jurisdictional differences in the categorization of fiduciary law have a relative importance. As argued by Goldmann, 'comparative law is about comparing functions, not terminologies'.[27] Though political, social, and economic contexts differ and may induce different ways of formulating the same ideas in legal instruments, these instruments ultimately have the same goals and

[23] E.A. Farnsworth, 'A Common Lawyers' View on His Civilian Colleagues' (1996) 57 Louisiana Law Review 234–5, 227.

[24] Though it is beyond the scope of this chapter, the legal cross-jurisdictional analysis of fiduciary duties' implementation should reveal various degrees of responsibility in the debt contracting process.

[25] Recent literature points to the convergence of fiduciary laws' implementation in civil and common law traditions. See e.g. T. Frankel, 'Towards Universal Fiduciary Principles', Boston University School of Law Working Paper No. 12-09 (2012) and V. Forti, 'Comparing American Trust and French Fiducie' (2010) 17 Colum. J. Eur. L.F. 28.

[26] A. Laby, 'SEC v. Capital Gains Research Bureau and the Investment Advisers Act of 1940' (2011) 91(3) B.U.L. L. Rev. 1051. See A. Laby, in 'Symposium: The Role of Fiduciary Law and Trust in the 21st Century, A conference inspired by the work of Tamar Frankel' (2011) 91 B.U.L. Rev. 1. in which the author shows how case law, under the influence of the agency doctrine, may have created a federal fiduciary duty on financial advisers despite the absence of a Federal Law.

[27] M. Goldmann, 'Responsible Sovereign Lending and Borrowing: the View from Domestic Jurisdictions', Study written for the United Nations Conference on Trade and Development, January (2012) 12, Max Planck Institute for Comparative Public Law and International Law, Heidelberg, Germany.

form part of the same legal family.[28] In fact, we will see in section C.II. that issues related to sovereign debt contracting are being dealt with using various tools that imply essentially equivalent fiduciary duties across various jurisdictions.[29]

In addition to arguments about jurisdictional differences, the question of the transferability of fiduciary principles between legal categories may be raised. For instance, if fiduciary duties emerge out of contract law in civil law countries, it is questionable whether the same duties are applicable in the context of administrative law regulating the employment of and the relationships between public agents. Two responses may be given. First, as will be seen in section C., in most countries, the separation of powers (legislative, executive, and judiciary) derived from constitutional laws gives rise to a delegation process running throughout sovereign debt contracting transactions. This process inevitably involves fiduciary relationships in the context of administrative law as well as any other law governing the actions of public officials in the pursuit of the public interest. Secondly, fiduciary relationships precede categories of law because they are first and foremost enshrined in social behaviours.[30] This means they can be regulated by any category of law that provides a control mechanism for the delegation of tasks assigned in the context of relations based on trust.

It follows from the previously-mentioned issues of categorization that if governmental fiduciary relationships (in the field of sovereign debt) can be recognized at the international level, the form of this recognition is yet to be determined. Soft law principles derived from domestic practices could be held to be customary international law and/or general principles of law. Although the origins of general principles of law are diverse, they are mostly produced by international judges. The common trait of these principles is their high level of abstraction and their generality. They effectively condense rules in the form of a simple formula, which may give rise to ambiguities.[31] Debates about these principles generally revolve around the autonomy of their existence.[32] Being the product of both states' enunciation[33] and international judges' use in support of their arguments,[34] these

[28] Goldmann (n. 8) 11, quoting Zweigert and Kötz: 'a legal family is characterised by common historic roots, a distinctive mode of legal thinking, comparable legal institutions, sources of law and underlying legal ideology'.

[29] Even if the remedies may differ. For instance, the use of specific performance could be more widespread in civil law countries, but in general the remedies will be damages in contract, tort law/civil responsibility, and/or prison in criminal law in most legal systems; H. Lando, 'The Myth Of Specific Performance in Civil Law Countries', American Law & Economics Association Annual Meetings, Paper No. 1014 (2004).

[30] T. Frankel, *Fiduciary Law* (Oxford University Press, 2011) 217–42, where the author explains why, despite the fact that fiduciary relations pervade human relations because trust is necessary for the functioning of any society, human beings need categories of law to deal with their environment.

[31] P-M. Dupuy and Y. Kerbrat, *Droit International public* (10th edn, Dalloz, 2010) 377.

[32] G. Scelle, *Manuel de Droit International Public* (Domat-Montchrestien, 1948) 400.

[33] Such principles include sovereign equality and its corollaries, the expression of which can be found in the UN Charter and subsequent resolutions (e.g. The Declaration on Principles of International Law concerning Friendly Relations and Co-operation among States, adopted by the General Assembly on 24 October 1970 (Resolution 26/25 (XXV)), among other sources.

[34] ICJ Statute, Art. 38 establishes that general principles of law of 'civilized nations' are one of the sources of International law; e.g. ICJ ruling in *Nicaragua v. US*, 27 June 1986, where the court based

principles do not have to be grounded in state practices, as opposed to international customary law.[35] This chapter thus examines state delegation practices in regard to sovereign debt contracting with a view to determining whether these practices reveal a customary existence of fiduciary relationships (and duties), and possibly also a general principle of law. To this effect, the criteria used for this assessment are that (a) there should be a procedural or substantive rule, (b) present in all types of legal systems, (c) and which may be applicable to the international order in the light of its general scope.[36] Of course, one could argue that the review of fiduciary relationships conducted in this chapter is not exhaustive and cannot provide the basis for the acknowledgement of either form of international recognition. Nevertheless, this study attempts to be as representative as possible of the various categories of states in regard to their political, economic, and social structures and it thus constitutes, at least in part, a contribution towards such recognition.[37]

Beyond issues related to the recognition of principles at the international level, a more substantial issue arises with regard to potential contradictions with existing international principles such as sovereign equality and its corollaries (i.e. the right to self determination, non-intervention in the affairs of other states, etc.).[38] It may be argued that, in the name of fiduciary relationships, states could be tempted to blame their fiduciaries in order to escape international responsibility.[39] In doing so, they would arguably threaten the basis of the principle of sovereign equality, which implies that sovereigns both control and embody their nation and consequently makes them responsible at the international level.[40] A weakening of these principles may theoretically tempt powerful states to breach the principle of non-intervention into other states' affairs. The answer to these questions must take into account that fiduciary relationships are ultimately designed to promote and protect citizens' general will.[41] Although a discussion about the merits of sovereign equality (and related principles) goes beyond the scope of this chapter, it is important to mention that an increasing number of scholars are questioning the application of these

its arguments on the fundamental concept of states' sovereignty, available at <http://www.icj-cij.org/docket/index.php?sum=367&code=nus&p1=3&p2=3&case=70&k=66&p3=5>.

[35] Dupuy and Kerbat (n. 31) 377, where it is argued that the difference between these two forms of international law is debatable because judges do not build theories out of nowhere, they condense principles that already exist and can be called customary.

[36] D. Carreau and F. Marella, *Droit international*, Vol. 1 (Pedone, 2012) ch. XI. The most commonly accepted interpretation of 'general principles of law' sees them as a set of principles common to all great current legal systems and applicable to the international order (see for instance the Statute of the International Criminal Court of Justice, Art. 21.1.C).

[37] Another contribution can be found in Goldmann (n. 27).

[38] Principle exemplified in the UN Charter, Art. 2, s. 1.

[39] See International Law Commission on State Responsibility, at <http://untreaty.un.org/ilc/guide/9_6.htm>.

[40] Dupuy and Kerbat (n. 31) 319, 320.

[41] For an in-depth discussion on the interaction of the fiduciary principle and other principles of international law, see Criddle & Fox-Decent (n. 13) 357, where the authors argue that *jus cogens* norms, such as sovereign equality and the right to self-determination, arise not from state consent at the international level but from a state-subject fiduciary relationship.

principles in various fields, including sovereign debt.[42] This questioning indeed bears particular relevance with respect to debts contracted by governments regarded as illegitimate by their successors.[43]

C. Integration of Fiduciary Relationships in Legal Frameworks Related to Debt Contracting

The sources of fiduciary relationships are enshrined in the legal framework regulating the parties to these relationships.[44] In the field of debt contracting, agency relationships characterize most of the interactions among the stakeholders. Sovereign debt contracting can involve several actors, identified in Table 10.1, who depend on each other for a coherent and orderly execution of governmental decisions. Dependency is indeed an essential attribute of a fiduciary relationship. This section examines the various aspects of these relationships by reviewing the strength of the delegation process, the presence and type of fiduciary duties, the existence of control mechanisms reinforcing trust among the parties, and the potential limits of fiduciary relationships.

I. State-government relationship (civil servants and politically appointed government officials)

The constitution of each country is the main legal reference pointing to a fiduciary relationship between governments and states.[45] Constitutions are the legal expression of state formation. They define the territory, the nature of citizenship, and the operational organs of the state, as well as the relations between these organs and the state and its citizens. The primary source of relation between these entities is the sovereignty of the state, i.e. the supreme authority without which it could not exist.[46]

The representation of citizens at the state level is thus generally expressed in constitutional laws.[47] Constitutions provide the legal basis for the agency relationship, which is the first component of the fiduciary relationship existing between the

[42] See for instance Buchheit and Gulati (n. 17); in the field of sovereign debt, see O. Lienau, *Rethinking Sovereign Debt: Politics, Reputation and Legitimacy in Modern Politics* (Harvard University Press, forthcoming 2014); in the field of human rights, see A. Peters, 'Humanity as the A and O of Sovereignty' (2009) 20 EJIL 513.

[43] The concept of odious debt has been debated at length in the sovereign debt literature (e.g. Buchheit, Howse, Lienau, Cheng).

[44] Fiduciary ties can be divided into vertical and horizontal relations. Vertical relations concern the relations that public officials have with citizens as represented by the state. Horizontal relations are found in inter-, intra-, and extra-governmental relations.

[45] For an academic discussion of the fiduciary foundations or administrative law, see E. Criddle, 'Fiduciary Foundations of Administrative Law' (2006) 54 UCLA L. Rev. 117.

[46] Although it is important in order to assess states' authority, the analysis of the foundation of sovereignty goes beyond the scope of this chapter.

[47] Detailed legal sources available from authors on request. Also see Peter (n. 3) 12–16.

Table 10.1 Fiduciary duties in selected countries

Legal duties pertaining to ethical considerations	
Respect hierarchy	Afghanistan, Algeria, China, Ecuador, France, Greece
Avoid conflict of interests and use of public means for personal gain	Afghanistan, Algeria, Australia, Brazil, Canada, China, France, Japan, Kenya, South Africa, United States
Confidentiality, reserve	Algeria, Australia, Canada, China, Greece, South Africa
Loyalty, honesty, integrity, good faith	Afghanistan, Algeria, Australia, Brazil, Ecuador, Kenya, South Africa, United States
Impartiality, neutrality	Afghanistan, Algeria, Brazil, France, Greece, Japan, South Africa, United States
Act in the public interest/uphold the public's trust	Canada, South Africa, Kenya, United States
Legal duties pertaining to considerations of performance	
Act with propriety in the service of public users (including impartiality, punctuality, dress code, politeness, availability, etc.)	Afghanistan, Australia, Canada, Greece, Kenya, South Africa, United States
Efficiency, effectiveness, competence, diligence	Algeria, Australia, Brazil, Canada, Ecuador, Kenya, South Africa, United States
Avoid being negligent, act conscientiously, professionally, with care	Afghanistan, China, Ecuador, Greece, United States
Enforce transparency	Brazil, Canada, United States
Recognition of the public's right of access to information, accountability	South Africa, Ecuador, France, United States

Source: J. R. Oyola and M. Sudreau, 2012 (based on observation from administrative laws and codes of conduct of the abovementioned countries)

state (representing present and future citizens) and governments. The degree to which power is delegated is high since the state agrees to relinquish its executive, legislative, and judiciary powers to operating organs composing the government. Through the process of elections (either parliamentary or executive), governments earn the state's trust to represent it. Though it may be argued that democracies alone may truly produce such fiduciary relationships, the process of delegation is also present in other political regimes. These regimes may not represent their citizens through an elective process but they are nonetheless tacitly representative of their people at the international level.[48] Moreover, where constitutions rely on

[48] H. Beran, 'In Defense of the Consent Theory of Political Obligation and Authority' (April 1977) 87(3) Ethics 260, 262, where the author argues that native born citizens implicitly consent to their membership of the state, implying that there is consent even in the absence of a democratic system.

The question of the existence of fiduciary relations in non-democracies touches upon criteria of sovereign legitimacy at international law. *De facto* sovereignty implies citizen representativeness

religious faith to legitimize their state (e.g. Saudi Arabia), fiduciary relationships are still present.[49]

The second component of fiduciary relations is the responsibilities that such relationhips entail for the 'fiduciary' (the government), with regard to the 'entrustor' (the state). From a rational point of view, governments are chosen and trusted by the citizens to act in their best interests. This will is sometimes expressed in the constitution. For instance, the constitutions of Algeria, Ecuador, and Japan explicitly assert that states are to act in the public interest. However, in order to determine the obligations of governments as acting agents of states, one has to look into the laws governing the actions of those who run governments and impersonate them, namely their administrators and political representatives.

The conduct of governments' administrators is generally regulated by civil servants and statutory laws. These exist in most jurisdictions reviewed in our sample. In addition, most countries have adopted codes of conduct and guiding manuals on how to implement these codes (e.g. Japan and South Africa). These codes have the effect of introducing considerations into the employment relationship that expose civil servants to legally enforceable controls and sanctions. The legal duties referred to in such legislation are of two types—ethical and performance-related. Interestingly, these two broad categories share similarities with the traditional common law categories of fiduciary duties, namely loyalty and care.[50] This categorization does not have any legal implications but provides a useful instrument to show the similarities of duties that exist in all legal systems (see Table 10.1).

As seen in Table 10.1, most countries have duties inscribed in their regulations concerning civil servants.[51] We find that ethical obligations are generally equivalent in terms of the conduct required of civil servants, with varying levels of detail.

deriving from control over the people of a territory and independence from other states but it does not automatically imply the legitimacy of this representativeness at the domestic or international levels. Fox-Decent argues that fiduciary relationships arise from the inherently authoritative nature of the state; see E. Fox-Decent, 'Fiduciary Nature of State Legal Authority' (2005) 31 Queen's L.J. 259. Scholars like Peters (n. 42) argue, however, that democracies are superior models of sovereign legitimacy because they promote governmental accountability towards citizens and humanity. This raises several objections to Western moral absolutism; see M. Walzer, 'The Moral Standing of States: A Response to Four Critics' (1980) 9 Philosophy and Public Affairs 209, 212 and 216.

49 Fiduciary relationships are recognized between God and a government or between believers of the same faith. This is exemplified under the Sharia law in Saudi Arabia; see Frankel (n. 30) 84, where the author identifies agency and trust in the Islamic Law.

50 Typically, loyalty is a concept that fits into the 'Ethics' category and care could fit into the 'performance-related' category. Frankel (n. 30) ch. 3, explains that loyalty and care are categories that include implementing duties such as duty to comply with rules of entrustment, duty to act in good faith in performing fiduciary services, duty to account, and duty not to delegate fiduciary duties for the duty of loyalty and different standards of care depending on situations.

51 Though they provide a good basis for assessing the existence of civil servants' duties, statutory laws or codes of conduct are not the only sources of principles guiding their conduct. Human rights charters and other instruments also have to be considered in order to establish a complete list of obligations.

After the obligation of compliance with the law, the most widespread obligations are those related to the avoidance of conflicts of interest and the prohibition against using public means for personal gain. Close to these come obligations of loyalty to the government, honesty, integrity, and good faith; impartiality and neutrality; and compliance with the hierarchy.

Performance-related obligations, on the other hand, are not always present (e.g. in the case of France), and when they are, there is a substantial disparity in detailed requirements, which tend to be more stringent in countries with codes of conduct (e.g. Canada, Kenya, South Africa, and the United States). Differences in legal frameworks do not seem to be influenced by the economic stage of development of the countries analysed (e.g. Kenya has included in its law the duty to improve performance, which is not found in other countries).

Whilst the analysis of civil servants' fiduciary duties is important because they are the executants of transactions leading to the creation of sovereign debt, the decision to contract a debt generally lies at the ministerial level and sometimes even with the head of state.[52] Politically appointed public officials have a 'short-term assignment' with the state and are in general not classified as civil servants;[53] hence, the aforementioned regulations may not apply to them. In an attempt to reinforce trust in the public service, some countries have adopted ministerial and parliamentary codes of conduct, which are non-binding in principle. Beyond codes of conduct, a requirement to disclose income and assets is generally imposed on politically appointed public officials, especially parliamentarians and ministers.

As with other cases of fiduciary relationships, an essential indicator is the presence of control mechanisms. The implementation of public officials' fiduciary duties generally implies that there are organizations in charge of interpreting codes and laws that differ according to their independence, oversight capacity, and decisional weight. They can take the form of commissions/agencies against corruption acting as a fourth branch of government (e.g. in Hong Kong) or operating with administrators of other agencies (including outside the public service, e.g. in France) or with the ability to hold agency or department heads accountable for their ethics programmes (e.g. in the United States).[54] Other agencies act like a service of a ministry (e.g. in Canada).[55] Disciplinary measures for civil servants are present in all of the countries reviewed.[56]

[52] For instance, 'le Grand Emprunt' in France, at <http://www.grandemprunt.net>.

[53] Except in Japan, where they are considered part of the 'special service'; see the National Public Service Act, No. 120 of 1947, art. 2.

[54] National Public Service Act (n. 53) art. 2.

[55] In our sample of countries, the oversight organizations include: Afghanistan (the General Independent Administration for Anti-Corruption), Algeria (forthcoming bureau of anti-corruption), Australia (Australian Public Service Commission), Brazil (Ethics Commission), Canada (Treasury Board), China (Ministry of Supervision), Ecuador (Anti-Corruption System of Ecuador Executive Committee), France (Service Central de la Prevention de la Corruption), Japan (National Public Service Ethics Board), Kenya (Kenya Anti-Corruption Commission), South Africa (Public Servants Commission), the US (Office of Government Ethics).

[56] Detailed legal sources available from authors on request.

II. Legislature-executive relations

Fiduciary relations between the legislature and the executive are found in the constitutions of most countries in relation to the adoption of budgets.[57]

By constitution, the parliament or congress has the ultimate power to borrow on behalf of the state. This power is carried out through the executive government, which proposes the budget and, once it is accepted, delegates its implementation to the various agents in charge of making disbursements on its behalf. Here, the agency relationship is clear despite the variation that may exist between one formulation and another in the allocation of responsibilities. For instance, in the case of Greece or Kenya, the Minister of Finance is identified as the one in charge of presenting the budget to the parliament, whereas in Japan this task is to be carried out by the government as a whole.

Although this agency relationship is well established, the powers that it entails are not always distributed in the same way. The parliament tends to have more power in countries that allow the initiative to present the budget to be shared between the government and that parliament.[58] In the United States, the constitution assigns to the Congress the power to borrow on the credit of the United States. Prior to 1917, Congress authorized each specific debt issuance, which guaranteed the control of Congress over borrowing. Presently, the US Treasury has the legal authority, pursuant to the President's approval, to issue bonds on the credit of the United States, subject to a debt limit.[59] In France, although the Parliament has the power to initiate the budget proposal, limitations are present as the proposals and amendments formulated by the members of Parliament cannot be received when their adoption would entail either a decrease in public resources or the creation or deepening of a public liability.[60]

The balance of power between the legislature and the executive also depends on the constitutional nature of the state.[61] For example, in parliamentary systems the legislature tends to play a less significant role in the formulation of the budget than in presidential systems. Because the executive's existence depends on the support of the legislature's majority, the legislature has no latitude to disagree with the budget proposed by the executive, or it would be equivalent to a vote of no confidence in the government.[62]

Fiduciary duties between the executive and the legislature in relation to sovereign contracting are related to the objective of voting on the budget to the satisfaction of all the stakeholders involved in the process. This objective is met when budgets are presented diligently and in a timely manner to the parliaments in accordance with national laws, and budget proposals are coherent and sustainable with respect to current and future citizens' ability to repay the debts created through the enactment

[57] Detailed legal sources available from authors on request.
[58] Stepenhurst, 'The Legislature and the Budget' (2004) World Bank Institute 3.
[59] Federal Reserve Act 1913 (Title 31 USCS §3102(a)).
[60] See articles of the French constitution, arts 39 and 40.
[61] Stepenhurst (n. 58) 5. [62] Stepenhurst (n. 58) 5.

of these budgets.[63] On a more general level, the institutions in charge of controlling the constitutionality of the laws enacted by the parliament, and thus their coherence with the nation's public interest, are the supreme courts or constitutional courts.[64]

III. Inter-ministerial relations: Ministry of Finance and Treasury, economic planning

The interrelation between ministries playing a role in debt contracting is closely linked with their involvement in the budget preparation process. As discussed earlier, this process mostly involves the department of the Ministry of Finance being in charge of proposing the budget and the parliament being in charge of voting and amending this proposal. The responsibility for preparing the budget usually lies with the Ministry of Finance, with input from the line ministries and some smaller spending agencies. This exercise is normally controlled by a central budget department located in the Ministry of Finance, or sometimes in a separate budget ministry. Organic laws on public financial management tend to be the main legal documents detailing the responsibilities of these departments in relation to the budget.[65]

Inter-ministerial fiduciary relationships are extremely intertwined as ministries rely on each other for specific actions which form part of a common effort to obtain a coherent budget proposal. Agency relations that are established as a result of a delegation of power enabling the execution of these actions depend on the distribution of tasks among the ministries. In some countries, a single organization is responsible for preparing the macro-economic framework (e.g. the United States, Kenya).[66] In other countries, the responsibility for macroeconomic projections is fragmented, with the Ministry of Finance being responsible for fiscal projections, the Ministry of Planning for projections for the real sector, and the Statistics Bureau for short-term projections for the real sector and price forecasts (e.g. Brazil).[67]

Inter-ministerial fiduciary relationships can be limited by a lack of coordination among ministries, which is crucial for the coherence of governmental action. Where planning/economy ministries are weak, governments cannot achieve their policy objectives.[68] Coordination between ministries is generally the task of the Prime Minister or the Presidential cabinet. In the United States, the Office of

[63] The Principles (4 November, draft version) suggest that the delegation from the legislative to the executive should be accompanied by specified long-term borrowing objectives (see Principle 10 on Transparency).

[64] e.g. the French Constitutional Court reviewed fiscal legislation with criteria such as respect for the general interest, proportionality, and coherence with the objectives of the law (see Decision No. 2004–511 DC, 29 November 2004, on the financial law 2005).

[65] Detailed legal sources available from authors on request.

[66] In Kenya, the Ministry of Finance, and in the US, the Office of Management and Budget.

[67] S. Schiavo-Campo and D. Tommasi, *Managing Government Expenditure* (Asian Development Bank, 1999).

[68] N. Caiden and A. Wildavski, *Planning and Budgeting in Poor Countries* (6th edn, Transaction Publishers, 2003).

Management and Budget (OMB) is a Cabinet-level office within the Executive Office of the President (EOP). In France, the Prime Minister initiates the budget preparation procedure by sending '*Lettres de Cadrage*', with budget ceilings, to the ministries, following the directions given by the President. The Prime Minister makes final decisions about budget allocation when needed.

With fiduciary relationships come fiduciary duties. With regard to budget preparation, these duties are created with a view to ensuring honest forecasting and a fair, transparent, and efficient allocation of resources. Several countries analysed in the sample incorporate duties in their financial legislation, such as the duty to respect spending limits or debt ceilings; to apply 'sound' (Australia) or 'efficient, effective and transparent' (South Africa) fiscal management, or even 'improve' budget management (China); to follow principles such as financial sustainability, coordination, respect for planning, transparency, and access to information (Ecuador); to be 'sincere' in the publication of information concerning the resources of the state (France); to respect the spending objectives set by law (Japan); and to ensure that resources are used in a way that is 'lawful, authorized, effective, efficient, economical and transparent'(Kenya).[69] Some countries like Brazil have gone further in this sense and adopted a Fiscal Responsibility Act, which goes into details on what it means to be fiscally responsible.

Control mechanisms governing the implementation of fiduciary duties between ministries when dealing with budgets, can be found in several sources. The first source of control is legislative, since the budget is voted by the Parliament. The second source of control is more political; if the collaboration among ministries does not run smoothly, the head of state is at liberty to demand the resignation of public officials. Interest groups can also be powerful in advocating where the budget should be allocated (e.g. in the United States and Canada).[70]

IV. Ministry of Finance—Debt Management Office (DMO)

Debt Management may be performed under different organizational structures. Generally, this function is carried out at the Treasury level under the supervision of the Ministry of Finance. In our sample this is the case for Afghanistan, Algeria, China, Brazil, Ecuador, France, Japan, the United States, and South Africa.[71] Some countries prefer to create an agency (also called a Debt Management Office) independent of the Ministry of Finance, though still under its supervision. Australia, Greece, and Kenya (where the process is under way)[72] have chosen this alternative. In Canada, debt management is performed under the organizational structure of the central bank.

[69] Detailed legal sources available from authors on request.

[70] <http://www.thestar.com/news/canada/politics/article/958962–interest-groups-react-to-federal-budget> (Canada); <http://www.nytimes.com/2011/11/04/us/interest-groups-seek-to-catch-debt-committees-ear.html> (US).

[71] Source: government internet portal of each country.

[72] <http://allafrica.com/stories/201108310125.html>.

The relationship between the Ministry of Finance and the Treasury or DMO can be established by decree and/or be specified in public finance legislation.[73] The tasks to be performed by debt managers are common to all structures, namely, to ensure that the state obtains sufficient funds at all times to pay maturing debts and pay for estimated budget deficits, while building sufficient cash reserves to smooth short-term fluctuations in the Treasury's cash account. In some countries, debt managers are also responsible for building sufficient borrowing capacity to absorb unexpected fiscal contingencies, such as a banking crisis or a natural disaster, and are building active debt strategies that explicitly seek to minimize risks by calculating trade-offs in risks and costs.[74]

Where the separation between the debt management unit and the Ministry of Finance is clear, the law clearly mentions the responsibilities incumbent on each party. The Australian Office of Financial Management states that it is 'part of the Treasury portfolio' and that it is 'accountable to the Treasurer and through him to the Australian Government, the Parliament and the public'.[75]

The main fiduciary duty stemming from the relationship here identified is linked with the objective of debt management, namely ensuring that the government always obtains sufficient liquid funds to meet current obligations. We found DMO staff to be subject to similar codes of conduct and administrative laws as other civil servants.

Similarly, controls on debt management practices are enforced by specific organizations involving internal and external public auditors. Regulations are prescribed by the Ministry of Finance to organize a debt management office into separate front, back, and middle offices. Regulations should prescribe a clear separation of approval of debt transactions and disbursement of funds. These controls should be examined periodically by internal and external audits. Personal liability for mistakes, negligent behaviour, and fraudulent actions, however, would be no different from the controls and penalties imposed on other government staff.

V. Fiscal relations between central and sub-national government

In performing their fiduciary role, sub-national governments enjoy various degrees of autonomy, depending on the organizational structure of their state, whether or not it opted for decentralization (and/or devolution), and if so, the extent to which this was achieved. In the last few decades, a rising consensus emerged as to the benefits of a certain degree of local autonomy as a way to increase efficiency.[76] Among the countries examined in this chapter, a significant number are federal states, namely, Australia, Brazil, Canada, South Africa, and the United States. Other countries, such as Afghanistan, Algeria, China, Ecuador, France, Greece,

[73] Detailed legal sources available from authors on request.

[74] Australia <http://www.aofm.gov.au>; Canada <http://www.fin.gc.ca/dtman/2010-2011/dmr-rgd1101-eng.asp>; Brazil <https://www.tesouro.fazenda.gov.br>.

[75] <http://www.aofm.gov.au>.

[76] E. Ahmad, G. Brosio, and V. Tanzi, 'Local Service Provision in Selected OECD Countries: Do Decentralized Operations Work Better?', IMF Working Paper WP/08/67 (2008).

and Japan, have also adopted a decentralized model but not to the same extent. Kenya is in the process of legislating on its decentralization process.[77]

With respect to the identification of fiduciary relationships, the delegation process that underpins agency also represents the means to achieve autonomy for sub-national governments. This process is closely tied to budget allocation, which goes hand in hand with the assignment of tasks to be executed by sub-national governments. Some states, like the United States, provide a lot of fiscal space for their sub-national governments, thereby indicating a high degree of delegation.[78] Others have chosen to keep central government involved in the allocation of expenditures and their borrowing capacities. These choices are largely influenced by the historical formation of these states.[79]

In terms of fiduciary relationships between a central government and its sub-national governments, the higher the capacity of the latter to make their own budget, control their expenditures, and make decisions as to their borrowing possibilities, the more trust is granted to them to perform their tasks and the stronger are fiduciary ties.[80] With these ties come responsibilities and control mechanisms, such as duties to manage finances efficiently in accordance with pre-determined policy orientations (e.g. as in Afghanistan or Ecuador),[81] duties to be transparent in the resource allocation process (e.g. South Africa),[82] duties to have a balanced budget and/or debt ceilings (e.g. Algeria, Brazil, China, France, or the United States),[83] the duty to promote the welfare of the citizens (e.g. Japan),[84] and the duty to respect the law and national interests (e.g. France).[85]

The legislation establishing relations between central governments and sub-national governments is generally the constitution.[86] However, responsibilities and control mechanisms tend to be found in local financial laws, sometimes at state/provincial levels for federal states and at other sub-national levels for regional and unitary states.[87] The fiduciary duties owed by sub-national governments to central governments are related to the management of revenues and expenditures. If not collected by the central governments themselves, sub-national revenues need to be transparent so as to enable their proper reallocation thereafter. In the same vein, expenditures and public borrowing need to be disclosed and included in

[77] The Intergovernmental Fiscal Relations Bill, 2011 is currently being examined.

[78] A. Plekhanov and R. Singh, 'How Should Sub-national Government Borrowing Be Regulated? Some Cross-Country Empirical Evidence', IMF Staff Papers 53/3 (2007).

[79] J. Kincaid, 'Comparative Observations' in J. Kincaid and G.A. Tarr (eds), *Constitutional Origins, Structure, and Change in Federal Countries* (McGill-Queen's University Press, 2005) 420.

[80] The level of autonomy is also assessed through the capacity of local governments to raise their own taxes, but this goes beyond the subject of analysis, see D. Sutherland et al., 'Les Règles Budgétaires s'appliquant aux collectivités territoriales' (2005/2) 41 Revue économique de l'OCDE 153.

[81] Afghanistan (Constitution, Ch. 8, art. 4), Ecuador (Constitution, arts 270, 272).

[82] South Africa (Public Finance Management Act, Ch. 3, Part 1, art. 17 and Ch. 6, Part 1, art. 57).

[83] Detailed legal sources available from authors on request.

[84] Japan, Local Autonomous Law 1946 (revised as of 1999), arts 1 and 2.

[85] France, Constitution, 1958, Titre XII, art. 72.

[86] Detailed legal sources available from authors on request.

[87] Detailed legal sources available from authors on request.

consolidated balance sheets to avoid confusion (off-balance sheet expenses pose a problem for some countries).

Reporting and intergovernmental cooperation provisions are key control mechanisms in legal frameworks seeking to ensure effective fiduciary relationships. Cooperation can be in the form of a budget council, as in South Africa, or of a loan council, as in Australia.[88] Parliamentary approval of the budget provides an additional layer of control. In Japan, the supervision of expenditures and borrowings by the central government (Ministry of Internal Affairs and Communications) is particularly intense; a system for fiscal rehabilitation is used to place local governments in danger of bankruptcy under the jurisdiction of the central government.[89] Also, in general, local officials are elected by citizens. This can constitute an additional control mechanism against fraud, misuse of public funds, or simply poor management.

VI. Ministry of Finance-central bank

The relations of central banks and other agencies are dictated by several sources of legislation. In some countries (e.g. in Brazil or Japan) the constitution establishes the powers of the central bank with respect to the government.[90] In most others, the source of this relationship is inscribed in either the statute or act of the central bank.

Central banks perform several tasks on behalf of the government as its fiscal agent, adviser, and depositor of the government.[91] This agency relationship is characterized by the delegation of powers from the government (the entrustor) to the central bank (the fiduciary) and is sometimes subject to contractual arrangements between them for the payment of the services provided by central banks.[92] The degree of autonomy of the central bank with respect to the government is key in the evaluation of the type of agency stemming from this relationship. According to the Bank of International Settlements: 'Central bank autonomy is high when the activities it performs for the government are clearly specified and exclude the obligatory financing of the government's activities and when the state cannot overturn its decisions.'[93] In our sample, Japan, Algeria, and Kenya give a specific mandate to their central banks to provide their governments with funding ('advances') when certain temporary adjustments are needed.[94]

[88] M. Sokhela, 'Intergovernmental Relations in the Local Sphere of Government in South Africa', PhD Thesis, University of Pretoria.

[89] N. Mochida, *Fiscal Decentralisation and Local Public Finance in Japan* (Routledge, 2008) 18.

[90] Japan also has the Bank of Japan Act (Act No 89 of 18 June 1997), which details the relationship of the Central Bank with the Government (art. 4).

[91] Detailed legal sources available from authors on request.

[92] For instance Canada (Reserve Bank Act, 1959, art 24), France (art. L141–7), Greece (Bank of Greece Statute, 2000, art 47), the US (Federal Reserve Board Annual Report, 2010), Saudi Arabia (Charter of the Saudi Arabian Monetary Agency No 23 dated 23-5-1377, art. 2).

[93] Bank of International Settlements (BIS), *Issues in the Governance of Central Banks* (2009) 58.

[94] Bank Statutes: Japan (art. 34(ii)), Algeria (art. 46), and Kenya (art. 46(1)).

A collaborative relationship between governments and central banks tends to be a good indicator of macroeconomic efficiency.[95] Fiduciary duties in this context involve paying specific attention to the mechanisms enabling the collaboration between these organizations. For example, the presence of high government officials in central banks' board meetings is sometimes stipulated in the central bank acts and statutes.[96] In terms of the professional conduct of the staff employed by central banks, some countries (e.g. Canada) include a requirement for oaths to be taken in their statutes.

Control mechanisms over the delegation process from the governments to central banks start with the appointment of governors and deputy governors by the heads of the executive and requirements for regular reports on monetary conditions and the central bank's performance.

VII. Legislature-auditors

Supreme Audit Institutions (SAIs) are government auditors with a sufficient degree of independence and technical capacity to perform three main fiduciary duties: (1) to enforce accountability and promote transparency in debt reporting; (2) to determine compliance with laws and loan contracts; and (3) to audit sovereign debt programmes to increase their effectiveness, reduce operational costs, and prevent fraudulent activities.[97] Depending on the country, these duties are defined in the country's constitution, in the organic laws, or in both.

The SAI's fiduciary activities are generally found in three main legal sources: the country's constitution, the SAI's organic law, and fiscal legislation. Constitutions are used to create the SAI and specify its duties in Algeria, Brazil, China, Ecuador, France, Japan, Kenya, and South Africa. Organic laws in Afghanistan, Australia, Canada and the United States have been used to create the SAI and to define its main duties. Fiscal responsibility laws have been used in both groups of countries to increase the SAIs' fiduciary responsibilities and powers, such as enforcing debt limits and conducting performance audits, respectively.

SAIs meet their fiduciary responsibilities by conducting financial, compliance, and performance audits. In financial audits SAIs scrutinize the reliability and usefulness of public debt information. In compliance audits SAIs determine whether the executive is complying with financial laws, loan contracts, and international agreements. In performance audits SAIs examine whether sovereign debt managers achieved their objectives (effectiveness); had low costs (efficiency); and adopted best management practices (economy).

But, how well do SAIs perform these fiduciary responsibilities? SAIs would normally enforce accountability by conducting audits of financial statements or public debt data, and enhance transparency by issuing objective reports to the legislature and the public, preferably through a medium that is free of charge and

[95] BIS (n. 93) 91. [96] Detailed legal sources available from authors on request.

[97] Most UN members have an SAI that belongs to INTOSAI. Members, websites, and key documents of SAIs are available at <http://www.intosai.org>.

easily accessible, such as their website. These two indicators can be used to measure whether SAIs met these fiduciary responsibilities. Table 10.1 shows that, in most countries in our sample, the SAIs are successful.

VIII. Primary dealers-governments

Primary dealers (PDs) are financial intermediaries which are selected by the government to: (1) participate in primary auctions of sovereign debt securities; (2) create a liquid secondary market in the same securities; and (3) provide advice to the government about the preferences of actual and potential buyers of debt securities. There is a legal agreement or understanding between the government and the PDs that defines their contractual duties as active participants in government securities markets in Brazil, Canada, France, Japan, South Africa, and the United States.[98]

PDs are not government officials and, therefore, they cannot be held to be in a fiduciary relationship with the citizens. The relationship between PDs and governments is nevertheless one of reliance (on the part of the state) on the competences of the other (PDs). Could PDs be regarded as fiduciaries to their client, the government? It is true that their contractual relationships with the state generally entail duties to not advise the government in their (the PDs') personal interest.[99] PDs perform a strategic role in countries whose main funding source is the sale of marketable government securities in regular auctions. In the United States, for example, the PDs are supposed to participate in all auctions in a meaningful way in order to avoid 'auction failures', which could happen if submitted bids are less than the securities offered by Treasury. However, PDs are buyers of government bonds and they are in charge of reselling to the secondary market at good prices. As such, they are not fiduciaries (they do not deal on behalf of the government), they are buyers (the title to property passes on to them).

IX. Multilateral lenders and monitoring institutions

Multilateral financial institutions (MFIs) have four main roles directly related to sovereign debt contracting, they are required to: (1) provide long-term concessionary loans; (2) provide expert advice and disseminate best practices; (3) conduct assessments and debt sustainability analyses; and (4) collect and report debt data for

[98] The European Union website provides links to the codes of conduct of primary dealers in 27 EU countries <http://europa.eu/efc>.

[99] In the US, the Securities and Exchange Commission (SEC) is responsible for monitoring actions by primary dealers and brokers who attempt to deceive investors through manipulative and deceptive practices in the trading of government securities. For example, in 2010 the SEC took action against the largest inter-dealer broker in the US Treasury market, for allowing its brokers to display fictitious trades on its screens and disseminating false trade information to the US Treasury secondary market. The company paid US$25m in disgorgement and penalties, and the supervisors of the brokers paid a US $100,000 penalty for negligence in their supervisory duties. See ICAP Securities, USLLC, Securities Act Rel No. 9097 (2010), at <http://www.sec.gov>.

Table 10.2 Supreme audit institutions: enforcing accountability and enhancing transparency

Countries	Fiduciary duties	
	Enforcing accountability	Enhancing transparency
	Does SAI audit public debt data published by government?	Are SAI reports available on SAI's website one year or less after publication?
Afghanistan, Algeria	N	N
Australia, Brazil, Canada, China, France, Kenya, Ukraine, United States	Y	Y
Ecuador, Japan, Greece	N	Y

Sources: authors' analysis. Websites of SAIs accessed in first three weeks of 2012.

surveillance purposes.[100] These roles have embedded in them a number of fiduciary relationships that affect both the institutional lender and the borrower country.[101]

In their role as lenders, MFIs are responsible for being leaders in promoting best loan practices, such as those proposed in the UNCTAD Principles. For example, the World Bank adopted in 2006 and revised in 2011 its *Guidelines on Preventing and Combating Fraud and Corruption in Projects Financed by the World Bank.*[102] Similarly, MFIs provide training, publish guides, and perform assessments using best practices in sovereign debt contracting.[103] The MFIs, as part of their surveillance activities, collect information on sovereign debt to monitor each country's debt position and monitor debt trends that can generate systemic risks to the world financial system.

The multiple roles of MFIs sometimes pose real or perceived conflicts of interest. For example, how does an MFI ensure that its loan agreements are drafted to ensure the best terms for the country as a borrower? Is there a fiduciary duty that should guide the MFIs when their staff promote specific debt management practices that have been developed by their own staff? What firewalls exist in MFIs between their advisers and the loan contracting officers? These sensitive issues are beyond the scope of this chapter, and can be addressed in future research.

[100] The original source of the rights and responsibilities of multilateral lenders and borrowers is found in the Articles of Agreement of their members. For example, see the World Bank's Articles of Agreement, art. 3—Provisions related to Loans and Guarantees, available at <http://web.worldbank.org>. MFIs are also parties to several conventions and agreements that are embedded in their loan contracts and practices, including multiple anti-corruption conventions, strict standards of procurement practices and financial transparency. MFIs also sign periodic accords that have a direct effect on their lending practices, such as the Monterrey Consensus, described in http://www.imf.org/external/np/pdr/FfD/2002/imp.htm.

[101] See n. 100.

[102] Guidelines on preventing fraud are available at <http://www.worldbank.org>.

[103] See Debt Management Performance Assessment (DeMPA) Guide (see n 16).

D. Conclusion

The establishment of fiduciary relationships between governments and citizens throughout the debt contracting process is of great importance not only to the fight against corruption but also to promote efficient debt management practices.

Fiduciary relationships arise naturally in sovereign debt contracting operations, starting at the highest level of the state, and running through parliaments to executive bodies. Two categories—ethical behaviour and performance-related duties—provide the analytical framework for the consideration of all legal duties owed to the state and its citizens. It is submitted here that the identification of these categories constitutes, to some extent, evidence as to the equivalence of fiduciary relationships across legal systems. Constitutions embody the main legal vehicle for the entrustment of powers to governments and parliaments. Other organic laws supplement constitutions, providing more precision on the nature of the fiduciary duties of each participant in the chain of operations of debt contracting and related debt management matters. Fiduciary relationships between public officials and states are embedded in administrative law and codes of conduct, which vary across countries depending on their legal systems and organizational structures.

As seen in this chapter, the recognition of fiduciary relations and resulting duties in the field is crucial to identifying responsibilities. This is especially important in times of crisis when cooperation between sovereign borrowers and lenders is most vulnerable and when the parties involved in sovereign indebtedness attempt to rid themselves of respective responsibilities. Agency patterns embedded in fiduciary relations facilitate the identification of the decision-makers and their executants because they provide a clear rule: the principal entrusts property and/or power to an agent, who acts in the sole interest of the principal.

The main finding of the chapter is that fiduciary relationships are pervasive and play a critical role in ensuring the effectiveness and efficiency of sovereign debt operations. Although widely present in our sample, fiduciary relationships can vary in terms of their strength and can be limited by a lack of coordination and ill-designed task allocation between the entrustor/principal and its agents. In this case, the enforcement of performance-related duties may be jeopardized. It is submitted here that these variations, however, do not prejudice the general principle of the existence of fiduciary relationships between the state and its governmental fiduciaries in the field of sovereign debt. Indeed, by their very nature, principles are abstract and flexible as to their application, and thus amenable to encompass such variations. This chapter has shown that fiduciary relationships in the field of sovereign debt contracting are the product of state practices such as delegation with a view to serving the public interest and the execution of control mechanisms entailing the enforcement of fiduciary duties. Such relationships thus imply a general rule stipulating that all states rely on their governments to act in their sole interest and that an infringement of this rule may give rise to legal defences.

This rule transcends legal systems and categories.[104] Legal systems have a clear impact on the legal categorization of fiduciary relations and duties. However, the objective of fiduciary relationships is equivalent in all countries, namely the establishment of fair and equitable practices with respect to the entrustor, which in this case is the state and can also be called the 'public interest'.[105] Though the importance of the concept of public interest lies more in its aspiration than in its substance, it embodies above all an interest against which public policy motivations may be assessed objectively.[106] This common objective provides for the basis of an international principle. Indeed, as the concept of public interest expands into the interest of the global community, especially in a field where the debts of one sovereign may have a substantial impact on the lives of neighbouring citizens, the transferability of the aforementioned rule at the international level seems vital.[107]

[104] See earlier discussion (n. 32) on the comparative legal functional approach adopted in this chapter.

[105] See earlier discussion (n. 5) about the public interest.

[106] Cases such as *Buck v. Bell* 274 U.S. 200 (1927), where the US Supreme Court explicitly approved the sterilization of the 'mentally retarded' in the name of the public interest, are a reminder that this concept must be used with caution. See Peter (n. 3) 11.

[107] This idea is supported by Criddle and Fox-Decent (n. 13) 357: 'Just as the fiduciary principle governs the domestic exercise of sovereign power, it may also be thought to underlie the authority of international law . . . for in both cases the dignity of the people subject to sovereign power is at stake.'

PART IV

CHINA AS A CASE STUDY

11

China's Governmental Preferential Loans and the Performance of its Lending Responsibility

Meibo Huang and Dandan Zhu

A. Introduction

Governmental preferential loans are long-term and low-interest loans provided by one government (usually a government of the developed and rich countries) to another government (usually a government of the developing countries).[1] Concessionality is achieved either through interest rates lower than those available on the market or by grace periods, or a combination of these.[2] Governmental preferential loans are an important form of international aid for developing countries, as they can ease capital shortage, finance imports of advanced technology and equipment and management expertise, boost the construction of infrastructure, facilitate stable and sustainable economic development, raise people's living standards, and promote the achievement of the Millennium Development Goals (MDGs).

In 1995, China initiated foreign aid structure reform, and preferential lending became a main form of Chinese foreign aid.[3] In recent years, Chinese preferential loans have been increasing rapidly while annual interest rates have been reduced from between 4–5 per cent to between 2–3 per cent, and maturities have been extended from between eight and ten years to between 15 and 20 years (including five to seven years' grace) at present.[4] By the end of 2009, China had provided preferential loans to 76 foreign countries, supporting 325 projects, of which 142 had been completed. Of China's preferential loans, 61 per cent has been used to help developing countries construct transportation, communications, and

[1] See *OECD glossary*, available at <http://stats.oecd.org/glossary/detail.asp?ID=5901> (accessed November 2011).

[2] See *OECD glossary* (n. 1).

[3] See G. Qi, 'Reform the Foreign Aid Work Further in New Situation-National Foreign Aid Reform Conference was Held in Beijing' (1995) 11 International Economic Cooperation 4–5.

[4] See Information Office of the State Council, *China's Foreign Aid White Paper* (2011), available at <http://english.gov.cn/official/2011-04/21/content_1849913.htm>.

electricity infrastructure, and 8.9 per cent to support the development of energy and resources, such as oil and minerals.[5]

China Export-Import Bank (hereinafter referred to as 'the Bank') declares that Chinese governmental preferential loans are conducted on the basis of mutual benefit and win-win cooperation. Such loans have effectively helped recipients to build a variety of productive projects with economic benefits and significant infrastructure projects, so as to create conditions for their sustainable development.[6] Recently the UNCTAD Principles on Promoting Responsible Sovereign Lending and Borrowing[7] have been formulated. The principles and practices of China's sovereign lending and borrowing are somewhat different from those international principles, especially in terms of the performance of its lending responsibility. Furthermore, by studying the practices of preferential loan-giving by developed countries, such as Japan, it can be seen that there are considerable differences in practice between China and the developed countries in many respects. Therefore, in order to improve the effectiveness of its preferential loans, we suggest that China should first examine the current principles and practices of its preferential loans, identify their characteristics and problems, and then make reference to the international principles (see Table 11.1) (especially those of UNCTAD) and the practices of developed countries. For example, China could increase the preferential degree, strengthen project financing, pay attention to identifying the legality and credibility of borrowers, take debt sustainability frameworks into account, improve data transparency, and so on.

In this chapter, we try to introduce international principles in responsible sovereign lending and borrowing, and the practices of preferential loans of developed countries (take Japan as a case in point). Then, based on the UNCTAD Principles, we analyse the situations and practices of China's preferential loans, covering the identification of the legality and credibility of borrowers' actions, preferential degree, project financing, debt sustainability, transparency, involvement in debt relief and restructuring, and so on. Finally, we propose some suggestions to China and international society for the improvement of the lending practices of China's preferential loans.

B. International Standards and Developed Countries' Practices

There are about 14 different international sets of rules, guidelines, or mere proposals (we use 'rules' instead of 'rules, guidelines or proposals' hereafter) on

[5] See *China's Foreign Aid White Paper* (n. 4).

[6] See the speech of the division chief of the department of preferential loans, Zh.Wang, China Export-Import Bank, available at <http://news.buildhr.com/1306473528/91536/1/0.html>.

[7] In 2009, UNCTAD launched an initiative to promote responsible sovereign lending and borrowing practices and develop a set of commonly accepted principles and practices on sovereign debt issues. UNCTAD established an Expert Group to draft the principles and the Principles on Promoting Responsible Sovereign Lending and Borrowing came into being on 10 January 2012. For the text of the Principles, see the Annex to this volume.

Table 11.1 International rules on sovereign lending and borrowing

		Relevant rules	Release agency/year	
Ex ante—Principles before debt comes into being		Equator Principles	IFC/2003	
		The Arrangement on Officially Supported Export Credits	OECD	1978
		The Principles and Guidelines to Promote Sustainable Lending Practices in the Provision of Official Export Credits to Low-Income Countries.		2008
Concurrent—initiatives of debt management	transparency	The Special Data Dissemination Standard (SDDS)	IMF/1996	
	effectiveness	Debt Management Performance Assessment (DEMPA) Tool	WB/2008	
	sustainability	Debt Sustainability Framework (DSF)	IMF/2005	
	responsibility	Responsible Financing Charter	Eurodad/2008	
Ex post initiative dealing with debt unsustainability	debt relief	Baker Plan and Brandy Plan	USA/1985 and 1989	
		Heavily Indebted Poor Countries (HIPC) Initiative	IMF and WB/1996	
		Multilateral Debt Relief Initiative (MDRI)	G8/2005	
	contractual way	Collective Action Clauses (CACS)— private creditor	G10/1996	
	legal way	Sovereign Debt Restructuring Mechanism (SDRM)—official creditor	IMF/2001	
	compromising way	Code of Good Conduct—private creditor	La Banque de France/2002	
	compromising way	Principles for Stable Capital Flows and Fair Debt Restructuring in Emerging Markets	IIF/2004	

sovereign lending or borrowing formulated by international organizations and other actors (see Table 11.1), which include standards before debt comes into being, standards of debt management, and standards of debt relief and restructuring. Their legal strength ranks from contractual agreements (collective action clauses, CACs), to moderate enforceability (such as the HIPC Initiative), and policy proposals without major repercussions in the official sector (Eurodad, Charter).

As stated previously, UNCTAD has recently formulated the Principles on Promoting Responsible Sovereign Lending and Borrowing (hereinafter referred to as 'the Principles'), based on the existing international rules stipulating standards on responsible sovereign lending and borrowing. In this part, we will analyse the existing international rules on sovereign lending and borrowing before focusing on the main points of the Principles on lending and examining various aspects of the practices of preferential loan-giving by developed countries, such as the legality and credibility of borrowers' actions, project feasibility investigation, debt sustainability, debt relief, and restructuring and transparency.

I. Possible international standards on sovereign lending and borrowing

Before UNCTAD initiated the discussion of the Principles, there were no definite international principles for guiding responsible sovereign borrowing and lending behaviour. Yet, the sovereign debt crisis has been a hot topic for discussion among the international community for a long time. With the outbreak of the Mexican debt crisis at the end of twentieth century, the discussion about sovereign debt crisis management reached a new peak. International organizations and other actors have launched a series of initiatives to deal with different aspects of sovereign debt issues. We have collected a total of 14 initiatives on sovereign lending and borrowing with a variety of legal statuses, though some of them are just policy proposals. Nonetheless, they all reflect international efforts to cope with sovereign debt issues before UNCTAD launched its initiatives on the Principles. Here we divide these initiatives into three categories, variously seeking: (1) to conduct *ex ante* examination before sovereign debts arise; (2) to improve debt management, thus being used to reduce debt costs and risks, which can be further divided into rules of debt transparency, debt management effectiveness, debt sustainability, and debt responsibility; and (3) to deal with debt sustainability, including debt relief and debt restructuring when sovereign debt cannot be repaid on time, with the latter being divided further based on the objects and characteristics of restructuring methods (see Table 11.1). Based on these, we then came up with a panoramic view of the overlappings and contradictions presented by these standards on debt crisis-prevention, debt management, and debt crisis present. After careful analysis of these possible standards, we have found that these initiatives are mostly used to restrain borrowers' actions, yet with little constraint of the actions of the lenders.

II. UNCTAD Principles and their purposes

In the light of this blatantly inconsistent framework, UNCTAD launched an initiative in 2009 to promote responsible sovereign lending and borrowing practices. The purpose of the initiative was to provide a forum for debate to develop a set of commonly accepted principles and practices relevant to sovereign debt issues. At present, the consolidated principles have been formed. These Principles determine the responsibilities of lenders and borrowers separately at the macroscopic level on the basis of current international rules on sovereign lending and borrowing. Under the Principles, the responsibilities of lenders include seven aspects: (1) agency; (2) informed decisions; (3) due authorization; (4) responsible credit decisions; (5) project financing; (6) international cooperation; and (7) debt restructurings. The first three stipulate that the sovereign lenders are responsible for the legality and credibility of sovereign borrowers' actions and principles; aspects 4, 5, and 7 refer to the responsible lending behaviour at different stages of sovereign debt, namely, project feasibility investigation, debt sustainability, and debt relief and debt restructuring.

III. Overall performance of governmental preferential loans in developed countries

In order to compare Chinese preferential lending with that of the developed countries in this section we will first analyse the overall performance of governmental preferential loans in developed countries.

1. Total sum of loans

On the whole, the average annual total sum of concessional loans of developed countries[8] in the past ten years has exceeded US$8 billion. Specifically, the years from 2002 to 2006, with the exception of 2005, saw a constant decrease, and the annual growth rate ranged from about -1 to -2 per cent; in the year 2006 there was a sharp drop of roughly 11.5 per cent compared with the year 2005, which was the lowest in those years. From 2006 to 2009, the total sum kept rising, with the growth rate changing significantly: 32.5 per cent in 2008, the highest in those years. Nonetheless, the growth rate declined noticeably in 2009, 16 per cent lower than that of 2008, owing to the financial crisis[9] (see Figure 11.1).

2. Loan conditions

The conditions of governmental preferential loans mainly involve maturity (including grace periods), interest rates, and the grant element. These conditions can

[8] This mainly refers to OECD/DAC bilateral member countries, rather than non-DAC member countries and multilateral organizations.
[9] OECD, StatExtracts, available at <http://stats.oecd.org>.

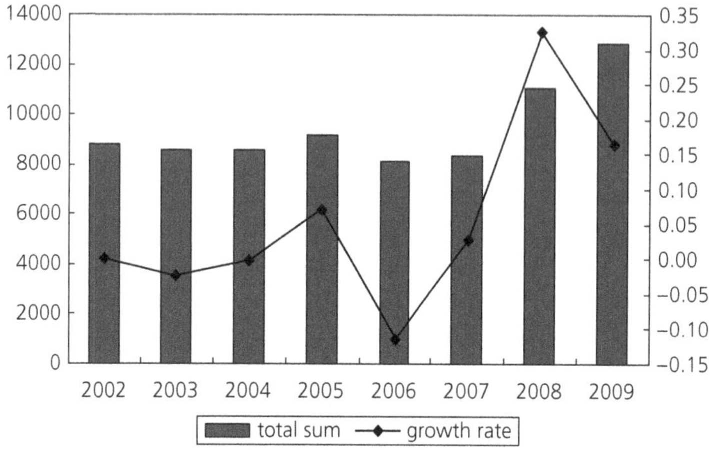

Fig. 11.1 Total sum of preferential loans from developed countries, 2002–2009
Source: based on data from OECD.StatExtracts, available at <http://stats.oecd.org>.

reflect the degree of concession of a country's preferential loans. The average loan term of preferential loans from developed countries was 30.7 years, plus a grace period averaging 9.2 years: a roughly 40-year maturity. The average annual interest rate from 2000 to 2009 was 1.3 per cent; the average interest rate has declined in recent years compared to that of 2004, which has been helpful in relieving the debt burden of the borrowers. By calculation,[10] the grant element of preferential loans from developed countries was up to 69.1 per cent; however, apart from the slight rise in the period 2003–2005 because of the lower interest rate, preferential loans in the form of grants decreased both in 2000–03 and in 2005–09, especially during the financial crisis in 2007–09 (see Table 11.2). The main reason for this situation was the financial crisis which led to global economic slowdown and lower than expected GNP growth in the major developed countries, which resulted in the decrease of the aid budget of donors.[11]

3. Sector distribution

In general, governmental preferential loans from developed countries are provided not for industrial projects, but for public projects, such as infrastructure, environmental protection, and poverty alleviation. From Figure 11.2, we can see that roughly 45 per cent of loans flow to infrastructure and services sector, fully reflecting the policy emphasized by developed countries of enhancing the ability of

[10] The formula of grant element is $GE=(1\text{-}i/q)(1\text{-}(E^{-qG}\text{-}E^{-qT})/q(T\text{-}G))$, whereby 'i' is the interest rate, 'q' the rate of return, 'T' maturity, 'G' grace period, and 'E' a natural logarithm.

[11] See OECD website, 'Aid statistics—Aid to poor countries slips further as governments tighten budgets', available at <http://www.oecd.org/development/stats/aidtopoorcountriesslipsfurtherasgovernmentstightenbudgets.html>.

Table 11.2 Loan Conditions of Preferential Loans from Developed Countries, 2000–09

	2000	2001	2002	2003	2004	2005	2006	2007	2008	2009	average
Loan term (years)	33.7	33.0	31.5	31.4	30.4	31.6	30.4	29.4	28.2	27.4	30.7
Grace period (years)	10.8	9.2	9.0	9.5	9.2	9.1	8.7	9.3	9.2	8.3	9.2
Average interest rate (%)	1.4	1.5	1.4	1.6	1.4	1.1	1.3	1.3	1.2	1.3	1.3
Grant element (%)	71.9	70.2	68.7	68.5	69	71.2	69.2	68.8	67.1	66.5	69.1

Source: OECD/DAC, *Development Cooperation Report*, 2001–2011.

borrowers to undertake independent development; 17 per cent of loans are destined for the social infrastructure and services sector, which covers issues concerning essential human rights and democracy, such as education, health, and government, as well as the much less prominent sectors of the borrowers, especially of the heavily indebted poor countries. Cross-department expenditure makes up about 12 per cent, mainly for environmental protection. In addition, distribution to the production sector, general programme assistance, and other debt-related areas take up 8 per cent, 9 per cent, and 7 per cent respectively.[12]

IV. Practices of governmental preferential loans from developed countries—taking Japan as a case in point

Japan, France, and Germany are ranked as the top three countries in terms of the total sum of governmental preferential loans in developed countries, exceeding a value of US$1 billion in 2009 (see Figure 11.3). Japan, as the biggest preferential loans provider in the world, pays a great deal of attention to the role of preferential loans in foreign aid. In 2009, Japan disbursed US$7.657 billion worth of Yen loans, accounting for 58.2 per cent of Japan's gross bilateral foreign aid, the highest in all Development Assistance Committee (DAC) member countries;[13] moreover, the grant element of Yen loans was about 72 per cent, higher than the average level of bilateral DAC member countries at 66.5 per cent. Yen loans have already formed a relatively thorough management mechanism, so a good understanding of the lending practices of Japan's preferential loans will be useful in understanding the principles and practices of loans from developed countries.

1. Legality and credibility of borrowers' actions

Japan's Official Development Assistance Charter stipulates explicitly that 'the government will implement appropriate measures to ensure data transparency,

[12] OECD, StatExtracts, available at <http://stats.oecd.org>.
[13] Aid data comes from OECD/DAC, *Peer Review of Japan* (2010), available at <http://www.oecd.org/dac/peer-reviews/45470028.pdf>.

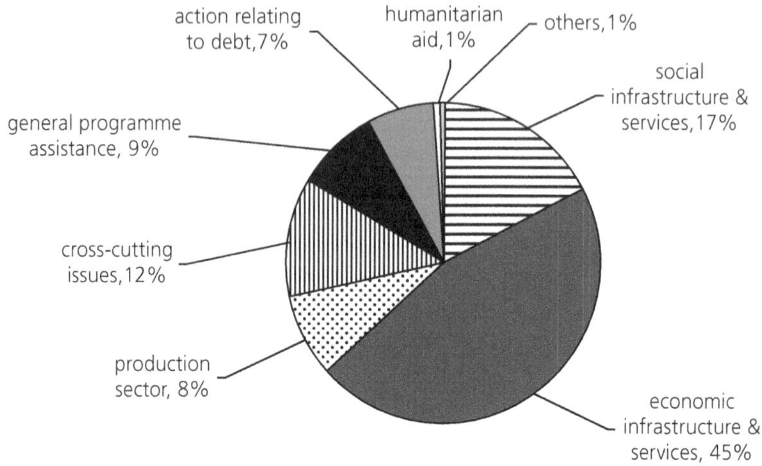

Fig. 11.2 Sector distribution of preferential loans of developed countries, 2009

Source: based on data from OECD.StatExtracts, available at <http://stats.oecd.org>.

Note: social infrastructure and services include: education, health, population, water supply and sanitation, government and civil society; economic infrastructure and services include: transport and storage, communications, energy, banking and financial services, business and other services; production sector includes: agriculture, forestry and fishing, industry, mining and construction; cross-cutting issues include: environmental protection; general programme assistance include: general budget support, food security assistance.

and to prevent fraud, corruption, and improper diversion of aid'.[14] The Japan Bank for International Cooperation (JBIC) conducts feasibility studies (F/S) involving the institutional, legal, and economic environment of borrowers during the preparation stage; meanwhile, JBIC requires borrowers to carry out due investigation and to provide timely and accurate information to ensure that the borrower's actions are in line with local law and public interest.[15]

2. *Feasibility investigation of projects*

Up to now, the Japan International Cooperation Agency (JICA) and JBIC have put forward three sets of guidelines for the evaluation and examination of the environmental and social effects of Yen loans; these include the *JBIC Guidelines for Environmental Considerations for ODA Loans*, published in 1999, the *JBIC Guidelines for Confirmation of Environmental and Social Considerations*, published in 2002, and the *JICA Guidelines for Environmental and Social Considerations*, published in 2010. The 1999 *Guidelines* introduced classification standards for Yen

[14] Government of Japan, Ministry of Foreign Affairs, Economic Co-operation Bureau, *Japan's Official Development Assistance Charter* (2003) 8, available at <http://www.mofa.go.jp/policy/oda/reform/revision0308.pdf>.

[15] JBIC, *Operational Guidance on Preparation for Japan's ODA Loan Projects* (2004), available at <http://www.jica.go.jp/english/our_work/types_of_assistance/oda_loans/oda_op_info/guidance/index.html>.

loans for the first time and conducted an environmental impact assessment (EIA) according to these standards, similar to the Equator Principles.[16] The 2002 *Guidelines* define four principles to follow in the environmental and social field regarding Yen loans: (1) ensure the implementation of guidelines through transparent procedures, for instance, by consulting with stakeholders, and so on; (2) disclose information positively, including categorization results, EIA reports, JBIC inspection results, and so on; (3) pay due attention to social impact; (4) introduce a target mechanism.[17] The 2010 *Guidelines* impose demanding requirements for environmental considerations, increase the involvement of an external advisory committee in environmental and social evaluations, and extend the degree and scope of information disclosure.[18]

The complete Yen loan project cycle has four stages: preparation, appraisal, implementation, and *ex post* evaluation and follow-up monitoring.[19] Japan requires relevant departments to inspect the environmental and social aspects of activities at every stage of the project cycle.

3. *Debt sustainability of borrowers*

Japan is one of the participants of the Debt Sustainability Framework (DSF) of the World Bank and the IMF, so it will conduct a debt sustainability assessment (DSA) of Yen loans. A Japanese DSA carefully studies and analyses all factors—including the borrower's exchange rates, foreign exchange reserves, trade balance, money supply and monetary policy, interest rates, government expenditures, revenues and fiscal policy, GDP growth, and of course the existing debt stock and its terms and conditions—by gathering information from stakeholders such as official agencies and civil societies to determine the future solvency of the borrower. Based on the results of the DSA, the government of Japan makes the decision as to whether the project is suitable for loan financing, and determines the total sum and terms of the loan. Generally speaking, Japan undertakes the DSA together with international or regional development banks, for example JICA, alongside the Asian Development Bank. From June to July of 2010, it undertook a joint DSA for East Timor.[20]

In addition, JICA adopted a Risk Management Policy to manage the risk of Yen Loans and to cope with debt unsustainability in borrowers.[21] The policy is used to

[16] Equator Principles classifies projects into A, B, and C categories on the basis of their potential environmental and social effects, to evaluate and manage environmental and social risk in project financing. The 1999 *Guidelines* also classify projects as A, B, or C and provides the specific sectors that each category includes. JICA, *JBIC Guidelines for Environmental Considerations for ODA Loans* (1999), available at <http://www.jica.go.jp/english/publications/jbic_archive/guidelines/>.

[17] JICA, *JBIC Guidelines for Confirmation of Environmental and Social Considerations* (2002), available at <http://www.jica.go.jp/english/publications/jbic_archive/environmental_guidelines/pdf/guide.pdf>.

[18] JICA, *JICA Guidelines for Environmental and Social Considerations* (2010), available at <http://www.jica.go.jp/english/operations/social_environmental/guideline/index.html>.

[19] See JBIC, *Operational Guidance* (n. 15) 4.

[20] See <http://www.jica.go.jp/usa/english/office/others/newsletter/2010/1006_07_06.html>.

[21] See JICA, *JICA Annual Report 2010* (2010) 172, available at <http://www.jica.go.jp/english/publications/reports/annual/2010/pdf/all.pdf>.

identify, measure, and monitor various risks to which Yen loans are exposed. Its major risks in management activities include credit risk management, market risk management, liquidity risk management, and operational risk management.

4. *Debt relief and restructuring*

Japan is a participant in the Heavily Indebted Poor Countries (HIPC) Initiative and Multilateral Debt Relief Initiative (MDRI), and its debt relief follows these two initiatives. That is to say, Japan will start debt relief with other creditors if the borrower reaches the 'decision point' and 'complete point' of structural adjustment set by the World Bank and the IMF. The Japanese government provides debt relief in the form of tied grant aid for recipients to encourage self-help development in order to then be able to repay Yen loans. Because this 'grant aid for debt relief' approach could cause debts to remain for an indefinite period and the recipients had to obtain hard currency for the repayment of loans, this method was abandoned. JBIC has adopted a waiver of loans for debt relief, and will take measures to keep a balance of account in providing debt relief. This means that JBIC will use its reserves and net earnings on the overseas economic cooperation account of the statutory financial statements to write off and provide an allowance for loans. Of course, as JBIC is only allowed to set aside a special reserve of 0.3 per cent of total loans, the debt relieved in this way is extremely limited.[22]

The JICA Annual Report 2010 indicates that when an indebted country is temporarily unable to service debt due to economic difficulties, debt rescheduling will take place among the creditors based on the Paris Club in order to ensure sustainable debt service. The debtor receiving this temporary support to overcome its liquidity problem will implement economic restructuring programmes agreed upon with the IMF to acquire sustainable debt service capacity.[23] Japan rescheduled the debt of the Central African Republic and Togo under the Agreement of the Paris Club in 2007 and 2008 respectively.[24] JICA discloses the loans rescheduled in the Paris Club, and the debtor countries are categorized as 'needs attention' in its self-assessments of asset quality, as loans are classified as 'Restructured Loans' or 'Special Attention Assets'.[25]

5. *Transparency*

From the first preparation stage to the final completion stage of Yen loans, all relevant information regarding loans and projects is published on the website of JICA or in other ways, and disclosure standards are in line with the Law Concerning Access to Information. Moreover, as Japan is one of the signatory countries of the Special Data Dissemination Standard (SDDS), it will publish its economic,

22 See <http://www.jica.go.jp/english/news/jbic_archive/autocontents/english/news/2002/000061>.
23 See JICA Annual Report 2010, 250.
24 See JICA Annual Report 2010, 204.
25 These two terms come from The Banking Law of Japan and The Revitalization Law respectively.

financial, fiscal, and other relevant information based on these standards and will ensure data quality and public access.

C. The Practices of China's Governmental Preferential Loans

China's governmental preferential loans differ from those of the developed countries in total sum, conditions, and sector distribution. Its practices, such as the evaluation of environmental and social effects, sustainability analysis, data transparency, and so on, also show some discrepancy from those of the developed countries.

I. Overall performance of China's governmental preferential loans

As in section B.III., we will again first analyse the overall performance of Chinese governmental preferential loans in total sum, conditions, and sector distribution.

1. Total sum of loans

As Figure 11.3 shows, the total sum of China's governmental preferential loans kept rising during the period 2002–09, exceeding US$0.1 billion (US$0.128 billion) for the first time in 2001, and continued to grow considerably, especially after 2006. In 2009, the total sum was more than US$3 billion, increasing about 333 per cent compared with US$0.693 billion in 2006, before the financial crisis. Specifically, the sum was less than the average level of OECD/DAC member countries, and lower than that of Japan, France, and Germany before 2006. In recent years, however, the growth rate of Chinese loans has been higher than that of DAC member countries as a whole, and the total sum of its loans surpassed the average level of DAC member countries in 2006, and Germany and France in 2007. China now ranks only second to Japan as a governmental preferential loan provider. In its *Foreign Aid White Paper 2011*, China promised to increase foreign aid gradually, with the development of its own economy, to promote the achievement of the MDGs.[26] Hence, we can anticipate that Chinese loans will grow even further in the future.

2. Conditions

As mentioned previously, governmental preferential loans from developed countries have an average annual interest rate of 1.3 per cent, and a 40-year maturity (including around ten years' grace period).[27] In its early years of lending, China's preferential loans had an interest rate of up to 4 or 5 per cent, while the loan term was merely eight to ten years, and the longest maturity less than 15 years, even with

[26] See *China's Foreign Aid White Paper* (n. 4).
[27] Data comes from OECD/DAC Development Cooperation Report in 2001–11.

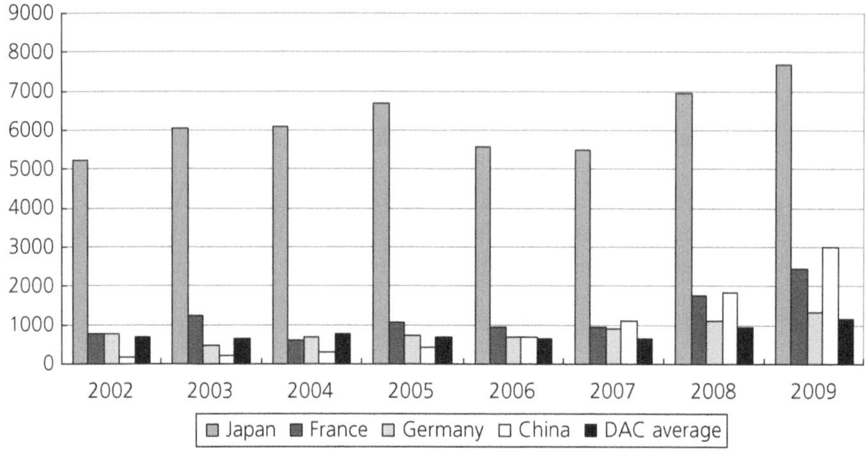

Fig. 11.3 The total sum of China's governmental preferential loans, 2002–09

Source: data on Japan, France, Germany, and DAC average level come from OECD.StatExtracts, data on the Export-Import Bank of China come from *The Dragon's Gift: The Real Story of China in Africa.*

a five- to seven-year grace period.[28] Calculations on the basis of these conditions find that the grant element of Chinese loans just meets the lowest standard of ODA defined by OECD. China's *Foreign Aid White Paper 2011* claimed that Chinese loans now have an interest rate between 2 and 3 per cent and a 15- to 20-year maturity (including a five- to seven-year grace period).[29] Even under these conditions, the grant element of Chinese loans is only 43.2 per cent, meaning that there is a considerable difference from the 69.1 per cent of the developed countries. Nevertheless, judging from an interview with an officer from the Ministry of Commerce, the future trend of Chinese preferential loans is quite certain: the concessional degree will increase gradually, with the continuous decreasing of interest rates on the one hand and a gradual extension of maturity on the other.[30]

3. *Sector distribution*

Figure 11.4 illustrates the sector distribution of Chinese loans. Evidently, about two-thirds of loans are used to help borrowers build economic infrastructure, for transport, communications, electricity, and so on, similar to loans from developed countries. It is worth noting that the infrastructure projects supported by China are mostly production projects of small and medium size with market-related, energy, and economic benefits, which stand in contrast to the public projects working in areas such as environmental protection and poverty

[28] See M. Huang and J. Hu, 'Development History and Prospect of China's Governmental Preferential Loans' (2010) 11 International Economic Cooperation 47.

[29] See *China's Foreign Aid White Paper* (n. 4).

[30] From an interview with an official who works in the Department of Aid to Foreign Countries, Ministry of Commerce of People's Republic of China on 29 February 2012.

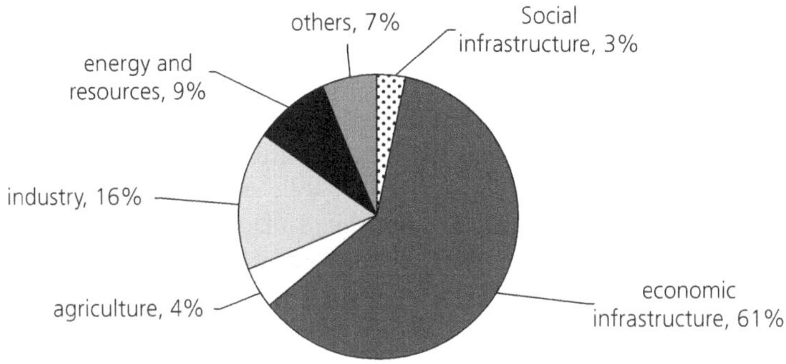

Fig. 11.4 Sector distribution of China's governmental preferential loans, by the end of 2009
Source: China's Foreign Aid White Paper, 2011.

alleviation, which are supported more frequently with loans from developed countries.[31] Social infrastructure input by China only accounts for 3.2 per cent of its loans, which is a long way from the 17 per cent of the developed countries. Furthermore, the expenditure of Chinese loans on production sectors such as industry and agriculture is higher than that of developed countries, reaching 20 per cent and 8 per cent, respectively.

II. The UNCTAD Principles and the practices of China's governmental preferential loans

Based on UNCTAD's lending principles and the practices of Yen loans, we will now discuss the principles and practices involved in China's governmental preferential loans.

1. Legality and credibility of borrowers' actions

The first three UNCTAD Principles concern the legality and credibility of borrowers' actions. In concrete terms, lenders should recognize that government officials involved in sovereign lending and borrowing transactions are responsible for protecting public interest (of the state and its citizens for which they are acting as agents) and have a responsibility to ensure that borrowers make informed decisions and that the decisions are authorized under applicable law. The process of the Export-Import Bank of China's preferential loans system largely consists of *ex ante* evaluation and review, management and monitoring on disbursement, *ex post* repayment, and a summary.[32] The *ex ante* evaluation and review stage is to ensure that the country to which the project belongs is politically stable, in a good

[31] Z. Yun and J. Han, 'International Comparation of China's Governmental Preferential Loans' (1997) 4 International Economic Cooperation 36.
[32] Summarized on the basis of China Export-Import Bank, *Interim Procedures of Preferential Loans of China Export-Import Bank* (1996, 2000).

economic situation, and is solvent, and that the borrower has a good credit rating and debt servicing capacity, while the guarantor is sound in compensation status.[33] It is thus clear that with Chinese loans, the main emphasis is on the profitability of projects, but little concern is shown for the legality and credibility of borrowers' actions. Before giving loans, China neither pays attention to the agency role of borrowers nor considers the governance and public support of borrowers. Provisions covering such issues are missing from the regulations of Chinese preferential loans, which is not in line with the Principles and also quite different from the practices observed in the granting of Yen loans, mentioned previously.

In fact, the greatest divergence between Chinese and Western aid is that loans from China are not bound by politics.[34] China and Western countries have different political systems, they are at different stages of economic development, and, at the same time, they have different histories and cultures. Thus they have different foreign policies, which lead to different foreign aid policies and principles. The principles of Chinese preferential loans are the same as the principles of Chinese foreign aid, both reflecting the '*Eight Principles for Foreign Aid*' put forward by former premier Enlai Zhou in 1964. China insists that it respects the right of recipients to choose their development methods and models, that it believes that the other developing countries can establish development methods that are appropriate to their national conditions, and that it does not wish to use foreign aid as a means of interfering other countries' internal affairs. On the contrary, developed donors always impose various conditions on recipient countries when providing aid. For instance, from the 1980s, DAC members thought that liberal economic reforms are the main engine for growth and that good governance, human rights, and democracy are the cornerstones of long-term sustainable development. Hence, to eradicate poverty, they always require developing countries to reform their economic and political systems according to these principles. Since the 1990s, DAC members have paid more attention to recipient countries' records on human rights and democracy, and ensured that their aid would bring about political, social, and economic progress.

2. *Feasibility investigation of projects*

The Interim Procedures of Preferential Loans of the Export-Import Bank of China[35] demonstrate that the Export-Import Bank will conduct a feasibility investigation of borrowers and projects in the *ex ante* evaluation and review stage, mainly reviewing the feasibility of projects and credit ratings, the financial situation, and the solvency of borrowers. The bank has also formulated a series of guidelines to solve the environmental and social problems that may be caused by projects.

[33] See Interim Procedures of Preferential Loans of China Export-Import Bank (2000) Art. 7.

[34] As W. He said, in an interview with the *Chinese Times Weekly*, 22 December 2011; she is the director of the African Research Office of West Asia and Africa Research Institution of the Chinese Academy of Social Sciences.

[35] China Export-Import Bank, *Interim Procedures of Preferential Loans of China Export-Import Bank* (1996, 2000).

The Bank adopted an environmental policy in 2004 to deal with environmental issues before, during, and after project implementation.[36] This policy requires environmental impacts to be studied in order for a project to receive funding, and states that 'projects that are harmful to the environment or do not gain endorsement or approval from environmental administration will not be funded' and 'once any unacceptable negative environmental impacts result during the project implementation, the Bank will require the implementation unit to take immediate remedial or preventive measures. Otherwise, they will discontinue financial support'.[37] In May and July 2007, the Bank signed two Memoranda of Understanding with the World Bank and the IFC respectively, and promised to cooperate with them in providing advisory services on environmental issues under the MOUs.[38] In August 2007, the Bank issued more specific guidelines on social and environmental impact assessment.[39] The guidelines require projects to comply with host country policies—but not international standards—regarding environmental impact assessment, resettlement, and consultation; they stipulate that the Bank can monitor environmental impacts throughout the project cycle, and has the right to cancel a loan if environmental problems are not properly solved.[40]

Although China has improved its practices in the feasibility investigation of projects, especially the evaluation of environmental and social effects, if we compare Chinese practices with the UNCTAD Principles or the practices of Yen loans, there is still a big gap in this regard. Article 5 of the UNCTAD Consolidated Principles stipulates that lenders financing a project in the debtor country have a responsibility to perform their own *ex ante* investigation into and, when necessary, post-disbursement monitoring of the likely effects of the project, including its financial, operational, civil, social, cultural, and environmental implications. However, Chinese preferential lending also emphasizes the feasibility investigation of projects on the one hand, but it hardly conducts any post-disbursement monitoring on the other. Meanwhile, its feasibility investigations place particular emphasis on analysing and evaluating the financial effects of projects, and pay more and more attention to environmental and social effects of projects with little concentration on operational, civil and, cultural implications. And with regard to Yen loans, the three *Guidelines* for Yen loans first set quite specific standards and implementation processes for the evaluation of environmental and social effects, as well as reference to international standards like the Equator Principles, while China just has ambiguous polices and guidelines, which are less operable and effective and fail to meet international standards. Secondly, Yen loans implement a specific Environmental Conservation Plan to prevent and reverse side-effects of projects, while China just reaches a point at which it will 'discontinue financial support', without any effective solutions. Thirdly, Yen loans emphasize the supervision of any environmental and other effects of financed projects after the accomplishment of projects and require recipi-

[36] See P. Bosshard, 'China's Environmental Footprint in Africa', Working Paper in African Studies Program at SAIS (2008) 12.

[37] See Bosshard (n. 36) 12.

[38] See Bosshard (n. 36) 13.

[39] See Bosshard (n. 36) 12.

[40] See Bosshard (n. 36) 12.

ents to submit relevant reports, while China has no regulation on this. Finally, Yen loans emphasize the disclosure of information about the feasibility investigation of projects and involve an external advisory committee, but this provision is also absent from Chinese loans.

3. Debt sustainability of borrowers

UNCTAD Principle 4 underlines that a lender is responsible for making a realistic assessment of the sovereign borrower's capacity to service a loan based on the best available information and objective and agreed technical rules on due diligence and national accounts. The Interim Procedures of Preferential Loans of the Export-Import Bank of China[41] referred to conducting a feasibility investigation of the solvency of borrowers, but made no mention of relevant standards and technical rules. At the same time, unlike Yen loans, Chinese loans do not carry out a debt sustainability assessment (DSA) under the DSF, neither do they have sound and systemic risk management plans. In fact, China has drifted away from the principles of the DSF since the World Bank and the IMF formulated the Debt Sustainabiltiy Framework in 2005. Additionally, China does not take any action to cooperate with other donors when providing loans, nor does it consider debt situations or the debt relief provided. Todd Moss and Sarah Rose describe Chinese loans as taking a 'free ride', that is, Chinese loans increase because of debt relief from other donors, so that the borrower falls once again into debt unsustainability.[42] However, in an interview, a Chinese officer from the Ministry of Commerce stated that, while providing governmental preferential loans, the Ministry of Commerce and the Ministry of Foreign Affairs of China are responsible for political aspects while the Export-Import Bank of China is interested in the economic aspects. Before providing loans, the bank does launch feasibility evaluations, including environmental evaluations and technical feasibility evaluations of projects, and assess loan risks and the solvency of borrowers.

4. Debt relief and restructuring

UNCTAD Principle 7 stipulates that in circumstances where a sovereign is manifestly unable to service its debts, all lenders have a responsibility to behave in good faith and with cooperative spirit to reach a consensual rearrangement of those obligations as early as possible. China forgave US$20 billion of loans to African heavily indebted poor countries (HIPCs) in the years up to 2010,[43] but it does not have a systemic framework for debt relief. China also lacks a framework for debt restructuring following debt unsustainability. Japan conducts the relief of Yen loans

[41] China Export-Import Bank, *Interim Procedures of Preferential Loans of China Export-Import Bank* (1996, 2000).

[42] See T. Moss and S. Rose, 'China ExIm Bank and Africa: New Lending, New Challenges', Center for Global Development (2006) 3, available at <http://www.cgdev.org/content/publications/detail/11116>.

[43] See <http://www.infzm.com/content/50494>.

based on the HIPC Initiative and the MRDI, and the restructuring of Yen loans conforming to the Paris Club principles, so it cooperates closely with other creditors. However, China does not conduct its debt relief under the framework of the HIPC initiative or the MDRI, so it does not involve structural adjustment, which makes it essentially different from developed countries in terms of debt relief. The debt relief provided by China usually includes postponing the payment of debt or relieving government interest-free loans while at the same time taking measures to strengthen bilateral trade and investment to boost the economic development of the borrower and thus to enhance its solvency.[44] An interview with an officer from the Ministry of Commerce indicated that China's debt restructuring usually consists of extending the maturity of governmental interest-free loans or unilateral debt relief, and that China rarely negotiates or cooperates with other donors.

5. Transparency

UNCTAD Principles 10 and 11 stipulate that borrowers must ensure the transparency of borrowing and disclose complete and accurate information on their economic situation relevant to their debt situation; yet the Principles do not mention the responsibility of lenders on this point. We believe that lenders' officials should also publish information on their economic situation and lending activities to the public and investors, which is responsible to taxpayers and investors and convenient for cooperation among lenders as well. As to transparency principles, China supports the General Data Dissemination System (GDDS) and the Special Data Dissemination Standard (SDDS) generally, but gives priority to the GDDS, and regards the SDDS as an objective framework to improve its data dissemination standards. China officially became a signatory country of the GDDS on 15 April 2002. The National Bureau of Statistics of China then published *China GDDS Work Rules* in April 2003 and drew up *Short-term Improvement Plan* and *Mid-term Improvement Plan* according to the rules, establishing the '(China) Leading Group for GDDS' and 'Office for GDDS'.[45] By implementing the GDDS, China made great strides in increasing the transparency of data formation and release, and improving the quality of data and extending statistical services. The statistical system of China meets the requirements of the GDDS on the whole, but still keeps some distance from the SDDS. The *Short-term Improvement Plan* and *Mid-term Improvement Plan* have some room for improvement before they can be adapted to the SDDS, which indicates that China has started to approach the SDDS. Nevertheless, the Export-Import Bank of China neither publishes its loan information like Japan or other donors, nor does it require borrowers to disclose borrowing information to the international community and the public. Consequently, it is hard to find out the total sum, conditions, and concessional degree of each loan, let alone make a comparison with other countries.

[44] From an interview with a Chinese officer from the Ministry of Commerce.

[45] See the website of the National Bureau of Statistics of China, at <http://www.stats.gov.cn/tjdt/zgjrgdds/t20031222_129061.htm> (2000).

From the foregoing analysis, we can see the total sum of Chinese loans has been growing, and that their conditions and concessional degree have been improved; moreover, China has adopted measures to improve its loan practices and to increase its effectiveness in responsible lending. The Chinese government believes that China's governmental preferential loans have facilitated the economic development of borrowers and enhanced the role and influence of China in the international lending and borrowing market. However, according to the UNCTAD Principles and compared with Yen loans, Chinese loans are of a lower concessional degree, while China's loan practices are not quite in line with the international principles on feasibility investigation, debt sustainability, debt relief and restructuring, and transparency.

D. Ways to Improve China's Governmental Preferential Loans

As mentioned earlier, Chinese preferential loans have achieved improvements on the one hand and yet suffered criticism from the international community on the other. In order to take the responsibility in sovereign lending and to improve the effectiveness of loans, China should recognize its divergence from the international principles and the developed countries' practices, and take measures to improve its lending behaviour. Based on its own situation, and with reference to the UNCTAD Principles and the practices of Yen loans, we suggest China's governmental preferential loans should be improved in at least the following respects.

I. Extend sources of loans and improve concessional degree

The sum available for loans should be closely related to the overall economic situation of lenders. China is a developing country at present, so, on the one hand, China should provide loans according to its abilities; on the other hand, with the development of its own economy, China is expected to increase the total sum of loans, lower the interest rate, and extend maturity (including the grace period) as much as possible.

In the event that the fund for loans cannot increase quickly, China must enhance the effectiveness of loans by improving their quality. Donors such as Sweden have reduced the number of recipients in recent years to maximize the effectiveness of foreign aid by using the limited funds in an intensive way.[46] Chinese loans could apply the same method of improving the country distribution of loans, differentiating between borrowers, and reducing lending to those countries that abuse loans or have low effectiveness, weak solvency capability, and bad governance, thereby increasing the economic and social benefits of the loans that they do grant.

[46] Sweden drew up new list of recipients in 2007 and intended to decrease its recipients from 67 to 33 to make intensive use of aid. The new list is available at <http://se.mofcom.gov.cn/aarticle/jmxw/200708/97801996743743.html>.

II. Improve transparency of preferential loans

To respond to the requirements of the international community on the transparency of data on Chinese foreign aid and to coordinate with other donors, China needs to take steps to increase the transparency of its lending and improve the timeliness and quality of the data. First, as a signatory country of the GDDS, China should bridge the gap between transparency of data dissemination and expected targets in the light of the standards, and strive to be a signatory of the SDDS soon. Secondly, as a lender government, China should publish the relevant contents of its loan agreements in a timely and fair manner by using, for example, the internet, press, and other media or other methods. Finally, China should require borrowers to publish their complete debt, fiscal, and economic data, precisely and in a timely fashion in the loan agreement, submit project progress reports, and inspect project progress, the use of funds, and other activities on the spot if necessary.

III. Pay attention to the legality and credibility of borrowers' actions

What is most important in identifying the legality and credibility of borrowers' actions is to collect information and evaluate projects at the feasibility investigation stage. Data can be obtained directly through extensive communication with local officials, NGOs, and other stockholders, or indirectly through local embassies, agencies, or through communication and cooperation with other donors in order to determine the credit rating of the borrower. When conducting legality and credibility evaluations, China must ensure the degree of involvement of relevant parties and the dissemination of and access to evaluation results, and can invite external bodies to provide consultation and guidance if necessary. When problems of corruption occur, China should adopt improvement measures in accordance with recognized solutions, as far as possible, rather than simply halting (or terminating) loans suddenly.

IV. Attach importance to the feasibility investigation of projects

To ensure that Chinese loans can achieve the expected economic and social benefits, and to avoid negative civil, cultural, environmental, and social effects on host countries, China should clearly define clauses on the evaluation of projects' effects and corresponding specific criteria and procedures in loan agreements, and supervise the whole operational process of projects, especially post-disbursement monitoring and post-supervision after the completion of projects. As for the evaluation of environmental and social effects, China could refer to the Equator Principles in drafting environmental and social standards applicable to its own financial industry. First, it could organize a research group on the basis of the Equator Principles with the guidance of the Industrial Bank of China, strengthen its communication and cooperation with such international financial organizations as the IFC, the World Bank, and the IMF, and draw lessons from their experiences of implementing the Equator Principles. Secondly, it should formulate an environmental and social impact evaluation standard suitable to Chinese loans by taking its own national conditions into account and developing detailed methods and procedures for its implementation. Finally, it could selectively adopt relevant standards according to the potential environmental and social impacts of projects, monitor the implementation of projects, and conduct evaluations of environmental and social impacts again after the completion of projects and produce a summary with suggestions for improvement. China could pay more attention to civil and cultural effects based on its technical level and capacity, further strengthen the evaluation of financial, environmental, and social effects of projects, and publish investigation reports and disseminate relevant information adequately and in a timely manner.

V. Emphasize analysis of debt sustainability of borrowers

When assessing the borrower's situation, China should consider the broad financial scenario, including direct and contingent liabilities according to the System of National Accounts adopted by the UN Statistical Commission. According to China's national conditions, the 'Chinese DSF' should, first, have a full understanding of its overall position. According to the Monterrey Agreement, it is the duty of developed countries to provide development aid for developing countries. As a developing country itself, China is willing to provide aid for other developing countries within its ability. However, China has no obligation or capabilities to provide loans according to the conditions of preferential loans from OECD countries, including degree of concession and level of un-tied aid, and does not need to provide loans in complete accordance with the requirements of the DSF.[47] Secondly, China should take an active part in coordination. With a good understanding of its overall position, China should participate in the revision of the DSF as far as possible and define exemptions for developing borrowers; and together with other developing borrowers, it should urge the World Bank and the IMF to improve the DSF and drive them to change their approach of merely controlling the volume rather than the quality of loans, so as to improve the effectiveness of such loans. Finally, China should enhance debt risk evaluation and monitoring, ensure the debt sustainability of borrowers, and at the same time, establish a risk fund for preferential loans and oversee investment guarantee systems by analysing the formation and transmission of Chinese preferential loans, so as to set up an insurance mechanism.

VI. Pay attention to involvement in debt relief and restructuring

China should realize that there could be situations where debt restructuring is necessary. At present, China can conduct debt relief independently by referring to the HIPC initiative and the MDRI; however, debt restructuring involves other

[47] See the website of News of Fiscal Bureau, Weihai city, 'DSF for low income countries', (2007), available at <http://www.whcz.gov.cn/default.asp?id=127325>.

lenders, so it is necessary to cooperate with them. The international community has not developed a uniform mechanism for sovereign debt restructuring up to now, and China could seize this chance to participate in the discussion of such a mechanism and to work towards safeguarding its rights with the new rules.

VII. Be moderately open and strengthen cooperation with financial institutions for international development

Chinese preferential loans have been operated mainly in an enclosed mode since their introduction, with little cooperation and coordination with other donor countries or agencies. This has undoubtedly maintained the independence of China's foreign aid policy, but has meant losing chances for cooperation with international and regional development financial agencies. In fact, China has been left out of the international aid architecture.[48] To achieve long-term development, Chinese loans could be moderately open in the context of global integration. China needs to have as good a comprehension as possible of the principles of preferential loans issued by development financial agencies, to take an active part in conferences and forums held by development financial agencies, to contribute to the discussion and formulation of their loan principles to the greatest extent, to strengthen cooperation with international development financial institutions in this field, to learn from and draw on their experiences in feasibility investigations of projects, debt management, debt relief and restructuring, and so on, so as to better promote the implementation of Chinese loans and to improve its loan effectiveness.

E. Conclusion

Since the outbreak of the Mexican debt crisis in the 1980s, the international community has paid close attention to the sovereign debt problem. International organizations and the international community have launched a series of rules or guidelines trying to prevent and solve the debt crisis. Before the formulation of the UNCTAD Principles, the existing international rules in this field were mostly used to restrain borrowers, rather than lenders. Developed countries have been lenders on the international sovereign lending and borrowing stage for a long time. Based on their own ideas of values and ideology, they have proposed relevant rules to restrain the activities of borrowers. It is arguable that it is not necessary to set up rules or guidelines for the developed lenders, but new developing lenders, like China, have sprung up in recent years. Their principles and practices in giving loans have the characteristics of south-south cooperation, and are quite different from those of developed countries. In response to these issues, UNCTAD launched an initiative to 'Promote Responsible Sovereign Lending and Borrowing' in 2009,

[48] Y. Zhang, 'Improvement of China's Governmental Preferential Loans referring to French Development Aid' (2002) 3 International Economic Cooperation 38.

aiming at restraining the practices of sovereign lenders and borrowers, and especially the irresponsible behaviours of new lenders.

After repeated discussions and revisions, UNCTAD issued the Consolidated Principles on Promoting Responsible Sovereign Lending and Borrowing in January 2012. It is necessary for China to analyse thoroughly the differences between its own principles and practices and the Principles and practices of loans issued by developed countries. This chapter has found that there are indeed some differences between the principles and practices of Chinese loans and UNCTAD Principles, as well as the practices of developed countries. We suggest that China should first fully recognize the differences and further understand the reasons causing these differences. As a new developing lender, the political system, economic development level, history, and culture of China differ from those of traditional developed lenders, which inevitably results in different principles and practices. China itself needs to study the content and effects of the UNCTAD Principles and the practices of developed countries with an open mind, and gradually to improve the practices of its governmental preferential loans according to the framework of the Principles and its lending behaviour, based on its own reality. For instance, China could take some measures to extend sources of loans; improve concessional degree and transparency; pay more attention to the legality and credibility of borrowers' actions, feasibility investigation of projects, analysis of debt sustainability of borrowers, and involvement in debt relief and restructuring; and be moderately open in strengthening cooperation with financial institutions for international development. But at the same time, we suggest that the international community should communicate with China in an encompassing manner and in a spirit of goodwill, rather than merely criticizing the principles and practices of Chinese loans in the manner of an international judge. The international community should give China enough time to understand the UNCTAD Principles and the different practices of developed countries, and to follow these in due course and under proper conditions.

12

Crisis Prevention for China as a Sovereign Creditor and the UNCTAD Principles

*Xiuli Han**

A. Introduction

UNCTAD launched a project to promote responsible sovereign lending and borrowing practices on 16 March 2009. The first working draft of a set of principles for promoting responsible sovereign lending and borrowing was reviewed at an UNCTAD conference on 'Developing Guidelines for Responsible Sovereign Lending and Borrowing' held in Xiamen, China on 8 September 2010. On 26 April 2011, UNCTAD published these 'Draft Principles on Promoting Responsible Sovereign Lending and Borrowing' (hereinafter the 'First Draft') which attempt to make clear respective responsibility in a holistic way, including both developed and developing countries as debtors, and private or public bodies as creditors, as well as multilateral lenders.[1] On 4 November 2011 and 10 January 2012, UNCTAD completed the 'Second Draft Principles on Promoting Responsible Sovereign Lending and Borrowing' ('Second Draft') and 'Consolidated Principles on Promoting Responsible Sovereign Lending and Borrowing' respectively (consolidated version).[2] This project is an important action taken by UNCTAD to deal with sovereign debt crises.[3] Although it is unlikely that the UNCTAD Principles will become 'hard law' in

* Thanks are owed to the Scientific Committee of the Conference on the Principles on Responsible Sovereign Lending and Borrowing in Madrid which was composed of professors Armin von Bogdandy, Rosa Lastra, Anna Gelpern, Francisco Garcimartín, Luis Hinojosa, Carlos Espósito, and Yuefen Li. Special thanks are due to the co-organizers of the Conference, Yuefen Li, Carlos Espósito, and Juan Pablo Bohoslavsky, for their helpful suggestions and encouragement on this chapter. The author also wishes to thank Deborah Reynolds for her helpful and extensive proofreading. All errors are mine. I can be contacted at hanxiu777@xmu.edu.cn.

[1] Sovereign creditors in the current market consist of a diverse group of institutions, including hedge funds, institutional investors, creditor nations, commercial banks, investment banks, and even individuals, which can be termed diversification of sovereign creditors.

[2] Consolidated Principles on Promoting Responsible Sovereign Lending and Borrowing, UNCTAD Project on Promoting Responsible Sovereign Lending and Borrowing, reproduced in the Annex to this book.

[3] On 22 December 2011, the United Nations General Assembly approved its annual resolution on external debt highlighting the relevance of UNCTAD's initiative on responsible sovereign lending and borrowing, which:

international economic law in the near future, due to their wording and lack of enforcement mechanisms,[4] they can, however, serve as significant guidance for sovereign debtors and creditors. China has become the second largest sovereign creditor in the world.[5] However, its sovereign lending practices remain unsophisticated[6] and the safety of its sovereign lending has become a serious concern requiring attention, with sovereign debt crises and defaults frequently occurring. Numerous factors, either systemic or random, can lead to a sovereign debt crisis. The reckless conduct of sovereign debtors and creditors or the malpractice of other actors can tip sovereign debtors into insolvency. The sovereign state could also be involved in or affected by the passive or active default of the sovereign debtor, no less than other creditors. As the world's second largest creditor, China cannot control all of these contributing factors and escape the adverse effects of sovereign debt default. In reality, China has been harmed by the lowering of some countries' sovereign credit rating and concomitant sovereign debt crises. China must seriously consider what it can do to prevent crisis from the creditor's perspective. This chapter focuses on China's duties as a responsible lender, and attempts to integrate the UNCTAD Principles with China's position as the second largest creditor nation in the world.

B. China as a Sovereign Lender

I. Status of China as a sovereign lender

At present, the global economy, mired in recession, is still unbalanced. A 'double circulation' system exists, which is based on a financial and industry/trade division.

> ... stresses the importance of responsible lending and borrowing, emphasizes that creditors and debtors must share responsibility for preventing unsustainable debt situations, and encourages Member States, the Bretton Woods institutions, the regional development banks and other relevant multilateral financial institutions and stakeholders to continue the ongoing discussions on this issue, inter alia, within the framework of the initiative of the United Nations Conference on Trade and Development to promote responsible sovereign lending and borrowing.

See GA Resolution A/RES/66/189, 14 February 2012, para. 3.

[4] International financial rules, though technically non-binding, are often relied upon. The predominance of international soft law in finance does not, however, imply that it is without flaws, especially when compared to the hard law and institutions of international trade, such as WTO law, which allows members to supervise compliance from their trading partners. See C. Brummer, 'Why Soft Law Dominates International Finance—and Not Trade' (2010) 13 J. Int'l Econ. L. 623, 642.

[5] Many Chinese scholars argue that China is the largest creditor nation. See e.g. Y.D. Yu, 'China is the Biggest Victim Facing Global Central Banks Making Banknotes', available at <http://news.cnstock.com/sdfx/201203/1911023.htm> (accessed 4 September 2012); H. Ping, 'Long-term Negative Income and the Distress of the Largest Creditor Nation', available at <http://www.21fd.cn/a/fengmianbaodao/2012042845358.html> (accessed 4 September 2012). However, China is in fact the second largest creditor nation in the world and Japan is the world's top creditor nation according to the IMF; see L. Cuadra, 'List of World's Largest Creditor and Debtor Nations', available at <http://www.financialsense.com/contributors/leslie-cuadra/2011/08/31/list-of-worlds-largest-creditor-and-debtor-nations> (accessed 4 September 2012).

[6] S.S. Ba, 'The Status of Chinese Creditor Nation is Exaggerated Obviously', available at <http://finance.people.com.cn/GB/12322648.html> (accessed 4 September 2012).

On the one hand, the United States has continued to grow a huge current account deficit, and resource product exporting countries (primarily the oil exporting countries) and emerging market countries have held an increasing current account surplus; on the other hand, numerous financial assets issued by the United States and denominated in US dollars, are prevalent in the whole world. In particular, large government bonds issued by the United States have entered into the official foreign currency reserves and bond markets of almost all countries. Thus, global debt circulation between debtor nations and creditor nations is formed.[7] On this basis, there are a handful of 'saving/creditor' nations and a multitude of 'indebted/debtor' nations.[8] One of the most prominent features of the contemporary economy is that public debt in the advanced economies has surged to levels that have not been recorded since the end of the Second World War.[9] After the First World War, the United States and the United Kingdom were major creditor nations and the continental European countries were major debtor nations. In the early 1980s, the United States became one of the world's leading creditor nations. At that time, the leading creditor nations also included Japan, West Germany, Switzerland, and the United Kingdom. However, Japan had become the world's largest creditor nation by the mid-1980s[10] and the United States turned into the biggest debtor nation in the 1990s.[11]

Since the beginning of the twenty-first century, China's economy has made remarkable progress, and its foreign currency reserves have successively broken new records.[12] These reached $853.7 billion at the end of February 2006, surpassing Japan for the first time and ranking first in the world. China held $2.4 trillion of foreign-exchange reserves in 2009, $2.8 trillion in 2010, and in 2011 defended its title once again with foreign-exchange reserves exceeding $3.2 trillion.[13] The financial structure of China's foreign-exchange reserves is kept confidential, but it is generally known that the majority are sovereign bonds;[14] the dominant type is

7 See M.N. Zhang, 'China's Credit under the Imbalance of Global Fortune Distribution' (2010) 9 *China's Economy and Trade* 62–3.

8 See Cuadra (n. 5).

9 See C.M. Reinhart and K.S. Rogoff, 'A Decade of Debt', NBER Working Paper No. 16827 (2011).

10 Y. Shinkai, 'The Internationalization of Finance in Japan' in T. Inoguchi and D.I. Okimoto (eds), *The Political Economy of Japan* Vol. 2 (Stanford University Press, 1988) 249.

11 See D. Burnstein, *YEN! Japan's New Financial Empire and Its Threat to America* (Simon & Schuster, 1988), discussing the transformation of the US from a creditor nation to a debtor nation.

12 The foreign currency reserves and sovereign credits of Hong Kong, Macao, and Taiwan are not included here.

13 China's Foreign Exchange Reserve Over the Years, available at <http://wenku.baidu.com/view/7b8c32858762caaedd33d40d.html> (accessed 9 January 2012); The Foreign Exchange Reserve of Our Country, available at <http://app.finance.ifeng.com/data/mac/month_idx.php?type=016&symbol=01602> (accessed 9 January 2012).

14 Correspondingly, the main form of sovereign debt is bonds, and the percentage of loans is small. For example, bonds account for 79.3% of the euro area total sovereign debt, but only 18% are loans. The EU Firstly Published Quarterly debt data, available at <http://epaper.dfdaily.com/dfzb/html/2012-02/08/content_582681.htm> (accessed 26 February 2012).

US Treasury Securities,[15] which represents a figure approaching $1.2 trillion (making China the third biggest holder of US Treasury Securities after the US Social Security Fund and the Treasury Department). Eurozone Government bonds held by China amount to 800 billion euros. Together, these make China the second largest official creditor nation in the world. In addition, it is estimated that among China's foreign-exchange reserves, 70 per cent are in US dollars, 10 per cent in Japanese Yen, and 20 per cent in euros and pounds.[16]

China also actively offers aid loans to developing countries by using its fiscal revenue.[17] China's interest-free loans come purely from China's state finances and its concessional loans are provided by the Export-Import Bank of China, wholly owned by the Chinese government, through raising principal from the market. 'Since the concessional loan interest is lower than the benchmark interest of the People's Bank of China, the difference is made up by the State as financial subsidies.'[18] China's accumulated foreign aid funds have surpassed 170 billion Yuan in the last ten years.[19]

Its position as the second largest creditor nation determines that the world debt crisis is not only a paralysing force on the debtor nations, but also a grave problem and challenge for China. Most critically, the world debt crisis even endangers the security and stability of the entire international financial system.

II. What can be seen behind China's sovereign credit?

On the one hand, China's sovereign credit comes from foreign exchange reserves, and these reserves come mainly from its trade surplus. Under the existing international trade system, China's environment is being destroyed, resources are becoming exhausted, and natural disasters occur with increasing frequency.[20] The rapid development of China's economy is not only highly dependent on imports, but also relies on exports in order to achieve economic balance. It is generally known that the polarization of income distribution in China is still a

[15] The US Treasury issues government bonds on behalf of the federal government. Government bonds are also known as the national public debt, which is based on the country's credit, and creates a relation of debt and credit through raising social funds domestically and abroad in accordance with the general principles for debt.

[16] China's Foreign Exchange Reserves, available at <http://baike.baidu.com/view/301076.htm> (accessed 10 January 2012).

[17] H. Zhang, *Study on the Legal Problems in Sovereign Debt Restructuring* (China People's University Press, 2007) 3; Information Office of the State Council of the People's Republic of China, China's Foreign Aid, April 2011, Beijing, available at <http://english.gov.cn/official/2011-04/21/content_1849913.htm> (accessed 26 February 2012).

[18] Information Office of the State Council of the People's Republic of China, China's Foreign Aid, April 2011, Beijing, available at <http://english.gov.cn/official/2011-04/21/content_1849913_4.htm> (accessed 26 February 2012).

[19] J.T. Hu, 'Decade of China's Accession Benefits the 1.3 Billion Chinese People and All Peoples in the World', 12 December 2011, available at <http://finance.people.com.cn/GB/16571399.html> (accessed 29 January 2012).

[20] China Should Be Wary of Sovereign Debt Crises, 10 September 2010, available at <http://hk.jrj.com.cn/2010/09/1009108141075.shtml> (accessed 24 January 2012).

problem: some Chinese are notable consumers in the world luxury goods market, while some Chinese cannot afford basic necessities.[21]

On the other hand, China's sovereign credit also comes from its fiscal revenue, which is huge, even in comparison with advanced states. China's fiscal revenue, whose main source is tax, has increased exponentially, amounting respectively to 1.8 trillion Yuan in 2002, 2 trillion Yuan in 2003, 3 trillion Yuan in 2005, 5 trillion Yuan in 2007, 8 trillion Yuan in 2010, and 10.374 trillion Yuan in 2011. The scale of China's sovereign credit is huge in view of its huge fiscal revenue, despite the percentage of its foreign loans to its fiscal revenue being no higher than before.[22] It is generally recognized that the ratio of fiscal revenue to GDP is increasing in China, and correspondingly, the tax burden on Chinese enterprises and individuals is increasing, leading to a wealthy state, with less wealthy individuals.[23] Chinese social spending has not grown correspondingly with fiscal revenue, and Chinese people still have to pay a huge price for medical care, education, pensions and housing. In addition, politicians tend to promise a wide variety of benefits to the population in order to win elections in most electoral politics states. The electoral system makes it difficult to reduce these benefits. Present-day Greece is a typical example. If these governments reduce benefits to vested interests, they will be opposed by stakeholders; this means that governments systematically overspend and do not have the political will or ability to tax more and spend less on social welfare programmes. Over years of public spending, the social welfare systems in these European and American states have remained of high quality, but could also be said to have become a greater burden on, or even an obstacle to, their economic development.[24] However, the pace of China's national income growth is far slower than that of its fiscal revenue and economic growth.[25]

[21] There are many articles involving this issue, see e.g. M.D. Cheng and J.F. Jin, 'A Rational View on China's Current Polarization between the Poor and the Rich' (2012) 4 Contemporary World and Socialism 75; X.H. Wei, 'Understanding the Polarization Between the Rich and the Poor in China' (2012) 5 Journal of Northwest Normal University 1–9; G.G. Liu, 'Reflections on National Wealth, People Rich and Common Prosperity' 10 (2011) Jingji Yanjiu (Economic Research Journal) 1.

[22] The highest proportion of China's Foreign Aid to its fiscal revenue is nearly 7%. See S.H. Cheng et al., 'China's International Aid Policy and Its Implications for Global Governance', Indiana University Research Center for Chinese Politics and Business, Working Paper No. 29, June 2012.

[23] Since 2004, the per capita rate of real wage increases is 16.2%, but the per capita rate of GDP growth is 17.7%, in view of the possiblity of misrepresentation, the per capita rate of real wage increases may be more or less; See G.M. Shen, 'Wage's Inflation' in S.L. Hu (ed.), *Sustainable Growth, China and the World: Strategizing Sustainable Growth* (Jiangsu Art Publishing House, 2012), available at <http://tushu.junshishu.com/Book18742/Content879728.html> (accessed 13 October 2012). The tax ratio has been higher than the rate of GDP growth since 1997, reaching 18.47%. See L.C. Yu, 'Rational Reflection on China's Tax Revenue Surpassing GDP Growth', available at <http://www.chinavalue.net/Finance/Blog/2012-4-13/895361.aspx> (accessed 13 October 2012).

[24] One of the reasons for the European debt crisis is the high quality social welfare systems found in European countries.

[25] Z.W. Chen, 'Why Can Chinese People Not Keep Pace with the GDP Income Growth', 2 August 2008, available at <http://chenzhiwu.blog.sohu.com/96573564.html> (accessed 29 January 2012).

III. Potential risk assumed by China's sovereign credit

1. China's sovereign credits diminished

Sovereign credit and sovereign debt are inseparable. When a sovereign debt crisis arises, sovereign credit cannot escape its harmful effects. The credit currency becomes unstable, and thus causes devaluation risks to sovereign credit. For example, Chinese scholars generally believe that the United States is trying on the one hand to force the Renminbi to appreciate, and on the other to dilute its debt by using its power to print money and inject a large amount of base currency (over-issuing currency) into the market.[26] In short, the United States, with its US dollar hegemony system and ongoing Quantitative Easing (QE) monetary policy, also makes its national debt international. On 5 August 2011, one of the three major credit rating agencies, Standard & Poor's, downgraded the United States' sovereign credit rating from AAA to AA+,[27] which can also make China's credit rating shrink. US debt held by China reached $1164.3 billion as of 30 June 2012, according to the US Treasury Department[28] and thus, depreciation of the US dollar by 10 per cent would mean losses exceeding $100 billion for China. The majority of emerging economies, especially China, are therefore paying for this depreciation, although the other side of the coin is that as their debts denominated in the US dollar also shrink, these economies are mainly creditor countries. At the same time, the credit ratings of most Eurozone countries are also being continuously downgraded, and the euro is becoming increasingly weak and may even collapse.[29] The value of both currency and bonds in US dollars or euros held by China will shrink because of the devaluation of these currencies.[30] In times of sovereign financial crisis and default, the main resolution is sovereign debt restructuring; however, this reorganization will often diminish the value of sovereign credit with a haircut.[31] In short, in a case of sovereign debt crisis facing many countries at the same time, China is exposed to a significant sovereign credit risk of devaluation.

[26] See H. Sheng, 'China Has to Cooperate with the United States on the Wane', available at <http://www.china-review.com/sao.asp?sid=210&id=28624> (accessed 4 September 2012).

[27] See W. Brandimarte and D. Bases, 'United States Loses Prized AAA Credit Rating from S&P', available at <http://www.reuters.com/article/2011/08/06/us-usa-debt-downgrade-idUSTRE7746VF20110806> (accessed 4 September 2012).

[28] Scale and Types of the United States National Debt Market, 23 August 2012, available at <http://news.xinhuanet.com/futures/2012-08/23/c_123618820.htm> (accessed 4 September 2012).

[29] Sovereign Credit Ratings of France, Austria, Malta, Slovakia, Slovenia, Italy, Portugal, Spain, and Cyprus were Degraded by Standard & Poor's on 13 January 2012. See M. Sobolewski and D. Kyriakidou, 'S&P Downgrades Nine Eurozone Countries', available at <http://www.reuters.com/article/2012/01/14/us-eurozone-sp-idUSTRE80C1BC20120114> (accessed 29 January 2012).

[30] See Z.H. Hu, 'Quantitative Easing Aggravates Risk of Western Sovereign Debt Default' (2012) 342 *Chinese Social Sciences Weekly*.

[31] Sovereign debt restructurings (SDRs) are a change to debt contracts that are negotiated between creditors and the debtor state. SDRs or 'workouts' often take the form of reducing the face value of the debt or 'swaps', where new bonds with lower interest rates and longer maturities are exchanged for the defaulted bonds. Such workouts are usually highly discounted and result in a loss for bondholders. See Sovereign Debt Restructuring and International Investment Agreements, IIA Issues Note 2 (2011).

2. Odious debt defence risk

In recent years, the global situation has been unstable and turbulent, and regimes in some states have changed frequently. Certain new rulers wish to use the odious debts doctrine as a defence to refuse to repay the former government's debt. There has been no well-recognized definition of the odious debts concept until now,[32] but it is acknowledged to have originated in 1898 following the Spanish-American War, and it traditionally emphasizes the notions of consent of, and benefit to, the people, and creditor awareness of the odious nature of the debt.[33] At the end of the Spanish-American War, the Spanish insisted that Cuba's debts to Spain be repaid, however, the US government refused this on the basis of the odious debt doctrine. As far as the requirement of 'consent of the people' is concerned, the cases show that a dictatorship or the illegitimacy of a predecessor government does not necessarily lead to the identification of odious debt, but the non-public-interest purpose and utilization of sovereign debt and creditor awareness of the odious nature of the debt are relevant.[34]

The Paris Club of creditor nations (composed of 19 nations including Brazil, Canada, Japan, the United States, and various Western European nations), the international financial community, and creditor nations like the United States have systematically refused to acknowledge the odious debt doctrine in the past.[35] However, on certain occasions they have changed their attitude, which has led to the continued and even growing relevance of the legal doctrine of odious debt today.[36] Therefore, it is likely that the odious debt doctrine will continue to ask and even force lenders to forgive such debts—even if lenders do not think they have a moral, philosophical duty, or an actual legal duty to do so—due to pressure from the international community or for economic or political considerations.

For example, the United States supported Iraq's new regime in applying the odious debt doctrine to its Saddam-era debt, the Bush administration's concern

[32] C.G. Paulus, 'The Evolution of the Concept of Odious Debts' (2008) 68 Zeitschrift für ausländisches öffentliches Recht und Völkerrecht 391; V. Nehru and M. Thomas, 'The Concept of Odious Debt: Some Considerations', Policy Research Working Paper of the World Bank No. 4676 (2008).

[33] See M. Kremer and S. Jayachandran, 'Odious Debt' (2002) 103 *Brookings Policy Brief* (The Brookings Institution) 1; S. Jayachandran and M. Kremer, 'Odious Debt' in C. Jochnick and F.A. Preston (eds), *Sovereign Debt at the Crossroads: Challenges and Proposals for Resolving the Third World Debt Crisis* (Oxford University Press, 2006) 215.

[34] See *Dreyfus Brothers and Co. v. Peru (French Claims against Peru)*, 11 October 1921, Arbitration under Chapter IV of the Hague Convention of 18 October 1907 for the Pacific Settlement of International Disputes, Permanent Court of Arbitration, (1922) 16 AJIL 480–4; Tinoco Arbitration (Great Britain v. Costa Rica), 18 October 1923, (1924) 2 ILR 34–9.

[35] e.g. historically, after the creation of the Peoples' Republic of China in 1949, the Political Consultative Council of China announced, on 29 September 1949, that: 'The Central Government of the Peoples' Republic of China will examine the contracts and agreements entered into by the prior Governments with foreign Governments and then decide depending on their contents to acknowledge, annul, revise them, or to enter into new consultations.' But of course, China's claim was not supported by the Western creditor countries, and the result was an economic embargo lasting many years. However, the Paris Club is not monolithic. Norway recognized this problem and took action.

[36] See O. Lienau, *Rethinking Sovereign Debt: The Politics of Reputation in the Twentieth Century*, available at <http://www.nyls.edu/user_files/1/3/4/15/276/LienauPaper.pdf> (accessed 29 May 2013).

being that the Hussein government used the money to buy arms or build palaces. Under the guidance of this doctrine, US Congress agreed to cancel all of Iraq's $3.5 billion debt to the United States, after persuading other Paris Club and non-Paris Club creditor nations to cancel 80 per cent of their loans to Iraq.[37] China is not a member of the Paris Club, but considering these circumstances, also cancelled 80 per cent of its Iraq credit, and as a result, China's total debt relief to Iraq reached $6.8 billion.[38] Tunisia's new government has demanded an audit of Tunisia's external debts inherited from the Ben Ali regime to distinguish between legitimate external debts which should be honoured and the odious external debts which will be repudiated. Belgium has declared that it will cancel all the debts that are found to be odious following the debt audit.[39]

Libya's new regime has declared that it will not repay its debt if the contract was entered into by bribery,[40] and this declaration may have far-reaching implications for China's sovereign credits to Libya. Furthermore, some scholars and UNCTAD have also proposed that odious debt issues are relevant to Africa's debt.[41] Although this does not target China, it should remind China of this risk in view of its huge foreign loans to African countries. In short, China's sovereign credit in Africa may also face the risk of odious debt defence at present and in the future. Thus, the Chinese government must pay attention to the purpose and utilization of its loans, and be sure not to lend when it suspects the odious nature of its loan, i.e. use of the loan for an odious personal purpose or to oppress the people.

C. Assessment of the Sovereign Creditor's Principles

This part of the chapter examines the sovereign lending principles raised by UNCTAD with reference to China's practice as a lender to other states.

[37] 149 Cong. Rec. E2450, E2452 (daily edn. 23 November 2003), statement of Rep. Leach: 'we should press vigorously for Saddam-era debt . . . to be written off'; 149 Cong. Rec. H8470, H8470 (daily edn, 23 September 2003), statement of Rep. Maloney, speaking in support of H.R. 2482, the 'Iraqi Freedom from Debt Act'; Press Release, the White House, President's Statement on Iraqi Debt, 21 November 2004, encouraging non-Paris Club creditor nations to agree to debt reduction for Iraq.

[38] China's State Council Approved Releasing 80 per cent of Iraq's Debt to China, available at <http://www.china.com.cn/international/zhuanti/ylkdxycj/txt/2010-02/02/content_19356179.htm> (accessed 18 January 2012).

[39] See L. Ndikumana, 'Tunisia leading the fight against "Odious debts"', available at <http://triplecrisis.com/tunisia-leading-the-fight-against-odious-debts/> (accessed 7 September 2012).

[40] 'Beijing Was Stunned: Gadhafi Fell from Power, But New Regime of Libya Used This Tactic on China', available at <http://www.51junshi.com/article/201108/41023_3.html> (accessed 21 January 2012).

[41] Some scholars argue that African governments should repudiate these 'odious debts' from which their people derived no benefit, and that the international community should assist in this effort; see L. Ndikumana and J.K. Boyce, *Africa's Odious Debts: How Foreign Loans and Capital Flight Bled a Continent* (Radical International Publishing, 2011); see 'New UNCTAD Study Makes Case for African Debt Write-Off', UNCTAD/PRESS/PR/2004/031 30/09/04. Because the development objective was not implemented, the report argued that most official lending to Africa and much of the debt of countries with profligate regimes that were of geopolitical/strategic interest is considered 'odious'.

I. Agency and public interest

The core of the agency and public interest principle lies in two points: the first is that lenders should recognize that government officials who are responsible for sovereign borrowing represent their state, and an agency relationship exists between the government official and their country, in other words, the debtor nation. Therefore, in principle, a change in government of the debtor country should not affect repayment of the sovereign debt, because the legal consequences of the agent's action can be attributable to the principal, i.e. the state. The second is that lenders should confirm whether a government and its officials in fact have legal agency rights and are acting in the state's and its citizens' interests by due diligence, and not for their own benefit, otherwise the legitimacy of the debt will be challenged. The basic rationale behind this principle is the principal-agent theory.[42] Therefore, if the government and its officials do not have valid power (including overstepping their authority) to indebt their country, or if other irregularities are present such as instances of bribery or corruption, including complicity between creditors and sovereign debtor in the borrowing process, the principle of agency and public interest will be violated.[43] In cases of unauthorized agency or agency *ultra vires*, or agency against the interests of the principal, the act of agency is invalid between the principal and the third party without ratification by the principal. Therefore, if the agent signed a contract with the counterpart (third party) under such circumstances, *pacta sunt servanda* should be applied only if the principal recognizes agency behaviour at a later date.[44] However, when the counterpart has acted in good faith, for example they do not reasonably know that the agent has no authority or is acting in excess of their authority, or is violating the benefits of the principal, the contract will be regarded as effective in law.[45]

As previously mentioned, the traditional odious debts doctrine emphasizes that the odious debt has no consent from the people, provides no benefits to the people, and there is creditor awareness of the odious nature of the debt.[46] Therefore, once

[42] See J. Oyola and M. Sudreau, Ch. 10 of this volume.

[43] Regarding bribery and corruption, Buchheit and Gulati said that:

> ... lenders must not suborn or consciously ignore conduct inconsistent with the fiduciary duties of the government officials contracting the debt. The fact that a governing regime in the debtor country may control the law-enforcement and judicial functions in the country, thus making exposure of government corruption unlikely or inconsequential, does not diminish the lender's responsibility.

This will undoubtedly increase the burden on the lender. See L.C. Buchheit and G.M. Gulati, 'Responsible Sovereign Lending and Borrowing' (2010) 73 Law & Cont. Probs 63, 77.

[44] See Z.J. Wang, *Principles on Law of Obligation*, Vol. 1 (China University of Political Science and Law Press, 2001), 303–4.

[45] This kind of agency is known as 'apparent agency'. The Chinese Contract Law has a similar provision. e.g. 'If an actor has no power of agency, oversteps the power of agency, or the power of agency has expired and yet concludes a contract in the principal's name, and the counterpart has reasons to trust that the actor has the power of agency, the act of agency shall be effective.' See Contract Law of the People's Republic of China, art. 49. Date Issued: 15 March 1999; Effective date: 1 October 1999; Issuing authority: National People's Congress, available at <http://en.pkulaw.cn/display.aspx?cgid=21651&lib=law> (accessed 26 February 2012).

[46] See Kremer and Jayachandran (n. 33); Jayachandran and Kremer (n. 33) 215–16.

these factors have been confirmed, it will become difficult for the creditor to collect its money if the new regime of the debtor nation insists on not repaying. If creditors bribe the agent of the sovereign debtor, which would necessarily cause damage to the public interest of the sovereign debtor, the result is the same. The Second Draft of the UNCTAD Principles adds the wording 'public interest' in order to express its importance. In fact, 'public interest' simply means the benefits for the principal, i.e. the state and its people, in the process of sovereign borrowing.

Therefore, the agency and public interest principle urges the creditor to investigate and confirm not only whether the agent is properly appointed or has due authority and is acting for the public interest of the sovereign debtor, but also whether the borrowing benefits the principals (citizens of the debtor nation). In addition, bribery, corruption, or any complicity is not permitted between the creditor and the debtor. As mentioned before, it is not enough to argue that a debt is odious purely because it was lent to a so-called odious government, but it is feasible to argue that a debt is odious because the lender knows the illegitimate purpose and use of the loan.[47] Thus, the principle reminds sovereign lenders to modify their lending practices to help to ensure that they do not knowingly make loans to sovereigns who use loan proceeds for purposes that do not benefit their citizens. On the basis of Meron's research, Buchheit and Gulati brilliantly point out that 'questioning, sometimes years or decades after the fact, the authority of a government official to bind the state to a particular debt has been a popular method for sovereign borrowers to disavow obligations while attempting to preserve some shred of legal respectability'.[48] The most famous case in this respect in China is *Russell Jackson et al. v. The People's Republic of China*. Plaintiffs acting as bondholders made a claim to the People's Republic of China for bonds issued by the Qing Dynasty in 1911. One of China's defences was that:

> The loan was a foreign debt contracted by the Qing government on the eve of its collapse, or on 20 May 1911, with a banking syndicate of the four countries of Britain, France, Germany and the United States in the name of building the Huguang railroad, but actually was a last-ditch struggle to maintain its reactionary rule. It was also a product of an act of collusion between international imperialism and the Qing government and an intensified effort to oppress and exploit Chinese people.[49]

Certainly, the sovereign lender can voluntarily decide to cancel the debt instead of being urged to do so by the debtor nation. For example, on 2 October 2006, Norway unilaterally cancelled $80 million of debt for five developing countries (Ecuador, Egypt, Jamaica, Peru and Sierra Leone) because the debt was harmful to the development, or not beneficial to the public interest, of these countries.[50]

[47] See M. Waibel, *Sovereign Defaults before International Courts and Tribunals* (Cambridge University Press, 2011) 137.

[48] See Buchheit and Gulati (n. 43) 78.

[49] See J.V. Feinerman, 'Odious Debt, Old and New: The Legal Intellectual History of An Idea' (2007) 70 Law & Cont. Probs 193, fn 24.

[50] See 'Norway Sets Standard for Rich Countries', available at <http://www.jubileedebtcampaign.org.uk/Norway3720sets3720standard3720for3720rich3720countries+2423.twl> (accessed 2 January 2012).

Norway offered to lend these poor countries money to buy Norwegian-built ships during the 'Ship Export Campaign' between 1976 and 1980 in Norway, but many of the ships had no useful value to these countries, not to mention to their development. Therefore, the Norwegian government admitted the failure of its loans and assumed 'a shared responsibility for the debts that followed'.[51] Norway offered to accept responsibility for its irresponsible lending and its unilateral repudiation policies set a good example for creditor nations.

Moreover, it seems that the implications listed in the 'Consolidated Version' about the first principle are insufficient. The agency and public interest principle should also be considered from the creditor country's side, the responsibility of the creditor's agents (the government and its officials) to its state and its citizens should also be emphasized. As far as China's lending is concerned, the Chinese government should pay more attention to its state and public interest from this particular perspective.

It should be mentioned at this point, that the present author considers that Principle 3, namely 'Due authorization', could be covered by the first principle, and therefore will not repeat it as a separate principle here.

II. Due disclosure of information

According to Principle 2, the lender should fulfil the duty of disclosure of its own information to its sovereign debtor respecting due diligence standards. This principle is easy to understand for it aims to ensure that the sovereign borrower understands each of the terms of loan, and to guarantee that the decision of the sovereign borrower is a reasonable one based on full information about the loan.

Due disclosure of information is common practice of commercial banks in China. The Banking Supervision Law of the People's Republic of China further regulates that banks (including commercial banks and policy banks, such as the Export-Import Bank of China) 'failing to disclose the information as required' will be punished according to the circumstances of the case.[52] The deterrence of these punishments should guarantee the transparency of bank credit.

On this basis, the China Banking Regulatory Commission tailors the Measures for the Information Disclosure of Commercial Banks to the purpose of subjecting commercial banks to the regulation of the market, regulating commercial banks on their information disclosure behaviour, effectively safeguarding the legitimate rights and interests of creditors, and promoting the safe, stable, and highly efficient operation of commercial banks.[53] The Chinese Government White Paper on Foreign Aid was first published in April 2011 after 60 years of giving foreign aid,

[51] See Norway Sets Standard for Rich Countries (n. 50).

[52] Banking Supervision Law of the People's Republic of China, effective date 1 February 2004, amended date 31 October 2006, issuing authority Standing Committee of the National People's Congress, art. 46, available at <http://en.pkulaw.cn/display.aspx?cgid=80997&lib=law> (accessed 26 February 2012).

[53] Measures for the Information Disclosure of Commercial Banks, issued by China Banking Regulatory Commission, date issued and effective date 3 July 2007.

and represents an important measure to make Chinese sovereign loans in the form of foreign aid more transparent. For a specific loan, the sovereign lender must disclose loan information on the basis of the actual situation of the sovereign borrower, enabling sovereign borrowers to make reasonable decisions based on the disclosed information.

III. Responsible credit decisions based on assessing the borrower's repayment capacity

Principle 4 aims to guarantee that credit is based on the reasonable repayment capacity of the sovereign debtor and full economic considerations, thus avoiding excessive lending. In fact, the present author deems that this principle arises from both historical and current lessons. Industrialized nations were eager to lend during the Cold War in order to secure the political allegiance of corrupt and totalitarian regimes.[54] At least 70 developing countries took on too much debt (much of it at high interest rates) in the 1970s, and a very serious debt overload crisis squeezed many developing nations between 1982 and 1990.[55] Nowadays, instead, some developed states have also engaged in reckless or excessive borrowing, putting themselves heavily in debt. If the debt ratio is expressed in relation to GDP (debt/GDP), it is recognized that high debt ratios or excessive sovereign debt dominate most Eurozone governments, and the sharp increase of debt as a consequence of the financial crisis compared with those at normal times cannot change this argument. Eurostat published its statistics on 21 October 2011 and alleged that the debt to GDP ratio of the 17 Eurozone governments increased from 79.8 per cent in 2009 to 85.4 per cent in 2010, and to 87.4 per cent in the first three quarters of 2011. Greece has the highest debt ratio, at 144.9 per cent, while Italy's amounts to 118.4 per cent.[56] However, the internationally accepted normal standard of debt ratio to GDP is 60 per cent.[57] The debt ratio to GDP of the United States reached 115 per cent by February 2012,[58] but the Obama administration persuaded Congress to raise the federal debt ceiling by $2.1 trillion to $16.4

[54] R. Sarkar, *Development Law and International Finance* (Springer, 1999) 93–8.

[55] See W.A. Lovett, *World Trade Rivalry: Trade Equity and Competing Industrial Policies* (Lexington Books, 1987) 137–66; see also M.D. Bordo and B. Eichengreen (eds.), *A Retrospective on the Bretton Woods System: Lessons for International Monetary Reform* (University of Chicago Press, 1993) 443–4; P. B. Kenen (ed.), *Managing the World Economy: Fifty Years After Bretton Woods* (Institute for International Economics, 1994); A.F. Lowenfeld, *International Economic Law* (Oxford University Press, 2008), 668–99, 719–48.

[56] Euro-area Government Debt Ratio Ascends to 85.4 per cent in 2010, Rising to Record High, available at <http://international.caixun.com/content/20111021/NE03015j.html> (accessed 21 January 2012); EU Published Quarterly debt data for the first time, available at <http://epaper.dfdaily.com/dfzb/html/2012-02/08/content_582681.htm> (accessed 26 February 2012).

[57] The ratio of gross government debt to GDP must not exceed 60% at the end of the preceding fiscal year, see PROTOCOL on the excessive deficit procedure, Art. 1 in Treaty on European Union (92/C 191/01), available at <http://eur-lex.europa.eu/en/treaties/dat/11992M/htm/11992M.html#0001000001> (accessed 13 September 2012).

[58] See United States Public Debt, available at <http://en.wikipedia.org/wiki/United_States_public_debt> (accessed 26 February 2012).

trillion on 3 August 2011.[59] 'Historically, high leverage episodes have been associated with slower economic growth and a higher incidence of default or, more generally, restructuring of public and private debts.'[60] The irresponsible debtor nation governments encouraged excessive borrowing so that their short-term interest could be served in avoiding sovereign debt default, in other words, rolling over old debts with new borrowing. It is therefore not fair to place too much blame with the creditor nation; this principle should primarily be based on the disclosure and transparency of debtor nations, and their willingness to curb their debt size. Both the assessment of repayment capacity of the sovereign debtors and the final lending decision of the creditor nation depend on the due information disclosure of the sovereign debtor.[61]

If motivated exclusively by commercial objectives, the desire of the sovereign lenders was to receive more than the cost of the loan back from the sovereign borrower, and therefore, they should have every economic incentive to investigate and realistically assess the borrower's capacity and willingness to repay the debt. Whether sovereign debt restructuring or outright default, which may occur in both developing and developed countries, demonstrates that sovereign debt is even less secure than private debt, which is usually secured against housing and other collaterals, not only a credit guarantee.

However, as regards bilateral government-to-government credit which also may be granted for other motives—such as stimulating exports of capital goods from the creditor country, acquiring geopolitical influence over the debtor, assuring long-term access to raw materials or energy supplies, or inducing the borrower to purchase military hardware from the lender[62]—these objectives 'may induce the lender to perform a gauzier or more wishful assessment of the borrower's repayment capacity as the predicate for a loan that otherwise would not have been granted',[63] in other words, these measures may indebt the sovereign borrower excessively and cause it to go bankrupt. Principle 4 therefore advises that a lender should inquire into the debtor's overall debt servicing capacity prior to disbursement of the proceeds in case of over-lending or borrowing. The agent of the sovereign lender is uniquely responsible for ensuring the sovereign lender's best interests in the longer term, which means not lending excessively and ensuring that its loans can be repaid.

This Principle reminds us of China's foreign aid policy without political conditions on recipient countries. China's lending is not based on political conditions such as democracy, human rights, and good governance, because the Chinese government considers that the insistence on political conditions by creditor

[59] An Agreement on Debt Ceiling Concluded in the United States, Raising At Least $2.1 Trillion, available at <http://news.sina.com.cn/o/2011-08-02/154022920995.shtml> (accessed 12 January 2012).

[60] See Reinhart and Rogoff (n. 9) 2.

[61] Principle 11, Disclosure and publication, stipulates sovereign debtor's obligation on transparency.

[62] On the topic of government-to-government debt, also see A. Gelpern, 'Odious, Not Debt' (2007) 70 Law & Cont. Probs 81.

[63] See Buchheit and Gulati (n. 43) 78.

nations, known as 'conditionality', should no longer be viewed as appropriate in an international aid programme.[64] China adheres to equality and mutual benefit, paying attention to practical results from its loans, does not impose political conditions on recipient countries,[65] and any state friendly with China that is not subject to UN sanctions can be granted a loan. The disagreement lies in the political nature of some developed states' lending, where they hope to change political regimes and the human rights situation in recipient countries. But China's foreign aid lending is for the most part carried out with economic aims, in the hope that it will promote bilateral economic development. Comparatively, it seems that China has drawn lessons from previous instances of foreign aid to Vietnam and Albania which was made for purely political reasons, but failed to yield positive results.[66]

China's foreign aid lending includes interest-free loans and concessional loans as follows, which can show China's lending, rather than involving political interference, aims at promoting the economic development of the recipient countries:

> Interest-free loans are mainly used to help recipient countries to construct public facilities and launch projects to improve people's livelihood. The tenure of such loans is usually 20 years, including five years of use, five years' grace and ten years of repayment. Currently, interest-free loans are mainly provided to developing countries with relatively good economic conditions.
>
> Concessional loans are mainly used to help recipient countries to undertake productive projects generating both economic and social benefits and large and medium-sized infrastructure projects, or to provide complete plant, mechanical and electrical products, technical services and other materials... [T]he period of repayment is usually 15 to 20 years.[67]

On the premise of respecting the independence and sovereignty of other developing countries, China's foreign aid lending must be used to benefit people in the recipient country, and make a real contribution to long-term local development. On this issue, China is not necessarily in conflict with major countries offering foreign aid loans and multilateral financial institutions around the world. Therefore, it should be pointed out that China's foreign aid imposing no political

[64] See D. Haroz, 'China In Africa: Symbiosis or Exploitation?' (2011) 35 Fletcher Forum of World Affairs 65, 78; T. Cheng, 'The Reasons are not Complicated for China's Aid to Africa', *Global Times*, 27 August 2012, available at <http://news.xinhuanet.com/world/2012-08/27/c_123635783.htm> (accessed 13 September 2012).

[65] Information Office of the State Council of the People's Republic of China, China's Foreign Aid, April 2011, Beijing, available at <http://english.gov.cn/official/2011-04/21/content_1849913.htm> (accessed 26 February 2012).

[66] China's Foreign Aid 60 Years: Gain and Loss, 1 August 2012, available at <http://www.360doc.com/content/12/0801/10/2406619_227615151.shtml> (accessed 13 October 2012).

[67] Information Office of the State Council of the People's Republic of China, China's Foreign Aid, April 2011, Beijing, available at <http://english.gov.cn/official/2011-04/21/content_1849913.htm> (accessed 26 February 2012). One of the most famous foreign aid projects in Chinese history is the Tanzania-Zambia railway, which was based on the Agreement on Building Tanzania-Zambia Railway, signed by China, Tanzania, and Zambia on 5 September 1967. China provided interest-free loans of 988 m Yuan, without attaching any conditions. China finally exempted 50% of the debt. See Tanzania-Zambia railway, available at <http://baike.baidu.com/view/75336.htm> (accessed 29 January 2012).

conditions does not mean imposing no economic conditions, for example the recipient countries cannot violate the economic use of the aid loan.

China's foreign aid lending mainly and ultimately comes from China's taxpayers and/or surplus, thus, other principles should be emphasized to ensure the safety and legitimacy of its loans without any political conditions. The Chinese government should certainly make responsible credit decisions based on assessments of the borrower's repayment capacity and make sure that the aid it grants is used to benefit the people of the recipient country.

IV. Full investigation in project financing

Financing projects in the debtor country, particularly infrastructure projects, brings a special set of responsibilities for the lender. The lender's responsibility for full investigation and surveillance extends to the whole process of the financing of the project, including the reasonably foreseeable consequences. 'A lender is therefore under a duty to consider factors such as the likely environmental effects of the project, the consequence of the project for indigenous peoples in affected areas, possible damage to archaeological or culture heritage sites and so forth.'[68] In addition, details of how the loan will be used should be provided and the quality of the project itself should be guaranteed. The Chinese government devotes 60 per cent of its concessional loans to economic infrastructure projects.[69] Therefore, China must attach importance to the monitoring and assessment of lending effectiveness in order to achieve lending targets. This monitoring and assessment must be systematic and transparent. China should assess the combined effect of economic, social, and environmental aspects of the financed project during the whole process, which will help to decide whether the lending should be further increased.[70] At this point, the Export-Import Bank of China, one of its business activities being to offer Chinese government concessional loans to developing states, has made some useful explorations. For example, in 2007, the Export-Import Bank of China issued a document entitled 'Guidelines for Environmental and Social Impact Assessments of the China Export and Import Bank's Loan Projects', which has detailed and strict requirements on environmental impact assessment.[71]

[68] See Buchheit and Gulati (n. 43) 79. The two authors drew this conclusion from the Equator Principles, a list of standards created by the International Finance Corporation that should be applied to any project finance loans.

[69] Information Office of the State Council of the People's Republic of China, China's Foreign Aid, April 2011, Beijing, available at <http://english.gov.cn/official/2011-04/21/content_1849913.htm> (accessed 26 February 2012).

[70] There are indeed some reports complaining of violations of human rights and the environment of projects financed by China. See e.g. D. Smith, Workers claim abuse as China adds Zimbabwe to its scramble for Africa, World news, *The Guardian*, 3 January 2012, available at <http://www.guardian.co.uk/world/2012/jan/02/china-zimbabwe-workers-abuse> (accessed 29 January 2012); P. Bosshard, 'China's Environmental Footprint in Africa', SAIS Working Papers in African Studies (2008).

[71] China Export and Import Bank, Guidelines for Environmental and Social Impact Assessments of the China Export and Import Bank's Loan Projects, 28 August 2007, available at <http://www.globalwitness.org/sites/default/files/library/Chinese%20guidelines%20EN.pdf> (accessed 26 February 2012).

The 'Full Investigation in Project Financing' principle increases the lender's liability, but all things considered, is beneficial to both sides. The Chinese government should keep firmly in mind that: 'Observers of sovereign lending patterns have long recognized that credit financing of visibly beneficial projects in a debtor country stand a better chance of being repaid, particularly if the country undergoes a dramatic change in its governing regime between the date of disbursement and the maturity date.'[72]

V. Abiding by UN sanctions

According to Article 2.5 of the UN Charter, 'all Members shall give the United Nations every assistance in any action it takes in accordance with the present Charter, and shall refrain from giving assistance to any state against which the United Nations is taking preventive or enforcement action'.[73] With respect to the effect of sanctions imposed on a regime in terms of its lending practices, Buchheit and Gulati have argued that: 'If international economic sanctions are imposed on a debtor country, any lending transactions that violate those sanctions should be treated as void, regardless of whether the lender's own jurisdiction has implemented the sanctions into domestic law.'[74] In fact, the so-called international economic sanctions here are unclear. Different kinds of international economic sanctions exist, and are implemented by one or more countries, regional international organizations, or the UN Security Council, generally through adopting measures in fiscal, financial, commercial, marine, aerial, and petrolic fields.[75] Although UN sanctions must be adhered to by every member state, states are not obliged to follow unilateral sanctions even though it may be argued that the sanctioned regime is brutal and repressive because it 'does not evolve around a consensus-building process and therefore creates no legal norm or obligation for members of the international community'.[76] In addition, unilateral sanctions may also violate international law. For example, unilateral sanctions without authorization from the WTO Dispute Settlement Body are illegal within WTO law, and are also contentious or not advocated in other international law fields. Therefore, the Chinese government does not support unilateral sanctions on Iran and does not refuse to do business with Iran. In addition, the Chinese government considers the prevention of the proliferation of weapons, and normal economic and energy

[72] See Buchheit and Gulati (n. 43) 78.

[73] UN Charter, Art. 2.5, available at <http://www.un.org/en/documents/charter/chapter1.shtml> (accessed 26 February 2012).

[74] See Buchheit and Gulati (n. 43) 80.

[75] Y.L. Shao, 'International Economic Sanctions: Historical Development and Theoretical Analysis', Dissertation on file at Academy of Social Science, Shanghai (2008) 8.

[76] See The AALCO Secretariat 29 C, Rizal Marg, Diplomatic Enclave, Chanakyapuri, New Delhi—110 021 (India) 4, 'Extraterritorial Application of National Legislation: Sanctions Imposed against Third Parties', available at <http://www.aalco.int/51stsession/Sanctions%20Brief%202012.pdf> (accessed 13 September 2012).

cooperation to represent two separate issues that cannot be combined.[77] Therefore, China has backed UN Security Council resolutions calling on Iran to halt uranium enrichment activities, while resisting economic pressure arising from the unilateral sanctions of the United States.[78] Resolution No. 1929, adopted in 2010, is the most severe Security Council Sanction Resolution on Iran in history, but it does not include an oil embargo; just the opposite, it underlines that it is not intended to affect legal economic activities.[79] Therefore, China opposes the US Iran sanctions bill, signed by US President Barack Obama on 31 December 2011, calling for new sanctions against financial institutions doing business with Iran's state banking institutions.[80] Concretely, 'China will impose only those sanctions required by applicable UN Security Council resolutions, but not impose sanctions beyond those specifically mandated.'[81] In short, China must follow UN sanctions, including not lending to a regime that is suffering UN sanctions, but has no duty to follow extra sanctions by states outside UN authorization. The 'Abiding by United Nations Sanctions Principle' is very clear and operable, and therefore may represent explicit guidance for China on its lending.

All in all, violating the 'Abiding by United Nations Sanctions Principle' will mean violating international law obligations. The 'Abiding by United Nations Sanctions Principle' will influence the lending practice of creditor nations and punish those who make loans that violate this principle. But it needs to be clear that the creditor nation has no duty to abide by unilateral sanctions taken by states or organizations other than the United Nations.

The 'Abiding by United Nations Sanctions Principle', together with the 'Agency and Public Interest Principle' can 'position a new government of a state that has previously been victimized by irresponsible sovereign lending/borrowing to seek relief from those debts without sacrificing its (the new government's) reputation in the financial markets or provoking its bilateral creditors to withhold further credit'.[82] These two principles cause China to be careful when considering loaning funds to nations under UN sanctions or irresponsible debtor governments.

VI. Debt restructurings in good faith and with cooperative spirit

Although debt servicing is a high priority for most sovereign borrowers to legitimate debt, and the sovereign borrower would repay the money to avoid affecting its

[77] W.M. Liu, Foreign Ministry of China, 'China rejects U.S. unilateral sanctions on third country', 12 June 2012, available at <http://english.peopledaily.com.cn/90883/7843885.html> (accessed 13 September 2012).

[78] 'China's Wen Defends Iran oil, Warns on Nuclear', available at <http://ajw.asahi.com/article/asia/china/AJ201201200007> (accessed 23 January 2012).

[79] See UN Security Council Resolution 1929 (2010), adopted by the Security Council at its 6335th meeting, on 9 June 2010, S/RES/1929(2010), para. 18.

[80] 'China Says US Sanctions for Iran Ties "Unreasonable"', available at <http://www.banglanews24.com/English/detailsnews.php?nssl=23dd1052628bd01a4146b88619ec601e&nttl=2012011730780> (accessed 23 January 2012).

[81] See K. Katzman, 'Iran Sanctions', Congressional Research Service, 7–5700 (2011) 35.

[82] See Buchheit and Gulati (n. 43) 67.

reputation in the sovereign lending and borrowing market,[83] the phenomenon of sovereign borrowers unable to repay is also a frequent occurrence. In these circumstances, however, a sovereign borrower cannot go bankrupt in the same way as an enterprise,[84] but similarly, the terms of their credit may be modified through renegotiation to restructure the debt. This process is called 'sovereign debt restructuring'. There also exist creditors who refuse to consent to debt restructuring, creating what is known as the 'creditor-holdout problem'.[85]

This principle aims in particular at 'vulture funds', which purchase sovereign debt when it is of a very low value before or after restructuring, and then file suits to increase the value of their investment instead of attending sovereign debt renegotiating and restructuring. They demand that the debt instruments be honoured fully, with the threat that otherwise they will initiate the high costs of litigation.[86] This kind of action impedes sovereign debt restructuring. Kevin P. Gallagher notes, for example, that as many as 158 suits were filed in the United States by vulture funds before July 2010.[87] Many bondholders have initiated international arbitral proceedings under the Italy-Argentina BIT.[88] By this method they expect to obtain more than creditors attending sovereign debt restructuring, but their actions will probably impede sovereign debt restructuring and undermine the ability of nations to recover from financial crises. It should also be mentioned that state-to-state debt can be utilized by vulture funds. In 1979, Zambia borrowed $15 million from Romania to purchase tractors. Donegal International Ltd, a private investment fund, purchased Zambia's debt from Romania in 1998 and sued Zambia in a British court in 2005 for more than $55 million. The court finally awarded $15.5 Million to Donegal.[89]

The principle of debt restructuring in good faith and with cooperative spirit can also establish prompt and fair debt restructuring as an officially accepted option. It seems that this principle originates from domestic law and can be guaranteed to a greater extent when the borrowers are private entities in domestic law. For example, according to the 'Law of the People's Republic of China on

[83] See M. Kremer and S. Jayachandran, 'Odious Debt' (2006) 96 Am. Econ. Rev. 82, 85.

[84] 'LDCs (less developed countries) don't go bankrupt… the infrastructure doesn't go away, the productivity of the people doesn't go away, the natural resources don't go away. And so their assets always exceed their liabilities, which is the technical reason for bankruptcy. And that's very different from a company.' See W.B. Wriston, 'Was I exacting? Sure. Was I occasionally sarcastic? Of course' (1987) 21 *Institutional Investor* 6, 17.

[85] K.P. Gallagher, 'The New Vulture Culture: Sovereign debt restructuring and trade and investment treaties', the Ideas Working Paper Series, Paper No. 02/2011 (2011) 14, available at <http://ase.tufts.edu/gdae/publications/GallagherSovereignDebt.pdf> (accessed 27 February 2012).

[86] H. Thompson and D. Runciman, 'Sovereign Debt and Private Creditors: New Legal Sanction or the Enduring Power of States?' (2006) 11 New Political Economy 541.

[87] J. Hornbeck, 'Argentina's Defaulted Sovereign Debt: Dealing with the "Holdouts"', United States Congressional Research Service (July 2010).

[88] e.g. *Giovanna A. Beccara and ors v. Argentine Republic*, ICSID Case No. ARB/07/5. *Giovanni Alemanni and ors v. Argentine Republic*, ICSID Case No. ARB/07/8, and *Giordano Alpi and ors v. Argentine Republic*, ICSID Case No. ARB/08/9. See ICSID cases, Argentina as respondent, available at <http://icsid.worldbank.org/ICSID/FrontServlet> (accessed 26 February 2012).

[89] See *Donegal International Ltd v. Zambia* [2007] EWHC (Comm) 197, paras 1, 6, 23, and 82 (England).

Enterprise Bankruptcy', debt restructuring should be conducted under the supervision of the court hearing the bankruptcy case, and credits should be grouped in the draft debt restructuring plan.[90] The relevant creditors shall be grouped according to the specific classification and vote on the draft plan.[91] Where some voting groups do not agree to a draft of debt restructuring plan, the court can approve the plan in response to the debtor if the plan meets specific requirements.[92] Therefore, China has a relatively high success rate of debt restructuring in domestic law. A debt restructuring plan as approved by the court has binding force on the debtor and all the creditors.[93] By contrast, when sovereign debt restructuring involves a creditor nation, there is no international dispute settlement body to guarantee each creditor's participation and cooperation. Thus, there is challenge to implementing the 'Debt Restructurings in Good Faith and with Cooperative Spirit Principle' with reference to sovereign lending and borrowing.

D. Legalization of Sovereign Lending and Borrowing Dispute Settlement

I. From barbarism to civilization

Where sovereign lending and borrowing disputes arise, peaceful settlement of these disputes should be a fundamental principle under existing international law. As a creditor nation, China should consider how to settle this kind of dispute between it and the debtor nation. Historically, when a sovereign debtor defaulted on its debt, a creditor nation often resorted to war. In the nineteenth century, for example, European powers often used military might or direct administration of the local economy, typically under threat of force, so-called 'gunboat diplomacy', to enforce the payment of debts. Some authors describe such measures, used during the period 1870–1913, as 'supersanctions', namely, the use of direct military pressure or the direct imposition of foreign political or financial control.[94] As Mitchener and Weidenmier noted, 'it was estimated that such sanctions were imposed in roughly one third of cases of sovereign default in that period', and 'all nations that defaulted on sovereign debt ran the risk of gunboats blockading their ports or creditor nations seizing fiscal control of their country'.[95] History is full of such events. H.B. Samuel

[90] Law of the People's Republic of China on Enterprise Bankruptcy, art. 82, date issued 27 August 2006, effective 1 June 2007, issuing authority Standing Committee of the National People's Congress, available at <http://en.pkulaw.cn/display.aspx?cgid=78895&lib=law> (accessed 27 February 2012).

[91] Law on Enterprise Bankruptcy (n. 90) art. 84.2.

[92] Law on Enterprise Bankruptcy (n. 90) arts 87.5, 113.1, 109, 113.3.

[93] Law on Enterprise Bankruptcy (n. 90) art. 92.

[94] See K.J. Mitchener and M.D. Weidenmier, 'Supersanctions and Sovereign Debt Repayment', NBER Working Paper 11472 (2005); H.S. Scott, *International Finance: Law and Regulation* (Sweet & Maxwell, 2004) 550; N. Roubini and B. Setser, *Bailouts or Bail-ins? Responding to Financial Crises in Emerging Markets* (Peterson Institute for International Economics, 2004) 290; M. Rahnama-Moghadam et al., 'The Clubs of London & Paris' (1998) 53(4) Dispute Resolution Journal 73.

[95] Mitchener and Weidenmier (n. 94).

points out that 'Britain alone led debt-related military interventions or direct administration of the local economy in Mexico (1861), Egypt (1882), Greece (1887), Venezuela (1902), Serbia (1904), and Guatemala (1913)'.[96] Britain, France, and Spain carried out military interventions, and France even ultimately imposed direct re-colonization on Mexico due to the default of the Mexican Benito Juárez government.[97] Britain, Germany, and Italy shelled Venezuelan cities due to Venezuelan sovereign default.[98] This chain of events led to the principle of the Calvo and Drago Doctrines, which were not accepted by most Western countries at that time.

Article 2 of the UN Charter is generally viewed as a cornerstone of post-Second World War international order, and develops the principle of 'prohibiting threat of force and use of force' into a fundamental provision of international law.[99] According to Article 2 of the UN Charter, beyond all doubt, a creditor nation is prohibited from making threats of force and using force to collect a debt or to enforce awards. Therefore, in terms of debt, there has been a historical trend and progression from using force to employing legal means to solve disputes.

Western banks, the governments of creditor nations, and multilateral organizations such as the IMF, the Bank for International Settlements, and the World Bank have all made contributions to more 'peaceful' sovereign lending. Among others, the Paris Club, an informal group of creditor nations formed in 1956, 'is tasked with renegotiating sovereign debt on behalf of its member nations and has the authority to enter into agreements with debtor nations for debt relief and restructuring, contingent upon the "consensus" of its members'.[100] Although as an official but informal creditors' organization, the Paris Club has formed many debt-restructuring basic principles in its long-term practice, this system is non-compulsory and has been criticized for its inefficiency.[101] Historically, there are few restrictions on creditor nations' behaviour since the creditor nations consist mainly of advanced countries who make the rules and set the standards.

The effort towards setting up comprehensive principles of responsible sovereign financing behaviour was initiated by UNCTAD. The legal characteristics of the resulting Principles are strong and embody the intention of UNCTAD to legalize principles on sovereign lending and borrowing. A set of legal principles should be

[96] See H.B. Samuel, *The French Default: An Analysis of the Problems Involved in the Debt Repudiation of the French Republic* (Wilson, 1930) 101.

[97] See T.S. Woolsey, *Lectures on International Law in Time of Peace by J.N. Pomeroy* (Houghton, Mifflin & Co., 1886) 75.

[98] See A.S. Hershey, 'The Calvo and Drago Doctrines' (1907) 1 AJIL 26, 28–31.

[99] Especially UN Charter, Arts 2.3 and 2.4. Art. 2.3 states that: 'All Members shall settle their international disputes by peaceful means in such a manner that international peace and security, and justice, are not endangered'; Art. 2.4 states that 'All Members shall refrain in their international relations from the threat or use of force against the territorial integrity or political independence of any state, or in any other manner inconsistent with the Purposes of the United Nations'. Available at <http://www.un.org/en/documents/charter/chapter1.shtml> (accessed 15 January 2012).

[100] 'What Are the Main Principles Underlying the Paris Club Work?', available at <http://www.clubdeparis.org/sections/composition/principes> (accessed 27 May 2013).

[101] See A.M. Dickerson, 'A Politically Viable Approach to Sovereign Debt Restructuring' (2004) 53 Emory L.J. 997, 1008–12.

an integral part of international economic order, with sovereign lending and borrowing relationships based on legal principles. Sound law will reduce the occurrence of sovereign debt crisis and risk. However, it is not sufficient to establish a set of principles: the consequences of violating those principles must be accompanied by judiciary responsibility and the corresponding legal remedies.

Only a binding international system for responsible lending and borrowing which holds creditors and debtors liable can ensure debt sustainability and avoid reckless lending and borrowing in the future. Under such a system, both creditors and lenders have legal obligations to abide by the relevant principles. The violation of these principles may produce legal defence and legal liability. Thus, where such legal defences are available to a sovereign debtor or creditor, could they be raised in a domestic court or international dispute settlement system of competent jurisdiction?[102]

II. The implementation of the Principles: the role of international tribunals?

Buchheit and Gulati referred to the third objective of attempting to reach a consensus on the principles of responsible sovereign lending and borrowing, i.e. 'to see whether these principles can be framed in a manner that would allow a judge sitting in a national court to take them into account in a lawsuit with a commercial lender over the judicial enforcement of a sovereign debt instrument'.[103]

However, generally, domestic judicial mechanisms cannot play a big role in sovereign debt litigation because of the sovereign immunity principle. Early in the last century, some scholars pointed out that such difficulties encountered by sovereign lenders were compounded by a further problem: the inability to enforce any judgment rendered against the borrower. Even if the lender could obtain a judgment, the sovereign's assets were likely to remain immune from enforcement. Even now, many developed countries regard international loan agreements signed and implemented between governments as the country's commercial activity, and international bonds usually also stipulate that each bondholder has the right to proceedings against the sovereign debtor in the event of default; however, formal legal enforcement is virtually unavailable to sovereign lenders.[104]

In the past, private lenders looked to their own government for support and protection against defaulting sovereign debtors, but today the situation has changed, and private sovereign creditors can file arbitration with the International Centre for Settlement of Investment Disputes (ICSID) independently.

[102] See Principles on Promoting Responsible Sovereign Lending and Borrowing, United Nations Conference on Trade and Development, Amended and Restated as of 4 November 2011, 9. A proposal for an international bankruptcy court was put forward, see M.T. Hilgers, 'Debtor-States and An International Bankruptcy Court: The IMF Creditor Problem' (2003) 4 Chi. J. Int'l L. 257.

[103] See Buchheit and Gulati (n. 43) 67.

[104] Certainly, national courts can sometimes play a part in sovereign lending and borrowing. e.g. in May 2009, US Representative Eric Massa (D-NY) introduced the Judgment Evading Foreign States Accountability Act, which mandated that foreign states (and their corporations) be denied access to US capital markets if they had been in default for more than two years on US judgments exceeding $100m.

When the creditor is a sovereign state, it is inherently difficult to use domestic proceedings. If a creditor nation is still unable to seek legal remedy in an international forum as a private investor when its loan is violated, this would be unfair and put the creditor nation at a disadvantage. For example, 'strategic dialogue' solutions are used to settle sovereign debt disputes between the United States and China. This implies making a political settlement. Thus, the key is each other's power, and in this case, the creditor has to beg the debtor to repay or face a debtor threatening not to repay; this is reminiscent of the traditional Chinese story, where 'Yang Bailao' became 'Huang Shiren'.[105] Therefore, political means do not represent a positive solution for the sovereign creditor.

In fact, there are already various framework design discussions on the 'Dispute Resolution Forum' (DRF) under the system of the IMF 'Sovereign Debt Restructuring Mechanism' (SDRM). According to the provisions of the Proposed Features of a Sovereign Debt Restructuring Mechanism (SDRM draft), the Dispute Resolution Forum has the following functions: dispute resolution, management, suspending performance, and making the internal rules. Although the IMF's proposed 'international bankruptcy court' has not been further implemented because of certain defects in the proposal—for example it was going to be founded on Chapter 11 of the US Bankruptcy Act, political obstacles could not be overcome, and the IMF would have acted as both creditor and arbitrator[106]—an international tribunal remains an interesting potential mechanism for addressing sovereign debt disputes.

When talking about the odious debts doctrine, Sack, its 'inventor', was of the opinion that in order to avoid arbitrariness on the part of debtor states, who might be tempted to try to rid themselves of onerous debts by repudiating them as odious if that were easily possible, no unilateral repudiation of odious debts by debtor states should be allowed. Instead, the application of the odious debts doctrine should be the exclusive domain of an independent international tribunal.[107] While Iraq was in the process of debt restructuring, this raised the issue of the establishment of an international institution for judging odiousness. While the new Iraq government was working to restructure its obligations, a group of NGOs and individuals proposed that an independent tribunal should be created and given the responsibility of designating certain Iraqi debts as odious. They argue that 'the

[105] Yang Bailao and Huang Shiren are two roles in the classic Chinese film 'the White Haired Girl', where Yang Bailao is a tenant, and Huang Shiren is a landlord. Yang Bailao was forced to commit suicide on the Lunar New Year's Eve because of debt due to Huang Shiren. Therefore, 'Yang Bailao' and 'Huang Shiren' respectively became bywords for 'debtor' and 'creditor' in Chinese society. However, the irony is that today, in the 21st century, the Chinese government and the US government have put on a modern 'Huang Shiren' and 'Yang Bailao' play with mismatched parts.

[106] See A. Krueger, 'International Financial Architecture for 2002: A New Approach to Sovereign Debt Restructuring', Address before the American Enterprise Institute, 26 November 2001, available at <http://www.imf.org/external/np/speeches/2001/112601.HTM> (accessed 27 January 2012); Hilgers (n. 102) 265; C. Seavey, 'The Anomalous Lack of An International Bankruptcy Court' (2006) 24 Berkeley J. Int'l L. 499, 516.

[107] A.N. Sack, *Les effets de transformations desÉtats sur leur dettes publiques et autres obligations financières* (Recueil Sirey, 1927) 163.

debts which Saddam owes cannot be legitimately passed on to the Iraqi people without assessment by an arbitration tribunal employing the doctrine of odious debts to assess whether the Iraqi people benefited from these loans'.[108] Patricia Adams recommended that 'the new Iraq administration first determine which of the Saddam-era debts were indeed odious and then simply refuse to pay them until creditors submit proof of non-odiousness'.[109] However, Stiglitz 'calls for the establishment of an international bankruptcy court by the UN to enforce an odious debt principle'.[110] Therefore, while the need for an Iraqi debt tribunal is essentially moot after the country's debt restructuring, who has authority to decide the odiousness and settle the sovereign debt dispute is still an issue which needs considering and resolving. Kremer and Jayachandran have even proposed creating a new international tribunal or judicial body to evaluate the relative odiousness of existing regimes as opposed to the odiousness of particular debts.[111]

Moreover, the Second Draft of the UNCTAD Principles also states, 'where such legal defences are available to a sovereign debtor, these should be raised in a court of competent jurisdiction' (such as if the creditor breaches the agency and public interest principle or the UN sanction principle). The Second Draft does not make clear what kind of jurisdiction it is, but obviously municipal courts in either the creditor or debtor nation would not be suitable. In addition, 'invocation of the concept of odious debt in multiple forums in respect of diverse debt contracts involving the same debtor state risks inconsistent decisions'.[112]

The ideal mechanism for the promotion of the previously discussed principles is a permanent international tribunal. Dissenting creditors or debtor nations complaining of particularly harsh renegotiation terms could then bring their objections before the tribunal. Its function would be to either confirm the renegotiation plan or demand changes in it, and help to settle the sovereign debt dispute once and for all.

E. Conclusion

Introducing clear and impartial principles for sovereign lending and borrowing is beneficial to both lenders and borrowers because they would know the 'rules of the game in advance', and thus could follow them. The UNCTAD Principles are designed to find a fair way of sharing the burden, and an equitable balance between the interests of the debtor nation and those of the creditors, including creditor nations from the perspective of international law. Additional issues need to be considered, for example whether certain rights should be owned by the sovereign creditor—such as the right to request sovereign debt to be guaranteed by assets of

[108] A. Feibelman, 'Contract, Priority, and Odious Debt' (2007) 85 N.C. L. Rev. 744.

[109] J. Damle, 'The Odious Debt Doctrine after Iraq' (2007) 70 Law & Cont. Probs 141.

[110] Damle (n. 109) 142.

[111] Kremer and Jayachandran (n. 33) 7.

[112] R. Howse, 'The Concept of Odious Debt in Public International Law', UNCTAD Discussion Papers No. 185 (2007).

the debtor or third party beyond credit guarantee of the debtor, since national credit is not a sufficient security measure in view of a possible lack of honesty and good faith on the part of some governments,[113] or the right to raise interest rates on sovereign debt that no longer has a top or good sovereign credit rating, or the right to seek legal remedy from an international dispute settlement body due to non-compliance with the UNCTAD Principles. In addition, the UNCTAD Principles are only binding on sovereign debtors and creditors, imposing no obligation on other actors in the sovereign lending and borrowing process. However, the crisis in Greece illustrates that the reckless action of actors other than the creditors and debtor, such as investment banks like Goldman Sachs and credit rating agencies, also played an instrumental role, and therefore, additional principles should be drawn up to govern other actors during sovereign lending and borrowing.

The most fundamental principle during sovereign lending and borrowing should be that sovereign debt contracts are binding and must be honoured because *pacta sunt servanda* is the fundamental international law principle to keep international order,[114] and therefore, the rights of the creditors should normally prevail except in rare circumstances, including serious violations of the UNCTAD Principles. In these circumstances, a fair rebalancing among debtors and creditors should take place.

If China abides by the UNCTAD Principles, there is the potential for the state to prevent and reduce the prevalence of sovereign debt crises, prevent reckless sovereign lending, maintain its stable economic growth, and support the achievement of its peaceful rise. The UNCTAD Principles are not legally binding for sovereign states at the international level at present, but are playing a role in affecting and changing sovereign lending and borrowing practices.[115] As the second biggest creditor nation, China should take these Principles seriously and fully participate in the consensus process. China should try to become a mature sovereign creditor as soon as possible and the Principles would be helpful to this process.

[113] e.g. some sovereign debtors wantonly concealed their actual economic situation or manipulated audits.

[114] See J.W. Yackee, '*Pacta Sunt Servanda* and State Promises to Foreign Investors before Bilateral Investment Treaties: Myth and Reality' (2008) 32 Ford. Int'l L.J. 1550, endnote 202.

[115] It is remarkable that Norway has agreed to adopt UNCTAD principles on its own initiative, see Norway to audit debt on basis of UNCTAD principles, 23 August 2012, available at <http://unctad.org/en/pages/newsdetails.aspx?OriginalVersionID=231> (accessed 15 September 2012).

PART V

EUROZONE: PROBLEMS AND SOLUTIONS

13

Restructuring a Sovereign Debtor's Contingent Liabilities

*Lee C. Buchheit and Mitu Gulati**

A. Introduction

How should the contingent liabilities of sovereigns (like government guarantees of the debts of state-owned enterprises or even private sector entities) be treated in a general restructuring of the debt of that sovereign? This question has played only a minor role in the sovereign debt restructurings of the last 30 years because the aggregate size of such contingent liabilities—in comparison to the overall debt stocks—has in most cases been very small.[1] Slathering explicit government guarantees on third party obligations, however, has recently become the tool of choice for many countries in their efforts to quell an incipient panic in their financial markets.[2] In addition, implicit government guarantees (the warm-arm-wrapped-over-the-shoulder; the wink; the nod; the unvoiced 'all will be well in the end' glance in the direction of the creditors) are now ubiquitous. Systemically important financial institutions, state-owned or sponsored enterprises, and sub-sovereign political units may all borrow under the shadow of an implicit sovereign guarantee. Inevitably, some of those sovereigns will need to restructure their own debts one day and this component of their balance sheets, or perhaps better said their *off* balance sheets, will need to be addressed.

* For comments, thanks to Juan Pablo Bohoslavsky, Carlos Espósito, Anna Gelpern, Yuefen Li, Rodrigo Olivares-Caminal, and Ignacio Tirado.

[1] The primary treatises that address sovereign restructurings devote little attention to the matter of how to restructure sovereign guarantees. See e.g. M. Megliani, *Sovereign Debt: Genesis—Restructuring—Litigation* (2012 draft, on file with authors); R. Olivares-Caminal, *Legal Aspects of Sovereign Debt Restructuring* (Sweet & Maxwell, 2009); P.R. Wood, *International Bonds, Loans, Guarantees, Legal Opinions* (Sweet & Maxwell, 2007).

[2] Our primary source for data on this topic is a 2012 Report by Houlihan Lokey, available at the website of the Institute for International Finance <http://www.iif.com/events/recent>; see also D. Singh and J.R. Labrosse, 'Developing a Framework for Effective Financial Crisis Management' (2012) 2 OECD Journal 4, reporting data on the increase in contingent liabilities in the EU as a function of the 2007 financial crisis.

This problem is not limited to sovereigns. States, provinces, and municipalities can also issue guarantees, often with little or no public awareness that the local taxpayer's credit has been engaged to repay the debt until it is too late.[3]

B. The Motivations

The traditional motivation for issuing a sovereign guarantee is to allow the beneficiary to piggy-back on the credit standing of the sovereign. Entities that could not by themselves borrow in the credit market, or a project that would not, on a stand-alone basis, have been bankable, are thus given access to financing at tolerably low interest rates. The alternatives for the sovereign often boil down to two—finance the enterprise/project through a sovereign borrowing followed by a re-lending to the enterprise/project, or wrap a sovereign guarantee around a direct borrowing by the debtor. The former places the liability squarely on the shoulders and the balance sheet of the sovereign, driving up debt-to-GDP ratios and requiring compliance with legal restrictions (such as statutory debt ceilings) on sovereign borrowing. The latter can often be accomplished off-balance sheet and outside the ambit of legal restrictions.

The dangers of unrestricted sovereign guarantees, and the need for greater transparency in governmental accounting for these arrangements, are gradually receiving more attention. UNCTAD's recently issued Principles on Responsible Sovereign Lending and Borrowing expressly address the problem. Principle 11 'Disclosure and publication' states:

Relevant terms and conditions of a financing agreement should be disclosed by the sovereign borrower, be universally available, and be freely accessible in a timely manner through online means to all stakeholders, including citizens. Sovereign debtors have a responsibility to disclose complete and accurate information on their economic and financial situation that conforms to standardized reporting requirements and is relevant to their debt situation. Governments should respond openly to requests for related information from relevant parties. Legal restrictions to disclosing information should be based on evident public interest and are to be used reasonably.

And Implication 3 to Principle 11 explains:

Debtors should make public disclosure of their financial and economic situation, providing among others the following information: (i) accurate and timely fiscal data; (ii) level and composition of external and domestic sovereign debt including maturity, currency, and forms of indexation and covenants; (iii) external accounts; (iv) the use of derivative instruments and their actual market value; (v) amortization schedules and, (vi) *details of any kind of implicit and explicit sovereign guarantees*. Sovereign borrowers may wish to

[3] See M.W. Walsh, 'Crushed by Promises—Bonds Arranged in Obscurity Return to Haunt Taxpayers', *New York Times*, 26 June 2012, B1, B6: 'The "full faith and taxing power" of communities, a solemn pledge, was being used to guarantee revenue bonds for non-essentials like solar-power projects, apartment buildings and a soccer stadium—things bailout weary taxpayers might walk away from if the guarantees were called.'

consider disclosing information by way of international norms, such as the IMF's Special Data Dissemination Standard.[4]

The European Union Council issued a Directive in 2011 with this text:

> For all sub-sectors of general government, Member States shall publish relevant information on contingent liabilities with potentially large impacts on public budgets, including government guarantees, non-performing loans, and liabilities stemming from the operation of public corporations, including the extent thereof.
>
> Member States shall also publish information on the participation of general government in the capital of private and public corporations in respect of economically significant amounts.[5]

The eurozone financial crisis that started in 2009 added a new twist on the motivation for sovereign guarantees. Some of the eurozone peripheral countries, like Greece, began to experience heavy outflows of bank deposits. The resources of the local central banks were unable to supply adequate liquidity to the banking systems. The solution? Local banks would issue debt instruments to themselves, obtain a government guarantee, and then use the instruments as collateral for loans from the European Central Bank. The sovereign guarantee in this context does not serve the conventional purpose of persuading a creditor to lend to an otherwise credit-impaired debtor; after all, in these situations the creditor and the debtor are the same entity—the issuing bank. The guarantee is simply a passport into the ECB discount window.[6]

C. The Challenge

The central problem with contingent liabilities is that they are contingent. Neither the beneficiary of the guarantee (the creditor) nor the sovereign guarantor will ordinarily know at the outset whether the primary obligor (the borrower) will eventually be able to repay the debt on its own.[7]

[4] UNCTAD, Principles on Promoting Responsible Sovereign Lending and Borrowing (2012), Principle 11 (Disclosure and Reporting), Implication 3 (emphasis added). Other principles also touch upon the issue, such as Principle 4 (Responsible Credit Decisions), Implication 3, and Principle 13 (Adequate Management and Monitoring). The text of the Principles is available at <http://www.unctad.info/upload/Debt%20Portal/Principles%20drafts/SLB_Principles_English_Doha_22-04-2012.pdf>, and is reproduced in the Annex to this book.

[5] See Council Directive on 8 November 2011 on Requirements for Budgetary Frameworks of the Member States (23 November 2011, Art. 14, Pt 3).

[6] See 'ECB Caps Use of State-Backed Bonds as Collateral', Reuters, 3 July 2012, available at <http://uk.reuters.com/article/2012/07/03/uk-ecb-collateral-idUKBRE8620V920120703>; S. Sirletti and E. Martinussi, 'Italy Banks Said to Use State-Backed Bonds for ECB Loans', Bloomberg, 21 December 2011, available at <http://www.bloomberg.com/news/2011-12-20/italian-banks-are-said-to-use-state-guaranteed-bonds-to-receive-ecb-loans.html>.

[7] But sometimes they will know. In the Greek debt restructuring of 2012 described later, for example, 36 bonds guaranteed by the Hellenic Republic (but only 36 out of hundreds of state-guaranteed obligations) were declared eligible to participate in the restructuring of the Republic's debt. One criterion used in selecting these bonds was a general recognition that the primary obligors did not have the capacity to service the debts out of their own resources. For details on the Greek restructuring, including regarding the guaranteed bonds, see J. Zettelmeyer, C. Trebesch, and M. Gulati, 'The Greek

Therein lies the challenge for the sovereign debt restructurer. If one forces the beneficiary to call on the sovereign guarantee as a means of bringing the liability into the main restructuring in order to treat it in a manner identical to other debts, the sovereign may be taking on its own shoulders a liability that, left on its own, would never have emerged from the cocoon of contingency. Why? Because the primary obligor may have paid it at maturity without government assistance.

Leaving large contingent liabilities out of the main debt restructuring, however, may plant a landmine on the road to debt sustainability once the restructuring closes. Is the restructurer to assume that (i) some, (ii) all or (iii) none of those contingent liabilities will eventually wind up as direct claims against the sovereign? The answer to that question may dramatically affect whether the main debt restructuring will achieve its primary aim of returning the country to a sustainable debt position.

For its part, the creditor/beneficiary of a state guarantee has a right to feel more aggrieved about being dragged into a sovereign debt restructuring than does a direct creditor of the State. The beneficiary of such a guarantee by definition holds 'two name paper'; the beneficiary enjoys the credit of both the State *and* the primary obligor. By roping the beneficiary of a State guarantee into a debt workout, the additional credit protection resulting from the independent obligation of the primary obligor to pay the debt is lost.

D. The Options

There are at least four possible ways of treating explicit contingent liabilities in a debt restructuring of the sovereign:

(1) *Ignore them.* Under this approach, the sovereign deals only with guarantees that are actually called by the beneficiary before the debt restructuring closes. No pressure is put on beneficiaries to call the guarantees; no effort is made to force the liabilities into the restructuring.

(2) *Entice them.* The sovereign may declare that paper bearing its guarantee will be eligible to be tendered in the restructuring transaction. Naturally, this leaves it in the discretion of the holders whether to tender now or wait and take their chances when the scheduled maturity date of the paper arrives. The sovereign may attempt to entice holders into the restructuring by offering them a small premium over the consideration being offered to direct creditors. Such a sweetener can be justified as the consideration paid to the beneficiary of a State guarantee in return for the beneficiary's release of the primary obligor.

(3) *Pressure the beneficiaries to call.* Careening to the other extreme, the sovereign debtor could attempt to pressure the beneficiaries to call on their State

Debt Exchange: An Autopsy' (2012 draft), available at <http://papers.ssrn.com/sol3/papers.cfm?abstract_id=2144932>.

guarantees in order to bring the resulting—now actual, no longer contingent—liabilities into the sovereign's debt restructuring. Presumably, this could only be done by threatening to repudiate any post-closing call of the guarantee. In the case of guarantees that are governed by the law of the sovereign's own jurisdiction (and our research suggests that a surprising number of eurozone sovereign guarantees specify local law for the guarantee even where the underlying instrument is governed by foreign law), pressure can be applied by passing a law mandating the terms on which the guarantee will be settled.

(4) *Call or don't call; you will receive the same consideration.* The fourth option is to tell beneficiaries that they are free to call or not as they choose, but if they elect to call on the state guarantee *after* the debt restructuring closes, the sovereign will honour it by delivering consideration having a net present value equal to what the creditor would have received had the claim been brought into the main restructuring.

E. The Problems

Each of these options has its own set of problems.

Leaving the guarantees out of a restructuring altogether (Option 1) places the sovereign at risk that the financial predicates underlying the debt restructuring could be undone. A large slug of liabilities coming onto the balance sheet of the sovereign unexpectedly in the future could render obsolete the debt sustainability analysis upon which the financial terms of the main restructuring was based. This is a risk both to the sovereign debtor and to the other creditors that join the restructuring.[8]

But forcing the beneficiaries to call on the explicit guarantees (Option 4), even if legally possible (which it probably won't be), compels the beneficiaries to give up their claims on the primary obligors. As noted earlier, this causes particular hardship for guaranteed creditors in comparison with their direct creditor counterparts.

Enticing the beneficiaries to join the restructuring by offering them a sweetener (Option 2) may bring in some of the beneficiaries, but probably not all of them unless the sweetener is extremely sweet.

Finally, telling beneficiaries that they will receive the same consideration in settlement of their guarantees regardless of when they may call on those guarantees (Option 3) may not be a credible threat. If things begin to improve in the debtor

[8] The existence of guarantees that pop up after a debt restructuring has closed can be an embarrassment, or worse, for the debtor country. This happened in Belize shortly after that country's debt restructuring closed in 2007. See 'Belize Bank: A $10 m Mystery', *The Economist*, 15 May 2008, available at <http://www.economist.com/node/11377008>. A heated scandal ensued. Local activists in Belize sought to block payments on the guarantee (which had quickly become direct obligations of the sovereign because the underlying obligor was unable to pay). The creditor, Belize Bank, however, took the position that it was entitled to full payment and the government subsequently conceded this in arbitration proceedings in the UK.

country after the restructuring closes, will the government really be eager to default on an item of guaranteed debt soon thereafter? Probably not.

F. The Practice

There has been no consistent practice in previous sovereign debt restructurings on this issue. The workouts of commercial bank sovereign loans in the 1980s generally followed Option 1. Beneficiaries were not required, nor even encouraged, to call on their sovereign guarantees.[9]

In its 2012 debt restructuring, Greece invited, but did not attempt to coerce, holders of a small segment of state-guaranteed debt to participate in the restructuring (Option 2). See Section G. 'The Greek Case'.

When the Heavily Indebted Poor Country initiative got under way in the mid-1990s, the HIPC rules *required* that all contingent liabilities of the debtor countries be brought into the settlement (Option 3). To our knowledge, however, the HIPC rules did not confide to the sovereign debtors how they were to achieve this if a creditor/beneficiary simply declined the offer.

At least one country has chosen Option 4 (promise equal treatment of the creditor whenever the guarantee may be called). Grenada, in its debt restructuring of 2005, had outstanding government guarantees in an amount equal to 10 per cent of the country's total stock of debt. Grenada could not legally force the beneficiaries to call on the guarantees, but it did expressly warn the beneficiaries that they should expect no better treatment if they elected to stay out of the restructuring and call on the guarantee after the restructuring closed. As described in a 2006 article:

> Grenada's solution to this dilemma had three elements:[10]
>
> - Beneficiaries of all government guarantees were given the option to call upon their guarantees at any time prior to the expiration date of the [restructuring exchange] offer. The face amount of any guarantee called by a beneficiary would then be exchanged, at par, for the new bonds being issued in the exchange.
> - A beneficiary calling a guarantee in these circumstances was required to subrogate the Government to all of the beneficiary's claims against the primary obligor and any collateral securing the debt of the underlying project.
> - If a beneficiary elected *not* to call on a government guarantee during the offer period, however, the disclosure document for the exchange warned that any subsequent call on

[9] The telex sent by Mexico addressed to 'The International Banking Community' on 8 December 1982 (at the very beginning of the global debt crisis of the 1980s) contained draft 'Restructure Principles'. The debt subject to the restructuring referred to principal maturities falling due within a specified time period, 'but, in the case of any Debt which arises from a guarantee, endorsement, aval or similar instrument, only such payment obligations which are invoked and payable' during that time period. This practice appears to have been followed by the other sovereign debt restructurings of that era.

[10] See Lee C. Buchheit and E Karpinski, 'Grenada's Innovations' (2006) 4 Journal of International Banking and Regulation 227, 231.

the guarantee would be discharged by the delivery to the beneficiary of the same bonds being issued in the exchange on terms comparable to those reflected in the exchange offer (or, at the Government's option, by delivery of other consideration having an equivalent value).

G. The Greek Case

In the spring of 2012, the Hellenic Republic restructured approximately €206 billion of its bond indebtedness in the hands of private sector creditors, the largest sovereign debt restructuring in history. More than 130 separate series of bonds were declared eligible to participate in this restructuring, including 36 series of bonds bearing the express guarantee of the Hellenic Republic. The Hellenic Republic offered no special compensation (over and above the consideration offered to holders of direct Hellenic Republic bonds) to the holders of guaranteed bonds in return for the surrender of the holders' claims against the primary obligors, nor were any contractual measures taken to coerce the holders of the guaranteed bonds into participating in the transaction.

At the time of this debt restructuring, the Hellenic Republic had put its guarantee on hundreds of outstanding debt instruments (loans and bonds), but only 36 were declared eligible to participate in the 2012 restructuring. One of the criteria used by the Republic to select these 36 series of bonds was their classification by Eurostat (the statistical office of the European Union) as 'central government debt' for Eurostat reporting purposes.

H. Preventive Measures

What preventive measures could a sovereign take to deal with this problem? One possible step would be for the sovereign to insert into its standard form of guarantee a contractual provision to the effect that the guarantee will be deemed automatically called (or will be callable at the option of the sovereign guarantor) in the event of the announcement of a generalized debt restructuring by the sovereign. We have never seen such a provision, however, and we doubt whether it would be well received by prospective beneficiaries of the guarantees.

Alternatively, a sovereign could attempt to preserve the economics of 'two-name paper' by telling a beneficiary who joins the sovereign's debt restructuring that if the exercise by the sovereign of its subrogation rights against the primary obligor produces a recovery after the restructuring closes, the proceeds of that recovery will be paid first to the beneficiary up to the amount of the financial loss it realized by joining the restructuring, and thereafter to the sovereign. The exercise of these subrogation rights, however, ought logically to be placed in the hands of a third party such as a trustee. The sovereign cannot be trusted to pursue the primary obligor aggressively (particularly if it is a state-owned enterprise), while the beneficiary would have no economic incentive to pursue a primary obligor to recover anything more than the beneficiary itself could claim as its make-whole amount.

A third option would be for the sovereign to include in its guarantees some form of collective action clause that would permit a supermajority of the beneficiaries of that guarantee to agree to a settlement of the guarantee as part of the sovereign's main debt restructuring. A decision taken pursuant to such a collective action clause would then bind any dissenting beneficiaries of the guarantee.

14

Current EU Mechanisms to Confront Sovereign Insolvency

A Normative Analysis against the Benchmark of the UNCTAD Principles

Ignacio Tirado

A. Introduction

Since 2010, a number of peripheral Member States of the European Union (EU) have suffered financial crises with unprecedented consequences for the stability of the eurozone. With a view to staving off the risk of a break up, the EU has embarked on a process of legal and institutional overhaul that has produced its first results. As of the end of 2012, the EU—with particular regard to the eurozone—counts on an enhanced economic governance framework, a permanent crisis management mechanism, and instruments to facilitate the restructuring of sovereign debt, should the anti-crisis legislative and institutional settings fail.

This chapter purports to critically describe the new scenario and analyse its consistency with the benchmark of the UNCTAD Principles on Promoting Responsible Sovereign Lending and Borrowing. It will be argued that the safety net created by the system of controls and information duties, if adequately implemented, constitutes a legal and institutional framework that is consistent with the Principles. It will also be argued, however, that compliance with the Principles is less clear concerning the reactive mechanisms to avoid and to solve sovereign insolvency; and, in any case, that the path chosen by the EU to tackle sovereign crisis might be neither just nor efficient.

Not all UNCTAD Principles will be analysed. Due to the characteristics of the countries of the eurozone (comparatively high level economic and institutional development as well as political stability), the content of some of the duties included in the Principles do not pose real problems. This is not to say that there exist no cases of corrupt officials, impostor agents, government representatives acting *ultra vires*, or project-fund deviations within the EU Member States, but those cases can be considered relatively rare and they are properly addressed by the general civil and criminal legal systems alongside a relatively robust institutional setting.[1] In the following analysis, EU countries will be treated as sophisticated enough to understand the risks and benefits of financial products, disregarding their kind and nature. The probability of generating (as borrowers) a case of odious debt also seems unlikely enough not to be considered.

This chapter will concentrate on the 'black letter law'. The analysis will be normative and only in specific cases will the implementation and applications of the norms be considered.

B. The *Ex Ante* Mechanisms to Avoid Sovereign Insolvency

The eurozone countries are furnished with mechanisms to control the adequacy of borrowing and prevent a situation of sovereign insolvency, broadly defined as a default of the country's obligations with financial creditors.[2] Over the years—and particularly in recent times—the EU has built a system of barriers aimed at staving off the risk caused by the over-indebtedness of its Member States. The initial barriers, established with the creation of the Economic and Monetary Union (EMU), proved inadequate by failing to contain the recent financial crisis.[3] In order to amend this, the EU has recently strengthened the barriers considerably, both at European and national levels (in those countries that required it); but the strengthening is only one side of the coin. Since the crisis was already well under way when the new preventive framework was set up, the solution had to include mechanisms to manage and directly avoid sovereign default. Both the limits of the level of debt/deficit and the reactive mechanisms to crises are designed as solutions to avoid sovereign insolvency, which, in the EU jargon (as in IMF jargon), is treated as 'non-sustainable debt': a level of indebtedness that cannot be managed without a restructuring. The set of rules that seek a limitation in the level of debt/deficit has been labelled *Euro Area Economic Governance Framework*, while the regulation for solving the latter's failure would be the *Euro Area Crisis Management Framework*.[4]

In the following sections we will provide succinct descriptions of both frameworks, followed by an analysis of how the legal and procedural machinery fit with the optimal benchmarks established by the UNCTAD Principles. It will be argued that an adequate implementation of the new framework should foster compliance

[1] This assertion tends to be proved by the relatively comfortable position of most eurozone countries in international assessments concerning corruption or efficiency in the institutional setting. As an example, see Transparency International's Corruption Perception Index Annual report for 2012, which included 15 EU members among the 30 countries with the lowest levels of perceived corruption in the world, available at <http://www.transparency.org/whatwedo/pub/corruption_perceptions_index_2012>.

[2] The default of nations in the timely payment of operational creditors (i.e. suppliers of goods and services) normally happens before the crisis has spread to financial creditors. The belated payment of operational creditors is widespread even in times where there is no apparent threat of a general default in the country's obligations and therefore it cannot be taken as the beginning of sovereign insolvency.

[3] See 'The Reform of Economic Governance in the Euro Area—Essential Elements' (March 2011) ECB Monthly Bulletin 99.

[4] Both references can be found in the ECB's description of the first version of the ESM: (July 2011) ECB Monthly Bulletin 71–84.

with responsible sovereign lending and borrowing and hamper sovereign insolvency. It will also be argued that, should financial trouble arise anyway, the mechanisms put in place may not be optimal to generate an efficient and fair outcome.

I. The European Economic Governance Framework

1. The new framework

With the arrival of Economic and Monetary Union (EMU), the Member States of the EU realized the need to achieve a minimum level of fiscal policy coordination and economic convergence. Based on Articles 121 and 126 of the Treaty on the Functioning of the European Union (TFEU), the Stability and Growth Pact was approved. Pursuant to a two-sided dialectic that has remained the scheme of EU fiscal policy regulation up to the recent reforms, the Pact included a 'preventive arm', which established, *inter alia*, the cap of a 3 per cent deficit/GDP and a Public Debt/GDP ratio below 60 per cent;[5] and a 'corrective arm', known as Excessive Deficit Procedure, which provided mechanisms to sanction non-compliance.[6]

Full implementation of the Pact never happened. The framework for the coordination of national fiscal policies in the EMU proved politically inapplicable. Conspicuously, France and Germany repeatedly breached the deficit cap and no sanction was imposed as a consequence; thereafter, the ratios of public debt/GDP have been exceeded by a number of Member States.

In 2011, with the looming possibility of eurozone break up, it was evident that the existing legal and institutional framework was insufficient to confront the situation. In the final weeks of 2011 and in 2012, the euro area decided to advance in the integration with the approval of a number of legal instruments that sought to severely tighten the knots that had loosely tied the application of the national fiscal policies of the Member States. The most relevant measures consisted of the adoption of the 'Six Pack'[7] and the approval of the Treaty on Stability, Coordination and Governance.

The 'Six Pack' establishes the main lines of the new European Economic Governance Framework (EEGF), which has been designed as a continuation—by way of enhancement and strengthening—of the modes and institutions comprised in the Growth and Stability Pact. Again based on the duality prevention-reaction, the EEGF's main instrument is the Macroeconomic Imbalance Procedure. This mechanism has three different stages. The first stage is designed to identify macroeconomic shortcomings by an early-warning device consisting of ten selected macroeconomic indicators periodically registered for each eurozone Member State. The inadequacy of one or more of the indicators would trigger an in-depth study, based on which the Commission/Council could issue preventive recommendations

[5] Council Regulation 1466/97 of 7 July. [6] Council Regulation 1467/97 of 7 July.

[7] Regulations (EU) 1173/2011, 1174/2011, 1175/2011, and 1176/2011, all from 16 November; Regulation (EU) 1177/2011 of 8 November; and the Council Directive 2011/85/EU of 8 November.

(second stage). When the indicators present a more serious imbalance, the Member State must proceed to its swift correction. According to the procedure envisaged in the EEGF, the Member State has to submit to the Commission a detailed corrective action plan with a clear roadmap and deadlines for implementation. Compliance with the plan is to be monitored by the latter through—among other mechanisms—comprehensive, regular progress reports. The third stage, only applicable to eurozone jurisdictions, allows for the strict enforcement of the corrective plan by way of setting up an interest bearing deposit, the conversion of the deposit into fines, as well as other possible sanctions. In order to prevent sanctions from being easily blocked, the mechanism provides for a system of semi-automatic decision-making processes.[8]

This picture would be incomplete without two key additional references: Directive 2011/85/EU, which completes requirements and seeks to achieve formal homogeneity concerning budgetary frameworks; and the 'Golden Rule', established by the Treaty on Stability, Coordination and Governance, according to which the budget of eurozone members must be 'balanced or in surplus'.[9] The primary surplus rule must be made effective in the national law of each eurozone Member State within one year after the entry into force of the Treaty 'through provisions of binding force and permanent character, preferably constitutional, or otherwise guaranteed to be fully respected and adhered to throughout the national budgetary processes'.[10]

2. *The general EU framework*

Assessment of compliance with the UNCTAD Principles must also consider the general norms that confirm the basis for the orderly functioning of the internal market and the single currency.

The set of European rules and standards on accounting plays a most significant role in lowering the transaction costs in the European market and constitutes a requisite *sine qua non* for the efficient supervision of the Member State's economic performance. The mandatory European System of National and Regional Accounts tries to provide a uniform quantitative description of the national economies. The rules (last updated in 1995—ESA 1995) are fully consistent with the UN System of National Accounts and allow for the reliable cross-comparison of the members' accounts.[11]

EU Member States count on a network of norms that regulate the entire market spectrum. The rules on corporate law, banking law, or procurement, to mention only a few examples, are similar in substance. Public borrowers with corporate

[8] This could prove key to the adequate functioning of the new framework. The ease with which decisions could be blocked is what arguably rendered the system unworkable.

[9] Only 'exceptional circumstances' would justify a deviation from the golden rule (Art. 3.1.(c)).

[10] Some countries, like Germany and Spain, have incorporated the rule into their constitutions.

[11] The ESA is also complemented by a comprehensive set of mandatory harmonized statistics and, at the corporate level, a number of EU Directives and other norms that seek uniform, transparent financial reporting.

form, financial entities participating in public projects, or public entities entering into contracts with private parties are all subject to legislation that is consistent across the EU and which should, at least with regard to the 'law on the books', be in line with the objectives of the UNCTAD Principles.

3. The UNCTAD Principles and the EEGF

The framework described in the two previous sections constitutes an adequate base for Member States to borrow and lend in full compliance with a number of UNCTAD Principles.[12]

This would be the case with Principle 10 on transparency. All EU Member States must have in place legal regulations that establish procedures and assign responsibilities concerning the assumption of sovereign debt obligations. Loans and other financial obligations of each Member State must be part of the national budget, which is presented to and approved by Parliaments (therefore taxpayers are indirectly involved in the decision) and determined by the EU rules on budget elaboration, content, approval, and compliance. There have been concerns about the debt hidden in the corporate form of publicly-owned entities in certain Member States (state, regional, or municipally owned). The rules on national accounts (EU based) have holes that allow for uncontrolled borrowing, especially with operational creditors. Although this type of debt inevitably ends up rising to the surface, additional controls might need to be implemented to increase transparency in sovereign lending. Concerns have also arisen regarding the inclusion of contingent liabilities in national accounts. Although Article 14 of Directive 85/2011 should remove doubts, full implementation is still to be achieved.[13]

The issuance of bonds, notes, and other financial products is done thorough pre-established procedures and following harmonized, publicly available mechanisms. In the eurozone, bond issuances are ordinarily carried out by administrative decisions of the competent authority, and the regulation of the issuance is contained in the law and in subordinate legislation. If bonds or notes are issued by contract, the whole procedure is executed through sophisticated intermediaries and in full compliance with the standard practice of international financial markets. Thus, the EU-derived legal framework applicable to borrowing in financial markets is aligned with Principle 11.

[12] Member States lending to other sovereigns are also partially regulated by the European framework. Loans to other troubled EU members will normally be done by the ESM and channelled through strict procedures that should ensure compliance with UNCTAD Principles 1–6. Bilateral loans to other Member States can also be granted in coordination with the ESM (Recital 14 TESM). But fully independent bilateral financial assistance to other Member States and third parties is not specifically captured by a concrete regulation. Good practice will derive from the general controls and informative duties applicable to government budgets. The general rules on procurement and the compulsory audits should ensure adequate lending by EU Member States.

[13] The amount of private debt guaranteed by the governments of EU jurisdictions is, allegedly, enormous. For reference, see L. Buchheti and M. Gulati, Ch. 13 of this volume.

Information on the borrowing of Member States is reflected in standardized reporting and the accounting principles are common to all members. This should allow for cross-comparison and provide timely and reliable information to existing and prospective lenders. The amount of information shaped according to SAS 95 and collected, treated, and publicized through Eurostat and the disparate national treasuries and agencies should be enough to enable investors to adopt sound lending decisions. The adequacy and availability of information regarding not only levels of indebtedness but also macroeconomic figures as well as other relevant economic indicators places investors—normally sophisticated agents active in national and international markets—in a position to assess risk and, therefore, to account for losses should their investment fail. This consequence, however, is not consistent with the way in which the EU has shaped the crisis management framework.[14]

The EU framework and the EU-based national legislation create the bases for compliance with Principle 13: EU governments must elaborate a debt management strategy and make it public; and monitoring systems exist both at national and international levels (legislative control, internal audit bodies, and courts, etc.).[15] The assessment is less evident regarding Principle 14 (avoiding incidences of over-borrowing). The nature of this Principle is more difficult to assess since it involves subjective valuations that must be determined *ex ante* but can only be valued *ex post*. And yet, there are elements in the EU framework that would favour compliance with the rule, while others would seem to contradict it. The existence of severe budget controls and the 'golden rule', according to which Member States must run a primary surplus, are mandatory limitations that should push governments to adopt decisions based on a strict cost-benefit analysis; these rules should also, gradually, help countries to reduce the level of indebtedness and diminish the need to borrow solely to cover previously chronic budget deficits.[16] However, the strictly imposed EU controls and the limited autonomy to exert fiscal policy in the national interest curtail the possibility of adopting countercyclical measures, even if these are badly needed.[17]

[14] See section I.1. and 2.

[15] Directive 2011/85 makes express reference to the need for independent audits of public accounts (Recital 2, Art. 3) 'conducted by public institutions such as courts of auditors or by private auditing bodies'.

[16] Although this might be the correct assertion in a system that started anew, with not overly indebted countries, reality is quite different. In some Member States, the recent crisis and older public sector imbalances have created the need to borrow solely to cover existing debt. Some EU states suffer from an over-indebtedness 'path dependence' that is difficult to solve. This problem might dampen the countries' ability to resort to markets at sustainable rates soon enough.

[17] Another element of the EU legal framework that would seem to be aligned with the UNCTAD Principles (more precisely, with Principle 14) is Art. 125 TFEU, the famous 'no bail-out clause'. According to Art. 125 TFEU: 'The Union shall not be liable for or asume the commitments of central governments, regional, local or other public authorities, other bodies governed by public law, or public undertakings of any Member State . . . '. This provision originated in the Treaty of Maastricht and its objective was to foster the budget stability of Member States by establishing a principle of states taking responsibilty for their circumstances.

II. The European Crisis Management Framework

With a view to containing the threat to the eurozone's stability posed by the domino effect of the Greek crisis, the EU countries realized the urgent need for a legal framework that would provide ad hoc relief to Member States with liquidity problems and restricted access to financial markets. The first measures were adopted in the ECOFIN Council of 9 May 2010, with the creation of two non-permanent mechanisms: the European Financial Stability Facility (EFSF) and the European Financial Stabilisation Mechanism (EFSM).[18] This temporary, faltering reaction was insufficient to quell the fears of capital markets. Italy and Spain, the EU's fourth and fifth largest economies, were on the brink of collapse. On 17 December 2010, the European Council recognized the need for a permanent mechanism and the European Stability Mechanism (ESM) was created as a result. The ESM would replace the ESFS and the EFSM with an initial 'firepower' of €500 billion, to 'provide stability support under strict conditionality . . . to the benefit of the ESM Members which are experiencing, or are threatened by, severe financing problems, if indispensable to safeguard the financial stability of the euro area as a whole and of its Member states'.[19] The final regulation of the ESM is contained in the Treaty establishing the European Stability Mechanism (TESM), signed on 2 February 2012.[20]

1. The European Stability Mechanism (ESM)

The ESM is designed to work with a *modus operandi* which very closely resembles that of the IMF:[21] financial assistance is made subject to strict conditionality, with a

[18] Regulation 407/2010 of 11 May 2010.

[19] See Art. 3 TESM. The European Council of 25 March 2011 adopted Decision 2011/199/EU which amended Art. 136 TFEU to make room for the new permanent mechanism. The paragraph added to Art. 136 allows Member States of the eurozone to establish a mechanism which could be activated when 'indispensable to safeguard the stability of the euro area as a whole', subject to strict conditionality. Unlike the TESM, the TFEU only seemed to regard the general stability of the eurozone as cause to ground the ESM's activity. No reference is made to risks to the Member States (legal consequences are, however, uncertain).

[20] In a landmark decision of 27 November 2012, the Full Court of the ECJ (Case C-370/12, a preliminary ruling under Art. 267 TFEU from the Supreme Court of Ireland in the case of *Thomas Pringle v. Government of Ireland, Ireland and the Attorney General*) enshrined the validity of the TESM and its compatibility with EU Law. The ECJ established the adequacy of the simplified procedure used to amend Art. 136 of the TFEU based on its finding that the TESM is not a mechanism of monetary policy; that, as an instrument of economic policy, its objectives were not only fully coherent with the EU's aims but also complementary; and that the creation of a permanent stability mechanism does not constitute a enhancement of the competences of the EU.

In a way that would seem aligned with the prevention/reaction dichotomy used in this chapter to divide the new European frameworks, the ECJ established that the European Council decision 2011/199 amending the TFEU to make room for the ESM serves as a 'complement' to the regulatory framework for strengthened economic governance of the EU:

> . . . while the provisions of the regulatory framework . . . are essentially preventive, in that their objective is to reduce so far as possible the risk of public debt crises, the objective of establishing the stability mechanism is the management of financial crises which, notwithstanding such preventive action as might have been taken, might nonetheless arise.

[21] The first version of the TESM, signed on 11 July 2011, included several express references to the role of the IMF in the activities of the ESM. In its Recital 6, the 2011 version of the TESM affirmed

tight monitoring process of compliance, lending in tranches at high interest rates and with seniority in case of default (with the ESM's debt subordinate only to that of the IMF). The procedure is voluntary, and it must be initiated by the Member State seeking financial help. Before there is a decision about the support, the European Commission and the ECB must be satisfied that the situation meets a double test: the 'risk of contagion test' (the existence of a risk to the euro area as a whole or to its Member States) and the 'sustainability test' (an assessment of the sustainability of public debt).[22] Once the ESM's Board of Governors decides to grant the stability support, a detailed Memorandum of Understanding (MoU) is negotiated with the sovereign. The MoU will include the 'conditionality', i.e. the country's weaknesses to be addressed, as well as the type and amount of financial assistance granted.

Thus far, under the EFSF and EFSM, the 'financially assisted' Member States have been subject to severe austerity measures, touching almost every layer of public administration and reaching even the most essential public services and social safety nets; structural reforms affecting these countries' markets have been imposed; and the growth of public debt and reduction of the private sector have occurred in every case. The TESM provides the framework to continue with these types of conditionality measures.

The ESM may provide financial support through the following instruments (Articles 14–18 TESM):[23] (a) 'precautionary financial assistance', consisting of a credit line or an 'enhanced conditions' credit line; (b) financial assistance for the recapitalization of financial institutions through earmarked loans granted to the state;[24] (c) loans, subject to 'a macro-economic adjustment programme' (Article 16.2 TESM);[25] (d) a primary market support facility, consisting of the purchase of bonds of the Member State in the primary market; and (e) a secondary market support facility, which would imply the acquisition of bonds in the financial markets to address the risk of contagion. In the case of activity in the secondary

the active involvement of the IMF 'in all circumstances'. Although the IMF continues to be a relevant partner in the activities of the ESM, the current version of the Treaty has toned down its mandatory involvement.

22 The participation of EU institutions (the ECB, the European Commission, and the ECJ) in the functioning of the ESM was expressly agreed by all Members States. Its legality was analysed and affirmed by the ECJ in the *Pringle* case (paras 154–177).

23 The TESM lists the types of instruments, but it does not regulate them sufficiently to be operative. Express reference to 'detailed guidelines' approved by the Board of Directors for each mechanism is made. The list can be reviewed and amended by the Board of Directors (Art. 19 TESM).

24 This is one of the aspects of the TESM that has been subject to stronger criticism. If a country has a banking sector problem, channelling the assistance through the state inevitably raises the public debt and the deficit (to the amount of the year's interest payments). This will be likely to worsen the sovereign's situation and further jeopardize its access to the financial markets. The alternative would be to create a legal and institutional mechanism to allow for the direct provision of funds to the troubled financial institutions. This would work as an effective firewall and improve the country's position as borrower. The possibility is being considered.

25 The specific reference to a necessary macroeconomic conditionality in case of loans could be interpreted to imply that no such conditionality is mandatory in case of 'precautionary assistance'—letter 'a' in the text.

market, the ECB must have stated the existence of exceptional financial market circumstances and risks to financial stability.[26]

In all cases, the financial assistance is provided in tranches or operations, and it is made conditional on the persistence of the need and strict adherence to the MoU. The TESM sets two rules concerning the pricing of operations: they must aim to fully cover the ESM's financing and operating costs; and they must include 'an appropriate margin' (Article 20). The legal requirement of an 'appropriate' spread might be explained as an instrument to reduce moral hazard by troubled sovereigns: if the price is sufficiently 'unattractive', the borrower will have an incentive to carry out all necessary actions—as established in the MoU by the lender—to return to self-financing in international markets as soon as possible.

2. *The outright monetary transactions*

During 2012, market pressure on Spain and Italy continued to mount and both countries saw the spreads of their ten-year bond with the German equivalent soar to levels incompatible with medium-term sustainability. Markets started to consider the possibility of some Member States giving up the euro and this was reflected in their bond yields in the shape of an exit-risk premium. Doubts about the future of the euro itself and the general economic situation severely hampered the monetary policy transmission. In the light of this new situation, on 6 September 2012 the ECB announced the start of a new mechanism, designed to act alongside the ESM: the Outright Monetary Transactions (OMT) programme. The OMT will consist of the direct purchase by the ECB of short- and mid-term debt (one to three years) of the troubled Member States in the secondary markets. The ECB's intervention will only be executed against 'strict and effective conditionality' attached to an EFSF or ESM programme and provided they include the possibility of EFSF/ESM primary market purchases.[27] This mechanism, conceived to complement the ESM, is aimed at lowering the borrowing costs of eurozone sovereigns by sending to the market the credible message that the ECB is prepared to buy debt without any previous quantitative limits. This message might be especially convincing, given the ECB's announcement that their debt will not rank with priority over other bondholders.

[26] In the *Pringle* case, the ECJ gave careful consideration to the compatibility of the financial instruments of the ESM with the TFEU's 'no bail out' clause (Art. 125) as well as with the limitation envisaged in Art. 123. In summary, the Court rejected both arguments by stating that: (a) art. 125 does not prohibit all kinds of financial assistance; (b) that assistance is possible so long as the recipient of funds remains responsible for its commitments to its creditors and such assistance is subject to a conditionality that prompts the Member State to implement a sound budgetary policy (which is described as the main objective of Art. 125); (c) the design of the functioning of the ESM ensures that the ESM will not act as guarantor or in any way assume the debts of the Member State; and (d) the limitation included in Art. 123 refers only to the ECB and the central banks of the Member States, so the ESM is out of the scope of the norm. For an excellent (and seemingly influential) analysis of the subject matter, see A. de Gregorio, 'Legal Developments in the Economic and Monetary Union during the Debt Crisis: the Mechanisms of Financial Assistance' (2012) 49 CML Rev. 1613.

[27] For a summary of the OMT programme, see <http://www.ecb.int/press/pr/date/2012/html/pr120906_1.en.html>.

III. The European Crisis Management Framework and the UNCTAD Principles

This chapter has argued that the new EEGF and the general EU legal framework have created a preventive system that could be considered to be aligned with the UNCTAD Principles. The design of the reactive instruments is a different kettle of fish. It is at the least arguable that the EU framework has signalled a way out of the crisis that is neither just nor efficient.

According to UNCTAD Principle 7, it is the duty of all lenders to behave in good faith and with cooperative spirit to reach a rearrangement of the debts whenever 'a sovereign is manifestly unable to service its debts'; similarly, Principle 15 imposes on the sovereign debtor prompt, efficient and fair action 'if a restructuring... becomes unavoidable'. So the duty for both debtor and creditors is triggered when the restructuring cannot be avoided and there is a clear appearance of crisis. The 'Implications' of Principle 15 cast some further light on the threshold by seemingly linking 'unavoidability' with the sovereign being 'left with insufficient funds to *normally* service its debt'. The key to insolvency's entry gate seems then to be identified—at least as one of the possibilities—with a liquidity shortage that would impede the debtor from servicing its obligations.

The main difficulty posed by this definition lies in the use of the term 'normally'. There are two possible interpretations: it either refers to the origin of the funds used to service the debt or to the country's regular compliance with its current obligations. The first interpretation would leave out of the scope of the rule a sovereign debtor that is able to pay its obligations by resorting to mechanisms that are 'not normal' (for example borrowing funds at a higher-than-normal interest rate, or an asset fire sale). The alternative interpretation would be to understand that the sovereign should start a restructuring process when it does not have enough funds to pay its debts as they fall due (according to the 'normal' maturity of the obligations).

The former interpretation is a classic requirement of entry to insolvency proceedings in corporate insolvency: companies that must incur extra expensive borrowing costs or resort to a fire sale of assets should have the door open to petition for insolvency protection precisely to avoid the unnecessary destruction of value. But this standard 'collective action' logic does not work as smoothly for sovereign debtors, which do not run the risk of being fully wound up and which—to a certain extent—have the possibility to obtain new funds to satisfy extortionate borrowing agreements by increasing the taxation levels of their citizens/non-national taxpayers (unlike a corporate entity, that cannot bindingly demand new capital from its shareholders). The latter interpretation also seems more in line with the inclusion of the term 'unavoidable' in Principle 15: if the restructuring must be unavoidable to trigger the duties of debtors and creditors, there can be no practicable alternative solutions. Thus, if this second interpretation is adopted, *restructuring should only happen whenever the debtor manifestly does not have enough funds to service its debts as they mature.*

This threshold, far along the path of the crisis, coincides with the approach adopted in the European legal framework to confront the financial crisis of its Member States. The recently built ECMF consists of a number of mechanisms aimed at preventing the sovereign's default in financial markets. But not only so; it seems to be designed mainly as an alternative to debt restructuring, and only marginally—when insolvency is 'unavoidable'—as a possible complement to it. The European Stability Mechanism would be set in motion so long as debt is 'sustainable', in the sense of there being a possibility to satisfy all (financial) debts as they mature with the measures adopted by the ESM and its 'agents' (the European Commission, the ECB, and, when possible, the IMF). Recital 12 of the TESM expressly states that 'in accordance with IMF practice, in exceptional cases an adequate and proportionate form of private sector involvement shall be considered in cases where stability support is provided, accompanied by conditionality in the form of a macro-economic adjustment programme'. On the face of it, interpreting Principle 15's expression 'normally' in the first of the aforementioned meanings, would lead to the conclusion that the current EU crisis management framework contradicts the UNCTAD rule. It would seem difficult to argue convincingly that the financial assistance of the EU mechanisms (provided with 'non-concessional' interest rates) constitute 'normal' borrowing.

The European Crisis Management Framework mainly tackles financial crises of the eurozone's Member States by providing financial support in exchange for economic and regulatory reform and a 'non-concessional' interest rate. On the face of it, this approach, almost a facsimile of the IMF's standard procedure, might make sense: it would contain market disruption, allow for the full honouring of the sovereign obligations, and it would limit the contagion effects to other euro members. However, it could be argued that the system, which generally has important downsides, does not take into consideration the specific circumstances of the eurozone. Doubts as to the adequacy of the solutions affect both the pricing policy and the mandatory macroeconomic conditionality.

This classic IMF approach to justify the imposition of legal reforms and 'unattractive' interest rates might make sense in countries with uncontrollable governments, opaque public accounts, and inadequate regulatory frameworks; but it is at least doubtful that it is the correct policy for EU countries. Eurozone members have systems of national accounts that follow the ESA 95 and the Excessive Deficit Protocol, their national market regulation is already harmonized with that of other EU jurisdictions, and there already exist powerful mechanisms to avoid moral hazard: on the one hand, the financial support is to be disbursed in tranches, with each of the tranches withheld until the conditions are complied with; on the other hand, the EU has a detailed set of rules and a network of institutions in charge of monitoring compliance with EU regulations that would enhance the Troika's monitoring power.[28] The convenience of legal-market reform is absent; the need for a 'margin' is (arguably) not justified. The ESM is aimed at stabilizing the

[28] The 'Troika' is composed of the IMF, the ECB, and the European Commission.

eurozone, not at making profits. Experience has shown that the public debt crisis the solution of which is the ESM's main objective becomes the sovereign's main public cost in the form of interest payments. The 'assisted' economy substitutes productive/public services spending for the payment of interest rates, forming a vicious circle. Fortunately, the expression used in Article 20 TESM is general enough to allow for a change in this type of policy without a legal amendment to the Treaty: 'appropriate margin' could be close to no margin, if the circumstances make it appropriate.[29]

Concerning the imposition of austerity measures and strict economic conditions, the EU seems to be embarking on an unknown adventure. To the best of the author's knowledge, the strict simultaneous application of these types of policies to a number of states within the same currency has not been tested before. It is undisputed that severe austerity measures will depress economies even further, before they can thrive. Eurozone economies are highly intertwined and the depression caused to some countries will reduce their demand for goods and services from the richer Member States (with a inter-EU positive balance of payments), whose economies would be damaged thereby. The internal devaluation and the improvement in competitiveness of the troubled economies could then be written off to some extent. These risks exist and no justification of the measures has been provided. So far, the ESM and its mandatory scheme have granted the application of one uniform policy to a number of countries with different economic problems at the origin of their crises. At least so far, the results have been far from satisfactory.

It can be argued that the current situation, with excessive deficits and overwhelming amounts of public debt, can hardly be adequately handled by the ESM (and even less so by the ESM alone). This type of approach places all the burden on the taxpayers and confers an unjustified windfall on private creditors, in the vast majority sophisticated financial institutions that largely benefited from the growth years of the countries now in dire straits.

This overprotection of private creditors is not easy to explain convincingly and very difficult to justify: it alters market rules (the basic rule stating that investments can go wrong and investors then suffer the consequences) and possibly generates moral hazard. It could be convincingly argued that the creation of the ESM and its mechanics does not by itself generate perverse incentives for sovereign debtors: the amount of suffering they create and the political pressure exerted by taxpayers/

[29] According to Art. 20, 'when granting stability support, the ESM shall aim to fully cover its financing and operating costs and shall include an appropriate margin'. There can hardly be a more malleable expression than 'appropriate', which only means suitable or proper in the given circumstances. Thus, if the context so requires, the margin could be close to zero and the measure would be in full compliance with the rule. However, the meaning of art. 20 would not seem to be so discretionary if it is interpreted together with Recital 15, which states that:

> ESM lending conditions for Member states subject to a macroeconomic adjustment programme... should be consistent with the lending conditions of the Financial Assistance Facility Agreements signed between the EFSF, Ireland and the Central Bank of Ireland on the one hand and the EFSF, the Portuguese Republic and Banco de Portugal on the other.

In these cases, 'non-concessional' interest rates were included as the price for the financial assistance. For specific data, see <http://www.efsf.europa.eu/about/index.htm>.

voters on the political class of the Member States should make up for a somewhat ethereal idea that governments will over-borrow because they count on being bailed out.[30] Conversely, the perverse incentives created on the side of lenders (with particular regard to international investors) are more likely to materialize. Excessive lending and inadequate concentration of risk in a given sovereign will not be penalized because of the mere existence of the ESM which, as its founding Treaty expressly states, will only allow losses to the private sector under exceptional circumstances. Quite to the contrary, the existence of the ESM with the current mandate seems to pave the way for speculative manoeuvres by investors active in international financial markets aimed at keeping the most fragile Member States on the line in order to benefit from higher yields.[31]

C. The *Ex Post* Mechanisms to Solve Sovereign Insolvency

The eurozone legal framework includes two mechanisms aimed at solving the 'unsustainable' debt crisis of a Member State. The main one is the mandatory inclusion of collective action clauses (CACs) in all bond issues after 1 January 2013. The second is the residual use of the ESM as a funding source for EU countries undergoing a debt restructuring during the time the jurisdiction has no access to the financial markets.

Although it seems difficult to see how they could assist in solving the current euro crisis, both mechanisms might be useful instruments for future crises, and they would seem to be in line with the gist of UNCTAD Principles 7 and 15. Arguably, the framework envisaged for future debt restructurings will make it easier for the debtor to approach creditors to reach a consensual agreement; it fosters orderly and economically sound creditor behaviour; provides instruments to find a solution; and it is bound to dampen the misbehaviour of holdouts. In the following section we will analyse in some detail how the current model of euro CACs meets the requirements set out in the 'Implications' of Principles 7 and 15.

I. Mandatory collective action clauses (CACs)

The permanent anti-crisis regulatory framework generated by the European Council decision of 28 November 2010 included the mandatory incorporation of standardized, identical collective action clauses in all euro area government bonds (Euro Collective Action Clauses (ECACs)). On 26 July 2011, a first draft of a model ECAC was circulated for comments among the most relevant stakeholders.

[30] As an example of this approach, the ECB (ECB's Bulletin, July 2011) states that the conditions of the loans must be 'sufficiently unattractive' to create an incentive for the sovereign debtor to seek a hasty return to financial markets.

[31] In a most awaited recent paper, the IMF seems to be generally switching its approach to sovereign crises, moving towards private sector involvement as part of the solution; see IMF Paper of 26 April 2013, 'Sovereign Debt Restructuring—Recent Developments and implications for the Fund's Legal and Policy Framework', available at <http://www.imf.org>.

In parallel, the TESM was approved and amended. The final version, signed on 2 February 2012, established that 'collective action clauses shall be included, as of 1 January 2013, in all new euro area government securities, with maturity over one year, in a way that ensures that their legal impact is identical' (Article 12.3). The TESM explains in recitals that this measure is aimed at preserving market liquidity; and that ECACs would only be used in 'exceptional cases' whenever an 'adequate and proportional form of private sector involvement' was to be considered.

The UNCTAD Principles expressly recommend the incorporation of CACs. One of the 'Implications' of Principle 15 states:

> If the sovereign has proved that a debt restructuring is in fact necessary, the debtor should seek and propose an agreement with the supermajority of creditors to modify the original contractual terms. Collective action clauses can facilitate sovereign debt restructuring; therefore it is recommended that debtors and creditors should include them in multi-party debt instruments.

The UNCTAD reference to CACs seems at the same time broader and narrower than the euro CAC: broader, since Principle 15 refers generally to 'multi-party debt instruments', while the European text is only applicable to government issued bonds with maturity beyond one year; narrower, because the Principles seem to only conceive CACs as a mechanism to facilitate majorities, while the model CAC issued by the European authority includes a number of rules that go beyond the regulation of majorities to reach agreements over contractual terms.[32]

The ECACs have incorporated some of the most common clauses in bonds issued under US and UK law with a view to facilitating renegotiation of the terms of the original issuance. As is common practice, ECACs have a different regulation depending on the type of amendment that is sought by the sovereign. The possibilities are clustered in two groups of modifications: reserved matter and non-reserved matter modifications.

Reserved matters are those that affect the core elements of the bonds and the requirements for their amendment are therefore stricter. According to the ECAC Common Terms of Reference (general definition h), reserved matters are, among others, changes in the date of payment (rescheduling); the reduction of amounts payable under the bonds ('haircuts'); the method of calculation of the amounts payable, currency, or place of payment; the imposition of new conditions to payment; the release of guarantees or securities; amendments to the events of

[32] The interpretation of the fourth implication of Principle 15 is not clear. Its general wording allows for different possible meanings. It can be argued that a recommendation beyond supermajority clauses is envisaged in the text. Implication 4 creates the debtor's duty to 'seek and propose an agreement with the supermajority of creditors to modify the original contractual terms'; this duty is followed by the general assertion that 'collective action clauses can facilitate sovereign debt restructuring', and that they are therefore recommended for inclusion. It should be noted that the Implication does not say that CACs facilitate 'agreements with the supermajority of creditors', but the rather more general 'sovereign debt restructuring[s]'. In other words, the recommendation to implement CACs might then be taken to refer to all clauses that facilitate restructurings, even if not directly related to the formation of majorities. This is precisely what happens with some of the clauses included in the euro model of CAC, which would then be in line with UNCTAD's recommendation.

acceleration, of the ranking of bonds, or the law applicable; and forum to sue. All modifications that do not form part of the list included in the definition of reserved matter are to be considered non-reserved matter.

The ECACs also include two possible procedural paths to renegotiate the sovereign bonds: through the holding of bondholder meetings or by means of a written resolution. The modification of a reserved matter must be adopted with the consent of the issuer and of holders of 75 per cent of the aggregate principal amount of the outstanding bonds represented at a duly called meeting of creditors, or by the signature of the written contract by holders of no less than 66⅔ per cent of the aggregate principal amount of the bonds outstanding. For non-reserved matters, the aforementioned percentages are reduced to 50 per cent. In case of modification affecting a number of series of bonds and debt securities (cross-series modification), the ECACs include specific rules providing both the possibility to reach an agreement by aggregation and by the separate approval of the holders of bonds and securities of each of the series affected (Articles 2.2, 3, and 4). The ECAC does not include a pure aggregation clause. In order to enhance the chances of a debt restructuring, cross-series partial modifications are a possibility.

The ECAC incorporates a watered-down version of disenfranchisement clauses (Article 2.7c). Bonds will not be taken into account for the calculation of quorums and majorities if the bond 'is held by the issuer, by a department, ministry or agency of the issuer and . . . the holder does not have autonomy of decision'. The autonomy of decision is to be regarded as held (and therefore the holder is eligible to vote) if, according to applicable legislation, the holder may not take instruction from the issuer or the latter is required to act in accordance with an objective prudential standard, in the interest of all stakeholders or in its own interest. In order to increase transparency in the negotiation, the sovereign must publish a list identifying each legal entity that is controlled by the issuer and does not have autonomy of decision.

From a procedural standpoint, the ECAC provides for the mandatory appointment of a calculation agent, who will be in charge of calculating the majorities required to approve a modification (section 3). The task of the agent will be carried out with the information provided by the sovereign; although 'affected bondholders' can submit written objections, they must be submitted to the issuer, not to the agent, who must rely on the sovereign. The ECAC also leaves the way open for the objecting bondholder to apply to the competent jurisdiction.

The ECAC provides a basic legal framework for bondholder meetings and the adoption of written resolutions. The rules incorporated in the Common Terms of Reference are *de minimis* and need to be completed by the states, either by specific regulation or by reference to the existing regulation of bondholder meetings in the corporate sector. Although the rule is that a meeting of creditors be convened voluntarily by the sovereign, the latter can be forced to summon its creditors if an event of default has occurred, or is continuing, and bondholders having no less than 10 per cent of the aggregate outstanding amounts so request. The quorum for valid formation of a meeting of bondholders is set at 66⅔ per cent of the aggregate principal amount of the bonds outstanding for reserved matters and 50 per cent for non-reserved matters. In case of adjourned meetings, the quorum for reserved matters remains 66⅔ per cent and for non-reserved it is lowered to 25 per cent. The quorum necessary for reserved matters is large enough to ensure that no modification to bond issuances is ever attained with less than half of all the outstanding bonds (66⅔ per cent × 75 per cent). The amendments reached following the regulated procedure will be binding on all bondholders, whether or not the holder was present at the meeting, voted for or against the resolution, or signed the written resolution.

The model ECACs have neither prescribed mandatory inclusion of acceleration and rescission of acceleration clauses nor the necessary appointment of a trustee. Although these types of clauses are very common in Anglo-American law-based bond issuances, the EU Committee has decided not to make them part of the ECAC. The main reason for this is, allegedly, the lack of practice in European jurisdictions as well as the possible disruption it could cause in the respective domestic systems.[33] However, the inclusion of these clauses is 'recommended' to the Member States, and a basic model is incorporated in the Common Terms of Reference as 'Supplemental Provisions'.[34] The normative effect of the supplemental provisions is dubious. There is no doubt that Member States are not constrained to include acceleration, rescission of acceleration, or trustee (limitation of sole holder action) clauses in the issuances; but it remains to be clarified whether, if they decide to incorporate them, the models included in the Common Terms of Reference are mandatory.

II. ECAC and the UNCTAD Principles

The European legal framework created by the ECAC and summarized previously will facilitate consistency with some of the duties prescribed by the UNCTAD Principles on lenders and borrowers when the Member States are in a position to restructure their debts (Principles 7 and 15).

Upon the manifest insolvency of the debtor, Principle 7 urges lenders to (a) assume the possibility that under certain circumstances a restructuring of their debt can be inevitable, (b) confront the situation in good faith and with cooperative spirit, engaging in fair negotiations with the debtor and the rest of the creditors. An ECAC neither forces creditors into negotiation nor does it (obviously) impose on lenders a duty to reach an agreement. Lenders are free to pursue their own individual

[33] See EFC Sub-Committee on EU Sovereign Debt Markets' Model Collective Action Clause Supplemental Explanatory Note, 7–8, available at <http://europa.eu/efc/sub_committee/pdf/supplemental_explanatory_note_on_the_model_cac_-_26_march_2012.pdf>.

[34] The Supplemental Provisions of the Common Terms of Reference are four: a 'Manifest Error, Technical Amendments' clause, which allows the issuer to unilaterally modify manifest errors or clarify ambiguities and to make formal changes or improve the position of bondholders, all of which must be followed by adequate publicity; an 'Acceleration' clause, according to which no less than 25% of the aggregate principal amount of the outstanding bonds must concur to accelerate in event of default; the 'Rescission of Acceleration' clause, also known as 'reverse' acceleration, that empowers a majority of the aggregate outstanding bonds (50%) to avoid the notice of acceleration passed by the 25%; and, finally, the 'Limitation on Sole Holder Action', that deploys its effects in case the bonds provide for a trustee (or fiscal agent) to be appointed, and bans bondholders from instituting proceedings or enforcing rights against the issuer of the bonds unless the trustee has failed to do so within a reasonable time.

interest and it is expected that they will do so. But the existence of supermajority clauses, the provision of an institutional setting to negotiate and vote on restructuring agreements, the disenfranchisement of certain creditors with conflicts of interest, or the limitations in the litigating rights of free riders are all elements that foster mutually satisfactory solutions and hamper the misbehaviour of those who want to profit at the expense of the rest of the parties (hold-out creditors).

The alignment of ECACs with the UNCTAD Principles can be more easily realized by assessing the concrete clauses of the European Common Terms of Reference against the benchmark of Principle 15. According to this Principle, the restructuring of sovereign debt 'should be undertaken *promptly*, *efficiently* and *fairly*'. Each of those goals will be analysed individually.[35]

Time. According to the second implication of Principle 15: 'The sovereign borrower's first responsibility in this situation of substantive financial troubles is to move in a timely fashion to communicate with its creditors and commence the process and finding and implementing a transparent and consensual debt rearrangement'. ECACs make no reference to the moment at which the sovereign must start the procedure. Sovereigns can start the negotiations before or after defaulting on their financial obligations, although it is more common—and certainly desirable—that the restructuring serves precisely to avoid a disorderly non-compliance with the terms of the sovereign's financial obligations. In the case of the eurozone, the ECMF is designed to ensure that economically troubled states do not resort to debt restructurings until the country's finances are proved 'unsustainable' and cannot be sanitized through the financial assistance and conditionality of the ESM. Given this context, there is a strong chance that countries will only reach the negotiations after a long, arduous, and painful fight against default.[36]

The ECAC framework provides rules regarding the identification of creditors. Unlike in corporate insolvency, where the active participation of creditors in a long and often cumbersome process of filing of claims is the driving force of the final list of participants, under the ECAC regime the debtor bears the burden of determining who its creditors are and the amount of their claims (Articles 3.2–3.4).[37] The issuing institution must draft and publish a 'certificate' listing the total principal amount of bonds and debt securities outstanding, which will be the information used to calculate the quorum and majorities. If the Member State has complied with the rules that regulate the issuance of public debt in the eurozone, compiling the data and producing the certificate should be done in an efficient and speedy manner.

[35] Although the requirement that restructuring happens 'promptly' can be regarded as part of the efficiency requisite, they will be treated separately.

[36] As it was stated elsewhere, the fight against default is normally only referred to financial obligations. Operational creditors will have suffered long delays in a majority of cases before default is spread to bondholders and professional lenders.

[37] This solution, which would be unacceptable for corporate insolvency, does not seem so problematic in the case of EU sovereign debt crises. The reinforced informative duties, the public issuance of bonds, and the formal mechanisms of debt holding in organized financial markets (registers, trading through authorized intermediaries, etc.) make the risk of debtor manipulation slender.

With a view to renegotiating the terms of the bonds, the identification of the relevant creditors can be hampered by the widespread existence of credit default swap (CDS) derivatives related to the sovereign risk of the troubled Member State.[38] The proportion of CDS is expected to be higher the more troubled the country. Currently, CDS derivatives are traded over the counter and it is almost impossible to know who has bought them and for what amount. The EU legislation has recently adopted measures that should help to reduce the identification problem. Following the G20 agreement, in September 2010 the European Commission made public a proposal to regulate the trading of standardized OTC derivatives. After a long process of negotiation, the European Parliament passed Regulation 648/2012 (known as the European Market Infrastructure Regulation (EMIR)). As an EU Regulation, it is directly applicable in each Member State. Regarding the matter of concern to this chapter, the EMIR makes it compulsory to clear OTC derivatives which meet certain criteria through a previously authorized central counterparty, and the final say as to which contracts need to be cleared is conferred upon the European Securities and Markets Authority (ESMA). Independently of the clearing system, the new regulation establishes the duty for the parties to a transaction and the central counterparty to 'ensure that the details of any derivative contract they have concluded and of any modification or termination of the contract are reported to a Trade Repository . . . ' (Article 9.1 EMIR). And the reporting obligation is given retrospective effect, so that the outstanding contracts entered into before the coming into force of the regulation must also be reported. Furthermore, the EMIR reinforces the parties' informative duties by creating the obligation for each counterparty to keep a record of all derivative contracts concluded for a minimum of five years. This new EU regulation must be welcomed and will no doubt facilitate the task of sovereigns when it comes to renegotiating the terms of sovereign bonds.[39]

Efficiency. UNCTAD Principle 15 aims for an *efficient* restructuring of the debt. The ECACs include institutional and regulatory mechanisms apt to foster the efficient restructuring of the sovereign's financial debt.[40]

One institution that can help to streamline the restructuring process is the appointment of a calculation agent. The agent—only one, even in case of cross-series modification—is to be appointed by the issuer exclusively to calculate the

[38] For an in-depth analysis of the problems caused by the nature and origin of bondholders, with particular attention to the eruption of derivatives in the sovereign bond scenario, see A. Gerlpern, 'Domestic Bonds, Credit Derivatives and the Next Transformation of Sovereign Debt', available at <http://papers.ssrn.com/sol3/papers.cfm?abstract_id=1017175>.

[39] The identification of creditors is not the only problem than can arise as a consequence of CDS derivatives. Negotiations could be more difficult since those who have hedged the risk through a CDS (protection buyers) could be interested in the country's default rather than a voluntary agreement that solves the problem. In order to align the incentives and interests adequately, rules should be established to give protection buyers some sort of participation in the negotiations.

[40] The EEGF as well as the general institutional setting in place also provide a good basis to streamline the debt restructuring process. Currently, all Member States have debt management agencies (or equivalents) in charge of planning the country's public debt strategy and with the ability to collect, process, organize, and distribute the information needed. These agencies are in a position to act as focal point for the needs of the renegotiation of the debt.

requisite majorities. The listing of the total principal amount of the bonds, outstanding and non-outstanding, their identification and the publication of the listings as well as of the calculated majorities are left in the hands of the issuer. There is no regulation as to the criteria for appointment of the calculation agent or the existence of possible conflicts of interest. The work of the agent can be particularly important in case of cross-series modifications where the sovereign has issued bonds in multiple currencies or if there are index-linked obligations, to mention only some possible cases.

Arguably the most relevant contribution of the ECAC framework towards the efficiency of a debt restructuring is the creation of a procedure—basic though it may be—to facilitate the agreement. Mirroring the disparate practice applying to bonds issued under New York and UK laws, the Common Terms of Reference provide an alternative between an open written agreement and a meeting of bondholders. This duality also exists in the province of corporate and personal insolvency. Since the very origin of insolvency law, creditors gathered in assemblies have decided the fate of their common insolvent debtor. The evidence that meetings of creditors are cumbersome and inefficient in terms of decision-making, especially when there is a need for debate among several options, has not pushed the European corporate insolvency legislator to eliminate meetings of creditors, but rather to incorporate parallel written procedures, included in insolvency proceedings alongside the meetings.[41] Experience from corporate insolvency shows that adequately regulated written procedures can be more efficient and less costly than creditors' meetings. On the face of it, this would also seem to be the case—and to a higher degree—for sovereign insolvencies, with possibly hundreds or even thousands of creditors. Despite the existence of mechanisms to reduce the transaction costs of creditors' meetings (convening with adequate publicity, providing relevant information beforehand; the appointment of a Chair to organize the event; the possibility of using proxies and accumulating the votes), assemblies cannot stand a comparison with written agreements in terms of efficiency. The main feature of assemblies is the possibility to have an oral discussion about the different solutions proposed. In the case of sovereign restructuring of financial debts, such debate would seem all but chimerical.

The comparison made with the meetings of creditors in corporate law is not convincing for a number of reasons: first, because the majorities that need to be reached in a meeting of sovereign bondholders are 'supermajorities', and only in very exceptional circumstances does the approval of a plan in corporate insolvency demand such majorities (therefore, pre-meeting agreements between creditors are easier to reach, and oral explanations in an assembly may be used to convince smaller creditors without needing their vote to form a majority); besides, corporate insolvencies normally involve a 'middle class' of creditors, not sophisticated/interested enough to get involved in pre-meeting negotiations but bigger than individual—retail—bondholders, and this type of creditor (i.e. SME suppliers)

[41] The existence of a written procedure as an alternative to a meeting of creditors can be found in the Insolvency Laws of Spain or Italy, to mention only two examples of large jurisdictions.

may be influenced by the oral explanations of a meeting of creditors; furthermore, the type of information available to corporate insolvency creditors is much more accessible to the 'lower and middle classes' of creditors (individuals and SMEs), since they normally include less sophisticated accounts and detailed explanatory reports by insolvency practitioners (as opposed to the complicated numbers and explanations involved in a sovereign default's restructuring plan).

Finally, the comparison with the corporate bondholders' meetings does not stand either: those assemblies count on specific 'organs' that streamline the debate concerning the decision-making process of bondholders (i.e. syndicate of bondholders) and a focal point that acts in the interest of, and on behalf of, bondholders in the negotiations (a trustee). The ECACs have not included the appointment of a trustee with the mandate to act in the interest of creditors as a whole, a measure that could have improved the functioning of the meeting of creditors while solving the collective action problems caused by free-riders. One of the most difficult obstacles to successfully completing the restructuring of a sovereign's bonds lies in the negotiation of the agreement. In this regard, the ECAC regime offers no instrument to streamline the process. Both the written resolution and the bondholder meeting provide the framework to cast votes; but neither one by itself helps to solve the problem of negotiations. This loophole will probably be filled by the pro-activity of the sovereign debtor, the only party with enough information to start a process that can lead to a successful negotiation with a sufficient majority of creditors.[42]

Fairness. According to Principle 15, the restructuring must be fair. Fairness has many sides in the sovereign debt restructuring conundrum. One of the sides refers to the 'subjective' (relative) fairness of the agreement. The legal framework must provide mechanisms to prevent a reduced percentage of bondholders from 'hijacking' the agreement, which ought to be a 'fair' agreement in relative terms. This is partially expressed in the UNCTAD text by its reference to bad faith hold-out creditors: 'A creditor that acquires a debt instrument of a sovereign in financial distress with the intent of forcing a preferential settlement of the claim outside of a consensual workout process is acting abusively.' The ECAC framework devotes special attention to tackling the problem of hold-outs, which are the 'visible heads' of the 'collective action problem' and therefore, arguably, the main reason for collective action clauses to exist.

As described previously, the ECAC regime includes a mandatory system of supermajorities whose figures depend on the type of modifications sought with the agreement (reserved matters versus non-reserved matters), the scope of the restructuring (individual bonds versus cross-series modifications), and the procedure selected to restructure the debt (bondholder meeting versus written resolution). If the requisite majorities are reached, the agreement (written or in one or more

[42] The ECAC Common Terms of Reference level the information asymmetry between the debtor and its creditors to a certain extent by creating the debtor's duty to publish the most relevant data concerning the formation of majorities: the total principal amount of bonds or, especially, a list of the holders of disenfranchised bonds and the total amount of their holdings (albeit not the total amount of each holder).

meetings of bondholders) will be binding on all holders of bonds. The majorities envisaged by the Common Terms of Reference would seem to seek a balance between the need to make them high enough not to create instability (and therefore make bonds less attractive to investors) and the need to create a realistic possibility of restructuring when circumstances make it unavoidable. The majorities foreseen in the final version of the ECAC are higher than in the initial version of the text, following the comments of relevant stakeholders. They include aggregation clauses, they allow for the possibility of partial agreements in cross-series modifications under certain circumstances, and the sovereign is given flexibility to group bonds of different series in separate modification packages. This framework is bound to make life difficult for financial investors seeking to acquire debt at discounts and hold-out of the general agreement with a view to receiving a windfall.

Another element that needs to be taken into consideration when assessing the 'fairness' test included in the UNCTAD Principles is the inclusion of *disenfranchisement clauses*. The link between the inclusion of disenfranchisement clauses and 'fairness' is clear: the issuer can use its control or influence to manipulate the vote of the bondholder against the interests of the rest of the creditors that could be 'unfairly' prejudiced thereby. These types of clauses are common practice in sovereign bond issuances under New York and UK law,[43] although there is no unanimity as to the scope of the limitation: in some cases, the clause is worded so that virtually all entities related to the issuer are excluded from voting on a restructuring plan; in other cases, however, the delimitation of the clause is such that Central Banks and similar entities keep their voting rights intact. As it was mentioned earlier, ECACs include a general disenfranchisement clause (Article 2.7), which would include 'bonds held by the issuer, by a department, ministry or agency of the Issuer, or by a corporation, trust or other legal entity that is controlled by the Issuer . . . or by a corporation, trust or other legal entity of the Issuer', and in the case of a corporation, trust or legal entity, so long as it does not have 'autonomy of decision'. The article establishes that a bondholder has autonomy of decision 'if, under applicable law, rules or regulations . . . the holder may not, directly or indirectly, take instructions from the Issuer on how to vote on a proposed modification; or the holder . . . is required to act in accordance with an objective prudential standard, in the interest of all of its stakeholders or in the holder's own interest . . . '.

Arguably, the disenfranchisement clause included in ECACs is quite 'soft' on sovereigns. Such clauses are justified by the authors of the ECAC framework in the following terms:

> . . . disenfranchising an investor is a serious step with important legal consequences, and it should be taken only for good cause . . . neither an investor's interests or motives, nor the predictability of an investor's vote . . . constitutes adequate grounds for disenfranchising an investor. For the Committee, the litmus test remains: is a bondholder acting in its own

[43] For the numbers and a valuation of such clauses by the market, see C.M. Bradley and G.M. Gulati, 'Collective Action Clauses for the Euro zone: an Empirical Analysis' (2012), available at <http://papers.ssrn.com/sol3/papers.cfm?abstract_id=1948534>.

interest? If so, the bondholder should be enfranchised irrespective of whether the investor may also be directly or indirectly owned or controlled by the issuer...[44]

The Note then goes on to use the specifc example of Central Banks as a paradigm of related entities that should keep their voting rights.

In the author's opinion, the current version of the ECAC on disenfranchisement might be poorly received by investors and could cause some interpretative problems. The reasoning of the EFC Sub-Committee is not fully convincing. First, the criterion of the creditor's 'self-interest' seems difficult to apply to most cases. The Central Bank analogy is not a good example; precisely because it is an exemption: Central Banks must, according to EU legislation, act independently from their governments. But the Sub-Committee might find it hard to identify many more valid examples. In many European legal systems, institutions regulated by administrative law are subject to the general mandate of pursuing the 'public interest'. This broad and somehow elusive legal concept is elastic enough to override any short-sighted, own interest criterion. Arguably, most—if not all—public institutions and publicly-controlled legal entities will act in a 'public interest' that will be dictated by the general interest as defined by the government. And even those that are only indirectly controlled (or influenced) will, in practical terms, be subject to pressures that might be difficult to resist. In moments of national emergency (as are normally those when a sovereign debt restructuring is a possibility), it seems difficult to imagine one of those entities voting against the criterion of the issuer.

But there are further reasons why the current versions of the ECAC may create some trouble. For example, the drafting of Article 2.7 would seem to leave all subnational entities out of the norm's scope. All references are made to the issuer and entities forming part of, or controlled by, the issuer, but neither the regions nor the municipalities (and corporations at both subnational levels) would fit a literal interpretation of the clause. Similarly, there would seem to be no restriction on the national government voting on the restructuring plan of one of its subnational entities. This issue should be clarified in the legal transposition of the ECAC. The applicability of the disenfranchisement clause to nationalized banks or to financial institutions where the government bears direct influence in the management also seems doubtful. In some countries, like Ireland or Spain, the question could be paramount.[45]

Fairness, on the other hand, is described by the Implications of UNCTAD's Principle 15 as encompassing the following: non-arbitrary discrimination among creditors; respect for the voluntary basis of the process and seniority of debts;

[44] See EFC Subcommittee on EU Sovereign Debt Markets Model CAC Supplemental Explanatory Note, available at <http://europa.eu/efc/sub_committee/cac/cac_2012/index_en.htm>.

[45] As insolvency approaches, there seems to be a tendency towards the accumulation of sovereign debt in domestic financial institutions. This has indeed been the case for Spain and Italy after the ECB's LTRO. The decision to disenfranchise domestic banks that have received financial assistance and are thereby controlled by the governments could be extremely influential in the outcome of the restructuring process of Spain or Italy.

proportionality between the measures and the sovereign's needs; and the sharing of an equitable burden by all stakeholders, 'including citizens'.

The first danger is, at least to a certain extent, confronted by the Common Terms of Reference. In cross-series modifications, every amendment proposed concerning different series must be available to all holders of affected bonds. ECACs include the possibility of more than one alternative modification (a sort of menu of options for investors), so long as all alternatives are offered to any bondholder affected. Besides, the majorities required for cross series modifications allow bondholders of each series effectively to be masters of their own fate: if they do not reach the requisite percentage of the vote, the bonds of that series will not be affected by the agreement. This framework will indeed make it difficult for the sovereign to unduly mistreat a class of creditors.

Respect for the voluntary participation in the process is not regulated in any of the legal instruments or protected specifically by the institutional setting here analysed. However, the constitutional framework, the design of the powers of the public administration, and general principles of private law of all eurozone jurisdictions should provide sufficient instruments to prevent the coercive participation of bondholders.[46]

Finally, the last two 'tests of fairness' (proportionality between measures and needs and the equitable burden-sharing by stakeholders, 'including citizens') should be met by the euro area Member States in case of debt restructuring. The conditions for this do not derive from the Common Terms of Reference but from the euro area legal framework for the management of financial crises. Compliance with mandatory accounting standards would ensure the availability of sufficient macroeconomic information to allow creditors to reject restructurings that are disproportionate in relation to the country's economic situation. Concerning the last test, there can be little doubt that 'citizens' will bear a share of the restructuring. The current system of crisis management (ESM) is designed to demand extreme efforts from taxpayers. What remains to be seen is the extent to which private sector stakeholders will in fact share any of the citizens' efforts.

III. ECACs and the future: uncertainties and positive elements

The model ECAC will not be of any assistance to help solve the eurozone's current crisis. ECACs are only mandatory for euro-area government securities issued after 1 January 2013. Since the vast majority of bond issuances in eurozone countries (and certainly in the case of the most endangered states, Spain and Italy) are subject to domestic law and do not include CACs, bond restructuring could be achieved by the passing of a law with retroactive effect (as has recently been done with Greece).

[46] Principle 15 does not expressly state what is to be understood by 'voluntary participation' in the restructuring process. The author takes it to make reference to the inadequacy of a unilateral debt restructuring (i.e. the existence of an orderly negotiation and voting on a restructuring plan, e.g. via CACs) as well as to the absence of coercion regarding the vote on the restructuring plan. In the latter sense, the EU framework does provide some protection through the disenfranchisements clauses described previously.

It is clear that such law would not be bound by the terms of the ECAC concerning all bonds issued before 2013. But the solution is less evident if the restructuring was to be worked through an exchange of old bonds for new bonds with the amended conditions, since the new bonds would constitute a new issuance and they would therefore have to comply with the terms of ECAC. At least that could be the case for some of them.[47]

The efficacy of ECACs will depend on how they are incorporated into the legislatures of the Member States. The TESM provides a general mandate stating that 'collective action clauses shall be included . . . in all new euro area government securities, with maturity above one year, in a way that ensures that their legal impact is identical'. So the main rule established in the Treaty refers to an 'identical impact', but how that is to be achieved seems to be left open to each Member State. From a normative point of view, the ECACs are applicable law in each Member State of the eurozone, and no national law or regulation can contradict the European legal text. The reason for this is that the ECACs constitute a direct normative derivation of a mandate included in the TESM, which, as a treaty, is directly applicable and is hierarchically 'superior' to national legislation (i.e. it cannot be breached by a national legal instrument).

Another debate lies with the normative nature of the content of the ECACs, i.e. if they can be altered, so long as the amendment is made following the spirit and objective of the European norm. Arguably, ECACs are a primary legal instrument that need to be incorporated as they are, since they seek to strike a balance between the protections of different interests. This is clearly the case regarding supermajorities. A decrease in the percentage would make agreements easier; but it would undermine the legal certainty of investors that might regard that nation's bonds as too volatile. Obviously, this is not to say that all elements of the ECAC must be present in every issuance of bonds. The ECACs themselves expressly foresee the inclusion of certain clauses as voluntary: this would be the case for bonds issued with guarantees, with collateral, including acceleration and/or reverse acceleration clauses or bonds with the possibility to submit to a foreign jurisdiction. Those clauses can be included or not in a given bond issuance; but, if they are included, the clause must be drafted as stated in the text of the Common Terms of Reference.[48]

Another element that is paramount to the efficient application of ECACs is the consistent, uniform interpretation of the clauses. This could have been easily achieved by establishing the jurisdiction of one Member State or a supra-national

[47] The European Council decision of 24–25 March 2011 allowed Member States to 'tap' debt issuances already outstanding at the date of commencement of the mandatory ECACs. Eurozone countries can reopen outstanding bond issuances for a quantity that is a percentage of the total face amount of all central government debt securities issued that year, and those 'tapped' issuances would not be bound by the ECACs.

[48] This also seems to be the case for the clauses included in the ECACs Terms of Reference as 'Supplemental Provisions' (Manifest Error; Technical Amendments; Acceleration and Rescission of Acceleration; and Limitation on Sole Holder Action). The alternative would be to consider that the text of the supplemental provisions is included as a mere example, with no legal effect. Art. 4.3 TEU would, in the author's opinion, support the legally binding effect of the supplemental clauses.

European forum as applicable to all litigation disputes over ECACs. However, this solution has not been chosen by the drafters of the ECACs. The absence of a specific reference to the applicable jurisdiction can only imply that disputes will be solved according to the law that is applicable to the issued bonds. Unless recent practice in EU countries changes drastically, that will often mean that disputes will be solved at a national level. Consistent interpretation could be hampered. One way to achieve (*ex post*) homogeneous interpretation would be by appealing to the European Court of Justice. This could be done through preliminary rulings (ex Article 267 TFEU) or by way of appeals.

D. Conclusion

Developments in the financial crisis that hit Europe in 2010 have resulted in a real threat of eurozone break up. The EU has reacted by adopting deep reforms in the economic and legal framework. Arguably, the most effective set of measures consist of strengthening the controls, increasing transparency, and beefing up the powers of the European institutions. The robust European Economic Governance Framework, taken together with the previously existing legal and institutional framework, creates a powerful preventive mechanism capable of ensuring responsible borrowing and harnessing spendthrift Member States. Effective implementation and full compliance with the said framework should ensure that internal EU borrowing is consistent with the benchmark of the UNCTAD Principles.

The European Crisis Management Framework has created a permanent—reactive—mechanism to deal with the financial crises of Member States which pose a systemic risk for the eurozone. The ESM mirrors the IMF almost to last detail. But unlike the practice of the IMF in previous—mainly non-European—sovereign insolvencies, its European counterpart aims to tackle the crises by financial assistance with no private sector participation unless it is unavoidable. There are sound reasons to consider it both ineffective and unfair. It could be ineffective because automatic severe conditionality (austerity measures) with non-concessional interest rates has so far proven to worsen the economic situation of the Member States; and unfair because leaving the private sector out of the rescue confers a windfall upon largely sophisticated creditors at the expense of the European taxpayer.

The EU has also designed a system of *ex post* solution to the financial crisis of Member States. The system is partial (it only affects bonds), limited (it provides solutions only to certain elements of the collective action problem), and uncertain (its implementation must still be defined). However, it is a valid measure and a step forward in the process towards an adequate system of sovereign insolvency. The mandatory inclusion of CAC is in line with the implications of UNCTAD Principles 7 and 15.

The weak points of the *ex post* EU crisis management mechanisms (lack of centralized negotiations, partial scope, absence of an institutional framework to solve disputes) are, precisely, the strong points of a formal procedure. With the current environment, in the midst of arguably the most all-encompassing legal framework reform, this might well be the time for more audacious solutions: a full insolvency procedure applicable to the eurozone Member States.[49]

[49] In any case, any step towards the direction of an insolvency proceeding for sovereign insolvencies within the eurozone should be welcomed. For example, an immunity scheme (a type of stay of execution) has been suggested as a mechanism to make life more difficult for holdouts, preventing them from benefitting from the moneys of European taxpayers channelled though the ESM. See L.C. Buchheit, G.M. Gulati, and I. Tirado, 'The Problem of Holdout Creditors in Eurozone Sovereign Debt Restructurings' (2013), available at <http://papers.ssrn.com/sol3/papers.cfm?abstract_id=2205704>.

PART VI

OUTLOOK AND IMPLEMENTATION

15

Reforming Sovereign Lending Practices

Modern Initiatives in Historical Context

*W. Mark C. Weidemaier**

A. Introduction

Through its Principles of Responsible Sovereign Lending and Borrowing, the United Nations Conference on Trade and Development (UNCTAD) hopes to establish 'commonly accepted principles and practices' for sovereign loan transactions and sovereign debt restructurings. The Principles represent an important effort to identify and promote appropriate norms in the sovereign debt markets. Yet this ambitious goal is inextricably linked with more prosaic and technical questions about the design of sovereign loan contracts. For example, consider Principle 7, which observes that lenders '*have a duty to behave in good faith and with cooperative spirit*' in response to a sovereign's financial difficulty.[1] The sentiment may be universal, but such generalities are not likely to alter market participants' behaviour unless translated into more specific rights and duties and embodied in the terms of loan contracts (or imposed as a matter of mandatory law). For that reason, the Principles represent only a first step along the path to reform. Their ultimate ambition is to set a 'global standard for the contracting of sovereign debt, against which to assess the quality of contracts and the sustainability of debt'.[2]

The effort to develop the Principles occurs at what may be a critical juncture in the history of sovereign lending, but it is not unprecedented. Over the past century, a number of other initiatives have pursued similar goals. This chapter, based on a paper written for an UNCTAD-sponsored conference on the Principles, mines this historical context to unearth lessons relevant to the implementation and ultimate impact of the Principles. The chapter begins with three case studies. The first is the informal and largely unsuccessful effort by the League of Nations in the 1920s and

* For helpful comments I thank Adam Feibelman, Anna Gelpern, and Mitu Gulati.

[1] UNCTAD, 'Draft Principles on Promoting Responsible Sovereign Lending and Borrowing', Principle 7 (2012) (hereinafter 'the Principles'), reproduced in the Annex to this book.

[2] UNCTAD Press Release, 'UNCTAD unveils principles to guide responsible sovereign lending and borrowing', 4 May 2011.

1930s to introduce a range of innovations into sovereign loan contracts, including arbitration clauses and (to a lesser degree) collective action clauses (CACs). The second involves mid-twentieth century efforts to encourage market participants to rely on formal adjudication, including arbitration, to resolve sovereign debt disputes. The third revisits the late-twentieth century effort to encourage lenders and issuers to plan for restructuring *ex ante* through the use of model CACs. Drawing on a dataset of sovereign bonds issued in New York and London, the chapter demonstrates how contracts responded (or failed to respond) to these initiatives, often in ways reformers did not anticipate.

Several lessons emerge. Firstly, initiatives designed to change entrenched contracting practices may require coordinated and assertive leadership by governments and other international actors. Less direct methods—such as promulgating model clauses—often fail. One reason for this is that the officials involved may misread market sentiment. As an example, for most of the twentieth century governments tried to steer lending disputes, and other disputes between private investors and foreign sovereigns, into arbitration or litigation in national courts. So did the League of Nations, which proffered model arbitration clauses for this purpose. These efforts were premised on the belief that market participants wanted a viable forum for resolving sovereign lending disputes. Evidence from bond prices and contracts, however, suggests that this belief was mistaken. Investors, at least, had little interest in legal enforcement—perhaps because the existence of viable enforcement rights might have relieved some of the pressure on wealthy governments to protect bondholder interests. As a result, sovereign bonds almost uniformly omitted dispute resolution clauses until statutory changes late in the century made it impossible to ignore the subject any longer. One implication is that major shifts in contracting practices may require more explicit and coordinated official-sector guidance. It is, of course, a separate question whether public officials should intervene so directly in the terms of loan contracts.

A second lesson is that even successful initiatives can have unexpected results. In particular, efforts to encourage the use of uniform contract terms may have the paradoxical effect of provoking greater variation. For example, the successful effort to promote the use of CACs in bonds governed by New York law, initiated in the early 2000s by the US Treasury Department, seems to have prompted a flurry of innovation in other sovereign debt markets. Bonds governed by English law, which had previously employed standardized CACs, began to depart from the standard. A third lesson, then, is that uniformity in contract terms—assuming that is a desirable goal—may have to be mandated. Encouragement and suasion do not suffice, even when applied by esteemed and influential actors.

The chapter concludes by exploring further ways in which the Principles could shape sovereign debt practices. As the case studies highlight, it is hard to predict whether and how the Principles will affect contracts in the long term. Their most lasting impact may arise from the effort to crystallize general norms concerning appropriate borrower and creditor behaviour. As just one example, an increasingly diverse group of actors—including national courts, international tribunals, and ad hoc arbitration panels—must confront the question of whether creditors behave abusively in the context of a sovereign debt restructuring. Regardless of their impact on contracts, the Principles may play an important role in developing consensus on this and other questions.

B. Collective Action Clauses: the Early Models (1920–45)

Contract terms do not usually take centre stage in discussions of financial crises and macroeconomic policy, but CACs are an exception. For at least the past decade, much of the discussion about how to respond to sovereign debt crises has revolved around CACs,[3] and the discussion continues today with plans to mandate the use of standardized CACs in eurozone bonds.[4] Although the Principles do not often refer to specific contract terms, Principle 15 makes an exception for CACs and emphasizes their importance in facilitating restructuring negotiations.[5]

The term 'CAC' actually refers to a variety of clauses designed to ease the coordination problems that may complicate the restructuring of sovereign bond debt.[6] For example, *modification clauses* allow a defined percentage of bondholders to approve a restructuring proposal in a vote that will bind all holders of that bond, and *aggregation clauses* allow for a similar vote to occur across different bond issues.[7] The term 'CAC' is often used as shorthand for one or both of these clauses. On occasion, however, it is used to refer to other clauses. *Trustee clauses*, for example, empower a trustee to make decisions on behalf of bondholders as a group. *Bondholder committee clauses* provide for the formation of a committee to negotiate with the issuer after a default. *Collective acceleration clauses* prevent individual bondholders from demanding full payment after a default and instead condition acceleration on approval by a defined percentage of bondholders.[8] Although they work in different ways, these contract terms are functionally similar. Each enables

[3] For early proposals to use CACs, see B. Eichengreen and R. Portes, *Crisis? What Crisis? Orderly Workouts for Sovereign Debtors* (Centre for Economic Policy Research, 1995) 34–6; R. Macmillan, 'The Next Sovereign Debt Crisis' (1995) 31 SJIL 305, 356.

[4] Eurogroup, Statement by the Eurogroup of 28 November 2010, retrieved from <http://www.consilium.europa.eu/uedocs/cms_data/docs/pressdata/en/ecofin/118050.pdf>.

[5] The implications section to Principle 15 notes that: 'Collective action clauses can facilitate sovereign debt restructuring; therefore it is recommended that debtors and creditors should include them in multi-party debt instruments.'

[6] This is not to say that these CACs are *necessary* to overcome these problems. For a summary of restructurings during the period 1998–2010 and a comparison of exchange offers to CACs, see R. Bi, M. Chamon, and J. Zettelmeyer, 'The Problem that Wasn't: Coordination Failures in Sovereign Debt Restructurings', IMF Working Paper WP/11/265 (2011). Nor is there consensus as to whether CACs are the ideal solution to problems arising in the context of sovereign default. For a review of the issues and proposals for the creation of a sovereign bankruptcy mechanism, see P. Bolton and D. Skeel, 'Redesigning the International Lender of Last Resort' (2005) 6 Chi. J. Int'l L. 177; S. Schwarcz, 'Sovereign Debt Restructuring: A Bankruptcy Reorganization Approach' (2000) 85 Corn. L. Rev. 101.

[7] If a majority vote were required by holders of each bond issue, then a minority of the issuer's bondholders might block a restructuring if they comprised a majority of a particular bond issue. Aggregation clauses solve this problem.

[8] For further discussion of these clauses, see M. Bradley and M. Gulati, 'CACs for the Eurozone: An Empirical Analysis' (2011), available at <http://papers.ssrn.com/sol3/papers.cfm?abstract_id=1948534>; W.M.C. Weidemaier and M. Gulati, 'How Markets Work: The Lawyer's Version', Studies

bondholders to decide important questions collectively, thus making it harder for lone or small groups of bondholders to impede a course of action—such as a restructuring—that might benefit the group as a whole.[9]

Given their central place in modern debates, it is tempting to view CACs as recent innovations. But this is not the case. CACs have been around for over a century. What is true is that CACs did not enter widespread use in sovereign bonds until they were introduced into English-law bonds in the mid-1980s.[10] As is widely known, CACs later spread to bonds governed by New York law after a prominent issuer (Mexico) included a CAC in a 2003 bond issuance.[11] Mexico's issuance was preceded by an official sector initiative—often attributed primarily to the US Treasury Department—to encourage the use of CACs, and a widespread (but contested) narrative attributes the adoption of CACs in the New York market to this initiative.[12]

If that is so, then success was a long time coming. Since at least the 1920s, model CACs have been available for use in sovereign loan contracts. Wealthy governments included these clauses in loans they arranged or guaranteed for countries that would otherwise have been unable to access global capital markets. Major international banks underwrote these loans and clearly knew that the loan documents included the novel CACs. Indeed, the banks borrowed other innovations from these loans for use in other contexts. It seems, however, that CACs were quickly forgotten.

I. The League Loans

In the aftermath of First World War, reconstruction loans were arranged under the auspices of the League of Nations to a number of European countries that found themselves shut out of global capital markets. These included Austria, Bulgaria, Estonia, Greece, and Hungary.[13] The League's Financial Committee also provided less formal advice and assistance to other countries.[14] League member governments were heavily involved in negotiating the terms of these loans and worked closely with the participating banks to design the contracts.[15] Default on these loans was a very real possibility and would necessarily implicate League member states, which

in Law, Politics, & Society (n.d.), available at <http://papers.ssrn.com/sol3/papers.cfm?abstract_id=1886435>.

9 See H. Scott, 'A Bankruptcy Procedure for Sovereign Debtors' (2003) 37 International Lawyer 103, 116–18, summarizing holdout problems in sovereign bond lending.

10 On this point, see Weidemaier and Gulati (n. 8) 16–21.

11 The most complete analysis of this shift is A. Gelpern and M. Gulati, 'Public Symbol in Private Contract: A Case Study' (2006) 84 Wash. U. L. Rev. 1627. For empirical documentation of the shift, see Bradley and Gulati (n. 8) 11–16.

12 Gelpern and Gulati (n. 11) 1643–4, 1649–74; A. Feibelman, 'Contract, Priority, and Odious Debt' (2007) 85 N.C. L. Rev. 727, 755–7.

13 The League also arranged loans to the city of Danzig. For history on the League Loans, see M. Myers, 'The League Loans' (1945) 60 Political Science Quarterly 492.

14 See Myers (n. 13) 492.

15 Although it had of course declined to join the League, the US government also worked closely with participating banks. See M.P. Leffler, *The Elusive Quest: America's Pursuit of European Stability and French Security, 1919–1933* (University of North Carolina Press, 1979) 58–64.

in some cases had guaranteed the loans.[16] As a result, the contracts took pains to address the possibility of a future restructuring. In some cases, they did so in ways that would be immediately familiar to a modern-day lawyer.

Modification clauses: Modification clauses appeared in sovereign bonds as early as 1922, sometimes paired with clauses designating an official-sector representative of bondholder interests. For example, bonds issued in New York and London by Czechoslovakia were 'secured' by customs and other revenues[17] but contemplated that the issuer might default if these revenues proved insufficient to service the loan. In that event, the bonds established a process by which the loan might be restructured:

> 13 .... the Czechoslovak Government further undertakes that in the event it does not fulfil its obligations... the Council of the League of Nations shall be invited to nominate its Financial Committee or any other Committee or a Representative who shall be empowered to make the best arrangement for the protection of the Bondholders, provided that the previous consent of the majority in value of the Bondholders at a meeting as provided [below], shall be obtained before any arrangement is accepted or the intervention of the Council of the League of Nations is invited.
>
> ...
>
> 15. Should circumstances arise hereafter in which it may be necessary or expedient to obtain the sanction of the Bondholders to any exercise of their rights or... any proposal which may be made to them by the Czechoslovak Government,... [the bankers may convene a meeting in London] and the decision of the holders of the majority in nominal value of Bonds present at such meeting, either in person or represented by proxy, shall be binding upon all Bondholders... but such majority must be comprised of not less than fifty per cent. of the Sterling Bonds and not less than fifty per cent. of the Dollar Bonds outstanding...[18]

These bonds are noteworthy for the extent to which they anticipate modern practices. They allow a majority of bondholders to appoint a representative to act on their behalf and to approve 'any proposal' made to them by the issuer. Any vote had to occur at a meeting—a requirement that remained standard in English-law bonds with modification clauses until at least 2003.[19] And they offer assurance against unequal treatment of similarly situated bondholders by requiring a majority vote from holders of both New York and London issues.[20]

[16] See Myers (n. 13) 494–505.

[17] It is something of a euphemism to use the term 'secured' in the context of sovereign loans. In general, secured sovereign loans pledge some revenue stream, such as customs duties, to the service of a particular bond issue. For further discussion, and evidence of the prevalence of these clauses in the pre-Second World War era, see M. Weidemaier, R. Scott, and M. Gulati, 'Origin Myths, Contracts, and the Hunt for *Pari Passu*' (2013) 38 Law and Social Inquiry 72.

[18] Listing Application for the Czechoslovak State $14,000,000 Eight Per Cent. Bonds (11 January 1923); Listing Application for the Czechoslovak State $9,250,000 Eight Per Cent. Bonds (3 February 1925).

[19] Bradley and Gulati (n. 8) 18–19. The Czechoslovakian bonds, however, differ in that they require holders of at least 50% of the outstanding debt to approve a modification. In the modern era, many English-law bonds allow modification upon a much lower vote. See generally Weidemaier and Gulati (n. 8) 21–6; Bradley and Gulati (n. 8) 16–18.

[20] Modern aggregation clauses often contain similar protections. They allow a supermajority of all bondholders (say, 85%) to bind holders of every bond issue, but only if a certain percentage of bondholders in each issue (say, 66.7%) vote favourably. See Bradley and Gulati (n. 8) 21.

Collective acceleration and 'reverse' acceleration clauses: After a default, many sovereign bonds allow each bondholder to accelerate future payments due under their bonds. This complicates restructuring, for it allows holdout creditors to demand payment in full immediately instead of suing only to recover missed coupon payments. As noted previously, collective acceleration clauses condition acceleration on the approval of a certain percentage of bondholders (typically, 25 per cent). Some modern clauses go a step further and allow a majority of bondholders to reverse a decision to accelerate. Thus, even if a holdout creditor obtained a 25 per cent stake, the majority could override its decision to accelerate the loan.[21]

As with modification clauses, these seemingly modern innovations have been used sporadically for nearly a century. Consider the following clause from a 1923 issuance by the Kingdom of the Serbs, Croats, and Slovenes, which conforms almost exactly to modern acceleration and 'reverse' acceleration clauses:

> In case [of default] . . . the Bankers shall, if requested so to do by a writing signed by the holders of twenty-five per cent. in amount of the bonds then outstanding, declare the principal of all the bonds then outstanding to be due and payable immediately . . . This provision, however, is subject to the condition that if within one year after such declaration the default on the part of the Government shall have been made good to the satisfaction of the Bankers, then and in every such case the holders of a majority in amount of the bonds then outstanding, by written notice to the Bankers, may waive such default and rescind and annul such declaration of maturity . . .[22]

Similar clauses appear in bonds issued in foreign markets by provinces, municipalities, and other sub-sovereign entities.[23] These provisions are curious—the standard justification for an acceleration clause is that the clause prevents holdout creditors from using litigation to disrupt restructuring efforts.[24] But when these bonds were issued, both the United Kingdom and the United States recognized the absolute theory of sovereign immunity, under which foreign sovereigns were immune from suit in national courts.[25] The presence of such clauses in bonds issued in the 1920s implies that, even in a world without strong legal enforcement rights, there may be benefits to treating the decision to accelerate as one to be made by the bondholders collectively.

[21] For discussion of these clauses, see Bradley and Gulati (n. 8) 24.

[22] Listing Application, Kingdom of the Serbs, Croats, and Slovenes, Forty-Year Eight Per Cent. Secured External Gold Coupon Bonds (9 April 1923).

[23] See e.g. Listing Application, Province of Upper Austria (Land Oberosterreich) External Secured Sinking Fund Six and One Half Per Cent. Bonds (16 April 1928); Listing Application, Hungarian Consolidated Municipal Loan (21 September 1927).

[24] S.J. Galvis and A.L. Saad, 'Sovereign Exchange Offers in 2010' (2005) 6 Chi. J. Int'l L. 219, 226–7. Whether the clause does so effectively is another question. For a sceptical view, see H.S. Scott, 'A Bankruptcy Procedure for Sovereign Debtors?' (2003) 37 International Lawyer 103, 120–1.

[25] In some European countries, by contrast, the principle of absolute immunity began to break down as early as the mid-19th century. French, German, and Swiss courts, for example, enforced *ex ante* waivers of state sovereign immunity under some circumstances, though typically only when the loan had some connection to the forum. See Harvard Law School Research in International Law, 'Competence of Courts in Regard to Foreign States' (1932) 26 AJIL Supp. 473, 548–80; G.R. Delaume, 'Jurisdiction of Courts and International Loans: A Study of Lenders' Practice' (1957) 6 AJIL 189, 203–4.

Trustee clauses: Some modern bonds provide for a trustee to make important decisions on behalf of bondholders, including whether to accelerate the loan and whether to sue. These clauses, too, have historical roots dating back at least to the League Loans. For example, unable to tap global capital markets on its own after the First World War, the Austrian government issued bonds guaranteed by a number of League of Nations member governments. The bonds called for the appointment of a trustee responsible both for ensuring that bondholders were paid out of Austrian customs duties set aside for that purpose and for enforcing the guarantee, if necessary.[26] Similar clauses appeared in bonds issued by Estonia,[27] Hungary,[28] and by Germany in connection with the Dawes (1924) and Young (1930) reconstruction plans.[29]

II. The Committee for the Study of International Loan Contracts

It is likely that League of Nations officials played a significant role in introducing these innovations into sovereign bond contracts. League officials, after all, were intimately involved in negotiating and documenting the loans and in ensuring their marketability.[30] But during the 1920s, they made no concerted effort to encourage widespread use of particular contract terms. By the mid-1930s, however, League officials had responded to the growing financial crisis by launching a more formal campaign to reform the terms of sovereign loan contracts. A 1935 resolution sponsored by the Netherlands created the Committee for the Study of International Loan Contracts, which was expressly charged with 'examin[ing] the means for improving contracts relating to international loans issued by Governments . . . and, in particular, [with preparing] model provisions . . . which could, if the parties so desired, be inserted into such contracts'.[31]

The Committee comprised leading figures from central banks, international financial institutions, and private bondholder associations.[32] Much of the Committee's attention was focused on the possibility of creating a system of international arbitration for resolving sovereign debt disputes.[33] Yet the Committee was

[26] Listing Application, Austrian Government Guaranteed Loan, 1923–1943 (29 May 1924). Guarantor states deposited their own bonds into an account in the trustee's name. After a default, the trustee was entitled to demand payment from each guarantor in exchange for surrendering bond coupons of equivalent value.

[27] See Listing Application, Republic of Estonia (Banking and Currency Reform) 7 Per Cent. Loan (29 October 1928).

[28] See Listing Application, Kingdom of Hungary Seven and One-Half Bonds (4 February 1925).

[29] See Listing Application, German External Loan 1924 (14 October 1924); Listing Application, German Government International 5½ per cent Loan 1930 (6 March 1931).

[30] For contemporaneous history, see Sir Arthur Salter, 'The Reconstruction of Austria' (1924) 2 *Foreign Affairs* 630; Sir Arthur Salter, 'The Reconstruction of Hungary', (1926) 5 *Foreign Affairs* 91–102. For a retrospective history, see G.A. Olivares Marcos, *The Legal Practice of the Recovery of State External Debts* (Institut universitaire de hautes études internationals, 2005) 125–30.

[31] League of Nations, *Report of the Committee for the Study of International Loan Contracts* (1939) 5 (hereinafter '*Report on Loan Contracts*').

[32] League of Nations, *Report on Loan Contracts* (n. 31) 5.

[33] On the committee's activities generally, see M. Waibel, *Sovereign Defaults Before International Courts and Tribunals* (Cambridge University Press, 2011) 324–6.

clearly aware that loan contracts could be improved by facilitating bondholder coordination. Its report, released in 1939, extensively discussed the potential benefits of trustee clauses and bondholder representatives[34] and proffered a mechanism for obtaining bondholder assent to a restructuring.[35] The Committee was also explicit about its concern that individual bondholders might undercut the collective good, especially through litigation: 'Too many lawsuits would be a bad thing; not only would they be unpleasant for the debtors, but their Stock Exchange effects would be disastrous.'[36] To limit this risk, the Committee discussed the merits of centralizing the power to initiate litigation in the hands of a bondholder representative.[37]

The report did not provide model clauses appointing a trustee or bondholder representative, but it did include a model clause providing for ad hoc arbitration.[38] In the Committee's view, its model clause neatly solved a recurring problem in the sovereign debt markets: the difficulty in finding a tribunal 'whose decisions will have legal and moral force in cases of dispute'.[39] The lack of such a tribunal, the Committee suggested, was what had kept previous sovereign debt disputes from being 'easily settled'.[40] Reflecting the Committee's fear of '[t]oo many lawsuits', the model clause provided that an arbitration could be initiated only by a bondholder representative or by a bondholder or group of bondholders holding at least 10 per cent of the outstanding debt.[41]

III. The market's (lack of) response

As these early bond issues make clear, many 'modern' innovations in the sovereign debt markets are not especially modern. Modification, acceleration, and trustee clauses have been in use for nearly a century, along with a range of other clauses that facilitate collective bondholder action. Many of these clauses appeared in loans arranged by the League of Nations to high-risk countries otherwise unable to access the capital markets. Major international banks—such as Rothschilds, Barings, and JP Morgan—were involved in these loans and were thus well aware of the benefits supposedly attributable to CACs. Furthermore, although the Committee for the Study of International Loan Contracts had only provided one model clause concerned primarily with arbitration, the League Loans provided models for modification clauses, acceleration clauses, and clauses providing for the appointment of a trustee.

[34] League of Nations, *Report on Loan Contracts* (n. 31) 17–21, 32–7.

[35] League of Nations, *Report on Loan Contracts* (n. 31) 33–4, proposing mechanics for conducting a meeting to vote on a restructuring proposal negotiated by the issuer and a bondholder representative.

[36] League of Nations, *Report on Loan Contracts* (n. 31) 33.

[37] League of Nations, *Report on Loan Contracts* (n. 31) 32.

[38] For extensive discussion, see Waibel (n. 33) 324–5.

[39] League of Nations, *Report on Loan Contracts* (n. 31) 24.

[40] League of Nations, *Report on Loan Contracts* (n. 31) 25.

[41] League of Nations, *Report on Loan Contracts* (n. 31) 26. The debtor government could also initiate an arbitration.

With respect to CACs, however, the League Loans seemingly had little impact on general market practices. In the course of other work, I and others have compiled a dataset of over 1,800 contracts and disclosure documents for sovereign bonds issued between 1823 and 2011.[42] The dataset consists primarily of bonds issued in London and New York and thus only permits inferences about these markets. Nevertheless, it provides little reason to believe these early CACs ever spread beyond a small subset of issues. Compared to their heyday in the nineteenth and early twentieth centuries, the bond markets were relatively dormant between 1930 and the mid-1980s.[43] Nevertheless, sovereigns continued to issue bonds during this era, and the dataset includes 380 issues between 1930 and 1985.

As Figure 15.1 indicates, the number of bonds in this era that included any form of CAC was small both as an absolute number and as a proportion of total issuances. The figure includes only bonds issued by countries in foreign markets. By contrast, CACs made occasional appearances in bonds issued by sub-sovereign entities, such as cities and provinces, as early as the 1920s.[44] But they did not appear with any frequency in bonds issued by countries until bonds governed by English law began to adopt modification clauses in the mid-1980s.[45]

The absence of CACs from government bonds cannot have been inadvertent. Banks were not shy about borrowing clauses found in League Loan documentation and putting them to use in other loan contracts. For example, Rothschilds, JP Morgan, and other banks appear to have copied arbitration clauses from some League Loan contracts nearly verbatim in other loan contracts.[46] The more plausible inference is that the bankers saw little reason to include CACs in the vast majority of government loans. Perhaps they were short-sighted. But it is also possible that policy-makers were focused on contract innovations that had little resonance for market actors. The effort to promote sovereign debt arbitration, discussed later, lends some credence to this view.

[42] For a more detailed description, see Weidemaier, Scott, and Gulati (n. 17); Bradley and Gulati (n. 8) 30–1.

[43] Y. Cassis, *Capitals of Capital: A History of International Financial Centres, 1780–2005* (Cambridge University Press, 2006) 192–3; R. Macmillan, 'Towards a Sovereign Debt Work-Out System' (1995) 16 Nw. J. Int'l L. & Bus. 57, 80–4.

[44] See e.g. Listing Application, Province of Buenos Aires 6 per cent Loan (31 July 1928), including a clause permitting acceleration and reversal by a majority of bondholders.

[45] See Weidemaier and Gulati (n. 8) 17–21.

[46] e.g. an arbitration clause was included in the contract for a loan to Czechoslovakia in 1922. See Agreement Between the Czechoslovak State and Baring Brothers & Co. (5 April 1922), para. 19. Very shortly thereafter, a nearly identical clause appeared in the contract for a loan to Brazil. See Agreement Among the Government of the Republic of the United States of Brazil, NM Rothschild & Sons, Baring Brothers & Co., and J. Henry Schroder & Co. (2 May 1922) para. 21. The clause, or a variant of it, was then repeated in contracts for loans to Argentina (in 1925) and Hungary (in 1926). See Agreement Among the Government of the Argentine Nation, JP Morgan & Co., and the National City Company (25 May 1925), section 5; Agreement Among the Government of the Kingdom of Hungary, NM Rothschild & Sons, Baring Brothers & Co., and J. Henry Schroder & Co. (23 July 1926), para. 30.

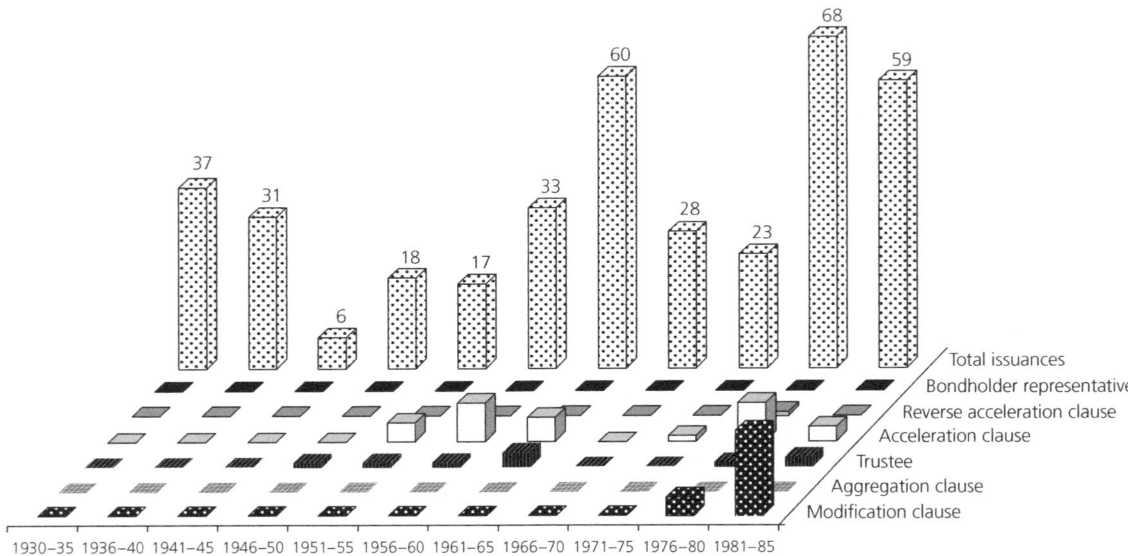

Fig. 15.1 Use of CACs in sovereign bonds, 1930–1985

C. The (Mostly Ignored) Effort to Facilitate Legal Enforcement

This section examines efforts to promote the use of adjudication to resolve sovereign lending disputes. The previous section discussed efforts by the Committee for the Study of International Loan Contracts to promote arbitration as a means of solving sovereign lending disputes. That early effort was followed by two important mid-century initiatives. The first was the effort to create multilateral treaty regimes to promote the use of international arbitration. The second was the gradual relaxation of the formerly strict approach to foreign sovereign immunity in the United Kingdom and United States. Despite the predictions of reformers, however, the evidence suggests that participants in the sovereign debt markets viewed these developments as largely irrelevant.

I. The mid-century effort to promote arbitration and litigation

If the report issued by the Committee on the Study of International Loan contracts had no perceptible impact on the use of CACs, it had an equally negligible impact with respect to its primary goal of encouraging arbitration. As noted previously, the Committee seemingly viewed its model clause as a sensible and uncontroversial solution to a problem that had bedeviled market participants: how to find an adjudicatory forum whose decisions would have 'legal and moral force'. If that were true, one would have expected market participants to eagerly embrace the model clause prepared by the Committee or to adapt for their own purposes one of the arbitration clauses used in the League Loan contracts in the 1920s.[47]

In the nineteenth and early twentieth centuries, arbitration was used to resolve a number of sovereign debt disputes, and arbitration clauses made rare appearances in sovereign bonds.[48] As I have noted elsewhere, however, many of these arbitration agreements were not genuine efforts to facilitate arbitration between bondholders and the borrower government.[49] Instead, many were designed to provide a legal pretext for the United States to intervene in the borrower's affairs—by force if necessary—in the event of a default.[50] But the United States and other capital-exporting countries grew increasingly unwilling to intervene so directly to protect their citizens' foreign investments. This fact goes some way towards explaining their newfound interest in legal enforcement. By encouraging creditors to rely on

[47] On several occasions, in fact, banks did adapt League Loan arbitration clauses for use in new contracts. Examples are cited in n. 46. They often did so, however, only to resolve disputes between the banks and the issuer. In those cases, the arbitration clause appeared in the loan contract between these parties, rather than in the bond itself, and referred only to disputes involving the banks.

[48] See Waibel (n. 33) 157–62. For an argument in favour of establishing an arbitration mechanism for managing sovereign restructurings, see K. Raffer, 'Debt Workout Mechanisms: Debt Arbitration' in F. Cheru and C. Bradford, Jr (eds), *The Millennium Development Goals, Raising the Resources to Tackle World Poverty* (Zed Books, 2005) 156–80.

[49] W.M.C. Weidemaier, 'Contracting for State Intervention: The Origins of Sovereign Debt Arbitration' (2010) 73 Law & Cont. Probs 335.

[50] Weidemaier (n. 49) 347–50.

arbitration or litigation, these countries may have hoped to deflect pressure to intervene in more direct and costly ways.[51]

In fact, over the course of the twentieth century, the United States and other governments adopted policies designed to channel their citizens' foreign investment disputes into arbitration or litigation.[52] Some of these efforts were multilateral, such as the New York Convention on arbitration in 1959 and the 1966 creation of the International Centre for Settlement of Investment Disputes.[53] Governments also tried to facilitate litigation against foreign sovereigns in national courts. Most notably, in the latter half of the twentieth century, the United States and United Kingdom abandoned the doctrine of absolute sovereign immunity in favour of the restrictive theory of immunity. As a result of this change, national courts gained limited power to hear lawsuits and enforce judgments against foreign sovereigns. In the United States, the shift to the restrictive theory of immunity began in 1952, when the State Department announced that, as a matter of Department policy, foreign sovereigns would no longer enjoy absolute immunity from suit in US courts.[54] Later in the century, both the United Kingdom (1978) and the United States (1976) formally adopted the restrictive theory of immunity by statute.[55]

For present purposes, several aspects of this (truncated) history are noteworthy.[56] First, governments actively promoted arbitration and litigation as methods of resolving disputes between private parties and sovereign entities. Secondly, they did so in part to insulate themselves from pressure to intervene more directly in these disputes. Thirdly, although debates at the time were not focused on sovereign loans, government officials were aware that sovereign lending disputes might be resolved through litigation or arbitration and viewed that as a positive development.[57] In this sense, these government policies were a natural extension of the efforts made by the Committee for the Study of International Loan Contracts.

[51] Weidemaier (n. 49) 350; Waibel (n. 33) 163.

[52] For a version of this argument, see W.M.C. Weidemaier, 'Sovereign Immunity and Sovereign Debt' (2012), available at <http://papers.ssrn.com/sol3/papers.cfm?abstract_id=2180228>.

[53] United Nations Convention on the Recognition and Enforcement of Foreign Arbitral Awards, 10 June 1958, 330 U.N.T.S. 3; Convention for the Settlement of Investment Disputes Between States and Nationals of Other States, Art. 55 (14 October 1966). Neither convention purports to address all of the issues that arise in the context of legal enforcement against sovereign states, and indeed the New York Convention does not address the subject of sovereign immunity.

[54] See Tate Letter, (1952) 26 Department of State Bulletin 984.

[55] See Foreign Sovereign Immunities Act, 28 U.S.C. §§ 1602ff.; State Immunity Act, 1978, c. 33 (UK).

[56] For an extensive treatment of these developments and their impact on loan contracts, see Weidemaier (n. 52).

[57] e.g. the State Immunity Act permits lawsuits against foreign sovereigns arising out of their commercial activities and includes in its definition of commercial activity 'any loan or transaction for the provision of finance'. State Immunity Act, 1978, c. 33, § 3(3). And while early drafts of the Foreign Sovereign Immunities Act proposed to retain immunity in cases arising out of a foreign sovereign's 'public debt', this was controversial and these provisions were removed. Explaining the decision to remove them, the relevant report of the House of Representatives flatly states that sovereign loans 'are activities which are of a commercial nature . . . [and] would not otherwise give rise to immunity'. House Report (Judiciary Committee) No. 94-1487, 1976 U.S.C.C.A.N. 6604, 6609. The Report also states the authors' belief that loan contracts would immediately adopt contract terms waiving the borrower's immunity from suit.

In each case, government officials and international actors acted on the belief that participants in the sovereign debt markets would embrace an adjudicatory process that could provide decisions with 'legal and moral force'.

II. Again, contracts do not respond

As with CACs, however, market participants seemingly viewed these innovations with indifference. It is true that sovereign loan contracts have occasionally included arbitration and other dispute resolution clauses.[58] But it is easy to overstate the frequency with which these clauses appeared, at least in bonds issued in New York and London. Until relatively late in the twentieth century, in fact, most sovereign bonds issued in these markets ignored the subject of dispute resolution altogether.[59]

Focusing on each decade from 1930 to the present, Figure 15.2 shows the total number of bond contracts in the dataset, the number that included waivers of the issuer's immunity from suit in foreign courts, and the number that included arbitration clauses. As the Figure indicates, arbitration clauses have never been common, and clauses submitting to the jurisdiction of foreign courts did not appear with any frequency until the 1970s, when both the United States and United Kingdom embraced the restrictive theory of sovereign immunity by statute. (Recall that the United States had embraced the restrictive theory as a matter of policy by 1952.)

It is not surprising that arbitration clauses rarely appear in sovereign bonds. Cross-border commercial loans, for example, rarely include arbitration clauses, a fact sometimes attributed to lenders' fear that arbitrators will not rigorously enforce loan obligations.[60] When modern sovereign bonds do include arbitration clauses, it

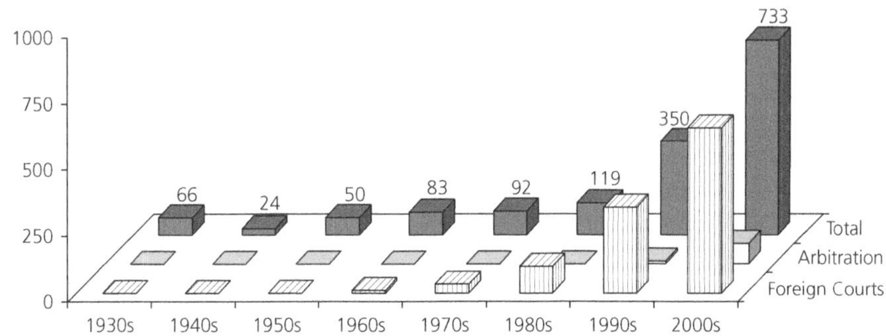

Fig. 15.2 Dispute resolution clauses, 1930–present

[58] See Waibel (n. 33) 160–8.

[59] Moreover, some early arbitration clauses were limited to disputes between the underwriting banks and the issuing government; bondholders themselves could not invoke the clause.

[60] See W.M.C. Weidemaier, 'Disputing Boilerplate' (2009) 82 Temple L. Rev. 1, 14.

is often because there is some reason to doubt the enforceability of foreign court judgments in the borrower's domestic courts.[61] Figure 15.2 is perhaps most noteworthy, then, for what it reveals about pre-1970s efforts to encourage sovereign bond contracts to include dispute resolution terms: they did not work.

In a private loan, the possibility of legal enforcement helps to assure the lender of repayment. Because sovereigns have traditionally been immune from suit and even now enjoy a variety of practical immunities, legal enforcement plays a much lesser role.[62] Nevertheless, sovereign bonds evolved in the late 1970s to include terms designed to facilitate litigation in national courts. How and why this evolution came to pass is discussed extensively elsewhere.[63] For present purposes, two aspects of the evolution are noteworthy. First, despite efforts to promote the use of arbitration clauses in sovereign bonds, and despite efforts to facilitate litigation against foreign sovereigns in national courts, very few bond contracts addressed the subject of dispute resolution until after major enforcement jurisdictions *codified* the restrictive theory of sovereign immunity.[64] The report issued by the Committee for the Study of International Loan Contracts, the adoption of the New York and ICSID Conventions promoting international arbitration, the 1952 adoption in the United States of the restrictive theory of sovereign immunity as a matter of policy—these developments had no discernible impact on the terms of sovereign bonds.[65]

Secondly, after the restrictive theory of immunity was codified in the United States and the United Kingdom in the 1970s, bonds issued in these jurisdictions almost uniformly incorporated terms waiving the sovereign's immunity from suit in national courts. But this change did *not* correspond to a major shift in lenders' dismissive attitude towards legal enforcement. In the United States, for example, bond prices did not react to the introduction or enactment of the Foreign Sovereign Immunities Act, suggesting that investors did not believe these statutes materially improved their position in the event of a default.[66]

Twentieth-century efforts to promote the use of arbitration and litigation were premised on the belief that investors wanted legal enforcement rights, or at least would take advantage of these rights once they were granted. But for much if not all of the century, this seems not to have been true. Sovereign bonds ignored the subject of dispute resolution despite decades of encouragement. It took major statutory developments to produce change in the terms of sovereign bond contracts, and there remains little evidence to suggest that bondholders viewed their newfound enforcement rights as meaningful.

[61] See Weidemaier (n. 60) 29–32.

[62] U. Panizza, F. Sturzenegger, and J. Zettelmeyer, 'The Economics and Law of Sovereign Debt and Default' (2009) 47 J. Econ. Lit. 1, 2–9, 20.

[63] See Weidemaier (n. 52).

[64] Because Figure 15.2 includes only bonds issued in New York and London, the US and UK would have been the primary (but not exclusive) sites of enforcement litigation.

[65] Some sub-sovereign issuers agreed to waive their immunity from suit and submit to the jurisdiction of foreign courts. So did Malaysia in 1965. See Weidemaier (n. 52) 26. But these were the rare exceptions.

[66] See Weidemaier (n. 52).

D. CACs, Reprised

This section returns to efforts to promote the use of CACs—in particular, modification clauses allowing bondholders to amend payment-related terms without a unanimous vote. As noted,[67] bonds governed by English law began to incorporate modification clauses in the mid-1980s, but bonds governed by New York law typically required unanimous assent to any modification. Beginning in 2003, a major shift occurred in which New York-law bonds also began to incorporate modification clauses. The story of this shift is widely known. As Gelpern and Gulati have documented, a prominent narrative attributes the shift to a combination of official sector pressure, the desire to pre-empt the introduction of a statutory sovereign bankruptcy regime, and innovation by leading market players.[68] In what follows, I accept the validity of that narrative, including its emphasis on the official sector's role in producing the change. I focus primarily on sovereign bond contracts after 2003.

The years leading up to the shift encompassed not only official-sector initiatives to promote the use of modification clauses, but also a range of efforts to promote the use of standardized CACs. These efforts went beyond modification clauses and encompassed trustee and bondholder representative clauses, acceleration clauses, and others. For example, at the behest of governments which made up the G-10, a working group of bankers, finance officials, and prominent lawyers proposed model clauses to be used 'as a package' in sovereign bonds.[69] An industry trade group, the International Capital Markets Association (ICMA), also proposed model clauses.[70] These models differed, but they reflected the widespread belief that contracting practices with respect to CACs would soon crystallize around a common standard. Indeed, some market participants believed that standardization was critical and that the 'least desirable outcome' would be for CACs to become 'a source of competition'.[71]

Yet bond contracts are hardly standardized in their use of CACs. After 2003, to be sure, virtually all bonds issued under New York or English law include modification clauses.[72] Almost all bonds governed by New York law, moreover, impose

[67] See text accompanying n. 45.

[68] See Gelpern and Gulati (n. 11) 1649–73; A. Gelpern and M. Gulati, 'Innovation After the Revolution: Foreign Sovereign Bond Contracts Since 2003' (2009) 4 Cap. Mkts L.J. 85, 86–90.

[69] See Group of Ten, 'Report of the G-10 Working Group on Contractual Clauses' (2002), available at <http://www.bis.org/publ/gten08.pdf>.

[70] See International Primary Market Association (now ICMA), 'Standard Collective Action Clauses (CACs) for the Terms and Conditions of Sovereign Notes, English Law, Fiscal Agent Structure' (2004), available at <http://www.icmagroup.org>.

[71] Robert B. Gray, Chairman, International Primary Market Association, 'Remarks Prepared for Delivery at UNCTAD Fourth Inter-Regional Debt Management Conference' (2003), available at <http://r0.unctad.org/dmfas/pdfs/Gray_Dammers.pdf>.

[72] As noted, a widely-accepted explanation for the shift emphasizes the combination of pressure by the US Treasury Department and the belief by some market participants that, by adopting modification clauses, they could deflect attention away from a solution they perceived as less desirable: the proposed sovereign debt restructuring mechanism. See text accompanying n. 68.

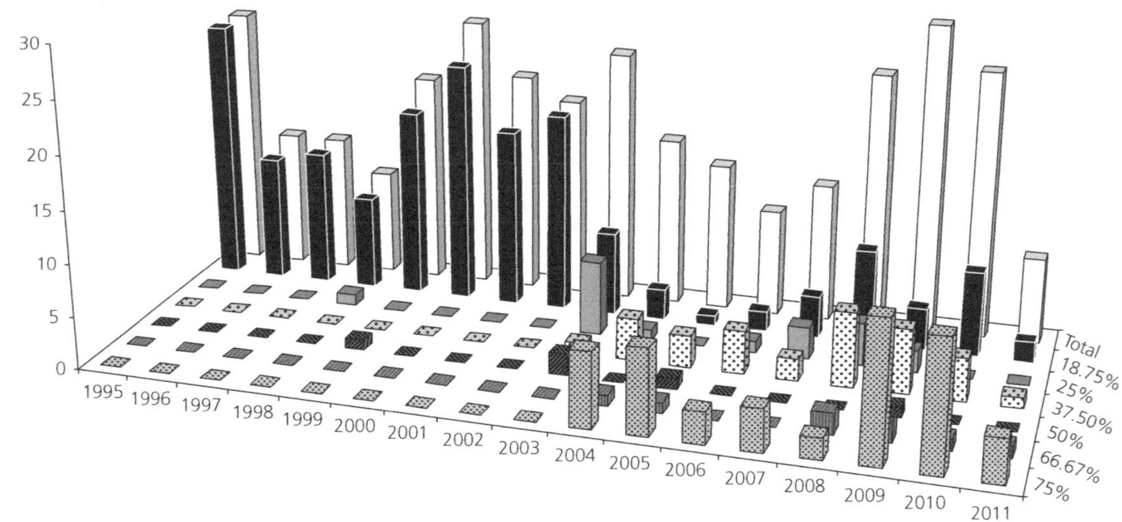

Fig. 15.3 Minimum vote to modify payment terms in English-law bonds

the same voting threshold for modifying payment-related terms. A modification must be approved by holders of 75 per cent of the aggregate principal amount of the outstanding debt, and this vote need not take place at a meeting.[73] In the wake of this relatively uniform shift in New York-law bonds, however, bonds governed by English law began to adopt new voting thresholds. Before 2003, virtually all English-law bonds allowed modification upon a much lower vote—typically 18.75 per cent.[74] Since 2003, however, English-law bonds have adopted a much wider range of voting thresholds, as Figure 15.3 shows. It is as if the shift in New York destabilized the standard that had prevailed in English-law bonds, although of course the causation remains unclear.

In part, the change in English-law contracting practices reflects the presence of new issuers in the market.[75] But a number of established issuers also adopted new voting thresholds.[76] Figure 15.3, moreover, focuses on only one source of variation: the vote required to modify payment-related bond terms. Additional variation persists in how sovereign bonds employ CACs. Recall that the term 'CAC' encompasses a variety of contract terms. These include, among others, modification clauses, aggregation clauses, trustee clauses, collective acceleration and reverse acceleration clauses, and clauses allowing for the appointment of a bondholder committee or representative. As a rough measure of how comprehensively sovereign bonds address collective action concerns, one can ask how *many* of these terms a given bond incorporates.

Using that measure, Figures 15.4 and 15.5 track the evolution over the past decade in bonds governed by New York and English law. As Figure 15.4 shows, before 2003, many bonds issued under New York law contained none of these terms ('No CAC'). Those that had CACs generally included only a restriction on the right of individual bondholders to accelerate the loan ('Acceleration Clause Only').[77] The few remaining bonds had modification clauses but did not include any other CAC ('Modification Clause Only'). After 2003, many bonds incorporated modification clauses but did not otherwise address collective action concerns. In many other cases, however, bonds addressed these concerns more comprehensively, often incorporating two, three, or even four of the CACs just listed.

Bonds governed by English law follow a similar pattern. Before 2003, most included modification clauses (unlike bonds governed by New York law), but only a handful contained other terms designed to address bondholder collective action

[73] See Bradley and Gulati (n. 8); Weidemaier and Gulati (n. 8).

[74] See Bradley and Gulati (n. 8); Weidemaier and Gulati (n. 8). This low voting threshold only applied when the vote was taken at an adjourned meeting, at which a lower quorum requirement applied.

[75] See Gelpern and Gulati (n. 68) 92.

[76] Often this was accomplished by eliminating the mandatory meeting requirement. Under the new bonds, the voting threshold must be satisfied by bondholders holding the requisite percentage of the outstanding debt, whereas the old bonds allowed modification if approved by the requisite percentage of bondholders *present or represented at a meeting*. The latter percentage is, of course, much lower, as only a subset of bondholders will attend or give proxies for a meeting. See Bradley and Gulati (n. 8) 17–19.

[77] The 'Acceleration Clause Only' category includes bonds with collective acceleration clauses as well as bonds that also include a 'reverse' acceleration clause.

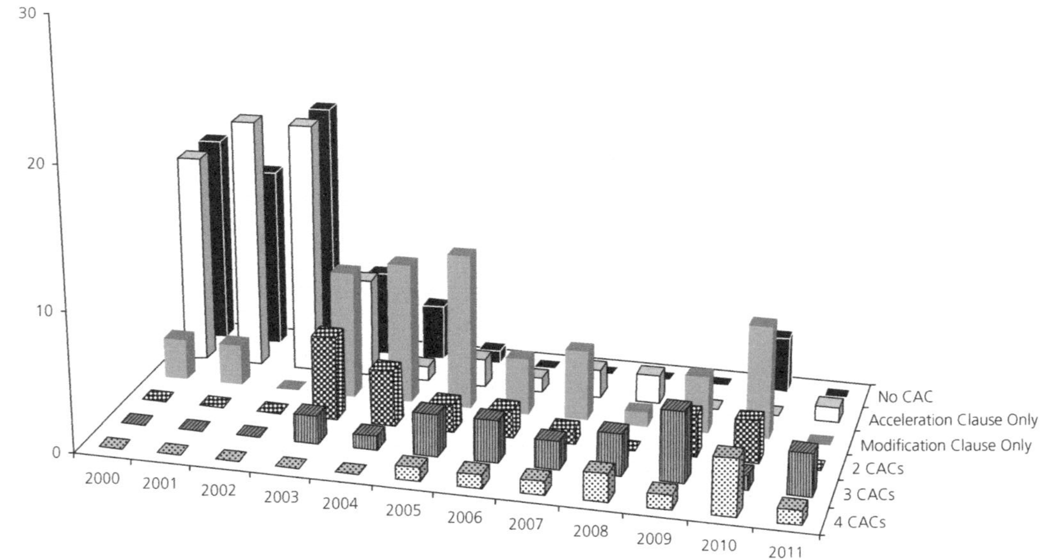

Fig. 15.4 Different types of CAC; number of New York-law bonds (2000–present)

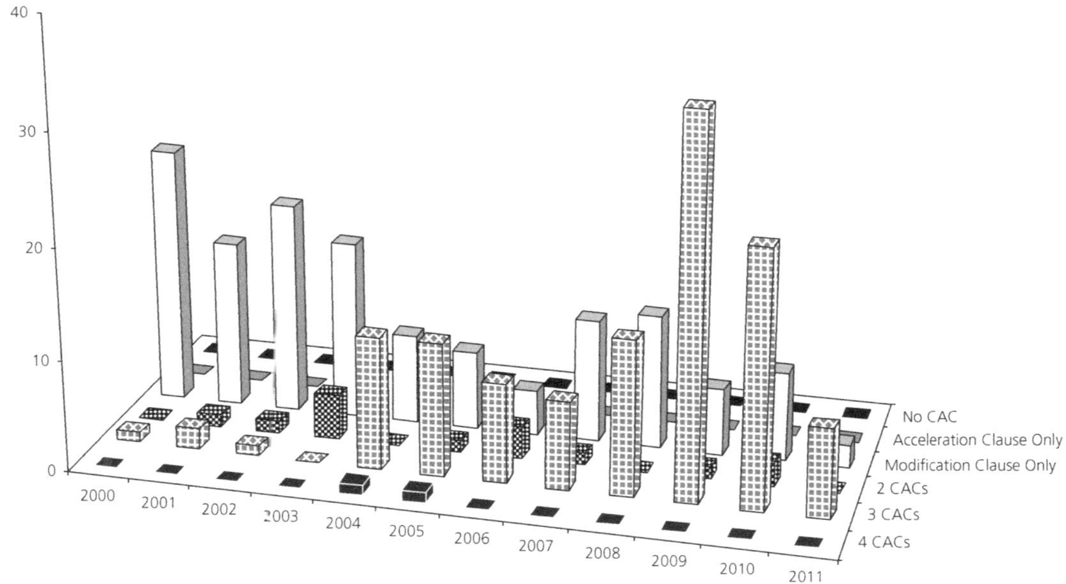

Fig. 15.5 Different types of CAC; number of English-law bonds (2000–present)

problems. Since 2003, however, bonds have often combined several of the CACs mentioned.

Admittedly, Figures 15.4 and 15.5 paint with broad strokes. They show that bonds issued after 2003 often include multiple terms designed to address bondholder collective action problems. Much of the attention in the sovereign debt world has been focused on the post-2003 shift to modification clauses in bonds governed by New York law. But in fact, what took place was more significant and had ramifications outside New York. In both markets, bonds began to address bondholder coordination problems more comprehensively. One issuance, for example, might include a modification clause that allow for aggregation across all of the issuer's bonds, provide for a trustee, and allow for collective decisions on whether to accelerate the loan and whether to reverse a decision to accelerate. Yet contracts did not conform to any of the available standards—such as the G-10 or ICMA model clauses. Instead, drafters adopted a range of approaches. Indeed, Figures 15.4 and 15.5 understate the variance by collapsing different approaches into a single category. Thus, the '3 CACs' category includes every bond that uses *any* three of the CACs listed earlier. Since 2003, in fact, English-law bonds have employed at least 11 different combinations of these terms, while New York-law bonds have employed at least 16.

It is not clear why sovereign bonds have adopted such varied approaches or whether bond prices are sensitive to all of these differences. The evidence does indicate that bond prices are sensitive to CACs, although the results sometimes point in different directions.[78] In the light of this evidence, it is plausible to assume that market participants have heterogeneous preferences with respect to these clauses. Certainly there is no obvious preference for standardization. And if that is so, it is not surprising that efforts to promote standardization have not succeeded.

E. The Long-Term Impact of UNCTAD's Principles

This section returns to UNCTAD's present effort to develop principles and best practices for the sovereign debt markets. As noted at the outset, the long-term impact of the Principles will be judged in part by whether they have a significant impact on loan contracts. This is not by any means the best or only way to judge their success. The Principles also aim to shape the behaviour of market participants in ways that might not be directly reflected in the terms of loan contracts. For example, if the Principles induce lenders to assess more seriously the ability of sovereign borrowers to repay (Principle 4), they will have had a profoundly positive impact.

[78] Bradley and Gulati (n. 8), find generally that CACs are associated with lower borrowing costs for higher-risk issuers, while earlier studies reach contrary results or find no association. Earlier studies include, among others, B. Eichengreen and A. Mody, 'Do Collective Action Clauses Raise Borrowing Costs' (2004) 114 Econ. J. 247–64, and M. Gugiatti and A. Richards, 'Do Collective Action Clauses Influence Bond Yields? New Evidence from Emerging Markets' (2003) 6 Int'l Fin. 415–47.

It is clear, however, that the Principles also aim to influence contracts. Sovereign bond contracts vary in significant ways, but in many respects they remain standardized and resistant to change. Efforts to prompt change must therefore overcome the natural inertia that characterizes such contracts.[79] A sizeable body of contract theory suggests ways in which this might happen. Of particular relevance here, some theories emphasize that governments and official sector actors can play an important role in overcoming barriers to innovation.[80] As this chapter has demonstrated, the history of sovereign lending is filled with such initiatives.[81]

This history does not yield definitive lessons. It suggests, however, that efforts to build consensus, or to provide model terms for market participants to adopt, may have only minimal impact. As examples, consider the range of initiatives to introduce new terms into sovereign bond contracts. The Financial Committee of the League of Nations introduced CACs into loan contracts in the 1920s—arguably legitimizing their use and providing a model for others to follow. Somewhat later in the century, the Committee for the Study of International Loan Contracts—a group comprising esteemed lawyers and finance officials—emphasized the need to facilitate coordinated bondholder action through the appointment of trustees and bondholder representatives. The Committee also sought to encourage the use of arbitration clauses and proffered a model clause for that purpose. Its efforts were aided by a range of government initiatives to promote arbitration and litigation in national courts. Yet none of these efforts had an appreciable effect on loan contracts. It took heavy-handed government pressure (in the case of CACs in New York) and formal statutory change (in the form of dispute resolution clauses) to prompt the introduction of new terms.[82] Efforts to encourage the use of standardized contract terms have also had limited impact.

What explains the limited impact of these initiatives? Without offering a full explanation, I offer several observations. First, official sector actors sometimes misread market sentiment. The assumption underlying many contract initiatives is that market participants would prefer a different set of terms but cannot overcome barriers to innovation.[83] If true, this would offer a compelling basis for intervention. In some cases, however, market participants do not *want* the terms offered. This seems to explain investors' historic indifference to legal enforcement rights, which investors seemingly dismissed as having no material impact on the

[79] O. Ben-Shahar and J. Pottow, 'On the Stickiness of Default Rules' (2006) 33 Fla. St. U. L. Rev. 651.

[80] See generally R.B. Ahdieh, 'Between Mandate and Market: Contract Transition in the Shadow of the International Order' (2004) 53 Emory L. J. 691.

[81] See Feibelman (n. 12) 757, noting that 'the official sector... can play an instrumental role in prodding market participants to embrace new contractual approaches'.

[82] I do not mean to imply that government pressure is required before sovereign bonds will introduce new terms. As just one example, English-law bonds began to incorporate modification clauses in the mid-1980s. See Weidemaier and Gulati (n. 8) 16–21. The point, rather, is that official sector efforts to introduce new terms are often unsuccessful.

[83] They have been abetted in this assumption by a body of contract theory emphasizing the stickiness of standardized terms. For a discussion of relevant theories, see Ben-Shahar and Pottow (n. 79). For discussion in the context of sovereign bonds specifically, see Ahdieh (n. 80).

likelihood of default.[84] A similar explanation may explain resistance to CACs. Some investors may prefer terms that increase the likelihood of a taxpayer-funded bailout if the sovereign encounters financial difficulty, and CACs often are seen as bailout substitutes.[85]

I am not suggesting that official sector actors should refrain from attempting to influence bond contracts. As the CAC example suggests, investors may prefer a world of bailouts to a world where investors bear the cost of improvident loans.[86] There is no reason why official sector actors should respect that preference. The point, rather, is that encouragement, suasion, and other non-coercive methods often will fail to dislodge entrenched contracting practices. To put it starkly, we should not be surprised when market participants do not eagerly embrace model clauses that achieve results they do not want to achieve. In such cases, change must be mandated—a fact that eurozone leaders appear to recognize in their stated plan to mandate the use of standardized CACs.[87]

The second observation relates to efforts to standardize bond contracts. Many debates in the sovereign debt world begin with the assumption that sovereign bonds are standardized in all material ways.[88] The assumption is valid to a degree, but if accepted uncritically it obscures the fact that bond contracts also vary in significant ways.[89] Despite a professed aversion to 'competition' in bond terms,[90] investors seem to have heterogeneous preferences. As a result, efforts to promote standardization—such as the introduction of model contract terms—may have limited impact.

Thirdly, contract change often follows some disruptive event. In many cases, the event is a financial crisis. For example, Choi, Gulati, and Posner document the introduction of new terms into sovereign bonds in the wake of financial crises from the 1980s to the present.[91] In other cases, the event may be the passage of a law making a particular contract term salient—as appears to have been the case with the passage of statutes adopting the restrictive theory of sovereign immunity in the United States and United Kingdom.[92] After enactment in each jurisdiction, bonds quickly incorporated waivers of sovereign immunity, even though these clauses arguably did little to improve enforcement prospects.[93]

[84] See the discussion accompanying nn. 58–66.

[85] Many observers, of course, believe that CACs are inadequate to solve the problems associated with sovereign default. See e.g. Patrick Bolton and D. Skeel, 'Inside the Black Box: How Should a Sovereign Bankruptcy Framework Be Structured?' (2004) 53 Emory L.J. 763; Schwarcz (n. 6).

[86] Bolton and Skeel (n. 85) 765.

[87] Statement by the Eurogroup (n. 4).

[88] Examples include, among others, J. Fisch and C. Gentile, 'Vultures or Vanguards?: The Role of Litigation in Sovereign Debt Restructuring' (2004) 53 Emory L.J. 1043, 1111; R. Ahdieh, 'The Role of Groups in Norm Transformation: A Dramatic Sketch, in Three Parts' (2005) 6 Chi. J. Int'l L. 231, 231.

[89] See text accompanying nn. 74–78.

[90] Gray (n. 71).

[91] S. Choi, M. Gulati, and E. Posner, 'Political Risk and Sovereign Debt Contracts' (2011), available at <http://papers.ssrn.com/sol3/papers.cfm?abstract_id=1962788>.

[92] Weidemaier (n. 52).

[93] Weidemaier (n. 52).

More broadly, contract change itself may be a disruptive event, one that begets further contract change. When contracts are standardized, parties who wish to depart from the standard may fear that they will send an unwanted signal to the markets if they bargain for their preferred term.[94] Before 2003, for example, an issuer considering adopting a non-standard CAC might have worried that investors would conclude that it posed an increased risk of default. After all, why else would it modify a term whose primary function is to facilitate a restructuring? By the end of 2003, however, contracts were in flux in one major market—New York—and this may have reduced the barriers to innovation in other markets. The post-2003 variation in English-law CACs is consistent with this explanation. The introduction of modification clauses in New York was a significant and disruptive event, and it was quickly followed by similar innovation in the English-law market.

These observations suggest that the Principles may have only a limited impact on bond contracts unless they receive substantial support from the official sector.[95] If the goal is to directly influence contracts, it will first be necessary to identify the concrete implications of the Principles' general, normative language. Even if a consensus on this difficult question is reached, experience with past initiatives teaches that bond contracts will not adjust automatically and that methods of 'soft' persuasion—such as promulgating model clauses—will have little effect. On the contrary, change may require fairly assertive, official-sector intervention. Yet this kind of intervention may have the effect of provoking other, unanticipated changes in bond contracts. As it turns out, the near future may offer a test of this prediction. Eurozone officials have mandated the use of standardized CACs, perhaps in the belief that other markets will follow. If the post-2003 experience with CACs is any guide, however, it is also possible that this intervention will prompt experimentation in other markets.

Of course, the Principles may have a significant impact even if they do not directly influence bond terms. Their primary aspiration is less concrete, if no less important: to 'identif[y], harmoniz[e], and systematiz[e] the basic principles and best practices applied to sovereign lending and borrowing', with the ultimate goal of preventing 'undisciplined, ineffective, abusive or non-cooperative behavior' by borrowers and creditors alike.[96] This aspiration can be pursued without altering the language of bond contracts. Principle 7, for example, reflects deep scepticism about

[94] See Ben-Shahar and Pottow (n. 79) 657–9.

[95] Governments have publicly expressed support for the Principles. See e.g. UNCTAD Press Release, 'Principles on Sovereign Lending and Borrowing: UNCTAD Kick Starts Endorsement Process', 23 April 2012, available at <http://www.unctad.info/en/Debt-Portal/News-Archive/Our-News/Principles-on-sovereign-lending-and-borrowing-UNCTAD-kick-starts-endorsement-process-Doha-22-April->. Such endorsements can play a role in a coordinated strategy for implementing the Principles. See A. Gelpern, 'Hard, Soft, and Embedded: Implementing Principles on Promoting Responsible Sovereign Lending and Borrowing' (2012), available at <http://papers.ssrn.com/sol3/papers.cfm?abstract_id=2041027>. For the reasons I have discussed, however, it is unlikely that mere expressions of support will prompt changes to established contract drafting conventions.

[96] UNCTAD, Preamble: Second Draft Principles on Promoting Responsible Sovereign Lending and Borrowing (2011).

investors who buy a distressed sovereign's debt for the purposes of demanding preferential payment terms. Such a creditor, the 'Implications' section declares, is 'acting abusively'.[97]

Holdout litigation may take place before many different courts and tribunals—including national courts, international tribunals, and ad hoc arbitration panels. Although the doctrinal questions may differ, each of these tribunals may confront arguments that creditors are behaving abusively in the context of a sovereign debt restructuring. For example, certain aspects of Greece's restructuring could prompt litigation before the European Court of Human Rights, before national courts in creditor countries, and before arbitration tribunals (assuming there are arbitration clauses in Greece's bilateral investment treaties).[98] In particular, Greece's decision to retroactively impose collective action clauses on its local law contracts might prompt legal challenge.[99]

By itself, the assertion that holdout creditors who demand preferential payment terms are 'acting abusively' cannot resolve these disputes. But if the Principles succeed in garnering widespread support, they may prove influential in less direct ways. For instance, governments who accept this view of creditor behaviour may wield significant influence over national courts, causing them to view some creditor claims with scepticism. As an example, an amicus brief filed in 2004 on behalf of the US government is widely credited with reducing the perceived risk associated with holdout litigation.[100] (The risk had been caused by fear that US courts would adopt a Belgian court's unexpected interpretation of a commonly-used contract term, the *pari passu* clause). One can imagine the principles having a similar, indirect impact on any litigation arising out of a Greek restructuring. If that were to happen, the Principles would have succeeded in rewarding restructuring negotiations conducted 'in good faith and with cooperative spirit', even if they do not succeed in changing the terms of bond contracts.

[97] UNCTAD, Draft Principles on Promoting Responsible Sovereign Lending and Borrowing (2012) 8, reproduced in the Annex to this book.

[98] See 'Hedge Funds May Sue Greece if it Tries to Force Losses', *New York Times*, 18 January 2012, noting the possibility of suit before the European Court of Human Rights.

[99] See L.C. Buchheit and G.M. Gulati, 'How to Restructure Greek Debt' (2010) 10–13, available at <http://papers.ssrn.com/sol3/papers.cfm?abstract_id=1603304>. For an analysis of the issues involved in such a restructuring, see M. Boudreau, 'Restructuring Sovereign Debt Under Local Law: Are Retrofit Collective Action Clauses Expropriatory?' (2012), available at <http://papers.ssrn.com/sol3/papers.cfm?abstract_id=1979238>.

[100] See M. Bradley, J. Cox, and M. Gulati, 'The Market Reaction to Legal Shocks and Their Antidotes: Lessons from the Sovereign Debt Market' (2010) 39 J. Legal Stud. 289.

16

Hard, Soft, and Embedded

Implementing Principles on Promoting Responsible Sovereign Lending and Borrowing

Anna Gelpern[1]

A. Introduction

Sovereign debt exists in a sparse legal space. Debt contract enforcement is uncertain.[2] There are no formal bankruptcy procedures to guide debt adjustment in distress, and create incentives for sound debt management in bankruptcy's shadow.[3] Informal restructuring procedures are entrenched and well known in a narrow circle of repeat players, but scattered across legal regimes and unintelligible to the public. National regulation, ubiquitous in other areas of finance, is limited at best in sovereign debt, where market participants are presumed to be sophisticated and in no need of protection. Treaty-based institutions for rule-making and adjudication, so salient in trade, are lacking in finance.[4] Elsewhere in finance, transnational regulatory coordination has sought to fill the gaps in the formal treaty fabric; however, even as it has grown in the wake of financial crises, the regulatory machinery has bypassed sovereign debt. There are good reasons for excluding sovereign debt from each of these regulatory domains; however, the resulting regime is fraught with bad incentives and destructive outcomes.

Agency problems, time inconsistency, information asymmetries, and moral hazard are perennial risks in sovereign lending and borrowing. Public officials

[1] I am grateful to Juan Pablo Bohoslavsky, Chris Brummer, Barry Carter, Esther Cho, Jennifer Locke Davitt, Carlos Espósito, Ryan Farha, Amanda Giglio, Mitu Gulati, Heather Hughes, David Hunter, Yuefen Li, Breanna Peterson, Mabel Shaw, Jodi Short, Andy Stamm, Brian Stewart, Katherine Wright, to the anonymous reviewers for this volume, and the participants in UNCTAD and UAM conferences for their help with this chapter.

[2] J. Eaton and M. Gersovitz, 'Debt With Potential Repudiation: Theoretical and Empirical Analysis' (1981) 48 Rev. Econ. Stud. 289, 289, noting: 'Unless the governments of private creditors are willing to coerce debtor governments into repaying loans, there is no explicit mechanism deterring a government from repudiating its external debts.'

[3] P. Bolton and D.A. Skeel, Jr, 'Inside the Black Box: How Should a Sovereign Bankruptcy Framework Be Structured?' (2004) 53 Emory L.J. 763.

[4] C. Brummer, 'Why Soft Law Dominates International Finance—and not Trade' (2010) 13 J. Int'l Econ. L. 623, 623, discussing a lack of formal procedures in international finance generally.

borrow in the name of the people, but not in their interest.[5] Future generations are saddled with unsustainable debts. Disclosure is faulty, particularly when it comes to contingent liabilities of the sovereign.[6] Lenders who expect to be rescued by third-country taxpayers—or to be repaid before others of equal rank—keep credit flowing to insolvent debtors.[7] When default comes, its worst effects fall on innocent bystanders, populations and future generations that had no say in the borrowing decisions. Banking, currency, and political crises go hand in hand with sovereign debt default.[8]

The Principles on Promoting Responsible Sovereign Lending and Borrowing ('Principles') contribute to filling the legal and institutional void in three ways. First, they attempt to generalize and systematize from the law and practice of sovereign debt, to propose a unified normative framework for law-making in this area. Secondly, the Principles initiative aims to diffuse this knowledge, and broaden the consensus around what constitutes responsible behaviour in sovereign finance. Thirdly, the Principles engage diverse stakeholders to create constituencies for responsible practices.

Successful implementation of the Principles should result in a durable change of behavior among sovereign borrowers and their lenders. The goal is not a change in the law, but a shift in economic and social outcomes. Formal law reform can help, but is neither necessary nor sufficient to bring about such a shift.

Four core characteristics of the Principles enhance the prospects of implementation defined in this way. First, the Principles do not claim to make new law, but rather to harness and elaborate existing best practices and general principles.[9] Even where this claim has been questioned, the task of the Principles is one of adaptation, not invention.[10] The core values and methods of the Principles are well established in national legal systems.[11] This should minimize the need for formal changes in national law, and the associated political and procedural obstacles to implementation.

Secondly, the Principles aspire to be comprehensive, inclusive, and even-handed: they address both debtor and creditor practices and both public and private creditors across a broad range of instruments. They also contemplate an active role for civil society stakeholders. Other recent efforts to promote responsibility in international finance have focused on discrete sectors, practices, constituencies, and

[5] Symposium, 'Odious Debts and State Corruption' (Summer 2007) 70 Law & Cont. Probs 1. See also J.A. King, 'Odious Debt: The Terms of the Debate' (2007) 32 N.C. J. Int'l L. & Com. Reg. 605, generally discussing and defining the odious debt principle.

[6] L.C. Buchheit and G.M. Gulati, Ch. 13 of this volume.

[7] Bolton and Skeel (n. 3) 767.

[8] C.M. Reinhart and K.S. Rogoff, *This Time Is Different: Eight Centuries of Financial Folly* (Princeton University Press, 2009).

[9] UNCTAD, Principles on Promoting Responsible Sovereign Lending and Borrowing, 10 January 2012.

[10] M. Goldmann, 'Responsible Sovereign Lending and Borrowing: The View from Domestic Jurisdictions', UNCTAD Working Paper (2012).

[11] L.C. Buchheit, G.M. Gulati, and R.B. Thompson, 'The Dilemma of Odious Debts' (2007) 56 Duke L.J. 1201.

forms of finance.[12] Partial regimes pose a greater risk of inequitable regulation and regulatory arbitrage. The Principles' ambitious reach promises to boost legitimacy and dissuade arbitrage in regulatory outcomes. By integrating diverse interests in a common programme, the Principles also suggest input legitimacy, which should contribute to effective implementation.

Thirdly, the process of drafting the Principles is another source of input legitimacy. They are a product of broadly-based consultations with diverse governments, multilateral institutions, civil society groups, market associations, and legal and economic experts. Building on these links as the content of the Principles is elaborated and specified should enhance acceptance among the actors ultimately responsible for implementation.

Fourthly, by improving risk management and accountability in sovereign finance, the Principles should become a force for financial stability. They contribute to crisis prevention by focusing on due diligence, transparency, and clear lines of authority *ex ante*. The Principles should improve the handling of sovereign debt distress by identifying the locus and standards of responsibility *ex post*. The Principles' emphasis on disclosure should facilitate the constructive operation of market mechanisms at all stages of sovereign debt management. Together, these features contribute to the output legitimacy of the Principles, which should build support for sustained implementation and diffusion.

Mindful of these strengths, I propose a three-pronged implementation strategy: locking in the gains, establishing foundations for institutionalization, and building enduring constituencies for implementation.

The first prong of the strategy requires locking in the gains already embodied in the Principles, with public endorsement by key groups of stakeholders: states, civil society groups, and market participants. This can be done without altering the soft law character of the Principles. At the outset, it is important to cement and broaden public acceptance of the essential goals and core values of the Principles. Without a signal of broadly-based ownership, the initiative may come to be portrayed as ineffectual or partisan. A diverse group of endorsers defines the Principles' ambitious constituency, and demonstrates demand for regulation[13] in this area.

In contrast, attempting to negotiate a formal treaty based on the Principles is both unfeasible and undesirable at this stage. It is unfeasible because treaty negotiation and ratification would take many years—putting off the task of implementation into the far future—and might result in weaker substantive commitments.[14] The treaty form

[12] See section B. of this chapter.

[13] W. Mattli and N. Woods, 'In Whose Benefit? Explaining Regulatory Change in Global Politics' in W. Mattli and N. Woods (eds), *The Politics of Global Regulation* (Princeton University Press, 2009), explaining demand for regulation.

[14] e.g. work on the Convention on the Succession of States in Respect of State Property, Archives and State Debts began in 1967. The convention opened for signature in 1983, but is yet to enter into force. See United Nations Conference on Succession of States in Respect of State Property, Archives and Debts, 1983, United Nations Diplomatic Conferences, available at <http://untreaty.un.org/cod/diplomaticconferences/succ-stateprop-archivesdbt-1983/succ-stateprop-archivesdbt-1983.html> (last visited 20 February 2012); International Law Association, Economic Aspects of State Succession: Final Report (2006).

cannot bind non-state actors, such as private creditors, except by the consent of their states.[15] As a result, a treaty may detract from the horizontal, multi-stakeholder character of the Principles that is their principal strength. No alternative formal commitment vehicle is available to bind diverse public and private actors under international law. Even if it were possible, formalization might be undesirable at this stage. It would risk freezing the current limited consensus and stymie further development of the Principles to reflect rapid changes in the financial markets and political participation.[16] Paradoxically, early formalization may weaken the compliance pull of the Principles by shifting resources away from generating information and improving organizational practices, to sanctioning bad behaviour[17] in an area where information is scarce, political tensions run high, and consensus on what constitutes compliance is only emerging.

The second prong of the implementation strategy would leverage support for the overall approach of the Principles, as evidenced by early endorsements, to begin institutionalization. Again, this does not require 'hard law' or treaty-based organizations. Instead, the focus should be on designing institutions to supply an open, accountable regulatory process and mobilizing constituencies to demand disclosure, monitoring, and assessment. Making information on sovereign lending and borrowing publicly accessible should enhance democratic accountability and market discipline alike. Creating institutions for monitoring information and fostering competition among them, can help to develop expertise, entrench good practices, and create conditions for continuous improvement.[18] Put differently, successful implementation of the Principles requires technology to disseminate information about sovereign lending and borrowing, and people with the skills and incentives to collect, distribute, and interpret such information. Both the monitored and the monitors are pushed to do better when there is a robust information flow, and competition to provide credible and transparent assessment of the information. Monitoring mechanisms may be stand-alone and brand new, part of existing public, private, or civil society institutions, or a combination.

Thirdly, successful implementation of the Principles requires constituents with a stake in compliance.[19] Many civil society, official, and market actors have been

[15] K.W. Abbott and D. Snidal, 'Strengthening International Regulation Through Transnational New Governance: Overcoming the Orchestration Deficit' (2009) 42 Vand. J. Transnat'l L. 501.

[16] Potentially a more flexible 'hard law' implementation strategy, which relies on judicial enforcement and the Principles' status as general principles of international law, is promising, but risky if pursued in isolation. Unfavourable court rulings may set back implementation, while a litigation-focused approach would mobilize interest groups and legal strategies opposed to the Principles. See Goldmann (n. 10); see also discussion in section B.I of this chapter.

[17] Data from environmental regulation suggests that coercive state sanctions weaken compliance with self-regulatory commitments, but robust regulatory surveillance improves it. J.L. Short and M. W. Toffel, 'Making Self-Regulation More Than Merely Symbolic: The Critical Role of the Legal Environment' (2010) 55 Admin. Sci. Q. 361.

[18] C. Sabel, D. O'Rourke, and A. Fung, 'Ratcheting Labor Standards: Regulation for Continuous Improvement in the Global Workplace', KSG Working Paper No. 00-010 (May 2000), available at <http://ssrn.com/abstract=253833>.

[19] This is related to the concept of demand for regulation; however, constituents can also include 'suppliers' such as rulemaking and monitoring institutions. Mattli and Woods, 'In Whose Benefit?' (n. 13).

there from the earliest days of devising the Principles. More constituents can emerge in an iterative process of elaborating and refining the Principles, and assessing compliance. Interpretation and revision of the Principles to reflect the evolving economic and political context, as well as implementation experience, should foster durable 'ownership' of the Principles among different stakeholders. Although interpretation and revision institutions should be inclusive, they need not be centralized. Decentralization can preserve the space for generating and contesting ideas[20] about the regulation of sovereign lending and borrowing, and also enhance legitimacy. Local, regional, and interest group bodies may be most effective in channelling different constituents' concerns, so long as there is an effective coordination mechanism among them. On the down side, multiple interpretation and assessment bodies can produce fragmentation and confusion, opening opportunities for arbitrage—or simply make the Principles so malleable that they lose all normative content. This is an argument for more centralization and even a hierarchy of interpretation.

Throughout, it is important to consider the relationship of the Principles to the existing machinery of 'hard law'—international organizations, national regulators, national and international dispute resolution fora, treaties, and contracts—as well as the established 'soft' infrastructure for cooperation, including the G-20 and the Financial Stability Board.[21] Linking the Principles to existing mechanisms taps into established institutional supply, promoting their institutional embeddedness, and making them part of the fabric of international law and financial regulation. Whether this leads to a 'hardening' of the Principles into custom, treaty, or other formal and binding law, and to the creation of new formal institutions, is a question for another day. Implementation need not wait until then.

The remainder of this chapter proceeds as follows. In section B., I put the Principles in the context of sovereign debt governance and international economic regulation. I describe the work of hard law, soft law, and new governance in sovereign debt. Section B. surveys experience from recent initiatives to govern aspects of the international financial system, including project finance, extractive industries, foreign aid, sovereign investment, and capital markets borrowing. I also consider the evolution of anti-corruption law from soft initiative to multilateral treaty. Although these experiences offer valuable lessons, none serves as direct precedent for the Principles. Section C. synthesizes the theoretical literature and the experiences described in section B., to offer recommendations for implementation.

As the first step, I suggest securing the endorsement of governments, but just as importantly, market and civil society groups. It is important to secure endorsements from different regions and parts of the national income spectrum. These should be unequivocal with respect to the overarching goals and methods of the Principles, but need neither adopt nor exclude specific principles and their

[20] Mattli and Woods, 'In Whose Benefit?' (n. 13).

[21] C. Brummer, *Soft Law and Global Financial System: Rule Making in the 21st Century* (Cambridge University Press, 2012).

implications. I recommend simultaneously reaching out to existing public fora, including the IMF, the Financial Stability Board, the Bank for International Settlements (BIS), and the Paris Club, some of which have been involved in the creation of the Principles, to explore incorporation in surveillance, technical assistance, and other aspects of their operations. Trade associations, such as the International Capital Market Association (ICMA), the Securities Industry and Financial Markets Association (SIFMA), and the Institute of International Finance (IIF), should be consulted for endorsement, but also to explore linkages with their best practice guidance and monitoring mechanisms. National debt management agencies can be tapped to consider incorporating the Principles in their debt contracts[22] and operational practices. Secondly, civil society groups, academics, and market participants should be encouraged to design monitoring and assessment mechanisms and publicize their proposals.[23] Finally, I recommend forming a Principles governance body to coordinate disclosure, monitoring, interpretation, and elaboration issues. The body should meet regularly and report to UNCTAD—which would assume an 'orchestration' role in support of informal regulation[24]—but also to the public on a dedicated website. Among other tasks, it should synthesize the compliance metrics developed by civil society, academic, market, and official participants; promote coordination among constituents; evaluate implementation; and support the adaptation of the Principles to ensure their continued relevance.

B. Hard Law, Soft Law, and New Governance in Sovereign Debt

I. Hard law in sovereign debt

At the time of writing, sovereign debt stands at over $40 trillion.[25] Considering its size, national and global importance, and the multitude of diverse international actors in this market, the apparent dearth and fragmentation of law in it is

[22] See E. Helleiner, 'Filling a Hole in Global Financial Governance? The Politics of Regulating Sovereign Debt Restructuring' in W. Mattli and N. Woods (eds), *The Politics of Global Regulation* (Princeton University Press, 2009), reporting on the successful reform of boilerplate sovereign debt contracts as an instance of entrepreneurial regulation. But see W.M.C. Weidemaier, 'Reforming Sovereign Lending Practices: Modern Initiatives in Historical Context', UNC Legal Studies Research Paper No. 1996763 (2012) 1–2, available at <http://ssrn.com/abstract=1996763>, suggesting that government efforts to prompt private contract reform have been ineffective or have brought about unforeseen results.

[23] Consideration of funding options to encourage effective civil society input is beyond the scope of this chapter.

[24] Abbott and Snidal (n. 15) 558–60, describing the orchestration function and 'orchestration deficit' in transnational governance.

[25] Estimate based on Bank for International Settlements, BIS Securities Statistics December 2011, Tables 12D (September 2011), 16A (June 2011), and Joint External Debt Hub data. The vast majority of this debt comprises domestic instruments issued by wealthy states in the capital markets. External debts owed by low and middle-income countries, and debts owed to bilateral and multilateral lenders, account for a small part of the total. In recent years, the boundaries between domestic and external debts, public and private creditors, have blurred: foreign residents participate in domestic debt markets, and central banks and sovereign investment funds are important creditors to foreign governments.

remarkable. In one sense, this state of affairs is par for the course in international finance. Scholars often contrast international finance—governed informally, through coordination networks among national regulators—and international trade, where formal and binding treaties and institutional structures of the WTO prevail.[26] But sovereign debt is exceptional even within international finance.

Private financial institutions and capital markets are subject to formal regulation at the national level, coordinated in fora such as the Basel Committee for Bank Supervision, and more recently, the Financial Stability Board. Market participants' contracts are routinely enforced in domestic courts. When they become insolvent, most can avail themselves of statutory bankruptcy or resolution procedures, which in turn create incentives for debt management in good times.

Virtually none of these features is present in sovereign debt. Sovereign immunity and the difficulty of reaching sovereign assets make debt contract enforcement unpredictable.[27] Some countries refuse to abide by repayment promises—yet others are forced to repay when they cannot and should not.[28] There is no bankruptcy procedure for sovereigns.[29] Debt adjustment takes place in a constellation of informal processes dominated by elite insiders, as discussed in more detail in the next section. From the perspective of the regulators, sovereign debt markets are generally the province of sophisticated issuers and investors, who need little by way of consumer protection.[30] As a result, sovereign debt is not just a zone where treaties, custom, and adjudication[31] are rare—it appears to be a law-free zone.

To be sure, most countries have laws and institutions governing their own debt issuance; courts do occasionally rule on foreign sovereign debt contract disputes;

[26] e.g. Brummer (n. 4).

[27] The immunity is codified in many jurisdictions, including the US and the UK. Foreign Sovereign Immunities Act of 1976, 28 U.S.C. § 1605(a)(2) (2006); State Immunity Act 1978, c. 33 (UK), available at <http://www.legislation.gov.uk/ukpga/1978/33>. This enforcement challenge is at the heart of economic theories about sovereign debt. See J. Eaton and M. Gersovitz, 'Debt With Potential Repudiation: Theoretical and Empirical Analysis' (1981) 48 Rev. Econ. Stud. 289; see also F. Sturzenegger and J. Zettelmeyer, *Debt Defaults and Lessons from a Decade of Crises* (MIT Press, 2007) 31–47, summarizing the literature. Litigation in the wake of Argentina's 2001 default is illustrative: the only creditor attachment came nearly a decade after the initial default, and involved obscure debates about trust law. *EM, Ltd v. Republic of Argentina, NML, Ltd v. Republic of Argentina*, Nos 03 Civ. 2507(TPG), 03 Civ. 8845(TPG), 05 Civ. 2434(TPG), 06 Civ. 6466 (TPG), 07 Civ.1910(TPG), 2009 WL 2568433 (S.D.N.Y. 18 August 2009), aff'd, *EM, Ltd v. Republic of Argentina*, 389 Fed. Appx. 38 (2d Cir. 2010), cert. denied, 131 S. Ct. 1474 (2011). See also A. Frankel, 'U.S. Walks Dangerous Line to Support Argentina in Bond Cases', Thompson Reuters, 9 April 2012, available at <http://newsandinsight.thomsonreuters.com/Legal/News/2012/04_April/U_S__walks_dangerous_line_to_support_Argentina_in_bond_cases>, US position in the latest round of creditor lawsuits against Argentina undermines already weak sovereign debt enforcement.

[28] See e.g. *Donegal International Ltd v. Republic of Zambia*, [2007] EWHC (Comm) 197 (Eng.).

[29] For an account of the most recent attempt to establish a statutory sovereign bankruptcy regime, see S. Hagan, 'Designing a Legal Framework to Restructure Sovereign Debt' (2005) 36 Geo. J. Int'l L. 299.

[30] Cases where retail investors are a big factor are rare—Argentina's default in 2001 was exceptional for involving numerous retail investors in Italy.

[31] For the widely accepted statement of the sources of 'hard' law, see Statute of the International Court of Justice, art. 38, 26 June 1945, 59 Stat. 1031, 33 UNTS 993.

and some national laws attempt to influence foreign sovereign debt practices.[32] There have been treaty initiatives to govern aspects of the market.[33] The steady evolution of sovereign immunity doctrines and, at the other end of the spectrum, the recently-revived debate about odious debt, testify to the potential of customary international law in this area.[34] However, such examples stand out as exceptions: they are few, and have a limited or contested record of implementation.

Scholars have considered why formal and binding international law plays such a limited role in international finance.[35] Some of their explanations apply to sovereign debt. Treaties take a long time to negotiate; may be diluted outright and through piecemeal reservations; and are hard to amend—though amenable to exit.[36] They seem ill-suited for a field characterized by the speed of technological and financial innovation.[37] By some accounts, customary international law is even more problematic for its combination of uncertainty and inflexibility. Custom can take a long time to emerge; the precise content and moment of its emergence are uncertain; and changing or opting out of custom is even harder than changing treaties.[38] None of these reasons would rule out recourse to treaties and custom as means of implementing the Principles, but at a minimum, they suggest caution in relying on these mechanisms as principal vehicles for implementation.

Different concerns apply to another potential avenue for hard international law: locating responsible lending and borrowing in 'the general principles of law recognized by civilized nations'.[39] Where such shared principles apply, courts are bound by them as by other sources of international law. Extrapolating to the implementation of the Principles, to the extent they are found to reflect widely accepted domestic law, courts may be asked to apply them as such.

As a source of hard sovereign debt law, general principles raise three challenges: identification, fragmentation, and constituency-building. Identifying general

[32] e.g. Debt Relief (Developing Countries) Act 2010, c. 22 (UK), available at <http://www.legislation.gov.uk/ukpga/2010/22/contents>.

[33] UNCTAD initiatives in the 1960s and 1970s are a prominent example. For a description, see L. Rieffel, *Restructuring Sovereign Debt: The Case for Ad Hoc Machinery* (Brookings Institution Press, 2003) 132–48; see also Hagan (n. 29).

[34] S. Michalowski, *Unconstitutional Regimes and the Validity of Sovereign Debt: A Legal Perspective* (Ashgate, 2007) 33–96.

[35] For a comprehensive account of the soft governance of international finance, see Brummer (n. 21); for a critique of the predominant explanations of the softness, see P-H. Verdier, 'Why Regulate International Finance?', Working Paper (2012).

[36] L.R. Helfer, 'Exiting Treaties' (2005) 91 Va. L. Rev. 1579, discussing unilateral exit clauses in treaties.

[37] R.S. Karmel and C.R. Kelly, 'The Hardening of Soft Law in Securities Regulation' (2009) 34 Brook. J. Int'l L. 883, 885.

[38] C. Bradley and G.M. Gulati, 'Opting Out of Custom' (2010) 120 Yale L.J. 202; see also A. Guzman, 'Saving Customary International Law' (2005) 27 Mich. J. Int'l L. 115, 165–6, discussing the difficulties of withdrawing from emerging custom.

[39] Statute of the International Court of Justice, Art. 38(1)(c), 26 June 1945, 59 Stat. 1031, 33 UNTS 993. Similarly, the Restatement of the Foreign Relations Law of the United States refers to: 'General principles common to the major legal systems.' Restatement of the Foreign Relations Law of the United States (Third) § 102 (1987). See M.N. Shaw, *International Law* (2008) 98–105; A. von Bogdandy, 'General Principles of International Public Authority: Sketching a Research Field' (2008) 9 German L.J. 1909.

principles can become a complex inquiry of comparative law. Where the inquiry is inconclusive or jurisdictions differ, courts may shy away from applying the law, or may apply it narrowly.[40] An academic study of 15 jurisdictions undertaken in connection with Principles implementation concludes that while many of the Principles are generally accepted, others reflect and adapt current trends.[41] It follows that an implementation argument based on general principles would be more successful with respect to some of the Principles than others, and in some courts more than in others, potentially contributing to the fragmentation of sovereign debt law. Finally, governing sovereign debt from 'hard' general principles relies importantly on litigation. In this context, some powerful interest groups will invest in legal strategies against hardening standards of responsibility. At a minimum, if such groups are also involved in the multi-stakeholder implementation strategies discussed in section C., they may find it more difficult to litigate in opposition.

Finally, hard law faces structural fit problems in sovereign finance, most of which is built on horizontal contracting between private creditors and states as market participants. This hybrid quality makes sovereign lending and borrowing a tricky subject for traditional public regulation. While national law may face enforcement constraints when applied to sovereigns, hard international law does not comprehend states and non-state actors in a horizontal relationship. A state may enter into a treaty to bind itself and its subjects; industry and NGO representatives may influence a state's position in treaty negotiations; states may even establish hybrid tribunals;[42] however, in all these arrangements, non-state participants enter indirectly and courtesy of their states.

The dearth of hard law in sovereign debt may have an optimistic explanation: the current constellation of formal institutions and informal practices, including the IMF, the World Bank, and the Paris Club, described in the next section, do a fine job of managing the space. A more sceptical view might be that the informal and ad hoc approach maximizes policy flexibility for the strongest private and state creditors at the expense of weaker actors.[43]

In summary, the role of formal domestic and international law in the sovereign space is limited. Even if it were easy to negotiate a treaty or spur the formation of custom in this field, it is likely to be an awkward fit. Relying solely on general principles of law in sovereign debt may contribute to fragmentation, and mobilize litigation strategies against standards of responsibility. The next two sections,

[40] R.E. Brooks, 'Law in the Heart of Darkness: Atrocity and Duress' (2003) 43 Va. J. Int'l L. 861, discussing judicial treatment of general principles in a case where a survey of 15 jurisdictions determined that civil and common law jurisdictions differed; see also Judgment, *Prosecutor v. Erdemovic*, Case No. IT-96-22-A (ICTY, Appeals Chamber, 7 October 1997), available at <http://www.un.org/icty/erdemovic/appeal/judgement/erd-aj971007e.htm>.

[41] Goldmann (n. 10). Most of the general principles concerned were not limited to sovereign debt, but rather debt and financial responsibility more broadly.

[42] The International Centre for Settlement of Investment Disputes is an example <https://icsid.worldbank.org>.

[43] See Helleiner (n. 22), describing how NGOs were out-manoeuvred by creditor groups and creditor country governments. cf. Verdier (n. 35).

B.II. and B.III., investigate soft law and new governance approaches to sovereign debt. While hard and soft law may lay on a continuum of qualitative attributes, such as formality, new governance is a matter of method—for law-making and implementation alike.

II. Soft law in sovereign debt and international financial regulation

Soft law hovers between hard law and aspiration. Although definitions abound, most focus on the absence or weakness of legal obligation, and on informality.[44] For some international law scholars, soft law hardly adds up to law at all.[45] Others appreciate its capacity to secure compliance by other means, and suggest that it may be as good as hard law in most pertinent respects—at least in international finance.[46] Examples of soft law in international finance range from high level commitments of the G-7 and the G-20, to the rule-making of the Basel Committee and the Financial Stability Board. None is formally binding, each exerts compliance pull.

In sovereign debt, the role of soft law is readily apparent in the prevailing system for dealing with debt distress. Traditionally, a country that has trouble paying its foreign debts might approach the IMF for financing. In most cases, such financing would be conditional on implementation of economic reforms, designed among other things to ensure that the Fund is repaid. The resulting economic programme would include an assessment of debt sustainability and financing need during the programme period. To fill the 'financing gap', the country would next go to the Paris Club, where creditor states will negotiate the relief of bilateral debts, usually based on one of a menu of formulas. They would then send the country to obtain 'comparable' terms from other creditors, including private commercial banks and bondholders.[47]

Figure 16.1 is a stylized representation of the external sovereign debt restructuring process. Bordered shapes stand for entities with legal personality under domestic or international law. Although the protagonists in the process are states, international organizations, and firms, the process itself—in the middle row—is overwhelmingly soft.

The Paris Club and the London Club are informal coordination mechanisms with no legal personality. They mediate between the sovereign and its creditors. The Paris Club emerged as a forum for official bilateral creditors in the mid-1950s; it meets regularly at the French finance ministry to negotiate debt restructuring

[44] e.g. A. Guzman, 'The Design of International Agreements' (2005) 16 Eur. J. Int'l L. 579, 583–4, defining soft law in terms of states' intent to be bound.

[45] e.g. J. d'Aspremont, 'Softness in International Law: A Self-Serving Quest for Legal Materials' (2008) 19 Eur. J. Int'l L. 1075; see also e.g. A. D'Amato, 'Softness in International Law: A Self-Serving Quest for Legal Materials: A Reply to Jean d'Aspremont' (2009) 20 Eur. J. Int'l L. 897; J. d'Aspremont, 'Softness in International Law: A Self-Serving Quest for Legal Materials: A Rejoinder to Tony D'Amato' (2009) 20 Eur. J. Int'l L. 911.

[46] Brummer (n. 21).

[47] 'What Does Comparability of Treatment Mean?', The Paris Club, available at <http://www.clubdeparis.org/sections/composition/principes/comparabilite-traitement/switchLanguage/en> (last visited 20 February 2012).

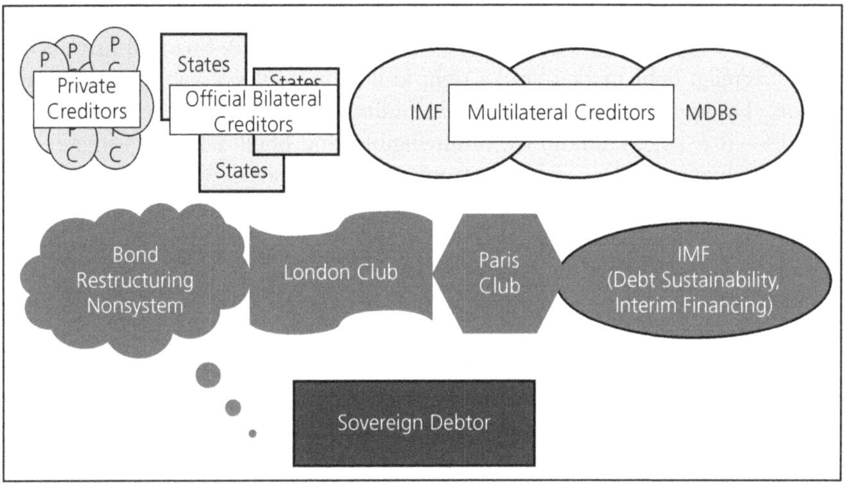

Fig. 16.1 Informality and fragmentation in sovereign debt restructuring

terms for government-to-government debt. Although its procedures and outcomes are quite regimented, the Paris Club has no charter and no personality under domestic or international law, and was relatively late to launch a website.[48] The London Club is even less formal. The term refers to a system of bank advisory committees that renegotiated syndicated loan contracts with low and middle-income sovereigns during the debt crisis of the 1980s. Although the workings of the London Club, like the Paris Club, are reasonably predictable, it has no permanent home, secretariat, or website.[49] The bond restructuring 'non-system' came to the forefront of sovereign debt management in the 1990s. Although it features a certain repertoire of restructuring tools,[50] the system lacks the institutional structure of the other fora. It is essentially a subset of capital markets transactions. Multilateral creditors traditionally have been excluded from restructuring, though they have scrupulously avoided claiming formal preference.[51] Initiatives for poor heavily indebted countries launched in the late 1990s are a partial exception to this treatment.

[48] The timing is ironic: the Paris Club became more transparent just as its relevance in international debt matters was beginning to decline in the wake of deep debt reduction initiatives that ended some countries' iterative relationship with the club.

[49] A. Mudge, 'Sovereign Debt Restructure: A Perspective of Counsel to Agent Banks, Bank Advisory Groups and Servicing Banks' (1984) 23 Colum. J. Transnat'l L. 59, 64–6.

[50] R. Bi, M. Chamon, and J. Zettelmeyer, 'The Problem that Wasn't: Coordination Failures in Sovereign Debt Restructurings', IMF Working Paper WP/11/265 (November 2011) 7–8, available at <http://www.imf.org/external/pubs/ft/wp/2011/wp11265.pdf>, describing sovereign bond exchange techniques.

[51] R.S.J. Martha, 'Preferred Creditor Status under International Law: The Case of the International Monetary Fund' (1990) 39 ICLQ 801, 811.

The sovereign debt restructuring process is routinized and well known to countries and institutions that participate (many repeatedly), financial firms active in the sovereign debt market, and a tight-knit cadre of lawyers in New York and London. However, to the outsider—including citizens of debtor and creditor countries—it is largely unknown, unintelligible, and potentially illegitimate. The system is hierarchical[52] and far from comprehensive. Already convoluted, Figure 16.1 would become hopelessly cluttered if regional authorities, trade creditors, suppliers, and domestic creditors—all of whose claims are addressed separately—were added in.

The record of this system in delivering debt relief, and more importantly, fostering responsible borrowing and lending *ex ante*, is vigorously contested. Some writers point to the dozens of cases where countries obtained deep debt relief without formal bankruptcy procedures as *prima facie* evidence of success. Yet others focus on the inadequate volume and slow provision of relief, and the persistence of problematic debt accumulation as evidence of system failure. Like most soft law systems, sovereign debt restructuring has shown flexibility over time—visible in the evolution of Paris Club membership and terms, the incorporation of bond restructuring techniques, and the introduction of multilateral debt relief in response to civil society initiatives—however, it has also suffered from deficits of transparency, democratic accountability, and efficacy.

It is useful to compare briefly the workings of soft law in sovereign debt and other areas of international finance. The existing literature on soft law in international finance is dedicated almost entirely to international financial regulation (IFR). On the whole, the assessment of soft law's role in IFR is positive, although the financial crisis has tempered some of the enthusiasm.[53]

Proponents describe soft law-making as more expert, flexible, and efficient; more cooperative and less threatening to regulatory sovereignty than old-style hard law.[54] With these advantages, soft law operating through transnational networks has blossomed, and has begun to develop a record of accomplishment in coordinating regulatory enforcement and harmonizing certain regulatory standards.[55] States adopt and implement the strictures of Basel capital accords, collaborate in enforcing securities laws, and fight money laundering even though (or precisely because) no one forced them to. In this telling, networks of similarly minded regulators[56] have succeeded where generations of diplomats have come up short.

[52] Debtor agency in the process is limited, defined essentially by the government's willingness to default. In 2000, efforts by private creditors to secure 'reverse comparability'—or press the Paris Club into debt restructuring on private creditors' terms—were decisively rebuffed. e.g. J. Gallardo, 'Cracks in the New Financial Architecture', *Euromoney*, April 2001, 50.

[53] See D. Zaring, 'International Institutional Performance in Crisis' (2010) 10 Chi. J. Int'l L. 475, discussing the impact of the financial crisis.

[54] This is a functionalist set of explanations for the success of soft law in international finance. A constructivist approach might emphasize socialization into compliance.

[55] cf. K. Raustiala, 'Transnational Networks: Past and Present' (2009) International Lawyer 205; D. Zaring, 'Three Challenges for Regulatory Networks' (2009) International Lawyer 211; with Verdier (n. 35).

[56] A-M. Slaughter, *A New World Order* (Princeton University Press, 2003).

This joyful take on transnational regulation has always had its critics, and has come under intense scrutiny in the aftermath of 2008.[57] Today's view of soft law is less inclined to presume cooperation and community of interest. It allows that national regulators may seek to promote domestic competitiveness ahead of regulatory harmony, resist the high domestic costs of adhering to global rules, and may pursue 'mock compliance' to mask substantive divergence.[58] The task is to explain what substantive compliance takes place despite these pressures.[59] But even where the system achieves compliance, problems remain. IFR networks are hardly comprehensive; IFR's strengths—decentralization and horizontality—also make it prone to arbitrage and capture. And the flipside of cooperative epistemic communities of regulators[60] is regulatory 'groupthink', which can magnify and spread individual regulatory errors in crisis.[61] The cosier the community—the more opaque, the more shielded from outside intervention—the higher the downside risk. Perhaps most importantly, an informal technocratic system deliberately insulated from politics is constantly defending its democratic legitimacy.

Many of these criticisms of IFR parallel criticisms of the soft system for sovereign debt restructuring earlier in this section. Some scholars of soft law have taken these shortcomings of IFR as a basis to prescribe hard law. For sceptics, soft law may be structurally incapable of raising regulatory standards and generating credible commitments. Soft law works best to promote liberalization and enforcement cooperation, both of which serve the interests of dominant actors in the global economy, rich states and large financial firms. Soft law's dominance of IFR may just be a by-product of power politics and regulatory capture.[62] If this argument is right, the IFR experience is a cautionary tale for Principles implementation.

On the other hand, the flaws of soft law are not in themselves a robust argument for hard law. The alternative to soft law in many instances is not a WTO-style regime, but a vacuum of legality. If the policy objective is better standards and deeper compliance, it makes sense to revisit in more detail the mechanics that make soft law bind.

Two broad categories of tools that promote compliance with soft law in IFR hold promise for Principles implementation. The first of these is disclosure and reporting, which can be leveraged to enhance reputational sanctions and market discipline.[63] Secondly, institutional linkages can help to anchor new and develop-

[57] e.g. P-H. Verdier, 'Transnational Regulatory Networks and Their Limits' (2009) 34 Yale J. Int'l L. 113; Zaring (n. 53); Brummer (n. 21) 263: 'the Basel process . . . viewed until recently as the apogee of international financial cooperation, has consistently failed to prevent bank failures and global economic crises, even with its ostensibly more stringent rules'.

[58] A. Walter, *Governing Finance: East Asia's Adoption of International Standards* (Cornell Univeristy Press, 2008) 171.

[59] Verdier (n. 35) 17–25 and sources cited (literature survey).

[60] e.g. P.M. Haas, 'Introduction: Epistemic Communities and International Policy Coordination' (1992) 46 *International Organization* 1.

[61] Brummer (n. 21) 220–33.

[62] Verdier (n. 35). The debate about the efficacy of soft law in international finance mirrors similar debates in national and transnational regulation. See e.g. literature surveys in Short and Toffel (n. 17) and Mattli and Woods, 'In Whose Benefit?' (n. 13).

[63] Verdier (n. 35).

ing soft law in established legal regimes, soft and hard, domestic and international. The two categories are complementary; the second may blend soft and hard law approaches. In the first instance, non-binding commitments are embedded in monitoring and reporting procedures. Monitoring and reporting may be linked to more formal surveillance by existing institutions, such as the IMF, the development banks, and the various regulatory fora. The initial standards may be refined, elaborated, and revised in the course of periodic surveys of 'core principles' and 'best practices'. Divergence from the standards may be subject to hard and soft sanctions, including name-and-shame strategies, conditionality, market exclusion, and abridgement of membership privileges in the various fora.[64] Although the most potent sanctions may be difficult to invoke and sustain, their ultimate availability and potential linkages among them exert a measure of discipline.

In summary, the debate about soft law in IFR is instructive for efforts to reform sovereign borrowing and lending. Soft law prevails in both fields, along with its collateral benefits and challenges: flexibility and potential for horizontality, but also uncertainty, incompleteness, fragmentation, lack of transparency and accountability. While the parallels between IFR and sovereign debt should not be overstated (for one, sovereign debt is very thinly regulated), some of the tools that promote compliance in IFR hold promise for the implementation of the Principles. In the next section, B.III., I briefly consider these tools from the perspective of the literature on new governance, which helps to enhance explanations of their effectiveness.

III. The new governance dimension

Contemporary scholarship on soft law in finance is anchored in debates about sources and compliance in public international law and international relations. Soft law also plays an important role in the literature on new governance, which emerged in the 1990s as an alternative vision of domestic administrative regulation.[65]

The core normative insight of new governance is that an open and collaborative approach to regulation—where subjects participate in law-making alongside government agents—produces better law and improved compliance. In this view, successful regulation is open-ended, to allow elaboration over time; iterative, to foster information flow and participatory law-making; and accountable, with all stakeholders responsible for the outcome.[66] 'Soft' codes, consultation, and

[64] Brummer (n. 21) 147–56.

[65] But see Mattli and Woods, *The Politics of Global Regulation* (n. 13); Abbott and Snidal (n. 15), adapting domestic new governance theory for transnational regulation. See also K.W. Abbott and D. Snidal, 'The Governance Triangle: Regulatory Standards Institutions and the Shadow of the State' in *The Politics of Global Regulation* (Princeton University Press, 2009).

[66] C.L. Ford, 'New Governance, Compliance, and Principles-Based Securities Regulation' (2008) 45 Am. Bus. L.J. 1, 5, description of new governance in finance. For theories of new governance and related perspectives, see S. Sturm, 'A Normative Theory of Public Law Remedies' (1991) 79 Geo. L. J. 1355; I. Ayres and J. Braithwaite, *Responsive Regulation: Transcending the Deregulation Debate* (Oxford University Press, 1992); J. Freeman, 'Collaborative Governance in the Administrative State' (1997) 45 UCLA L. Rev. 1; M.C. Dorf and C.F. Sabel, 'A Constitution of Democratic Experimental-

monitoring arrangements are common examples. Regulators might turn to this new approach for a number of reasons, including substantive conviction, limited public sector resources, or limited information about the regulated industry. Theory predicts that the approach should work because the resulting regulation is based on better information, and because regulatory subjects that to help make the law are more likely to follow it.

Despite obvious overlaps, soft law and new governance are distinct. Soft law's softness stands in contrast to the formal attributes and binding force of treaties and custom. The novelty of new governance is in the process, emphasizing public-private collaboration, adaptive problem-solving, experimentalism, open-endedness, and shared accountability. Its foil is 'command and control' regulation, where governments make fully articulated static rules, and enforce private actors' compliance with them. Soft law can be (but is not necessarily) an instrument of new governance—and new governance techniques can be important in promoting compliance with soft law. Flexibility, horizontal and decentralized law-making may be among the by-products and advantages of softness, but they are not universal, nor essential to its definition.[67] For example, the prevailing regime for sovereign debt restructuring is certainly soft, but rarely horizontal. In contrast, such characteristics are at the heart of new governance. Linkages between soft law and hard institutions of the sort described in the preceding section are prominent in new governance methodology.

The distinct perspectives on accountability in soft law and new governance are revealing. In soft law, accountability—understood as law-making governments answering to the people—is a perennial challenge that attends informality and law-making by expert networks. New governance replaces the challenge with the concept of 'decentralized accountability'—open, participatory law-making, where state and non-state actors answer to one another. The ideal of legitimacy in new governance might be one where regulation is accepted as a shared community norm, internalized as 'appropriate and justified' in the absence of top-down authority or sanction.[68]

Legal scholarship in the field tends to be expressly prescriptive: arguing for or against the adoption of new governance models in lieu of, or to complement,

ism' (1998) 98 Colum. L. Rev. 267; C.F. Sabel and W.H. Simon, 'Destabilization Rights: How Public Law Litigation Succeeds' (2004) 117 Harv. L. Rev. 1016; J. Black, 'Constructing and Contesting Legitimacy and Accountability in Polycentric Regulatory Regimes' (2008) 2 Reg. & Gov. 137. For different perspectives on the scholarly field, see O. Lobel, 'The Renew Deal: The Fall of Regulation and the Rise of Governance in Contemporary Legal Thought' (2004) 89 Minn. L. Rev. 342; and B. Karkkainen, '"New Governance" in Legal Thought and in the World: Some Splitting as Antidote to Overzealous Lumping' (2004) 89 Minn. L. Rev. 471; for an account situating new governance in the broader context of 'new realism' scholarship, see V. Nourse and G. Shaffer, 'Varieties of New Legal Realism: Can a New World Order Prompt a New Legal Theory?' (2009) 95 Cornell L. Rev. 61.

67 These elements resonate with the constructivist view of soft law: law emerges from collaborative iteration, and socialization into shared values.

68 S. Bernstein and B. Cashore, 'Can Non-State Global Governance Be Legitimate? An Analytical Framework' (2007) 1 Reg. & Gov. 347, 348–9, putting forward a 'logic of appropriateness' as an alternative source of legitimacy in non-state market driven governance systems, in contrast to the traditional 'logic of consequences' in state regulation).

traditional regulation. Other disciplines put more emphasis on identifying, classifying, and explaining the proliferation of governance initiatives. Scholars have found examples of new governance in labour, environmental, healthcare, corporate, criminal, and many other fields of law. These include stakeholder consultation requirements in rule-making, codes of social responsibility, corporate monitors, and regulatory exemptions linked to internal procedures at private firms. Typologies and histories abound. Some accounts trace the progressive development of first-, second-, and third-person private regulation, from voluntary commitments at isolated firms, to industry-wide codes of conduct, to independent certification regimes.[69] Others focus on actors, and the ways in which they come together to produce and implement regulation. Abbot and Snidal's 'Governance Triangle' is an elaborate actor-centred representation of new governance by combinations of states, firms, and NGOs, occupying the triangle's vertices.[70] In this view, some initiatives emerge from the combined efforts of firms and states, others from firms and NGOs, yet others from states and NGOs. Some, though not many, reside in the centre of the triangle, channelling all three sets of actors.

The Principles fit comfortably on the new governance spectrum both for the collaborative process that produced them, as well as for their emphasis on common interests and non-coercive implementation. On the other hand, they are somewhat atypical for the literature, because in sovereign borrowing and lending, states appear first and foremost as transaction participants and regulatory subjects, with little by way of regulatory background where states traditionally predominate. The ambiguous role of the states would make the 'Governance Triangle' an uneasy fit.

As a school of thought, new governance claims a large cadre of prominent academics, and has had a measure of policy influence.[71] Yet others have criticized its theories as ill-defined. New governance prescriptions, particularly with respect to accountability, have faced scepticism familiar to students of soft law: putting unelected private actors in charge of regulation risks regulatory capture by powerful elites, and may undermine electoral democracy and government capacity.[72]

Empirical studies of the effectiveness of new governance are still sparse and inconclusive.[73] This is not surprising for a field that is relatively new, and

[69] e.g. F. Mayer and G. Gereffi, 'Regulation and Economic Globalization: Prospects and Limits of Private Governance' (2010) 12(3) *Business and Politics* 6–7.

[70] Abbott and Snidal (n. 15) 512–19; Abbott and Snidal (n. 65).

[71] See Symposium, 'New Governance and the Transformation of Law' (2010) 2 Wisconsin Law Review 227.

[72] C. Scott, 'Regulation in the Age of Governance: The Rise of the Post Regulatory State' in J. Jordana and D. Levi-Faur (eds), *The Politics of Regulation: Institutions and Regulatory Reforms for the Age of Governance* (Elgar, 2004) 145; J.M. Conley and C.A. Williams, 'Global Banks as Global Sustainability Regulators?: The Equator Principles' (2011) 33 Law & Policy 542. But on tripartism as a capture-mitigant, see Ayres and Braithwaite (n. 66).

[73] For examples in law journals, see Conley and Williams (n. 72); C. Ford and D. Hess, 'Can Corporate Monitorship Improve Corporate Compliance?' 34 (2009) J. Corp. L. 680; L.T. Alexander, 'Stakeholder Participation in New Governance: Lessons from Chicago's Public Housing Reform Experiment' (2009) 16 Geo. J. on Poverty L. & Pol'y 118; F. Houle, 'Consultation During Rule-Making: A Case Study of the Immigration and Refugee Protection Regulation' (2010) 28 Windsor Y. B. Access Just. 395; U. Feldman and O. Lobel, 'The Incentives Matrix: The Comparative Effectiveness

(depending on your perspective) either radically heterogeneous or ill-defined. Much of the empirical research agenda has focused on documenting the phenomenon of the new governance in regulation. Qualitative studies in particular tend to focus on the informants' experience of new governance, and are cautious in their efficacy assessments. However, several go further, to consider the success of new governance schemes in achieving their stated goals, or to tease out the factors that contribute to the impact of particular initiatives.

No study finds unqualified success. There is evidence that corporations excel at formal compliance and new governance rhetoric, with limited or inconsistent effect on their behaviour.[74] However, the same studies find palpable changes in institutional culture and awareness. Another notable finding is that weak non-state actors (such as poor people) may be at a disadvantage in a purely informal governance regime, and need a hard law backstop to bolster their bargaining position.[75]

Even so, asking whether new governance 'works' may be beside the point: successful or not, new governance phenomena are pervasive.[76] Just as treaties may not be a practical alternative to soft law, old-style regulation is not always a practical alternative to new governance.[77] For the purposes of implementing the Principles, the relevant inquiry would identify more and less successful strategies for achieving compliance, find ways to link soft and hard law, and help to establish realistic goals.

So far, theory and experience with new forms of regulation suggests that at a minimum, they help to change the way firms talk about responsible behaviour, and the way in which they interact with civil society and government actors. This affects firm culture and holds out the potential of changing behaviour.[78] Empowering civil society participation in the regulatory process through fostering awareness and opening access may help to reduce the risk of capture.[79] The presence of hard law in the background—notably in the form of induced competition and information-forcing surveillance, as alternatives to coercive sanctions[80]—can help soft law to succeed in a new governance framework. This poses a special challenge for international law-making, where hard law is scarce. Scholars who have considered the problem recommend more active 'orchestration' and capacity-building

of Rewards, Liabilities, Duties, and Protections for Reporting Illegality' (2010) 88 Tex. L. Rev. 1151. In social science journals, see e.g. Short and Toffel (n. 17).

74 J.M. Conley and C.A. Williams, 'Engage, Embed, and Embellish: Theory Versus Practice in the Corporate Social Responsibility Movement' (2005) 31 J. Corp. L. 1; see also Conley and Williams (n. 72); Ford and Hess (n. 73).

75 Alexander (n. 73).

76 cf. K. Raustiala (n. 55).

77 e.g. states may lack economic or political resources to implement effective top-down regulation.

78 This reflects Mattli and Woods' view that both supply (access, process) and demand must be present to avoid capture. Particularly where transparency and access to the regulatory process are limited, select NGOs and corporate monitors may be co-opted, becoming 'legitimators'.

79 Ayres and Braithwaite (n. 66), discussing tripartism and 'enforced' self-regulation.

80 Sabel, O'Rourke, and Fung (n. 18); Short and Toffel (n. 17).

by international organizations, using tools such as conditionality and technical assistance.[81] The academic literature on new governance also emphasizes the need for context-specific approaches, and frequent adjustment as the context evolves and more information becomes available.

In section B., I have sought to situate the Principles in the existing legal landscape of sovereign borrowing and lending, and in the context of theories about soft law and new governance. In summary, domestic and international 'hard law' play a small role in sovereign debt compared to most other fields. The sovereign debt restructuring regime is dominated by soft law coordination, fragmented and poorly understood by the public. This regime in turn creates the incentives for borrowing and lending, which occur 'in the shadow' of restructuring expectations.

Academic writing and experience with soft law and new governance suggest that informal and non-binding mechanisms such as the Principles can improve regulation and compliance in some circumstances. However, they must be properly designed to minimize the risks of error, capture, and illegitimacy. To get a better sense of the optimal design features before turning to implementation recommendations, section C. briefly considers five new governance-style codes in international finance and development. In conclusion, I review the evolution of anti-corruption law from national legislation to transnational 'soft' governance, and later international treaty. These case studies, where the actors addressed similar or overlapping problems, will help to contextualize the prescriptions for Principles implementation.

C. Ancestors and Analogues

The Principles have no direct precedent, and are in many ways more ambitious than the existing codes of best practices in international finance: they seek to cover more instruments and discipline more diverse actors than the initiatives that have come before; they are also more substantively prescriptive than others in the field. However, the past decade has produced a wealth of experience with codes and practices, which together shed light on potentially promising strategies and pitfalls in Principles implementation. This section offers a brief survey of five new governance initiatives, chosen to reflect different aspects of the Principles. All came about within the past decade, and are notable for their multi-stakeholder approach—especially when compared to the standards and codes of the 1990s, which were predominantly devised by the official sector to improve regulation in low and middle-income countries. The first two case studies, the Equator Principles and the Extractive Industries Transparency Initiative, seek to enhance social and environmental responsibility and promote accountability in discrete privately financed sectors. In the next two case studies, the Paris

[81] Abbott and Snidal (n. 15) 570–3.

Declaration and the Santiago Principles, the authors and subjects of regulation are states or state instrumentalities. The final case study is most closely related to the UNCTAD Principles: the Principles for Stable Capital Flows and Fair Debt Restructuring seek to govern sovereign borrowing and debt restructuring in the capital markets. The later set of principles targets government debtor and private creditor behaviour. In conclusion, I discuss an earlier experience with anti-corruption initiatives for an illustration of soft law hardening into international treaty, while maintaining features of new governance.

I. The Equator Principles

The Equator Principles (EPs) are a framework for managing social and environmental risk from project finance by commercial banks. Adopted in 2003 and substantially revised in 2006, the EPs reflect a combination of diminished official participation in large-scale infrastructure in developing countries, sustained NGO advocacy, and a heightened perception of risk on the part of the banks.

Although they articulate substantive social and environmental sustainability goals, the ten principles are essentially procedural: they commit banks to require their borrowers (project sponsors) to adopt responsible practices, focusing on projects in developing countries. Participating banks, or Equator Principles Financial Institutions (EPFIs), pledge to (1) review and categorize projects over $10 million according to social and environmental impact, and to require their borrowers to (2) conduct impact assessments, (3) use International Finance Corporation (IFC) standards in such assessments, (4) develop plans for managing the associated risks, (5) engage in consultations with, and provide disclosure to, stakeholders, (6) establish a grievance procedure, (7) secure independent review of the project assessment in higher risk projects, (8) covenant to comply with applicable host country laws, IFC standards, disclosure and decommissioning procedures, and (9) secure independent monitoring of risky projects over the life of the loan. (10) In addition, the EPFIs themselves agree to report at least once a year on their EP practices and experience. Like many initiatives of this sort, the EPs contain a disclaimer to the effect that they concern internal procedures of the participants, and do not create rights or binding obligations.[82] Nevertheless, the mechanism hinges on a mix of organizational practices and a network of enforceable contractual commitments, which the EPFIs pledge to extract from their counterparties.

Membership has grown from ten EPFIs in 2003, to 73[83] at the time of writing, which accounts for over 70 per cent of all international project financing in the developing world. In 2010, the EPFIs formed the EP Association, a 'soft,' unincorporated grouping of all member institutions, which operates under a set of rules

[82] Equator Principles, 'The Equator Principles' (June 2006) 6, available at <http://www.equator-principles.com/resources/equator_principles.pdf>.

[83] This includes two 'Associate Members' (JP Morgan Chase and Wells Fargo), who have adopted the EPs and abide by EP reporting requirements, but are not 'active in project finance' according to the EP definition.

promulgated by the membership. The Association appears to have been a response to the challenge of coordinating a growing body of stakeholders; it also helps to preserve and promote the EP brand. (The stated rationale was 'to ensure long-term viability and ease of management'.) Subject-matter working groups are coordinated by a 14-member Steering Committee. A two-person EP Secretariat, based in the United Kingdom, staffs the Association on a day-to-day basis. The EPs were revised in 2006 to incorporate new, more stringent IFC standards, and are undergoing another round of revision following a strategic review in 2011.[84]

The EPs are an established example of soft law and new governance. They are among the more institutionally developed initiatives of this sort. Several design features of the EPs are worth noting in the context of Principles implementation:

- *Financial institutions as principal subjects and law-makers.* The EPs originated as pre-emptive self-governance among a core group of financial institutions, which approached the IFC. EPFIs are both members and principal subjects of regulation.
- *Risk mitigation/defensive motive.* Like other initiatives in this space, the EPs responded to what was perceived as a common set of risks (or threats) and sought to mitigate them in flexible and evolving ways.
- *Adoption and membership.* The EPs contain bright-line criteria for adoption and membership. Even though the EPs themselves are adopted voluntarily and do not, by their terms, create rights in members or other stakeholders, the clear act of joining, paying membership fees, and signing up to specific standards, serves as a commitment and community-defining device.
- *Recruiting.* Comprehensive coverage of the project finance industry is an explicit objective of the EPs. Members, together with IFC representatives, actively recruit new EPFIs, paying attention to country and regional representation.
- *Constituency definition and outreach.* The EP consultation and governance process expressly seeks to balance regional, sector, and interest group representation. Project-specific consultation under the EPs should include a broad range of stakeholders.
- *Elaboration and adaptation.* The EPs are regularly elaborated and periodically revised, including most recently as part of a high-profile strategic review. Subsidiary and interpretive documents and guides refine and augment the code.
- *Harmonized disclosure and reporting.* The EPs mandate disclosure at multiple levels of both the EPFIs and their borrowers, and promulgate standards for disclosure to promote comparability.

[84] See 'Launch of Equator Principles III Delayed to July 2012', PRIZMA, 10 January 2012, available at <http://prizmablog.com/2012/01/10/launch-of-equator-principles-iii-delayed-to-july-2012>.

- *Decentralized dispute resolution.* There is no centralized dispute resolution or binding interpretation process for the EPs. Each EPFI commits to require its borrowers to establish project-specific and 'culturally appropriate' grievance procedures for the stakeholders.
- *Capacity building.* The EPs provide for a transitional period and technical assistance for new members.
- *Linkages with 'hard' law and institutions.* The EPs originated in bank consultations with the IFC, with the IFC coming to play a coordinating role. The banks explicitly adopt IFC standards, as well as some World Bank and OECD nomenclature, and advocate compliance with national legislation where it equals or exceeds IFC standards. Since its recent establishment, the EP Association has taken on the role of engaging with international organizations on behalf of the membership.
- *Branding.* The 'Equator Principles' name was designed to signal North-South balance. Because so much of the payoff to EPFIs is reputational, the process has a highly developed branding and public relations strategy, including a current and generally informative website.

As with virtually all new governance initiatives, assessments of the EPs' efficacy are inconclusive. In one sense—membership and industry coverage—the EPs have been a resounding success. However, quantitative studies of development outcomes are few, and those that exist supply no definitive answers. Some proponents claim that the EPs have changed the behaviour of large firms; however, even optimistic assessments note that smaller firms lack the resources to comply.[85] Critics stress the absence of a demonstrable shift in environmental and social outcomes on the ground.[86] In a detailed qualitative study, one team of scholars has noted that participation in the EPs affects firm culture at the EPFIs, and potentially promotes awareness and better practices within these banks beyond their project finance portfolio.[87] In this sense, EP banks have the capacity to diffuse standards of responsibility both within the project finance industry and elsewhere in the banks' business. Nevertheless, this research also casts doubt on the true sources and viability of the commitment pull: although the EPs are expressly framed as bank risk management, most of the bankers interviewed were ambivalent about the business case for the EPs, and justified participation in terms of responding NGO pressure. Such findings echo stories of pre-emption, self-preservation, and cosmetic compliance in other industries. To be sure, different firms might have looked to the EPs for different business benefits ranging from project risk mitigation, to learning green best practices ahead of the curve, to reputation-cleansing under NGO

[85] See C. Langdon, 'The Impact of the Equator Principles on Mining and Metals Finance in Emerging Markets', White & Case LLP (March 2007).
[86] See N. Mathiason, 'Green Protocol 'Failing To Curb Damaging Bank Lending', *The Guardian*, 15 January 2010, 38.
[87] Project finance accounts for about 5% of the large institutions' portfolio. Conley and Williams (n. 72) 546.

pressure. Each firm's reasons for participating might evolve over time. And the affected communities' interest in the EPs is altogether distinct, beyond the scope of the studies.

II. Extractive Industries Transparency Initiative

The Extractive Industries Transparency Initiative (EITI) emerged at about the same time as the EPs, in 2003, with strong leadership of the UK authorities and NGOs, such as the Publish What You Pay Coalition. EITI promotes transparency and accountability in the extractive industries through public disclosure of 'all material oil, gas, and mining payments' by firms to governments, and all material government revenues from oil, gas, and mining companies. The focus of the six EITI Criteria appears to be even more targeted and procedural than that of the EPs: it is all about disclosure. However, the 12 EITI Principles articulate a much broader set of objectives, ranging from sustainable development and responsible stewardship of natural resource wealth, to improving public finance management and accountability.[88]

The structure of EITI is quite different from that of the EPs:

- *Governments as subjects of regulation.* Although the overall framework is expressly and emphatically 'multi-stakeholder', and includes major extractive firms and civil society participation, the parties principally charged with compliance are countries. EITI countries are held responsible for the reporting of firm payments in their jurisdiction, and creating structures for such reporting.
- *Private firms as 'supporting investors'.* Private firms are invited to participate in the EITI process by signing onto a statement of support, engaging in certain publicity and outreach, and paying an annual fee of US$1,500; however, 'supporting' status does not trigger reporting requirements. According to the EITI factsheet, supporting the initiative helps to demonstrate investor compliance with Principles 3 and 5 of the UN Principles for Responsible Investing.[89]
- *Other supporters.* Civil society organizations, industry associations, non-member countries, and international organizations may all become supporters of EITI. For the most part, supporter status involves no or minimal undertakings.
- *Graduated membership structure.* Countries must have at least a two and a half year record of compliance with EITI criteria to qualify for full membership. This structure can support capacity building, but also sanction non-compliance. Regular reviews validate continued membership. Yemen and Madagascar have had their membership suspended.

[88] Extractive Industries Transparency Initiative, 'EITI Rules' (November 2011), available at <http://eiti.org/files/2011-11-01_2011_EITI_RULES.pdf>.

[89] Extractive Industries Transparency Initiative, 'How to Become a Supporting Investor', available at <http://eiti.org/files/2009-11-23_How_to_Support_Investors%5B1%5D.pdf>.

- *Emphasis on tripartism.* EITI explicitly requires tripartite governance of country EITI participation, including governments, extractive firms, and civil society representatives in ongoing consultations. In other words, EITI expressly aspires to occupy the centre of the 'Governance Triangle'.
- *External independent evaluation.* A team of independent consultants provided a strategic evaluation of EITI in 2011.
- *Formal corporate structure, funding, and IO linkages.* The EITI is organized as a non-profit association in Norway. Since the mid-2000s, it has had a 20-member Board, a Secretariat, and access to a multi-donor trust fund managed by the World Bank. Most of its funding comes from member governments, supporting firms, and NGOs; however, the government of Norway provides fully 20 per cent of the fund.[90] The Multi-Donor Trust Fund provides technical assistance to implementing countries.
- *Global conferences.* The biennial EITI Global Conference is an important component of EITI governance. The Board is appointed at the conferences. During the conference, EITI also conducts constituency meetings with countries, firms, and civil society.
- *Further linkages and related initiatives.* The IMF has published a Guide to Resource Revenue Transparency. The World Bank has published the Extractive Industry Review. In 2010, US legislation mandated disclosure of extraction-related payments by firms applying to register securities with the SEC.[91]

As with other case studies, academic empirical studies of EITI are hard to come by. Country membership and supporter lists have grown, and now include major portions of the global extractive industry. Liberia became the first country to expand EITI beyond extractive industries, to include forest management. A strategic evaluation conducted for EITI by independent consultants from Scanteam in 2011 has found that the initiative has had some success in establishing tripartite governance and reporting mechanisms in the member countries. However, according to the report: 'While *transparency* has improved, *accountability* does not appear to have changed much.' The reviewers attribute the limited societal and global effects on the targeted focus of the initiative, weak institutions in member countries, limited linkages, and a lack of a broader vision of how improved reporting would leverage social change.[92] NGO critics are less charitable. According to Oxfam America, there is a 'yawning gap' between the actions and rhetoric of oil companies supporting EITI.[93] Others argue that EITI shields

[90] Extractive Industries Transparency Initiative, 'How We Are Funded', available at <http://eiti.org/about/funding>.

[91] The Dodd-Frank Act, Pub. L. No. 111-203, § 1504, 124 Stat. 1376 (2010) (codified at 15 U.S.C. § 78m).

[92] Extractive Industries Transparency Initiative, 'Achievements and Strategic Options: Evaluation of the Extractive Industries Transparency Initiative' (May 2011), available at <http://eiti.org/files/2011-EITI-evaluation-report.pdf>.

[93] I. Gary, 'The Transparent Hypocrisy of Big Oil', Oxfam, 9 February 2012, available at <http://politicsofpoverty.oxfamamerica.org/index.php/2012/02/09/the-transparent-hypocrisy-of-big-oil>.

companies from criticism while they fight disclosure rules on extraction-related payments by the US securities regulators.[94] NGOs have also criticized national EITI chapters for failing to live up to the initiative's transparency standards.[95]

An academic synthesis of implementation assessments acknowledges EITI's shortcomings, while pointing out that some of the development impacts of transparency would be hard to measure.[96] On the other hand, the authors note design failures that reduce constituent ownership and, with it, development impact. For example, countries' EITI disclosure appears to be geared disproportionately to external audiences. Domestic constituents have scant economic, technical, and political capacity to process and use the information generated from EITI.

It appears that the focus on government-led implementation at a minimum makes it difficult to assess the effect of EITI on the behaviour of private actors. The international prominence of the initiative has contributed to its external focus, which in turn potentially reduces domestic ownership. However, to the extent that the primary concern of the initiative is public finance reform and accountability, rather than reform of a broader set of extractive industry and development practices, it may be unfair to hold EITI responsible for the limited or uncertain effect it has had on the industry.

III. The Paris Declaration on aid effectiveness

Unlike the initiatives in the preceding case studies, which sought to affect to varying degrees the behaviour of both public and private actors, the 2005 Paris Declaration is a purely intergovernmental undertaking, albeit one that invites civil society participation. The Declaration comprises five fundamental principles of aid effectiveness: ownership by recipient countries, alignment of the donors and use of local systems, harmonization of procedures and information-sharing among donors, a focus on measurable development results, and mutual accountability of donors and recipients for such results. Flowing from these principles, the Declaration provides for over 50 commitments, monitored by 12 indicators. The Accra High Level Forum adopted an Agenda for Action in 2008 to accelerate the implementation of the Declaration. This timing proved challenging with the onset of the global financial crisis, which strained aid resources.

The Paris Declaration's use of tiered, open-ended principles elaborated in ongoing consultation and evaluation procedures, generally administered under the auspices of the OECD's Development Co-operation Directorate, recalls

[94] A. Powell, 'Anti-Corruption Views—Transparency is for life, not just for PR', TrustLaw, 9 February 2012, available at <http://www.trust.org/trustlaw/blogs/anti-corruption-views/transparency-is-for-life-not-just-for-pr>; P. Kollipara, 'Oil Industry Battles SEC Rules on Disclosure', *Houston Chronicle*, 15 February 2012, available at <http://www.chron.com/business/article/Oil-industry-battles-SEC-rules-on-disclosure-3334841.php>.

[95] N. Ezeah, 'NGO Tasks NEITI on Transparency, Accountability,' Vanguard (31 January 2012), available at <http://www.vanguardngr.com/2012/01/ngo-tasks-neiti-on-transparency-accountability>.

[96] A. Gillies and A. Heuty, 'Does Transparency Work? The Challenges of Measurement and Effectiveness in Resource-Rich Countries' (2011) 6 Yale J. Int'l Aff. 25, 36.

familiar soft law and new governance forms. Invocation of mutual accountability and collaborative programme development is also consistent with the paradigm. However, the initiative essentially uses existing intergovernmental and institutional channels to promote improved aid effectiveness.

OECD-led assessments of the Declaration's impact show progress in establishing and reforming recipient country institutions for policy development and aid administration.[97] There is also some evidence of increased aid volumes. However, an independent audit completed in 2011 suggests that changes on the donor end have been very limited.[98] Whether this is a structural deficiency or a function of the crisis is difficult to assess at this time.

It is also too early to draw lessons from the Paris Declaration for implementation of the Principles. Although the Declaration has articulated ambitious goals, and has proceeded to elaborate them in successive meetings, it did not emphasize institutional innovation in the way the more hybrid public-private initiatives have done.

IV. The Santiago Principles[99]

The Generally Accepted Principles and Practices for Sovereign Wealth Funds, unveiled in Santiago, Chile, in August 2008 (hence Santiago Principles), are essentially a public sector initiative like the Paris Declaration. However, the Santiago Principles bring together very different kinds of government actors—international investment vehicles of surplus countries—and for a very different purpose than the traditional aid enterprise.

State-owned investment vehicles or Sovereign Wealth Funds (SWFs) proliferated in the mid-2000s, but also faced an increasingly hostile investment environment in Europe and the United States. At the outset, many SWFs saw one another as competitors and were not inclined to collaborate. The idea of a best practices code emerged in G-20 discussions in 2007, and received a boost from the development of academic, commercial, and think tank assessments of the SWFs.[100] The goal was to improve the transparency and accountability of the SWFs, and thereby to make them seem less threatening to the host countries. Because SWF sponsors had no need for official funding, conditionality was not available as a lever to change individual SWF behaviour. Any resulting code would have to be 'soft', or non-binding. Members of the International Working Group refrained from describing their work product as 'best' practices—but rather as generally accepted

[97] OECD, 'Aid Effectiveness 2005–10: Progress in Implementing the Paris Declaration' (2011), available at <http://www.oecd.org/dataoecd/25/30/48742718.pdf>.

[98] OECD, 'The Evaluation of the Paris Declaration, Phase 2', Final Report (2011), available at <http://pd-website.inforce.dk/content/content-en.html>.

[99] Portions of this section were previously published in A. Gelpern, 'Sovereignty, Accountability, and the Wealth Fund Governance Conundrum' (2011) 1 Asian J. Int'l L. 289.

[100] e.g. E.M. Truman, 'A Scoreboard for Sovereign Wealth Funds', Peterson Institute for International Economics (2007), available at <http://www.iie.com/publications/papers/truman1007swf.pdf>.

practices suitable for countries across the national income spectrum.[101] The IMF was invited to facilitate the development of the principles and serve as the initial International Working Group secretariat based on its macroeconomic and technical expertise, without explicit programme or surveillance links. Participants in the development of the Santiago Principles over the first half of 2008 report that a community of interests gradually emerged among disparate SWFs.

The two dozen Santiago Principles address the structure and objectives of SWFs ('legal, institutional and macroeconomic' factors), their governance practices (especially decision autonomy from the home government), and their investment and risk management policies, focusing on financial stability. The document is suffused with accountability rhetoric, which is cited in support of all but a few of the two dozen principles. At the same time, the Santiago Principles take a particular view of accountability that is distinct from earlier public statements by SWFs and host governments: SWFs promise to act and be accountable as market actors, not political entities. They go the farthest in answering to their narrow stakeholders under the terms of their constitutive arrangements,[102] abiding by the laws their hosts made applicable to similarly situated investors,[103] and participating in the global financial markets in the manner of profit-driven private investors.[104] The most significant disclosure is made to the owner, not the domestic public, effectively relying on general government channels to inform the populace and the world at large.[105] Domestic political sensitivities trumped transparency in important instances: for example SWFs are not required to disclose the size of their asset holdings.[106]

Because the objective of SWFs was to demonstrate their commercial essence despite their public ownership, the Santiago Principles seek to distance the signatories from the social responsibility agenda: SWFs are in the business of maximizing 'risk-adjusted returns' and operate solely 'based on economic and financial grounds'. Any social, ethical, or religious motive is a deviation from the group norm (albeit one in which some important members like Kuwait and Norway engage), which must be specifically disclosed. Disclosure obligations elsewhere in the document are justified in terms of dispelling 'concern about potential noneconomic or nonfinancial objectives'.[107] The funds' contribution to global financial

[101] International Working Group of Sovereign Wealth Funds, 'Sovereign Wealth Funds: Generally Accepted Principles and Practices "Santiago Principles"' (October 2008) (hereinafter GAPP), available at <http://www.iwg-swf.org/pubs/eng/santiagoprinciples.pdf>; GAPP 5.

[102] GAPP (n. 101) 6–10.

[103] GAPP (n. 101) 15. A press report went so far as to designate compliance with host country disclosure laws as 'the most significant of the 24 guidelines' in the Santiago Principles. 'Cash in Hand', *The Economist*, 19 June 2010, 68. This characterization is somewhat puzzling since, unlike some of the other GAPP items, GAPP 15's non-binding exhortation to abide by already-binding legal rules yields no new content and uncertain additional commitment.

[104] GAPP (n. 101) 2, 17, 19.

[105] GAPP (n. 101) 5.

[106] See e.g. E.M. Truman, 'A Blueprint for Sovereign Wealth Fund Best Practices' (Peterson Institute for International Economics Policy Brief 08-3 (2008) 27; E.M. Truman, *Sovereign Wealth Funds: Threat or Salvation?* (Peterson Institute for International Economics, 2010) 112.

[107] GAPP (n. 101) 21; see also e.g. GAPP 6; GAPP 16, Explanations and Commentary.

stability comes not from a sense of public duty, but rather from their capacity—by virtue of their economic objective and structure—'to take a long-term view in their investments and ride out business cycles'.[108]

When the International Working Group announced agreement on the Santiago Principles, its members were at pains to disassociate them from the IMF surveillance process: they insisted that everything about the principles was voluntary. Perhaps as a matter of pre-emption, the Santiago Principles incorporated a periodic internal review mechanism.[109] In theory, nothing prevents the IMF from considering the Generally Accepted Principles and Practices (GAPP) criteria in its assessment of home and host policies implicating SWFs, just as nothing prevents a host government from using GAPP as part of its investment screen.[110] But doing so may undermine the Principles' legitimacy in the home countries, and scuttle cooperation between new and old powers and institutions.

Shortly after releasing the principles themselves, the International Working Group secretariat released an SWF survey, answering calls for transparency while seizing the initiative and asserting control in a field where authoritative information was scarce and analysis was dominated by private investment banks and consultancies.[111] Six months after presenting the Principles to the IMFC, the group released the Kuwait Declaration establishing a standing forum of SWFs. The International Working Group's successor, the International Forum of Sovereign Wealth Funds is 'a voluntary group of SWFs' whose membership is open to funds that meet the GAPP definition of SWF and, significantly, 'endorse' the Principles. It is a soft institutional counterpart to the emphatically soft law of the Santiago Principles.[112] The International Forum has met periodically in member capitals, has issued statements advocating open investment, and has brokered a code of 'good practices' on investment risk management, conducting member surveys as part of the process.[113]

The following features of the Santiago Principles process merit attention for purposes of Principles Implementation:

[108] Santiago Principles: Objective and Purpose; GAPP 3.

[109] International Working group of Sovereign Wealth Funds, Press Conference Call Transcript No. 08/01, 2 September 2008, available at <http://www.iwg-swf.org/tr.htm>.

[110] Some members of the US Congress have suggested using CFIUS review to encourage SWF compliance with best practices, albeit omitting specific reference to GAPP. See House Financial Services Committee, 'Frank, Maloney, Gutierrez Call on Treasury to Address Sovereign Wealth Funds in FINSA Regulations', Press Release, 13 March 2008, available at <http://democrats.financialservices.house.gov/press110/press0313082.shtml>; Truman (n. 106) 100.

[111] International Working Group of Sovereign Wealth Funds, 'Sovereign Wealth Funds: Current Institutional and Operational Practices', 15 September 2008, available at <http://iwg-swf.org/pubs/swfsurvey.pdf>; B.W. Setser, 'Sovereign Wealth and Sovereign Power: The Strategic Consequences of American Indebtedness', Council on Foreign Relations CSR No. 37 (2008), noting a decline in transparency.

[112] International Working Group of Sovereign Wealth Funds, '"Kuwait Declaration": Establishment of the International Forum of Sovereign Wealth Funds', 6 April 2009, available at <http://www.iwg-swf.org/mis/kuwaitdec.htm>.

[113] International Forum of Sovereign Wealth Funds, 'Sovereign Wealth Funds Issue "Baku Statement" Reaffirming the Need for Maintaining Open Investment Environment', 9 October 2009, available at <http://www.ifswf.org/pr/pr2.htm>.

- *Membership criteria.* In the case of SWFs more than any other, a common definition of regulatory subjects was missing—SWFs were just too diverse and contested as a phenomenon. Defining the category, and requiring members to formally endorse the Santiago Principles as a condition of joining, established a community, a code of behaviour, and a sanction[114] in one step. This is similar to the concepts of EPFIs and EITI member countries.
- *Common defence motive.* Diverse SWFs were ultimately prodded into cooperation by common fears about protectionist laws in host countries. The code is unlikely to have emerged without this background risk. In this respect, SWFs are not unlike some of the banks adopting the Equator Principles; at least at the outset, codes emerge from a marriage of convenience.
- *Elaboration, reporting, and institutionalization.* The initial code of behaviour was quickly supplemented by information release and more inward-looking best practice efforts for the benefit of SWF members.
- *Limited emphasis on disclosure and civil society collaboration.* In one important respect, the Santiago Principles are unlike other new governance initiatives. Although transparency and SWF-host collaboration are important objectives, the funds' commitment to these goals is carefully circumscribed owing in large part to domestic political constraints. Civil society participation and social consciousness are de-emphasized.
- *Involving international organizations as facilitators.* The IMF's role in the Santiago Principles process may be akin to UNCTAD's role in the preparation of the Principles.
- *Role of non-governmental monitors.* The presence and continued reporting by think tanks and industry observers contributed to the content and implementation of the Santiago Principles. There is ample evidence of competing outside metrics influencing the content of the Santiago Principles, of SWFs tracking and seeking to improve their 'scores' (sometimes by lobbying the scorekeepers), and trying to pre-empt outside monitoring by supplying their own information.

The Santiago Principles' implementation record is limited—they are just over three years old. However, judging by outside assessments, many SWFs have improved their disclosure to varying degrees in the process of negotiation and early implementations. Because the objectives of SWFs are limited and commercial, they also face a lower assessment bar than the development-focused initiatives discussed in the three preceding case studies.

V. Principles for stable capital flows and fair debt restructuring

The Principles for Stable Capital Flows and Fair Debt Restructuring (until 2012, Principles for Stable Capital Flows and Fair Debt Restructuring in the Emerging

[114] e.g. limitations on membership.

Markets) (Capital Markets Principles) were developed under the auspices of the Institute for International Finance (IIF) in 2004, partly responding to the controversy surrounding Argentina's debt crisis in 2001 and the ensuing debate about sovereign bankruptcy and sovereign debt contract reform. Like the EPs and the Santiago Principles, the Capital Market Principles were adopted partly as 'market self-defence': large issuers and creditors felt threatened by the prospect of a statutory sovereign bankruptcy regime, but were amenable to a code of conduct, especially if adopting it would help to defeat the bankruptcy proposal.[115]

The Capital Markets Principles exhibit the familiar characteristics of soft law and new governance: they are non-binding, open-ended and specified over time, and designed to secure parallel undertakings from borrowers and creditors. They only apply to a subset of debt instruments, and are thus narrower in scope and have fewer constituents than the Principles for Responsible Lending and Borrowing.

The Capital Markets Principles have four basic prongs: transparency and timely flow of information, debtor-creditor cooperation to avoid restructuring, good-faith actions, and fair treatment. At the outset, they were adopted by major financial institutions and supported by emerging markets borrowers. Elements of the official sector, including the G-20 and the International Monetary and Financial Committee of the IMF, have 'noted' and 'welcomed' the Capital Markets Principles, but have stopped short of robust endorsement.

The Principles Consultative Group (PCG), comprising 31 representatives of sovereign borrowers and leading financial institutions, meets periodically as the governance organ of the Emerging Markets Principles. The Group of Trustees of the Principles, comprising 'elder statesmen' in sovereign finance, consider the overall development of the Capital Markets Principles in the context of the international financial system, and may recommend modifications. The IIF (an industry group representing large financial institutions) was the leading force behind the Capital Market Principles and serves as the secretariat. While other financial industry groups have indicated co-sponsorship and support for the Capital Market Principles, none is as vocal in proclaiming their relevance. In the run-up to publication and since, there have been reports of dissent within financial industry ranks with respect to the content and application of the principles.[116]

Like the other initiatives considered here, the Capital Markets Principles come with periodic reporting and self-assessment, elaboration and refinement by the PCG, staffed by the IIF. Unlike some of the others, the Capital Markets Principles have a discrete view of their constituents: major financial institutions and governments in major emerging market countries. Like the Santiago Principles, the Capital Markets Principles do not aspire to civil society participation, or a broader social reform agenda. Nor have there been large-scale independent audits of the sort that more development-focused initiatives, such as EITI, have undergone.

[115] Helleiner (n. 22). [116] Helleiner (n. 22).

Critics of the initiative point to the prominent role of IIF, infighting and defections among private creditor constituents, and the apparently provisional engagement by both the developing countries and the official sector, as evidence that the Capital Markets Principles are unlikely to succeed on their own relatively circumscribed terms.[117] The Capital Markets Principles were tested in Greece, where the IIF took the lead in negotiating on behalf of private creditors through much of 2011 and early 2012, and invoked the Capital Markets Principles. In an October 2012 report focusing on the Greek experience, the Joint Committee on Strengthening the Framework for Sovereign Debt Crisis Prevention and Resolution declared victory on the Principles' behalf—and quietly expanded their reach by removing the phrase 'Emerging Markets' in their title. Most outside observers agree that the Greek restructuring was an immensely impressive transaction; consensus is harder to come by on other measures of success (Greek debt is still unsustainable) as well as the role of the Principles and the IIF.

The Capital Markets Principles initiative can claim the largest measure of success in fostering professionalized investor relations, such as the *ex-ante* establishment of debt management offices and improving disclosure practices among emerging markets countries. It is difficult to tell to what extent these changes might have happened absent the Capital Markets Principles.

This section has surveyed five case studies of soft law and new governance initiatives in development finance. The key insight is that while all five are informal and nonbinding, they take rather different institutional forms, which may in turn help predict or explain their performance. To be fair, none of the five can boast a deep record of implementation, especially as measured by development outcomes on the ground.

The Equator Principles appear to have a robust infrastructure for engaging direct participants in project finance, and the tightest link between the professed goals and the methods used to achieve them. The EP initiative has a discrete set of objectives, is controlled by the primary subjects of regulation (EPFIs), and benefits from linkages to the IFC, which supplies the content of the standards. Contracts between the EPFIs and their clients become delivery vehicles for the content; in this sense, the initiative hinges on the enforceability of private contracts. On the other hand, placing financial institutions at the centre of the initiative and relying on contractual mechanisms for stakeholder access and public awareness potentially raises the risk of capture. The IFC's orchestration role becomes more important in this context, as does early and vigorous oversight by civil society constituents.[118]

The EITI has a more formal and elaborate structure than the EPs, and a more formal connection with the official sector. However, its emphasis on government

[117] B. Herman, 'Why the Code of Conduct Falls Short' in B. Herman, J.A. Ocampo, and S. Spiegel (eds), *Overcoming Developing Country Debt Crises* (Oxford University Press, 2010).

[118] Mattli and Woods, 'In Whose Benefit?' (n. 13), theorizing the risk of capture; Abbott and Snidal (n. 15) 570, 575, proposing an orchestration role for international organizations. For an example of civil society oversight, see Bank Track at <http://www.BankTrack.org>.

accountability to govern public and private actors, the indirect commitment of the private extractive industry, as well as the gap between the immediate objective of disclosure and the larger goals of development, creates risks for implementation. On the other hand, independent and public audits and information dissemination practices create incentives for public monitoring, even in the absence of direct obligations on non-government stakeholders.

The Paris Declaration is the case study closest to the 'old governance' model: it has articulated ambitious goals on aid effectiveness, but has largely eschewed radical institutional innovation in pursuing them. Even so, it has helped to secure important improvements in recipient aid management, despite relatively weak performance on the part of the donors.

Like the EPs, the Santiago Principles benefit from a delimited constituency, narrowly set goals, and the perception of business risk. The Santiago Principles do not aspire to change the world, but to make it safe for SWF investment. The most interesting element of this initiative for Principles implementation is the role of outside indices and scoreboards, which became an important foil and driver of the Santiago Principles.

The Capital Markets Principles similarly do not set ambitious development policy goals. They may have played a role in improving *ex ante* debt management and monitoring on the part of emerging market countries; however, their effect on debt restructuring practices is uncertain. Their close association with a subset of creditors has exposed them to criticism for limited legitimacy.

In conclusion, it is worth considering a much older initiative, which culminated in the 2003 UN Convention on Corruption. Beginning with the enactment of the Foreign Corrupt Practices Act in the United States in 1977, US officials tried to persuade counterparts to adopt similar measures, so as not to put US firms at a disadvantage. However, such efforts largely failed. The campaign got a new lease of life with the formation of Transparency International in 1993, based in Germany, which began with promoting transparency pacts between governments and bidders for public contracts, and expanded to monitoring and rating countries for public corruption indicators. US negotiators had given up on securing hard law commitments on bribery; however, they enthusiastically supported Transparency International's soft law campaign. The civil society campaign led to a series of soft law instruments (guidelines and recommendations) promulgated by the OECD, a formal international organization, followed by classic hard law—the 1997 OECD Anti-Bribery Convention. Scholars credit the strategic, purposeful collaboration and iterative process between state and civil society actors with the success of the effort in changing domestic legislation and norms of behaviour in many jurisdictions.[119]

Echoes of this 'hardening' trajectory may be found in some of the case studies in this part of the chapter (section C.), including the incorporation of EITI concerns in the Dodd-Frank Act and national legislation in Liberia and Nigeria. However,

[119] R.S. Karmel and C.R. Kelly, 'The Hardening of Soft Law in Securities Regulation' (2009) 34 Brook. J. Int'l L. 883, 916–24.

one must be cautions in implying a necessary and unidirectional relationship between soft and hard law from this case: while some scholars have emphasized complementarity between soft and hard initiatives, others have shown ways in which states and market participants can play soft law and hard law against each other, weakening both in the process.[120] With these lessons in mind, section D. contains recommendations for Principles implementation.

D. An 'All of the Above' Implementation Strategy

The central premise of this chapter has been that the goal of implementation goes beyond formal adoption or widespread endorsement. The implementation of the UNCTAD Principles should be measured by compliance: a drop in unsustainable, unauthorized, and exploitative sovereign debt. Compliance here may take years, in some cases decades, to ascertain. This fact should not detract from the overarching goal. It does raise distinct implementation challenges and tempers expectations of assessment. None of the initiatives discussed in the case studies in section C. can claim to have developed a robust record of compliance in the course of the past decade.[121]

The implementation recommendations that follow draw on the theories of soft law and new governance sketched out in section B., and on the case studies in section C. They fall into three categories: endorsement and membership, monitoring and information flow, and institutional linkages. More specifically, the implementation strategy should (a) maintain the non-binding character of the Principles; (b) secure clear endorsement from diverse constituents, with diversity measured both geographically and by sector (states, financial firms, civil society); (c) continue to elaborate and adapt the Principles to build support; (d) promote regular monitoring and publicly accessible reporting, using both internal and external mechanisms; (e) forge institutional links with multiple stakeholders and connections to other best practices regimes; and (f) create a governance body to maintain oversight, review and adapt the Principles, reinforce ties with stakeholders, and potentially administer membership sanctions. I elaborate in the following:

First, it makes little sense to turn the Principles into a treaty instrument. Especially to the extent that they reflect elements of existing law, their best promise lies in their capacity to reach out to diverse audiences, expand the consensus, and adapt to fast-changing circumstances. This feature would be lost to a multi-year process of treaty negotiation, with membership and compliance being highly uncertain in the end. Moreover, even where a treaty is in place, remedies for breach

[120] G.C. Shaffer and M.A. Pollack, 'Hard vs. Soft Law: Alternatives, Complements, and Antagonists in International Governance' (2010) 94 Minn. L. Rev. 712.

[121] This is not unusual for new governance initiatives. Most are in the early stages of development. For a theoretical explanation, see Bernstein and Cashore (n. 68).

may be inaccessible, uncertain, or ineffective. This stands in contrast to the general viability of retaliation in trade. Recent literature suggests that soft law has had success in the realm of international financial regulation when it engages new governance techniques; there is untapped potential for both soft law and new governance in sovereign debt.

Secondly, formal adoption or endorsement of the Principles by governments, G-groups, international financial institutions, civil society and private creditor groups, contract counterparties, and others, is important, but not sufficient. It would of course be useful to have all the stakeholders formally adopt the Principles. Adoption creates a community of interest, channels for information exchange, and moral suasion, and ultimately reputational sanctions for not complying with group norms. However, adoption does not correlate perfectly with compliance, and may even mask non-compliance. Selective adoption and implementation of the Principles may be a way to jump-start endorsements; however, it is also fraught with risks of dilution and fragmentation. In particular, it is important to gain broadly-based agreement on what constitutes the substantive core of the Principles, which should be protected from variation to the extent possible, even at a cost to formal participation. One possible way to reconcile the need for endorsement now and the strength of commitment down the line is to 'tier' elements of the Principles, much like some of the initiatives in section C., case studies: a general and rarely-changed core could be adopted up front, with more specific implications to be further developed by the participants.

Thirdly, the Principles would benefit from substantive and technical elaboration over time. This process can be used to broaden acceptance of the Principles and keep them relevant. For example, if a group of experts from different jurisdictions prepared a report on how sovereign debt contracts or debt management practices might better reflect the goals of the Principles, this would create an implementation vehicle, demonstrate the ongoing vitality of the Principles project, and secure ownership in an important constituency. Export credit and development agencies, and national debt management offices, are key constituents that could contribute to elaboration, fostering ownership. Other practical reports could address subjects such as interpreting sovereign fiduciary duty across jurisdictions, due diligence and post-disbursement monitoring, domestic legislative implications, the role of the judiciary in implementing the Principles, a 'best practices bank', and even debt data collection. Preserving the open and contested character of the Principles is important in order to continue generating new implementation ideas, and new opportunities for broadly-based acceptance. The process of elaboration should be open, with reports being publicly available and inviting public comment.

Ultimately, the elaboration process may consider whether the Principles should harden, and if so, in what form. Elaboration may take place in multiple stakeholder settings; it may also be centralized in a multi-stakeholder governance forum. Where it is decentralized, coordination is key.

Fourthly, monitoring is an essential component of Principles implementation. Apart from promoting accountability, monitoring and reporting may help to create positive feedback loops: better due diligence, better risk-management systems, and more generally a 'race to the top' among borrowers, lenders, and monitors. For monitoring to be effective, it must be user-friendly and relevant both to external and internal constituents. It would help to develop specific compliance benchmarks. Different forms of monitoring and reporting could be useful; they are not mutually exclusive. Public monitoring and reporting by civil society groups specifically referencing the Principles and any relevant elaboration would promote the public accountability and diffusion of the Principles. Facilitating and encouraging such monitoring would put pressure on governments to disclose more, especially with respect to direct and contingent liabilities, and the terms of their debt contracts. At least one dedicated independent monitor with periodic (at least annual) reporting duties to the consultative group, UNCTAD, and/or another organ, would promote better governance for the Principles.

The role of competition in monitoring should be actively considered. Multiple private sector, NGO, and public monitors, at least at the outset, can contribute to improved assessment standards, and create broader demand for regulation and information. It is not necessary to decide at the outset on a single rating or compliance certification process. Single compliance metrics would be particularly difficult to articulate in sovereign finance, as distinct from the more traditional context of supply-chain certification. A multi-layered assessment, akin to the SWF scoreboard, would be more appropriate.

Fifthly, institutional and operational linkages can help to promote durable compliance. For example, incorporating the Principles into the monitoring agenda of existing groups and institutions, and cross-referencing and linking to other best practices in public and private instruments, would help to support wider acceptance of the Principles. Embedding the Principles among the standards monitored by international organizations such as the IMF, the Financial Stability Board, sector and regional groupings, and bilateral creditors, would leverage existing institutional competence to support implementation. In forging such links, it is important to engage all relevant stakeholders and create meaningful expectations for their respective roles.

Sixthly, a dedicated institutional framework for the Principles, soft or hard, would help to coordinate the monitoring and elaboration functions discussed earlier, entrench constituencies for implementation, and embed the Principles in the fabric of sovereign lending and borrowing practice. Institutionalizing broadly-based consultations, even after the Principles are substantially fleshed out, should enhance acceptance and ultimately help to boost compliance. It bears emphasis that all of the initiatives discussed in section C resulted in the establishment of a governance body, some more formal than others, within a few years of their launch. At the outset, a rotating advisory group including representatives of sovereign borrowers, official and private creditors, and civil society, would support the continuing legitimacy and relevance of the Principles. Such a group could oversee their elaboration, adaptation, and refinement. It may make sense to consider two distinct advisory groups: one for lenders, the other for borrowers. Splitting the groups might better channel expertise; on the other hand, this would detract from the valuable holistic character of the Principles, and would require an additional coordination framework. Other institutional forms to consider include a secretariat and a periodic general meeting. These would be in addition to the advisory body. If the Principles enjoy any measure of success, questions of interpretation, standards, membership sanctions, and eventual 'hardening' may come up. It would be useful to consider up front a framework for handling such questions.

E. Conclusion

This chapter has discussed strategies for the implementation of the UNCTAD Principles, along with theoretical and pragmatic grounds for the proposed implementation path. These are anchored in the particular qualities of the Principles. The Principles are distinctly ambitious in terms of trying to govern both debtor and creditor practices, including public and private creditors, covering a broad range of instruments, and actively involving civil society stakeholders. This is ultimately a key source of strength for the Principles: it is likely that they would be seen as even-handed, and therefore more legitimate. The true constituency of the Principles is the global economic system. Properly implemented, they should promote stability and equity within it.

The Principles are also a product of broadly-based consultations with diverse government, private sector, multilateral, and civil society groups. Formal and informal outreach is an important source of input legitimacy for the Principles, especially as the content is elaborated and made more specific. The diversity of constituents for the Principles presents an additional process opportunity. The Principles may be 'tested' in discrete fields, where they could demonstrate their usefulness and win broader adherence based on experience. The presence of multiple constituencies presents opportunities for targeted outreach, where proponents may emphasize the Principles' utility to such constituencies, and ultimately, the shared interest in compliance.

The Principles are a mix of well-established principles of national and international law, and an effort at systematization and progressive development of international law governing sovereign lending and borrowing. The Principles do not claim to make new law, but rather to harness and elaborate existing best practices and general principles. Done in the right way, the process of adaptation could create acceptance at the national level at moderate political cost.

By charting both *ex ante* and *ex post* debt management practices, the Principles frame a comprehensive debt management regime that enhances financial stability. By focusing on due diligence, transparency, and authority, the Principles contribute to crisis prevention. The emphasis on disclosure should facilitate the constructive operation of market mechanisms at all stages of the process. Finally, by clarifying the locus and standards of responsibility, the Principles contribute to the sound management of debt distress.

All that said, a strategy emphasizing soft law and new governance is by definition uncertain: success is a function of active and purposeful engagement by the participants, some of whom may have limited incentives to cooperate beyond cosmetic compliance. Political buy-in, technical and financial resources are hard to come by, and constant revision is burdensome. Nevertheless, none of the 'hard' alternatives by itself can ensure implementation. A parallel-track process with thought-out linkages among the tracks stands the best chance of changing borrowing and lending behaviour—along with producing good outcomes for development and financial stability.

CONCLUSIONS

17

Concluding Remarks in the Light of International Law

Robert Howse

From a legal perspective, the UNCTAD Principles make two important contributions to shaping the international normative order as it concerns sovereign debt. The first is to qualify or limit a sovereign debtor's obligation to repay the debt in full, where there is a situation of economic necessity. The second is to contribute to the evolution of the odious debt doctrine by establishing the norm that valid sovereign debt obligations are those contracted by publicly interested state officials for purposes of serving the public good. Neither of these contributions depends on the Principles themselves being transformed into a hard law international instrument, such as a treaty, or acquiring the status of custom. Rather, the Principles offer new normative tools for reshaping legal relationships between sovereign debtors and both official and private creditors in the absence of a centralized international institution or tribunal (see Chapter 16, by Anna Gelpern, in this volume). In these brief concluding remarks, I will discuss each of these contributions in turn.

Going back to the 1980s debt crisis, the *Grundnorm* on the basis of which the various institutions and actors, including the Paris and London Clubs and the IMF, addressed the payment difficulties of sovereigns was that of the sanctity of the obligation to repay the debt in full, principal and interest, regardless of the economic inefficiency of not marking the debt to market, and regardless of social consequences. While sometimes presented as the hard law obligation of *pacta sunt servanda* (as Michael Waibel points out in Chapter 5 of this volume), *pacta sunt servanda* applies to treaties, not contractual obligations, and in any case not to obligations to private parties. The *Grundnorm* of an absolute obligation to repay in full thus could not be upheld on the basis of international law; rather it gained its force from being the norm that the institutional actors in the international community all adhered to in their dealings with creditors and debtors. By the 1990s one started to see cracks in the facade—inventive methods of reducing obligations or discounting them surreptitiously, whether Brady bonds, or debt-for-nature, or debt equity swaps at questionable pricing. Eventually and begrudgingly, international financial institution (IFI) creditors acceded to highly conditional programmes of debt relief for poor, heavily indebted countries.

In fact, the norm of an absolute obligation to repay in full has faced two radical challenges that I believe have shaken confidence in its viability as the *Grundnorm* for addressing the sovereign debt crisis. The first is the human rights revolution. As Armin von Bogdandy and Matthias Goldmann suggest in Chapter 3 of this volume, as an exercise in public authority, any institutionalized international settlement of a sovereign debt crisis must be tested against the computability of that settlement with the capacity of a debtor state to fulfil its social and economic rights obligations to its own population.

Secondly, as we have seen with Greece, and with the demonstrations in some Latin American countries, how to approach sovereign debt crises is now a matter of intense public contestation and debate. It is no longer a negotiation among a small group of elite actors, governmental and private sector managers, lawyers, and IFI officials, where the broader social consequences are marginalized, and the solutions are regarded as 'technical', based on economic formulas for structural adjustment or conditionality. The significance of publicity is also well developed in the Bogdandy and Goldmann essay. (When I was involved many years ago in a Paris Club rescheduling, working for an official creditor, the only Paris Club that had a visible public presence was an adult entertainment facility.) Anna Gelpern, in Chapter 16, gives a good flavour of the dominance of a rather closed epistemic community here.

Finally, and perhaps of most significance, there is Argentina's decision to bypass the traditional institutional framework and impose a unilateral restructuring of its debt on its creditors. If full repayment and the kind of arrangements associated with reconciling full repayment with inability to service debt in the short term were losing their normative legitimacy, Argentina's experiment has arguably resulted in a great loss of empirical legitimacy. While holdout creditors continue to pursue legal actions against Argentina, sometimes with initial success (but without yet being able to go the full distance in getting their money back), the punishment that was always supposed to be forthcoming if a sovereign debtor challenged the *Grundnorm* has not been forthcoming. Argentina remains part of the international financial system, the IMF still deals with it, and while the United States has rapped it on the knuckles with some trade measures, this is hardly the same thing as effective community enforcement of a supposed sacred community *Grundnorm*. I do not wish to be misunderstood: I am not suggesting that what Argentina did was equitable or justified in the particular circumstances of its economic situation. On balance, I think the contrary. I am merely suggesting that Argentina has made an important contribution to shaking confidence in the viability of the received *Grundnorm* of absolute obligation to repay in full.

If on the one hand, this received *Grundnorm* is no longer credible, it is hard to imagine the institutional frameworks that deal with sovereign debt crises, or the actors within them, operating effectively without some kind of normative framework or principle in the shadow of which negotiations are conducted, directly and indirectly, across the public/private divide. Institutions cannot easily operate with unbounded struggle and contestation of the applicable norms; such struggle creates enormous transaction costs and uncertainty, and interferes with the functionalist mission of getting out of crisis and re-establishing confidence in the debt markets. And here is exactly where the UNCTAD Principles move in to fill the gap.

It is arguable that Principles 9 and 15 taken together can constitute the basis of a new *Grundnorm*. Principle 9 indicates that while: '*A sovereign debt contract is a binding obligation and should be honored. Exceptional cases nonetheless can arise. A state of economic necessity can prevent the borrower's full and/or timely repayment.*' The reference to the prevention of 'full' and not just 'timely' repayment indicates the departure of Principle 9 from the old *Grundnorm*. It implies a legitimate claim not just to debt rescheduling (the time frame of repayment) but to relief from the obligation of paying the obligation in full. This is elaborated in Principle 15, which refers to the notion that 'the restructuring should be proportional to the sovereign's need and all stakeholders (including citizens) should share an equitable burden of adjustment and/or *losses*' (emphasis added). The requirement that creditors share the burden equitably by taking some 'losses' represents a clear departure from the received and now tattered *Grundnorm* of absolute obligation to repay in full. As noted, under that *Grundnorm*, any debt restructuring would entail the debtor fully compensating the creditor for the transaction costs of rescheduling (fees) and for the extension in the time of repayment (interest).

The significance of Principles 9 and 15 in the establishment of a new *Grundnorm* is somewhat blunted or obscured in my view by looking at the concept of necessity in Principle 9 as simply echoing or repeating the notion of 'necessity' in the ILC Articles on State Responsibility. To the extent that a state's obligation to repay in full is an obligation under international law (more problematic than is often assumed, as mentioned) it may be limited by 'necessity' within the meaning of Article 25 of the ILC Articles of State Responsibility. Unlike Michael Waibel, I think there are important differences in the concept of 'necessity' from customary international law codified in the ILC Articles and the principles expressed in UNCTAD Principles 9 and 15. First of all, Article 25 only allows for the suspension or delay (not elimination) of secondary obligations-state responsibility. It provides no basis for the limitation or modification of the underlying primary obligation. Thus Article 27 states that the invocation of Article 25 is 'without prejudice to: (a) Compliance with the obligation in question, if and to the extent that the circumstance precluding wrongfulness no longer exists; (b) The question of compensation for any material loss caused by the act in question'. The difference between this understanding of 'necessity' and those in Principles 9 and 15 is considerable. Principle 9 suggests that economic necessity could prevent 'full' repayment, which, as noted, means that it could legitimately entail altering the underlying primary obligation, and not just a suspension of the performance of the obligation during a defined period of a 'state of necessity'. Secondly, Article 27(b) of the ILC Articles clearly indicates that it is the state that is invoking 'necessity' that must, afterwards, based on general principles of state responsibility, pay in full the costs of its suspension of the performance of its obligation during the period of 'necessity', while UNCTAD Principle 15 provides for equitable sharing of burdens, including 'losses'. Thus, I find it impossible to agree with Waibel's suggestion that 'as worded, the UNCTAD Principles . . . do not increase the scope of the defence of necessity, but defer to the strict limits of the defence in general international law'. Further, Principle 9 indicates that a state of necessity may be a circumstance giving rise to a legal defence before a 'competent judicial authority', i.e. regardless of whether there is an interstate dispute. This extends the role of 'necessity' beyond the context of state responsibility in pubic international law, to a principle that may affect rights and obligations under private law.

The other contribution of the UNCTAD Principles that I would like to emphasize concerns odious or illegitimate debt. The Principles articulate a set of standards that is very helpful to assessing claims that debt is odious or illegitimate. This relates to the notion that if the lender was aware of these features, they may be held accountable and perhaps even lose the entitlement to full repayment. First of all, the Principles, in their implications, identify conduct that is 'wrongful': 'Any attempt by a lender to suborn a government official to breach [their duty to the State and its citizens for which they act] (Principle 1) and 'any form of self-interest or peculation on the part of government officials involved in the borrowing' (Principle 8). These standards, which relate to existing norms concerning corruption, may be helpful in applying illegality or public policy defences against debt obligations, and may also be useful in guiding audits of sovereign debt, especially in a transitional context. The broader notion that '*when they contract debt obligations, [governments] have a responsibility to protect the interests of their citizens*' carries with it, logically, the possibility of some remedy when this obligation is breached, although the remedy itself is not explicitly stated in the UNCTAD Principles. However, the Principles also emphasize that '*Lenders should recognize that government officials involved in sovereign lending and borrowing transactions are responsible for protecting the public interest*' (Principle 1) and this raises the issue of whether there is breach of lender responsibility where the lender is aware that the officials are in violation of their duty to protect the public interest. Consider Principle 3: '*Lenders have a responsibility to determine, to the best of their ability, whether the financing has been appropriately authorized*' which implies 'that the government officials are authorized under applicable law to enter into the transaction'. The question is whether officials could ever be truly 'authorized' by the state or its citizens to enter into transactions that do not protect the public interest; thus, Principle 3 needs to be read together with Principle 1 on Agency. The approach of the UNCTAD Principles would seem to push in the direction of defining an odious regime as one where, habitually or generally, the acting officials of the regime fail to protect the public interest. This seems to converge with the evolving concept of human security in international legal and policy discourse, and the related notion of Responsibility to Protect (R2P).[1] As Xiuli Han illustrates, in Chapter 12 of this volume, claims concerning 'odious' debt are arising more and more, especially in transitional contexts (recently, Tunisia and Libya), and the Principles can operate as standards that help make more concrete and coherent

[1] R. Teitel, *Humanity's Law* (Oxford University Press, 2011) ch. 6.

related international law doctrines, as well as structuring negotiations with official and private creditors after political transition.

This brings me back to the theme of how to conceive of the Principles in terms of international law. In our work on 'Beyond Compliance',[2] Teitel and I question the adequacy of the vocabulary of 'compliance' or enforcement or implementation in accounting for the way in which international legal normativity has effects in the world. We point out that sometimes 'soft law' can have stronger and wider normative effects than hard law. We need, without any prejudice in favour of hard law, to understand why a certain kind of legal material is able to gain a significant normative effect. What is the underlying nature of legitimacy that makes it possible for the material to have certain particular normative effects rather than fewer or less or different normative effects. So that is an abstract statement. Concretely here, I think what it means is that we have to be imaginative: for example why couldn't sovereign borrowers simply include the principles in the contract, to say that this debt contract shall be interpreted and applied in accordance with the UNCTAD Principles on Responsible Sovereign Lending and Borrowing. Once you get a few sovereign borrowers who are doing that, you may start a trend. This is norm entrepreneurship. The Principles are clearly intended to relate to and affect legal norms even if they are explicitly stated not, as such, to constitute a change to international law; they are full of legal categories and notions, such as agency, due diligence, collective action, and so forth. Even with respect to Argentina alone, there are many claims going through the investment regime that relate to sovereign debt and it would greatly surprise me if one or more arbitrators over the next two years,[3] trying to grasp how to apply a very general standard in an investment treaty, like the standard of fair and equitable treatment, would want to grab off the shelf any useful international standards relevant to the area of sovereign debt, in order to apply the very broad treaty provisions in question in the sovereign debt context. So I think these Principles have a bright future and they may be more effective than new hard law initiatives in normatively shaping an area of international controversy where, as noted, the actors are multiple and diffuse (from private corporations to domestic courts to international arbitrators and IFIs) and the institutional context is highly fragmented.

[2] R. Howse and R. Teitel, 'Beyond Compliance: Rethinking Why International Law Really Matters' (2009) 1 *Global Policy* 127.

[3] See *Ambiente Ufficio S.p.A. and others v. Argentine Republic*, ICSID Case No. ARB/08/9 (formerly *Giordano Alpi and others v. Argentine Republic*), dissenting opinion of Santiago Torres Bernárdez, 2 May 2013, <http://www.italaw.com/cases/1750>.

Annex: Principles on Promoting Responsible Sovereign Lending and Borrowing

United Nations Conference on Trade and Development

JANUARY 2012, GENEVA BACKGROUND OF THE UNCTAD INITIATIVE

The causes and widespread negative effects of the global financial and economic crisis prompted UNCTAD to launch an initiative in 2009 to promote responsible sovereign lending and borrowing practices. The purpose of UNCTAD's initiative is to provide a forum for debate on responsible practices and to develop a set of commonly accepted principles and practices relating to sovereign debt.

The annual United Nations General Assembly resolution on external debt has repeatedly stressed the importance of promoting responsible sovereign lending and borrowing. In December 2010, it emphasized the need for creditors and debtors to share responsibility for preventing unsustainable debt situations and encouraged Member States, the Bretton Woods institutions, regional development banks and other relevant multilateral financial institutions and stakeholders to pursue the ongoing discussions within the framework of UNCTAD's Initiative to promote responsible sovereign lending and borrowing, while taking into account the work on this issue that is carried out by other organizations and forums.

Identifying agreed principles to guide sovereign lending and borrowing is the first step in this process. Thus, UNCTAD aims to build consensus around a set of internationally agreed principles to prevent irresponsible sovereign financing.

These Principles are still open for discussion and debate. The endorsement process aims to be transparent and inclusive of all UN member states. The consolidated version is a result of extensive international consultations, but may still be subject to finer refinements.

An expert group was established to contribute to the process of drafting these Principles. The group is composed of world renowned experts in law and economics, private investors and NGOs. Senior representatives from the IMF, the World Bank and Paris Club participate as observers of this group. After several formal meetings and exchanges of ideas, these Principles emerged.

UNCTAD is now reaching out to get national and regional feedback on the design and the possible and voluntary implementation process from UN Member States, essentially through Consultative Regional Meetings.

UNCTAD is grateful for the contributions provided by members and observers of the Expert Group, UN member states, external consultants and UNCTAD staff who worked in their professional capacities. The views expressed here do not necessarily represent the views of their institutions or organizations. UNCTAD is also grateful for the generous financial support from the Government of Norway.

PREAMBLE

Sovereign insolvencies occur due to systemic and/or extraordinary reasons and due to lenders' and/or borrowers' behavior. Both developing and developed countries—as well as bilateral, multilateral, and private lenders—have been involved in or affected by sovereign defaults.

Undisciplined, ineffective, abusive or non-cooperative behavior on the part of both creditors and sovereign debtors should be prevented in order to minimize sovereign insolvencies and their negative consequences. Sovereign lending and borrowing conducted in a prudent and disciplined manner can promote growth and development; but irresponsible financing can have harmful consequences for the debtor country, its citizens, its creditors, its neighbors and its trading partners. These effects can extend well beyond the territory of the sovereign debtor itself.

Encouraging responsible sovereign borrowing and lending practices is therefore a matter of truly international concern. Sovereign lending and borrowing are intrinsically linked to the feasibility of the Millennium Development Goals. Each side of a sovereign lending transaction—the borrower and the lender—is accountable for its own conduct in these transactions. Neither side can wholly shift to the other the duty of ensuring that the agreement is economically beneficial, financially sound, legally authorized, appropriately documented and carefully monitored.

These principles aim to promote more responsible behavior and provide economic benefit to both sovereign borrowers and their lenders. They are also conceptualized in a holistic way and are thus meant to be applied to sovereign borrowers, developed or developing countries alike, as well as their lenders.

Principles identified in this document are already followed by some sovereign borrowers and lenders. The normative contribution of these Principles lies not in the creation of new rights nor obligations in international law but in identifying, harmonizing and systematizing the basic principles and best practices applied to sovereign lending and borrowing and in elaborating the implications of these standards and practices for lenders and borrowers at the international level. This set of principles should apply without prejudice of other international rules concerning the action of lenders or borrowers.

The first step of this Initiative has been to shape a robust and well grounded set of principles and build consensus around them respecting the sovereigns' priorities and preferences.

The responsibilities of lenders and borrowers are presented separately in these Principles. Each Principle is accompanied by bullet points that clarify its meaning and highlight some relevant implications of the Principle.

I. RESPONSIBILITIES OF LENDERS

1. Agency

Lenders should recognize that government officials involved in sovereign lending and borrowing transactions are responsible for protecting public interest (to the State and its citizens for which they are acting as agents).

Implications:

- Lenders to sovereign borrowers are dealing with agents (the government officials directly involved in the borrowing process) who owe responsibility to the State and its citizens for which they act.
- Any attempt by a lender to suborn a government official to breach that duty is wrongful (for example, instances of bribes or corruption).

2. Informed Decisions

Lenders have a responsibility to provide information to their sovereign customers to assist borrowers in making informed credit decisions.

Implications:

- Applicable due diligence standards should be followed by lenders including taking reasonable steps to ensure that the sovereign understands the risks and benefits of the financial product being offered.
- The level of financial sophistication among sovereigns differs widely. Some are well informed about markets and financial techniques, others less so. The lender's responsibility increases when dealing with an unsophisticated sovereign counterparty.

3. Due Authorization

Lenders have a responsibility to determine, to the best of their ability, whether the financing has been appropriately authorized and whether the resulting credit agreements are valid and enforceable under relevant jurisdiction/s.

Implications:

- A lender has an independent duty to ensure to the best of its ability, that the government officials are authorized under applicable law to enter into the transaction and that the arrangement is otherwise consistent with such law.
- Should the lender determine that these conditions do not exist, it should desist from concluding the agreement.

4. Responsible Credit Decisions

A lender is responsible to make a realistic assessment of the sovereign borrower's capacity to service a loan based on the best available information and following objective and agreed technical rules on due diligence and national accounts.

Implications:

- Lending beyond a borrower's reasonable capacity to repay not only risks a default on the loan in question, it adversely affects the position of all other creditors of that sovereign debtor.
- When assessing the borrower's situation, lenders should consider the broad and real financial scenario, including direct and contingent liabilities according to the System of National Accounts adopted by the United Nations Statistical Commission.
- In a transaction in which a lender is motivated solely by commercial considerations, the lender should have a direct economic interest in assessing the borrower's repayment capacity.
- Credits extended to sovereign borrowers as a means of enhancing a bilateral (government-to-government) lender's geopolitical influence, however, will involve other motivations. The financing of military exports from the creditor country falls in this category. The desire to realize such benefits from a financing transaction should not replace a serious assessment of the borrower's repayment capacity.
- Lending decisions are critically dependent on the willingness of the sovereign borrowers to provide timely and accurate information (see Principle 11 below).

5. Project Financing

Lenders financing a project in the debtor country have a responsibility to perform their own ex ante investigation into and, when applicable, post-disbursement monitoring of, the likely effects of the project, including its financial, operational, civil, social, cultural, and environmental implications. This responsibility should be proportional to the technical expertise of the lender and the amount of funds to be lent.

Implications:

- In the context of project financing, a lender carries some of the responsibility for the reasonably foreseeable effects of the project and the host government shares a corresponding responsibility.
- When applicable, this investigation will normally include post-disbursement monitoring of the use of the proceeds of the loan (see Principle 12 below). This monitoring should be transparent and not affect any sovereign's faculty to decide on its developmental priorities.

6. International Cooperation

All lenders have a duty to comply with United Nations sanctions imposed against a governmental regime.

Implications:

- UN sanctions are imposed against a state in order to maintain or restore international peace and security. In instances of serious misconduct where sanctions are deemed to be necessary, lenders should not participate in financial transactions that violate, evade or hamper such sanctions.

7. **Debt Restructurings**

In circumstances where a sovereign is manifestly unable to service its debts, all lenders have a duty to behave in good faith and with cooperative spirit to reach a consensual re-arrangement of those obligations. Creditors should seek a speedy and orderly resolution to the problem.

Implications:

- To date, no universal sovereign debt restructuring mechanism has been established. A sovereign borrower facing severe financial distress therefore has no choice but to approach its creditors for a consensual rearrangement of its debt burden.
- Although the presumption is that contracts will be performed according to their terms, lenders should recognize the possibility that circumstances may arise in the future that may require the restructuring of sovereign debt. The sovereign debtor's responsibilities in this situation are summarized under Principle 15 (below).
- Lenders should be willing to engage in good faith discussions with the debtor and other creditors to find a mutually-satisfactory solution.
- A creditor that acquires a debt instrument of a sovereign in financial distress with the intent of forcing a preferential settlement of the claim outside of a consensual workout process is acting abusively.

II. RESPONSIBILITIES OF SOVEREIGN BORROWERS

8. **Agency**

Governments are agents of the State and, as such, when they contract debt obligations, they have a responsibility to protect the interests of their citizens. Where applicable, borrowers should also consider the responsibility of lenders' agents toward their organizations.

Implications:

- Sovereign debts that are contracted by governments bind the continuing legal entity of the State, including its future administrations and future generations of its citizens. The government officials who authorize and execute such borrowings therefore carry responsibilities vis-à-vis the people who must ultimately repay the money.
- This status makes wrongful any form of self-interest or peculation on the part of government officials involved in the borrowing. National laws as well as international and regional conventions against corruption are relevant in assessing the legality of this behavior.
- Codes of Ethics applicable to the circumstances of debt management that address the significant risks in this area should also be adopted and enforced.

9. Binding Agreements

A sovereign debt contract is a binding obligation and should be honored. Exceptional cases nonetheless can arise. A state of economic necessity can prevent the borrower's full and/or timely repayment. Also, a competent judicial authority may rule that circumstances giving rise to legal defense have occurred. When, due to the state of economic necessity of the borrower, changes to the original contractual conditions of the loan are unavoidable, Principles 7 and 15 should be followed.

Implications:

- A sovereign's inability to continue normal debt servicing is typically caused by acute financial distress. Sometimes the sovereign will have been the author of its own difficulties (for example, by pursuing imprudent macroeconomic policies); occasionally a sovereign predicament will have been abetted by reckless creditor behavior. In other cases the crisis may have been precipitated by events beyond the sovereign's control (natural disasters or a general deterioration in international markets).
- In some cases the circumstances surrounding the incurrence of a sovereign loan may give rise to a legal defense pertaining to the performance of that contract by the sovereign borrower. Creditor complicity in the corruption of government officials in the borrowing process is one. Transactions that hamper or directly imply violations of sanctions imposed by the United Nations Security Council is another case. Where such legal defenses are available to a sovereign debtor, these should be raised in a court of competent jurisdiction.

10. Transparency

The process for obtaining financing and assuming sovereign debt obligations and liabilities should be transparent. Governments have a responsibility to put in place and implement a comprehensive legal framework that clearly defines procedures, responsibilities and accountabilities. They should particularly put in place arrangements to ensure the proper approval and oversight of official borrowings and other forms of financing, including guarantees made by State-related entities.

Implications:

- Because the taxpayers of a country will ultimately be responsible for the repayment of the sovereign's debt, their representatives in the legislature should ideally be involved in the decisions about whether and how to incur the debt. This may take the form of legislatively-specified debt ceilings, borrowing objectives, legislative oversight of government finances, the ability to conduct post-disbursement audits of specific transactions, or any other kind of legislative intervention.
- Transparency should operate at the level of specific transactions and at the aggregate government sector level. The reporting standards to be followed depend on the type of stakeholder for whom the report is made.

- Transactions or accounting techniques that have the effect of misrepresenting the true nature or extent of a sovereign's debt picture are inconsistent with a sovereign's duty of candor to its citizens and its creditors.

11. Disclosure and Publication

Relevant terms and conditions of a financing agreement should be disclosed by the sovereign borrower, be universally available, and be freely accessible in a timely manner through online means to all stakeholders, including citizens. Sovereign debtors have a responsibility to disclose complete and accurate information on their economic and financial situation that conforms to standardized reporting requirements and is relevant to their debt situation. Governments should respond openly to requests for related information from relevant parties. Legal restrictions to disclosing information should be based on evident public interest and are to be used reasonably.

Implications:

- If lenders are expected to bear the risk of their sovereign investment decisions, it is necessary that they be given the information required to analyze that risk properly before making the investment. A sovereign borrower that does not provide full disclosure—subject only to a very limited category of exceptions involving national defense—or misrepresents its information at the time it incurs a debt, will be ill-positioned to argue that its creditors have a moral responsibility to participate in any necessary workout of the loan down the road.
- In the same spirit, the material terms (financial and legal) of a sovereign's outstanding debt issuances should at least be made publicly available in the official language(s) of the country.
- Debtors should make public disclosure of their financial and economic situation, providing among others the following information: (i) accurate and timely fiscal data; (ii) level and composition of external and domestic sovereign debt including maturity, currency, and forms of indexation and covenants; (iii) external accounts; (iv) the use of derivative instruments and their actual market value; (v) amortization schedules and, (vi) details of any kind of implicit and explicit sovereign guarantees. Sovereign borrowers may wish to consider disclosing information by way of international norms, such as the IMF's Special Data Dissemination Standard.

12. Project Financing

In the context of project financing, sovereign borrowers have a responsibility to conduct a thorough ex ante investigation into the financial, operational, civil, social, cultural and environmental implications of the project and its funding. Borrowers should make public the results of the project evaluation studies.

Implications:

- The debt incurred to finance a project will remain payable even if the sovereign borrower comes later to regret the design or commissioning of the project. Project assumptions should be based on an honest and careful technical assessment.

- Traditional project financing (where the lenders take the credit risk of the project, rather than that of a sponsor of the project such as the host State) is often kept off the balance sheet of the host State. Ill-designed or underfunded projects, however, must often be taken over by the State before completion which then results in unexpected public sector liabilities.
- Borrowers should ensure that project funds are not used for purposes other than those agreed upon.
- When applicable, lender's responsibility to investigate a project that is being funded with public monies (see Principle 5) does not relieve the sovereign borrower of its independent responsibilities in this regard. Recent history offers many examples of lenders that have tempted sovereigns to commission unnecessary or even harmful projects to access the hard currency loans on offer to finance the project.

13. Adequate Management and Monitoring

Debtors should design and implement a debt sustainability and management strategy and ensure that their debt management is adequate. Debtor countries have a responsiblity to put in place effective monitoring systems, including at the sub-national level, that also capture contingent liabilities. An audit institution should conduct independent, objective, professional, timely and periodic audits of their debt portfolios to assess quantitatively and qualitatively the recently incurred obligations. The findings of such audits should be publicized to ensure transparency and accountability in debt management. Audits should also be undertaken at sub-national levels.

Implications:

- Many countries have suffered from undisciplined practices with respect to the incurrence of debt obligations by sovereign and other public sector borrowers. In the absence of a centralized approval and monitoring process, loans can be contracted without regard to the country's overall debt sustainability. As a result, the application of the proceeds of such loans may remain opaque and the terms—both legal and financial—of such borrowings may be inconsistent and ill-advised.
- Federal and unitary constitutional structure of the country should be considered when carrying out an audit. Auditors should have the power to duly access all information needed to perform debt audits according to the standards established in this Principle.
- The establishment of an efficient debt management office (DMO) can address many of these concerns. DMOs exist in many countries, both developed and developing, and technical assistance is available from international financial institutions to help countries in the establishment of a DMO.

- A DMO should be involved in both the pre- and post-disbursement aspects of any credit for which the State or one of its instrumentalities will be liable. DMO should have sound processes in place to develop an effective medium-term debt strategy (including procedures to review the strategy periodically, to monitor emerging risks, to monitor interest costs, to take into account other liabilities that could impact on the government budgetary position, to monitor performance and to report clearly and transparently the outcome of the strategy).
- A thorough knowledge, understanding and publication of the current and future implications of the sovereign debt portfolio are keys to both the public interest relationship between governments and their citizens and the financial relationship between States and their lenders. Audits should follow commonly agreed principles in this field.

14. Avoiding Incidences of Over-Borrowing

Governments have a responsibility to weigh costs and benefits when seeking sovereign loans. They should seek a sovereign loan if it would permit additional public or private investment, with a prospective social return at least equal to the likely interest rate.

Implications:

- Sovereigns should borrow if the alternative would involve cutting back investment with a return greater than the interest rate.
- A sovereign can legitimately borrow to finance consumption (i.e. a cut in saving) rather than an increase in investment where macroeconomic stability and private investment is endangered. When necessary, preventive and defensive countercyclical measures should be allowed.
- The calculations described above should be performed after internalizing relevant social and environmental costs and benefits.
- Engaging in borrowing to solely cover large chronic budget deficits could eventually erode the debtor country's credit standing, impair its ability to obtain loans on favorable terms in the future and effectively impose a tax on subsequent generations of citizens. Borrowing for this purpose, when not justified by a national emergency, could therefore be inconsistent with a sustainable economic policy.
- In calculating prospective social returns and likely interest rates one should take account of the danger that outcomes may not be favorable as expected ex ante.
- This principle should allow countries to design and implement adequate medium and long term debt strategies.

15. Restructuring

If a restructuring of sovereign debt obligations becomes unavoidable, it should be undertaken promptly, efficiently and fairly.

Implications:

- Although debt servicing should be a high priority for governments, there may be occasions in which, by state of economic necessity, the sovereign borrower will be left with insufficient funds to normally service its debt.
- The sovereign borrower's first responsibility in this situation of substantive financial troubles is to move in a timely fashion to communicate with its creditors and commence the process of finding and implementing a transparent and consensual debt rearrangement. Protracted debt restructurings are generally injurious to all concerned parties, both the debtor and its creditors. The sovereign debtor should therefore seek to conclude the operation as efficiently as possible.
- The sovereign borrower should provide the necessary information which would demonstrate that the sovereign is unable to normally service its debt.
- If the sovereign has proved that a debt restructuring is in fact necessary, the debtor should seek and propose an agreement with the supermajority of creditors to modify the original contractual terms. Collective action clauses can facilitate sovereign debt restructuring; therefore it is recommended that debtors and creditors should include them in multi-party debt instruments.
- The borrower should avoid opportunistic behavior and arbitrary discrimination among creditors; and it should respect the voluntary basis of the process and the seniority of debts. The restructuring should be proportional to the sovereign's need and all stakeholders (including citizens) should share an equitable burden of adjustment and/or losses.

Index

ability to pay 34, 56, 133, 191
abusive credits 132, 176
ad hoc solutions 40, 57, 88, 91
ADB 193
Africa
  AfDB 174
  bankruptcy legislation 65
  capital flight 168
  Central African Republic 248
  China 250, 252, 253, 254, 268, 275
  corruption 193
  fiduciary relations 214, 22–3, 227–32,
  Mobutu 31
aggregation clause 309, 315, 325, 327, 332, 339
Argentina
  arbitration 52, 66, 68, 107, 108, 141
  bilateral Investment Treaties 144–54, 278, 389
  bond 331
  comparative law 119, 123, 124, 130
  constitution 165
  debt 166, 167, 179
  default 23, 136, 375, 386
  Ecuador 189
  emergency law 67
  figures 25
  Greece 198
  Grundnorm 386
  hold-outs 67
  IACHR 210
  IMF 176
  litigation 63, 68, 159, 160, 353
authority to sign 165, 167, 172,
  Chapter 9 (US Chapter 9, Title 11) 40, 65, 85, 137, 166,
audit
  Belgium 268
  capital Markets Principles 375
  corruption 202, 204
  donors 371
  Ecuador 97, 179
  EU 299, 300
  external public auditors 228
  fiduciary relation 214 , 231
  general principle 133
  incentives 377
  manipulation 284
  principles 35, 75, 83, 89, 388, 396, 398, 399
  supreme audit institutions 12, 231, 233
  Tunisia 268

Belgium 56, 63, 67, 101, 107, 146, 208, 268,
Bilateral Investment Treaties (BITs) 61, 69, 110, 144–8, 278, 284, 346
bona fide
  creditors 9, 163, 167, 176, 180, 181
  Discrimination 185, 186
Brazil
  Brazilian Loans Case 93, 84, 107
  chamber of deputies 123
  comparative law 65, 119, 124, 214
  constitution 127
  contract 331
  debt ceiling 128
  domestic law 4
  fiduciary relations 222, 226–33
  fiscal projects 226
  oversight 224
  Paris Club 267
  ratio 130

capacity to pay 89, 101, 165, 186
China
  Export-Import Bank of China 240, 250–2, 254, 255, 264, 271, 275
  preferential loans 9, 239, 240–6, 248–54, 256–60
civil society
  China 246, 247
  firms 363
  initiatives 358
  participation 368–70, 374–81
  principles 112, 348–52
  working group 88
comparative law
  fiduciary relation 218
  general principles 116, 355
  legal source 77, 114
  methodology 84, 118 31, 215
compliance pull 350, 356
complicity 191, 206, 207, 269, 270, 396
conflict of interest 11, 222
contingent liability/ies
  Chile 129
  China 258
  debt restructuring 9, 287–94
  disclosure 348
  EU 299
  Principles 22, 35, 380, 394, 398
contracta sunt servanda 103, 105
cost
  economic 16
  social 27, 29, 37
Costa Rica 66, 96, 165, 167, 184, 267 *see also* *Tinoco* case
credit markets 171, 288

debt restructuring (haircut) 66, 68, 85, 155, 175–7, 308
deformalization of international law 47, 86
domestic debt/borrowing 4, 20, 50, 68, 130, 352
domestic insolvency law
  comparative law 135, 136
  Principles 8, 58, 137, 143, 149, 160
Drago-Porter Convention 92

EBRD 175
economic governance framework 295, 296, 297, 301, 319
Ecuador
  arbitration 146, 147, 149
  audit 97, 179
  comparative law 214
  debt restructuring 155, 180
  fiduciary relations 222–4, 227–31, 233
  IACHR 210
  Norway 270
Elliot Associates 67, 68, 141, 159, 183–5
ethical obligations 223
EU Law 154, 200, 301,
expert group 6, 12, 74, 75, 84, 240, 391
Extractive Industries Transparency Initiative 190, 364, 368–70, 374–7

fiduciary responsibilities/duties chapter 10
Financial Stability Board 351–353, 356, 380
fiscal policy 8, 22–7, 113, 120–6, 131–3, 297
fiscal transparency 8, 121

G-20 351, 356, 371, 375
German Reich 101
Germany
  bonds 329
  budget balance 22
  China 270
  comparative law 119, 123,124, 128, 130
  courts 65
  creditor nation 263
  deficit 21, 297, 298
  legal method 54
  legislation 66
  North Sea Continental Shelf 89
  preferential loan 245, 249, 250
  Transparency International 377
  Tripartite Commission on German Debt 101
  Venezuela 92, 280
global administrative law 45, 46, 48, 58, 69, 73
global governance 4, 7, 41–6, 48, 49, 53
global legal good 7, 4
Grundnorm 104, 385–7
guarantor of debt 173, 252, 289, 293, 303, 329

haircut *see* debt restructuring
Heavily Indebted Poor Countries Initiative 43, 52, 181, 241–8, 254–8
hold-out creditors 311, 314, 315

ICSID 70, 61–9, 83, 107–8, 144–52, 278, 281, 336
implementation of the Principles chapter 16
internationational financial regulation 356–60
international investment law 8, 135, 160
international law sources *see* sources on international law
international public authorities 5, 7, 8, chapter 3, 115
  procedural requirements 41, 45, 56, 58
  substantive issues 41, 42, 45, 51, 55, 60, 61, 62, 64, 70
international surveillance 131
Iraq
  odious debt 97, 267–8, 282–3
  UN Security Council Resolution 1483 (2003) 109
  US invasion 87–8
Italy
  origins of debt crisis 21–4

jus cogens 76–7

League Loans 326–33
legitimacy
  of debt restructurings 40–1
  input 349
  and international public authority 44–9, 53–5
  and new governance 361
  normative/empirical 386
  procedural 58
lenders
  bilateral 28–9
  multilateral 29, 232–3
  private 90
loan conditions 243–4
local government 124–5, 130
London Club 51, 58–9, 90, 356–7
London Debt Conference 110

necessity *see* economic necessity and state of necessity
new governance 360–4
normativity 47, 81, 86, 389
Norway 83, 270–1

obligation to repay 385–7
odious debts 167, 267–8, 282–3
OECD Anti-Bribery Convention 98–9, 377
opinio juris 89, 90, 93, 98, 103, 110, 111
over-borrowing 22–3, 26–9, 177–8, 300
over-lending 28–9, 32–3

pacta sunt servanda 103–5, 385
Palmerston, Lord (British Foreign Secretary) 92
pari passu 68, 110, 184, 346
Paris Club 49–51, 55–62, 102, 109–10,181–2, 355–8
Paris Declaration 370–1

Peru 97, 183–4, 185
Poland
  Balcerowicz Plan 88
Portugal
  origins of debt crisis 21–4
principles for stable capital flows and fair debt restructuring 374–8
procyclical 29–30
public interest 95–9, 269–71

regulators 33–4
Ricardian Equivalence 17–19

Santiago Principles 371–4
soft law 46–7, 80–5, 117, 190–1, 360
sources of international law *see generally* chapters 5 and 6
  case law 77
  customary international law 76
  and generally chapter 5
  and generally chapter 6
  general principles of law 114–20
  treaties 76, 353–4
sovereign bonds dataset chapter 15
Soviet Union
  Czarist debt 105
Spain
  origins of debt crisis 21–4
state of necessity 76, 103–9, 151–3, 387–8
  Russian Indemnity Case 106
state practice
  the UNCTAD Principles and
  role of international organizations, in generally chapter 5, 90–1

Tinoco case 96, 165–9
transparency
  and China 255–6, 257
  and credit borrowing procedures 202–3
  and the EEGF 299
  and the EITI 368–70
  and fiscal policy 120–5
  and legitimacy 60
  negative effects of 28
  and progressive development of international standards on sovereign debt 111–12
  and Yen loans 248–9
Tripartite Commission on German Debt 101
Turkey
  Ottoman Empire 106
  Russo-Turkish War 106

United Nations
  General Assembly 7, 11, 79, 83–4, 88, 98, 110–11
  Member states 5, 12, 123, 178, 262, 391
  Security Council 44, 88, 92, 109, 276, 277, 396

Venezuela
  use of force 92
vulture funds 9, 64, 67, 141, 145, 160, 178

wartime loans 100
World War Foreign Debt Commission 101

The manufacturer's authorised representative in the EU for product safety is Oxford University Press España S.A. of El Parque Empresarial San Fernando de Henares, Avenida de Castilla, 2 - 28830 Madrid (www.oup.es/en or product.safety@oup.com). OUP España S.A. also acts as importer into Spain of products made by the manufacturer.
Printed and bound by CPI Group (UK) Ltd, Croydon, CR0 4YY
14/09/2026
02216308-0016